International Humanitarian Law Series

VOLUME 37

Editors-in-Chief
H.E. Judge Sir Christopher Greenwood
Professor Timothy L.H. McCormack

Editorial Advisory Board
Professor Georges Abi-Saab
H.E. Judge George H. Aldrich
Madame Justice Louise Arbour
Professor Ove Bring
Professor John Dugard
Professor Dr. Horst Fischer
Dr. Hans-Peter Gasser
H.E. Judge Geza Herczegh
Professor Frits Kalshoven
Professor Ruth Lapidoth
Professor Gabrielle Kirk McDonald
H.E. Judge Theodor Meron
Captain J. Ashley Roach
Professor Michael Schmitt
Professor Jiří Toman

The International Humanitarian Law Series is a series of monographs and edited volumes which aims to promote scholarly analysis and discussion of both the theory and practice of the international legal regulation of armed conflict.
The series explores substantive issues of International Humanitarian Law including,
- protection for victims of armed conflict and regulation of the means and methods of warfare
- questions of application of the various legal regimes for the conduct of armed conflict
- issues relating to the implementation of International Humanitarian Law obligations
- national and international approaches to the enforcement of the law and
- the interactions between International Humanitarian Law and other related areas of international law such as Human Rights, Refugee Law, Arms Control and Disarmament Law, and International Criminal Law.

The titles published in this series are listed at brill.nl/ihul

What Is War?

An Investigation in the Wake of 9/11

Edited by

Mary Ellen O'Connell

MARTINUS

NIJHOFF

PUBLISHERS

LEIDEN • BOSTON
2012

Library of Congress Cataloging-in-Publication Data

What is war? : an investigation in the wake of 9/11 / edited by Mary Ellen O'Connell.
    p. cm. -- (International humanitarian law series)
  Includes index.
  ISBN 978-90-04-17234-0 (hardback : alk. paper) 1. War (International law) 2. War
(Philosophy) 3. Terrorism--Prevention--Law and legislation. 4. Politics and war. I.
O'Connell, Mary Ellen, 1958-
  KZ6385.W48 2012
  341.6--dc23

                                    2012014079

ISSN 1389-6776
ISBN 978 90 04 17234 0   (hardback)
ISBN 978 90 47 42581 6 (e-book)

Copyright 2012 by Koninklijke Brill NV, Leiden, The Netherlands.
Koninklijke Brill NV incorporates the imprints BRILL, Global Oriental, Hotei Publishing,
IDC Publishers and Martinus Nijhoff Publishers.

Printed on acid-free paper.

Printed by Printforce, the Netherlands

We note with sadness the passing of two esteemed members of our Editorial Advisory Board – Antonio Cassese (01 January 1937 - 21 October 2011) and Leslie C Green (06 November 1920 - 27 November 2011). Antonio and Leslie were outstanding scholars and enthusiastic supporters of the IHL Series and both will be sorely missed.

Table of Contents

Preface

President Obama declared that 'Justice has been done' with respect to the killing of Osama Bin Laden by United States military forces on Sunday 1 May 2011 in a compound where he was living in Abbottabad, Pakistan. While many of the circumstances of Bin Laden's death remain unclear, what is certain is that there was no arrest followed by legal proceedings. The UN Human Rights Council Special Rapporteurs on extrajudicial, summary or arbitrary executions and on the promotion and protection of human rights and fundamental freedoms while countering terrorism, responded with the following statement:

> Acts of terrorism are the antithesis of human rights, in particular the right to life. In certain exceptional cases, use of deadly force may be permissible as a measure of last resort in accordance with international standards on the use of force, in order to protect life, including in operations against terrorists. However, the norm should be that terrorists be dealt with as criminals, through legal processes of arrest, trial and judicially decided punishment.
>
> Actions taken by States in combating terrorism, especially in high profile cases, set precedents for the way in which the right to life will be treated in future instances.[1]

In seeking further details of the events surrounding Bin Laden's death, the two special rapporteurs did not mention the word 'war'. In contrast, in his statement to the American people on announcing the death of Bin Laden, President Obama referred on a number of occasions to 'our war against al-Qaida', fought 'in order to protect our citizens, our friends, and our allies.'[2] The international legal regime regulating when and who it is permissible to kill during armed combat is very different from that with respect to permissible violence against

---

[1]   UN Office of the High Commissioner on Human Rights, press statement, 'Osama bin Laden: statement by the UN Special Rapporteurs on summary executions and on human rights and counter-terrorism', 6 May 2011.

[2]   Barack Obama's full statement on the death of Osama bin Laden, the Guardian 2 May 2011 available at http://www.guardian.co.uk/world/2011/may/02/barack-obama-statement-bin-laden.

suspected criminals. The existence or otherwise of a 'war' against al-Qaida is therefore an important factor in assessing the legality under international law of the death of Bin Laden.

On 17 February 2011 mass demonstrations erupted against the government of Libya in Benghazi, Tripoli and other cities in Libya, which were repressed with extreme force, resulting in escalating violence and killings, and heavy casualties within the civilian population. In demanding a ceasefire and compliance by the Libyan authorities with their obligations under international law, the United Nations Security Council referred to international humanitarian law (applicable in international or non-international armed conflict) as well as human rights law.[3] It thereby implied that at some unidentified moment the character of the events had evolved from protest to some form of armed conflict. On 16 May the Prosecutor of the International Criminal Court applied to a pre-trial chamber of the Court for the issuance of arrest warrants against Muammar Mohammed Gaddafi, Saif-al-Islam Gaddafi and Abdullah al-Senussi for the crimes of murder and persecution as crimes against humanity.[4] There is no requirement that crimes against humanity – widespread and systematic crimes committed against a civilian population – be committed during war. At the same time the prosecutor indicated that investigations would continue, including into allegations of war crimes 'during the armed conflict that started towards the end of February.'[5]

These events in the early months of 2011 show that the central question explored in this important and ambitious book – *What is War?* – is as important and topical and as difficult to answer as it was when Professor Mary Ellen O'Connell proposed the topic to me in the wake of the aftermath of 9/11 as ripe for examination by an international committee of the International Law Association. Without an understanding of what forms of violence constitute 'war' (or in contemporary international legal parlance 'international or non-international armed conflict', although still popularly known as 'war') legal regulation of its incidence and conduct must be impeded. The Committee was set up in May 2005 by the Executive Council of the ILA under the able and energetic leadership of Professor O'Connell (as Chair) and Professor Judith Gardam as rapporteur. It was mandated to report on the definition of war in international law. This book traces the evolution of the Committee's thinking and work on the subject. In 2006 the Committee determined to tackle the subject through standard international law (and ILA) methodology, drawing upon the discipline's accepted sources. It accordingly combines scholarly analysis by Committee members drawn from 13 ILA Branches with extensive examination of multiple instances of state practice and *opinio juris* from 1945-2010. The result

---

3   UNSC Resolution 1973, 17 March 2011.

4   Situation in the Libyan Arab Jamahiriya, ICC-01/11, 16 May 2011.

5   International Criminal Court, Statement ICC Prosecutor Press Conference on Libya, 16 May 2011.

is an outstanding volume. It brings together background papers on international law with papers that go 'beyond international law', examining the topic from the perspectives of political science, military history, journalism, ethics and peace studies. It includes the successive reports of the Committee presented to the ILA's biannual conferences at Rio de Janeiro (2008) and The Hague (2010).

As Director of Studies of the International Law Association I am proud that this book has been published during my term of office and honoured to have been asked to write this Preface. The main objectives of the ILA are the study, clarification and development of both public and private international law. This volume makes an important contribution both to the fulfilment of those objectives and more broadly to international law.

Christine Chinkin
Director of Studies,
International Law
Association

Acknowledgements

This book developed over the years that the International Law Association's Use of Force Committee researched and drafted its Report on the Meaning of Armed Conflict in International Law. Throughout this time, I have had the opportunity to work with a number of exceptional people who deserve special thanks. The person who deserves the greatest thanks is Professor Judith Gardam who served as the Committee's rapporteur. It is owing to Judith's hard work, expertise, wisdom, and sense of humor that the Committee produced its Report. It was a privilege to work with her.

At Notre Dame, I had help from three outstanding office assistants: Nicole Bourbon, Layla Krog, and Andy Mason. Many student research assistants did essential work, especially Jolie Schwarz and Lenore VanderZee. Patti Ogden, of Notre Dame's Kresge Law Library supported every phase of this project.

Lindy Melman of Martinus Nijhof has been a great source of encouragement. I am grateful for her patience and professionalism.

Oxford University Press gave permission to reprint: Mary Ellen O'Connell, *Defining Armed Conflict*, 13 JOURNAL OF CONFLICT AND SECURITY LAW (Winter 2008).

The Kroc Institute for International Peace Studies at the University of Notre Dame and The Ohio State University's Mershon Center for the Study of International Security provided generous funding for the September 2007 conference at Notre Dame, "What is War?" Gerard Powers of the Kroc Institute and Richard Herrmann and John Mueller of the Mershon Center assisted in the overall design and organization of the conference.

Finally, my husband, the photographer Peter Bauer, a highly decorated combat veteran, deserves thanks for many things related to this project but most of all for regularly reminding me of the service international law scholars can provide to the men and women who serve in our armed forces.

Contributors

(Biographies as of the September 2007 Conference:
What Is War?)

These are the biographies of the contributors to the volume as of the date of the conference, September 2007, when preliminary chapters were presented. At the end of the contributor list are the biographies of other speakers at the conference who were unable to contribute to the book but whose participation in the conference was important to the outcome of the Final Report.

Masahiko Asada is Professor of International Law at the Graduate School of Law, Kyoto University. He is a member of the International Relations Committee of Japan's Atomic Energy Commission, the Subcommittee on Security and Trade Control of the Industrial Structure Advisory Council in the Ministry of Economy, Trade and Industry, the Editorial Board of *Journal of Conflict and Security Law* (Oxford) and the *Japanese Annual of International Law*. A former Senior Associate at St. Antony's College, Oxford, he has served as legal adviser to several Japanese delegations to arms control conferences and meetings. Professor Asada is the author of numerous articles in the *Journal of Conflict and Security Law*, the *Kyoto Journal of Law and Politics*, and other publications.

Jeremy Black is Professor of History at the University of Exeter. After graduating from Cambridge, he did postgraduate work at Oxford and then taught at Durham before moving to Exeter in 1996. He has lectured extensively all over the world and has held visiting chairs at West Point, Texas Christian University, and Stillman College. A past council member of the Royal Historical Society, he is a Fellow of the Royal Society for the Encouragement of Arts, Manufactures and Commerce, and a Senior Fellow of the Foreign Policy Research Institute. His books include *War and World 1450-2000* (Yale), *The British Seaborne Empire* (Yale), *Maps and History* (Yale), *George III* (Yale) and *European Warfare in a Global Context, 1660-1815* (Routledge).

Jutta Brunnée is Professor of Law and Metcalf Chair in Environmental Law at the University of Toronto. Previously, she served on the faculties of law at McGill University and the University of British Columbia. She is co-editor of the *Oxford Handbook of International Environmental Law* (Oxford) and author of *Acid Rain and Ozone Layer Depletion: International Law and Regulation*, as well as numerous articles. She is a member of the ILA's Committee on the Use of Force and of the World Conservation Union's Environmental Law Commission and was a member of the U.N. Environment Programme's International Expert Group for the Montevideo Programme (III). She holds an LL.M. from Dalhousie University, Canada, and a Doctorate in Law from Johannes Gutenberg University, Germany.

John Darby is Professor of Comparative Ethnic Studies at the Joan B. Kroc Institute for International Peace Studies at the University of Notre Dame. He was founding director of INCORE, a joint program of the Tokyo-based United Nations University and the University of Ulster in Northern Ireland. He has held visiting positions at Harvard and Duke Universities and has been a fellow of the Rockefeller Foundation in Bellagio, the Woodrow Wilson Center in Washington, the United States Institute of Peace, and the Fulbright New Century Scholars' Program. He has written or edited fourteen books and more than 100 other academic publications, including *The Effects of Violence on Peace Processes*; *Contemporary Peacemaking*; *Violence and Reconstruction*; and *Peacebuilding after Peace Accords*.

Michael W. Doyle is the Harold Brown Professor of International Affairs, Law and Political Science at Columbia University. In 2006-07, he was the Georges Lurcy Visiting Professor of Law at Yale Law School. His current research focuses on preventive self-defense. His publications include *Ways of War and Peace* (W.W. Norton), *Empires* (Cornell University Press), *Making War and Building Peace* (Princeton Press), and study of U.N. peacekeeping written with Nicholas Sambanis. He served as Assistant Secretary-General and Special Adviser to former U.N. Secretary-General Kofi Annan, where his responsibilities included strategic planning, outreach to the international corporate sector (the "Global Compact"), and relations with Washington. He has recently been named the U.N. Secretary-General's representative on the Advisory Board of the U.N. Democracy Fund.

Judith Gail Gardam teaches Public International Law at University of Adelaide Law School in South Australia. Her areas of expertise include International Humanitarian Law and the law regulating the use of force in international law. Her latest monographs are *Proportionality, Necessity and Force in International Law* (Cambridge) and *Women, Armed Conflict and International Law* (Kluwer). Her recent work focuses on the challenges posed to the application of proportionality in response to the forceful activities of terrorists, and she has written on this issue in the *Nordic Journal of International Law* and in *Essays in Honour of Professor Igor Blischenko* (forthcoming). Professor Gardam is an expert on the law regulating the treatment of women in times of armed conflict and is the author of *International Humanitarian Law and Human Rights Law Applicable to*

Women and Girls in Times of Armed Conflict, a study commissioned by the U.N. Secretary-General.

James Thuo Gathii is the Associate Dean for Research and Scholarship and the Governor George E. Pataki Professor of International Commercial Law at Albany Law School, in New York. He is also a member of the Global Faculty of the Trade Policy Training Institute (TRAPCA) in Arusha, Tanzania. He has published over fifty articles and book chapters on international economic and trade law as well as on public international law and on good govern-ance in Africa. He is a founding member of the Third World Approaches to International Law network and currently the Co-Chair of the African Interest Group of the American Society of International Law. He is also a member of the International Law Association's Study Committee on the Meaning of War.

Professor Gathii has published two books: African Regional Trade Agreements as Legal Regimes, Cambridge University Press,2011 andWar, Commerce and International Law, 2010 published by Oxford University Press. Professor Gathii received his LL.B. from the University of Nairobi and his LL.M. and S.J.D. from Harvard Law School.

Thomas B. Grassey is the first James B. Stockdale Professor of Leadership and Ethics at the U.S. Naval War College. He teaches professional ethics, decision theory, intelligence and U.S. military operations, and strategic leadership. A 1967 NROTC graduate of Villanova University, he served two years aboard the destroyer USS *MASSEY* (DD 778) and then was officer-in-charge of the Naval Weapons Orientation Group, Camp Pendleton Marine Corps Base, provid-ing weapons training for Navy and Coast Guard personnel assigned to duty in Vietnam. Professor Grassey earned his M.A. and Ph.D. in philosophy at the University of Chicago. In 1987 he was appointed academic director of the intelli-gence studies program at the Naval Postgraduate School. He has served as editor of the *Naval War College Review* and director of the Naval War College Press and has held National Endowment for the Humanities faculty fellowships in law, history, and humanities, and a Carnegie Council fellowship in ethics. He retired from the U.S. Naval Reserve intelligence program as a captain.

Christine D. Gray is Professor of International Law at the University of Cambridge and a Fellow of St John's College. She was a Research Fellow at Selwyn College, Cambridge, from 1978-1980, a Fellow of St Hilda's College, Oxford, and a Lecturer at the University of Oxford from 1980-1996. She has been a visiting fellow in the Max Planck Institute in Heidelberg, as well as visit-ing professor at Duke and other U.S. universities. She is a member of the edito-rial board of several journals, including the *British Yearbook of International Law,* the *European Journal of International Law* and the *Cambridge Law Journal.* Her main publications are *Judicial Remedies in International Law* and *International Law and the Use of Force* (three editions).

James Gordon Meek is an investigative reporter who covers national news, politics and terrorism for the *New York Daily News*. He reported on the 9/11 attacks from the Pentagon and has traveled to Afghanistan and embedded with U.S. special operations forces. He covered the trials of Zacarias Moussaoui and Lewis "Scooter" Libby. He has broken countless stories, including the 2006 plan by Lebanese militants linked to Al Qaeda in Iraq to blow up tunnels in New York City and flood lower Manhattan, and has authored a series of stories about abuses of inmates in Guantanamo Bay, Cuba. Previously, Meek worked for UPI, APBnews.com, and the *Los Angeles Daily Journal*. He contributed reporting to CNN terrorism analyst Peter Bergen's book, *The Osama Bin Laden I Know* and was the first cyberjournalist accredited by Congress and the White House.

Elzbieta Mikos-Skuza is a Lecturer in Public International Law at the University of Warsaw. She graduated from the Faculty of Law, University of Warsaw (Poland), earned degrees from two post-graduate programs in international law, development, and social justice at the Institute of Social Studies in The Hague, and a Ph.D. in law from the University of Warsaw. An expert in international law and international humanitarian law, Professor Mikos-Skuza has authored numerous books and articles and, since 1981, she has volunteered with the Polish Red Cross. She serves as an expert to the Polish Ministry of Foreign Affairs and is a vice-president of the PRC, member of its national board, and president of its Commission for International Humanitarian Law. She is also a member of the San Remo International Institute of Humanitarian Law and of the ILA Committee on the Use of Force. In 2001 she was elected a member of the International Humanitarian Fact-Finding Commission, and has served as its vice-president since 2002.

John Mueller holds the Woody Hayes Chair of National Security Studies at the Mershon Center for International Security Studies and is Professor of Political Science at the Ohio State University, where he teaches international relations. He is the author of *Overblown: How Politicians and the Terrorism Industry Inflate National Security Threats, and Why We Believe Them*, as well as *War, Presidents and Public Opinion* (Wiley), *Retreat from Doomsday: The Obsolescence of Major War* (Basic Books), *Policy and Opinion in the Gulf War* (University of Chicago Press), *Quiet Cataclysm: Reflections on the Recent Transformation of World Politics* (HarperCollins), *Capitalism, Democracy, and Ralph's Pretty Good Grocery* (Princeton), and *The Remnants of War* (Cornell), which was awarded the Lepgold Prize for the best book on international relations in 2004. Professor Mueller has been a visiting fellow at the Brookings Institution, the Cato Institute, the Hoover Institution, and the Norwegian Nobel Institute in Olso.

Williamson Murray is Senior Fellow at the Institute of Defense Analyses and Distinguished Visiting Professor at the U.S. Naval Academy. After graduating from Yale, he served five years as an officer in the U.S. Air Force, including a tour in Southeast Asia with the 314th Tactical Airlift Wing (C-130s). He then returned to Yale to earn his Ph.D. and taught for two years before moving to the Ohio State University. He received the Alumni Distinguished Teaching Award in 1987 and, in 1995, retired as Professor Emeritus of History. He has also taught at the Air War College, the U.S. Military Academy, and the Naval War College, where he was Secretary of the Navy Fellow. He served as the Centennial Visiting Professor at the London School of Economics, the Matthew C. Horner Professor of Military Theory at the Marine Corps University, the Charles Lindbergh Chair at the Smithsonian's Air and Space Museum, and the Harold K. Johnson Professor of Military History at the Army War College. Murray has written and edited numerous books on history and the military, and his articles have appeared in *The National Interest*, *Strategic Review*, *Orbis*, *Joint Forces Quarterly*, and other publications.

Mary Ellen O'Connell is the Robert and Marion Short Professor of Law at Notre Dame Law School. Previously, she was the William B. Saxbe Designated Professor of Law at the Moritz College of Law at the Ohio State University. She earned her B.A. in history from Northwestern University, an M.Sc. in International Relations from the London School of Economics, and an LL.B. from Cambridge University. She earned her J.D. from Columbia University in 1985, then practiced with Covington & Burling in Washington, D.C., before teaching at Indiana University School of Law, the Bologna Center of Johns Hopkins University, the Paul H. Nitze School of Advanced International Studies in Bologna, Italy, the George C. Marshall European Center for Security Studies in Germany, and the University of Cincinnati College of Law. She is the author of three casebooks, four edited collections, and more than sixty articles and book chapters.

Gerard F. Powers is Director of Policy Studies for the Joan B. Kroc Institute for International Peace Studies at the University of Notre Dame and Chairman of the Steering Committee and Coordinator of the Catholic Peacebuilding Network. He earned a J.D. and an M.A. in theology from Notre Dame and a B.A. from Princeton. He previously served as director of the Office of International Justice and Peace of the U.S. Conference of Catholic Bishops and was its foreign policy advisor specializing in European affairs, religious liberty, and the ethics of the use of force. He has been an adjunct faculty member at the National Law Center of George Washington University and the Oblate School of Theology. Professor Powers' recent articles have examined the ethics of the use of force in Iraq, nuclear weapons, humanitarian intervention, and economic sanctions. He has also written on religion and U.S. foreign policy, the right to self-determination, and the role of religion in the conflicts in Northern

Ireland and Bosnia-Herzegovina. He is co-editor of *Peacemaking: Moral and Policy Challenges for a New World*.

General Sir Michael Rose was educated at Cheltenham College, the Sorbonne, and St. Edmund Hall, Oxford. He is an honorary fellow of his College and a Senior Associate Research Fellow at King's College, London (International Policy Institute). He joined the Reserve in 1957 and was commissioned as a Regular Officer into the Coldstream Guards in 1964. Following attendance at the Staff College in 1973, his appointments took him to the Middle and Far East as well as the Falkland Islands. He attended the Royal College of Defence Studies in 1986 and became Commandant of the Staff College in 1991. He was Commander of the UK Field Army and Inspector General Territorial Army from 1993 to 1994, when he took command of the U.N. Protection Force in Bosnia-Herzegovina. In January 1995, he was appointed to the Army Board as Adjutant General. General Sir Rose retired from the Army in 1997. He has since written and lectured extensively on peacekeeping and leadership around the world. He is the author of two books; *Fighting for Peace*, about the UN in Bosnia, which was published in 1998 in London, and *Washington's War*, comparing the American War of Independence and the current war in Iraq, which was published in London in 2007 and in New York in 2008.

Peter Wallensteen is the Richard G. Starmann Research Professor of Peace Studies at Notre Dame's Joan B. Kroc Institute for International Peace Studies and the Dag Hammarskjöld Professor in the Department of Peace and Conflict Research at Sweden's Uppsala University, where he directs the Uppsala Conflict Data Program and the Special Program on the Implementation of Targeted Sanctions. Professor Wallensteen is the author of *Understanding Conflict Resolution: Peace, War, and the Global System*. His interest in targeted sanctions resulted in an edited volume, *International Sanctions: Between Wars and Words*, in 2005. He was also involved with *Making Targeted Sanctions Effective*, the outcome of a large international process for improving sanctions and presented to the U.N. Security Council in February 2003. He published an edited volume on Nobel Peace Prize Laureate Alva Myrdal, *Alva Myrdal in International Affairs*.

Todd David Whitmore is Associate Professor of Social Ethics in the Department of Theology at the University of Notre Dame. He is also the Director of the Program in Catholic Social Tradition and a Faculty Fellow in the Kroc Institute for International Peace Studies. His current work takes him to northern Uganda and Southern Sudan, where he is researching the impact of the 21-year conflict between the Lord's Resistance Army and the government of Uganda.

Other Participants

Richard K. Herrmann is Professor of Political Science and Director of the Mershon Center for International Security Studies at the Ohio State University. He has written widely on international security, American foreign policy, and politics in the Middle East. His research has appeared in the *American Political Science Review, International Organization, World Politics,* and the *Journal of Politics.* His most recent piece is entitled "From Prediction to Learning: Opening Expert's Minds to Unfolding History," *International Security* (Spring 2007). From 1991-1996, Professor Herrmann served as coeditor of *International Studies Quarterly,* the flagship journal of the International Studies Association. Previous to that, he served on Secretary of State James Baker's Policy Planning Staff at the U.S. Department of State.

George A. Lopez is the Theodore M. Hesburgh, CSC, Professor of Peace Studies at the Joan B. Kroc Institute for International Peace Studies at the University of Notre Dame. Working with David Cortright since 1992, he has written more than twenty articles and book chapters, as well as five books on economic sanctions, including *The Sanctions Decade: Assessing UN Strategies in the 1990s,* with special reference to U.N. sanctions on Iraq. Lopez and Cortright's research detailing the unlikely presence of WMDs in Iraq was featured before the war in "Disarming Iraq," *Arms Control Today* (Sept. 2002), and further articulated after the war began in "Containing Iraq: the Sanctions Worked," *Foreign Affairs* (July/August, 2004). Their most recent volume, *Uniting Against Terror* was just published by MIT Press. Professor Lopez has served as a senior research associate at the Carnegie Council on Ethics and International Affairs.

Darrin D. Mortenson is a Visiting Scholar in Journalism at the Mershon Center for International Security Studies at The Ohio State University. He covered the first three years of the war in Iraq for the *North County Times* at Camp Pendleton, California. He was embedded with U.S. Marines during the initial invasion of Iraq in 2003 and during the siege of Fallujah in early 2004, and covered the first general elections from Kufa, Karbala, and Najaf, sending more than 150 dispatches and contributing reports to *Time,* Nightline, and ABC World News Tonight. As the Mershon Center's first-ever journalist-in-residence, he completed a manuscript on the U.S. Marines during the invasion of Iraq and most of a manuscript on the Marines' experience in Fallujah. He is the author of *A Thousand Miles to Baghdad,* a book of images and impressions from the invasion of Iraq.

Major General William L. Nash has been a Senior Fellow at the Council on Foreign Relations since 2001. He is also a lecturer at Georgetown University, a visiting lecturer at Princeton, and a military consultant to ABC News. Previously, he served as Director of the Center for Preventive Action and the

John W. Vessey Senior Fellow for Conflict Prevention, where he led efforts to work with governments, international and non-governmental organizations, and the business community to anticipate international crises and recommend preventive action. Major General Nash served in Vietnam and in Operation Desert Storm; from 1995-1997, he commanded the U.S. Army's 1st Armored Division. In 1995 he led American troops in Bosnia as the Commander of Task Force Eagle, a multinational division of 25,000 soldiers from 12 nations charged with enforcing the military provisions of the Dayton Peace Accords. In 2000 he led a joint civilian-military peacekeeping operation and, at the request of the U.S. government, became the Regional Administrator for the U.N. in northern Kosovo. He was the Director of Civil-Military Programs at the National Democratic Institute for International Affairs. After retiring from the Army in 1998, he was a Fellow and Visiting Lecturer at the John F. Kennedy School of Government at Harvard.

Sir Michael Wood, KCMG, is a Senior Fellow of the Lauterpacht Centre for International Law, University of Cambridge, and a barrister at 20 Essex Street. He was Legal Adviser to the Foreign and Commonwealth Office and was a member of the UK delegation to many international conferences, including the Third U.N. Conference on the Law of the Sea, the Lancaster House Conference on Rhodesia, the "Two-plus-Four" negotiations on German Unification, the Cambodia Peace Conference, and the Dayton and Rambouillet Conferences on the former Yugoslavia. His postings included the British Embassy in Bonn and the UK Mission to the U.N. in New York, dealing chiefly with Security Council matters. He was Agent for the UK for several years before the European Commission and Court of Human Rights, an Agent in the *Lockerbie* and *Legality of Use of Force* cases before the International Court of Justice, as well as in the *MOX Plant* proceedings before the International Tribunal for the Law of the Sea.

Part I

The ILA Decision to Study the Meaning of "War" in International Law

Chapter 1

Introduction:
Defining Armed Conflict in the Decade after 9/11

Mary Ellen O'Connell

Humanity has sought for millennia to control war, armed conflict, and other significant armed violence through the mechanism of legal regulation. The effort to develop legal controls on war has resulted in an impressive collection of institutions, rules, norms, and principles. We can find law relevant to almost every issue associated with intergroup violence from the general prohibition on resort to armed force agreed to in the 1945 United Nations Charter to the types of care packages that must be provided to prisoners of war under the 1949 Geneva Conventions. This law has had some discernable positive impacts. Certain types of armed conflict have been declared unlawful and have, subsequently, declined in number and even disappeared. For example, States no longer fight wars to collect contract debts. They rarely fight wars of conquest. The law of war has also led to widely held normative precepts such as the prohibited nature of intentionally targeting civilians during combat or of abusing prisoners.[1] On the other hand, much remains to be done in the struggle to suppress resort to armed force and toward mitigating the suffering of those caught up in war. Hundreds of unlawful wars have been fought since the adoption of the UN Charter. Civilian casualties continue to be higher than military casualties in most wars. Progress toward new laws or renewed commitment to current law will require new leadership and a renewed vision of what law can accomplish against war.

---

1   Protocol Additional to the Geneva Conventions of 12 August 1949, and relating to the Protections of Victims of International Armed Conflicts (Protocol I), *adopted* June 8, 1977, 1125 U.N.T.S. 3 [hereinafter AP I]; Protocol Additional to the Geneva Conventions of 12 August 1949, and relating to the Protections of Victims of Non-International Armed Conflicts (Protocol II), *adopted* June 8, 1977, 1125 U.N.T.S. 609 [hereinafter AP II] (according to art 51(3) of Additional Protocol I and art 13(3) of Additional Protocol II to the 1949 Geneva Conventions, civilians are immune from direct attack "unless and for such time as they take a direct part in hostilities").

Mary Ellen O'Connell (ed.), What Is War? An Investigation in the Wake of 9/11.
© *2012 Koninklijke Brill NV. Printed in The Netherlands. ISBN 978 9004 17234 0. pp. 3 – 11.*

Given both the success of law in the control of war and the obvious need for more progress, international law has contained a curious gap in its large body of rules related to international violence. Until 2010, international lawyers could not easily point to international law's definition of war. This may seem surprising but, in fact, before 2001 there was little need for a definition. Much war was obvious: Situations of major fighting between the armed forces of sovereign states or well-organized fighting forces within states was commonly known as war. Since the end of the Second World War, we have seen the Korean War, the Vietnam War, the Gulf War, the Ethiopian-Eritrean War, the Iraq War, and others. These examples involve international armed conflict. We have as many or more examples of civil war or non-international armed conflict since 1945, including in Afghanistan, Congo, Ethiopia, Lebanon, Sri Lanka, Sudan, and Yugoslavia. In situations involving less violence than in these examples, however, governments have often attempted to avoid having the violence labeled "civil war." When a war occurs on a state's territory, governments have often attempted to deflect attention from what is plainly a major government failure. Inter-group fighting amounting to armed conflict means the state is the scene of terrible suffering, displacement, and economic crisis. It means investors and trading partners look elsewhere; the UN and human rights organizations begin to scrutinize government conduct. The International Committee of the Red Cross (ICRC) will demand access to conflict zones and prisons.

It is understandable that governments will try to avoid these negative repercussions by avoiding the label "war." The records of the ICRC contain many such examples where governments have denied the organization access claiming that violence was below the threshold of war and, therefore, below the threshold of the ICRC's jurisdiction to monitor compliance with law relevant to war. While the ICRC has pressed governments to recognize war or armed conflict,[2] as a matter of international law, there is in fact no persuasive reason for governments to recognize war. When a government denies that violence amounts to war, it must respect the normal human rights standards that prevail outside of war. Thus, when a government denies that armed conflict is occurring on its territory, the situation for individuals should be better than when a government declares war. Outside of war, all human rights prevail. Within war, some of the

---

2   *See* Robert K. Goldman, *International Humanitarian Law: Americas Watch's Experience in Monitoring Internal Armed Conflicts* (1993) 9 AM. U. J. INT'L L & POL'Y 49, 89 (discussing the situation in El Salvador); INTERNATIONAL COMMITTEE OF THE RED CROSS, ICRC ANNUAL REPORT 1996 140-42 (1997) [hereinafter ICRC ANNUAL REPORT] (discussing the situation in Sri Lanka); Barbara Hintermann, *ICRC action to protect and assist the victims of armed conflict in Colombia*, ICRC April 2, 2008, http://www.icrc.org/eng/resources/documents/report/colombia-report-02042008.htm (discussing the situation in Colombia).

most important human rights may be curtailed, including such basic rights as
the right to life, the right to a trial, and respect for private property.[3]

On 9/11, however, the world saw a dramatic exception to the tendency by
governments to deny the existence of war. On that day, the government of the
United States declared war even before it had confirmed against whom the
war was being waged. Understandably, the government was in a state of alarm.
Almost 3000 persons perished that day when members of the al-Qaeda terrorist
group hijacked three planes and flew them into the World Trade Center towers
in New York City, the Pentagon in Washington, D.C., and a farm field in
Pennsylvania. Within hours of the attack, President George W. Bush declared
a "global war on terrorism."[4] By November 2001, it was clear that for the Bush
administration declaring a "war" against terrorism was a basis for asserting wartime privileges, including the right to kill without warning, to detain without trial, and search and seize cargo on the high seas.[5] In November 2001,
President Bush issued the first public legal document based on the new position that the United States was in a worldwide war against al-Qaeda and other
terrorist groups and their associates. In an executive order titled "Detention,
Treatment, and Trial of Certain Non-Citizens in the War Against Terrorism"
President Bush confirmed that the U.S. would be claiming wartime privileges
wherever it found terrorism suspects, regardless of the situation in which the
U.S. found the suspects.[6] The lawyers further argued that, given their claim that
the United States was at war with these individuals, the U.S. was not legally
required to extend human rights or U.S. Constitutional protections to them so
long as they were outside the United States. For this reason, the U.S. created a
military prison at Guantanamo Bay, Cuba, where the U.S. has a Navy base but
where the territory is Cuban. By January 2002, the President's lawyers were also
arguing against extending the usual law of war protections to members of al-
Qaeda or others. They drafted documents concluding that al-Qaeda members
and others did not qualify for such protections.[7]

---

3   *See* Special Rapporteur on extrajudicial, summary or arbitrary executions, *Study on
    Targeted Killings,* ¶ 28, HRC, U.N. Doc A/HRC/14/24/Add.6 (May 28, 2010) (by
    Philip Alston) ("Whether or not a specific targeted killing is legal depends on the
    context in which it is conducted: whether in armed conflict, outside of armed con-
    flict, or in relation to the inter-state use of force." Citing UN Doc A/61/311, ¶ 33-45
    (detailed discussion of 'arbitrary' deprivation of life under human rights law)).

4   President's Address to the Nation on the Terrorist Attacks, 37 WEEKLY COMP.
    PRES. DOC. 1301 (September 11, 2001).

5   Mary Ellen O'Connell, *Ad Hoc War, in* KRISENSICHERUNG UND HUMANITÄRER
    SCHUTZ – CRISIS MANAGEMENT AND HUMANITARIAN PROTECTION 405 (Horst
    Fischer et al, eds., 2004).

6   Exec. Order, Detention, Treatment, and Trial of Certain Non-Citizens in the War
    Against Terrorism, 66 Fed. Reg. 57833 (Nov. 16, 2001).

7   *See* Memorandum from Jay Bybee, Asst. Atty Gen., for Alberto Gonzales, Counsel

These three sets of inter-locking arguments resulted in the infamous "legal black hole." Being in a war limited human rights obligations, keeping detainees outside of the U.S. did so as well, and labeling suspects in the war "unlawful" enemy combatants, limited even law of war protections. By June 2004, hundreds of pages of legal memoranda began surfacing arguing over and over that in the "global war on terror" the U.S. could claim wartime privileges afforded by international law but did not owe its enemies international law's basic legal protections.

Ironically, the very evidence U.S. government lawyers used to argue that al-Qaeda members and others were not lawful combatants was evidence that demonstrated they were not combatants at all. The evidence showed that, in many cases, members of al-Qaeda had participated in criminal conduct that warranted criminal charges, arrest, trial, and punishment in the civil criminal justice systems. Many of these persons had not participated in any war or armed conflict.[8]

The media began to report on the memoranda and what had followed from them: secret prisons, harsh interrogation, prosecutions lacking in fundamental due process of law, and targeted killing.[9] In the secret prisons, as well as at the prisons at Bagram, Afghanistan, Abu Ghraib, Iraq, and Guantánamo Bay, Cuba, detainees were subjected to waterboarding and other forms of torture and cruel, inhuman and degrading treatment to attempt to extract information from them. Persons were detained far from any armed conflict zone and held without trial. In addition to detention without trial, the U.S. also practiced killing without warning even in places where the U.S. was plainly not involved in armed conflict hostilities, including in Yemen, Pakistan, and Somalia.[10] With respect to search and seizures on the high seas, the U.S. backed away from exercising this wartime privilege under pressure from allies, in particular, the

---

to the President and William J. Haynes II, General Counsel of the Dept. of Defense, *available at* http://www.justice.gov/olc/docs/memo-laws-taliban-detainees.pdf.

8   Exec. Order, *supra* note 6 (stating that terrorist suspects would be tried before military tribunals and subjected to military detention, irrespective of where the person was captured).

9   Raymond Bonner et al., *Questioning Terror Suspects in a Dark and Surreal World*, N.Y. Times (March 9, 2003), http://www.nytimes.com/2003/03/09/world/threats-responses-interrogations-questioning-terror-suspects-dark-surreal-world.html; David Johnston and James Risen, *Aides Say Memo Backed Coercion Already in Use*, N.Y. Times (June 27, 2004), http://www.nytimes.com/2004/06/27/world/reach-war-interrogations-aides-say-memo-backed-coercion-already-use.html.

10   Scott Shane, *U.S. Approves Targeted Killing of Radical Muslim Cleric Tied to Domestic Terror Suspects*, N.Y. Times, April 7, 2010, at A10.

United Kingdom, which maintained that the vessel's master or flag-state had to give consent to searches.[11]

In March 2010, the U.S. administration of Barack Obama made clear that it would, in general, adopt its predecessor's global war paradigm. The State Department Legal Adviser, Harold Koh, explained that the Obama administration had rejected the label, "global war on terror." Instead, it would base its actions on its view that the U.S. was in an "armed conflict with al-Qaeda, the Taliban and associated forces."[12] While the name is different, the Obama administration continued to conduct missile strikes in areas where no armed conflict was occurring, to detain persons captured far from any hostilities for suspected membership in certain organizations, and to deny civilian trials or any trials at all to persons not involved in hostilities.[13]

A decade after the paradigm of global war was first declared, it appears that only one or two other states take a similar legal position respecting terrorist suspects. India, the scene of several serious terrorist attacks since 9/11, has not used military force against Pakistan, which it believes bears at least some responsibility for the attacks. India has used law enforcement measures and diplomacy.[14] The same has been true of others states, even those in which al-Qaeda members have carried out terrorist attacks or have planned to do so. This has been true of Egypt, Kenya, Tanzania, Spain, Indonesia, Germany, and the United Kingdom. Indeed, in the United States itself, with only a few short-lived exceptions, peacetime law has prevailed.[15]

The one important source of support for the U.S. position that terrorism could amount to war is found in commentary to the 1949 Geneva Conventions. To promote wide application of the Conventions, a comment drafted in the

---

11 Mary Ellen O'Connell, *Ad Hoc War, supra* note 5, at 418-21. U.S. Ambassador John Bolton apparently changed his position from 2002 to 2003 when he argued that post-9/11 the United States and its allies could stop and search shipping on the high seas without consent of the ship's master or flag state pursuant to his "Proliferation Security Initiative." *See id.* Thereafter, the U.S. signed cooperation agreements with major flag states, including Panama and Honduras.

12 Harold Hongju Koh, Address at the Annual Meeting of the American Society of International Law: The Obama Administration and International Law (March 25, 2010).

13 For details on U.S. drone use, *see* Mary Ellen O'Connell, *Unlawful Killing with Combat Drones: A Case Study of Pakistan, 2004-2009, in* SHOOTING TO KILL, THE LAW GOVERNING LETHAL FORCE IN CONTEXT (Simon Bronitt ed., forthcoming), *available at* http://papers.ssrn.com/sol3/papers.cfm?abstract_id=1501144.

14 *Mumbai attacks: One year on*, 26 November 2009. Available at http://news.bbc.co.uk/2/hi/8379828.stm.

15 *See* Ronald Reagan, Letter of Transmittal, January 29, 1987 *reprinted in* 81 AM. J. INT'L L. 910, 911 (1987) (explaining that terrorists should be treated as criminals); Mary Ellen O'Connell, *Enhancing the Status of Non-State Actors Through a Global War on Terror*, 43 COLUM. J. TRANSNAT'L. L. 435 (2005).

1950s urges application of the Conventions in the event of *any* exchange by the militaries of states party to the Convention.[16] The International Committee of the Red Cross, the international organization that is the guardian of international humanitarian law, in particular, the Geneva Conventions, has continued to promote this position that low levels of violence or even non-violent exchanges may trigger the Conventions.[17] The comment is not a definition of war or armed conflict. It is an expression of a policy preference, which the ICRC has supported since 1949. The ICRC did not wish for states to quibble over definitions, but wished the protective provisions of the Conventions to be applied broadly.

By 2005, however, the international community could no longer muddle through without a widely recognized definition. The negative impacts of the extensive claims to wartime privileges by the U.S. in the absence of any obvious war were raising concerns around the world. The International Law Association as the leading scholarly organization devoted to the study of international law was the obvious organization to take up the question, "what is war?"

The International Law Association is described on its website as follows:

> The International Law Association was founded in Brussels in 1873. Its objectives, under its Constitution, are "the study, clarification and development of international law, both public and private, and the furtherance of international understanding and respect for international law". ...
>
> The activities of the ILA are organised by the Executive Council, assisted by the Headquarters Secretariat in London. Membership of the Association, at present about 3700, is spread among Branches throughout the world. The ILA welcomes as members all those interested in its objectives. Its membership ranges from lawyers in private practice, academia, government and the judiciary, to non-lawyer experts from commercial, industrial and financial spheres, and representatives of bodies such as shipping and arbitration organisations and chambers of service.
>
> The Association's objectives are pursued primarily through the work of its International Committees, and the focal point of its activities is the series of Biennial Conferences. The Conferences, of which 72 have so far been held in different locations throughout the world, provide a forum for the comprehensive discussion and endorsement of the work of the Committees.[18]

---

16   I *Commentary on the Geneva Conventions of 12 August 1949* at 32 (footnote omitted) (Jean Pictet ed., 1952).

17   *See* Goldman, *supra* note 2; ICRC Annual Report, *supra* note 2; Hintermann, *supra* note 2.

18   International Law Association, http://www.ila-hq.org/en/about_us/index. cfm.

In 2005, the ILA Executive Council tasked its Committee on the Use of Force with reporting on the definition of war in international law. The first document in this collection is the Executive Council's Mandate to the Committee. Mary Ellen O'Connell of the University of Notre Dame, USA, chaired the Committee and Judith Gardam of the University of Adelaide, Australia, was its rapporteur. By the time of the conclusion of the work, the Committee consisted of 18 members from 15 countries with widely recognized expertise in the areas of international law in general, the law of war, law on resort to war, and human rights. The Committee met informally several times and formally twice – in Berlin (2006) and at Notre Dame (2007) in preparation of an initial report delivered at the 2008 ILA Biennial meeting in Rio de Janeiro. The Initial Report is included in Part III of the book. Following the submission of the Initial Report, the Committee worked for two additional years with several new members toward a final report, also included in this book in Part III. The Committee presented its Final Report in The Hague at the 2010 ILA Biennial where it was adopted along with a resolution to seek wide dissemination and respect for the definition. The Resolution is also included in Part III.

The primary purpose of this book is to fulfill the ILA Resolution to seek recognition and respect for international law's definition. The book contains the background research papers prepared by the international lawyers of the Use of Force Committee for the Berlin meeting and by members of other, non-law disciplines for the meeting at Notre Dame. The background papers of this book have not been updated since first submitted to the editor. They are intended as a record of the drafting history of the ILA's Final Report on the Meaning of Armed Conflict in international law. Not all members of the Committee or all participants at the Notre Dame Conference could contribute to the book. Nevertheless, the papers here are the ones the Committee relied upon most extensively because it had the texts or formal comments that later became texts for this book. The contributor list and the list of Committee members included with each report demonstrate the extensive and inter-disciplinary approach the Committee took to researching the international community's definition of war. Excerpts from memos from the Committee's Chair, the editor of this collection, are also included throughout as statements of the Committee's methodology, working assumptions, and preliminary conclusions on the path to The Hague in 2010.

What became clear through all of this work is that the international community has a definition. It no longer uses the term "war" as the critical label but the broader term, "armed conflict." The situations that may be treated for purposes of international law as armed conflict is not a matter that a national leader may simply decide as a matter of his discretion. It is not a political question or a policy issue. It is a legal question of the greatest importance. Armed conflict is a situation that can be distinguished from peace where peacetime human rights and other law prevails. The Committee found that in international law armed conflict exists only when there is intense exchange of fighting by organ-

ized armed groups.[19] It is not the case that *every* engagement of armed forces
– no matter how minor – is an armed conflict. Nor is it the case that terrorist
attacks or other one-off attacks are armed conflict. Intense exchange of fighting
by organized armed groups is the minimum requirement of all armed conflicts
as the Report explains in detail. The Committee also found that international
law's definition of armed conflict is less stringent than that used by political
scientists and peace studies scholars where definitions range from a requirement of 1000 deaths per year to 25 deaths per year. These definitions often also
require that fighters have a certain purpose for the fighting – political change,
for example. These definitions stand in stark contrast to the ICRC position that
an armed conflict could exist even in the absence of any fighting.

While other disciplines do not share the definition found in international
law, considering how other disciplines define armed conflict encouraged the
members of the ILA Use of Force Committee to see the evidence relevant to
international law in a realistic light. The reality is that low-level exchanges of
the armed forces of sovereign states where no damage or deaths occur are not
armed conflict. International law's own central organizing principles of order
and protection for human rights equally guides scholars to the conclusion that
the privileges of armed conflict must be restricted to actual armed conflict and
the exigencies of the chaos and social breakdown created by actual intense and
organized armed fighting.

Most international lawyers will undoubtedly agree that clarifying the definition of armed conflict in international law was an important and useful effort.
They may believe that its most important use was during the years of the Bush
administration in Washington, 2001-2009, but in fact the idea that armed conflict privileges may be claimed outside of armed conflict has persisted in the
administration of President Bush's successor, Barack Obama. In fact, only a
small shift has been made from the Global War on Terror to the Global War
on al-Qaeda. According to U.S. State Department Legal Adviser Harold Koh:

> As recent events have shown, al-Qaeda has not abandoned its intent to attack
> the United States, and indeed continues to attack. Thus, in this ongoing armed
> conflict, the United States has the authority under international law, and the
> responsibility to its citizens, to use force, including lethal force, to defend
> itself, including by targeting persons such as high-level al-Qaeda leaders who
> are planning attacks.[20]

---

19   *See* International Law Association, Final Report of the Use of Force
     Committee, The Meaning of Armed Conflict in International Law
     (forthcoming, June 2010), *available at* http://www.ila-hq.org/en/committees/index.
     cfm/cid/1022 and Part III *infra*.

20   Koh, *supra* note 12.

Journalists and others continue to refer to the "war" on terrorism. For example, Peter Bergen, a reporter for CNN, published a book in 2010, titled, *The Longest War, Inside the Enduring Conflict between America and al-Qaeda*.

A clear definition of armed conflict is needed as much in 2011 as in 2001. In 2011, ten years after the 9/11 attacks, the U.S. may be the sole state advocating a *sui generis* definition of armed conflict. The editor of this volume hopes that its publication will persuade even the U.S. to join the world in its common understanding, an understanding that armed conflict is an exceptional situation – a rare occasion in which modifications of the human right to life and to a trial are justified.

Chapter 2

Proposal to Study the Meaning of War in International Law (May 2005)

ILA Committee on the Use of Force

Since at least the time of Hugo Grotius and his seminal work, THE LAW OF WAR AND PEACE (1625), international law has been organized around the existence of the two categories he refers to: war and peace. Of course there is no immutable, scientifically-definable line between these socially-constructed concepts, and, therefore, a perennial challenge for international law has been understanding what armed conflict is and determining when the rules relevant to armed conflict apply.[1] The challenge might have been somewhat less during the age of legal formalism when governments formally declared war, and, upon that declaration, the law relevant to war was triggered. But even then, the challenge remained where states were plainly engaged in warfare but did not declare it – or declared it where it was plainly not occurring.

With the adoption of the United Nations Charter, the law relevant to armed conflict[2] is triggered upon facts of fighting, not declarations. With this change the challenge has shifted away from the problem of declarations to the problem of understanding what facts amount to armed conflict. We have a number of examples of governments denying that fighting on their territory amounts to armed conflict, arguing instead it is criminal activity that the government has under control and that the rules of war are therefore not applicable. With the September 11 attacks on the United States, however, we have a reversal of that more common issue – now we have an example of a government declaring war where many would call it crime.

One explanation for these controversies is that international law does not today contain an accepted definition of armed conflict. A definition or understanding can be built from a number of legal sources,[3] but no widely-accepted

---

1   Nathaniel Berman, *Privileging Combat? Contemporary Conflict and the Legal Construction of War*, 43 Col. J. Trans. L. 1 (2004).

2   Also, with the adoption of the Charter, the term "armed conflict" was widely substituted for "war."

3   Mary Ellen O'Connell, What is War?, http://jurist.law.pitt.edu/forum/oconnell1.php.

Mary Ellen O'Connell (ed.), What Is War? An Investigation in the Wake of 9/11.
© 2012 *Koninklijke Brill NV. Printed in The Netherlands.* ISBN 978 9004 17234 0. *pp. 13 – 15.*

standard exists against which to measure government claims. We lack such an accepted definition despite the fact that so much in the law turns on the meaning of armed conflict. In particular, a state's right of response under the *jus ad bellum* is determined, in part, by whether it is confronting an armed conflict or a lesser provocation. The *jus in bello* is in its entirety triggered by the existence of an armed conflict. With the passage from peace to armed conflict, the right to life becomes circumscribed by the combatant's right to kill; in armed conflict the enemy may be detained without trial until the end of hostilities, but those of the enemy who fight according to the laws and customs of war, should arguably be treated as prisoners of war, not criminals. Many other rights, such free navigation on the high seas, free trade, and asylum rights may be circumscribed in armed conflict but not in peace. Treaty obligations may be terminated or suspended by armed conflict. The obligations of neutral states are determined by the existence of armed conflict.

The lack of a widely-accepted definition may not have been a serious impediment to the proper functioning of the law when the problem was under-inclusion of armed conflicts. When a government contended it was not involved in armed conflict, it had to comply with the laws of peace, including the full panoply of human rights protections. True, some who should have been declared POWs were labeled common criminals, but that inequity pales in comparison to the rights violations that occur when a government claims the rights and privileges of wartime in non-war situations. In wartime, government forces have "combatant immunity" to kill without warning. They may detain enemy forces until the end of the conflict without the requirement to provide a speedy and fair trial.

The United States and other states, for example Russia, have claimed combatant immunity to kill suspected terrorists anywhere and the right to detain suspects indefinitely. Under this view the US – or any other state – has the legal right to target and kill an Al Qaeda suspect on the streets of Hamburg, Germany, or any other peaceful place. While numerous governments have protested America's detention policies, few have protested the killing of six persons in Yemen in 2002 as an exercise of the "combatant's privilege." It is not clear whether there is an emerging pattern of state practice and if so whether it is having a modifying effect on the meaning of armed conflict and/or the rules relevant to armed conflict. Antonio Cassese, in a short article published soon after September 11, decried what was being done to the categories of international law in the name of fighting terrorism.[4] More recently Thomas Franck has written suggesting a new legal status for persons accused of terrorism – somewhere between the peacetime status of criminal and the wartime status of combatant.[5] Judith Gardam has long held that we need no war/peace distinction,

---

4   Antonio Cassese, *Terrorism is Also Disrupting Some Crucial Legal Categories of International Law*, 12 EJIL 993 (2001).

5   Thomas Franck, *Criminals, Combatants, or What? An Examination of the Roles of Law in Responding to the Threat of Terror*, 98 Am. J. Int'l L. 686 (2004).

but that all uses of violence be governed by the principles of necessity and proportionality.

The International Law Association created a study committee to produce a report on the meaning of war. The committee will consider the law as it existed on September 11, 2001 and consider changes that have possibly occurred since that date. The committee has four years to complete the study. It submitted its work plan in June at the ILA meeting in Toronto (5-9 June 2006). The Committee held a preliminary drafting session in Berlin in December 2006. It plans it primary drafting session for Notre Dame, Indiana in September 2007 and will submit its final report at the biennial meeting in Rio de Janerio in 2008.

Part II

Background Papers for the Study: International Law
(2006)

Chapter 3

International Law's Changing Terms:
"War" becomes "Armed Conflict"*

Elzbieta Mikos-Skuza

1. "War" and "Armed Conflict"

1.1 Different meanings of "war"

There are numerous meanings of the term "war" – from a flexible expression used as a **figure of speech** ("war of nerves") or an allusion to a **social campaign** ("war on narcotic drugs") to a "war" as a **legal term** having a special legal connotations.

As for a second meaning mentioned above (social campaigning with the use of the word "war"), it is noted that "the 'war on' pattern dates from the turn of the 20th century, when people adapted epidemiological metaphors to describe campaigns against social evils such as alcohol, crime and poverty – endemic conditions that could be mitigated but not eradicated".[1]

If one looks at the expressions used, one draws an easy parallel between the war on social phenomena like a crime and the "war on terror". The latter one suggests:

> "a campaign aimed not at human adversaries but at a pervasive social plague. At its most abstract, terror comes to seem as persistent and inexplicable as evil itself, without raising any inconvenient theological qualms. And in fact, the White House's use of 'evil' has declined by 80 percent over the same period that its use of 'terror' has been increasing.
>
> Like wars on ignorance and crime, a 'war on terror' suggests an enduring state of struggle – a 'never-ending fight against terror and its relentless

---

*   Editor's Note: A longer version of this Chapter is on file with the author and the editor. It includes a review of relevant Russian language literature.

1   G. Nunberg, *The war of words: 'terror' and 'terrorism'*, International Herald Tribune, 22 July 2004.

Mary Ellen O'Connell (ed.), What Is War? An Investigation in the Wake of 9/11.
© *2012 Koninklijke Brill NV. Printed in The Netherlands.* ISBN 978 9004 17234 0. pp. 19 – 29.

onslaughts', as Albert Camus put it in *The Plague*, his 1947 allegory of the rise and fall of Fascism."[2]

"It has been suggested that wars against proper nouns (e.g., Germany and Japan) have advantages over those against common nouns (e.g., crime, poverty, terrorism), since proper nouns can surrender and promise not to do it again."[3]

A lot of confusion relating to the "war on terror" results from the efforts aiming at investing a special legal meaning to an expression that otherwise would be considered a rhetorical flourish. Actually "war on terror" is not a "war" in the legal sense, but a series of armed conflicts of international or non-international character or of other types of situations.

1.2   *War as a legal term*

"War" as a legal term might have different meanings under national and international law. There are examples of **national laws** labeling "war" situations that do not amount even to a common understanding of war. For example, when martial law was introduced in Poland in 1981 to prevent the "Solidarity" workers' movement from overthrowing the communist regime, the regime officially proclaimed a "state of war."[4] This qualification was based on the Polish Constitution in force at that time that in the case of a "state of war" authorities had the power to undertake more drastic steps against the population than those that were allowed in case of a "state of emergency." State of emergency would have been more appropriate from the point of view of an internal situation with demonstrations, social unrest and tensions, but without armed force being used either before or after the proclamation. Fatalities occurred after the proclamation resulting from the use of firearms by police, and not military, forces.

Under public international law there is no binding definition of war contained, for instance, in a multilateral convention in force or in another document of legal value. Instead, there are definitions drafted by scholars and judges of various nations.[5]

---

2   *Idem.*

3   G. Rona, *Interesting Times for International Humanitarian Law: Challenges from the "War on Terror"*, The Fletcher Forum of World Affairs, vol. 27:2, Summer/Fall 2003, p. 60.

4   In Polish: "stan wojenny".

5   In Russian language Soviet era books "war" and "armed conflict" are considered to be synonymous with some preference for the term "armed conflicts" due to the outlawing of 'war' in the UN Charter, e.g. textbooks: I. N. Arcibasov, V. A. Egorov, *Vooruzonnyj konflikt: pravo, politika, diplomatia (Armed Conflict: Law, Politics,*

1.3   Definitions drafted by scholars

End of the XIXth and beginning of the XXth centuries:

K. von Clausewitz: "War is a struggle of an extensive scale designed by one party to compel its opponent to fulfil its will".[6] It was developed in a case *Driefontain Consolidated Gold Mines v Janson:* "When differences between States reach a point at which both parties resort to force, or one of them does acts of violence, which the other chooses to look upon as a breach of the peace, the relation of war is set up, in which the combatants may use regulated violence against each other, until one of the two has been brought to accept such terms as his enemy is willing to grant."[7]

Middle and end of the XXth century:

I.A.Shearer: "There must now be distinguished:

1. A war proper between states.
2. Armed conflicts or breaches of the peace, which are not of the character of war, and which are not necessarily confined to hostilities involving states only, but may include a struggle in which non-state entities participate.

It is significant that coincidentally with the development of the second category (...) the nature of war itself has become more distinctly clarified as a formal status of armed hostility, in which the intention of the parties, the so-called animus belligerendi, may be a decisive factor. This is consistent with Clausewitz's view that war is not merely of itself a political act, but serves as a real political instrument for the achievement of certain ends. Thus a state of war may be established between two or more states by a formal declaration of war, although active hostilities may never take place between them. (...) Moreover, the cessation of armed hostilities does not, according to modern practice, necessarily terminate a state of war."[8]

L. Oppenheim: "War is a contention between two or more States through their armed forces, for the purpose of overpowering each other and imposing such conditions of peace as the victor pleases."[9]

Diplomacy), Moskva, 1989, p. 19; N.T. Blatova, *Mezdunarodnoe pravo (International Law)*, Moskva 1987, p. 477; F.I.Kozevnikov, *Mezdunarodnoe pravo (International Law)*, Moskva 1987, p. 528; A. I. Poltorak, A. I. Savinskij, *Vooruzonnye konflikty i mezdunarodnoe pravo (Armed Conflicts and International Law)*, Moskva 1976, p. 79; *Slovar mezdunarodnogo prava (Dictionary of International Law)* Moskva 1982, pp. 23 – 25; G. I. Tunkin (ed.), *Mezdunarodnoe pravo (International Law)*, Moskva 1982, chapter 22.

6   Quoted after I.A.Shearer, *Starke's International Law*, Butterworths, 11th Edition, 1994, p. 478.

7   *Idem.*

8   *Ibidem*, p. 480.

9   L. Oppenheim, *International Law* – H. Lauterpacht ed., 7th ed., 1952, p. 202.

Y. Dinstein, analyzing this definition in detail, points out that "One element seems common to all definitions of war.... War is a contest between states. Some qualifying words should nevertheless be appended. International law recognizes two disparate types of war: inter-State wars (waged between two or more States) and intra-State wars (civil wars conducted between two or more parties within a single State).... Many of the rules applicable to and in an intra-State strife are fundamentally different from those relating to an inter-State war. Hence, Oppenheim was entirely right in excluding civil wars from his definition". [10]

Dinstein's definition reads as follows: "War is a hostile interaction between two or more States, either in a technical or in a material sense. War in the technical sense is a formal status produced by a declaration of war. War in the material sense is generated by actual use of armed force, which must be comprehensive on the part of at least one party to the conflict". [11] He also accepts the existence of a "status mixtus" – a state of 'intermediacy' between war and peace.

Ch. Greenwood: "At one time ... 'war' ... was a formal legal concept which only came into being when there was a declaration of war or some other indication by one of the parties to a conflict that it regarded itself as being at war with its adversary; there could be war without actual fighting and fighting without war. Determining whether a conflict constituted a war, in this sense, was therefore never easy; contrary to popular belief, most conflicts did not start with a declaration of war even in the eighteenth and nineteenth centuries (in a footnote: out of 117 conflicts between 1700 and 1870, only ten had begun with a declaration of war)..... Since 1945, declarations of war have been almost unknown with most States engaged in hostilities denying that they were at war. Since the duty to treat prisoners or civilians in a humane fashion should not depend upon such formalities, in 1949 Article 2 of the Geneva Conventions provided that the Conventions should apply to any armed conflict between states parties, even if a state of war was not recognized by one of them. Thus, servicemen captured in a conflict in which both sides denied that they were at war ... were nevertheless prisoners of war". [12]

Nowadays, one should disagree with definitions attaching any importance to a declaration of war. Such a declaration would not be valid, if one takes into consideration the UN Charter and the *ius cogens* concept. The Hague Convention III of 1907, relative to the Opening of Hostilities, should be considered as void and terminated under a customary rule codified in Art. 64 of the Vienna Convention on the Law of Treaties.

---

10   Y. Dinstein, *War, Aggression and Self-Defence,* 3rd edition, Cambridge 2002, p. 5.

11   *Ibidem*, p. 15.

12   Ch. Greenwood, *The Law of War (International Humanitarian Law)* (in:) M.D.Evans (editor), *International Law*, 1st Edition, Oxford, 2003, pp. 791-792.

1.4   International practice

In the period preceding World War II, there were **international hostilities** taking place that were not deemed to be **of the nature of** war, but of **non-war armed conflicts**, e.g.:
a)   Sino-Japanese hostilities in Manchuria, 1931-1932;
b)   Russo-Japanese hostilities at Changkufeng in 1938;
c)   Armed operations involving Outer Mongolian and Inner Mongolian forces at Nomonhan in 1939.[13]

In the period after World War II most of the conflicts were not called wars but **armed conflicts**. A good example is provided by the comment by the British Lord Privy Seal of 1 November 1956 with regard to the Suez Canal zone hostilities: "Her Majesty's Government do not regard their present action as constituting war.... There is no state of war, but there is a state of conflict".[14]

There is one example of a conflict called "war", namely the Vietnam conflict, particularly after early stages and the struggle escalated from about 1965 onwards. The Paris Agreement of 27 January 1973 concluded for the purpose of terminating the conflict, bore the title "Agreement on Ending the War and Restoring Peace in Vietnam".

1.5   Development "from war to armed conflict" in international documents

This development was clearly visible in the following documents:
a)   **United Nations Charter** – replacement of Art. 16 of the Covenant of the League of Nations referring to a "recourse to war" by a Covenant–breaking state by Art. 39 of the Charter referring to "threat to the peace, breach of the peace, or act of aggression" by a Charter-breaking state.
b)   **Four Geneva Conventions of 1949** use both the terms "war" and "armed conflict" indicating that "armed conflict" comprises "war", but is of a broader scope: common Article 2 provides that "...the Convention shall apply to all cases of declared war or of any other armed conflict which may arise between two or more of the High Contracting Parties, even if the state of war is not recognized by one of them." The Fourth Geneva Convention relates "to the Protection of Civilian Persons in Time of War", but the section on the status of aliens (Arts. 35-46) relates to "Aliens in the Territory of a Party to the Conflict"...
c)   First document that in a consistent way uses the phrase "armed conflict" only and exclusively – from its title and preamble through its final provi-

---

13   Examples after I.A.Shearer, *op.cit.*, p. 478.
14   Quoted after I.A.Shearer, *op.cit.*, p. 478.

sions – is **The Hague Convention of 14 May 1954 for the Protection of Cultural Property in the Event of Armed Conflict.**

d)   Consolidation of this terminology in the two Protocols Additional of 1977, the Certain Conventional Weapons Convention of 1980 and its Protocols, Ottawa Convention of 1997, ICC Statute of 1998 as well as in treaties regulating other branches of international law, like the Vienna Convention on Diplomatic Relations of 1961, Art. 44 and 45.

This shift in terminology might be explained by the content of the UN Charter – not only its Art. 39, but above all Art. 2, paragraphs 3 and 4 that prohibit the resort to force by states in their international relations. An example of the impact of the Charter on thinking was seen in 1949 by the **International Law Commission** when the ILC was drafting a program of its work:

> "18. The Commission considered whether the laws of war should be selected as a topic for codification. It was suggested that, war having been outlawed, the regulation of its conduct had ceased to be relevant. On the other hand, the opinion was expressed that, although the term "laws of war" ought to be discarded, a study of the rules governing the use of armed force – legitimate or illegitimate – might be useful.... The majority of the Commission ... considered that if the Commission, at the very beginning of its work, were to undertake this study, public opinion might interpret its action as showing lack of confidence in the efficiency of the means at the disposal of the United Nations for maintaining peace".[15]

Other arguments raised with relation to the replacement of the term "war" by "armed conflict" refer to efforts to localize conflicts and prevent them attaining the dimension of a general war as well as to some problems generated by a formal status of neutrality that is possible only in a case of a formal status of war.[16]

Finally, the ICRC Commentary to the First Geneva Convention of 1949 contains this: "The substitution of this much more general expression ("armed conflict") for the word "war" was deliberate. One may argue almost endlessly about the legal definition of "war". A State can always pretend, when it commits a hostile act against another State, that it is not making war, but merely engaging in a police action, or acting in legitimate self-defense. The expression "armed conflict" makes such arguments less easy. Any difference arising between two States and leading to the intervention of armed forces is an armed conflict ... even if one of the Parties denies the existence of a state of war".[17]

---

15   *Yearbook of the International Law Commission*, 1949, p. 281.

16   I.A.Shearer, *op.cit.*, p. 479 – 480.

17   J.S.Pictet, *Commentary to the First Geneva Convention for the Amelioration of the Condition of the Wounded and Sick in Armed Forces in the Field*, ICRC, Geneva, 1952, p. 32.

The evolution of terminology presented above related to the use of force in inter-state relations. The terms for "civil war" – force between two or more parties within a single State were found in common language but not in legal terminology. Civil war was not regulated until 1949. Actually the inclusion of common Article 3 to the four Geneva Conventions of 1949 was one of the reasons for preferring the term "armed conflicts" to "war." Article 3 starts with the phrase: "In the case of armed conflict not of an international character occurring in the territory of one of the High Contracting Parties, each Party to the conflict shall be bound to apply....". There are two additional references to the notion of "the Parties to the conflict".

Hence, in legal terms, hostilities within the boundaries of one state were called "armed conflict" – "armed conflict not of an international character" (common Article 3 to the four Geneva Conventions of 1949, Article 19 of The Hague Convention of 1954 for the Protection of Cultural Property in the Event of Armed Conflict, Article 22 of the 1999 Second Protocol to the Hague Convention of 1954) or "non-international armed conflicts", with the adoption in 1977 of the Protocol Additional II to the Geneva Conventions of 1949.

2.   Non-international armed conflicts

There are three factual situations of violence enumerated under international law to which the following legal regimes apply:
–   international armed conflicts – both national and international law applies, including the whole body of international humanitarian law and international human rights law ("hard core" provisions and other rules that have not been derogated from);[18]
–   non-international armed conflicts – basically same legal regimes apply, but international humanitarian law to a much more limited extent than in case of international armed conflicts;
–   internal disturbances and tensions – national (including criminal) laws and international human rights law regulations apply; international humanitarian law does not apply to such situations.

2.1   *Threshold – internal disturbances and tensions and a non-international armed conflict*

Article 1(2) of Additional Protocol II of 1977 to the Geneva Conventions of 1949 clearly states that it "shall not apply to situations of internal disturbances and

---

18   As for the applicability of human rights law, the case-law of ICJ is of particular importance – Advisory Opinion of 8 July 1996 on the *Legality of the Threat or Use of Nuclear Weapons*, para. 24 and the Advisory Opinion of 9 July 2004 on the *Legal Consequences of the Construction of Wall in the Occupied Palestinian Territory*, paras. 102 – 113, 127 – 130.

tensions, such as riots, isolated and sporadic acts of violence and other acts of a similar nature, as not being armed conflicts".

The notions of internal disturbances and tensions have been defined by the International Committee of the Red Cross in its Commentary to Article 1(2) of Additional Protocol II:

> "**Internal disturbances** ... involve situations in which there is no non-international armed conflict as such, but there exists a confrontation within the country, which is characterized by a certain seriousness or duration and which involves acts of violence. These latter can assume various forms, all the way from spontaneous generation of acts of revolt to the struggle between more or less organized groups and the authorities in power. In these situations, which do not necessarily degenerate into open struggle, the authorities in power call upon extensive police forces, or even armed forces, to restore internal order. The huge number of victims has made necessary the application of a minimum of humanitarian rules. As regards **internal tensions**, these could be said to include in particular situations of serious tension (political, religious, racial, social, economic, etc.), but also the sequels of armed conflict or of internal disturbances. Such situations have one or more of the following characteristics, if not all at the same time:
> — large scale arrests;
> — a large number of "political" prisoners;
> — the probable existence of ill-treatment or inhumane conditions of detention;
> — the suspension of fundamental judicial guarantees, either as part of the promulgation of a state of emergency or simply as a matter of fact;
> — allegations of disappearances."[19]

As for the non-international armed conflict's perspective on the threshold, Article 3 common to the four Geneva Conventions of 1949 does not offer a clear definition on the notion of non-international armed conflict (... in the case of armed conflict not of an international character occurring on the territory of one of the High Contracting Parties...). Article 1 of Protocol Additional II of 1977 to the four Geneva Conventions of 1949 does offer a definition of non-international armed conflict, but only for the purpose of this Protocol – "armed conflicts which take place in the territory of a High Contracting Party between its armed forces and dissident armed forces or other organized armed groups which, under responsible command, exercise such control over a part of its territory as to enable them to carry out sustained and concerted military operations and to implement this Protocol". As mentioned earlier, this definition does not cover situations of internal disturbances and tensions.

---

19   Paras. 4475-4476.

As noted by M. Sassòli and A. Bouvier "this fairly restrictive definition applies only to Protocol II. The definition does not apply to Article 3 .... Practically, there are thus situations of non-international armed conflicts in which only Article 3 will apply, the level of organization of dissident groups being insufficient for Protocol II to apply."[20]

The ICC Statute provides an intermediary threshold of application in Article 8(2)(f). There is no longer a requirement for the conflict to take place between governmental forces and rebel forces, for the latter to control part of the territory, nor for them to be a responsible command. The conflict must however be protracted and the armed groups must be organized, which is a clear allusion to the Tadić definition of an armed conflict: "An armed conflict exists whenever there is resort to armed force between States or protracted armed violence between governmental authorities and organized armed groups or between such groups within a State".[21]

The Tadić definition was repeated by, among others, the International Commission of Inquiry on Darfur that noticed that "Modern international humanitarian law does not legally set out the notion of armed conflict. Additional Protocol II only gives a negative definition which, in addition, seems to narrow the scope of Article 3 common to the Geneva Conventions". It deducted *a contrario* from Article 2 common to the Geneva Conventions that "a non-nternational armed conflict is a conflict without the involvement of two states."[22]

2.2   *Threshold – a non-international armed conflict and an international armed conflict*

This issue is dealt with by other members of the ILA Study Committee.

2.3   *Difference between legal regimes for non-international and for international armed conflicts*

From a humanitarian point of view there is no difference between victims of international and non-international armed conflicts, therefore, the same rules should protect them and to ensure to them the right to assistance. However, States have never accepted that both categories of conflicts could be treated equally. It would be incompatible with the very concept of contemporary international society made up of sovereign States. "No State is ready to accept that

---

20   M. Sassòli, A. Bouvier, *How Does Law Protect in War?*, Vol. I, ICRC, Geneva, 2006, p. 110.

21   ICTY, The Prosecutor v. Dusko Tadić, Appeals Chamber, Decision of 2 October 1995, para. 70.

22   *Report of the International Commission of Inquiry on Darfur to the United Nations Secretary-General*, Geneva 25 January 2005, para. 74.

its citizens would wage a war against their own government. In other words no government would in advance renounce to punish its own citizens for their participation in the rebellion. Such a renunciation, however, is the essence of the combatant status as prescribed by the law of international armed conflicts."[23]

It means that the basic, insurmountable (for the time being) difference between the regime of international and non-international armed conflicts is the existence or lack of the "combatant status" and, consequently, the existence or lack of the "protected person status", like the prisoner of war status.

As for other issues, during the last decade the regulations relating to non-international armed conflicts are drawing closer to the regulations on international armed conflicts. The evidence could be found in:
–   recent treaties on weapons and on cultural property:
    a)   Protocol II to the Convention on Certain Conventional Weapons of 1980, as amended in 1996 (in order to, among others, extend it to non-international armed conflicts);
    b)   2001 Amendment to Article 1 of the Convention on Certain Conventional Weapons of 1980, in Order to Extend it to Non-International Armed Conflicts;
    c)   Ottawa Convention on Landmines of 1997;
    d)   1999 Second Protocol to the Hague Convention of 1954 for the Protection of Cultural Property in the Event of Armed Conflict.
–   war crimes defined in the Statute of the International Criminal Court, especially if one compares Article 8 (2) (a) and (b) with Article 8 (2) (c) and (e);
–   case-law of the International Criminal Tribunals for the former Yugoslavia and Rwanda, e.g. ICTY, The Prosecutor v. Dusko Tadić, Jurisdiction, Appeals Chamber, 2 October 1995, paras. 96-136, relating to customary rules of international humanitarian law governing internal armed conflicts as well as to individual criminal responsibility in internal armed conflicts;
–   reports by fact-finding missions, e.g. Report of the International Commission of Inquiry on Darfur to the United Nations Secretary General of 25 January 2005, paras. 154-167;
–   2005 study on customary international humanitarian law that identifies 161 customary rules of international humanitarian law. Of the 161 rules identified, 159 apply in international armed conflicts and 149 apply in non-international armed conflicts. As for the latter category, two rules apply in non-international armed conflicts only and exclusively which means that 147 apply in both categories of conflicts. They are catalogued in six chapters: principle of distinction, methods of warfare, weapons, specific protections, treatment of persons, accountability and implementation.[24]

---

23   M. Sassòli, A. Bouvier, *op. cit.*, p.250.
24   J.M. Henckaerts, L. Doswald-Beck, *Customary International Humanitarian Law*, Vol. I & II, Cambridge, 2005.

2.4 Different types of non-international armed conflicts

The category of non-international armed conflicts is not a uniform one – there are different types of such conflicts:

a) Conflicts to which common Article 3 is applicable, like in Nicaragua[25] or Rwanda;[26]

b) Conflicts covered by common Article 3 and Article 8 (2) (e) of the ICC Statute;

c) Conflicts to which, in addition, Protocol II of 1977 is applicable, like in Chechnya in the mid-1990s, in accordance with the Judgement of the Constitutional Court of the Russian Federation of 31 July 1995;[27]

d) Conflicts to which international humanitarian law as a whole is applicable following:

  – recognition of belligerency by the government, like in Colombia in accordance with the Ruling of the Constitutional Court of 1995;[28]

  – special agreements among the Parties, like special agreements in the former Yugoslavia of 1991 and 1992 concluded between representatives of Bosnia-Herzegovina and Bosnian Croats and Serbs.[29]

There might be also **problems of qualification** in case of internationalized internal armed conflicts, conflicts of secession or foreign intervention not directed against governmental forces.

To conclude

– The old concept of "war" has been abandoned and replaced by a concept of "international armed conflicts";

– Activities referred to as the "war on terror" in political rhetoric are not to be considered as a "war" in the legal sense, but as a series of armed conflicts of international or non-international character or of other types of situations;

– There is no universally adopted definition of non-international armed conflicts;

– The law of non-international armed conflicts should be applied to any conflict of certain intensity and duration where military operations are conducted;

– The law of non-international armed conflicts is not limited to treaty law.

---

25   ICJ Nicaragua v. USA , *Military and Paramilitary Activities in and against Nicaragua,* Merits, Judgement of 27 June 1986, para. 219.

26   ICTR, The Prosecutor v. Jean-Paul Akakyesu, Judgement of 1998, pras. 619 – 621.

27   *Rossijskaja Gazeta,* 11 August 1995, p. 3.

28   M. Sassòli, A. Bouvier, *op. cit.,* vol. II, pp. 2266 – 2281, paras. 14 – 15 at pp. 2269 – 2271.

29   *Ibidem,* pp. 1761 – 1769.

Chapter 4

The Meaning of Armed Conflict and the *Jus ad Bellum*

Jutta Brunnée

At the center of the legal framework governing the use of force under the UN Charter is a sweeping prohibition of threat or use of inter-state force (Article 2(4)). This prohibition must be understood against the background of two devastating world wars and the Charter's ambition to protect succeeding generations from the scourge of war (Preamble). As is well-known, under the Charter individual states may resort to military force only in self-defense. In all other cases, recourse to military means is legal only if authorized by the UN Security Council pursuant to Chapter VII of the UN Charter.

This background paper is concerned with the triggers of a state's *jus ad bellum*,[1] the geographical scope of that right, and its duration. For the purposes of this text, it is assumed that the trigger, geographical scope and termination of UN authorized military action under Chapter VII are determined by relevant Security Council resolution(s). With respect to "humanitarian intervention," it is assumed that no *jus ad bellum* for individual states currently exists at international law. Any protective intervention would have to be authorized by the Security Council under Chapter VII, with the abovementioned consequences for trigger, geographical scope and duration. Therefore, this paper focuses only on unilateral resort to force in pursuit of the right to self-defense. It approaches the topic by considering several inter-related concepts that must be carefully distinguished.

1.   Intervention

International law prohibits intervention in the affairs of a sovereign state. Illegal intervention can take a number of forms and, in extreme cases, can involve mili-

---

[1]   The *jus ad bellum* is "the law governing the initial resort to force between two states". See Eritrea Ethiopia Claims Commission, Partial Award, *Jus Ad Bellum*, Ethiopia's Claims 1-8 (December 19, 2005), footnote 1. And see, generally, Robert Kolb, "Origin of the Twin Terms of *Jus ad Bellum* and *Jus in Bello*," (1997) 320 *International Review of the Red Cross* 553.

Mary Ellen O'Connell (ed.), What Is War? An Investigation in the Wake of 9/11.
© 2012 Koninklijke Brill NV. Printed in The Netherlands. ISBN 978 9004 17234 0. pp. 31 – 50.

tary intervention. It is important to bear in mind that, for present purposes, intervention constitutes an umbrella term. Specifically, even where a given military action does not constitute an "armed attack" (see below) that would entitle a state to take self-defense measures, and even in cases in which a *de minimus* military action may not violate Article 2(4), it may still amount to illegal intervention in the affairs of a state. The victim of that intervention would be entitled to invoke the responsibility of the intervening state and demand cessation, reparation, etc., and may be entitled to take countermeasures (short of military measures).

2.   Use of Force

Article 2(4) prohibits the threat or use of force between states. Today, it is generally accepted that "force" for the purposes of Article 2(4) means military force. Other coercive actions by one state against another (e.g. economic or political pressure) may violate the non-intervention principle but do not constitute force within the meaning of Article 2(4).[2] The reference to "territorial integrity or political independence" of states in Article 2(4) was intended by the drafters to strengthen the prohibition, rather than allow for the subsequently made argument that use of force does not violate the provision unless it is aimed at undermining these two aspects of sovereignty.[3]

Article 2(4) is violated where pressure is exerted through a threat of military force (including, potentially, a declaration of war),[4] so long as the threatened force is not *de minimus* or would be justified as self-defense. Such a threat would trigger the law of state responsibility and may entitle the victim state to resort to countermeasures (again short of military action). Only an illegal use of force that constitutes an "armed attack" (see below) entitles the victim to take military action in self-defense.

In the Charter scheme, all uses of force are prohibited unless explicitly permitted by the Charter.[5] However, it appears that military action must rise to a certain threshold to transgress Article 2(4), and that *de minimus* actions do not violate the provision. O'Connell observes that "numerous examples of states using armed force can be found that are not treated as violations of Article 2(4)" (providing example of "Red Crusader" incident between UK and Denmark; see also *Corfu Channel* case).[6]

---

2   Yoram Dinstein, *War, Aggression and Self-Defence*, 4th ed. (Cambridge: Cambridge University Press, 2005) at 86.

3   Thomas Franck, *Recourse to Force, Action Against Threats and Armed Attacks* (Oxford: Oxford University Press, 2002) at 12; Dinstein, *ibid*, at 87.

4   Christopher Greenwood, "The Concept of War in Modern International Law," (1987) 36 *ICLQ* 283 at 302.

5   Dinstein, *supra*, note 2, at 87.

6   Mary Ellen O'Connell, *International Law and the Use of Force, Cases and Materials* (Foundation Press, 2005) at 14.

3.   Armed Attack

Whereas Article 2(4) bars member states from the "threat or use of force" against other states, Article 51 of the UN Charter, which outlines states' right to self-defense, makes reference to the occurrence of an "armed attack" against a member state. Four major issues are raised by these differences in terminology.

a.   Attacks by Non-State Actors

First, whereas Article 2(4) clearly prohibits only inter-state use of force, Article 51 appears to cast the notion of armed attack more widely, suggesting that the concept encompasses attacks by non-state actors.[7] After the massive terrorist attacks of September 11, 2001, there appears to be growing acceptance of the wider understanding of "armed attack" for purposes of Article 51.[8] Indeed, if one evaluates the nature of the relationship between the Taliban regime in Afghanistan and Al-Qaeda as *not* sufficiently close to deem the 9/11 attacks an armed attack by Afghanistan (as many observers would), then the international response to the self-defense justification offered by the United States and the United Kingdom for military action in Afghanistan suggests that the broader concept of armed attack has taken hold in international law.[9] For some observers, this broader concept has always been part of the law of self-defense. For example, the facts in the *Caroline* case did not revolve around actions by the United States against British interests, but by non-state actors operating from US territory.[10] Nonetheless, the International Court of Justice (ICJ), in recent decisions, could be read as asserting that Article 51 is concerned with only

---

7   See e.g. Nico Schrijver, "Responding to International Terrorism: Moving the Frontiers of International Law for 'Enduring Freedom'?" (2001) XLVIII *Netherlands Int'l L. R.* 271, at 284-285.

8   See e.g. Elizabeth Wilmshurst, "The Chatham House Principles of International Law on the Use of Force in Self-Defence," (2006) 55 *ICLQ* 963, at 969-971.

9   For a detailed evaluation of state reactions and academic commentary, see Tal Becker, *Terrorism and the State: Rethinking the Rules of State Responsibility* (Oxford: Hart Publishing, 2006) 211-238 (suggesting the wider concept has gained acceptance). But see also André Nollkaemper, "Attribution of Forcible Acts to States: Connections Between the Law on the Use of Force and the Law of State Responsibility," in N. Blokker and N. Schrijver, eds., *The Security Council and the Use of Force: Theory and Reality – A Need for Change?* (Leiden: Martinus Nijhoff Publishers, 2005) 133, at 168-171 (questioning that conclusion).

10   See e.g. discussion in Sean Murphy, "Terrorism and the Concept of "Armed Attack" in Article 51 of the U.N. Charter" (2002) 43 *Harvard Int'l L. J.* 41, at 50; Christopher Greenwood, "War, Terrorism, and International Law," (2003) 56 *Current Legal Problems* 505, at 517.

inter-state force,[11] a view that is shared by a number of commentators.[12] Others appear to take a middle position, suggesting that self-defense measures can be taken against attacks by non-state actors so long as this can be done without violating the territorial sovereignty of another state (e.g. on the High Seas or with the consent of a state in which the attackers are found).[13] In all other cases, however, there must be a sufficient link between the attacks and the state that is to be subject to self-defense measures within its territory, let alone against it.[14]

b.   *Relationship between States and Non-State Actors*

Second, assuming that even after 9/11 only an armed attack by another state triggers the right to self-defense, or assuming that a given attack by non-state actors is in fact in some way connected to a state, what must be the nature of the relationship to justify either deeming the state's involvement to amount to an armed attack, or to be able to impute the non-state actors' attack to the state? The approach of the ICJ has been to require substantial involvement by the state; the standard set out by the International Criminal Tribunal for the Former Yugoslavia in *Tadić* was somewhat wider.[15] Either way, under a substantial involvement standard, logistical or financial support, or "harbouring" of terrorists or other armed bands, would not rise to the level of an armed attack

---

11   Advisory Opinion on the *Legal Consequences of the Construction of a Wall in the Occupied Palestinian Territory*, ICJ Reports 2004, paras. 138-139. But see e.g. Declaration of Judge Buergenthal, para. 6. See also the Separate Opinion of Judge Higgins, para. 33; and the Separate Opinion of Judge Kooijmans, para. 35. See also *Case Concerning Armed Activities on the Territory of the Congo (Democratic Republic of the Congo v. Uganda)* (19 December 2005), paras. 146-147. However, as in the *Wall* case, some of the judges disagreed with the Court's holding on this issue. See Separate Opinions by Judge Kooijmans, paras. 26, 28; and Separate Opinion of Judge Simma, para.12. For a discussion, see Christine Gray, "The Bush Doctrine Revisited: The 2006 National Security Strategy of the USA," (2006) 5 *Chinese Journal of International Law* 555, at 570-572.

12   See Christine Gray, *International Law and the Use of* Force, 2d ed. (Oxford: Oxford University Press, 2004) at 109-110 (observing that "the Court's description of the scope of armed attack is consistent with state practice and with the practice of the Security Council"); Eric P.J. Myjer & Nigel D. White, "The Twin Towers Attack: An Unlimited Right to Self-Defence?" (2002) 7 *J. Conflict & Security L.* 5.

13   See, e.g., Waldron Davis, "The Phantom of the Neo-Global Era: International Law and the Implications of Non-State Terrorism on the Nexus of Self-Defense and the Use of Force", in Russell Miller and Rebecca Bratsies (eds), *Progress in International Law* (Leiden: Martinus Nijhoff Publishers, 2008), at 637, n. 19.

14   See e.g. Mary Ellen O'Connell, "Lawful Self-Defense to Terrorism," (2002) 63 *U. Pitt. L. Rev.* 889, at 899.

15   See Case No IT-94-1-A *Prosecutor v Tadić*, reprinted in (1999) 38 ILM 1518.

by the state in question.[16] However, after 9/11, the view appears to be gaining ground that such lesser forms of involvement may put a state in the cross-hairs of a military response, so long as it can be justified as a necessary and proportional exercise of the right to self-defense.[17] It has been suggested that a crucial factor in such circumstances will be whether the defending state is acting against the target state, or merely within its territory.[18]

A closer assessment of the manner in which the legal relationship between the non-state actor and the state is constructed may also be helpful. It would appear that two broad approaches are being employed. The ICJ and a significant number of commentators treat the "relationship" issue as a matter of the primary rule set out in Article 51. In other words, the question for this mode of analysis is (as set out above) whether or not the state's involvement suffices to meet the "armed attack" threshold (note that this also appears to be the analytical approach that underlies the UN General Assembly *Definition of Aggression*),[19] and whether use of force against a state is necessary and proportional to defend against a non-state actor attack. By contrast, a significant number of commentators treat the issue as a matter of secondary rules. This approach becomes particularly important when one assumes that the attack itself, for purposes of Article 51, can be one perpetrated by non-state actors. In that scenario, the next question is whether, in keeping with the rules of the law of state responsibility, the attack can be imputed to a state. Arguably, lower-level assistance or harboring situations are problematic for this approach, as they do not rise to the imputation threshold set out in the Draft Articles on the Law of State Responsibility.[20]

Suffice it for now to simply highlight these difficult questions. It is premature to explore them further, as the conclusion may well be that no such shift in the law has occurred in the first place. Still, the questions are crucial, precisely because the *jus ad bellum* is affected – the question when one state can validly assert a (unilateral) right to take military action against (or in) another state. Here lies one of the dilemmas – it is all very well to say the statist outlook of the rules on the use of force is ill-suited to the threats posed by global terrorist networks. But how to adequately deal with the fact that, in most cases, military measures against terrorists will involve attacks on or within another state?

Be it in the context of a wider notion of armed attack or attribution of armed attack, or in situations were terrorists are simply found in the territory of a given state, the issues of necessity and proportionality of a military response

---

16 See e.g. Gray, *supra*, note 12 at 165.

17 See e.g. Nollkaemper, *supra*, note 9, at 136; Wilmshurst, *supra*, note 8, at 970.

18 See Kimberley N Trapp, "Back to Basics: Necessity, Proportionality, and the Right to Self-Defence Against Non-State Terrorist Actors," (2007) 56 *ICLQ* 141.

19 See Nollkaemper, *ibid*, at 145-148. Becker *supra*, note 9, at 176-182.

20 An excellent discussion of these questions is provided by Becker, *ibid.*, Chs. 5 and 6.

will of course be crucial.²¹ Whether or not military action in or against another state is necessary and proportional will depend on the degree of involvement of that state in the attack (if any), its responsiveness to diplomatic steps or non-military pressure, and the urgency of self-defence action.²²

c. Gravity

Third, it is widely held that not all illegal recourse to force necessarily amounts to an armed attack. The dominant opinion remains that only when an attack involves military force of some gravity does it amount to an "armed attack" in the sense of Article 51. In the *Nicaragua* case, the International Court of Justice (ICJ) stressed the need to "distinguish the most grave forms of the use of force (those constituting an armed attack) from other less grave forms."²³ In commenting on the activities of certain irregular forces, the ICJ went on to observe that the central question was whether or not the operation, "because of its scale and effects, would have been classified as an armed attack rather than as a mere frontier incident had it been carried out by regular armed forces."²⁴ More recently, the Ethiopia-Eritrea Claims Commission concluded, with respect to the operations of regular forces, that "[l]ocalized border encounters between small infantry units, even those involving loss of life, do not constitute an armed attack for the purposes of the Charter."²⁵ One legal implication of this approach is that the victim of an illegal use of force that does not rise to the level of an armed attack is limited to responding by non-forcible countermeasures. In other words, the view that the right to self-defense is triggered only by an armed

---

21   See e.g. G. Travalio and J. Altenburg, "State Responsibility for Sponsorship of Terrorist and Insurgent Groups: Terrorism, State Responsibility and the Use of Military Force," (2003) 4 *Chicago J Int'l L* 97.

22   See Tarcisio Gazzini, *The Changing Rules on the Use of Force in International Law* (Manchester: Manchester University Press, 2005), at 193-197. And see examples of state practice in Trapp, *supra*, note 18, especially at 146 et seq.

23   Military and Paramilitary Activities In and Against Nicaragua (Nicaragua v. U.S.), [1986] ICJ Rep 14, at para. 191 [hereinafter *Nicaragua*]; and *Case Concerning Oil Platforms (Islamic Republic of Iran v. United States of America)* [2003] ICJ Rep, para. 51 [hereinafter *Oil Platforms*]. See also Dominic Raab, "'Armed Attack' After the *Oil Platforms* Case" (2004) 17 *Leiden J Int'l L* 719, at 724 (observing that the Court's approach to the gravity issue was novel in that, in the *Nicaragua* case, it had used this criterion to determine whether non-state actor attacks could amount to armed attacks. By contrast, in the *Oil Platforms* case, the criterion was applied to the actions of a State's regular forces).

24   *Nicaragua* case, ibid., at para. 195.

25   Eritrea Ethiopia Claims Commission, Partial Award, *Jus Ad Bellum*, Ethiopia's Claims 1-8 (December 19, 2005), para. 11. For a critical assessment of the ruling, see Christine Gray, *The Eritrea/Ethiopia Claims Commission Oversteps Its Boundaries: A Partial Award?* (2006) 17 *EJIL* 699, at 719-720.

attack of some gravity goes hand-in-hand with the view that armed reprisals are no longer permitted by international law.[26]

However, as Gardam observes, "State practice is not consistent on this point, and commentators differ, with some regarding any armed action as amounting to an armed attack."[27] The central legal implication of this view is that forcible self-defense against such actions is said to be possible. Dinstein concludes, more pointedly, that armed reprisals remain lawful so long as they can be justified as necessary and proportional self-defense measures. For Dinstein, then, each situation must be evaluated to determine whether an armed reprisal meets the requirements of self-defense. In any case, the right to self-defense in such circumstances will be limited to measures "short of war."[28]

In state practice, the preference has been to avoid arguments based on the lawfulness of armed reprisals and to justify military responses to smaller scale attacks on the basis of self-defense. Typically, the argument is that several smaller scale attacks or cross-border incursions, even if none amounts to an armed attack individually, can accumulate to an extent that, taken together, they do constitute an armed attack that justifies forcible self-defense measures. This line of argument has been used on numerous occasions by the United States and Israel, notably to justify 'surgical strikes' or other responses to state-sponsored terrorist attacks. Legally speaking, this line of reasoning presupposes the legitimacy of certain forms of anticipatory self-defense (see below). Since the attacks to which the measures are responding are by definition complete, the justification of a military response turns on the prevention of further attacks. In other words, the claim is that several smaller attacks are in fact an ongoing attack, and that self-defense is available so as to prevent a continuation through further attacks. It is this argument that is meant to distinguish the response action from (unlawful) armed reprisals. The difficulty is that, no matter the legal justification, it is often hard to see the response action as anything but retaliatory.[29]

---

26   See also the approach of the International Law Commission (ILC), Draft Articles on Responsibility of States for Internationally Wrongful Acts, in ILC, *Report of the International Law Commission on the Work of Its Fifty-third Session*, UN GAOR, 56th Sess., Supp.No. 10, 43, UN Doc. A/56/10 (2001) (explaining that "[t]he term "countermeasures" covers that part of the subject of reprisals not associated with armed conflict.") And see condemnation of armed reprisals by UN SC and by UNGA in 1970 *Friendly Relations Declaration*, cited in Dinstein, *supra*, note 2, at 229.

27   Judith Gardam, *Necessity, Proportionality and the Use of Force by States* (Cambridge: Cambridge University Press, 2006) at 144; Wilmshurst, *supra*, note 8, at 966 (an "armed attack means any use of armed force, and does not need to cross some threshold of intensity"); and Raab, *supra*, note 23, at 725 (pointing to "substantial academic support for the view that 'gravity' is irrelevant to the question of whether there has been an armed attack by regular military forces").

28   See Dinstein, *supra*, note 2, 222-230.

29   The difference between a theory of 'cumulative' attack and a focus on each individ-

d.   *Anticipatory or Preventive Self-Defense*

Fourth, whereas Article 2(4) clearly proscribes threats of recourse to military force (so that mere threats would trigger the law of state responsibility – see above), the language of Article 51 suggests that only an actual armed attack triggers the right to self-defense. One of the most controversial issues in the law of self-defense is the question whether and, if so, to what extent, states may resort to force to pre-empt an armed attack. There are four broad themes in the debate.

A significant number of states and commentators give Article 51 a strict reading and reject the possibility of anticipatory self-defense. Since Article 51 specifically provides that self-defense is available "if an armed attack occurs", runs the argument, there is no room for pre-emptive action. Whether or not a right to anticipatory self-defense existed when the UN Charter was adopted, it is said to have been superseded by the explicit language of Article 51. Indeed, it was the United States that saw to it that the phrase "if an armed attack occurs" was inserted after the reference to states' "inherent right to self-defense". The leader of the American negotiating team confirmed that this phrasing was designed to have a limiting effect because the United States "did not want exercised the right of self-defence before an armed attack had occurred."[30] For Franck, therefore, it is "beyond dispute that the negotiators deliberately closed the door on any claim of 'anticipatory self-defence'".[31] Although the ICJ concluded in the *Nicaragua* case that customary and Charter rules on the use of force, including self-defense, co-existed, adherents of the narrow view on self-defense maintain that state practice since 1945 does not support claims of a right to anticipatory self-defense.[32]

However, the opposite view appears to be increasingly widely held. Some proponents of this view argue that the idea of anticipatory self-defense has existed at least since the 1837 *Caroline* case. At the time of adoption of the UN Charter, states did have a customary law right to anticipatory self-defense when

---

ual attack is well illustrated in the Iranian and US arguments in the *Oil Platforms* case. Iran asserted that each incident in question had to be considered individually, that none amounted to an armed attack, and that the US responses therefore were unlawful reprisals. The United States asserted that it was taking lawful self-defense measures against future threats that resulted from a series of incidents. The ICJ did not pronounce itself on the issue but could be seen as supportive of the idea. See Gray, *supra*, note 25, at 720; and Raab, *supra*, note 23, at 724 and at 732, pointing to some ambiguity in the Court's ruling, given that it observed that "even taken cumulatively" the incidents in question could not be qualified as the 'most grave' form of the use of force and thus as an armed attack on the United States (para. 64). See also ICJ in *DRC v. Uganda*, *supra*, note 11 (para. 146).

30   Quoted in Franck, *supra*, note 3, at 50.
31   Ibid. See also Dinstein, *supra*, note 2, at 185-187.
32   See e.g. Gray, *supra*, note 12, at 129-134 (commenting on the practice before 2001).

faced with immediate and pressing threats and so long as the use of force was a necessary and proportionate means to avert the threat.[33] Article 51, according to this view, was not intended to provide an exhaustive statement of the right. Rather, as the *travaux préparatoires* reveal, it was intended to clarify that regional organizations can take defensive (as opposed to enforcement) military action without Security Council authorization.[34] This intention was confirmed by the reference to the "inherent" right (*droit naturel*) to self-defense in Article 51 and, in any case, the Charter does not take away the pre-existing rights of states without clear language.[35]

Adherents of this view point to the state practice since 1945, which they maintain leaves room for anticipatory self-defense arguments. For example, Thomas Franck, who maintains that Article 51 did supersede custom that existed when the Charter was adopted, also argues that a customary right to anticipatory self-defense has evolved since.[36] It appears that, in the aftermath of the September 11th attacks, there is growing acceptance of at least limited scope for anticipatory action.[37] In the context of recent UN reform debates, the High-Level Panel on Threats, Challenges and Change, which the UN Secretary General had convened to assess whether the Charter's collective security framework was still viable, came out in support of the concept. The panel concluded that, notwithstanding the restrictive language of Article 51, "a threatened State, according to long established international law, can take military action as long as the threatened attack is *imminent*, no other means would deflect it and the action is proportionate."[38]

However, it also appears that a more extreme view, advanced after September 11th, notably by the United States, has not taken hold. In its 2002 National Security Strategy, the United States asserted a right not just to use force to pre-empt imminent attacks, but also to act preventively to avert longer-

---

33 Wilmshurst, *supra*, note 8, at 967 (referring to "a circumstance of irreversible emergency").

34 See Dinstein, *supra*, note 2, at 177.

35 See discussion of the academic debate in Gray, *supra*, note 12, at 98-99.

36 Franck, *supra*, note 3, at 97-108.

37 See e.g. Stefan Talmon, "Changing Views on the Use of Force: The German Position," (2005) 5 *Baltic Yearbook of International Law* 41.

38 See *A more secure world: our shared responsibility*, Report of the High-level Panel on Threats, Challenges and Change, UN Doc. A/59/565 (29 November 2004), para. 188 [emphasis in original]; at http://www.un.org/secureworld [hereinafter HLP Report]. See also response by the UN Secretary General to the HLP Report, *In Larger Freedom: Towards development, security and human rights for all*, Report by the Secretary-General, UN Doc. A/59.2005, 21 March 2005, para. 124 (noting that "[i]mminent threats are fully covered by Article 51"). But see also opposing statements by various state representatives in the General Assembly discussions of *In Larger Freedom*, UN Doc. A/59/PV.85 – A/59/PV.90, *passim*.

term threats posed by terrorists and 'rogue states'. However, even at this stage, the Legal Advisor to the US State Department took pains to bring the "Bush Doctrine" within the parameters of anticipatory self-defense, stressing that "a preemptive use of proportional force is justified only out of necessity."[39] He added that "necessity includes both a credible, imminent threat and the exhaustion of peaceful remedies." Indeed, "[w]hile the definition of imminence must recognize the threat posed by weapons of mass destruction and the intentions of those who possess them, the decision to undertake any action must meet the test of necessity... in the face of overwhelming evidence of an imminent threat, a nation may take preemptive action to defend its nationals from unimaginable harm."[40] In the meantime, while some states appear to have adopted the concept in their own policy statements, the United States seems to have stepped back from the most expansive claims of preventive self-defense rights.[41]

The international response to the concept has been generally negative.[42] In any case, to the extent that there has been support for the concept (India, Israel, Russia and Australia), it has not been sufficient to allow the conclusion that there has been a shift in customary international law.[43] The abovementioned High-Level Panel also addressed the question whether a state can claim a right to act "in anticipatory self-defense, not just pre-emptively (against an imminent or proximate threat) but preventively (against a non-imminent or non-proximate one)?"[44] Its unequivocal answer was that no such right existed. Indeed: "[T]he answer must be that, in a world full of perceived potential threats, the risk to the global order and the norm of non-intervention on which it continues to be based is simply too great for the legality of unilateral preventive action, as distinct from collectively endorsed action, to be accepted."[45]

---

39   See William H. Taft IV, "Memorandum: The Legal Basis for Preemption," 18 Nov 2002, at 1; at www.cfr.org/publication.php?id=5250].

40   Ibid., at 3.

41   See discussion in W. Michael Reisman & Andrea Armstrong, "The Past and Future of the Claim of Preemptive Self-Defense" (2006) 100 *AJIL* 525.

42   See e.g. Michael Byers, "Not yet havoc: geopolitical change and the international rules on military force" (2005) 31 *Review of Int'l Studies* 51, at 62.

43   See e.g. Colleen Swords (then Legal Adviser to the Canadian Department of Foreign Affairs and International Trade), Address to Canadian Bar Association Conference on International Law, Ottawa, June 5, 2003 (observing that "given the quite divergent views of governments, it seems unlikely that any of the views could be considered as representing state practice sufficient to have evolved into customary international law").

44   HLP Report, *supra*, note 38, para. 189.

45   Ibid., para. 191. And see *e.g.* Lord Goldsmith, Statement in the U.K. House of Lords, 21 April 2004, cited in Philippe Sands, "International Law and the Use of Force," in U.K. House of Commons Foreign Affairs Committee, *Foreign Policy Aspects of the War Against Terrorism, Vol. II: Oral and written evidence*, Seventh

Finally, it should be noted that there is also a line of reasoning that attempts to bring some instances of anticipatory self-defense within Article 51. Indeed, it has been observed that the difference between the strict reading of Article 51 and the reading that considers anticipatory self-defense as encompassed "should not be overstated."[46] Thus, some commentators maintain that an armed attack can be said to "occur" when it is underway, but that an expansive view can be taken of when that is the case. For example, mine-laying "may be interpreted as the commencement of the commission of an armed attack."[47] In addition, in cases involving a series of attacks, it is said that state practice supports anticipatory action that is a necessary and proportional means of preventing further attacks. In fact, it is on this basis that the United States justified its military intervention in Afghanistan, an intervention that was widely supported by other states.[48] A more difficult question is how to interpret the criterion of "imminence." A recent study concludes that the factors to be taken into account include gravity of the threatened attack, capability of the attacker (e.g. possession of WMD), nature of the attack, geographical location of the attacker and its past record of attacks.[49]

4. Armed Reprisals

Dinstein observes that "armed reprisals are prohibited unless they qualify as an exercise of self-defence under Article 51. Only defensive armed reprisals are allowed." "They must come in response to an armed attack ... in circumstances satisfying all the requirements of legitimate self-defence."[50] For Dinstein, armed reprisals differ from other measures of self-defence "short of war" in that they occur "at a time and a place different from those of the original armed attack". Nonetheless, these measures, like all measures "short of war" must comply with the requirements of the *jus in bello*.[51] To meet the requirements of self-defense, Dinstein considers that armed reprisals must be necessary (thus must be preceded by non-forcible attempts at resolution) and must meet the test of immedi-

---

Report of Session 2003-04 (29 July 2004), Ev 91, at Ev 92-93 ("...international law permits the use of force in self-defence against an imminent attack but does not authorize the use of force to mount a pre-emptive strike against a threat that is more remote"). And Memorandum prepared by Christopher Greenwood, "The Legality of Using Force Against Iraq," in U.K. House of Commons Foreign Affairs Committee, *Foreign Policy Aspects of the War Against Terrorism*, Second Report of Session 2002-03 (24 October 2002) Ev 17, at Ev 20.

46 Wilmshurst, *supra*, note 8, at 965.

47 See Raab, *supra*, note 23, at 730.

48 See Gardam, *supra*, note 25, at 147.

49 See Wilmshurst, *supra*, note 8, at 970.

50 Dinstein, *supra*, note 2, at 222.

51 Ibid.

acy – "an inordinate procrastination is liable to erode the linkage between force and counter-force."[52] Dinstein canvasses the spectrum of opinion, citing various scholars who share his assessment. But, as he acknowledges, "most writers deny that self-defence pursuant to Article 51 may ever embrace armed reprisals."[53] Indeed, since the adoption of the Charter, armed reprisals (or forcible coun-termeasures) are seen by most observers and virtually all states as prohibited by international law.[54] Both sides of the academic debate point to the same instances of state practice, each finding support for their respective positions in the incidents and justifications in question.

5.   Aggression

Neither the term "armed attack" nor the term "aggression" has acquired settled meaning in international law. Although the UN General Assembly adopted Resolution 3314 (1974) intended to provide a *Definition of Aggression* (for the purposes of assisting the Security Council in its determinations under Chapter VII),[55] the concept of aggression remains controversial (as the efforts to agree on a definition of the crime of aggression in the Rome Statute of the International Criminal Court) attest.[56] It remains also unclear to what extent there is overlap between the concepts of aggression and armed attack. In the *Nicaragua* case, the ICJ drew upon the *Definition of Aggression* to clarify the concept of armed attack. However, it would appear as if the notion of aggression is broader than that of armed attack. According to Dinstein, an armed attack is, "of course, a type of aggression" (armed aggression). But aggression "in its generic meaning may be stretched to include mere threats."[57]

6.   Armed Conflict

By definition, all armed conflicts involve recourse to military means. However, a minimal cross-border transgression is not an armed conflict,[58] nor does

---

52   Ibid, at 225. See also Derek W. Bowett, "Reprisals Involving Recourse to Armed Force" (1972) 66 *AJIL* 1, at 17-23.

53   Dinstein, *supra*, note 2, at 226.

54   See Gardam, *supra*, note 27, at 49; Gray, *supra*, note 12, at 163; Byers, *supra*, note 42, at 53; Ian Brownlie, *International Law and the Use of Force by States* (Oxford: Clarendon Press, 1963) at 281. And see ILC, text accompanying *supra*, note 24.

55   UNGA Resolution 3314 (XXIX).

56   See Article 5 (2) Rome Statute of the International Criminal Court. And see Rev. Conf. of the Rome Statute, May 31-June 11, 2010, ICC Doc. RC/11/Res.6 (The Crime of aggression) (11 June 2010).

57   Dinstein, *supra*, note 2, at 184. See also discussion in Becker, *supra*, note 9, at 176-185.

58   See O'Connell, *supra*, note 6, at 3.

even an armed attack necessarily give rise to an armed conflict. According to Greenwood, "many isolated incidents, such as border clashes and naval incidents, are not treated as armed conflicts. It may well be, therefore, that only when fighting reaches a level of intensity which exceeds that of such isolated clashes will it be treated as armed conflict to which the rules of international humanitarian law apply."[59]

No armed conflict will arise unless the victim of an armed attack opts for a military response.[60] And, even if an attack by non-state actors, such as a terrorist group, were to constitute an armed attack for the purposes of the right to self-defense (see above), response action against the terrorists would not normally give rise to an armed conflict. For some, then, armed conflicts must have a territorial dimension, so that non-state actors cannot engage in an armed conflict unless they control territory.[61] In *Prosecutor v. Tadić*, the International Criminal Tribunal for the Former Yugoslavia (ICTY) defined "armed conflict" as existing "whenever there is resort to armed force between States or protracted armed violence between governmental authorities and organized armed groups or between such groups within a state."[62]

7. War

a. Definition / Legal Concept

In Oppenheim's classic definition, war was "a contention between two or more States through their armed forces, for the purpose of overpowering each other and imposing such conditions of peace as the victor pleases."[63]

While the term "armed conflict" appears to have displaced the concept of "war" for most practical purposes,[64] it would appear that it remains possible for states to find themselves in a state or war,[65] or to make formal declarations of war.[66] Indeed, it has been argued that even before the intervention in Afghanistan, "the United States was engaged in a war. We were at war at 0845 on 11 September 2001, a war "declared" by the Commander-in-Chief in his 20 September address before a joint session of Congress. Congress swiftly fol-

---

59   Christopher Greenwood, "Scope of Application of Humanitarian Law", in Dieter Fleck, ed., *The Handbook of Humanitarian Law in Armed Conflict* (1995) at 42.

60   O'Connell, *supra*, note 6, at 11.

61   Greenwood, *supra*, note 4, at 283.

62   *Tadić, supra*, note 15, para. 70. See also Greenwood, *supra*, note 10, at 527.

63   L. Oppenheim, *International Law* (1906) 56.

64   Few conflicts since 1945 have been characterized by the protagonists as wars. See Greenwood, *supra*, note 4, at 290-294.

65   Ibid., at 305.

66   Eritrea Ethiopia Claims Commission, *supra*, note 1, para. 17.

lowed his declaration with a joint resolution supporting the use of force against terrorists."[67]

However, a declaration of war alone would not suffice to trigger a state of war. It is generally understood today that factual circumstances determine whether or not states are at war.[68] The central factor is the extent of military confrontation. According to Dinstein, "there is no warfare in the material sense without some acts of warfare." "An economic boycott or psychological pressure is not enough. A 'Cold War', threats to use force, or even a declaration of war (unaccompanied by acts of violence), do not warrant the conclusion that war in the material sense exists."[69]

And, as with the concept of armed conflict, an armed attack or even a state's recourse to force in self-defense, do not necessarily give rise to "war".[70] According to Dinstein, "[i]ncidents involving the use of force, without reaching the threshold of war, occur quite often... Border patrols of neighbouring states may exchange fire; naval units may torpedo vessels flying another flag; interceptor planes may shoot down aircraft belonging to another state;" etc. "In large measure, the classification of a military action as either war or a closed incident ('short of war') depends on the way in which the two antagonists appraise the situation."... "Once one of the parties elects to engage in war, the other side is incapable of preventing that development."[71] "A legal analysis of the true state of affairs ... hinges on a perception of the use of force as comprehensive."[72]

In this context, note also that the right to self-defense arose in part against the background of states' unlimited right to resort to war. To avoid the legal consequences of a state of war, states began to define instances of use of force "short of war". This endeavor picked up speed once limits began to be placed on resort to war.[73] Recourse to war or declarations of war, are rare in part because of the prohibition on the threat or use of force contained in the UN Charter.[74] For

---

67   See Gary D. Solis, "Are we really at war?" (2001) 127 *Proceedings Magazine* 34.

68   Therefore, "[t]here ought to be no doubt that October 7th – and not September 11th – is the date of the beginning of the war between the United States and Afghanistan." See Dinstein, *supra*, note 2, at 31. See also O'Connell, *supra*, note 6, at 2-3.

69   Dinstein, *supra*, note 2, at 10.

70   See Mary Ellen O'Connell, "When is a War not a War? The Myth of the Global War on Terror" (2005) 12 *ILSA J. Int'l & Comp. L* 1, at 4.

71   Dinstein, *supra*, note 2, at 11.

72   Ibid., at 12.

73   Note also the significance of the fact that the prohibition on the use of force in the UN Charter is much more sweeping that the limitations on resort to war (in the technical sense of the term at the time) contained in the 1919 Covenant of the League of Nations, and then the prohibition of war in the 1928 Kellogg-Briand Pact. See Franck, *supra*, note 3, at 10-11.

74   See review in Dietrich Schindler, "State or War, Belligerency, Armed Conflict," in Antonio Cassese ed., *The New Humanitarian Law of Armed Conflict* (1979) 3.

example, the United States has not formally declared war since World War II.[75] Note also that, given that prohibition, a declaration of war would not render an otherwise illegal use of force legal. Indeed, for "the purpose of applying Article 2(4), it is unnecessary to consider whether a conflict amounts to war."[76] "Similarly, a State which uses force in response to an armed attack ... cannot enlarge its rights by characterizing the conflict as war. The right of self-defence permits only the employment of such force as is reasonably necessary."[77] Note that, in the final analysis, the US did not actually justify its recourse to force in Afghanistan in terms of a 'war on terror'. Instead, it relied on a claim of self-defense.[78]

Historically, "war has been seen as a relationship between States."[79] "It was considered by most international lawyers and governments that only States had the right to wage war, so that the resort to force without the authority of the State was an act of lawlessness. More importantly, only States had the legal capacity to wage war; for example, the laws of war are built around the assumption that the belligerents are States and have the apparatus of States (such as a criminal justice system) to draw upon."[80]

The trigger, geographical scope and duration of individual states' *jus ad bellum* are determined by the question whether they have a right to use force in self-defense.

b.   *Relationship between "War" and* Jus ad Bellum *("Self-Defense")*

It has been suggested that, due to the restrictions imposed in the UN Charter in general and Article 51 in particular, even a state that resorts to force in self-defense may not create a state of war.[81] The argument runs that the creation of a state of war would only in the rarest of circumstances satisfy the requirement of proportionality (in view of the comprehensive goals inherent in warfare – overthrowing the opponent).

According to Dinstein, the "essence of self-defence is self-help: under certain conditions set by international law, a State acting unilaterally ... may respond with lawful force to unlawful force."[82] Therefore, "... an aggrieved State may resort to non-forcible measures..." In addition, "... legitimate self-help ...

---

75   O'Connell, *supra*, note 6, at 7.

76   Greenwood, *supra*, note 4, at 301.

77   Ibid., at 302.

78   Greenwood, *supra*, note 10, at 524.

79   Ibid., at 511.

80   Ibid., at 512 (the exceptions being civil wars within countries and hostilities waged by national liberation movements).

81   See Greenwood, *supra*, note 4, at 289.

82   Dinstein, *supra*, note 2, at 175.

may take the shape of forcible measures" but today these measures must meet "the requirements of self-defence."[83] Again according to Dinstein, self-defence can consist in measures 'short of war' (see above) as well as 'war'.[84] "War as an act of self-defence denotes comprehensive counter-force in response to an armed attack."[85]

Controversially, Dinstein argues that "once a war is properly stamped with the legal seal of self-defence, this legal characterization is indelible regardless of the vicissitudes of the hostilities."[86] In his view, once begun in self-defense, "the entire ... war is painted in the colour of self-defence". Therefore, once a war is legal as a necessary and proportional response to the attack, there is no room for continuous assessment of necessity and proportionality.[87] Indeed, according to Dinstein, "[o]nce war is raging, the exercise of self-defence may bring about 'the destruction of the enemy's army', regardless of the condition of proportionality."[88]

While most commentators might agree that war can be conducted within the parameters of lawful self-defense, most would also insist on adherence to these parameters. In other words, the requirements of self-defense determine not only whether war-fare (as opposed to a lesser form of military action) is legal in the first place, but also how long it so remains. The answer to both questions, in the majority view, depends on the requirements of necessity and proportionality.[89] Thus, Greenwood notes that "a State which uses force in response to an armed attack ... cannot enlarge its rights by characterizing the conflict as war. The right of self-defence permits only the employment of such force as is reasonably necessary."[90] Elsewhere, Greenwood elaborates:

> "Prior to 1945 – or at least to 1919 – the outbreak of war meant that a State
> was no longer subject, vis-à-vis the other belligerent, to any restraints which
> international law imposed on the recourse to force (the *jus ad bellum*)... The
> Charter..., however, introduced a marked change... Under the Charter it is
> plain that an aggressor cannot free itself from the effect of the prohibition of
> resort to force by the expedient of declaring war on its victim, but nor can the

---

83   Ibid. 176.

84   Ibid., 219.

85   Ibid., 235.

86   Ibid.

87   Ibid., 237.

88   Ibid., 238. For Dinstein, cease-fires (which merely suspend hostilities) do not alter this fact so that the Gulf War remained a war of self-defense even after a lengthy cease-fire period.

89   See e.g., Gardam, *supra*, note 27; Christopher Greenwood, "The Relationship Between the *Ius Ad Bellum* and *Ius In Bello*" (1983) 9 *Rev. Int'l Stud.* 221, at 223.

90   Greenwood, *supra*, note 4, at 302.

victim, free itself of the limitations which international law places on the right of self-defence ... by declaring war on the aggressor."[91]

In stark disagreement with Dinstein's claim, Greenwood notes (in relation to the so-called 'war on terror') that "even the existence of a war in the formal sense of international law, i.e. a war between two or more States at least one of which possesses *animus belligerendi*, does not automatically justify resort to military action; even where such a state of war exists, the legality of resort to force depends on the State which takes that step being able to meet the conditions of the United Nations Charter."[92] Note also that, in the final analysis, US actions confirm this view. The US did not actually justify its recourse to force in Afghanistan in terms of a "war on terror." Instead, it relied on a claim of self-defense.[93]

What is more, at "international law there is no basis for speaking of a war on Al-Qaeda or any other terrorist group, for such a group cannot be a belligerent, it is merely a band of criminals, and to treat it as anything else risks distorting the law."[94] The bottom line is that "reference to a war on terrorism would add nothing to the debate on the legality of recourse to force."[95]

c.   *Geographical Scope of "War"/*Jus ad Bellum

Whether or not military action in or against another state is necessary will depend on the degree of involvement of that state in the attack (if any), its responsiveness to diplomatic steps or non-military pressure, and the urgency of self-defence action.[96] The necessity requirement, therefore, also restricts the *geographic scope* of lawful self-defence action. For example, a state could not use force against terrorists found within the territory of another state unless that military action could be shown to be necessary, and proportional.

---

91   Greenwood, *supra*, note 10, at 514.

92   Ibid., at 515.

93   See *supra*, note 69 and accompanying text.

94   Greenwood, *supra*, note 10, at 529.

95   Ibid., at 525.

96   See Gazzini, *supra*, note 22, at 193-197. And see examples of state practice in Trapp, *supra*, note 18, especially at 146 et seq.

Bibliography

Books:

ROBERTA ARNOLD AND GEERT-JAN ALEXANDER KNOOPS, PEACE SUPPORT OPERATIONS AND THEIR LEGAL IMPLICATIONS (2006)

TARCISIO GAZZINI, THE CHANGING RULES ON THE USE OF FORCE IN INTERNATIONAL LAW (2005)

CUSTOMARY INTERNATIONAL LAW ON THE USE OF FORCE (Enzo Cannizzaro & Paolo Palchetti eds., 2005)

REDEFINING SOVEREIGNTY, THE USE OF FORCE AFTER THE COLD WAR (Michael Bothe et al eds., 2005)

YORAM DINSTEIN, WAR, AGGRESSION AND SELF-DEFENCE (4th ed. 2005)

FRITS KALSHOVEN, BELLIGERENT REPRISALS (2005)

THE TORTURE PAPERS, THE ROAD TO ABU GHRAIB (Karen J. Greenberg and Joshua L. Dratel eds., 2005)

MARY ELLEN O'CONNELL, INTERNATIONAL LAW AND THE USE OF FORCE, CASES AND MATERIALS (2005)

CHRISTINE GRAY, INTERNATIONAL LAW AND THE USE OF FORCE (2d ed. 2004)

KRISENSICHERUNG UND HUMANITÄRER SCHUTZ – CRISIS MANAGEMENT AND HUMANITARIAN PROTECTION (Horst Fischer et al, eds., 2004)

A.P.V. ROGERS, LAW ON THE BATTLEFIELD (2004)

YORAM DINSTEIN, THE CONDUCT OF HOSTILITIES UNDER THE INTERNATIONAL LAW OF ARMED CONFLICT (2004)

THOMAS FRANCK, RECOURSE TO FORCE, ACTION AGAINST THREATS AND ARMED ATTACKS (2002)

LINDSAY MOIR, THE LAW OF INTERNAL ARMED CONFLICT (2002)

WILHELM G. GREWE, THE EPOCHS OF INTERNATIONAL LAW (trans.& rev'd, Michael Byers 2000)

KARL P. MAGYAR & EARL CONTEH-MORGAN, PEACEKEEPING IN AFRICA, ECOMOG IN LIBERIA (1998)

A. MARK WEISBURD, USE OF FORCE: THE PRACTICE OF STATES SINCE WORLD WAR II (1997)

STANIMIR ALEXANDROV, SELF-DEFENSE AGAINST THE USE OF FORCE IN INTERNATIONAL LAW (1996)

THE HANDBOOK OF HUMANITARIAN LAW IN ARMED CONFLICT 42 (Dieter Fleck ed., 1995)

THE LAWS OF WAR (Michael Howard et al. eds., 1994)

HILAIRE McCOURBREY & NIGEL WHITE, INTERNATIONAL ORGANIZATIONS AND CIVIL WARS (1995)

ENFORCING RESTRAINT: COLLECTIVE INTERVENTION IN INTERNAL CONFLICTS (Lori F. Damrosch ed. 1993)

THE GULF WAR 1990-1991, IN INTERNATIONAL AND ENGLISH LAW (Peter Rowe ed., 1993)

HILAIRE MCCOUBREY & NIGEL WHITE, INTERNATIONAL LAW AND ARMED CONFLICT (1992)

LAW AND FORCE IN THE NEW INTERNATIONAL ORDER (Lori F. Damrosch & D.J. Scheffer eds., 1991)

BELATCHEW ASRAT, PROHIBITION OF FORCE UNDER THE U.N. CHARTER, A STUDY OF ART. 2(4) (1991)

N.D. WHITE, THE UNITED NATIONS AND THE MAINTENANCE OF INTERNATIONAL PEACE AND SECURITY (1990)

MIGHT V. RIGHT, INTERNATIONAL LAW AND THE USE OF FORCE 45 (Louis Henkin et al. eds., 1989)

INTERNATIONAL INCIDENTS, THE LAW THAT COUNTS IN INTERNATIONAL AFFAIRS (W. Michael Resiman & Andrew R. Willard eds., 1988)

DIETRICH, SCHINDLER & JIRI TOMAN, THE LAW OF ARMED CONFLICT (1988)

THE CURRENT LEGAL REGULATION OF THE USE OF FORCE (A. Cassese ed., 1986)

PETER MACALISTER-SMITH, INTERNATIONAL HUMANITARIAN ASSISTANCE: DISASTER RELIEF ACTIONS IN INTERNATIONAL LAW AND ORGANIZATION (1985)

CLAUDE PILOUD ET AL., COMMENTARY ON THE ADDITIONAL PROTOCOLS 647 (1987)

GEOFFREY BEST, HUMANITY IN WARFARE (1980)

LAW AND CIVIL WAR IN THE MODERN WORLD (John Norton Moore ed., 1974)

QUINCY WRIGHT, A STUDY OF WAR (1964)

IAN BROWNLIE, INTERNATIONAL LAW AND THE USE OF FORCE BY STATES (1963)

C. H. M. Waldock, *The Regulation of the Use of Force by Individual States in International Law*, 81 RECUEIL DES COURS 451 (1952 II)

Articles:

Kimberley N Trapp, *Back to Basics: Necessity, Proportionality, and the Right to Self-Defence Against Non-State Terrorist Actors*, (2007) 56 *ICLQ* 141.

Carsten Stahn, "'*Jus ad bellum*', '*jus in bello*' ... '*jus post bellum*'? – Rethinking the Conception of the Law of Armed Force," (2006) 17 *EJIL* 921

William Abresch, *A Human Rights Law of Internal Armed Conflict: The European Court of Human Rights in Chechnya*, 16 EUR. J. INT'L L. 741 (2005)

Mary Ellen O'Connell, *Enhancing the Status of Non-State Actors Through a Global War on Terror*, 43 COL. J. TRANS. L. 435 (2005)

Christopher Greenwood, *War, Terrorism and International Law*, 56 CURR. LEG. PROBS. 505 (2004)

Nathaniel Berman, *Privileging Combat? Contemporary Conflict and the Legal Construction of War*, 43 Col. J. Trans. L. 1 (2004)

Marco Sassoli, *Use and Abuse of the Laws of War in the "War on Terrorism,"* 22 LAW & INEQ. 195 (2004)

Mary Ellen O'Connell, *What is War?*, Mar. 17, 2004 http://jurist.law.pitt.edu/forum/oconnell1.php

Gabor Rona, *Interesting Times for International Humanitarian Law: Challenges from the "War on Terror"*, 27 FLETCHER FORUM OF WORLD AFFAIRS 55 (2003)

Norman G. Printer, Jr., *The Use of Force Against Non-State Actors Under International Law: An Analysis of the U.S. Predator Strike in Yemen*, 8 UCLA J. INT'L L. & FOR-EIGN AFF. 331 (2003)

William A. Schabas, *Punishment of Non-State Actors in Non-International Armed Conflict*, 26 FORDHAM INT'L L.J. 907 (2003)

Anthony Dworkin, *Law and the Campaign Against Terrorism: The View from the Pentagon*, Dec. 16, 2002, http://www.crimesofwar.org/print/onnews/pentagon-print. html

Mary Ellen O'Connell, *Lawful Self-Defense to Terrorism*, 63 U. PITT. L. REV. 889 (2002)

Gary D. Solis, *Are We Really at War?*, 127 U.S. NAVAL INST. PROC. 34 (Dec. 2001)

Frédéric Mégret, *'War'? Legal Semantics and the Move to Violence*, EJIL (2001)

Oren Gross & Fionnuala Ni Aolain, *Emergency, War and International Law – Another Perspective*, 70 NORDIC J. INT'L L. 29 (2001)

Alain Pellet, *No, This is Not War*, EUR. J. INT'L L., Oct. 3, 2001, http://www.ejil.org/forum_WTC/ny-pellet.html

Robert Kolb, "Origin of the Twin Terms of *Jus ad Bellum* and *Jus in Bello*," (1997) 320 *International Review of the Red Cross* 553.

Judith Gardam, *Legal Restraints on Security Council Military Enforcement Action*, 17 MJIL (1996) 285

Stephen C. Neff, *Towards a Law of Unarmed Conflict: A Proposal for a New International Law of Hostility*, 28 CORNELL INT'L L.J. 1 (1995)

Christopher Greenwood, *The Concept of War in Modern International Law*, 36 INT'L & COMP. L.Q. 283 (1987)

Oscar Schachter, *The Right of States to Use Armed Force*, 82 MICH. L. REV. 1620 (1984)

Helmut Rumpf, *The Concepts of Peace and War in International Law*, 27 GER. YBK. INT'L L. 429 (1984)

Christopher Greenwood, *The Relationship Between the* Ius Ad Bellum *and* Ius In Bello 9 REV. INT'L STUD. 221 (1983)

Dietrich Schindler, *State of War, Belligerency, Armed Conflict, in* THE NEW HUMANITAR-IAN LAW OF ARMED CONFLICT 3 (Antonio Cassese ed., 1979)

Tom Farer, *Humanitarian Law and Armed Conflicts: Toward the Definition of "International Armed Conflict"*, 71 COLUM L. REV. 37 (1971)

Elihu Lauterpacht, *The Legal Irrelevance of the "State of War"* in Proceedings of the American Society of International Law at its Sixty-Second Annual Meeting 58 (1968)

Philip C. Jessup, *Should International Law Recognize an Intermediate Status Between Peace and War?*, 48 AM. J. INT'L L. 98 (1954)

Chapter 5

The Concept of "Armed Conflict" in International Armed Conflict

Masahiko Asada

Introduction

There are a number of treaties of quasi-universal application that govern the conduct of belligerents in international armed conflict. They include, *inter alia*, the 1949 Geneva Conventions and the 1977 Additional Protocol I to the Geneva Conventions. In all these treaties, the concept of "armed conflict" is of vital importance for their actual application. Common Article 2, paragraph 1, of the Geneva Conventions stipulates as follows:

> In addition to the provisions which shall be implemented in peacetime, the present Convention shall apply to all cases of declared war or of any other *armed conflict* which may arise between two or more of the High Contracting Parties, even if the state of war is not recognized by one of them. (emphasis added).

For its part, Additional Protocol I in Article 1, paragraph 3, provides that "this Protocol, which supplements the Geneva Conventions of 12 August 1949 for the protection of war victims, shall apply in the situations referred to in *Article 2 common to those Conventions*" (emphasis added).[1]

---

*   Editor's Note: Professor Asada requested this version of his chapter despite the fact the Committee did not rely on this version because it omits certain significant facts, for example, that the British vessel *HMS Troubridge* engaged the Danish vessel in the *Red Crusader* incident, and that the UK government took no position on the application of the Geneva Conventions to Iran's detention of British sailors in 2007. Despite the omissions, this version still demonstrates that Professor Asada found *no* examples of states applying the 1949 Geneva Conventions to low intensity engagements of armed forces.

1   The scope of application of Additional Protocol I is also provided in Article 1, paragraph 4, regarding the so-called national liberation conflict, which will not be specifically addressed in this chapter. Protocol Additional to the Geneva Conventions of 12 Aug. 1949, and Relating to the Protection of Victims of International Armed Conflict art. 1, June 8, 1977, 1125 U.N.T.S. 17513.

Mary Ellen O'Connell (ed.), What Is War? An Investigation in the Wake of 9/11.
© *2012 Koninklijke Brill NV. Printed in The Netherlands.* ISBN *978 9004 17234 0. pp. 51 – 67.*

Thus, "armed conflict" is the trigger concept that gets the rules of international humanitarian law to operate and to override some of the peacetime rules of international law.[2] Indeed, as Professor Vaughan Lowe says, "War – armed conflict – has a radical legal effect."[3]

However, no definition is given to the term "armed conflict" in the Geneva Conventions,[4] the Protocol, or in any other international humanitarian law trea-

---

2   *See* International Covenant on Civil and Political Rights art. 4, Dec. 16, 1966, 999 U.N.T.S. 171. In the *Legality of the Threat or Use of Nuclear Weapons* Case of 1996, the International Court of Justice (ICJ) discussed the relationship between the ICCPR and the law of armed conflict. It pointed out that "the protection of the International Covenant of [sic] Civil and Political Rights does not cease in times of war, except by operation of Article 4 of the Covenant whereby certain provisions may be derogated from in a time of national emergency." It further pointed out, in relation to Article 6 of the ICCPR on the right not arbitrarily to be deprived of one's life, that this right applies also in hostilities, but added that "[t]he test of what is an arbitrary deprivation of life, however, then falls to be determined by the applicable *lex specialis*, namely, the law applicable in armed conflict which is designed to regulate the conduct of hostilities." Legality of the Threat or Use of Nuclear Weapons, Advisory Opinion, 1996 I.C.J. 226, 240 (July 8). The ICJ observed in the *Israeli Wall* Case of 2004 that "[a]s regards the relationship between international humanitarian law and human rights law, there are ... three possible situations: some rights may be exclusively matters of international humanitarian law; others may be exclusively matters of human rights law; yet others may be matters of both these branches of international law." However, the Court did not elaborate on this point any further. Legal Consequences of the Construction of a Wall in the Occupied Palestinian Territory, Advisory Opinion, 2004 I.C.J. 136, 178 (July 9). For the views of human rights treaty bodies on the relationship between human rights law and international humanitarian law, see Int'l Covenant on Civil and Political Rights [ICCPR], Human Rights Comm., *General Comment No. 31: Nature of the General Legal Obligation Imposed on States Parties to the Covenant*, ¶ 11, U.N. Doc. CCPR/C/21/Rev.1/Add.13 (May 26, 2004); Decision on Request for Precautionary Measures (Detainees at Guantanamo Bay, Cuba), Inter-Am. C.H.R., 41 I.L.M. 532, 533 (2002). They affirm that both human rights law and humanitarian law are applicable in situations of armed conflict. For the response of the United States to the decision by the IACHR, criticizing, among other things, that in applying humanitarian law the Commission has acted without authority, see Response of the United States to Request for Precautionary Measures – Detainees in Guantanamo Bay, Cuba, Inter-Am. C.H.R., 41 I.L.M. 1016, 1020-21 (2002).

3   Professor Lowe goes on to write that: "Combatants in States' armed forces may kill and destroy property within the laws of war without fear of facing trial for murder or criminal damage." VAUGHAN LOWE, INTERNATIONAL LAW 282-83 (2007).

4   It is obvious from the phrase at the end of Common Article 2, paragraph 1, of the Geneva Conventions, that there is no longer any need for a formal declaration of war or for a recognition of the state of war as preliminaries to the application of the Geneva Conventions (or Additional Protocol I). In this connection, a question may be asked about whether the Conventions are applicable, when a State declares

ties.[5] The absence of a definition sometimes makes it difficult to determine which group of rules applies to a particular situation at a particular point in time. This holds especially true with internal conflicts,[6] but it also applies to international armed conflicts.[7] It is to fill this gap that the International Law Association mandated the Use of Force Committee to look into international law to discern what definition the law supports. (See Chapter Two of this volume.)

This chapter tries to identify possible parameters with which to determine when the rules applicable in international armed conflicts apply, particularly whether they apply when only low intensity fighting has occurred. It will examine legal texts, State practice and judicial decisions, as well as legal doctrines.

1.   The ICRC Commentaries and the ICTY Decisions

1.1   Two Often-Cited Statements

Although no definition of "armed conflict" is provided in relevant international treaties, there are a few instances in which the application of international armed conflict rules is discussed. Thus, for example, the International

---

war against another State, but neither conducts armed hostilities nor participates in such against the other State. On this question, Professor Dietrich Schindler argues that the Conventions apply to such cases, because Common Article 2 declares explicitly that the Conventions shall apply to all cases of declared war. Dietrich Schindler, *The Different Types of Armed Conflicts according to the Geneva Conventions and Protocols*, 163 RECUEIL DES COURS [Collected Courses] 131, 131-32 (1979).

5   Christopher Greenwood, *The Development of International Humanitarian Law by the International Criminal Tribunal for the Former Yugoslavia*, 2 MAX PLANCK Y.B.U.N. L. 114 (1998). The UN International Law Commission has been developing draft articles on the effects of armed conflicts on treaties. Draft Article 2 (b), adopted by the Commission on first reading in 2008, defines "[a]rmed conflict" as "a state of war or a conflict which involves armed operations which by their nature or extent are likely to affect the application of treaties between States parties to the armed conflict or between a State party to the armed conflict and a third State, regardless of a formal declaration of war or other declaration by any or all of the parties to the armed conflict." *Report of the International Law Commission to the General Assembly*, 60 U.N. GAOR Supp. (No. 10) at 83, U.N. Doc A/63/10 (2008). Not only is this definition merely for the purposes of the draft articles, as the chapeau of Article 2 provides, but it does not seem to provide insight for purposes of this chapter either.

6   In this chapter, the terms "internal armed conflict" and "non-international armed conflict" are used interchangeably.

7   Arne Willy Dahl & Magnus Sandbu, *The Threshold of Armed Conflict*, 45(3-4) REVUE DE DROIT MILITAIRE ET DE DROIT DE LA GUERRE [REV. DR. MIL. DR. GUERRE] 369 (2006).

Committee of the Red Cross (ICRC)[8] in its Commentary on the 1949 Geneva Conventions mentions the scope of application of these Conventions – an indication of what an armed conflict is:

> The Convention becomes applicable as from the actual opening of hostilities. The existence of armed conflict between two or more Contracting Parties brings it automatically into operation.
>
> It remains to ascertain what is meant by "armed conflict." ... *Any difference arising between two States and leading to the intervention of armed forces is an armed conflict* within the meaning of Article 2, even if one of the Parties denies the existence of a state of war. *It makes no difference how long the conflict lasts, or how much slaughter takes place.* The respect due to human personality is not measured by the number of victims. ... If there is only a single wounded person as a result of the conflict, the Convention will have been applied as soon as he has been collected and tended ... (emphasis added).[9]

The International Criminal Tribunal for the Former Yugoslavia (ICTY) looked into the definition of armed conflict more recently in *The Prosecutor v. Tadić* Case (Jurisdiction, Appeals) in 1995. In that case, the issue in part was whether an armed conflict had existed as the appellant asserted that "there did not exist a legally cognizable armed conflict – either internal or international – at the time and place that the alleged offences were committed."[10] The case related, therefore, to international internal armed conflict. The Appeals Chamber reached the following determination:

> [W]e find that an armed conflict exists whenever there is *a resort to armed force between States* or *protracted armed violence between governmental authorities and organized armed groups or between such groups within a State*. International humanitarian law applies from the initiation of such armed conflicts and

---

8   Although the ICRC has been given a special status by the Geneva Conventions and their Additional Protocols as a guardian of humanitarian law and for other functions, its status under international law is, strictly speaking, no more than a non-governmental organization. Nonetheless, such legal status of the ICRC becomes scarcely relevant, when its views are adopted by an international court or tribunal, as we will see in the text below (the *Delalic* Case).

9   COMMENTARY ON THE GENEVA CONVENTION FOR THE AMELIORATION OF THE CONDITION OF THE WOUNDED AND SICK IN ARMED FORCES IN THE FIELD 32 (Jean S. Pictet ed., 1952). In its Commentary on the Prisoners of War Convention (the Third Geneva Convention), the ICRC further states that "[e]ven if there has been no fighting, the fact that persons covered by the Convention are detained is sufficient for its application." COMMENTARY ON THE GENEVA CONVENTION FOR THE AMELIORATION OF THE CONDITION OF THE WOUNDED AND SICK IN ARMED FORCES IN THE FIELD 23 (Jean S. Pictet ed., 1960).

10   Prosecutor v. Tadić, Case No. IT-94-1-T, Jurisdiction, ¶ 66 (Oct. 2, 1995).

extends beyond the cessation of hostilities until a general conclusion of peace is reached; or, in the case of internal conflicts, a peaceful settlement is achieved. Until that moment, international humanitarian law continues to apply in the whole territory of the warring States or, in the case of internal conflicts, the whole territory under the control of a party, whether or not actual combat takes place there (emphasis added)."

From these two often-cited statements about when international armed conflict rules are triggered, we could identify at least two elements that are common to them. One is related to the intensity and duration of the conflict; and the other concerns the participants who perform the relevant armed activities. This chapter will focus on the former element.

1.2 ICRC Commentaries

On that element, the ICRC Commentary indicates that the Geneva Conventions are triggered regardless of the intensity or duration of fighting. This interpretation is maintained in the ICRC's Commentary on Additional Protocol I to the Geneva Conventions. It states in Article 1, paragraph 3, of the Protocol

---

11   *Id.* at ¶ 70. In the same paragraph, the decision goes on to state, in applying the concept of armed conflict quoted in the text to the hostilities in the former Yugoslavia: "These hostilities [i.e., fighting among the various entities within the former Yugoslavia] exceed the *intensity requirements* applicable to *both international and internal* armed conflicts. There has been protracted, large-scale violence between the armed forces of different States and between governmental forces and organized insurgent groups" (emphasis added). *Id.* These sentences may suggest that intensity requirements apply both to international and internal armed conflicts, notwithstanding the fact that the *concept* of armed conflict formulated by the ICTY a few sentences earlier does not refer to intensity. But Mary Ellen O'Connell and others conclude that the ICTY is discussing the definition of armed conflict throughout the paragraph. She emphasizes that "the Court uses the qualifier 'protracted' for conflicts other than those between two states, but also refers to an 'intensity' standard for both internal and international armed conflicts." MARY ELLEN O'CONNELL, INTERNATIONAL LAW AND THE USE OF FORCE: CASES AND MATERIALS 9 (2005). In my view no clear, immediate answer can be found to the question as to how one can interpret the whole paragraph (¶ 70) in a consistent manner. However, it should be emphasized that the ICTY in the *Delalic* Case, as we will see later, quoted only the part shown in the text and did not refer to the above-cited latter part of paragraph 70 from the *Tadić* decision. Prosecutor v. Delalic, Case No. IT-96-21-T, Judgment, ¶ 183 (Nov. 16, 1998) (hereinafter cited as *"The Prosecutor v. Delalic* (Trial)"). Likewise, the Statute of the International Criminal Court (ICC), as again we will see later, does not refer to the intensity or duration requirement at all in relation to *international* armed conflict, while it does mention both requirements in relation to *non-international* armed conflict (Art. 8, para. 2 (f)).

concerning the scope of application that: "the [Geneva] Conventions are not applicable only in cases of declared war ... [A]s will most often be the case in practice, humanitarian law also covers any dispute between two States involving the use of their armed forces. *Neither the duration of the conflict, nor its intensity, play a role ...*" (emphasis added). [12]

The ICRC's most recent opinion on this question is generally in accord. According to the ICRC's opinion paper entitled, "How is the Term 'Armed Conflict' Defined in International Humanitarian Law?," dated March 2008, it is said that: "International armed conflicts exist whenever there is *resort to armed force between two or more States*" (emphasis in original). [13] It does not repeat the phrase from the earlier Commentaries: regardless of intensity or duration. However, the 2008 paper follows the wording of the ICTY's *Tadić* decision and does not seem to have deviated from its earlier position. This can be confirmed by the ICRC's definition of "non-international armed conflicts" in the same paper, which reads that: "Non-international armed conflicts are *protracted armed confrontations* occurring between governmental armed forces and the forces of one or more armed groups, or between such groups arising on the territory of a State [party to the Geneva Conventions]. The armed confrontation must reach *a minimum level of intensity* and the parties involved in the conflict must show *a minimum of organization*" (emphasis and square brackets in original). [14] The phrases as originally emphasized by the ICRC support the interpretation here that the ICRC position remains unaltered. Indeed, the paper clearly states in its body that: "An IAC [International armed conflict] occurs when one or more States have recourse to armed force against another state, regardless of the reasons or the intensity of this confrontation."

1.3   *ICTY Decisions*

In the *Tadić* Case, the ICTY stated that "an armed conflict exists whenever there is a resort to armed force between States or protracted armed violence between governmental authorities and organized armed groups or between such groups within a State." This so-called "*Tadić* test" for determining the existence of an armed conflict has been applied consistently by the same Tribunal. [15] It has also

---

12   COMMENTARY ON THE ADDITIONAL PROTOCOLS OF 8 JUNE 1977 TO THE GENEVA CONVENTIONS OF 12 AUGUST 1949, 40 (Yves Sandoz et al. eds., 1987).

13   Int'l Comm. Of the Red Cross [ICRC], Opinion Paper, *How is the Term 'Armed Conflict' Defined in International Humanitarian Law?*, 5 (2008). But see, Jelena Pejic of the ICRC who writes that "[i]nternational humanitarian law is the body of rules applicable when armed violence reaches the level of armed conflict, whether international or non-international."

14   *Id.* at 5.

15   Prosecutor v. Milošević, Case No. IT-02-54-T, Decision on Motion for Judgment of Acquittal, ¶ 16-17 (June 16, 2004) (hereinafter cited as "*The Prosecutor v.*

been applied by other courts such as the International Criminal Tribunal for Rwanda (ICTR).[16]

With the contrasting descriptions in the *Tadić* test of *international* armed conflict as being "a resort to armed force between States," and *internal* armed conflict as involving *"protracted* armed violence" (emphasis added), the ICTY seems to have differentiated between the two types of armed conflict at least in terms of the duration of hostilities ("protracted"), and dismissed the importance of the armed force used between States being protracted in the case of international conflicts.

The correctness of this interpretation of the *Tadić* test was confirmed by the ICTY itself in *The Prosecutor v. Delalic* Case (Trial) in 1998. The Tribunal, after citing the above part of the *Tadić* decision, stated as follows:

> In the former situation [i.e., international armed conflict], the existence of armed force between States is sufficient of itself to trigger the application of international humanitarian law. In the latter situation [i.e., internal armed conflict], in order to distinguish from cases of civil unrest or terrorist activities, the emphasis is on the protracted extent of the armed violence and the extent of organisation of the parties involved.[17]

It seems that the concept of "protracted armed violence" in the *Tadić* test, which apparently refers only to the *duration* of a conflict, in fact encompasses the element of *intensity* as well. It could even be said that the emphasis has been placed more on the intensity aspect than the duration of the conflict in subsequent decisions of the ICTY, including the *Tadić* Case itself. The Tribunal held in the merits stage of the *Tadić* Case that "[t]he test applied by the Appeals Chamber to the existence of an armed conflict for the purposes of the rules contained in Common Article 3 [on non-international armed conflict] focuses on two aspects of a conflict; the *intensity* of the conflict and the *organization* of the parties to the conflict" (emphasis added).[18] This was a statement under the heading of *"Protracted* armed violence between governmental forces and organized armed groups" (emphasis added). This approach of referring especially to the intensity of a conflict in relation to the concept of "protracted armed violence"

Slobodan Milošević (Acquittal)"); Prosecutor v. Limaj, Case No. IT-03-66-PT, Trial Chamber, ¶ 84 (Nov. 30, 2005) (hereinafter cited as *"The Prosecutor v. Limaj* (Trial)").

16   See, e.g., Prosecutor v. Akayesu, Case No. ICTR 96-4-T, Trial Chamber, ¶ 619 (Sept. 2, 1998); Prosecutor v. Rutaganda, Case No. ICTR-96-03-T, Judgment and Sentence, ¶ 92 (Dec. 6, 1999).

17   *The Prosecutor v. Delalic* (Trial), ¶ 184.

18   Prosecutor v. Tadić, Case No. IT-94-1-T, Opinion and Judgment, ¶ 562 (May 7, 1997).

has been followed by the ICTY in subsequent cases.[19] Thus, it could be said that, in the above-cited contrasting definitions of international and internal armed conflict, the ICTY dismissed the importance not only of the duration but also and especially of the intensity of conflict in the case of international armed conflict. This seems in harmony with how the ICRC sees the Geneva Conventions and Additional Protocol I.

Again, in the *Delalic* Case, the ICTY explicitly indicated that it followed the views of the ICRC downplaying the importance of the intensity and duration of a conflict by saying that: "[i]n its adjudication of the nature of the armed conflict ..., the Trial Chamber is guided by the Commentary to the Fourth Geneva Convention, which considers that '[a]ny difference arising between two States and leading to the intervention of members of the armed forces' is an international armed conflict and '[i]t makes no difference how long the conflict lasts, or how much slaughter takes place'."[20]

Turning to the international court with more general jurisdiction in geographical and temporal terms, it is worth mentioning that the Statute of the International Criminal Court (ICC) in Article 8, paragraph 2 (f), provides that:

> Paragraph 2 (e) [on other serious violations of the laws and customs applicable in non- international armed conflicts] applies to armed conflicts not of an international character and thus does *not apply* to situations of *internal disturbances and tensions, such as riots, isolated and sporadic acts of violence or other acts of a similar nature.* It applies to armed conflicts that take place in the territory of a State when there is *protracted* armed conflict between governmental authorities and organized armed groups or between such groups (emphasis added).[21]

---

19   See, e.g., *The Prosecutor v. Slobodan Milošević* (Acquittal), ¶ 17; *The Prosecutor v. Limaj* (Trial), ¶ 84, 93.

20   *The Prosecutor v. Delalic* (Trial), ¶ 208.

21   Rome Statute of the International Criminal Court art. 8 (2)(f), July 12, 1998, 2187 U.N.T.S. 3. It may be interesting to note the slight difference in approach that exists between the first and second sentences of this sub-paragraph in that the first sentence carves out certain situations from the concept of "armed conflict" while the second sentence excludes non-protracted "armed conflict" from the scope of application. The second sentence does not literally incorporate the relevant part of the *Tadić* decision, which referred to "protracted armed *violence* between governmental authorities and organized armed groups or between such groups within a State" (emphasis added). The phrase "protracted armed *conflict*," used in place of "protracted armed *violence*," had already appeared in the Sierra Leone proposal that ultimately resulted in the inclusion of the phrase in Article 8, paragraph 2(f). *See also* Anthony Cullen, *The Definition of Non-International Armed Conflict in the Rome Statute of the International Criminal Court: An Analysis of the Threshold of Application Contained in Article 8(2)(f)*, 12(3) J. CONFLICT & SEC. L. 419, 432-34 (2007).

The first sentence of this sub-paragraph copies almost *verbatim* the provision of Article 1, paragraph 2, of Additional Protocol II applicable to non-international armed conflicts;[22] and the second sentence comes from the *Tadić* decision quoted above.[23] There is no comparable provision stipulated in relation to international armed conflict in the Statute. Thus, it is said that the ICC has adopted different thresholds of application between international and internal armed conflicts in line with what we have discussed above.[24] It should also be noted that the ICC in its 2007 decision in the *Lubanga* Case referred to the above cited ICRC Commentary statement on what constitutes an international armed conflict.[25]

---

22   However, the first sentence has not incorporated Article 1, paragraph 1, of Additional Protocol II that requires that the conflict take place between governmental forces and rebel forces, for the latter to control part of a territory, and for there to be a responsible command. For an argument that this exclusion was intentional, see Cullen, *supra* note 21, at 436-37; Theodor Meron, *Crimes under the Jurisdiction of the International Criminal Court, in* REFLECTIONS ON THE INTERNATIONAL CRIMINAL COURT 54 (Herman A.M. von Hebel et al. eds., 1999). Professor Meron further points out that "[t]he reference to protracted armed conflict was designed to give some satisfaction to those delegations that insisted on the incorporation of the higher threshold of applicability of Article 1(1) of Additional Protocol II." *Id.* Regarding Additional Protocol II, it may be worth noting here that in the *Tadić* Case, the ICTY held that "[m]any provisions of this Protocol [i.e., Additional Protocol II] can now be regarded as declaratory of existing rules or as having crystallised emerging rules of customary law or else as having been strongly instrumental in their evolution as general principles." *The Prosecutor v. Tadić* (Jurisdiction, Appeals), ¶ 117. *See also* Jean-Marie Henckaerts, *Study on Customary International Humanitarian Law: A Contribution to the Understanding and Respect for the Rule of Law in Armed Conflict*, 87 INT'L REV. RED CROSS 175, 188 (2005); Emily Crawford, *Unequal before the Law: The Case for the Elimination of the Distinction between International and Non-international Armed Conflicts*, 20(2) LEIDEN J. INT'L L. 441, 456 (2007).

23   The ICTY itself holds this view by saying that "Article 8 is not only consistent with the *Tadić* test, but also incorporates part of the *Tadić* Jurisdiction Appeals Decision into its own definition of 'war crimes'." *The Prosecutor v. Slobodan Milošević* (Acquittal), ¶ 20. *See also* COMMENTARY ON THE ROME STATUTE OF THE INTERNATIONAL CRIMINAL COURT: OBSERVERS' NOTES, ARTICLE BY ARTICLE 285 (Otto Triffterer ed., 1999); Darryl Robinson & Herman von Hebel, *War Crimes in Internal Conflicts: Article 8 of the ICC Statute*, 2 Y.B. INT'L HUMANITARIAN L. 193, 204-05 (1999).

24   Michael Bothe, *War Crimes, in* THE ROME STATUTE OF THE INTERNATIONAL CRIMINAL COURT: A COMMENTARY 418 (Antonio Cassese, Paolo Gaeta, & John R.W.D. Jones eds., 2002).

25   *Prosecutor v. Lubanga*, Case No. ICC-01/04-01/06 Decision on the Confirmation of Charges, Pre-Trial Chamber I, ¶ 207 (Jan. 29, 2007).

2.   Legal Scholarship

2.1   *Objective Criteria: Intensity and Duration of Conflict*

Writers have different views on whether intensity and duration of conflict matter in triggering the application of rules of *international* armed conflict.

For instance, Jelena Pejic, writes that "[i]nternational humanitarian law is the body of rules applicable when armed violence reaches the level of armed conflict, whether international or non-international."[26] By saying that, she indicates that the threshold of armed conflict is the same for both international and internal armed conflict. Professor Karl Josef Partsch provides a similar position in a commentary on Article 1 of Additional Protocol I. He writes that certain situations mentioned in Article 1 of Additional Protocol II (i.e., internal disturbances and tensions) "should also be excluded from the concept of armed conflict as this term is used in Art. 1 of the first Protocol."[27] Professor Partsch cannot mean literally that internal disturbances are excluded as it is difficult to imagine that there exist such situations as "internal" disturbances in "international" conflict to which Protocol I applies. Presumably he means interstate conflicts involving only low-level armed violence and tensions. This reading comports with his reasoning "that the concepts used in both Protocols [i.e., armed conflict] have the same meaning."[28]

However, this reasoning is not very convincing to me. Although the same term "armed conflict" is used in both Protocols, they are different treaties dealing with entirely different situations. Indeed, the situations to which the two Protocols apply are mutually exclusive (See Art. 1, para. 1, of Additional Protocol

---

26   Jelena Pejic, *Terrorist Acts and Groups: A Role for International Law?*, 75 BRIT. Y.B. INT'L L. 71, 73 (2004). Several scholars refer to objective criteria, including the presence of a certain level of intensity, as a threshold of application of international humanitarian law. However, they tend to discuss it only in the context of *non-international* armed conflict. See, e.g., Roberta Arnold, *Terrorism and IHL: A Common Denominator?*, in INTERNATIONAL HUMANITARIAN LAW AND THE 21ST CENTURY'S CONFLICTS: CHANGES AND CHALLENGES 11 (Roberta Arnold & Pierre-Antoine Hildbrand eds., 2005); ROBERTA ARNOLD, THE ICC AS A NEW INSTRUMENT FOR REPRESSING TERRORISM 113-17 (2004); A.P.V. Rogers, *Unequal Combat and the Law of War*, 7 Y.B. INT'L HUMANITARIAN L. 3, 7-10 (2004).

27   MICHAEL BOTHE, KARL JOSEF PARTSCH, & WALDEMAR A. SOLF, NEW RULES FOR VICTIMS OF ARMED CONFLICTS: COMMENTARY ON THE TWO 1977 PROTOCOLS ADDITIONAL TO THE GENEVA CONVENTIONS OF 1949 46 (Nijhoff, 1982). Other writers who advocate the same threshold for both international and internal armed conflict include Arne Willy Dahl and Magnus Sandbu. Dahl & Sandbu, *supra* note 7, at 369-82. However, they tend to downplay the importance of the intensity factor of armed struggle.

28   Bothe, Partsch & Solf, *supra* note 26, at 46.

II).[29] In addition, it is important to note the conspicuous fact that Additional Protocol II excludes certain low intensity violence (i.e., internal disturbances and tensions) from its scope of application, while Additional Protocol I does not. This suggests that in the case of international armed conflict, there is no comparable requirement in terms of intensity of conflict.

A second school of thought[30] has been led by Professor Dietrich Schindler, who argues that "[t]he existence of an armed conflict within the meaning of Article 2 common to the [Geneva] Conventions can always be assumed when parts of the armed forces of two States clash with each other. Even a minor frontier incident is sufficient. Any kind of use of arms between two States brings the Conventions into effect."[31] More recently, Professor René Provost asserts that: "The threshold of applicability [of the Geneva Conventions] is clearly intended to be very low, and to include all situations where humanitarian law may provide some protection to the victims of military operations." He presents a couple of cases that support his argument.[32]

Although they do not provide specific reasons for the differentiated treatment between international and non-international armed conflicts, Article 1, paragraph 2, of Additional Protocol II seems to reveal the reasons. It provides that the Protocol shall *not* apply to "situations of internal disturbances and tensions, such as riots, isolated and sporadic acts of violence and other acts of a similar nature, as not being armed conflicts." By so providing, it excludes from the scope of application of Protocol II those situations that are to be regarded as internal affairs of the State concerned.

---

29   Protocol Additional to the Geneva Conventions of 12 August 1949, and Relating to the Protection of Victims of Non-International Armed Conflicts (Protocol II), June 8, 1977, *available at* http://www.icrc.org/ihl.nsf/FULL/475?OpenDocument. Article 1, paragraph 1, of Protocol II provides that: "This Protocol ... shall apply to all armed conflicts which are not covered by Article 1 of [Additional Protocol I]."

30   Other writers belonging to this school include Hans-Peter Gasser. Gasser argues that according to State practice, *"any use of armed force* by one State against the territory of another triggers the applicability of the Geneva Conventions between the two States" (emphasis added). He continues by stating that: "as soon as the armed forces of one State find themselves with wounded or surrendering members of the armed forces or civilians of another State on their hands, as soon as they detain prisoners or have actual control over a part of the territory of the enemy State, then they must comply with the relevant convention. The number of wounded or prisoners, the size of the territory occupied, are of no account, since the requirement of protection does not depend on quantitative considerations." Hans-Peter Gasser, *International Humanitarian Law: An Introduction, in* Hans Haug et al., Humanity for All: The International Red Cross and Red Crescent Movement 510-11 (Paul Haupt Publishers, 1993).

31   Schindler, *supra* note 4, at 131.

32   René Provost, International Human Rights and Humanitarian Law 250 (Cambridge U.P., 2002).

Internal conflicts had long been treated, unless the recognition of belligerency was granted to the insurgents, as outside the scope of application of any international law of war or armed conflict. They had essentially been internal affairs of a State. Even today the same considerations seem to contribute to making the application of rules of humanitarian law for internal conflicts subject to certain conditions and limitations, and excluding from the scope of application such situations as fall under internal affairs of a State. This can be seen as safeguards on the part of the States against excessive intrusion of international law into their inherently domestic sphere and their freedom of action.[33] Article 3, paragraph 1, of Additional Protocol II confirms this by providing that no provision of the Protocol "shall be invoked for the purpose of affecting the sovereignty of a State or the responsibility of the government ... to maintain or re-establish law and order."[34]

By contrast, no such considerations are required to play a role in the case of international armed conflicts. There is no obstacle that would prevent the rules of humanitarian law from applying to those conflicts upon resort to armed forces by States, irrespective of the intensity or duration of violence.

3.   State Practice: Relevant and Irrelevant Cases

3.1   Fisheries Cases

Recall that some authors argue that for a conflict to constitute an "armed conflict" for the purpose of applying the law of international armed conflict, it must satisfy certain criteria, including the threshold similar to the one provided in Additional Protocol II applicable to non-international armed conflict. In fact, there are fairly numerous cases where, despite the fact that shots were fired, the law of armed conflict was not applied, thus apparently supporting the above argument.

For instance, in 1929 the *I'm Alone,* a British schooner registered in Canada, was ordered to heave to by a US Coast Guard vessel on suspicion of smuggling liquor at the time of the prohibition in the United States. When the *I'm Alone* refused to heave to, she was fired upon by another Coast Guard vessel and sunk more than 200 miles off the coast of the United States.[35]

---

33   *See* Yves Sandoz, *International Humanitarian Law in the Twenty-First Century*, 6 Y.B. Int'l Humanitarian L. 3, 14 (2003).

34   Similarly, Article 8, paragraph 3, of the ICC Statute provides that: "Nothing in paragraph 2 (c) and (e) [on war crimes in non-international armed conflicts] shall affect the responsibility of a Government to maintain or re-establish law and order in the State or to defend the unity and territorial integrity of the State, by all legitimate means." Rome Statute of the International Criminal Court art. 8 (3), July 12, 1998, 2187 U.N.T.S. 3.

35   S.S. "I'm Alone", 3 Rep. int'l Arb. Awards 1609, 1609-18 (1935). *See also* D.J.

In 1962, the *Red Crusader,* a Scottish trawler, was arrested by a Danish fisheries inspection vessel, the *Niels Ebbesen,* and ordered to proceed to the Faroes (Danish territory) for trial for fishing in a prohibited area. After obeying for a while, the *Red Crusader* sought to escape. Since she did not heed to the warnings to stop, she was fired upon directly with solid shot and damaged (but not sunk). All of the firing occurred in Faroese territorial waters. [36]

In these cases, the law of armed conflict was not applied. The doctrinal arguments have centered on the question of whether the use of force was within the reasonable and necessary limit, and not the applicability of the law of armed conflict. This is because of the following self-evident reasons. The use of force by the US Coast Guard or the Danish fisheries inspection vessels was both directed against ships that were not owned or operated by a State, so that there was no State-to-State use of force in these cases. If there is no State-to-State use of force, there will be no possibility, basically, for the law on the use of force in international relations or for the law of armed conflict to apply. The use of force in these cases should better be understood as police actions or domestic law enforcement measures. As Professor Howard Levie correctly points out, "police actions in conflicts such as fisheries conflicts [are] not matters involving armed conflict."[37]

In a more recent case occurring on March 9, 1995, in which Canadian government vessels seized a Spanish fishing vessel, the *Estai,* some 245 miles from the Canadian coast, Spain argued before the International Court of Justice (ICJ) that "the use of force by one State against a fishing vessel of another State on the high seas is necessarily contrary to international law," and said that "the particular use of force directed against the *Estai* ... amounted to a violation of Article 2, paragraph 4, of the [UN] Charter." Speaking generally of the relevant Canadian legislation, and rejecting the Spanish arguments, the Court held that "the use of force authorized by the Canadian legislation and regulations falls within the ambit of what is commonly understood as *enforcement* of conservation and management measures"[38] (emphasis added). Similarly, in the *Saiga* (No. 2) Case of 1999, involving an oil tanker conducting commercial activities (selling oil to fishing vessels) 22 miles from the Guinean island, the International Tribunal for the Law of the Sea (ITLOS) described the Guinean patrol boat's use of force against the *Saiga* as "law enforcement operations."[39]

HARRIS, CASES AND MATERIALS ON INTERNATIONAL LAW 437-39 (Sweet & Maxwell, 5th ed. 1998).

36   The Red Crusader (Denmark v. United Kingdom), 35 I.L.R. 485 (Comm. of Inquiry 1962).

37   Neutrality, the Rights of Shipping and the Use of Force in the Persian Gulf War (Part II), 82 AM. SOC'Y INT'L L. PROC. 609 (1988).

38   Fisheries Jurisdiction Case (Spain v. Canada), 1998 I.C.J. 432, 465-66 (Dec. 4).

39   M/V Saiga (No. 2) (Saint Vincent v. Guinea) 38 I.L.M. 1323, 1355 (Int'l Trib. L. of the Sea 1999).

It is true that one cannot completely exclude the possibility that even a use of force by a governmental vessel against private ships might be viewed as a use of force in international relations. The Definition of Aggression of 1974[40] provides in Article 3, paragraph (d), that "[a]n attack by the armed forces of a State on the land, sea or air forces, or *marine and air fleets* of another State" qualifies as an act of aggression (emphasis added). The "marine fleet" mentioned there must be a fleet of privately-owned (merchant or fishing) ships because it is stipulated side by side with, and in addition to, the "sea forces" of a State in the same paragraph.

It should, however, be borne in mind that the attack on a marine fleet here is, according to the drafting history,[41] to be in such a large scale that it could be equated with a blockade of the ports or coasts of a State, the latter being provided as another example of aggression in Article 3, paragraph (c), of the Definition. Hence, the attack on a marine fleet as an example of aggression should be viewed as an extreme case.[42] More importantly, all this does not conflict with our idea that the concept of *inter-State* armed conflict basically does not carry any particular threshold of intensity. Rather, the above-quoted provision of the Definition of Aggression should be seen as a good illustration that the use of force by a State against privately-owned ships, as opposed to governmentally-owned ships, has to reach a considerably high level of intensity in order to qualify as an aggression and, arguably, as an armed conflict as well.

Thus, it could schematically be said that as far as the use of force between vessels is concerned, it is only the use of force between vessels of two or more governments that could amount to an international armed conflict, with the above-mentioned rare exceptions.

---

40 G.A. Res. 3314(XXIX), art. 3(d), U.N. Doc. A/RES/3314(XXIX) (Dec. 14, 1974).

41 *See*, Benjamin B. Ferencz, Defining International Aggression: The Search for World Peace vol. 2 549, 570-71 (Oceana Pub., 1975).

42 There were doubts expressed during the drafting of the Definition of Aggression as to whether to retain the words "marine and air fleets" in paragraph (d) as an example of aggression. It was argued that their retention would allow countries possessing modern fishing fleets to deplete at will the fishing resources of less advanced countries, which would be deprived of the right to defend themselves. General Assembly Annex A/9411, 10 December 1973, p. 10, ¶ 20, reproduced in Ferencz, *supra* note 41, at 549. As a result, it was agreed at the Sixth Committee of the UN General Assembly that "nothing in the Definition of Aggression, and in particular article 3 (d), shall be construed as in any way prejudicing the authority of a State to exercise its rights within its national jurisdiction, provided such exercise is not inconsistent with the Charter of the United Nations." Report of the Sixth Committee to the General Assembly A/9890, 1-2, ¶ 10, (Dec. 6, 1974) reproduced in Ferencz, *supra* note 41, at 599-600.

3.2   Low Intensity (and Short Duration) Armed Conflicts

As discussed above, the ICTY apparently accepted in the *Delalic* judgement the concept that any conflict involving armed forces of two States is an international armed conflict, irrespective of its duration, and triggers the application of international humanitarian law. The author is not aware of any cases in which the Tribunal has changed this finding of law.

In addition, there are at least a couple of instances where one of the States concerned claimed the applicability of the law of international armed conflict to a very low intensity (and short duration) conflict. One such example is the "Lieutenant Goodman" incident. When Lieutenant Goodman in a US plane was shot down by Syria on 4 December 1983, he was held by the Syrians for about a month. The day following his downing, a US spokesman made a statement that he was considered to be a prisoner of war.[43]

This is one of the cases that Professor Provost cites when he asserts that: "The threshold of applicability [of the Geneva Conventions] is clearly intended to be very low."[44] On the other hand, Professor Levie questions if this particular incident is really a case of armed conflict. After pointing out that "[i]solated incidents can result in a state of armed conflict," but "usually nations don't elect to do that unless the intent of the incident was to create a basis for saying that there is an armed conflict," he indicates that he doesn't believe that is how that incident can be interpreted.[45] However, it is noteworthy that he was not advocating an intensity requirement for international armed conflict in this statement. Rather, he was in fact admitting that international humanitarian law can be applied to isolated incidents. What's more, commenting on the ICRC Commentary statement regarding the irrelevance of intensity and duration of conflict in international armed conflict, Professor Levie states that the ICRC statement does not necessarily apply in 100 percent of the cases but will be applicable in "99 percent of all cases."[46]

---

43   Neutrality, the Rights of Shipping and the Use of Force in the Persian Gulf War (Part II), 82 Am. Soc'y Int'l L. Proc. 598 (1988) [hereinafter cited as *"Neutrality,* 82 Am. Soc'y Int'l. L. Proc. 598"]. A week later, US President Ronald Reagan made a statement indicating that the lieutenant was not a prisoner of war by saying that "I don't know how you have a prisoner of war when there is no declared war between nations. I don't think that makes you eligible for the Geneva Accords." However, this was a dubious statement from an international legal perspective, as Professor Levie correctly points out, in that it made the application of Geneva Conventions conditional on the existence of a declared war. *Id.* at 598, 610.

44   Provost, *supra* note 31, at 250. The other case Professor Provost cites is a clash between Mexico and the United States in 1916 involving 250 soldiers and lasting for thirty minutes. *Id.*

45   *Neutrality,* 82 Am. Soc'y Int'l L. Proc. 598, *supra* note 45.

46   *Id.*

A more recent instance of low intensity conflict in which one of the parties to the conflict claimed the application of international humanitarian law was that of the Iranian capture and detention of 15 UK navy personnel. On 24 March 2007, Iran captured at gunpoint the crew of a small British navy vessel, constituting part of the occupation forces in Iraq under UN auspices and having just completed their routine inspection activity. Iran claimed that the vessel was in Iranian waters, while the British argued that they were in Iraqi waters. When the captives appeared on Iranian television, a spokesman for UK Prime Minister Tony Blair complained that doing so was a violation of the Third Geneva Convention relative to the Treatment of Prisoners of War.[47] This complaint premised itself on the application of the law of international armed conflict, though there is conflicting information that the United Kingdom did not take an official position as to whether the Convention applied.[48]

While others may view these cases differently, they are indeed cases in which one of the States concerned claimed the application of the law of international armed conflict to situations of a very low intensity (and short duration) conflict between States. Although the number is small, the existence of these examples requires us to hesitate to conclude that international humanitarian law rules do not apply in low-intensity conflicts between States.

Conclusion

Whether a given conflict is an "armed conflict" or not would affect very much the legal relationship between those involved. This is because with the passage from peace to armed conflict, the applicable rules dramatically change. In addition, whether a given armed conflict is "international" or "non-international" would also make a big difference.

Rules for international armed conflict have steadily developed since the 19th century, while those for non-international armed conflict have not matched them. Until the mid-20th century, internal fighting had been outside the scope of international law, however severe the fighting was, unless the recognition of belligerency was granted to the insurgents, which was extremely rare. It is only in Common Article 3 of the 1949 Geneva Conventions that international law started to regulate non-international armed conflict.

Even now, if violence occurs within a State's territory (non-international conflict), it will not be treated as "armed conflict," unless the violence reaches at a certain level of intensity. The reason for this is that low intensity internal con-

---

47   Commentary, *An International Kidnapping*, L.V. REV. J., March 30, 2007, at 12B; Matthew B. Stannard, *What Law Did Tehran Break?: Capture of British Sailors a Gray Area in Application of Geneva Conventions*, S.F. CHRON., Apr. 1, 2007, at A-1.

48   International Law Association Committee on the Use of Force, *Initial Report on the Meaning of Armed Conflict in International Law* 20 (2008) *available at* http://www. ila-hq.org/en/committees/index.cfm/cid/1022.

flicts have been regarded and treated as internal affairs of the State concerned, and thus blocked to international law by the sovereignty of the State.

In the case of international conflict between States, any difference arising between States leading to the intervention of their armed forces is, in principle, an international armed conflict to which international humanitarian law applies. It makes little difference how long the conflict lasts or how much slaughter takes place, as the ICRC states in its Commentary on the Geneva Conventions. This is because in inter-State conflict, there is no room for the concept of sovereignty to play a role in order to exclude minor disturbances as "internal affairs of a State." Additional Protocol I applicable to international armed conflict contains no comparable provision excluding riots or sporadic acts of violence that is found in Additional Protocol II applicable to non-international armed conflict. In international judicial practice, both ICTY and ICC seem to follow the above idea put forward by the ICRC. In State practice, too, there are some very low intensity conflicts to which a State concerned claimed the application of the law of armed conflict, which suggests that the traditional *opinio juris* has not been lost.

Chapter 6

The Meaning of Armed Conflict: Non-International Armed Conflict

Christine Gray

Introduction

Non-international armed conflicts – and in particular internal armed conflicts, as will be defined below – are the most common type of conflict; in the period 1995-2005 95% of armed conflicts have taken place within states.[1] There was a dramatic increase in the number of civil wars after the Second World War, and an equally dramatic decline in their numbers in the 1990s, but they still constitute the vast majority of conflicts.[2]

It is only comparatively recently that treaty provision has been made for such conflicts, though an early attempt to regulate the American Civil War was made in the 1863 *Lieber Code*.[3] This civil war code subsequently influenced the development of *ius in bello* on international armed conflict. Recently we have seen attempts to achieve the converse, to ensure that the law applicable to international armed conflict applies in full (or almost) to non-international armed conflict.

The crucial factors in establishing the existence of a non-international armed conflict, and the threshold to be reached for the application of IHL, are the identity and degree of organization of the parties, the intensity of the conflict; and the related questions as to start, finish and area of the conflict. Until recently the question of the definition of a non-international armed conflict was a more sensitive question than the definition of international armed conflict. The ICRC did not deal with this issue in its recent Commentary. So there is a clear need for the ILA to study the question.

---

1   HUMAN SECURITY REPORT 2005: WAR AND PEACE IN THE 21ST CENTURY viii (2005).

2   *Id.* at 1-2, 146.

3   *See* George D. Haimbaugh Jr., *Introduction to Panel II: Humanitarian Law: The Lincoln-Lieber Initiative*, 13 GA. J. INT'L & COMP. L. 245 (1983).

Mary Ellen O'Connell (ed.), What Is War? An Investigation in the Wake of 9/11.
© 2012 *Koninklijke Brill NV. Printed in The Netherlands.* ISBN 978 9004 17234 0. *pp. 69 – 95.*

Threshold: Treaty provisions

Common Article 3 of the four 1949 Geneva Conventions was a revolution-ary provision in that it was the first international treaty to attempt to regulate non-international armed conflict.[4] However, it offers no definition. Common Article 3 provides only: "In cases of armed conflict not of an international char-acter occurring in the territory of one of the High Contracting Parties;" thus it offers only a negative formula. Some commentators were critical of this, saying that the desire for maximum breadth of application had overridden the desire for that element of certainty which legal norms demand if they are to be effec-tive. "The value of the individual rules of restraint in conflict is lost if the scope of the provision lacks certainty."[5] Others regarded the lack of any more rigorous definition as an advantage in that it provided flexibility.[6]

The ICRC commentary on Common Article 3 suggests criteria for deter-mining the existence of an armed conflict:[7]

1. That the party in revolt against the de jure Government possesses an organ-ized military force, an authority responsible for its acts, acting within a determinate territory and having the means of respecting and ensuring respect for the Convention.

2. That the legal Government is obliged to have recourse to the regular mili-tary forces against insurgents organized as military and in possession of a part of the national territory.

3. (a) That the de jure Government has recognized the insurgents as bellig-erents; or

    (b) That it has claimed for itself the rights of a belligerent; or

    (c) That it has accorded the insurgents recognition as belligerents for the purposes only of the present Convention; or

    (d) That the dispute has been admitted to the agenda of the Security Council or the General Assembly of the United Nations as being a threat to international peace, a breach of the peace, or an act of aggres-sion."

4. (a) That the insurgents have an organization purporting to have the char-acteristics of a State.

    (b) That the insurgent civil authority exercises de facto authority over per-sons within a determinate portion of the national territory.

---

4   194 parties, more than the 192 members of the UN.

5   G.I.A.D Draper, *Humanitarian Law and Internal Armed Conflicts*, 13 GA. J. INT'L & COMP. L. 253, 264 (1983).

6   LINDSAY MOIR, THE LAW OF INTERNAL ARMED CONFLICT 32-33 (Cambridge University Press 2002).

7   Convention (IV) Relative to the Protection of Civilian Persons in Time of War, Aug. 12, 1949, *available at* http://www.icrc.org/ihl.nsf/com/380-600006.

    (c)   That the armed forces act under the direction of an organized authority and are prepared to observe the ordinary laws of war.

    (d)   That the insurgent civil authority agrees to be bound by the provisions of the Convention.

The Commentary said that these criteria were useful to distinguish a genuine armed conflict from mere acts of banditry or unorganized and short-lived insurrection.[8]

    The 1977 *Additional Protocol II* (APII) sets a much higher threshold than Common Article 3;[9] this was done in order to make its more detailed and demanding rules acceptable to states.[10] APII applies to "all armed conflicts which are not covered by Article 1 of the Protocol Additional to the Geneva Conventions ... and which take place in the territory of a High Contracting Party between its armed forces and dissident armed forces or other organized armed groups which, under responsible command, exercise such control over a part of its territory as to enable them to carry out sustained and concerted military operations and to implement this Protocol." Article 1(2) provides that "this Protocol shall not apply to situations of internal disturbances and tensions, such as riots, isolated and sporadic acts of violence and other acts of a similar nature, as not being armed conflicts." That is, APII applies only to conflicts which resemble traditional inter-state conflict, between the government and armed groups; it requires control over territory by organized armed groups. (Many commentators have expressed doubts as to whether this requirement of territorial control is appropriate to conflicts involving non-state actors; it is certainly not suitable for conflicts with terrorists. How far is armed conflict today aimed at control of territory rather then at winning the hearts and minds/will of the people?) APII does not cover the situation where there is no government. It requires sustained and concerted operations, and that the rebels be able to implement the protocol. Some commentators are critical of the narrower application of APII, given that the provisions are exclusively humanitarian in character, designed for the protection of civilians.[11]

    Thus, Common Article 3 provides wider but more limited protection. It is generally taken as customary international law. This initial provision was supplemented, but not replaced, by APII. "This Protocol, which develops and supplements Article 3 common to the Geneva Conventions of 12 August 1949

---

8   *Id.*

9   162 parties; these do not include the USA, Iran, Iraq or Afghanistan. Protocol Additional to the Geneva Conventions of 12 August 1949, and Relating to the Protection of Victims of Non-International Armed Conflicts (Protocol II), June 8, 1977, *available at* http://www.icrc.org/ihl.nsf/FULL/475?OpenDocument.

10   Draper, *supra* note 5.

11   Moir, *supra* note 6, at 103; Christopher Greenwood, *International Humanitarian Law and the Laws of War* (1999) at para 137.

without modifying its existing conditions of application." Thus there are two separate regimes for non-international armed conflict.

Do the statutes of international criminal tribunals offer any guidance on the meaning of "non-international armed conflict"? There is nothing in the statutes of the ICTY or the ICTR. Implicitly the Security Council characterized the conflict in Rwanda as internal and accepted that the conflict in the former Yugoslavia could be either internal or international.[12]

In contrast, the *Rome Statute* of the International Criminal Court does offer a definition, or rather more than one definition, of non-international armed conflict.[13]

Article 8(2)d: "Paragraph (2)(c) [on serious violations of Common Article 3] applies to armed conflicts not of an international character and thus does not apply to situations of internal disturbances and tensions, such as riots, isolated and sporadic acts of violence or other acts of a similar nature."

Article 8(2)(f) is narrower and is based on the ICTY decision in *Tadić*; it adds "Paragraph (2)(e) [on other serious violations of the laws and customs applicable in armed conflict not of an international character] applies to armed conflicts that take place in the territory of a State when there is protracted armed conflict between governmental authorities and organised armed groups or between such groups." This, although similar to APII, does not exactly reproduce its provisions: the Rome Statute is not limited to conflicts between governments and armed groups; it omits the condition that dissident armed forces or other organised groups should "be under responsible command or exercise such control over part of its territory as to enable them to carry out sustained and concerted military operations." This may be seen as a recognition that the requirement of territorial control is not realistic for conflicts against guerillas and other irregular forces.[14] Moreover the Rome Statute does not base the list of crimes that may be committed in non-international armed conflicts on APII, but makes a selection from Article 8(2)(b) on international armed conflict.[15]

12   Prosecutor v. Akayesu, Case No. ICTR 96-4-T, Trial Chamber, ¶ 606 (Sept. 2, 1998).

13   104 parties; entered into force 1 July 2002.

14   Deidre Willmott, *Removing the Distinction between International and Non-International Armed Conflict in the Rome Statute of the International Criminal Court,* 5 MELB. J. INT'L L. 196 (2004).

15   Heike Spieker, *The International Criminal Court and Non-International Armed Conflicts,* 13 LEIDEN J. INT'L L. 417 (2000).

Threshold: Cases
The Tadić definition

The most important case on this issue is *Tadić*. The ICTY Appeals Chamber[16] held that "armed conflict exists whenever there is a resort to armed force between States or protracted armed violence between governmental authorities and organized armed groups or between such groups within a State."[17] This has been followed in many later cases: see the list in *Limaj*.[18]

The *Tadić* formulation sets a generally low threshold for the existence of non-international armed conflict under Common Article 3: there is no requirement that the insurgents exercise territorial control, or actually meet obligations under Common Article 3, or that the government use its armed forces or that there be a recognition of belligerency.[19] There is no requirement that the government be involved in the conflict.

However, the formulation does require "protracted armed violence". Is this a restrictive approach? Most commentators argue that it is not and that it is best understood as little more than a restatement of the general rule excluding isolated and sporadic acts of violence from the scope of IHL.[20] In *Kordić and Cerkez* (Appeal Judgment at para 341) the Appeals Chamber said that the term "protracted" is significant in excluding mere cases of civil unrest or single acts of terrorism in cases of non-international conflicts. In applying this test the *Tadić* Trial Chamber (Judgment May 1997, para 562) said that it focused on two aspects of a conflict; the intensity of the conflict and the organization of the parties to the conflict. In an armed conflict of an internal or mixed character these closely related criteria are used solely for the purpose of distinguishing an armed conflict from banditry, unorganized or short-lived insurrections or terrorist activities which are not subject to IHL. Many other cases follow this approach.[21]

---

16   Prosecutor v. Tadić, Case No. IT-94-1-T, Jurisdiction, (Oct. 2, 1995).

17   *Id.* at 561-568.

18   Limaj, Trial Chamber 30 November 2005, at note 294.

19   MOIR, *supra* note 6, at 42-43.

20   Derek Jinks, *The Temporal Scope of Application of International Humanitarian Law in Contemporary Conflicts* (Harvard University Background Paper Prepared for the Informal High-Level Expert Meeting on the Reaffirmation and Development of International Humanitarian Law, Jan. 27-29, 2003).

21   *See* Prosecutor v. Blagojević and Jokić, Case No. IT-02-60-T, Trial Chamber, ¶536 (Jan. 17, 2005); Prosecutor v. Halilović, Case No. IT-01-48-T, Trial Chamber, ¶ 24 (Nov. 16, 2005); Prosecutor v. Galić, Case No. IT-98-29-T, Trial Chamber, ¶ 9 (Dec. 5, 2003); Prosecutor v. Stakić, Case No. IT-97-24-T, Trial Chamber, ¶ 560 (July 31, 2003).

Kosovo

The question as to whether there was a non-international armed conflict came up before the ICTY with regard to the conflict in Kosovo; the tribunal had to decide whether there was an actual non-international armed conflict or mere internal unrest. In *Milošević* an *amici curiae* motion was brought (under Rule 98 bis) that there was no armed conflict in Kosovo at the relevant times and so no case to answer for war crimes under Article 3 of the ICTY Statute.[22] It was argued that there was no armed conflict before 24 March 1999 when the NATO bombing campaign began: the conflict was not protracted armed violence; it was only "acts of banditry, unorganized and short-lived insurrections or terrorist activities." The Trial Chamber held that *Tadić* had set out the test for the existence of an armed conflict. The *Tadić* test was "not inconsistent" with the ICRC's Official Commentary to Common Article 3 GC. The ICRC commentary was of persuasive value only; although it does offer a more extensive list of criteria, these are not definitive or exhaustive. And the *Tadić* test is also consistent with the ICC Rome Statute Article 8 which incorporates part of the *Tadić* Jurisdiction Appeals decision into its own definition of war crimes. The *Tadić* test is also consistent with APII. Thus the more restrictive criteria of the ICRC are dismissed in favour of the broader approach in *Tadić*.

The Trial Chamber found that the KLA was sufficiently organized; it did not apply the requirement from the ICRC commentary put forward in the Amicus Brief that the insurgents should have "the means of respecting and ensuring respect for the Convention." On the intensity of the conflict the Chamber considered a large body of evidence: the size of the Serbian response to the KLA actions was treated as evidence of the nature of the conflict; account was taken of the spread of the conflict over territory, the increase in number of government forces and of the weapons used. The Chamber said that control over territory by insurgents was not a requirement for the existence of a non-international armed conflict; but nevertheless it found that there was such control over 50% of the territory in summer 1998. It did not, however, decide exactly when the conflict started.

This difficult question came up again in *Limaj* (31 May 2004).[23] The Pre-Trial brief argued that there was no internal armed conflict in Kosovo at the time of the alleged crimes, May – July 1998. The Prosecution had said that there was an armed conflict between the FRY and the KLA but had not specified exactly when such armed conflict actually began. The Pre-trial Brief relied on the ICRC criteria, and argued that not every use of arms in defiance of a government could be said to give rise to an armed conflict and make Common Article 3 applicable.

---

22   Prosecutor v. Milošević, Case No. IT-02-54-T (June 16, 2004).
23   Prosecutor v. Limaj, Case No. IT-03-66-PT, Trial Chamber, ¶ 294 (Nov. 30, 2005).

The Trial Chamber judgment rejected these defence arguments.[24] Applying the *Tadić* test for the existence of an armed conflict, it assessed the intensity of the conflict and the organisation of the parties.[25] The Defence had argued that the Chamber should consider a list of extra factors based on the ICRC Commentary to Common Article 3: insurgents' control of territory, the government's use of the army against the insurgents, the insurgents' status as belligerents, whether they have a state-like organisation and authority to observe the rules of war. But the Commentary clarifies that the list is by no means obligatory and merely suggests convenient criteria. The drafting history also shows a clear rejection of more detailed criteria. And Article 8 of the Rome Statute of the ICC followed *Tadić*. The Defence also argued that the Tribunal had not yet defined the extent of organisation of the parties required or the level of intensity. In order to be bound by IHL a party must be able to implement international humanitarian law and must possess a basic understanding of the principles of Common Article 3, a capacity to disseminate rules and a method of sanctioning breaches. The Chamber rejected this view. The two elements – intensity and level of organisation – are used solely to distinguish an armed conflict from banditry, unorganised and short-lived insurrection or terrorist activities, which are not subject to IHL.

Therefore the Chamber applied the test in *Tadić* to determine whether the existence of an armed conflict had been established. It said that other Chambers had considered such factors as the seriousness of attacks and whether there had been an increase in armed clashes, the spread of clashes over territory and over a period of time, any increase in the number of government forces and mobilisation and the distribution of weapons among both parties to the conflict, as well as whether the conflict has attracted the attention of the Security Council and whether any resolutions have been passed.[26]

The Chamber found that the KLA did possess the characteristics of an organised armed group, despite some conflicting evidence. It had a general staff who appointed zone commanders, gave directions to units and issued public statements. Unit commanders gave orders and subordinate units generally acted in accordance with those orders. Steps had been taken to introduce disciplinary rules and military police and to recruit, train and equip new members. And there was also the requisite degree of intensity of the conflict. The Defence had argued that a series of regionally disparate and temporally sporadic attacks carried out over a broad and contested geographic area should not be held to amount to an armed conflict, but the Chamber found that they were not sporadic or dispersed. It also rejected the Defence argument that the use of force

---

24   *Id.*

25   *Id.* at 84.

26   Prosecutor v. Tadić, Case No. IT-94-1-T, Judgment, ¶ 567 (May 7, 1997).; Prosecutor v. Mucić, Case No. IT-96-21-T, Judgment, ¶ 190 (Nov. 16, 1998) [hereinafter Celebici case].

was one-sided. By the end of May 1998 KLA units were constantly engaged in armed clashes with substantial Serb forces in many areas.

ICTR[27]

The ICTR followed the approach of the ICTY on Common Article 3. The ICTR also had a wider jurisdiction to decide on international criminal responsibility under APII.[28] *Akayesu*[29] considered the nature of the conflict in Rwanda at some length; it treated Common Article 3 and APII separately.[30] First, what constituted an armed conflict under Common Article 3? The Chamber quoted *Tadić* on the definition of armed conflict; it also noted the ICRC commentary on Common Article 3 which ruled out mere acts of banditry, internal disturbances and tensions and unorganized and short-lived insurrections.[31] The ICRC specified that the conflicts referred to in Common Article 3 were armed conflicts with armed forces on either side engaged in hostilities: conflicts, in short, which are in many respects similar to an international armed conflict, but take place within the confines of a single country. Because the definition of an armed conflict is abstract, the question whether or not a situation can be described as an armed conflict, meeting the criteria of Common Article 3, was to be decided by a **case-by-case** approach. *Akayesu* suggested an "evaluation test" whereby it was necessary to evaluate the intensity of the conflict and the organization of the parties.[32] Intensity did not depend on the subjective judgement of the parties, it was objective.[33] On APII it adopted a four-fold list of criteria to determine the existence of a non-international armed conflict.[34]

---

27   *See* Human Rights Watch, Case Law of the International Criminal Tribunal for Rwanda (2004), *available at* http://www.hrw.org/reports/2004/ij/ictr/index.htm.

28   In so far as APII was not customary international law.

29   *Akayesu*, Case No. ICTR 96-4-T, Trial Chamber, ¶ 619-627 (Sept. 2, 1998).

30   *See also* Prosecutor v. Kayishema & Ruzindana, Case No. ICTR-95-1-A, Judgment, ¶ 170 (May 21, 1999).

31   See also *Akayesu*, Case No. ICTR 96-4-T; *Kayishema & Ruzindana*, Case No. ICTR-95-1-A ; Rutaganda v. Prosecutor, Case No. ICTR-96-03-R, Judgment (Dec. 8, 2006).

32   *Akayesu*, Case No. ICTR 96-4-A, Appeal Chamber, ¶ 91 (June 1, 2001).

33   *Akayesu*, Case No. ICTR-96-4-T, Trial Chamber, ¶ 603.

34   *Id.* at ¶ 622-627:
     i)   An armed conflict takes place within the territory of a HCP between its armed forces and dissident armed forces or other organized armed groups;
     ii) the dissident armed forces or other organized armed groups are under responsible command
     iii) the dissident armed forces or other organized armed groups are able to exercise such control over a part of their territory as to enable them to carry out sustained and concerted military operations; and

In *Rutaganda*, the first conviction for war crimes by the ICTR, the Trial Chamber (1999) followed the same approach.[35] In *Musema* the Trial Chamber (2002) said that non-international armed conflict is distinct from an international armed conflict because of the legal status of the entities opposing each other: the parties to the conflict are not sovereign states but the government of a single state in conflict with one or more armed factions within its territory. The expression "armed conflicts" introduces a material criterion: the existence of open hostilities between armed forces which are organized to a greater or lesser degree.

The significance of the classification of a conflict

The question of classification is not simply an abstract question; it is important in so far as it affects the application of the substantive law in IHL, human rights and use of force. Common Article 3 and APII distinguish between international and non-international armed conflicts. It is crucial to note that "non-international" is not limited to purely internal conflicts. In the past there has been some suggestion that Common Article 3 applies only to civil conflict on the territory of only one High Contracting Party. But this has generally been rejected as it would create a gap in the application of IHL; it also misconceives the policy behind Common Article 3 that rules on international conflicts apply also to non-international conflicts in order to protect the victims.[36] Rather "non-international armed conflict" is the residual category of all conflicts which are not between states, or between states and national liberation movements (NLM) under Article 1(4) API. This was recently affirmed in the US Supreme Court case of *Hamdan v Rumsfeld*.[37] The US government argued that Common Article 3 was not applicable to those Al-Qaida suspects detained in Guantanamo bay, Cuba, because the conflict with Al-Qaida being international in scope does not qualify as a conflict not of an international character. "That reasoning is erroneous. The term 'conflict not of an international character' is used here in contradistinction to a conflict between nations ... Although an important purpose of the provision was to furnish minimal protection to rebels involved in a civil war the ICRC commentaries also make clear that the scope of the Article must be as wide as possible."

---

iv)   the dissident armed forces or other organized armed groups are able to implement Additional Protocol II.

35   *Rutaganda*, Case No. ICTR-96-03-R, Judgment, at ¶ 93.

36   Jinks, *supra* note 20.

37   Hamdan v. Rumsfeld, 548 U.S. 557 (2006); see John Cerrone, ASIL Insight, *The Military Commissions Act of 2006: Examining the Relationship between the International Law of Armed Conflict and US Law*, Nov. 13, 2006 Vol 10 Number 30, *available at* http://www.asil.org/insights/2006/11/insights061114.html.

The most basic distinction is that between international and non-international conflicts. The difference is still important in IHL in that there are more detailed rules governing international conflicts. The only treaty provisions on non-international armed conflicts are the mini-convention of Common Article 3 and the 28 articles (15 of them substantive) of APII.

The main differences in the treaty provision – in outline only – are:
a)   on targeting; more limited on protection of civilians, on the principles of distinction and proportionality.[38]
b)   less detailed provisions on prohibited weapons, etc.[39]
c)   provisions on the protection of POW and civilians who have taken a direct part in hostilities.
d)   individual criminal responsibility. The grave breaches regime applies only in international armed conflicts. The Rome Statute makes a distinction between those crimes which can be committed in international/non-international armed conflicts.

Also **human rights law** is more important in non-international armed conflict than in international. There is growing discussion of the issue of the relation of IHL and human rights law. The ICJ has repeatedly held that "the protection offered by human rights conventions does not cease in case of armed conflict."[40] The traditional position is that IHL provides *lex specialis* in non-international armed conflict. The ICJ in its Advisory Opinion on the *Legality of the Threat or Use of Nuclear Weapons* said the protection of the ICCPR does not cease in times of war … In principle the right not arbitrarily to be deprived of one's life applies in hostilities. The test of what is an arbitrary deprivation of life, however, then falls to be determined by the applicable *lex specialis*, namely the law applicable in armed conflict which is designed to regulate the conduct of hostilities.[41] However, this traditional position is coming under challenge. Thus Abresch argues that as the IHL on internal armed conflict is not very developed the case for the application of human rights is strengthened. It should not be assumed that IHL necessarily constitutes *lex specialis*.[42]

---

38   James G. Stewart, *Towards a Single Definition of Armed Conflict in International Humanitarian Law*, 85 Int'l Rev. Red Cross 313, 320 (2003).

39   Willmott, *supra* note 14.

40   Legal Consequences of the Construction of a Wall in the Occupied Palestinian Territory, Advisory Opinion, 2004 I.C.J. 136, ¶ 102, 105, 106 (July 9); Armed Activities on the Territory of the Congo (Dem. Rep. Congo v. Uganda), 2005 I.C.J. 116, ¶ 216 (Dec. 19).

41   Legality of the Threat or Use of Nuclear Weapons, Advisory Opinion, 1996 I.C.J. 226, ¶ 24-25 (July 8).

42   William Abresch, *A Human Rights Law of Internal Armed Conflict*, 16(4) Eur. J. Int'l L. 741 (2005).

The Human Rights Committee is working to elaborate Fundamental Standards of Humanity which would apply in all situations.[43] The point at which situations of internal violence reach the threshold level required for the application of IHL is not always clear. Also in states of emergency the protection offered by human rights law may be limited by derogations. Therefore it is necessary to state principles to be derived from human rights and IHL to be applicable to everyone in all situations. It has concluded that there is no need to develop new standards; the aim is to strengthen practical protection.[44]

Human Rights tribunals have applied human rights law to various conflicts: in early cases (concerning conflicts with the IRA and the PKK) the European Court of Human Rights used the language of IHL; it is not clear how far it was actually applying IHL rather than human rights law to conflicts of various kinds.[45] More recently it took a different line; in two cases on the Chechen conflict it applied human rights law to the conduct of hostilities in internal ongoing armed conflict.[46] There are currently several cases before the European Court of Human Rights arising out of the conflict in Iraq.

Conversely the Inter-American Commission on Human Rights has asserted jurisdiction to decide on the existence of a non-international armed conflict and to apply IHL, despite the absence of any express legal basis for this.[47] It has affirmed that human rights and IHL complement each other in situations of armed conflict.

> "In certain circumstances, however, the test for evaluating the observance of
> a particular right ... in a situation of armed conflict may be distinct from that
> applicable in time of peace. In such situations, international law, including the
> jurisprudence of this Commission, dictates that it may be necessary to deduce
> the applicable standards by reference to international humanitarian law as the
> applicable *lex specialis*."[48]

---

43   Under its Resolution 2000/69. *See* The Secretary-General, *Report of the Secretary-General on the Promotion and Protection of Human Rights, delivered to the Economic and Social Council*, U.N. Doc.E/CN.4/2006/87 (Mar. 3. 2006).

44   Also the ICRC Customary International Humanitarian Law study identifies 18 fundamental guarantees in Chapter 32 that apply to all civilians in armed conflict.

45   Kenneth Watkin, *Controlling the Use of Force: A Role for Human Rights Norms in Contemporary Armed Conflict*, 98 Am. J. Int'l L. 1, 23 (2004).

46   Isayeva v Russia, no. 57950/00, Eur. Ct. H.R., 24 February 2005. *See also* Abresch, *supra* note 42.

47   Watkin, *supra* note 45. *See* Case 10.951, Coard and Others v. United States, 123 ILR 156 (Inter-Am. Commission report 1999) (USA objected to this assertion of competence by the Inter-American Commission.)

48   Precautionary Measures issued by the Commission on 12 March, 2002 in *Detainees of Guantanamo Bay, Cuba*.

It has asserted that it is competent to apply IHL and to determine the existence of an armed conflict.

Both contrasting approaches are problematic. Human rights bodies may not be qualified to decide on matters of IHL. Human rights accountability is one-sided in that it imposes responsibility on the government only. But some commentators have welcomed the application of human rights law as offering the chance of protection for civilians through human rights mechanisms when states are not willing to acknowledge the existence of an internal armed conflict and the applicability of IHL. The application of human rights in non-international armed conflict also avoids the need to make the difficult distinction between internal armed conflict and mere riots etc.

The question whether a conflict is international or internal may affect ius ad bellum.[49] The classification of a conflict as international affects the *ius ad bellum* on intervention. There should be no forcible intervention in a purely civil war – unless this is authorized by the UN Security Council. But if there is prior outside intervention on the side of the rebels then other states may assist the threatened government.

The question of the classification of a particular conflict is not always a straightforward choice between international and non-international armed conflict. The British Manual of the Law of Armed Conflict (2004) observes that in practice many conflicts since 1945 have had the characteristics of both international and non-international armed conflicts.[50] According to the jurisprudence of the ICTY there may be a mixed internal/international conflict within one state with both internal and international conflicts taking place at the same time in different areas with the result that different laws may apply between different parties. This has been criticised by some commentators.[51]

Also an internal conflict may subsequently become international, or an international conflict may become internal. Questions as to how to determine the start and end of international and internal armed conflicts then become crucial.

Finally, an internal conflict may be internationalized by third state intervention. The Human Security Report lists examples.[52] It includes proxy wars in the Cold War and internationalized conflicts where a civil war spills over into neighbouring states, as in the cases of Congo (DRC)/Uganda, Sierra Leone/Liberia. The NATO intervention in Kosovo also falls into this group.

---

49 Christine Gray, *Bosnia and Herzegovina: Civil War or Interstate Conflict? Characterisation and Consequences*, 67 BRITS. Y.B. INT'L L. 155 (1996).

50 MINISTRY OF DEFENCE, THE MANUAL OF THE LAW OF ARMED CONFLICT ¶ 15.1.1 (Oxford Univ. Press 2004).

51 Stewart, *supra* note 38.

52 HUMAN SECURITY REPORT 2005: WAR AND PEACE IN THE 21ST CENTURY 20 (2005).

Traditionally if a third state intervenes to help the government then this is a non-international armed conflict. An "internal" or non-international armed conflict is one where there is only one state involved or several states, but all on the same side.[53] But if a foreign government intervenes to help the rebels then this is an international armed conflict. But is it right that this distinction should affect the applicable law? Many commentators have been critical of this position.[54] Aldrich argues on the basis of his experience with Vietnam that, whichever side the state intervenes on, its intervention transforms the conflict into an international armed conflict.[55]

In practice this type of classification has proved extremely controversial, as may be seen with regard to the Soviet intervention in Afghanistan. Clearly in this and other cases there was doubt as to whether there was a genuine invitation and thus as to whether it was a non-international or international armed conflict.[56] Conversely the USA, after the 2001 invasion of Afghanistan, classified *Operation Enduring Freedom* as an international conflict, as part of the "war on terror", even after the end of the initial operations, the overthrow of the Taliban and the invitation to assist by the government of Afghanistan after the announcement of the end of the occupation.[57]

The question whether a conflict is internal or whether it amounts to an international armed conflict under API Article 1(4) on NLM is also difficult.[58] This distinction affects *ius ad bellum*, the law on intervention and *ius in bello*. But the question whether the Article 1(4) classification is customary international law is still controversial. And in practice no state has been willing to accept that a conflict on its territory constitutes a war of national liberation, as may be seen with regard to Kosovo, Chechnya, Palestine/Israel and Sri Lanka.

Decisions on type of conflict[59]

There have now been many decisions on classification by international criminal tribunals. Such decisions will determine whether an international tribunal has jurisdiction at all; or, less drastically, what crimes may be charged.

---

53 Jinks, supra note 20.

54 Stewart was also critical of the attempt to decide whether internationalized conflict should be classified as international or non-international.

55 George H. Aldrich, *The Laws of War on Land*, 94 Am. J. Int'l L. 42, 62 (2000).

56 Byron argues that this should be regarded as an international conflict. Christine Byron, *Armed Conflicts: International or non-international*, 6 J. Conflict & Sec. L. 63 (2001).

57 See below at 65.

58 166 parties.

59 See Stewart, *supra* note 38; Mohamed Bennouna, *The Characterization of the armed conflict in the practice of the ICTY*, in Essays on ICTY Procedure and Evidence in Honour of Gabrielle Kirk McDonald 55 (Richard May ed., 2001); Byron, *supra* note 56.

The question was dealt with in a summary manner by the ICTR, which is not willing to re-open the question. The issue came up in *Ntagerura* when the defence wanted to introduce evidence from expert witnesses that the conflict in Rwanda was actually international (because of Ugandan, US and British involvement) and that therefore the ICTR had no jurisdiction as its jurisdiction was only over non-international armed conflict. The judge rejected the request: "It is a matter of common knowledge that the conflict in Rwanda was of an internal non-international character."[60]

But the issue has proved much more difficult for the ICTY and its decisions have vastly complicated this area of the law. *Tadić* has proved a revolutionary case, but one which is in many ways complicated and problematic. In order to decide whether Tadić could be charged with grave breaches the tribunal had to decide whether the conflict was internal or international or mixed, and whether there had been a shift from an internal to an international armed conflict. It said, "In the case of an internal armed conflict breaking out on the territory of a State, it may become international (or, depending upon the circumstances, be international in character alongside an internal armed conflict) if (i) another State intervenes in that conflict through its troops, or alternatively if (ii) some of the participants in the internal armed conflict act on behalf of that other State."[61]

The difficulty is compounded as it follows from this that the tribunal has to adopt a case-by-case approach to determine whether at the time of the alleged offence the particular conflict in the former Yugoslavia was internal (between the Bosnian Serbs/Bosnian Croats /Bosnian Muslims) or international (between Croatia or the FRY and Bosnia). This was spelled out in *Kordić and Cerkez*: the Chamber understands the passages from *Tadić* to mean that the determination as to whether the conflict is international or internal has to be made on a case-by-case basis, that is each case has to be determined on its own merits and accordingly it would not be permissible to deduce from a decision that an internal conflict in a particular area in Bosnia was internationalised that another internal conflict in another area was also internationalised.[62] The case-law of the ICTY since *Tadić* follows this case-by-case approach and shows that each decision on classification depends on the particular time and place; there is thus only limited room for precedent in ICTY decisions as to classification.[63]

---

60   Prosecutor v. Ntagerura, Case No. ICTR-99-46-T, Oral Decision, ¶ 9 (July 4, 2002).

61   Prosecutor v. Tadić, Case No. IT-94-1-A, Appeal Judgment, ¶ 84 (July 15, 1999).

62   Prosecutor v. Kordić & Cerkez, Case No. IT-95-14/2-T, Judgment, ¶ 70 (Feb. 26, 2001); Prosecutor v. Kordić & Cerkez, Case No. IT-95-14/2-A, Appeal, ¶ 319-321 (Dec. 17, 2004).

63   Claire Harris, *Precedent in the Practice of the ICTY,* in ESSAYS ON ICTY PROCEDURE AND EVIDENCE IN HONOUR OF GABRIELLE KIRK MCDONALD 341 (Richard May ed., 2001); Bennouna, *supra* note 59.

According to the decision in *Tadić*, a conflict may be or become international, first, if there is direct intervention by a foreign state through its own troops. On this basis the Trial Chamber held in *Blaskić* (March 2000) that Croatia's direct intervention in Bosnia was enough to transform an internal conflict into an international one. Even though Croatia's regular army personnel were stationed outside the area of conflict between the BH army and Bosnian Croats. Foreign military intervention that indirectly affects an independent internal conflict is enough to render that conflict international.[64] The tribunal did not go into detail on the extent of direct military force needed.[65] This line was taken also in *Kordić and Cerkez* (Judgment February 2001) and *Naletilić* (Judgment March 2003). But this is problematic; how does this reasoning fit with the *Tadić* suggestion that an internal conflict could co-exist with an international conflict? Would a single use of foreign force in a civil war internationalize the conflict?[66]

The second type of internationalization in *Tadić* is equally problematic; a conflict may become international if some of the participants (the Bosnian Serbs) in the internal armed conflict act on behalf of another state (the FRY). The *Tadić* Appeals Chamber turned to the law on state responsibility and rejected the decision of the ICJ in *Nicaragua*: there would be an international conflict if a state was responsible for the acts of non-state actors under an overall control test. Subsequent cases all followed *Tadić* in this regard, with continuing dissent by some judges.[67] The dissenting judges preferred a simpler, global approach.[68] Many commentators are critical of the *Tadić* decision.[69]

According to *Tadić* there are also mixed conflicts. That is, the decision is not just whether the conflict is international or non-international; it is also possible to have a combination of both as in the conflict in the former-Yugoslavia.

---

64   *Kordić,* Case No. IT-95-14/2-T; Prosecutor v. Naletilić & Martinovic, Case No. IT-98-34-T, Judgment (Mar. 31, 2003). The two cases follow the same reasoning.

65   *See* Prosecutor v. Rajić, Case No. IT-95-12-T, Review of Indictment (Sept. 13, 1996) (held to be necessary for the troops to intervene significantly and continuously).

66   Stewart, *supra* note 38.

67   *See* Prosecutor v. Aleksovski, Case No. IT-95-14/1-A, Appeal (Mar. 24, 2000); *Celebici*, Case No. IT-96-21-A, Appeal (Feb. 20, 2001).

68   Prosecutor v. Aleksovski, Case No. IT-95-14/1-T, Judgment, (June 25, 1999) (Judge Rodrigues Dissenting opinion); *Tadić,* Case No. IT-94-1-A, Judgment (Judge Li Separate Opinion); Prosecutor v. Nikolic, Case No. IT-02-60/1-S, Judgment (Dec. 2, 2003); Prosecutor v. Karadzić & Mladić, Case No. IT-95-5/18, Judgment (July 5, 1996); Prosecutor v. Blaskić, Case No. IT-95-4, Judgment (Mar. 3, 2000) (Judge Shahabuddeen took the same approach in his separate opinion in this case as in the *Tadić* Appeal Judgment). *See* Byron, *supra* note 56. See also the US amicus brief in *Tadić,* Case No. IT-94-1-T, this approach was welcomed by some writers, such as Stewart and Aldrich.

69   *See* Bennouna, *supra* note 59; Stewart, *supra* note 38, at 326; Byron, *supra* note 56.

Tadić offered various possible classifications: conflicts "could have been characterized as both internal and international, or alternatively, as an internal conflict alongside an international one, or as an internal conflict that had become internationalized because of external support, or as an international conflict that had subsequently been replaced by one or more internal conflicts, or some combination thereof."[70]

The coexistence of two different types of armed conflict was accepted earlier in *Nicaragua* where the ICJ held that the conflict was both internal and international. The conflict between the contra forces and those of the government of Nicaragua was an armed conflict not of an international character; the actions of the USA in and against Nicaragua fell under the legal rules applicable to international conflict.[71] In *DRC v Uganda* the ICJ again accepted that the complex conflict involved both a civil war and outside intervention against the government.[72]

Tadić also raised questions about the shift from one type of conflict to the other. The conflict in Bosnia was said to have started as an international one; this ended when there was a cessation of hostilities when the external forces of the JNA withdrew in May 1992; then a distinct, self-contained internal conflict broke out between the government of Bosnia and organized armed groups within that state.[73] Finally the conflict became international again because of FRY involvement through the Bosnian Serbs.[74]

These questions of classification are difficult decisions for Tribunals, as is clearly shown by the different conclusions on classification reached by different tribunals and different judges – as in *Tadić* and *Kordić*.

---

70   *Tadić*, Case No IT-94-1-I, Decision on the Defence Motion for Interlocutory Appeal on Jurisdiction, ¶ 72 (Oct. 2, 1995); Willmott, *supra* note 14.

71   Armed Activities on the Territory of the Congo (Dem. Rep. Congo v. Uganda), 2005 I.C.J. 116, ¶ 219 (Dec. 19).

72   *Id.* at ¶ 165, 212.

73   *Celebici*, Case No. IT-96-21-T, Judgment.

74   Some commentators prefer the approach in the *Celebici* Trial Judgment with its aim to give wide protection. The tribunal said that it may be difficult to establish the point when an international conflict ended and became internal if there was no general conclusion of peace. However, there is a presumption that a link remains between the foreign state and a military force which used to be an organ of that state: "the relevant norms of international humanitarian law apply throughout its territory until the general cessation of hostilities, unless it can be shown that the conflicts in some areas were separate internal conflicts, unrelated to the larger international armed conflict." *Celebici*, Case No. IT-96-21-T, Judgment, ¶ 209. But this presumption was not adopted in the Appeal. *Celebici*, Case No. IT-96-21-A, Judgment, ¶ 45 (Feb. 20, 2001).

Many commentators are critical of the current state of affairs.[75] The ICRC is critical for humanitarian reasons: the aim of IHL is to extend protection to all victims and therefore the question of classification should not have a significant impact on the applicable law.

Others are concerned about the practical problems of multiple regimes. Thus the decision in *Tadić* meant that the ICTY had to determine the type of conflict in any prosecution for grave breaches. This determination could be avoided if the ICTY decided not to bring prosecutions for grave breaches. Murphy suggested that after *Tadić* the prosecution indeed withdrew some grave breaches cases precisely because of the added difficulty caused by the need to show the existence of an international armed conflict.[76] If a prosecution is brought only under Common Article 3 then it does not matter whether the conflict is international or internal.[77]

But now the ICC will have to face the problem of classification because of the different provisions in Article 8 of its Statute. The prosecution will have to establish the nature of the armed conflict in every case of prosecution of war crimes. The ICTY experience shows that this will be demanding.[78]

The issue may also arise for some of the new international or hybrid criminal tribunals in war crimes cases. Thus, the Cambodia and Sierra Leone tribunals may face this question. Also, in theory, this could have been an issue in the trial of Saddam Hussein.

Convergence

To the extent that there is convergence between the rules governing international and non-international armed conflicts it will be less important to classify the type of conflict. The jurisprudence of the ICTY, state practice and treaties all show that there has been some convergence.[79]

---

75   *See* Stewart, *supra* note 38.

76   Sean D. Murphy, *Progress and Jurisprudence of the International Criminal Tribunal for the Former Yugoslavia*, 93 Am. J. Int'l L. 57, 68 (1999); *see also* Harris, *supra* note 63, at 354.

77   Prosecutor v. Halilović, Case No. IT-01-48-T, Trial Chamber (Nov. 16, 2005); *Celebici*, Case No. IT-96-21-A, Judgment, ¶ 45 (Feb. 20, 2001); see also the discussion by Human Rights Watch, Genocide, War Crimes and Crimes against Humanity: A Topical Digest of the Case Law of the ICTY 63 (2006).

78   Willmott, *supra* note 14; Bennouna, *supra* note 59.

79   Sonja Boelart-Suominen, *Grave Breaches, Universal Jurisdiction and Internal Armed Conflict: Is Customary Law Moving Towards a Uniform Enforcement Mechanism for All Armed Conflicts?*, 5 J. Conflict & Sec. L. 63 (2000); M. Gandhi, Comment, *Common Article 3 of Geneva Convention, 1949 in the Era of International Criminal Tribunals*, 1 ISIL Y.B. Int'l Human. L. & Refugee L. 11 (2001).

First, as regards substantive law on weapons. Several conventions do not distinguish between international and non-international armed conflict.[80] Second, the Second Protocol to the 1954 Hague Cultural Property in Armed Conflict (1999) applies to all armed conflicts.

Thus there are a number of instruments showing the gradual extension to internal armed conflicts of rules and principles concerning international wars. *Tadić* made the famous statement in relation to means and methods of warfare: "Indeed elementary considerations of humanity and common sense make it preposterous that the use by States of weapons prohibited in armed conflicts between themselves be allowed when States try to put down rebellion by their own nationals on their own territory. What is inhumane, and consequently proscribed, in international wars, cannot but be inhumane and inadmissible in civil strife."[81] But there can be no wholesale transfer of rules: "[T]his extension has not taken place in the form of a full and mechanical transplant of those rules to internal conflicts; rather, the general essence of those rules, and not the detailed regulation they may contain, has become applicable to internal conflicts."[82]

Extending the rules governing conduct during armed conflict (on the means and methods of warfare) to internal conflicts does not mean extending the rules on the status of those individuals involved, and is therefore acceptable to states. Those rules which *do* relate to status of combatants are more controversial.[83]

There has also been convergence in the enforcement regime and in particular in the establishment of individual criminal responsibility in internal armed conflicts. The Statute of the ICTR was the first international instrument to provide for such responsibility. Also some states in their national legislation do not distinguish between international and internal armed conflict as regards IHL.[84] And international criminal courts have extended individual responsi-

---

80   Convention on the Prohibition of the Development, Production and Stockpiling of Bacteriological (Biological) and Toxin Weapons and on their Destruction, Mar. 26, 1975, 1015 U.N.T.S. 163; Convention on the Prohibition of the Development, Production, Stockpiling and Use Chemical Weapons and on their Destruction, Apr. 39, 1997, 31 I.L.M. 800; Convention on the Prohibition of the Use, Stockpiling, Production and Transfer of Anti-Personnel Mines and on their Destruction, Mar. 1, 1999, 2056 U.N.T.S. 211; Convention on Prohibitions or Restrictions on the Use of Certain Conventional Weapons Which May Be Deemed to Be Excessively Injurious or to Have Indiscriminate Effects, May 18, 2004, 1342 U.N.T.S. 137. *See* Steven Solomon, *Internal Conflicts: Dilemmas and Developments*, 38(3) GEO. WASH. INT'L L. REV. 579 (2006); Willmott, *supra* note 14.

81   *Tadić*, Case No IT-94-1-I, Decision on the Defence Motion for Interlocutory Appeal on Jurisdiction, ¶ 119.

82   *Id.* at ¶ 126 (Oct. 2, 1995).

83   *See* Solomon, *supra* note 80. But some rules such as those on belligerent occupation and enemy nationality can *not* be assimilated. Stewart, *supra* note 38.

84   *See* Gandhi, *supra* note 79; Stewart, *supra* note 38; Boelart-Suominen, *supra* note 79.

bility to non-international armed conflicts. The *Tadić Appeal Chamber* (1995) made the radical step of asserting individual criminal responsibility in internal armed conflicts.[85] This was still said to be controversial in the drafting of Rome Statute.[86]

Tadić even suggested that although the crime of grave breaches was currently only available in international armed conflict, this might change if state practice changed.[87] The USA amicus brief supported this position, and later cases suggested that there had been change in this regard.[88] But the Rome Statute of the ICC Article 8(2)(a) preserved the difference: crimes of grave breaches could be committed only in international armed conflict.

Start/End/Area

The questions of the identification of the beginning and end, and the area, of an armed conflict seem generally more difficult in regard to non-international than to international armed conflicts.

Start: As we have seen, *Tadić* requires a "protracted" armed conflict. At the start of a non-international armed conflict it is obviously not possible to say whether this criterion is satisfied,[89] and later it may be difficult to determine the exact starting point. The Kosovo cases show the problem with identifying the start of an internal conflict. ICTR decisions decide that armed violence over only a few months satisfies the protracted requirement. The *Tablada* case (1997) of the Inter-American Commission of Human Rights goes much further: a conflict lasting less than a day was said to be an internal armed conflict.[90] The ICRC also seems to take this approach; for example, recently in regard to Chad the ICRC called for compliance with IHL and determined that there was a situation to which the principles and rules of IHL applied even though the "particularly intense armed clashes" had taken place on only one day.[91]

---

85 *Tadić*, Case No. IT-94-1-A, Appeal Judgment, ¶ 128-129 (July 15, 1999).

86 M. Bothe, *War Crimes*, *in* THE ROME STATUTE OF THE INTERNATIONAL CRIMINAL COURT: A COMMENTARY 79 (Antonio Cassese, Paolo Gaeta, & John R.W.D. Jones eds., 2002).

87 *Tadić*, Case No IT-94-1-I, Decision on the Defence Motion for Interlocutory Appeal on Jurisdiction, ¶ 83 (Abi-Saab, J., separate opinion).

88 *Celebici*, Case No. IT-96-21-T, Judgment (Nov. 16, 1998).

89 Jinks, *supra* note 20.

90 Liesbeth Zegfeld, *The Inter-American Commission on Human Rights and International Humanitarian Law: A Comment on the* Tablada *Case*, 80 INT'L REV. RED CROSS 505 (1998) (was critical of this decision).

91 Press Release, International Committee of the Red Cross, Chad: ICRC Calls for Compliance with International Humanitarian Law (Apr. 15, 2006) (on file with author).

In those cases where there is a shift from international to internal armed conflict is the test the same as that for the end of an international armed conflict or is something more required?

End: In the 1949 Geneva Conventions the general rule is that (with some exceptions) armed conflict terminates at the "general close of military operations". There is no provision on this issue in APII.

According to *Tadić* (Appeals Chamber) IHL applies from the initiation of such conflicts and extends beyond the cessation of hostilities until a general conclusion of peace is reached; or, in the case of internal armed conflicts, a peaceful settlement is reached. The ICTR in *Akayesu* followed this approach. Many internal armed conflicts – even those involving terrorist organizations and even the violent campaigns by terrorist organizations such as the IRA and ETA – have been terminated by peace agreements, as in Sri Lanka (2002), Nepal (2006), and Sudan (2004, 2006).[92] But in many cases there are problems with the implementation of these peace agreements and there may be no final end to the fighting for many years, as for example in the cases of Liberia, Sri Lanka, and Sudan.

Area: *Tadić* established the approach that until the peaceful settlement is reached "IHL continues to apply … in the case of internal conflicts, [to] the whole territory under the control of a party, whether or not actual combat takes place there."[93] Common Article 3 applies outside the narrow geographical context of the actual theatre of combat operations. This seems straightforward – even though territorial control is not necessary for the existence of an armed conflict under Common Article 3 and even though the territorial control requirement of APII may be seen as inappropriate. There is no problem with this formulation as IHL simply applies to the whole territory under the control of a party; if rebels do not control the territory then the government would be presumed to be in control. The underlying policy is to ensure protection for civilians.

Thus in *Kunarac* the Appeals Chamber held that there is no necessary correlation between the area where the actual fighting is taking place and the geographical reach of the laws of war. "[The laws of war] apply in the whole territory of the warring states or, in the case of internal armed conflicts, the whole territory under the control of a party, whether or not actual combat takes place there and continue to apply … in the case of internal armed conflicts, [until] a peaceful settlement is achieved." A violation of the laws or customs of war may therefore occur at a time when and in a place where no fighting is actually taking place.[94]

---

92   Stewart, *supra* note 38, at 339 (asserts that such agreements are rare, but this does not seem to be supported by the practice).

93   *Tadić*, Case No IT-94-1-I, Decision on the Defence Motion for Interlocutory Appeal on Jurisdiction, ¶ 69, 70 (Oct. 2, 1995).

94   *Id.*

Moreover, in *Kunarac* it was held that "the Prosecutor did not have to prove that there was an armed conflict in each and every square inch of the general area. The state of armed conflict is not limited to the areas of actual military combat but exists across the entire territory under the control of the warring parties."[95] *Limaj* confirmed that the geographic and temporal framework of the *Tadić* test for the existence of an armed conflict was settled jurisprudence.[96]

Similarly, the ICTR held in *Akayesu* and *Rutaganda* that the requirements of Common Article 3 and APII apply in the whole territory where the conflict is occurring and are not limited to the war front or to the narrow geographical context of the actual theatre of combat operations.[97]

Failure to accept the existence of an internal armed conflict in practice

Traditionally states have resisted any acknowledgment that Common Article 3 and Additional Protocol II are applicable to a conflict on their territory, despite the provision in Common Article 3 that "the application of {Common Article 3} shall not affect the legal status of the Parties to the conflict". They do not want to confer protected status on rebels and insurgents. They see opposition groups as criminal and are not willing to exempt them from prosecution under domestic law or to acknowledge any kind of legitimacy. On the other side the insurgents themselves may not be keen to acknowledge the existence of an internal armed conflict. There may be no advantage to them from the application of these provisions: they will not have POW status; they can still be prosecuted for taking up arms against the government. It is often argued that there is little incentive for insurgents to comply with laws of war if they cannot claim POW status.

There are very few/no clear examples of the express acceptance of the application of Common Article 3 during an internal armed conflict. Moir gives a list of the limited practice: Algeria, Biafra, and Bosnia (and possibly also Congo and Yemen).[98] Currently Russia does not accept that there is an internal armed

---

95   Prosecutor v. Kunarac, Case No. IT-96-23-A, Appeal Judgment, ¶ 64 (June 12, 2002).

96   *Id.* at ¶ 84.

97   *See Akayesu*, Case No. ICTR 96-4-T, Trial Chamber, ¶ 635-36 (Sept. 2, 1998); *Kayishema & Ruzindana*, Case No. ICTR-95-1-T, Judgment, ¶ 182-83 (May 21, 1999). *See also* Prosecutor v. Musema, Case No. ICTR 96-12-T, Judgment (Jan. 27, 2000); Prosecutor v. Semanza, Case No. ICTR 97-20-T, Judgment (May 15, 2003); Prosecutor v. Bagilishema, Case No. ICTR 95-1A-T, Judgment (June 7, 2001). See HUMAN RIGHTS WATCH, CASE LAW OF THE INTERNATIONAL CRIMINAL TRIBUNAL FOR RWANDA (2004), *available at* http://www.hrw.org/reports/2004/ij/ictr/index.htm.

98   Moir, *supra* note 6, at 67.

conflict in Chechnya; Turkey rejected the argument that it was involved in an internal armed conflict with the PKK.[99] The CAR denied the existence of an internal armed conflict in 2006.[100] In 2006, the USA denied that there was a sectarian civil war in Iraq.[101]

Some special agreements providing for the application of IHL have been made between parties involved in internal armed conflict.[102] An example is that of Bosnia, referred to in the *Tadić* case.[103] It may be implicit in these agreements that there is an internal armed conflict, but not surprisingly the agreements do not go into questions of definition or specify the relevant criteria.

Similarly the Security Council in calling for the application of IHL to a conflict does not specify the classification of the conflict. Typically it just calls on all parties to apply the relevant human rights and humanitarian law; it may be implicit that there is a non-international armed conflict in some cases, but in the absence of any discussion of this or any indication of the criteria applied to determine the existence of such a conflict these resolutions cannot add to our understanding of non-international armed conflict. Typical resolutions are SC Resolution 1270 (1999) on Sierra Leone which calls upon all parties to respect strictly the relevant provisions of IHL and human rights law, and SC Resolution 788 (1992) on Liberia which calls upon all parties to the conflict and all others concerned to respect strictly the provisions of IHL.

Also the Security Council, the General Assembly and the Human Rights Commission have requested ICRC access in many conflicts, including those in Afghanistan, Chechnya, Rwanda, Tajikistan and the former Yugoslavia. Again the question of classification is avoided. The UN Secretary-General or the ICRC may occasionally make an assertion that a certain conflict is a civil war in passing but without explanation.[104] Thus, the large number of internal conflicts has not produced any significant guidance on the issue of definition. The ICRC also acts in situations of emergency and visits prisons.

---

99   Abresch, *supra* note 42, at 754-56.

100 *Religious Violence*, KEESING'S REC. OF WORLD EVENTS, Feb. 2006, at 47081.

101 See below at ¶ 67, 68.

102 The Secretary-General, *Report of the Secretary-General on the Promotion and Protection of Human Rights*, ¶ 41, *delivered to the Economic and Social Council*, U.N. Doc.E/CN.4/2001/91 (Jan. 12, 2001).

103 *Tadić*, Case No IT-94-1-I, Decision on the Defence Motion for Interlocutory Appeal on Jurisdiction, ¶73 (Oct. 2, 1995) (the parties agreed to the application of Common Article 3 and certain extra provisions).

104 *See* Press Release, Secretary-General, Secretary-General Deplores Escalation of Violence in Sri Lanka, U.N. Doc. SG/SM/10686 (Oct. 16, 2006); Press Release, International Committee of the Red Cross, Operational Update on Nepal (Sept. 30, 2006).

The "war on terror"

The rhetoric of the "war on terror" currently poses a challenge to the traditional classifications. The USA apparently sees itself as involved in a global war of indefinite duration; those who are not with it are with the terrorists. It claims to be acting in an armed conflict against Al-Qaida and related groups. President Bush and Prime Minister Blair have identified the enemy as one; they conflate different terrorist attacks and groups all over the world despite the different historical contexts. President Bush has also used the language of World War III.[105] As of 2006, the preferred term is "the long war".[106] According to the Pentagon's 2006 Quadrennial Defense Review Report, the long war is unlimited in time and space; it may be fought in many countries simultaneously and for many years to come.

The ICRC in a 2003 report summarises this position: the world is faced with a new kind of violence to which the laws of armed conflict should be applicable. According to this view, transnational violence does not fit the definition of international armed conflict because it is not waged among states, and does not correspond to the traditional understanding of non-international armed conflict because it takes place across a wide geographic area. Thus the law of armed conflict needs to be adapted to become the main legal tool in dealing with acts of transnational terrorism. It is claimed that such adaptation is taking place in practice. Some proponents of this view argue that persons suspected of being involved in acts of terrorism constitute "enemy combatants" who may be subject to direct attack and, once captured, may be detained until the end of active hostilities in the "war against terrorism".[107] Some in the Bush administration have even claimed that the 1949 Geneva Conventions are obsolete with regard to the "war on terror".[108]

Thus, the USA relies on this assertion of a "war on terror" to claim the right to target suspected terrorists and to detain combatants indefinitely as the armed conflict is not over, and possibly also to claim a wide right to intervene in civil

---

105   George W. Bush, President of the United States, Speech at Fort Bragg (June 28, 2005); George W. Bush, President of the United States, Speech at Salt Lake City (Aug. 31, 2006).

106   PENTAGON, U.S. DEP'T OF DEF., QUADRENNIAL DEFENSE REVIEW REPORT 9 (2006) (this is the term used by the Pentagon and President Bush adopted it in his 2006 State of the Union Address).

107   Int'l Comm. of the Red Cross, *International Humanitarian Law and the Challenges of Contemporary Armed Conflicts*, 03/IC/09, at 232, Dec. 2-6, 2003(document of the 28th international conference of the Red Cross and Red Crescent).

108   Mary Ellen O'Connell, *Enhancing the Status of Non-state Actors Through a Global War on Terror*, 43 COLUM. J. TRANSNAT'L L. 435 (2005); Christopher Greenwood, *War, Terrorism and International Law*, CURRENT LEGAL PROBS. 505 (2003). Both O'Connell and Greenwood are critical of this approach.

wars to assist governments against those it classifies as terrorists. But it does not acknowledge the protections provided to detainees by the laws of international armed conflict (and of human rights).[109] In March 2006 the USA set out its position in reply to the *Report of the Five UNCHR Special Rapporteurs on Detainees in Guantanamo Bay, Cuba*: "the USA is engaged in a continuing armed conflict against Al-Qaida, the Taliban and other terrorist organizations supporting them, with troops on the ground in several places engaged in combat operations. Certain laws of war govern the conduct of that conflict and related detention operations".[110]

Since the *Hamdan* case the US administration has purported to accept the application of Common Article 3 to detainees held in the conflict with Al-Qaida, but the classification underlying this is not clear.[111] The USA still does not characterise the conflict against non-state terrorists as non-international.

Others have rejected this US approach. The ICRC, and NGOs such as Human Rights Watch and Amnesty International argue that the "war on terror" is not an international armed conflict, because it is not between 2 states; nor is it a non-international armed conflict against non-state terrorist actors because sporadic outbreaks of violence and acts of terrorism do not amount to an armed conflict. Sporadic bombings and other violent acts which terrorist networks perpetrate in different places around the globe and the ensuing counter-terrorism measures, even if they are occasionally undertaken by military units, cannot be said to amount to an armed conflict in the sense that they trigger the applicability of IHL.[112]

The generally accepted view of the conflict in Afghanistan is that in the period immediately before *Operation Enduring Freedom* in 2001 there was an internal conflict between the Taliban forces of the government and opposition forces such as the Northern Alliance. The launching of *Operation Enduring Freedom* on 7 October 2001 meant that there was then an international armed

---

109   Initially the USA asserted in a 7 February 2002 Memorandum that those members of Al-Qaida and the Taliban detained were not entitled to the protection of the 1949 Geneva Conventions. This position was modified in the *Military Commissions Act of 2006*, 29 September 2006, which provided that Common Article 3 is applicable, but only as interpreted by the US President.

110   REPLY OF THE GOVERNMENT OF THE UNITED STATES OF AMERICA TO THE REPORT OF THE FIVE UNHCR SPECIAL RAPPORTEURS ON DETAINEES IN GUANTANAMO BAY, CUBA, 45(3) I.L.M. 742, 751 (2006).

111   *See* Cerrone, *supra* note 37.

112   Official Statement, International Committee of the Red Cross, The Relevance of IHL in the Context of Terrorism (July 21, 2005); HUMAN RIGHTS WATCH, AFGHANISTAN IN INTERNATIONAL LEGAL CONTEXT (2004). Amnesty Int'l, *USA Report, US Detentions in Afghanistan*, AI Index AMR51/093/2005, June 6, 2005; Eur. Consult. Ass., *Opinion on the International Legal Obligations of Council of Europe Member States in Respect of Secret Detention Facilities and Inter-State Transport of Prisoners*, 66th Plenary Session, Doc. No. 363/2005 (2006).

conflict between the USA and its allies against the Taliban. The Northern Alliance continued to operate and now cooperated with the US forces but was not always under the control of the coalition forces; so it may be that the conflict between them and government forces was partly internal. The end of the international conflict came by 19 June 2002 when a new government was established. Most commentators accept that there is now an internal armed conflict because the USA and other foreign states are helping the government of Afghanistan.[113] Therefore the UN-authorised forces of ISAF, present in Afghanistan to help the government to establish stability, are engaged in a non-international armed conflict.

But the position with regard to *Operation Enduring Freedom* is more controversial in that the USA apparently regards this as a continuation of the operation initiated under Congressional authorization after 9/11. The US *Operation Enduring Freedom* website does not go into this question. Little material is available from participating governments such as the UK, Germany, Canada, Australia and New Zealand. *Operation Enduring Freedom* is also conducted in the Horn of Africa and the Philippines. The applicable IHL is not clear.[114]

Further questions with regard to categorization arise with regard to Iraq. At first the operation which began in March 2003 was an international armed conflict. But when a new government was established and the end of the occupation was proclaimed after the handover of power on 28 June 2004[115] then it was generally accepted that the conflict became an internal one, with US and other foreign forces operating with the consent of the Iraqi government under Security Council Resolution 1511. The ICRC issued a statement to this effect on 8 August 2004: The current hostilities in Iraq between armed forces opposing the MNF and/or the newly established authorities amount to a non-international armed conflict.

However, the USA has also stated that this is the frontline of the "war on terror" and some of those who resist the presence of foreign forces are called terrorists. It is not entirely clear what the legal implications of this may be.[116] The USA also resists any suggestion that there is a civil war between different religious groups in Iraq.[117]

---

113 The USA and Afghanistan are not parties to APII.

114 The German Bundestag agreed to extend its participation in *Operation Enduring Freedom* on 10 November 2006.

115 SC Resolution 1546 (2006) determined that the Coalition Provisional Authority had transferred all government authority to the Iraqi Interim Government. The ICRC also accepted that the US occupation ended on 28 June 2004.

116 Nathan A. Canestaro, *Small Wars and the Law: Options for Prosecuting the Insurgents in Iraq*, 43 COLUM. J. TRANSNAT'L L. 73 (2004).

117 George W. Bush, President of the United States, Salt Lake City Speech (Aug. 31, 2006); *Iraq*, KEESING'S REC. OF WORLD EVENTS, Aug. 2006, at 47436. *See also* United Kingdom Secretary of State, RUSI Speech (May 24, 2006).

Lebanon

Questions arose as to whether this recent conflict should be seen as an international armed conflict against Lebanon (and possibly also Syria and Iran), or as a non-international armed conflict against a non-state actor – Hizbollah, or as part of an international "war on terror". Israel initially seemed to attribute responsibility for an armed attack to Lebanon, but it subsequently claimed that its attacks were not against Lebanon but against Hizbollah. This was not convincing to many states, who seemed therefore to regard the conflict as international rather than non-international. Israel's references to the laws of armed conflict have been general and they do not clarify this question of classification. However, it does accept the application of some of the rules in API and the Geneva Conventions.[118] The UN Security Council did not pronounce on this issue in Resolution 1701(2006). Human rights groups generally avoided the classification of the conflict: they were able to determine that there had been serious violations by Israel (and also by Hezbollah) without going into this issue.[119] However, the Commission of Inquiry on Lebanon established by the Human Rights Council reported firmly that there was an international armed conflict between Israel and Lebanon; and that Hezbollah as a non-state actor was bound by Common Article 3 applicable to non-international armed conflict.[120]

Many other conflicts could also give rise to the question as to whether they are mere domestic unrest, civil wars or part of the "war on terror". Thus the USA has recast certain conflicts such as those in the Philippines and Colombia as part of the war on terror. Others such as China, Russia (Chechnya) and Uzbekistan have also made similar claims that those acting in opposition to the government were terrorists, perhaps linked to Al-Qaida.

Conclusion

Historically there have been important differences between the regimes governing international and non-international armed conflicts with late and limited provision made for the latter. There is a growing perception that the existence of

---

118 Israeli Ministry of Foreign Affairs, Responding to Hizbullah attacks from Lebanon: Issues of Proportionality (July 25, 2006).

119 HUMAN RIGHTS WATCH, QUESTIONS AND ANSWERS ON HOSTILITIES BETWEEN ISRAEL AND HEZBOLLAH (2006) *available at* http://www.hrw.org/english/docs/2006/07/17/lebano13748.htm; Amnesty Int'l, *Lebanon: Deliberate Destruction or "Collateral Damage"? Israeli Attacks on Civilian Infrastructure*, AI Index MDE 18.007/2006, Aug. 23, 2006, *available at* http://www.amnesty.org/en/library/info/MDE18/007/2006.

120 Report of the Commission of Inquiry on Lebanon (Nov. 10, 2006), *available at* http://www.reliefweb.int/rw/rwb.nsf/db900SID/YA01-6VS3P3.

different regimes is not satisfactory, given the humanitarian concerns common to both. To the extent that the two regimes converge the questions of definition will be less important. There is growing pressure for assimilation/unity; in the Commentary on the Rome Statute the Tentative Assessment by the Board of Editors expressed the increasingly accepted view that there should be one set of rules for all armed conflicts.[121]

Tadić was in many ways a visionary decision, establishing criminal responsibility for war crimes during non-international armed conflicts under Common Article 3 and making it clear that there had been some assimilation of the two regimes. It established apparently clear tests for the classification of armed conflicts, but application of these rules in mixed conflicts or where there was a shift from one type of conflict to another was complex.

Serious practical problems remain. Classification is difficult for tribunals. In theory it is even more difficult for those actually involved in armed conflict, but in practice there is little or no question of classification affecting behaviour. The experience of the ICTY indicates that ex post facto decision-making by criminal tribunals is unlikely to increase the effectiveness of IHL in conflict.

But the main problem is that of getting governments/opposition groups to agree that there is a non-international armed conflict rather than mere unrest, and to accept that Common Article 3 or APII is applicable to a particular conflict. If the regimes for domestic unrest and internal armed conflict converge through the acceptance of fundamental humanitarian standards then the line between internal unrest and internal armed conflict will be less important.

---

121   THE ROME STATUTE OF THE INTERNATIONAL CRIMINAL COURT: A COMMENTARY
1904 (Antonio Cassese, Paolo Gaeta, & John R.W.D. Jones eds., 2002).

Chapter 7

Irregular Forces and Self-defense Under the UN Charter

James Gathii

Introduction

The traditional position that the right to self-defense under Article 51 of the Charter of the United Nations requires an armed attack by a State has come under increasing challenge in the recent past.[1] The question, under what circumstances the conduct of irregular non-State actors amounts to an armed attack to permit the use of self-defense under Article 51 of the UN Charter, was most recently addressed by the ICJ in *Congo v. Uganda*.[2] As I note below, the separate and dissenting opinions in that case illustrate the increasing challenge to the requirement of an armed attack attributable to a State prior to the exercise of the right of self-defense. With that challenge comes the possibility of lowering the barrier to the right to engage in armed conflict inconsistently with the UN Charter.

In addition to the ongoing debate among the ICJ's judges, recent Security Council Resolutions have been cited as evidencing a move towards expanding the right of self-defense where attacks by irregular forces could not be attributed to a State. Expanding the right of self-defense to include attacks by irregular forces whose conduct is not attributable to a State is inconsistent with earlier Security Council criticisms of self-defense, especially by occupying countries.[3] Although the Court's opinion in *Congo v. Uganda* specifically

---

1   See, e.g., Vincent-Joël Proulx, *Babysitting Terrorists: Should States be Strictly Liable for Failing to Prevent Transborder Attacks?*, 23 BERKELEY J. INT'L L. 615 (2005); Derek Jinks, *State Responsibility for Sponsorship of Terrorist and Insurgent Groups: State Responsibility for the Acts of Private Armed Groups*, 4 CHI. J. INT'L L. 83 (2003). See Tom Ruys & Sten Verhoeven, *Attacks by Private Actors and the Right of Self-Defence*, 10 J. CONFLICT & SECURITY L. 289 (2005).

2   Armed Activities on the Territory of the Congo (Dem. Rep. Congo v. Uganda), 2005 I.C.J. (Dec., 19) [hereinafter Congo v. Uganda].

3   Members of the Security Council disapproved Israel's claim in the 1960s and 70s that the call to arms or the implementation of force was justifiable as a response to

Mary Ellen O'Connell (ed.), What Is War? An Investigation in the Wake of 9/11.
© 2012 Koninklijke Brill NV. Printed in The Netherlands. ISBN 978 9004 17234 0. pp. 97 – 108.

declined to address the permissibility of a right to self-defense, even against large-scale attacks by irregular forces,[4] it nevertheless found Uganda not only to have occupied parts of Congolese territory but to have used force in violation of the prohibition of the use of force contained in Article 2(4) of the Charter. Since Uganda argued that it had suffered attacks from irregular forces which it sought to forcibly repulse, *Congo v. Uganda* ought to be read as affirming the prohibition of the use of force in the absence of an armed attack attributable to a State. The refusal by the Court to expand the right of self-defense to include cases involving attacks by irregular forces that cannot be attributed to a State is an acknowledgment that the acceptance of an expanded right of self-defense would need more than its judicial imprimatur. Indeed, while the *Nicaragua* decision affirmed self-defense as an inherent right,[5] this inherent right to self-defense "must" ultimately "be regarded as limited and not only legitimated by law."[6]

The Use of Force and Self-Defense under the UN Charter

Except in the case of self-defense or as mandated by the authority of the Security Council, Article 2(4) of the UN Charter prohibits the use of force. Article 2(4) requires that "[a]ll Members shall refrain in their international relations from the threat or use of force against the territorial integrity or political independence of any state, or in any other manner inconsistent with the Purposes of the United Nations."[7] The term "war" is not included within this prohibition, rather all uses of force whether equated to war or lesser actions are prohibited.[8] Under

---

the internal domestic instability in Lebanon, and its inability to curb and prevent terrorist attacks originating from its soil to Israel. *See* Ruys & Verhoeven, *supra* note 1, at 298; Christine Gray, International Law and the Use of Force, 132-39 (2008).

4   Congo v. Uganda, 2005 I.C.J., at 53, para. 147 (Dec., 19). Here, the ICJ having concluded that the evidentially accepted facts of the current case lacked the necessary circumstances for the justifiable exercise of the right to self-defense by Uganda, stated "[a]ccordingly, the Court has no need to respond to the contentions of the Parties as to whether and under what conditions contemporary international law provides for a right of self-defence against large-scale attacks by irregular forces." *Id.*

5   Military and Paramilitary Activities in and Against Nicaragua (Nicar. v. U.S.), 1986 I.C.J. 14, 94, para. 176 (June, 27) [hereinafter Nicaragua].

6   Oscar Schachter, *Self-Defense and the Rule of Law*, 83 AJIL 259, 277 (1989). *But see* W. Michael Reisman & Andrea Armstrong, *The Past and Future of the Claim of Preemptive Self-Defense*, 100 AJIL 525, 550 n.118 (2006) (suggesting that the world has "changed significantly since Schachter noted the potentially destabilizing effect of uncertainty and indeterminacy of evaluating unilateral claims to preemptive self-defense ...").

7   UN Charter, art. 2(4).

8   Mary Ellen O'Connell, International Law and the Use of Force 7 (2009).

Article 51, the use of force in self-defense is triggered by the existence of an armed conflict or an armed attack attributable to a State.[9] Lesser-isolated incidents, including minor quarrels across territorial boundaries, would not suffice as an attack or armed conflict and thus do not trigger the right of self-defense.[10]

Article 51 fails to mention that an armed attack must emanate from a State; which has, in turn, led some scholars and ICJ judges to conclude that the omission of such language means that attacks triggering self-defense could emanate from irregular forces, even if their conduct was not attributable to a State.[11] The argument is that the use of force as self-defense is permissible against irregular forces acting independently and on their own accord.[12] Those who make this argument support their view by virtue of the difference in the language used in Article 2(4) as opposed to Article 51. While Article 2(4) prohibits the use of force by one State against another, Article 51 contains no similar reference to a State in relation to the origin of an armed attack.[13]

This reading of Article 51 is buttressed by distinguishing the Security Council's condemnation of Israel's use of force as self-defense in the 1960s and 70s, from what they consider a proper case of self-defense following attacks by irregular forces. The claim is that the condemnation of Israel is distinguishable since it was influenced by the fact that Israel was illegally occupying the West Bank, Gaza and the Golan Heights when it claimed to use force in self-defense.[14] Similarly, Portugal's claims of self-defense in its African colonies against forces fighting for decolonization were criticized since "Portugal was using force to maintain its illegal colonial power. The right of self-defense could not be invoked to perpetuate colonialism and to flout the right to self-determination and independence."[15] Based on these contentions proponents of an expanded reading of Article 51 argue that, when the armed conduct of irregular forces is of such gravity and the scale and effects equals to an armed attack that

---

9   *Id.* Article 51 provides that "[n]othing in the present Charter shall impair the inherent right of individual or collective self-defence if an armed attack occurs against a Member of the United Nations, until the Security Council has taken measures necessary to maintain international peace and security." UN Charter, art. 51.

10   Nicaragua, 1986 I.C.J. at 103, para. 195 (June, 27).

11   *See infra* note 12.

12   *See* YORAM DINSTEIN, WAR, AGGRESSION, AND SELF-DEFENCE 204 (4th ed. 2005) (stating that "[t]he perpetrator of [the] armed attack is not identified necessarily as a State. An armed attack can therefore be carried out by non-State actors."); Sean D. Murphy, *Terrorism and the Concept of "Armed Attack" In Article 51 of the U.N. Charter*, 43 HARV. INT'L L.J. 41, 50 (2002) (claiming that "[t]here is nothing in Article 51 of the U.N. Charter that requires the exercise of self-defense to turn on whether an armed attack was committed directly by another state.").

13   Murphy, *supra* note 12, at 50; GRAY, *supra* note 3, at 128-40, 199.

14   *See* GRAY, *supra* note 3, at 132-39.

15   *Id.* at 138.

would have been undertaken by regular forces, then attribution of such conduct to a State is unnecessary to trigger the right of self-defense under Article 51.[16]

Interpretation of Article 51 By The ICJ

In *Nicaragua,* the ICJ held that the exercise of the use of force permitted by the right to self-defense "is subject to the State concerned having been the victim of an armed attack."[17] To arrive at this conclusion, the Court did not rely solely on the text of Article 51. Rather, the Court made reference to the Definition of Aggression as stated in Article 3(g) of General Assembly Resolution 3314 (XXIX), which the Court stated is a norm of customary international law.[18] In defining an armed attack, the Court held that, in addition to actions by regular armed forces, armed action by irregular forces, mercenaries and the like may constitute an armed attack if sent by a State or on its behalf, and if such activity "because of its scale and effects, would have been classified as an armed attack … had it been carried out by regular armed forces."[19] Thus, according to the Court, the armed conduct of irregular forces had to be attributable to a State directly or indirectly to permit the use of force in self-defense. The Court further opined that attribution of such conduct "to give rise to legal responsibility … in principle [requires proof] that the State had *effective control* of the military or paramilitary operations in the course of which the alleged violations were committed."[20] Thus, under *Nicaragua,* where the gravity of the armed conduct of irregular forces can be defined as an armed attack, the right of self-defense by the victim State is permissible only upon attribution of such conduct to a State under the effective control test.

Additional examples of international judicial interpretation of Article 51 include the ICJ's statement in its Advisory Opinion on *Legal Consequences of the Construction of a Wall in the Occupied Palestinian Territory* that "Article 51 of the Charter thus recognizes the existence of an inherent right of self-defence in the case of armed attack by one State against another State."[21] In *Congo v. Uganda,* the Court found there was no satisfactory proof of the direct or indirect involvement of the Government of the Democratic Republic of the Congo (DRC) in attacks against Uganda. The Court further held that "[t]he attacks did not ema-

---

16   *Id.* at 138–39.

17   Nicaragua, 1986 I.C.J. at 103, para. 195 (June, 27).

18   *Id.*

19   *Id.*

20   Nicaragua, 1986 I.C.J., at 103–04, para. 116 (June, 27) (*See also* para. 195 noting that the conduct of irregular forces attributable to a State could amount to an armed attack under Article 51).

21   Legal Consequences of the Construction of a Wall in the Occupied Palestinian Territory, Advisory Opinion, 2004 I.C.J. 136, 194, para. 139 (July, 9) [hereinafter Legal Consequences, Advisory Opinion].

nate from armed bands or irregulars sent by the DRC or on behalf of the DRC, within the sense of Article 3 (*g*) of General Assembly resolution 3314 (XXIX) on the definition of aggression, adopted on 14 December 1974."[22] These cases show that the ICJ continues to consistently require the existence of another State or at least attribution of the armed attack to such a State in order for the use of force as self-defense to be permissible under Article 51 of the Charter.

On the related question of the definition of an armed attack, it is notable that the Appellate Chamber of the International Criminal Tribunal of the Former Yugoslavia in the *Tadić* case found an "armed conflict" to exist "whenever there is a resort to armed force between States or protracted armed violence between governmental authorities and organized armed groups or between such groups within a State."[23] It has often been noted that the use of the term "armed conflict" by the Chamber suggests a much lower threshold than armed attack. However, *Tadić* was not really about the permissibility of the use of force in self-defense. But if *Tadić* is relevant in this context, it must be noted that the Chamber qualified the term armed conflict with the verb "protracted" thus signifying the necessity of a higher intensity of armed conflict. However, the Chamber's recognition of conflicts between non-State actors for the applicability of International Humanitarian Law made no reference to the necessity of attribution of the armed conflict to a State unlike under Article 51. In addition, in distinction to *Nicaragua,* the Chamber applied a lower threshold of control, i.e. *overall control* by a State "not only by equipping and financing the group, but also by coordinating or helping in the general planning of its military activity."[24] The Chamber noted that this overall control test may be limited to the specific facts of that case relating to circumstances where "armed forces fighting against the central authorities *of the same State* in which they live ... may be deemed to act on behalf of another State."[25] By phrasing the underlying inquiry in such terms, the overall control test may have been the tribunal's attempt to attribute the conduct of irregulars to a State whose existence was in the process of dissolution.

In the *Wall* decision, Judge Higgins, in her separate opinion, with reference to the requirement that an armed attack be attributable to a State argued that: "[t]here is, with respect, nothing in the text of Article 51 that *thus* stipulates that self-defence is available only when an armed attack is made by a State."[26] She further explained that, to the extent that this view of Article 51 is based on the Court's decision in *Nicaragua,* she had reservations about the tenability of

---

22   Congo v. Uganda, 2005 I.C.J., at 53, para. 146 (Dec., 19).

23   Prosecutor v. Tadić, Case. No. IT-94-1, Decision on the Defence Motion for Interlocutory Appeal on Jurisdiction, para. 70 (Oct. 2, 1995).

24   Prosecutor v. Tadić, Case. No. IT-94-1-A, Judgement, para. 131 (July 15, 1999).

25   *Id.* at para. 91.

26   Legal Consequences, Advisory Opinion, 2004 I.C.J., at 215, para. 33 (July, 9).

this proposition in *Nicaragua*.[27] In that same decision, Judge Buergenthal also expressed his dissatisfaction of the majority holding stating that, "the United Nations Charter, in affirming the inherent right of self-defence, does not make its exercise dependent upon an armed attack by another State, leaving aside for the moment the question whether Palestine, for purposes of this case, should not be and is not in fact being assimilated by the Court to a State."[28]

Lastly, the most recent critiques as to the necessity of attribution to a State of an armed attack by irregular forces was expressed in the Separate Opinions of the *Congo* case, where the Court, in failing to find a connection between the conduct of the irregular forces attacking Uganda from the Congo (the territory from which such attacks emanated) held against Uganda's self-defense argument. In response to this ruling, Judge Kooijmans noted that "[e]ven if one assumes (as I am inclined to do) that mere failure to control the activities of armed bands cannot in itself be attributed to the territorial State as an unlawful act, that in my view does not necessarily mean that the victim State is under such circumstances not entitled to exercise the right of self-defence under Article 51."[29] He continued by making reference to his dissenting position in the *Wall* case, and stated that "Article 51 merely 'conditions the exercise of the inherent right of self-defence on a previous armed attack without saying that this armed attack must come from another State even if this has been the generally accepted interpretation for more than 50 years.'"[30]

In agreement with Judge Kooijmans, Judge Simma also expressed his dissent noting "that the Court should have taken the opportunity presented by the present case to clarify the state of the law on a highly controversial matter which is marked by great controversy and confusion – not the least because it was the Court itself that has substantially contributed to this confusion by its *Nicaragua* Judgment of two decades ago."[31] Further, with reference to circumstances where a State is unable to curb the hostile conduct of irregular forces, Judge Simma, again in accord with Judge Kooijmans, concluded that "if armed attacks are carried out by irregular forces from such territory against a neighbouring State, these activities are still armed attacks even if they cannot be attributed to the territorial State, and, further, that it 'would be unreasonable to deny the attacked State the right to self-defence merely because there is no attacker State and the Charter does not so require so.'"[32] Thus, it is appar-

---

27   *Id.*

28   *Id.* at 242, para. 6.

29   Congo v. Uganda, 2005 I.C.J., at 6, para. 26 (Dec., 19) (Separate Opinion of Judge Kooijmans).

30   *Id.* at para. 28 (citation omitted).

31   Congo v. Uganda, 2005 I.C.J., at 2, para. 8 (Dec., 19) (Separate Opinion of Judge Simma).

32   *Id.* at para. 12 (citation omitted).

ent that, despite the consistent reiteration of the traditional understanding of Article 51 by the ICJ, there is growing debate about the continued tenability of the requirement an armed attack being attributable to a State as a precondition for the exercise of the right to self-defense.

The Resolutions Adopted by the Security Council and the General Assembly

Professor Dinstein has argued that "[i]rrespective of questions of State responsibility, the principal issue is whether acts of violence unleashed against Utopia from Arcadian territory by terrorists or armed bands – not sponsored by Arcadia – may amount to an armed attack within the meaning of Article 51...."[33] While he concludes that such conduct by irregular forces amounts to an armed attack irrespective of attribution to a State, he notes that "all lingering doubts on this issue have been dispelled as a result of the response of the international community to the shocking events of [11] September 2001 (9/11)."[34] Adopted one day after 9/11, Security Council Resolution 1368 (2001) explicitly recognized "the inherent right of individual or collective self-defence" and expressed the "readiness to take all necessary steps to respond to the terrorist attacks of 11 September 2001, and to combat all forms of terrorism" which it regards as a threat to international peace and security.[35] Notably, the Council also called on all States "to bring to justice the perpetrators, organizers and sponsors of these terrorist attacks" and also made provision for the accountability of those "aiding, supporting or harbouring" such perpetrators.[36] The preamble to the resolution expresses the Council's determination to combat threats to international peace and security caused by terrorist acts and then reaffirms the inherent right of self-defense. Nowhere in this resolution is the term armed attack ever used except in the Council's unequivocal condemnation of the "horrifying terrorist attacks."[37] There is also no mention that the tragic attacks of September 11, 2001 were attributable to a State. Rather, the resolution called on the international community to increase their efforts in the prevention and suppression of terrorist acts and in collectively aiding to bring the *perpetrators* to justice.

Resolution 1373 was adopted by the Security Council two weeks after Resolution 1368.[38] Resolution 1373 also reaffirmed the principle that "every State has the duty to refrain from organizing, instigating, assisting or participating in terrorist acts in another State or acquiescing in organized activities within its

---

33   DINSTEIN, *supra* note 12, at 206.

34   *Id.* at 206–07.

35   S.C. Res. 1368, UN Doc. S/RES/1368 (Sept. 12, 2001).

36   *Id.*

37   *Id.*

38   S.C. Res. 1373, UN Doc. S/RES/1373 (Sept. 28, 2001).

territory directed towards the commission of such acts[.]"³⁹ The resolution then follows this statement with an affirmative decision that States shall:

a)   Refrain from providing any form of support, active or passive, to entities or persons involved in terrorist acts, including by suppressing recruitment of members of terrorist groups and eliminating the supply of weapons to terrorists;

(b)   Take the necessary steps to prevent the commission of terrorist acts, including by provision of early warning to other States by exchange of information;

(c)   Deny safe haven to those who finance, plan, support, or commit terrorist acts, or provide safe havens;

(d)   Prevent those who finance, plan, facilitate or commit terrorist acts from using their respective territories for those purposes against other States or their citizens; ...

(g)   Prevent the movement of terrorists or terrorist groups by effective border controls and controls on issuance of identity papers and travel documents, and through measures for preventing counterfeiting, forgery or fraudulent use of identity papers and travel documents;⁴⁰

These two resolutions have been argued to license States to use their inherent or collective right to self-defense in combating terrorism. As already noted, the separate opinions discussed above strongly suggest the Security Council has opened the door to permit the use of force in self-defense against irregular forces even where their conduct was not attributable to a State. For example, in the *Wall* case decided in 2004, 3 years after the adoption of the above resolutions, Judge Buergenthal notes that "[i]n neither of these resolutions did the Security Council limit their application to terrorist attacks by State actors only, nor was an assumption to that effect implicit in these resolutions. In fact, the contrary appears to have been the case."⁴¹ Similarly, Judge Kooijmans concluded that:

Resolutions 1368 (2001) and 1373 (2001) recognize the inherent right of individual or collective self-defence without making any reference to an armed attack by a State. The Security Council called acts of international terrorism, without any further qualification, a threat to international peace and security which authorizes it to act under Chapter VII of the Charter. And it actually did so in resolution 1373 (2001) without ascribing these acts of terrorism to a particular State. This is the completely new element in these resolutions. This new element is not excluded by the terms of Article 51 since this conditions

---

39   *Id.*

40   *Id.* at para. 2.

41   Legal Consequences, Advisory Opinion, 2004 I.C.J., at 242, para. 6 (July, 9).

the exercise of the inherent right of self-defence on a previous armed attack
without saying that this armed attack must come from another State even if
this has been the generally accepted interpretation for more than 50 years. The
Court has regrettably by-passed this new element, the legal implications of
which cannot as yet be assessed but which marks undeniably a new approach
to the concept of self-defence.[42]

I address these calls for an expanded definition of the scope of Article 51 in the
conclusions. Suffice to say here what is most significant about these resolutions
as a question of international law is that they reinforce and increase a State's
affirmative duty of vigilance. Indeed, even the most recent statements by the
General Assembly, in the United Nations Global Counter-Terrorism Strategy
is consistent with these heightened duties. In the Global Counter-Terrorism
Strategy, the General Assembly required States to "refrain from organizing,
instigating, facilitating, participating in, financing, encouraging or tolerating
terrorist activities and to take appropriate practical measures to ensure that our
respective territories are not used for terrorist installations or training camps,
or for the preparation or organization of terrorist acts intended to be committed against other States or their citizens."[43] This statement, while encompassing
the obligations stated by the resolutions of the Security Council, also adds the
additional prohibition against tolerating terrorist activities. In *Congo v Uganda*,
the ICJ linked the toleration of rebels within a State's territory to a State's duty
of vigilance.[44] It noted this was a separate issue from active support of such
rebels. Thus, the increased responsibilities in these Security Council resolutions
impose affirmative international obligations on States irrespective of whether
the conduct of irregular forces may be attributed to the State itself. Such duties
add an additional form of accountability and further emphasize the point made
in the seminal article: "State Responsibility For Injuries to Aliens Occasioned
by Terrorist Activities," where Professors Lillich and Paxman concluded that
"[a] state is responsible for the acts of individuals only when it has failed to fulfill its international obligations to prevent such acts. [Thus], for a state to incur
responsibility it must be shown that, under the circumstances of the particular
case, the state failed to maintain the required level of vigilance or 'due diligence'
to prevent the injury."[45] Thus, rules of State responsibility determine when a

---

42   *Id.* at 230 para. 35.

43   Global Counter-Terrorism Strategy, http://www.un.org/terrorism/strategy-coun-
      ter-terrorism.shtml.

44   *Congo v. Uganda*, 2005 I.C.J., at 91, para. 300 (Dec., 19). *See also* Jonathan Somer,
      Acts of Non-State Armed Groups and the Law Governing Armed Conflict, 10 AM.
      Soc. INT'L L. INSIGHTS (Aug. 24, 2006), http://www.asil.org/insights/2006/08/
      insights060824.html.

45   Richard B. Lillich & John M. Paxman, *State Responsibility For Injuries to Aliens
      Occasioned by Terrorist Activities*, 26 AM. U. L. REV. 217, 230-31 (1977).

State is responsible for the conduct of non-State actors.[46] Attribution of the conduct of non-State actors to a State for purposes of the right to use force in self-defense still requires the much higher threshold of whether there was so much or complete dependence on one side, and control on the other such that the non-State actor would be regarded as acting on behalf of the State.[47] This test for establishing when a non-State actor can be regarded as an organ of a State was affirmed in the ICJ's judgment in the *Case Concerning the Application of the Convention on the Prevention and Punishment of the Crime of Genocide (Bosnia and Herzegovina v. Serbia and Montenegro).*[48] The views of individual judges of the ICJ who would eliminate the requirements of direction and control as prerequisites to attributing non-State actor conduct to a State cannot be a substitute to consent based norms of international law.[49]

---

46   Articles 8 and 9 of the International Law Commission's *Draft Articles on State Responsibility* (1996, amended in 2001), provide for circumstances under which attribution to the State of the conduct of persons acting in fact on behalf of the State is made. Under Article 8, "[t]he conduct of a person or group of persons shall be considered an act of a State under international law if the person or group of persons is in fact acting on the instructions of, or under the direction or control of, that State in carrying out the conduct." Additionally, under Article 9, "[t]he conduct of a person or group of persons shall be considered an act of a State under international law if the person or group of persons is in fact exercising elements of the governmental authority in the absence or default of the official authorities and in circumstances such as to call for the exercise of those elements of authority." State Responsibility, Art. 8-9, UN Doc. A/CN.4/L.602/Rev.1 (July 26, 2001). *See also* Mary Ellen O'Connell, *Enhancing the Status of Non-State Actors Through a Global War on Terror?*, 43 COLUM. J. TRANSNAT'L L. 435, 448-49 (2005).

47   Nicaragua, 1986 I.C.J., at 62, para. 109 (June, 27).

48   Application of the Convention on the Prevention and Punishment of the Crime of Genocide (Bosn. & Herz. v. Serb. & Mont.) 2007 I.C.J. 4 (Feb., 26). *See also* Antonio Cassese, *The Nicaragua and Tadić Tests Revisited in Light of the ICJ Judgment on Genocide in Bosnia*, 18 EJIL 649 (2007) (discussing Nicaragua's complete control test versus the overall control test of the Tadić judgment and the shortcomings of the judgment in definitively showing that the overall control test was no longer customary international law).

49   *See* J. Patrick Kelly, *Naturalism in International Adjudication*, 18 DUKE J. COMP. & INT'L L. 395, 402-03 (2008) (showing how customary international law has come to be articulated by scholars, non-governmental officials and international jurists rather than by practice by states based on their belief that they are legally bound. Prof. Kelly notes that such interpretations of customary international law have been used to support the unilateral use of force inconsistently with the prohibition of the use of force in the Charter of the United Nations).

Conclusions

The Security Council's extension of additional responsibilities on States in the anti-terrorism context is evidence of its emerging legislative role.[50] Resolutions 1368 and 1373 were, however, unnecessary to permit the US to use force in self-defense after the attacks of September 11, 2001 since the law on self-defense has not changed.[51] That these resolutions are now being cited as changing the law under Article 51 of the Charter to license States to use force in self-defense against irregular forces whose conduct is unattributable to a State is analogous to claims about how Security Council resolutions may be interpreted by individual States to permit the use of force without resort to explicit Security Council authorization in other contexts such as the 2003 Gulf War.[52]

As José Alvarez has argued, such claims "license recurrent projections of military force based on auto-interpretation and since they endorse *unilateral* military action, they are ideally suited to hegemonic sensibilities" (emphasis in original).[53] Notably, in *Congo v. Uganda*, the ICJ explicitly rejected Uganda's auto-interpretation of Security Council resolutions as authority to legitimate its armed activities in the Congo. The Court's rejection of Uganda's expanded claims of self-defense against irregular forces implicitly rejects this kind of auto-interpretation of Security Council resolutions by States as authority to use force inconsistently with Article 51 of the Charter.[54]

Indeed, it was precisely to limit and legitimate the use of force in self-defense as being justified only within the strict confines of Article 51 that the ICJ in *Congo v. Uganda* held that Article 51 "does not allow the use of force by a State to protect perceived security interests beyond these parameters."[55] In this

---

50 *See* Paul C. Szasz, *The Security Council Starts Legislating*, 96 AJIL 901 (2002).

51 Thomas M. Franck, *Terrorism and the Right of Self-Defense*, 95 AJIL 840 (2001). Notably, Judge Kateka's dissenting opinion in *Congo v. Uganda* argues that the use of force by irregular forces that falls below the threshold of an armed attack at least violates the principle of non-intervention. Congo v. Uganda, Dissenting Opinion of Judge Kateka, 2005 I.C.J., at 3-4, paras. 14-15 (Dec., 19).

52 One of the best instances of such a claim is William H. Taft IV & Todd F. Buchwald, *Preemption, Iraq and International Law*, 97 AJIL 557 (2003). *See also*, Gregory E. Maggs, *The Campaign to Restrict the Right to Respond to Terrorist Attacks in Self-Defense Under Article 51 of the U.N. Charter and What the United States Can Do About It*, 4 REGENT J. INT'L L. 149, 165-66 (2006).

53 Jose E. Alvarez, *Hegemonic International Law Revisited*, 97 AJIL 873, 881 (2003). *See also* Henry J. Richardson, III, *U.S. Hegemony, Race, and Oil in Deciding United Nations Security Council Resolution 1441 on Iraq*, 17 TEMPLE INT'L & COMP. L.J. 27 (2003).

54 *See* James Thuo Gathii, *Armed Activities on the Territory of the Congo (Democratic Republic of the Congo v. Uganda)*, 101 AJIL 142 (2007).

55 Congo v. Uganda, 2005 I.C.J., at 53-54, para. 148 (Dec., 19). The argument on the other hand is that limiting the use of force to situations where there has been an

case, although Uganda did not claim that its 'operation safe haven' initiative was an anticipatory or pre-emptive war to curtail the use of Congolese territory for launching anti-Ugandan attacks, the Court's finding can be read as precluding a reading of Article 51 as permitting the unilateral use of force in the context of the war against terrorism.[56] I have recently argued based on the number of States that supported unilateral exercises of the use of force in the period leading to the 2003 Gulf War, there is no evidence of widespread repudiation of the norm against the use of force[57] and I would argue that there has been no widespread repudiation of the requirement of an armed attack attributable to a State as a precondition of the exercise of the right of self-defense as well.

These conclusions are consistent with the view that the prohibition of the use of force is a norm of "higher normativity" which means that it ought to be maintained "even in the face of inconsistent practice."[58] It is widely recognized that "there is a category of norms that are part of 'general international law' which governments in general regard as obligatory despite violations, even if widespread" and that the prohibition on the use of force was one of them.[59] Further, State practice inconsistent with a rule of international law should not be treated as evidence of emergence of a new rule. Instead, such inconsistent practice should, according to the International Court of Justice be treated as a breach of that rule.[60]

armed attack encourages states to resort to 'surrogate warfare' through non-state actors, *see* THOMAS M. FRANCK, RECOURSE TO FORCE: STATE ACTION AGAINST THREATS AND ARMED ATTACKS 50 (2002).

56   Judge Simma makes it clear he had the 'Bush doctrine' of preemptive war in mind in his separate opinion. Congo v. Uganda, Separate Opinion of Judge Simma, 2005 I.C.J., at 3, para. 11 (Dec., 19). *See also* James Thuo Gathii, *Assessing Claims of a New Doctrine of Pre-emptive War Under The Doctrine of Sources*, 43 OSGOODE HALL L. J. 67 (2005).

57   Gathii, *supra* note 56.

58   Oscar Schachter, *Entangled Treaty and Custom, in* INTERNATIONAL LAW AT A TIME OF PERPLEXITY: ESSAYS IN HONOUR OF SHABTAI ROSENNE 717, 733-34 (Yoram Dinstein & Mala Tabory eds.,1989). This part of my analysis is based on Gathii, *supra* note 56.

59   Oscar Schachter, *New Custom: Power, Opinio Juris and Contrary Practice, in* THEORY OF INTERNATIONAL LAW AT THE THRESHOLD OF THE 21ST CENTURY: ESSAYS IN HONOUR OF KRZYSZTOF SKUBISZEWSKI 539 (Jerzy Makarczyk ed., 1996).

60   Nicaragua, 1986 I.C.J., at 98, para. 186 (June, 27).

Chapter 8

United Nations Peacekeeping and the Meaning of Armed Conflict

Mary Ellen O'Connell and Ania Kritvus

> The point is that the Geneva Conventions cannot be said to apply to a peace-keeping operation unless there is an *actual* armed conflict applicable to the United Nations forces themselves.[1]

As this quotation indicates the application of international humanitarian law (IHL) to United Nations peacekeeping involves understanding what actual armed conflict is. The authors' intent in this quotation is to emphasize that the Geneva Conventions and IHL apply to peacekeeping missions when this law applies for the UN, as opposed to when it applies for troop contributing states. For purposes of determining whether IHL applies to a UN mission, we look to the circumstances of that mission and the UN's obligations, not what the obligations might be if the troop contributing state were itself involved in the action. This is an interpretation of the law that has evolved as UN peacekeeping has evolved. Peacekeeping began as an activity that did not involve troops in armed conflict. Thus, some have argued that IHL does not apply to peacekeepers. That position was never uniformly shared and has now been officially abandoned by the UN, which acknowledges that UN forces must comply with IHL when circumstances warrant.[2]

For purposes of understanding the meaning of war in international law generally, the case of UN forces is helpful. The ICRC has long taken the position that the Geneva Conventions are triggered whenever the armed forces of the High Contracting Parties engage in any level of violent exchange.[3] The Conventions themselves say that they are triggered when there is an "armed conflict." An implication of the ICRC position, therefore, is that "armed con-

---

[1]   Garth J. Cartledge, *Legal Constraints on Peacekeeping Operations, in* THE CHANGING FACE OF CONFLICT AND THE EFFICACY OF INTERNATIONAL HUMANITARIAN LAW 128 (Helen Durham and Timothy L. H. MacCormack eds., 1999) (emphasis added.)

[2]   *See infra.*

[3]   *See infra.*

Mary Ellen O'Connell (ed.), What Is War? An Investigation in the Wake of 9/11.
© *2012 Koninklijke Brill NV. Printed in The Netherlands. ISBN 978 9004 17234 0. pp. 109 – 118.*

flicts" can range from World War II to the exchange of a few bullets by the armed forces of two high contracting parties. It is understandable that the ICRC would seek to have states respect IHL in the widest possible circumstances, but there may be unintended consequences of this goal when we consider that the rights to life and to a fair trial are circumscribed in armed conflict. If armed conflicts are found in the most minimal situations of violence, these rights are significantly undermined.

The case of UN forces indicates, however, that the meaning of armed conflict derived from the ICRC position is not consistent with the meaning of armed conflict in international law. National authorities considering the application of IHL to their troops involved in peacekeeping have looked for significant armed violence before concluding that IHL applies. Unfortunately, the author quoted above does not spell out what an *actual* armed conflict is. Indeed, despite the evident importance of having a definition for the purposes of knowing when international humanitarian law (IHL) applies to peacekeeping, the literature is mostly silent on the matter. Yet, on at least one aspect of this question, the consensus is strong. International law continues to recognize two distinct legal situations: armed conflict and peace. The application of the law of human rights, international criminal law and other important matters turns on the distinction.

This paper begins by tracing the evolution of UN peacekeeping and applicable international law. The second part of the paper looks at several national decisions on the application of IHL to wrongdoing by peacekeepers in Bosnia, Somalia and Rwanda.

I.   UN Peacekeeping and IHL

The legal framework of UN peacekeeping has evolved in significant respects since the end of the Cold War. Mandates and rules of engagement for the use of force have expanded dramatically. Along with this expansion has come the recognition that IHL forms a critical part of the law governing peacekeeping operations.

The term "peacekeeping" does not appear in the UN Charter; the Security Council has no express authority to send peacekeepers.[4] UN lawyers have, nevertheless, long argued that as long as peacekeeping actions have the consent of all the parties to the particular conflict, act impartially, carry only defensive weapons, and intervene only following a cease-fire, there could be no real legal challenge to their deployment.[5] Under Chapter VI of the Charter, the Security Council has authority to recommend to states a variety of measures for peaceful

---

4   *See* Mary Ellen O'Connell, International Law and the Use of Force, chap. 8 (2005).

5   Carl-August Fleischhauer, *Remarks* Proc. 86 Am. Soc. Int'l Law 586-88 (1992); *see also*, Trevor Findlay, The Use of Force in UN Peace Operations (2002).

settlement of disputes and under Chapter VII it can send troops of the member states to conflict areas. Putting these provisions together, international lawyers believe the authority can be found. If the peacekeepers have the consent of all parties, where a ceasefire is in place, and use limited force, the UN would be able to avoid interfering in the political struggle behind such conflicts.

Before the end of the Cold War, seventeen peacekeeping missions were organized. These missions aided compliance with cease-fires by literally impos- ing blue-helmeted soldiers between warring factions or setting up observer posts to report breaches of the cease-fire. Peacekeepers were not, however, peace enforcers – they did not take coercive action to compel compliance with a cease- fire.

With the formation of the first peacekeeping mission, a debate began about the relevance of IHL for peacekeeping.[6] Derek Bowett pointed out that "[i]t is not accepted that UN Forces, absent other legal considerations, are released from … the law of war because of the legal status of its opponent."[7] Yet, peacekeeping is different from the action of armed forces of states contending for a military objective with each other or with organized armed groups within a state.[8] At the time of the 1977 Diplomatic Conference on the Reaffirmation and Development of International Humanitarian Law Applicable in Armed Conflicts the UN Secretary-General took the formal position that IHL does not apply to UN peacekeepers. Some had advocated the position that IHL should apply to peace- keepers as it would if their states of nationality were involved instead of the UN. The traditionalist response was that "peacekeepers are not normally engaged in armed conflict and the Geneva Conventions, therefore, do not apply to them, however, desirable this may be."[9] This remained the official position until it was formally modified with the adoption in 1999 of the Secretary General's *Bulletin on Observance by United Nations Forces of International Humanitarian Law*.

This change came almost eight years after the Security Council had begun authorizing "peace enforcement" missions. With the end of the Cold War, the Security Council began authorizing missions where force beyond personal self- defense by peacekeepers was contemplated. Following the successful enforce- ment action in the 1990-1991 Gulf War, Security Council members and the UN Secretary General, began to think more expansively about the UN's role

---

6   William J. Bivens, *Report of Committee on the Study of the Legal Problems of the United Nations, Should the Laws of War Apply to United Nations Enforcement Action?* 46 ASIL Proceedings 216 (1952).

7   Derek Bowett, United Nations Forces 496 (1964).

8   New Zealand's Military Manual (1992) in para. 1904 stresses that the UN peace- keeping forces have no combat function, they are not present in state territory in any hostile capacity, not engaged in any sort of armed conflict either – as a result the Geneva Conventions I-III do not govern their activities or protect them.

9   Cartledge, *supra* note 1, at 128.

in world peace.[10] The Council began to authorize missions to respond to human rights crises – situations that did not fit easily in the UN Charter's reference in Article 39 to the Council's authority to take measures to restore international peace. Human rights crises had not traditionally been interpreted as breaches of the peace.[11] The missions themselves were given authority to use force to actually enforce the peace or end the crisis in contrast with traditional peacekeeping missions that could only use force in personal self-defense. The new missions have come to be called "peace enforcement." The Security Council typically refers to "Chapter VII" of the Charter in authorizing them, and it usually states the mission has the right to use "all necessary means" to carry out their actions. Despite these significant changes, the troops in the field carrying out the missions still wear the UN blue helmet and are still typically referred to as "peacekeepers."

With this expansion of the mandates, the evident need for rules regulating the use of force by peacekeepers became manifest. A concept known as "limited application of IHL" began to develop. Early proponents of limited application suggested that the laws of war should apply "to the extent commensurate with the amount of force necessary to permit effective self-defense and accomplishment of [the] mandate".[12] In 1999, the Secretary General adopted this approach, recognizing that UN forces would have to respect IHL if engaging in armed conflict. He published a "bulletin" on 6 August 1999, which sets out the fundamental principles of IHL applicable to peacekeepers. The principles read like a list of the agreed customary international law principles of IHL. Section 1 sets out the "Field of Application":

> 1.1   The fundamental principles and rules of international humanitarian law set out in the present bulletin are applicable to United Nations forces when in situations of armed conflict they are actively engaged therein as combatants, to the extent and for the duration of their engagement. They are accordingly applicable in enforcement actions, or in peacekeeping operations when the use of force is permitted in self-defense.
>
> 1.2   The promulgation of this bulletin does not affect the protected status of members of peacekeeping operations under the 1994 Convention on the Safety of United Nations and Associated Personnel or their status as non-combatants, as long as they are entitled to the protection given to civilians under the international law of armed conflict.

---

10   *See* the Secretary General's Agenda for Peace, U.N. Doc. S/24111-A/47/277 (1992).

11   The Security Council took measures with regard to Rhodesia in the 1960s and South Africa in the 1970s. S. C. Res. 418 (1977). While the real motive for action may not have been international peace, the Council found such breaches before issuing resolutions.

12   R. SIMMONDS, LEGAL PROBLEMS ARISING FROM THE UNITED NATIONS MILITARY OPERATIONS IN THE CONGO 174-177 (1968).

The limited application approach also addresses traditional peacekeeping missions where the "essentially peaceful situation degenerates to one where the peacekeeping forces become involved in actual fighting with organized armed units existing on the territory of the state".[13]

II.   Applying IHL in the Cases

The Secretary General's *Bulletin* recognizes that UN peacekeepers must respect IHL's "fundamental principles and rules."[14] Significantly for this paper, the *Bulletin* says that the application of IHL to UN-mandated operations has to be "determined in accordance with the facts on the ground."[15] On that much there is agreement. What exactly those facts are, is less well understood.

Peacekeepers are under the authority of IHL "to the extent and for the duration of their engagement"[16] in fighting of a certain intensity. Recent international criminal law statutes also reflect that the law changes for peacekeepers when they engage in fighting of a certain intensity. Intentionally attacking peacekeepers is a crime, but only "as long as they are entitled to the protection given to civilians or civilian objects under the international law of armed conflict".[17]

The formula "to the extent and for the duration of their engagement" seems to imply that IHL becomes effective only when peacekeepers are engaged in fighting and ceases to apply immediately after a particular engagement is over. The logic behind this provision is similar to the "revolving door" argument in the case of civilians taking direct part in hostilities, which means that they can become lawful targets only at the moment of "direct participation."[18] If they

---

13   Dieter Fleck, The Handbook of the Law of Visiting Forces 501 (2001).

14   Secretary-General's Bulletin, ST/SGB/1999/13, 6 August 1999. s. 1.

15   ICRC Report on the Expert Meeting on Multinational Peace Operations, Application of IHL and International Human Rights Law to UN-mandated Force 208, December 2003.

16   Secretary-General's Bulletin, ST/SGB/1999/13, 6 August 1999. s. 1.1.

17   Rome Statute art. 8 2 (b) (iii) and (e) (iii). Similar language is employed in art. 4 (b) of the Statute of the Special Court for Sierra Leone (2002); sections 6 (1) (b) (iii) and (e) (iii) of the UNTAET Regulation No. 2000/15 (2000) for the East Timor Special Panels. Burundi's Draft Law on Genocide, Crimes against Humanity and War Crimes (2001) art. 4 (B) (c) and (D) (c); German Law Introducing the International Crimes Code (2002) art. 1 para 10 (1) (1); and Mali's Penal Code (2001) art. 31 (i) (3). For more examples *see* Customary International Humanitarian Law 640 *et seq.,* (J-M. Henckaerts and Louise Doswald-Beck eds., (2005) [hereinafter the ICRC Customary IHL Study].

18   *See* J-F Queguiner *Direct Participation of Civilians in Hostilities under International Humanitarian Law*, Nov. 2003, www.ihlresearchorg/portal/ihli/alabama.php.

leave hostilities or the hostilities end, civilians may no longer be the lawful target of attack. (They may be subject to arrest and trial for unlawful participation in hostilities.)

Similarly, IHL applies to peacekeepers in situations of intense fighting. The question remains as to whether this is the same triggering situation that applies to other armed groups or do peacekeepers have a specific threshold for them? The general threshold of IHL application hinges on criteria of intensity, organization of the parties, nature and character of armed violence and varies in international and internal conflicts.[19] Are these the factors relevant to the triggering of IHL for peacekeepers?

Christopher Greenwood observes that there is a tendency to identify the threshold for UN peacekeeping as somewhat higher than may be the case for states.[20] In other words, fighting would need to be more intense for IHL to became applicable for peacekeepers. There is no express authority for this position. It is rather based on several arguments. One argument is that in practice we find that the UN and troop contributing states are quite reluctant to recognize that their forces are engaged in armed conflict.[21] The tendency, therefore, may be that IHL is not being applied in as many situations as would be the case if those involved in the fighting were not UN forces.

A second argument regarding the situations triggering IHL for peacekeeping, concerns the Convention on the Safety of the United Nations and Associated Personnel of 1994.[22] The Convention generally requires respect for UN personnel, but also provides a so-called "combat exception". Article 2(2) of the Convention stresses that the humanitarian law of international armed conflict covers only peacekeeping operations authorized under Chapter VII as enforcement actions "in which any of the personnel are engaged as combatants against organized armed forces". It also states, however, that nothing in the Convention shall affect the applicability of IHL as concerns the protection of peacekeepers (Article 20 (a)). This would appear to contradict Article 2(2), which incorporates a determination of the Security Council regarding Chapter VII as the basis for triggering IHL, rather than an assessment of facts on the ground.

Another argument for a higher UN threshold concerns the ICRC's position that the Geneva Conventions are triggered by even the most minimal armed exchanges by High Contracting Parties. If IHL is triggered at such a low threshold for states, the UN, not being a party to the Conventions, is not held to the same low threshold. *Pictet's Commentary* says "the existence of an international armed conflict should not be regarded as contingent upon hos-

---

19   Other papers by Use of Force Commitee Member deal with this question in detail.

20   Christopher Greenwood, *International Humanitarian Law and UN Military Operations*, 1998 Yearbook of International Humanitarian Law, 24.

21   *See* Greenwood *supra* note, at 24.

22   UN GA res. 49/59, 49 UN GAOR Supp. (No. 49) at 299, UN Doc. A/49/49 (1994).

tilities reaching a particular level of intensity"[23] before the Conventions apply among the parties.

It should be noted, however, that Pictet's comment is not entirely consistent with the plain terms of the Geneva Conventions. The existence of an "armed conflict" indicates that fighting between organized armed groups has reached a particular level of intensity. The Geneva Conventions only apply in armed conflict and occupation, not in every violent exchange, regardless of Pictet and the policy of the ICRC that the Conventions should apply as widely as possible. State practice supports the view that "armed conflict" is, at the least, referring to armed exchanges of a certain intensity. Most States do not regard an isolated incident or limited exchange of fire, as an armed conflict, bringing into operation the full panoply of the Geneva Conventions.[24]

The International Court of Justice in the *Nicaragua Case* also distinguished minor armed exchanges from attacks that give rise to the right of self-defense. Similarly, such incidents are too insignificant to be labeled an armed conflict.[25] In 2005, the Ethiopia-Eritrea Claims Commission also referred to incidents too insignificant to trigger self-defense. If they cannot trigger the right of self-defense, such incidents are too insignificant to be armed conflicts. "[M]any isolated incidents, such as border clashes and naval incidents, are not treated as armed conflicts. It may well be, therefore, that only when fighting reaches a level of intensity which exceeds that of such isolated clashes will it be treated as an armed conflict to which the rules of international humanitarian law apply."[26]

Indeed, states are reluctant to acknowledge that conflicts on their territory, especially internal armed conflicts, are serious enough to trigger IHL. Thus, rather than finding a higher threshold must be reached to trigger IHL for the UN, it would appear to be the same threshold as for states, just higher than the ICRC might like. That leaves the question of where the threshold is, whether for the UN or states?

National courts in the United Kingdom, Canada, Italy and Belgium have struggled with cases turning on the legal status of peacekeeping operations and the applicability of traditional IHL to their conduct. In *R. v. Ministry of Defence, ex parte Walker*[27] an UNPROFOR officer applied unsuccessfully for

---

23   *Commentary on Geneva Convention III* 23 (Jean S. Picket ed., 1960).

24   INTERNATIONAL LAW 792 (Malcolm D. Evans ed., 2003).

25   Military and Paramilitary Activities In and Against Nicaragua (Nicaragua v. U.S.), 1986 I.C.J. 14, 102-03 (June 27) [hereinafter Nicaragua]. *See also,* INTERNATIONAL INCIDENTS: THE LAW THAT COUNTS IN WORLD POLITICS (W. Michael Reisman & Andrew R. Willard eds., 1988.

26   Christopher Greenwood, *Scope of Application of Humanitarian Law, in* The HANDBOOK OF HUMANITARIAN LAW IN ARMED CONFLICT 39, 42 (Dieter Fleck ed., 1995)(footnotes omitted.)

27   *R. v. Ministry of Defence, ex parte Walker,* House of Lords [2000] 2 All ER 917, 6 April 2000.

compensation under the British Criminal Injuries Scheme. Originally the Scheme excluded compensation for acts of violence committed by an enemy when a state of war existed or a war-like situation was declared to exist. "War operations" and "military activity by warring factions" were later added to the list of excluded acts. The applicant argued that he was injured as a result of a crime in the form of an attack on an UNPROFOR building. He argued the attack was not military activity by a warring faction. The court determined that the attack was an excluded act under the Scheme in terms of domestic law, if not international law.[28]

In the *Brocklebank* case,[29] the Canadian Court Martial Appeal Court considered the torture and beating to death of a Somali teenager during Canada's participation in the UN peacekeeping mission in Somalia. The Court did not find evidence of an armed conflict in Somalia at the material time and, on that basis, found the criminal counts inapplicable because they were based on the Fourth Geneva Convention, which does not apply to peace operations. However, other authorities, such as the Commission of Inquiry of 1995[30] and the Simpson Study of the law applicable to Canadian forces in Somalia in 1992–1993,[31] arrived at the opposite conclusion. Unlike the court, the Simpson Study did find evidence of an armed conflict:

> In the common ordinary meaning of the expression, there surely was available information – although apparently not presented in evidence – of 'armed conflict' in Somalia at the relevant time. Not only was it noted in reports of the Secretary General of the UN to the Security Council in 1992 and 1993, but hundreds of shooting deaths of members of other contingents of UNITAF and Somalis attested to serious and persistent armed conflict.[32]

---

28   T. M. C. ASSER INSTITUUT, YEARBOOK OF INTERNATIONAL HUMANITARIAN LAW 600, Hague, The Netherlands (2000).

29   *Regina v. Brocklebank*, CMAC of Canada, 2 April 1996, 106 Canadian Criminal Cases (3d) at p. 371 of T. M. C. ASSER INSTITUUT, YEARBOOK OF INTERNATIONAL HUMANITARIAN LAW, Hague, The Netherlands (1998).

30   Although the Commission of Inquiry did not reach any definitive conclusions on the issue of applicability, 87% of its general recommendations were supported and implemented by the Department of National Defence.

31   James M. Simpson, *Law Applicable to Canadian Forces in Somalia 1992/93: A study prepared for the Commission of Inquiry into the Deployment of Canadian Forces to Somalia*, Ottawa: Minister of Public Works and Government Services Canada (1997).

32   Robert M. Young and Maria Molina, *International Humanitarian Law and Peace Operations: Sharing Canada's Lessons Learned from Somalia*, T. M. C. ASSER INSTITUUT, YEARBOOK OF INTERNATIONAL HUMANITARIAN LAW, Hague, The Netherlands 365 (1998), quoting Simpson Study *supra* note 30, at 28.

The Simpson Study found that Canadian peacekeepers were surely bound in Somalia by the IHL principle of humanity, even if the government argued that Common Article 3 of the Geneva Conventions and Additional Protocol II did not apply.[33] The Study concluded,

> in any event, it is illogical that combatants are subject to the laws of armed conflict as members of national forces, whereas as members of armed forces in the same armed conflict acting as UN peacekeepers are exempt from the obligation to respect rights of protected persons.[34]

Canadian rules of engagement[35] indirectly supported this conclusion where they stated that "forces are to deal with hostile acts, intentions, force and terrorist attacks by armed civilians, military and paramilitary groups". The Rules of Engagement allow response using all necessary force, including deadly force,[36] and are to be implemented in accordance with domestic and international law.[37]

An Italian Commission of inquiry looking into the conduct of Italian peacekeeping troops in Somalia apparently also found it difficult to define the nature of the conflict:

> It appears evident from the Report that it is truly difficult to ascertain whether the events reported can be set within a legal context of war or within that of a police operation aiming at restoring public order. Therefore, the Commission failed to express any legal evaluation of the facts, particularly from the perspective of international humanitarian law.[38]

Similarly the Belgian Military Court denied the applicability of IHL in Somalia and Rwanda. It found that IHL did not apply to operations with humanitarian aims in situations of internal conflicts, instituted under Chapter VII of the UN

---

33   *Simpson Study* (1997); *See* the Universal Declaration of Human Rights 1948; Martens Clause, and "elementary considerations of humanity" according to the ICJ *dicta* in *Corfu Channel*, Merits, I.C.J. Reports 1949, p. 22.

34   *Simpson Study*, para 24.

35   *See also* The Laws of Armed Conflict at the Operational and Tactical Level, Office of the Judge Advocate General B-66-005-0027/AF-020, available at www.dnd.ca.

36   Katia Boustany, *A Questionable Decision of Court Martial Appeal Court*, T. M. C. ASSER INSTITUUT, YEARBOOK OF INTERNATIONAL HUMANITARIAN LAW, 372 (1998).

37   *See* Boustany *supra* note 211 at 374. See also Daphna Shraga, *The United Nations as an Actor Bound by International Humanitarian law, in* THE UNITED NATIONS AND INTERNATIONAL HUMANITARIAN LAW 315-338, (Luigi Condorelli and Sylvie Scherrer eds., 1996).

38   T. M. C. ASSER INSTITUUT, YEARBOOK OF INTERNATIONAL HUMANITARIAN LAW 375, 379 (1998).

Charter. Consequently it rejected the argument that Belgian troops were either "combatants" or "occupying forces" in either crisis.[39]

The evidence collected here is not overwhelming, but tends toward the conclusion that IHL is triggered for UN peacekeeping operations in the same situations as for states.[40] It also indicates that the key factor in triggering IHL is the intensity of fighting. No other factors, such as organization of enemy forces, control of territory, duration of fighting, or the like seemed relevant. Nevertheless, intensity of fighting has important consequences. It impacts the applicable law and thereby criminal liability of individuals.

---

39   Belgium, Military Court, Violations of IHL in Somalia and Rwanda Case Nr. 54 A. R., Nov 20 and Dec. 17 1997. The French report on military engagement in Rwanda also does not offer any practical solutions. www.assemblee-nationale.fr/2/2rwanda.html. However, Indonesia's report on investigations and prosecution of atrocities in East Timor seems to be different; excerpts are available at www.indonesia-ottawa.org/news. T. M. C. ASSER INSTITUUT, YEARBOOK OF INTERNATIONAL HUMANITARIAN LAW (1998).

40   *See also* M. ZWANENBURG, ACCOUNTABILITY UNDER INTERNATIONAL HUMANITARIAN LAW FOR UNITED NATIONS AND NORTH ATLANTIC TREATY ORGANIZATION 201-204 (2004).

Part III

Background Papers for the Study:
Beyond International Law (2007)

A. Political Science

Chapter 9

Silence of the Laws?
Conceptions of International Relations and International Law in Hobbes, Kant, and Locke

Michael Doyle and Geoffrey Carlson[1]

Introduction

Inter armes silent leges? In international law war is traditionally seen as a unique condition. Insurance policies are overridden, property becomes liable to seizure and destruction, and civilians have lost some rights including, for example, habeas corpus and the right to a civilian trial, as when President Lincoln suspended during them the Civil War.[2] In war, soldiers are given certain immunities, provided they obey the laws of war.[3] With the rise of undeclared wars and ambiguously declared wars, whether and why this should be the case has become subject to debate. In this essay, we would like to explore what international political theory can add to explaining the state of war and its implications for the legal character of the decision to begin a war (*jus ad bellum*) and the manner in which war is conducted (*jus in bello*) in light of the theories of

---

1   Michael W. Doyle is the Harold Brown Professor of International Affairs, Law and Political Science at Columbia University. Geoffrey S. Carlson is a judicial law clerk in the U.S. District Court for the District of Columbia. This paper appeared in the *Columbia Journal of Transantional Law* 46, 3, pp. 648-66 (2008); reprinted with permission. We are grateful for comments from José Alvarez and Mary Ellen O'Connell and other participants at the Notre Dame Conference on "What is War?"

2   *United States v. Averette*, 41 C.M.R 363 (1970) for a discussion of military trials of civilians in time of war. Many constitutional law scholars now think that Congressional authorization is also needed to legalize a suspension during a time of rebellion or invasion. In current debates, "time of war" is being controversially expanded to cover the more ambiguous situations of "peace operations" and, for some, the "war on terror."

3   For good surveys of pre-UN Charter law see Arnold McNair, *The Legal Meaning of War, and the Relation of War to Reprisals*, 11 TRANSACTIONS OF THE GROTIUS SOC'Y 29 (1925), and the for the post-UN Charter period, John A. Cohan, *Legal War: When Does it Exist, and When Does it End?*, 27 HASTINGS INT'L & COMP. L. REV. 221 (2004).

Mary Ellen O'Connell (ed.), What Is War? An Investigation in the Wake of 9/11.
© *2012 Koninklijke Brill NV. Printed in The Netherlands. ISBN 978 9004 17234 0. pp. 123 – 140.*

Hobbes, Kant, and Locke. And taking advantage of the themes that attend this discussion, we take the analysis a step further and ask what the implications of these theories are for compliance with the laws of war and with international law more generally.

International political theory presents numerous visions of the states of war and peace,[4] but we focus on three distinct ones. One, called Realist, inspired by Hobbes, portrays war as a condition natural to anarchy. "Out of civil states," Thomas Hobbes famously concluded, "there is always war of every one against every one."[5] Lacking a global common sovereign, inter-state relations is thus a constant "state of war," whether actual or potential. Another, Liberal Republican, inspired by Kant, explores the pacifiying effects of liberal principles and republican institutions on relations among liberal states. Amongst themselves, liberal republics can establish a reliable separate self-enforcing peace. A third, Liberal Legalism, inspired by Locke, bridges Hobbes and Kant. Unlike Hobbes, Locke portrays war as an act, a choice creating a specific condition. "Men living together according to reason," John Locke announced, "without a common superior on earth, with authority to judge between them, is *properly the state of nature*. But force, or a declared design of force, upon the person of another, where there is no common superior on Earth to appeal for relief, *is the state of war*."[6] Nonetheless, unlike Kant, Locke sees international peace as troubled; without authoritative international institutions (courts, etc.) rivalries can escalate into war.

While the two Liberals seem the more obvious foundations of international law, all three can lay claim to key features of the modern law of war and peace, while curiously upsetting modern international law conventions. Despite his rejection of the possibility of an international law of peace, Hobbes accepts the modern view of sovereign equality. Kant's scope for the international rule of law, while deep among liberal republics, is also narrow, rejecting the prospect of a full state of law among nonrepublics and between republics and nonrepublics. And Locke, notwithstanding the fact that he laid the foundation for laws of peace and war, introduces more occasions for the just use of force.

Hobbes, Kant, and Locke share similar modern foundations in rational individualism, which makes their international law differences all the more interesting. Curiously, it is Locke that offers the most complete, indeed modern, understanding of compliance with international law in general and the laws of war in particular. Lockean international law is both a genuine condition affect-

---

4   Michael W. Doyle surveys Realist, Liberal, and Socialist theories of war and peace, intervention and nonintervention, and just and unjust distributions of international income in WAYS OF WAR AND PEACE (1997). Some of these remarks draw on arguments presented there.

5   THOMAS HOBBES, LEVIATHAN, 100 (Michael Oakeshott ed., Collier 1962) (1651).

6   JOHN LOCKE, *Second Treatise, in* TWO TREATISES OF GOVERNMENT 321 (Peter Laslett ed., Cambridge University Press 1988) (1690).

ing all states and yet is not a fully reliable political framework for order for any of them.

II.   Compliance with International Law: Concepts and Framework

Louis Henkin articulated the single most famous statement on compliance with international law: Almost all states comply with almost all international law almost all of the time. But "almost all" might mean a compliance rate of less than 75%. So what is the significance of compliance? It is important to distinguish, as George Downs and colleagues have, between deep cooperation and shallow coordination as illustrated by the difference between accurately playing "hard" versus "easy music."[7] States engage in deep cooperation when they forego immediate material advantages or make costly changes in preferences in order to achieve the benefit of long run cooperation or avoid the costs of sanctions imposed by others. They engage in shallow coordination when they make minor changes to pursue current national preferences that are already clear and widely recognized.

Shallow and deep compliance seem to vary according to issues and scope. Stanley Hoffmann, for example, distinguished between three kinds of international law: First, the "law of political **framework**" identifies international actors and provides the basic rules of their interaction, such as sovereignty and nonaggression. Second, the "law of **reciprocity**" defines the rules of interstate relations in areas in which states have a mutual and lasting interest in cooperation, such as trade or investment law. And finally, the "law of **community** ... [concerns] problems of a technical or scientific nature for which borders are irrelevant."[8] Hoffmann believed that levels of contestation (and by implication compliance) would differ across these three types of law in any given international system. He further believed international systems – whether "moderate" or "revolutionary" – would differ in the overall levels of compliance. In his view, the law of political framework, which closely relates to the distribution of power, would be the most highly contested. By contrast, the law of reciprocity and even more fundamentally the law of community would elicit significant compliance because they involved mutual interests.[9]

We want to identify two other dimensions of compliance that arise in the contemporary debate in international law and politics. The first dimension tracks **indiscriminate** versus **discriminate** compliance. This asks whether states

---

7   George W. Downs, David M. Rocke, & Peter N. Barsoom, *Is the Good News about Compliance Good News about Cooperation?*, 50 INT'L ORG. 379, 382 (1996) (comparing playing "Haydn rather than Maher or Stravinsky").

8   Stanley Hoffmann, *International Systems and International Law*, 14 WORLD POLITICS 205, 210–13 (1961).

9   *Id.* at 233.

comply equally with all states or selectively with states of a particular kind. The interesting exchanges between Anne-Marie Slaughter and José Alvarez – focusing on whether and to what extent liberal states differ in their creation of, enforcement of, and compliance with international law between themselves and liberal and non-liberal states – is perhaps the most salient scholarly debate concerning this issue.[10] Second, compliance could be distinguished according to whether its scope was **wide** or **narrow**. That is, whether it covered many areas or subjects, from the law of force through trade and other regulation, or just a few. Hoffmann's three levels overlap here, but in this dimension the focus is on the range of law-governed interdependence and above on the difficulty of achieving cooperation.

III.   International Theory and International Law

a.   Hobbesian Realism

Thomas Hobbes, the great seventeenth-century Realist philosopher, explained how insecurity and anarchy were inherently linked.[11] Hobbes argued that states, like individuals prior to the formation of states, are basically similar, self-interested actors. They are driven by the competition for material goods, contests over prestige, and fear of conquest. The first motive leads to war when one state is considerably stronger and does not expect costly resistance to its predation; the second and third when power is more-or-less equal as neither state is likely to defer to the prestige of the other or know whether its power is sufficient to deter the other from attacking. Given the likely uncertainties about other states' motivations, rational states rarely experience security. They may clash even when each thinks it is seeking security but, absent a global Leviathan, cannot

---

10   *See* Anne-Marie Burley, *Law Among Liberal States: Liberal Internationalism and the Act of State Doctrine*, 92 COLUM. L. REV. 1907 (1992) (identifying a "zone of law" between liberal states and a "zone of politics" between liberal and non-liberal states in the context of U.S. court adjudications using states' domestic laws); Anne-Marie Slaughter, *International Law in a World of Liberal States*, 6 EUR. J. INT'L L. 503 (1995) (discussing processes, peculiar to inter-liberal state interactions, that will influence how international law operates between them) [hereinafter Slaughter, *Liberal States*]; Anne-Marie Slaughter, with a Comment from José E. Alvarez, *A Liberal Theory of International Law*, 94 AM. SOC'Y INT'L L. PROC. 240 (2000) (summarizing their respective positions on this issue); José E. Alvarez, *Do Liberal States Behave Better? A Critique of Slaughter's Liberal Theory*, 12 EUR. J. INT'L L. 183 (2001) (elaborating on potential shortcomings on Slaughter's liberal theory) [hereinafter Alvarez, *Critique*].

11   This view is identified with the writings of philosophers from fifth-century BCE Athenian general Thucydides to contemporary conservative thinkers Henry Kissinger and – at least before she became President Bush's national security adviser – Condoleezza Rice.

know whether the security of other states is compatible with its own. War then is a constant possibility in the international system.

The implications of Hobbesian Realism for international law are complex. On the one hand Hobbes famously declared the "covenants, without the sword, are but words."[12] The globe lacks an armed global Leviathan and so international law would lack hierarchical enforcement. But that does not mean that law would have no role. Hobbes's logic constitutes the legal foundation of both the doctrines of sovereign equality and the voluntary, positivistic character of modern, post-Westphalian international law. Making international agreements would be an equal right of each and every sovereign, and these agreements would have equal standing as law. But states' self-interests would still animate international law. So the law would not constrain self-interest, but perhaps refine it by clarifying ambiguity and thus solving coordination problems in which states have a mutual interest in compliance.[13] For example, while sovereigns have promised and have clear incentives not to harm innocent subjects, foreign "innocents" (noncombatants) in war are not protected unless a specific covenant requiring protection has been negotiated and it is likely for reasons of mutual advantage (the threat of retaliation) that state parties to the covenant will comply.[14]

The *jus ad bellum* and the *jus in bello* reflect these Hobbesian limits. Hobbesians would expect that states would continue to go to war driven by the Hobbesian trinity of fear, advantage, and glory, unrestrained by any international law forbidding armed conflict. And much of the modern international law of war and peace reflected this logic. States retained the discretion to declare war (*jus ad bellum*), at least prior to the Covenant of the League of Nations, which required the recourse to peaceful settlement procedures before declaring war, and the Kellogg-Briand Pact, which outlawed the aggressive use of force. Humanitarian law (*jus in bello*) from the Hague agreements onwards restricted how war could be fought, protecting noncombatants and outlawing some needlessly cruel forms of warfare. But throughout most of the twentieth century, as a Hobbesian realist would predict, these restrictions were enforced primarily by the self-interested fear of immediate retaliation, or by victors over the vanquished as at Nuremberg and Tokyo, and in the ICTY and ICTR.[15] Reputation plays a limited role, constraining a self-interested and publicly declared defec-

---

12   HOBBES, *supra* note 5, at 129.

13   Hobbesian international law would thus resemble the model of international law's limits recently advanced by Jack L. Goldsmith and Eric A. Posner in their influential THE LIMITS OF INTERNATIONAL LAW (2005) or Robert H. Bork's *The Limits of International Law*, 18 THE NAT'L INTEREST 3 (Winter 1989–90).

14   HOBBES, *supra* note 5, at 324. Relatedly, subjects that rebel are of course liable to punishment; and so are their children even to the "third and fourth generation." *Id.*

15   These are the International Criminal Tribunal for the Former Yugoslavia, and the International Criminal Tribunal for Rwanda.

tion from an alliance, for example, only when doing so would leave the defector so notorious as to be shunned by future alliance partners that it is likely to need for survival.[16]

For a Hobbesian, the wider reach of international law would be limited by self-interest, unless coerced, but available to all states. The range of subjects ripe for legal agreement could in principle be either wide or narrow, depending on how interdependent the interests of potentially benefiting states were. Security interests would tend to constrain that cooperation, along with multipolar balances of power. Their greater uncertainty would limit international cooperation because differences in benefits, even if both do experience a pareto improvement, can be utilized to tilt the security balance. In contrast, bipolar balances allow for more interdependence, because the area of common benefit is larger when states are stably aligned against a common enemy. This produces more intra-alliance coordination and cooperation of interests, but only within the larger alliances and under the shadow of each polar hegemon.[17]

States would be most likely to comply with international law in the Hobbesian world with respect to community issues where the common interests of states in, for example, aviation safety or the efficient delivery of the mails would prevail.[18] These issues would be limited by national egoism and the degree to which material common interests overlap. Hobbes's conception of international law would also succeed in advancing reciprocal interests when retaliation was a clear means of enforcement, as it would be in simple prisoner's dilemma games when iterated over an uncertain future, as Robert Axelrod has argued.[19] Thus, trade negotiations under the World Trade Organization (WTO) enforced with the expectation that the retaliation would be authorized for violations bear the clear mark of Hobbesian rationality.[20] So, too, would the negotiation of

---

16   HOBBES, *supra* note 5, at 115.

17   For this argument with examples from international monetary relations, see FRED HIRSCH, MICHAEL W. DOYLE & EDWARD MORSE, ALTERNATIVES TO MONETARY DISORDER (1977).

18   The Universal Postal Convention, *amended by* Sixth Additional Protocol to the Constitution of the Universal Postal Union, with General Regulations and the Universal Postal Convention, Sept. 15, 1999 (entered into force Jan. 1, 2001), at http://www.upu.int (last visited May 8, 2008) has 191 state members. *See also* Constitution of the Universal Postal Convention, July 10, 1964, 16 U.S.T. 7, 611 U.N.T.S. 7. The Convention for the Unification of Certain Rules for International Carriage by Air, May 28, 1999, S. Treaty Doc. 106-45 (2000) had 68 parties – which includes only one entry for the European Community nations – as of 2006. *See* U.S. Department of State, U.S. Multilateral Treaties and Other Agreements, http://www.state.gov/documents/organization/66287.pdf (last visited Mar. 4, 2008).

19   Robert Axelrod, *The Emergence of Cooperation among Egoists*, AM. POLITICAL SCI. REV. 75, 306 (1981).

20   For example, when a WTO member state wins a case before the WTO Dispute Settlement Body, the method of enforcement granted to the state is the ability

bilateral investment treaties, even ones that involved circumscribed delegations of sovereignty. But Hobbes is least likely to provide firm foundation for the law of the framework, the rules of sovereign political independence, and territorial integrity. It is not that retaliation fails to enforce those rules, as it would among equal states. Rather, the rules would lack fundamental support or enforcement in protecting weak states from strong ones.

The key message of Hobbesian Realism is that law is weak, but relevant. Any law that reflects the material, prestige, or security interests of a state would be complied with. Moreover, even when those interests dictate defection, states will be reluctant to acquire the reputation of faithlessness when they rely on cooperation for survival.[21]

b. Kantian Liberalism

Immanuel Kant's 1795 essay, "Perpetual Peace,"[22] offers a coherent explanation of two important trends in world politics: The tendencies of liberal states to be peace-prone among themselves and war-prone in their relations with nonliberal states. Kant's theory held that a stable expectation of self-sustaining peace among states would be achieved once three conditions were met. He calls them the "definitive articles" of the hypothetical peace treaty he wants states to sign. We can rephrase them as:

- Representative, republican government, which includes an elected legislature, separation of powers, and the rule of law. Kant argued that together those institutional features lead to caution because the government is responsible to its citizens. This does not guarantee peace, but selects for popular wars.
- A principled respect for human rights all human beings can claim. This should produce a commitment to respect the sovereignty of fellow liberal republics because they represent free citizens who constrain their state and thus those states represent individuals' rights who deserve our respect. It also produces a distrust of non-republics because if they cannot trust their own citizens to rule, why should we trust them?[23]

---

to impose countermeasures against the products of the breaching state that are "equivalent to the level of the nullification or impairment." Understanding on Rules and Procedures Governing the Settlement of Disputes, Marrakesh Agreement Establishing the World Trade Organization, art. 22(4), Annex 2, 1869 U.N.T.S. 401, 33 I.L.M. 1226 (Apr. 5, 1994).

21 HOBBES, *supra* note 5, at 115.

22 IMMANUEL KANT, *Perpetual Peace, in* KANT's POLITICAL WRITINGS (Hans Reiss ed., H. B. Nisbet trans., Cambridge University Press 1970) (1795).

23 The individual subjects of autocracies, of course, do not lose their rights. It is just that the autocrats cannot legitimately claim to speak for their subjects. Subjects retain basic human rights, such as the rights of noncombatants in war. The terror

–   Social and economic interdependence. Trade and social interaction gener-
    ally engender a mix of conflict and cooperation. A foreign economic policy
    of free trade tends to produce material benefits superior to optimum tariffs
    (if other states will retaliate for tariffs, as they usually do). Liberalism pro-
    duces additional material incentives to bolster cooperation because, among
    fellow liberals, economic interdependence should not be subject to security-
    motivated restrictions ("Trading with the Enemy" acts) and, consequently,
    will be more extensive, varied, and robust.

Kant suggested that each was necessary to secure a zone of peace among fellow
liberals.[24] The first principle specifies representative government responsible to
the majority; the second and third specify the majority's ends and interests.
Kantian Liberalism thus shapes foreign policy in democracies either because
public opinion is liberal and demands it or the political elite has liberal values
and implements it.

With regard to the *jus ad bellum* and the *jus in bello*, republics in Kant's view
abide by the laws of war unless it is extremely costly. There should be next to no
wars with fellow liberals, as the empirical record confirms. Although relations
between liberals and nonliberals would be Hobbesian, there should be more
restraint in the *jus in bello*, reflecting Kantian commitment to human rights.
Indeed, ratification of humanitarian law by a "democracy" does enhance compliance, as compared with ratification by a non-democracy.[25]

Kantian international law is discriminate compared to Hobbesian international law. There is special commitment to fellow republican states to respect
human rights and cooperate economically. Because law will animate and regulate those obligations, creation of[26] and compliance with those laws is embedded
in the Definitive Articles. Professor Slaughter also hypothesizes higher levels of
international law compliance among liberal states, resulting from, *inter alia*, the
denser networks of interactions between them and subsequent channeling of
disputes into domestic courts – i.e. "vertical enforcement."[27] Outside of the lib-

---

bombing of civilians – as in the bombings of Dresden, Tokyo, Hiroshima, and
Nagasaki – constitute, in this view, violations of these rights and of liberal principles and demonstrate weaknesses of liberal models in these cases.

24   These three points are developed in Michael W. Doyle, *Kant, Liberal Legacies, and
     Foreign Affairs*, 12 PHILOSOPHY & PUB. AFFAIRS 205 (1983); Michael W. Doyle,
     Kant, Liberal Legacies, and Foreign Affairs Part II, 12 PHILOSOPHY & PUB. AFFAIRS
     323 (1983); DOYLE, *supra* note 4, at 251–300.

25   *See* James D. Morrow & Hyeran Jo, *Compliance with the Laws of War: Dataset and
     Coding Rules*, 23 CONFLICT MGMT. & PEACE SCI. 91 (2006).

26   We note, however, that this chapter does not purport to address the differences
     between how liberal and non-liberal states create international law *per se*, although
     this is a major point of contention between Slaughter and Alvarez.

27   *See* Slaughter, *Liberal States*, *supra* note 10, at 532–34. This enhanced creation and

eral peace, Kant shares some of Hobbes's skepticism. He also thinks that immediate self-interest will govern relations, and that states will develop law outside
the pacific union as they would if they were Hobbesians. The many examples of
international law creation and compliance between liberal and nonliberal states
that Professor Alvarez identifies provide examples of this.[28] But in addition to
sharing Hobbesian assumptions about the dangers of international relations
outside the pacific union, Kantians have deep moral commitments to treating
individuals as ends (i.e. respecting human rights) that shape the policies they
adopt and the treaties they make.

Kantian international law is the most legalized regime, but only within
the liberal peace. The framework of international law is secured by "Perpetual
Peace," itself a peace treaty. Its three definitive articles are legally binding obligations – most centrally the obligation to maintain peace respecting the territorial integrity and political independence of fellow liberal states. This is the
deepest cooperation envisaged by the three theories, covering not just shared
common interests and reciprocity reinforced by retaliation (as with Hobbes)
but a legal framework ("constitution") that defines members and their obligations.[29] This is not global government (the Hobbesian route to peace). It is self-
enforced international law, enforced by a mutual restraint and respect among
liberal republics that is produced by the domestic institutions and the interests
and ideas of the citizenry those institutions reflect. And there is considerable
evidence demonstrating that liberal states actually do abide by non-aggression
against fellow liberal states.[30]

But within the pacific union where cooperation on peace is deep and complete, the range of subjects for legal agreement is narrowed by a continuing
commitment to independence. In order to avoid the pacific union becoming
tyrannical, exercising governing authority without representation over independent polities, Kant limits its scope to peace and hospitality (e.g., permit-

---

compliance are two of several results stemming from several "attributes" of liberal
states, which include "peace," "market economies," and "a dense network of transnational transactions." *Id.* at 509–14. *But see* Alvarez, *Critique, supra* note 10 (calling into question the consequences of these attributes).

28   *See* Alvarez, *Critique, supra* note 10.

29   This deep cooperation forms the basis for the "zone of law" that Burley – now
Slaughter – identifies. *See* Burley, *supra* note 10, at 1918–19. ("This core of common
values and institutions ensures that in most cases states can disagree with the specific policy choices embedded in each other's national laws but nevertheless respect
those laws as legitimate means to the same ultimate ends.").

30   For the debate on the empirical tendency of democracies to remain at peace with
each other see DEBATING THE DEMOCRATIC PEACE (Michael E. Brown, Sean
M. Lynn-Jones & Steven E. Miller eds., 1996) that includes essays by Michael
W. Doyle, Bruce Russett, and John Owen and critiques by Henry Farber, Joanne
Gowa, David Spiro, and others. The debate is predominantly over the reasons for
the tendency, not its existence.

ting free trade).[31] Kantian republics would comply with community interests and these interests might well be broader than those envisaged by Leviathans simply because security-motivated restrictions would be absent. When it comes to the law of reciprocal cooperation, the liberal regime would be cross-pressured. It respects the law among liberals, but it also responds to representative politics, electoral coalitions, and whims.[32] Thus, liberalism promotes the rule of law domestically and discounts long-run commitments in favor of interests of present coalitions.

These interpretations not only affirm the views of both Professor Alvarez and Professor Slaughter in their valuable exchange on the significance of liberal states for international law, but also recognize the common ground between them. With Professor Alvarez, we agree that international law shapes the relations of both Hobbesian Leviathans and Kantian republics when it comes to community and reciprocal interests. Moreover, although it will be relatively easy to identify which "engine" is driving law between states (based on their liberal or nonliberal character) predicting differences between the quality and character of those laws will be difficult because in community and reciprocal law Hobbesian self-interest can easily overlap with cross-pressured Kantian commitments.[33] Indeed, sometimes the former may be more powerful than the latter. With Professor Slaughter we agree that liberal states are different, given their special commitments and political character. Thus, we should still be able to identify special avenues of law formation, cooperation, and compliance between liberal states, most importantly in framework law (the liberal peace itself) and becoming increasingly discernable within the fields of human rights and deep economic cooperation.

Liberal states are different first and most importantly because the framework law of sovereign independence is genuinely secure among them. The most significant effect that appears to follow from this is a particular form of transnational law. As noted above, it is not that transnational law does not exist among nonliberal states. But it appears so far to be only liberal republics that have

---

31   Kant believes that these limits are natural results of nations' desires to retain their own cultural character, which will be embedded in, *inter alia*, languages, institutions, and ideals (see *Perpetual Peace, supra* n. 22). But while Kant's reasoning appears fundamentally sound, he may have underestimated the ability of people to find sufficient common ground that would result in a polity like the European Union, which has particularly strong supra-national governance law and institutions.

32   As Beth Simmons and Miles Kahler have noted liberal democracy is a dual factor. Beth A. Simmons, *The Legalization of International Monetary Affairs*, 54 INT'L ORG. 573 (2000); Miles Kahler, *Conclusion: The Causes and Consequences of Legalization*, 54 INT'L ORG. 661 (2000).

33   Thus, the "burden ... to prove that a liberal/non-liberal distinction exists" will be difficult to satisfy. *See* Alvarez, *Critique, supra* note 10, at 123.

formed genuine transnational political spaces. No common market has evolved into an integrated political and economic union other than the one among liberal European democracies. The common markets elsewhere have either collapsed (East Africa) or remained limited to trade preferences (the Andean and Central American and South East Asian associations). Not all liberals form economic unions, because the interdependence is not strong enough. Yet only liberals have succeeded in forming economic unions.

Second, liberals have a special affinity to compliance with human rights. In the era of Abu Ghraib, these clearly must be taken as far less than an iron law. Nonetheless, linkages between commitment and tendency toward compliance in human rights are special to democracies, according to various studies by Oona Hathaway. Liberal democracies are not only more likely to comply if they ratify but also less likely to ratify a treaty merely for reputational gain, irrespective of whether they plan to comply, because their reputations are more fixed. [34]

And, third, no Alien Tort claim[35] cases (listed in the ALR report on the ATCA[36]) have been successfully filed against another liberal government or government official – although some plaintiffs have tried it against, e.g., the

---

34 Oona Hathaway, *Do Human Rights Treaties Make a Difference?*, 111 YALE L.J. 1935, 2000 (2002) ("[F]ull democracies appear to be more likely to comply with their human rights treaty obligations than the group of nations as a whole and more likely when they ratify treaties to have better practices than otherwise expected."). Similarly, Hathaway also finds that democratic countries are less likely to commit torture and more likely to join the Convention on Torture than nondemocratic countries. Moreover, ironically reflecting a respect for law and expectation that it will be enforced, democratic countries that do engage in torture are less likely to join the convention, unlike nondemocratic countries that are more likely to join the convention the more they torture. Oona Hathaway, *The Promise and Limits of the International Law of Torture, in* TORTURE: PHILOSOPHICAL, POLITICAL AND LEGAL PERSPECTIVES (Sanford Levinson ed., 2004).

35 The Alien Tort Claims Act ("ATCA") provides that "[t]he District Courts shall have original jurisdiction of any civil action by an alien for a tort only, committed in violation of the law of nations or a treaty of the United States." 28 U.S.C. § 1350.

36 Russell G. Donaldson, *Construction and Application of the Alien Tort Statute*, 116 A.L.R. FED. 387 (1993).

United States,[37] Israel, and Germany.[38] These cases could not overcome obstacles such as the political question doctrine, a finding that the alleged activity did not breach the law of nations, and sovereign immunity.

c.   Lockean Liberalism

Like Kantian Liberalism, Lockean Liberalism focuses less on capabilities and more on *intentions* as embodied in institutions and legal/moral commitments. Locke explicitly analogizes the international system's condition to that of equal, rational, and independent men in the state of nature.[39] And like the Hobbesian Realist's and Kantian Liberal's natural state, it is anarchic. Locke differs in his emphasis on the natural rights of life, liberty, and property that all men are bound to respect even in the state of nature, creating a degree of mutual trust. These duties elevate the state of nature out of Hobbesian war and into a peace – albeit a troubled one fraught with "Inconveniences." These Inconveniences are:

a)   That bias and ignorance can cause war among well-meaning liberals, Locke warns us, is the first "Inconvenience" of the state of nature. Even though the laws of nature are clear, we will fail to reflect on their implications or be biased in their consideration in our own case.

b)   That partiality, passion, and revenge can corrupt the adjudication of even clear law in one's own interest, is the second. Negligence will make them remiss in the consideration of the others. Both will lack, therefore, adequate authority to make adjudication effective.

c)   That weakness and fear will erode effective execution of the law is the third, Locke concludes. The power to enforce just judgments will thereby be absent.

Men in Locke's state of nature create states to overcome inconvenience and protect their natural rights. But unlike Hobbes's conception of the state of nature,

---

37   The closest anyone seemed to come to a successful claim was *Jama v. United States INS*, 22 F. Supp. 2d 353 (D.N.J. 1998) where alien asylum-seekers sued the Immigration and Naturalization Service ("INS"), INS officials, and INS contractors alleging they were detained under awful conditions and tortured. While dismissing the ATCA claims against the INS on sovereign immunity grounds, the court refused to dismiss the ATCA claims against the individual INS officials and allowed the case to reach summary judgment. But the Supreme Court's decision in *Sosa v. Alvarez-Machain*, 542 U.S. 692 (2004), came down before the case finished, and the court then dismissed the ATCA claims against the INS officials saying the claims could not satisfy the *Sosa* standard for a breach of the law of nations. *Jama v. United States INS*, 343 F. Supp. 2d 338 (2004).

38   *See Hirsh v. State of Israel*, 962 F. Supp. 377 (S.D.N.Y. 1997) (dismissing plaintiff's claim against Germany and Israel that the ATCA provided a basis for recovery of reparations they alleged were due to them under treaty).

39   LOCKE, *supra* note 6, at 14, 95.

people are not so terrified that they will submit to just any government; they must consent to civil society for it to be legitimate. They chose a form of government – democratic, oligarchical, or monarchic – and allocate functions among a supreme "legislature" and subordinate "executive" (administrative) and "federative" (foreign relations) powers. Individuals agree to obey the laws and cede the right to punish to the state, as long as the state protects the fundamental rights of individuals and abides by its constitution. And although the specific form of the state makes little difference to its legitimacy, Locke prefers and praises representative government. Any illegal exercise of force, whether within the state of nature or within a tyranny, creates a right to reenter a state of war, a right to rebel.

The same natural rights and duties apply between Lockean states as between men. And it is these duties that lead just commonwealths to want to maintain peace with each other. Their public principles and their institutionalization of fundamental rights enable them to establish and signal reputations that encourage cooperation. Adhering to international law is a strategy for doing exactly that, and thus layers a positivist duty to abide by international law on top of states' natural duties. But, unlike the Kantian republican peace, the signaling is unreliable. Natural partiality and the poorly institutionalized character of world politics can overcome their duties to try to resolve disputes peacefully, resulting in imprudent aggression and complaisance.

Thus, Locke's international condition is an anarchic state of nature, a troubled peace fraught with Inconveniences that could deteriorate into war through the combined effects of bias, partiality, and the absence of a regular and objective system of adjudication and enforcement.[40] That Locke – unlike Kant – is prepared to delegate foreign policy ("federative") power to the executive alone might magnify such inconveniences by removing checks.[41] But war must still be a clear act of aggression violating rights to life, liberty, or property or a stated declaration of intent to do so. All else is peace. And in peace, natural law – now, international law – should rule. In short, the foreign relations of liberal commonwealths differ from Realists' only in that they remain constrained by the duty not to violate natural or international law. Rather than Rational Egoists, they are Legal Leviathans.

---

40   Richard Cox in LOCKE ON WAR AND PEACE (1960) argues that Locke's state of nature would resemble Hobbes's, but we advance reasons below to suggest that we take Locke's own label, "inconveniences", as just that.

41   But Locke's statespersons, like his citizens, are still governed by the duties of natural law – life, liberty, and property. Lockean executives and their states are thus distinguished by a commitment to mutual trust under the law. In the literature explaining the logic of negotiation, trust is crucial for stable agreements, and all rational egoistic bargainers will want to cultivate a reputation for it. *See generally* Philip B. Heymann, *The Problem of Coordination: Bargaining and Rules*, 86 HARV. L. REV. 797 (1973); JOHN DUNN, LOCKE (1984).

Lockean *jus ad bellum* and *jus in bello* reflect those distinctive features of Lockean international law. Going to war is neither discretionary (Hobbes) nor precluded (inside Kant's liberal peace). Instead, for a Lockean, just war is limited to self-defense, as in Articles 2(4) and 51 of the UN Charter, against attacks on a state's life, liberty, or property.[42] One exception, however, to the non-use of force (except in self-defense) involves cross-border enforcement of basic rights. In the original state of nature we all have the right to enforce our natural rights to life, liberty, and property against transgressors. So, too, in international law, Lockean states have rights derived from our own: political independence from our life and liberty, and territorial integrity from our property.

Aggressor states that violate natural rights make themselves targets of just wars (*jus ad bellum*) of defense and even conquest. Just conquerors have the right to punish transgressors (for murder, slavery, and theft) to deter future aggression and to exact just reparations. Transcending the traditional legal standards of sovereign immunity, Locke advocated what are now the modern standards of individual accountability – the post-Nuremberg principles of international criminal law. Indeed, Lockean standards are if anything more demanding. They apply to the crimes of war (*jus in bello*) and conquest, but also to infringements on property rights. The first two are punishable by death,[43] the latter by some lesser penalty. And the penalties apply to all those who have "assisted, concurred, or consented" in the act of war, which widens the "circle of responsibility" from conspirators to anyone who merely concurred. That means Nazi voters could be punished if the Nazi Party plan were known in 1933.[44]

That said, Locke's restrictions on just punishment are even more important for the modern conception of the right of self-determination and the *jus in bello* rights of noncombatants. Conquest, even just conquest, gives no title to territory. Territory is worth more than any due compensation and the people retain their right to self-government and self-determination.[45] Moreover, no one who did not plan, assist, or concur can be harmed. He thus bars all collective punishment and explicitly excludes reprisals against women and children. Although property may be seized to exact reparations, property belonging to wives may not be. The rights of legatees to subsistence thereby limits what reparations may be justly seized from a war criminal.[46]

So while Locke provided a powerful foundation for the precepts of contemporary international humanitarian law, ambiguities in his principles illustrate a contemporary dilemma in it. Violation of natural law inflicted on anyone, any-

---

42   *See* Alexander Moseley, *John Locke's Morality of War*, 4 J. Mil. Ethics 119 (2005).

43   Locke, *supra* note 6, at 178.

44   For a contemporary discussion, see Michael Walzer, Just and Unjust Wars ch. 18 (2000).

45   As Locke noted, the Greeks retained a right of rebellion against the Turks despite the centuries of imperial occupation. Locke, *supra* note 6, p. 441. para. 192.

46   *Id.* at pp 436-438 paras. 181–83.

where in the original condition can be punished by anyone. We cede the right of punishment to the state. Can one state then punish the violations of natural law inflicted by another state on the second state's own population? Is there a right of forcible "humanitarian intervention"?

Lockean "federative power" and "tacit consent" further complicate this question. Although violations should be punished, only the members of a Commonwealth have a right to rebel against their state. Short of rebellion we must presume tacit consent and tacit consent delegates the federative power to the state which would then have the right to call upon its citizens to defend itself from the foreign humanitarian intervention. Of course, the citizens who think their state has violated natural law have a right to refuse the call, and a foreign power could justly support them. But citizens holding different views would have a right and a duty to defend the state against the same foreign intervention.[47] The "appeal to heaven" (i.e. war) would be made. Prudent sovereigns, we hope, would refrain from intervention until it was evident by a "long (and large) train of abuses" or mobilization of popular resistance that a just revolution was underway. And thus we see again why the international condition is full of Inconveniences.

Lockeanism's implications for compliance in the context of international law are substantial. As it is for Hobbes, international law is universally applicable; but, as with Kant, it is embedded in the rights to life, liberty, and property. Rather than just immediate interest and retaliation, Lockean states have commitments and reputations that they want to maintain for human rights, property rights, and the rule of law. These reputations allow law to be more influential, encouraging cooperation even when immediate costs accrue.[48] Lockean liberalism thus tends to deepen cooperation beyond immediate self-interest and fear of retaliation to provide foundations for a wider scope of legal commitments. At the same time, Lockean commitments to protecting human rights and punishing violations could make the international system's foundations in sovereign equality more contested, rather than more stable, as Lockeans seek to enforce rights globally. And even though Lockeans engage indiscriminately with all

---

47 In Kosovo, for example, the Albanian Kosovars welcomed NATO's intervention; the Serbian Kosovars opposed.

48 *See* Andrew Guzman, *A Compliance-Based Theory of International Law*, 90 Cal. L. Rev. 1823 (2002). A commitment to the rule of law also makes compliance more likely in the expected reciprocity governing monetary commitments. Compliance with Article VIII of the IMF's Articles of Agreement, which spells out general obligations of members and prohibits restrictions of the making of payments and transfers for current international transactions, is enhanced by making a formal legal commitment when that commitment is made by states that measure high on their domestic rule of law (as would a Lockean state). Beth Simmons, *International Law and State Behavior: Commitment and Compliance in International Monetary Affairs*, 94 Am. Pol. Sci. Rev. 819 (2000).

states that are prepared to make legal commitments, their better foreign relations will be with similar rule-of-law states.

Judith Kelley recently took advantage of the advent of the International Criminal Court (ICC) to explore the reasons behind states' compliance with treaties.[49] Following the ICC's creation, the United States sought to secure bilateral agreements with other nations pledging that they would not surrender U.S. personnel to the court, which essentially meant that the other country would refuse to honor their ICC treaty obligations vis-à-vis the United States.[50] Using quantitative analysis, Kelley discovered a number of interesting patterns among nations in this context. First, states with a "high rule of law"[51] were not especially likely to sign onto the ICC relative to "low rule of law" states. Yet if they had ratified the ICC treaty, the former were significantly more likely to decline to sign the bilateral agreements with the United States than the latter.[52] Second, low rule of law states were actually more likely to sign the bilateral treaties with the United Sates if they had ratified the ICC than if they had not.[53] And third, Kelley concludes that the states that refused to sign the U.S. bilateral agreements did so for one or two reasons: respect for the ICC itself and respect for their treaty compliance in general.[54] In sum, a general respect for the rule of law impelled many states to rebuff U.S. requests.

In a similar vein, Beth Simmons has analyzed commitment and compliance with international monetary law, specifically the obligations under Article VIII of the IMF Articles of Agreement.[55] With respect to international commitments, Simmons argues that "governments are much more likely ... to

---

49 Judith Kelley, *Who Keeps Commitments and Why? The International Criminal Court and Bilateral Nonsurrender Agreements*, 101 AM. POL. SCI. REV. 573 (2007).

50 *See* Rome Statute of the International Criminal Court art. 89(1), July 17, 1998, 2187 U.N.T.S. 90 ("States Parties shall, in accordance with the provisions of this Part and the procedure under their national law, comply with requests for arrest and surrender.")

51 Kelley uses two measurements to determine the "rule of law" in a state. First, she uses the International Country Risk Guide (PRS Group 2004) which measures "the peaceful implementation and use of adjudication through law and established institutions." Kelley, *supra* note 49 at 578. Second, she uses the World Bank's Worldwide Governance Research Indicators Dataset for 2002 which measures the "quality of contract enforcement, the police, and the courts, as well as the likelihood of crime and violence." *Id.* at 579 (quoting Daniel Kaufmann, Aart Kraay & Massimo Mastruzzi, GOVERNANCE MATTERS IV: GOVERNANCE INDICATORS FOR 1996–2004, 4 (2005)).

52 Kelley, *supra* note 49, at 574.

53 *Id.* at 582.

54 *Id.* at 586.

55 Specifically, Simmons analyzes nations' commitments to and compliance with obligations under Article VIII of the IMF Articles of Agreement. *See* Simmons, *supra* note 32, at 573.

commit ... [when] such a commitment would be credible, but that commitment is also conditioned on other countries' willingness to commit."[56] And because the IMF agreement lacks any enforcement body, Simmons asserts that "the desire to avoid reputational costs is crucial" to explain compliance.[57] That is, nations want to "send a costly signal to market actors" that they will maintain certain economic conditions, even when this "involve[s] domestic political costs."[58] Compliance is especially enhanced when reinforced by high universal compliance, and especially influenced by high regional compliance patterns.[59] But Simmons sharply distinguishes two explanatory variables: "democracy"[60] and the "rule of law." While she finds that states with a high rating in the latter have correlatively high rates of compliance,

> Surprisingly for those who view the international behavior of democracies as somehow distinctive with respect to law and obligation, the more democratic the Article VIII country, the more likely it may have been ... to place restrictions on current account. On the other hand, regimes that were based on clear principles of the rule of law were far more likely to comply with their commitments. This finding indicates that rules and popular pressures can and apparently sometimes do pull in opposite directions when it comes to international law compliance. There is no reason to think, based on these findings, that democracy itself is a positive influence on the rule of law in international relations.[61]

Kantian republics should qualify on both fronts, being committed to both representative government and the rule of law, but not all democracies would clearly qualify.

Conclusion

These comparisons are purely speculations, illustrated but not proven. Their significance lies only in the logical coherence between the literature on the laws of war and peace, the general compliance with international law and the causal arguments of the international political theorists. Realist-inspired states in the

---

56   Simmons, *supra* note 32, at 574.

57   *Id.*

58   *Id.* at 583.

59   *Id.* at 589.

60   Simmons functionalizes "democracy" by using numerical scores derived from POLITY III set data, which measures the existence of democratic institutions in each country, ranking "competitiveness of political participation, the openness and competitiveness of executive recruitment, and the level of constraints on the chief executive." *See* Simmons, *supra* note 48, at 833.

61   Simmons, *supra* note 32, at 599-600.

balance of power, liberal states committed to life, liberty, and property, or liberal republics establishing a separate peace make real-world compromises and particularize the commitments and institutions that manage those commitments. But to the extent that the debates on law rest on the logics the theories develop, these observations are likely to have significance as frameworks for explaining compliance with international law.

Of Hobbes, Kant, and Locke, it is Locke who provides the firmest theoretical foundations for an international law open to all states that are willing to abide by it. Hobbes makes it clear that there are no states outside the zone of law, if we are prepared to include self-interested behavior as sufficient for lawful compliance. Locke adds a commitment to law for its own sake, by any state prepared to make the commitment. He includes both democratic and and nondemocratic states within the zone of law – to the extent they are prepared to respect life, liberty, and property. Locke overlooks the secure foundations of the Kantian republican peace, but in doing so, devises an international rule of law resting on sovereign equality.

Chapter 10

War, Crime, and Terrorism: Distinctions and Implications

John Mueller

Terrorism and crime are similar in that they are violent activities carried out sporadically by small groups and individuals. Terrorists and criminals differ primarily in their goals and in their willingness to risk death. Terrorists operate in pursuit of a political goal and are frequently willing to die in the effort, while criminals are in the game for fun and profit and are distinctly unwilling to die in the process.

When criminal bands become significant enough in size and in their predations or when governments enlist significant numbers of criminals into their military forces, criminal warfare ensues. Something similar holds for the relation of terrorism to disciplined warfare. When disciplined methods are applied sporadically and by individuals or small groups, the process can be designated "terrorism." When such violence is perpetrated by substantial groups and becomes continuous or sustained enough, it will look like, and be called, "war."

This essay explores and extrapolates from these distinctions.

Differentiating between disciplined and criminal warfare

Broadly speaking, there seem to be two methods for developing combat forces – for successfully cajoling or coercing collections of men into engaging in the violent, profane, sacrificial, uncertain, masochistic, and essentially absurd enterprise known as war. The two methods lead to two kinds of warfare: criminal warfare and disciplined warfare.

Intuitively, it might seem that the easiest (and cheapest) method for recruiting combatants would be to enlist people who revel in violence and routinely seek it out or who regularly employ it to enrich themselves, or both. We have in civilian life a name for such people – criminals – but the category would also encompass people popularly known as bullies, hooligans, toughs, goons, and thugs. Violent conflicts in which people like that dominate can be called criminal warfare, a form in which combatants are induced to wreak violence primarily for the fun and material profit they derive from the experience.

Mary Ellen O'Connell (ed.), What Is War? An Investigation in the Wake of 9/11.
© 2012 Koninklijke Brill NV. Printed in The Netherlands. ISBN 978 9004 17234 0. pp. 141–163.

Criminal armies arise from a couple of processes. Sometimes criminals – robbers, brigands, freebooters, highwaymen, hooligans, thugs, bandits, pirates, gangsters, outlaws – organize or join themselves together in gangs, bands, or mafias. When such organizations become big enough, they can look and act a lot like full-blown armies.

Criminal armies can also form when a government or ruler needs combatants to prosecute a war and concludes that the employment or impressment of criminals and thugs is the most sensible or direct method for accomplishing this. In this case, criminals and thugs essentially act as mercenaries.

As it happens, criminals and thugs tend to be undesirable warriors, however much they may be drawn to combat by their inclination to relish violence or to find profit in it. To begin with, they can be trouble-makers: unruly, disobedient, and mutinous, often committing unauthorized crimes while on duty (or even off duty) that can be detrimental or even destructive to the military enterprise. This natural unruliness is often enhanced by the deprivation and boredom that commonly envelop the long periods between military actions.

Most importantly, criminals can be disinclined to stand and fight when things become dangerous, and they often simply desert when whim and opportunity coincide. Ordinary crime, after all, preys on the weak – on little old ladies rather than on husky athletes – and criminals often make willing and able executioners of defenseless people.[1] However, if the cops show up they are given to flight. The motto for the criminal, after all, is not a variation of "semper fi," "all for one and one for all," "duty, honor, country," "Banzai," or "remember Pearl Harbor," but "take the money and run."

Indeed, for a criminal to perish in battle (or in the commission of a bank robbery) is essentially absurd. In general, then, although they seem to be more willing to accept risk than ordinary people and although they can be induced to engage in battle by the appeal of pay or booty and by the prospect of inflicting violence, they will tend to fight only when the probability of being killed is low enough or when they are massively coerced. In addition, the presence of such people in the ranks can affect the fighting morale of non-criminals in the combatant forces. Non-criminals routinely avoid criminals and other social undesirables in civilian life, and they may sensibly distrust their reliability in combat (McPherson, 1997, 8-9, 116).

The discovery of these problems with the employment of criminals as combatants has historically led to efforts to recruit ordinary men as combatants – people who, unlike criminals and thugs, commit violence at no other time in their lives (though they may watch a lot of it on television). Combat studies, in fact, generally find performance positively correlated with social class,

---

1   See Valentino (2004), chapter five, on the use of jailed criminals in the Turkish massacres of Armenians in 1915. See Kaldor (1999), 55, on the use of mostly criminal paramilitaries to carry out the massacre at Srebrenica in Bosnia in 1995.

education, intelligence, and personal stability (Grinker & Spiegel, 1945, 11-12; McPherson, 1997, 9; Stouffer et al., 1949, 36-38; Watson, 1978, 49).

The result has been the development of disciplined warfare in which men primarily inflict violence not for fun and profit, but because their training and indoctrination has instilled in them a need to follow orders, to observe a carefully contrived and tendentious code of honor, to seek glory and reputation in combat, to love, honor, or fear their officers, to believe in a cause, to fear the shame, humiliation, or costs of surrender, or, in particular, to be loyal to and to deserve the loyalty of their fellow combatants.[2]

Differentiating disciplined war from terrorism

The distinction between terrorism and disciplined war is essentially quantitative. Terrorism is a relatively petty event – an incidental, isolated act of mayhem perpetrated by individuals or by small groups, violence that generally does a comparatively limited amount of damage. If such acts become common and sustained – and therefore become much more significant – we no longer call the process terrorism, but insurgency, guerrilla or unconventional warfare, or, simply, war.

Thus, it seems reasonable to consider the Irish Republican Army – whose activities, together with those of its opponents, resulted in the deaths of less than 100 people per year – to be a terrorist force. But by the same token the sustained and far more murderous activities of antigovernment and anti-Soviet forces in Afghanistan in the 1980s continue to be best classified as warfare.

The current situation in Iraq also illustrates the point. For sound political reasons, President George W. Bush frequently refers to the violence going on there as "terrorism," but most observers prefer "insurgency." In fact, if the sustained warfare committed by the insurgents in Iraq is considered to be terrorism, a huge number of what have been called civil wars in the past would have to be reclassified as exercises in terrorism, including the decade-long conflict in Algeria in the 1990s in which perhaps 100,000 people perished. Most "primitive warfare" would have to be reclassified as well. Primitive warfare, like irregular warfare more generally, relies mostly on raids rather than on set-piece battles

---

2   The most reliable quality inspiring people to risk deadly combat is a quality variously known as small group loyalty, unit cohesion, primary group solidarity, male bonding, or the buddy system. To a very significant degree, all you need to fight a war is love. See Dyer (1985), chapter five; Guilmartin, (1997), 37-40; Grinker & Spiegel (1945), 25; Hauser (1980), 188-95; Hedges (2002), 38, 40; Holmes (1985), 270-385; Keegan (1987), 197; McPherson (1997), chapter six; Shils & Janowitz (1948), 283-88. See also Bourke (1999), chapter five; Smith (1949); Valentino (2004). Peer pressure may motivate at least some criminal warfare as well – showing off one's viciousness, prowess, and daring to one's buddies helps motivate some ordinary crime. Criminal combatants, however, are far less likely to carry this to the point of being willing to die for each other.

(Keeley, 1996). Indeed, the concept of civil war might have to be retired almost entirely. Most of the mayhem in the American Civil War took place in set-piece battles between uniformed combatants, but that conflict was extremely unusual among civil wars in this respect – the rebels in most civil wars substantially rely on tactics that are indistinguishable from those employed by the terrorist. Moreover, any genocide, massacre, or ethnic cleansing carried out by insurgents in civil wars would now have to be reclassified as an instance of terrorism.

Countering terrorism and crime

If criminal or terrorist activity, following the processes discussed above, becomes widespread and continuous enough to be labeled war, the goal for those engaged in opposing them is to stop and reverse the process by reducing the activities to more bearable levels. When successful, "war" – whether disciplined or criminal – will cease to exist, although crime and terrorism may still persist. Reducing disciplined and criminal war to lower levels generally requires military, or a combination of military and policing, methods.

Then, if criminal or terrorist activity is repressed below warlike levels, policing methods are primarily required. That is, the rules of policing, rather than those of warfare, apply – or, to put it another way, "wars" on terrorism or on crime become oxymoronic and are likely to have counterproductive results if the metaphor is taken seriously.

In neither case does it make much sense to seek to eliminate the violence entirely; because criminal and terrorist violence can be accomplished at any time by individuals or by very small groups, there is no way it can be completely eradicated. This is fully appreciated in the case of crime where police chiefs seek to achieve a low and essentially bearable crime rate and do not even pretend to be able to reduce the frequency to zero. In the case of terrorism, however, the impossible goal of complete eradication is very often sought, or, at any rate, proclaimed. Since terrorism, unlike crime, is often an exceedingly rare activity in many areas, this goal may seem achievable. However, this goal is essentially illusory because there is no way to guarantee an individual or small group might not from time to time launch another attack.

Policing terrorism and crime presents major challenges to those opposing them. It is most important to prevent policing measures from becoming counterproductive by enhancing criminal and terrorist ranks. Thus, because the police have sometimes used, or appear to have used, methods that have been unacceptably brutal and indiscriminate, some residents may turn to crime or terrorism because they come to believe that they are no less likely to be persecuted by the police if they refrain from such activities than if they commit them. Moreover, hostility toward or fear of the police may make residents reluctant to cooperate with the authorities, effectively making them into criminal or terrorist accomplices. Brutal and excessive efforts by governments to forcefully put down incipient criminal or terrorist insurgencies have repeatedly served to enhance the ranks of the criminal or terrorist elements to the point where the authorities become confronted with a full scale civil war. (Mueller, 2004, 172-74)

The issue of "collateral damage" may be illustrative. To blow up a building filled with innocent people in order to kill combatants hiding among them may be accepted as a sometimes necessary element (if often unwise or counterproductive) of military practice. However, it is unacceptable for police to do so to eliminate a band of criminals or terrorists. The act would be condemned not only for its immorality and illegality, but because it would create more problems than it would solve and therefore would be foolish policing.

Terrorism, crime, and the provocation of overreaction

The dangers of counterproductive policing and of overreaction are especially acute when dealing with terrorism. In general, criminals are not out to provoke overreaction by the authorities – though it sometimes works to their benefit. However, the provocation of overreaction by their foes is very often central to the terrorist enterprise.

Thus, as Osama bin Laden put it mockingly in a videotaped message in 2004, it is "easy for us to provoke and bait.... All that we have to do is to send two mujahidin...to raise a piece of cloth on which is written al-Qaeda in order to make the generals race there to cause America to suffer human, economic, and political losses" (bin Laden Speech, 2004). His policy, he extravagantly believes, is one of "bleeding America to the point of bankruptcy" (*Ibid.*) and it is one that depends on overreaction by the target. He triumphantly points to the fact that the terrorist attacks of September 11, 2001 (hereinafter: 9/11) cost al-Qaeda $500,000 while the attack and its aftermath inflicted, he claims, a cost of more than $500 billion on the United States. (*Ibid.*)

Although insurgencies have often been militarily successful, terrorists have only occasionally succeeded in gaining their political goals through terrorism alone – that is, without moving to the larger insurgency stage of disciplined warfare. When they have proved successful using terrorism alone, this usually has come about because of the counterproductive reaction, or overreaction, terrorism often inspires.

Terrorist impact: assassination, situations of low casualty tolerance

There are two classes of events in which terrorism has sometimes had a significant, even crucial, impact by itself: political assassination and situations where the terrorized have a very low tolerance for casualties.

Assassination. If terrorism were defined as mayhem directed at political innocents, assassination would be regarded as an entirely separate sort of event, not as a form of terrorism. If assassination is considered to a special subset of terrorism, however, there seem to be instances where it has had, or could have had, a notable historical impact.

For an assassination to be significant, the figure removed must also be significant. Where individual people are of considerable, even decisive, historical consequence, assassination could be similarly decisive. The person of Adolf Hitler was probably a necessary cause of the World War that erupted in Europe in 1939 (Mueller, 2004, 54-65). Consequently, had he been violently removed from the scene earlier, history would likely have been substantially altered (Turner, 1996). The deaths of Mao and especially of Stalin seemed to change history considerably (and for the better) (Valentino, 2004, 60-64), and it seems reasonable to assume that their earlier removal by unnatural means would also have been significant.

Among assassinations that actually did happen, the murder of John F. Kennedy in 1963 violently removed from office a man who, some people argue, was less likely than his successor, Lyndon B. Johnson, to enter and to sustain the catastrophe of the Vietnam War. There are historians skeptical of this speculation, but it is a plausible one. On the other side, one might also note that the political skills of Johnson, combined with the emotional reaction to the Kennedy assassination, were vital ingredients in getting historic civil rights legislation passed in 1964.

The assassination of Yitzhak Rabin in 1994 in Israel might have had some notable negative effect on the peace process, one of the goals of the assassin, because the leader who replaced him had less prestige and was less politically skillful. Significant consequences probably also flowed from the assassinations of Indira Gandhi in 1984 or of her son, Rajiv in 1991.

The assassination in Sarajevo in 1914 removed a notable opponent to war from the governmental decision-making apparatus. However, as will be discussed below, that fact alone was unlikely, by itself, to have led to war.

Low casualty tolerance. If the terrorized entity has a low tolerance for casualties, relatively small acts of terrorism can be important, even decisive, in changing its policy. American forces sent to Lebanon in 1982 and to Somalia in 1992 were engaging in peacekeeping, a venture few considered to be worth very many lives. Thus, when terrorist bombs in the first case, or a wild firefight in the second (possibly something that could be labeled terrorism), took the lives of a significant number of those forces, American policy shifted, and the troops were withdrawn.

Before U.S. troops were committed to Bosnia in late 1995, some 67 percent of the American public said it would favor sending the troops if none were killed, but this figure plunged to 31 percent if it was suggested 25 might die (Mueller, 2002, 212; Larson, 1996; 2000). This phenomenon seems to be general. By 1997, Spanish troops had suffered 17 deaths policing the deeply-troubled situation in postwar Mostar, and the government indicated that this was enough for them, withdrawing from further confrontation, something that greatly encouraged the Croat gangs in the city (Hedges, 1997). Similarly, Belgium abruptly withdrew from Rwanda – and, to save face, urged others to do so as well – when ten of its policing troops were massacred and mutilated early in the genocide (African Rights, 1995, 1112; Des Forges, 1999, 618-20; Gourevitch, 1998, 114).

Zionist terrorism may have influenced the British to leave Palestine in 1947 (Simon, 2001, 43-46). To the degree that it did so, however, an important element in the process was the British government's low tolerance for casualties in its onerous and unsung protectorate duties.

Terrorist impact: overreaction

Beyond these rather limited cases, terrorism's impact seems to have derived not so much from the act itself, but from the reactions, or overreactions, of states and electorates to that act. Sometimes these reactions are self-defeating or even self-destructive and very often they play into the hands of the terrorists.

Governmental overreaction as a political ploy. There is an important caveat – or semi-caveat. In some cases terrorist acts have had consequences because they are used as an excuse for – or seized upon to carry out – a policy desired for other reasons. The terrorist acts do not "trigger" or "cause" these historically-significant ventures, but rather facilitate them by shifting the emotional or political situation, potentially making a policy desired for other reasons by some political actors possible, but no more necessary than it was before the terrorist act took place.

An important case in point is the reaction of Austria and Germany to the assassination in Sarajevo in June 1914. It is frequently suggested that this terrorist act "triggered" or even "caused" the cataclysm that soon came to be known as the Great War. It seems clear, however, that rather than causing the massive (and, in the end, spectacularly counterproductive) Austrian and German overreaction, the violence in Sarajevo merely gave some Austrian leaders an excuse to impose Serbia-punishing policies they were seeking to carry out anyway. In an extensive discussion, Richard Ned Lebow concludes of the episode:

> the Sarajevo assassinations changed the political and psychological environment in Vienna and Berlin in six important ways, *all of which* were probably necessary for the decisions that led to war. First, they constituted a political challenge to which Austrian leaders believed they had to respond forcefully; anything less was expected to encourage further challenges by domestic and foreign enemies. Second, they shocked and offended Franz Josef and Kaiser Wilhelm and made both emperors more receptive to calls for decisive measures. Third, they changed the policymaking context in Vienna by removing the principal spokesman for peace. Fourth, they may have been the catalyst for Bethmann-Hollweg's *gestalt* shift. Fifth, they made it possible for Bethmann-Hollweg to win the support of the socialists, without which he

never would have risked war. Sixth, they created a psychological environment in which Wilhelm and Bethmann-Hollweg could proceed in incremental steps toward war, convincing themselves at the outset that their actions were unlikely to provoke a European war, and at the end, that others were responsible for war (Lebow, 2003, emphasis added).

Except for the third, all of these apparently necessary consequences deal with reactions, emotional or calculated, none of which were necessary results of the event itself. Because a terrorist gets lucky with a couple of shots in a distant province does not mean important decision-makers are required to shift beliefs or to give in to emotions to embrace risky (and, as it turned out, catastrophically foolish) policies they had previously rejected.

Similarly, many people in the Bush Administration had long been yearning for a war to depose Saddam Hussein in Iraq. Many of these immediately moved into operation after 9/11 in the belief, correct it now seems, that that dramatic event, even though it had nothing to do with Iraq, might well have cleared the air sufficiently to allowed them to carry out the policy they had been longing for. As Zbigniew Brzezinski bluntly put it, "The war of choice in Iraq could never have gained the congressional support it got without the psychological linkage between the shock of 9/11 and the postulated existence of Iraqi weapons of mass destruction" (Brzezinski, 2007).

Similarly, in 2004 Vladimir Putin seized the political opportunity afforded by some Chechen terrorist acts (and by some incompetent policing measures taken by the Russian police). He abruptly enhanced his control over the Russian political system – something that had absolutely nothing at all to do with the acts themselves. To say that the acts of terrorism caused this power grab would be absurd. Rather, they simply facilitated it.

Regimes have frequently allowed their participation in peace talks to be importantly affected by terrorists. By stating that they will not negotiate as long as terrorist attacks continue, both the Israeli government over the Palestinian Territories and the British government over Northern Ireland effectively permitted individual terrorists to set their agendas. However, of course, if those governments actually did not want to negotiate anyway, the terrorist acts simply supply a convenient excuse.

Governmental overreaction as an expression of rage or fear. Sometimes states react or overreact to terrorist events not so much out of a contrived or opportunistic effort to advance a pre-existing agenda, but rather out of rage, fear, or a desire to exact revenge. Once again, the historically consequential development derives from the reaction, not from the terrorist act itself, because the responder always could simply ignore or fail to give in to the provocation.

It is common to lash out impetuously at the perceived threat without much in the way of careful analysis. In 1999, for example, responding to several vicious acts of terrorism apparently perpetrated by Chechens, the Russian government reinstituted a war against the breakaway republic, a war that resulted in far more destruction of Russian (and, of course, Chechen) lives and property than the terrorists ever brought about.

When two American embassies in Africa were bombed in 1998, killing over 200, including a few Americans, President Clinton retaliated by bombing a suspect pharmaceutical factory in Sudan, the loss of which may have led to the deaths of tens of thousands of Sudanese over time (Daum, 2001, 19). Also bombed were some of Osama bin Laden's terrorist training camps in Afghanistan. These bombings appear to have caused the Afghan government, the Taliban, to renege on pledges to extradite bin Laden to Saudi Arabia, made him into an international celebrity, essentially created his al-Qaeda organization by turning it into a magnet for funds and recruits, and converted the Taliban from reluctant hosts to allies and partners (Burke, 2003, 167-68; Byman, 2005, 201-3; Coll, 2004, 400-2, 414-15; Cullison & Higgins, 2002; Kepel, 2002, 420 n. 50; Lake, 2002; Wright, 2006, 267-68, 287-89).

Eager to "do something" about terrorism in 1986, Ronald Reagan bombed Libya with planes launched from Britain after terrorists linked to Libya had blown up a Berlin discotheque killing two people, one of them American. After the bombing, in which one plane crashed and scores of people were killed (none of them Libya's leader, Muammar Qaddafi), Reagan triumphantly proclaimed, "no one can kill Americans and brag about it. No one. We bear the people of Libya no ill will, but if their Government continues its campaign of terror against Americans, we will act again" (Simon, 2001, 199). The bombing raid, notes Ray Takeyh, "only enhanced Qaddafi's domestic power and led to his lionization in the developing world" (Takeyh, 2001, 64). Moreover, although other countries became more wary about cooperating with Qaddafi and although he reined in his rhetoric and ceased to "brag about it," he continued to kill Americans. In rather short order Libyan agents had murdered an American and two Britons held hostage in another country and launched several other attacks including an attempted bombing of a U.S. officers' club in Turkey and the attempted assassination of an American diplomat in Sudan (Simon, 2001, 199). Then, two years later, Libya participated in the bombing of a Pan Am airliner over Lockerbie, Scotland, that killed 270 people, 187 of them Americans, and toppled the airline company into bankruptcy (*Ibid.*, 197-200).

Outraged by a series of terrorist attacks and shellings perpetrated by Palestinian forces based in bordering Lebanon, the Israelis moved in with massive force in 1982. By the time Israeli forces withdrew in 2000, vastly more Israelis had perished as a result of harassing Arab attacks than had been killed by terrorists before 1982.

Similarly, the Indian government massively overreacted to Sikh terrorism in 1984 by attacking the Sikh's holiest place, the Golden Temple, and engaged in other excessive military behavior. The result was a huge escalation in the conflict as large numbers of Sikhs were outraged. Among the consequences was the assassination of the Indian prime minister by two of her Sikh bodyguards and the explosion of an Air India plane in which 329 perished – the largest death toll caused by a terrorist attack until 9/11 (Pape, 2005, 156-60; Simon, 2001, 186).

Reactions to terrorism have also often led to massive and hugely unjustified persecution, some of considerable historic consequence. The Jewish pogroms in Russia at the end of the 19th century, for instance, were impelled in major part because Jews were notable in terrorist movements at the time.[3]

The impact of terrorism on elections. Not only have governments overreacted, often foolishly and sometimes self-destructively, to acts of terrorism, but so have electorates. In Israel, Arab terrorists have apparently had the goal of sabotaging Israeli-Palestinian peace talks. In both 1996 and 2001, Israeli voters responded to Arab terrorism at the time by obligingly electing to office parties and prime ministers, Benjamin Netanyahu and Ariel Sharon, who were, like the terrorists, hostile to the negotiations.

Terrorism in Spain in 2004 was almost immediately followed by the election of a party committed to withdrawing Spanish troops from the American war in Iraq. However, the election results are probably more nearly attributable to the incompetent way the ruling government reacted to the terrorist acts than to the acts themselves. In addition, the Spanish troops committed to Iraq were so small in number that their removal scarcely made much difference to the war effort. Moreover, the new Spanish government actually increased its commitment to the effort in neighboring Afghanistan, an act that probably compensated for any negative military effects caused by its withdrawal from Iraq.

The economic and human costs of overreaction. Other common reactions to terrorism are over-protection and overspending on defense. Sometimes, victim countries can become so fearful and self-protective (cutting off their borders or expelling a significant set of residents, for example) that significant consequences, particularly economic ones, ensue.

The costs of overreaction outweigh those imposed by the terrorists even for the attacks of 9/11, which were by far the most destructive in history. The direct economic losses of 9/11 amounted to tens of billions of dollars, but the economic costs in the United States of the much enhanced security runs several times that. The yearly budget for the Office of Homeland Security, for example, is approaching $50 billion per year while state and local governments spend additional billions.[4] Moreover, safety measures carry additional consequences:

---

3   For more on this, see Rapoport (2004), 68; see also Ignatieff (2004), 63. On the often deadly and indiscriminant overreaction to anarchist terrorism in the United States and elsewhere, see Jensen (2002).

4   For more on this, see Friedman (2004), 35; Gorman (2004); see also Pillar (2003), 25-27. And, not surprisingly, much of this hasty spending has been inefficient by any standards as porkbarrel and politics-as-usual formulas have been liberally applied: Peterson (2004), 116-17. See also Mueller (2006), chapter two.

economist Roger Congleton calculates that strictures effectively requiring people to spend an additional half-hour in airports cost the American economy $15 billion per year while, in comparison, total airline profits in the 1990s never exceeded $5.5 billion per year (Congleton, 2002, 62; Applebaum, 2005). The reaction to the 2001 anthrax attacks will cost the United States Post Office alone some $5 billion dollars – that is, one billion for every fatality inflicted by the anthrax attacks (Rosen, 2004, 68).

The reaction to 9/11 has even claimed more – far more – human lives than were lost in the terrorist attacks. Out of fear, many people canceled airline trips and consequently traveled more by automobile than by airline after the event, and one study has concluded that over 1000 people died in automobile accidents in 2001 alone between September 11 and December 31 because of this (Sivak & Flannagan, 2004). If a small percentage of the 100,000-plus road deaths subsequent to 2001 occurred to people who were driving because they feared to fly, the number of Americans who have perished in overreaction to 9/11 in automobile accidents alone could well surpass the number who were killed by the terrorists on that terrible day. In addition, it appears that there have been more than 400 auto deaths each year of people who have abandoned short-haul air flights because of the increased costs and waiting time imposed after 9/11.[5] Moreover, the reaction to 9/11 included two wars that are yet ongoing – one in Afghanistan, the other in Iraq – neither of which would have been politically possible without 9/11 Pillar, 2003, xv). The number of Americans who have died in those ventures far surpasses the number killed on September 11.

In addition, there have been great opportunity costs: the enormous sums of money being spent to deal with this threat have in part been diverted from other, possibly more worthy, endeavors. Thus, almost 75 percent of the appropriations for first responders has gone for terrorism rather than for natural disasters, and Justice Department resources have been greatly re-directed toward terrorism away from the prosecutions of mobsters, white-collar criminals, environmental crimes, and civil rights infractions (Eggen & Solomon, 2007; Manjoo, 2005).

Is overreaction to terrorism required politically?

In many respects, then, the way for states and peoples to defeat terrorism is refusal to play into the hands of the terrorists by restraining their reactions and, in particular, their desires or instincts to overreact.

It is often argued, however, that there is a political imperative that public officials "do something" (which usually means overreact) when a dramatic terrorist event takes place: "You just can't not do anything." By contrast, history clearly demonstrates that there may not really be a compelling political require-

---

5   For more on this, see Ellig, et al. (2006), 35. In comparison, some 200 or 300 people have been killed each year since 9/11 throughout the entire world outside of war zones by al Qaeda and its imitators and wannabes. Mueller 2007.

ment to overreact. Sometimes, in fact, leaders have been able to restrain their response. Even more important, restrained reaction – or even capitulation to terrorist acts – has often proved to be entirely acceptable politically. That is, there are many instances where leaders did nothing after a terrorist attack (or at least refrained from overreacting) and did not suffer politically or otherwise.

Consider, for example, the two instances of terrorism that killed the most Americans before September 2001. Ronald Reagan's response to the first of these, the suicide bombing in Lebanon in 1983 that resulted in the deaths of 241 American Marines, was to make a few speeches and eventually to pull the troops out. The venture seems to have had no negative impact on his re-election a few months later. The other was the December 1988 bombing of a Pan Am airliner over Lockerbie, Scotland, in which 187 Americans perished. Perhaps in part because this dramatic and tragic event took place after the elections of that year, the official response, beyond seeking to obtain compensation for the victims, was simply to apply meticulous police work in an effort to apprehend the culprits, a process that bore fruit only three years later and then only because of an unlikely bit of luck (Simon, 2001, 227-34). That cautious, even laid-back, response proved to be entirely acceptable politically.

Similarly, although President Clinton responded with (apparently counterproductive) military retaliations after the two U.S. embassies were bombed in Africa in 1998 as discussed earlier, his administration did not have a notable response to terrorist attacks on American targets in Saudi Arabia (Khobar Towers) in 1996 or to the bombing of the U.S.S. Cole in 2000, and these non-responses never caused it political pain. President George W. Bush's response to the anthrax attacks of 2001 included a costly and wasteful stocking-up of anthrax vaccine and, as noted above, enormous extra spending by the U.S. Post Office. Beyond that, however, Bush's response was the same as Clinton's had been to the terrorist attacks against the World Trade Center in 1993 and in Oklahoma City in 1995, and the same as the one applied in Spain when terrorists bombed trains there in 2004 or in Britain after attacks in 2005 and 2007: the dedicated application of police work to try to apprehend the perpetrators. This approach was politically acceptable even though the culprit in the anthrax case (unlike the other ones), owing to a suspect's suicide in 2008, may never be confirmed.

The demands for retaliation are somewhat more problematic in the case of suicide terrorists since the direct perpetrators of the terrorist act are already dead, thus sometimes impelling a vengeful need to seek out other targets. Nonetheless, the attacks in Lebanon, Saudi Arabia, Great Britain, and against the U.S.S. Cole were all suicidal, yet no direct retaliatory action was taken.

Thus, despite short-term demands that some sort of action must be taken, experience suggests politicians can often successfully ride out this demand after the obligatory (and inexpensive) expressions of outrage are prominently issued.

Even in an extreme case like 9/11, it seems likely that a communicative leader could have pursued more patient and more gradual policies. The requirement after 9/11 to "do something" would need to be fulfilled. However, a policy emphasizing agile coordination with other countries (almost all of them, including the crucial one, Pakistan, very eager to cooperate after the shock) and one stressing pressure on the Afghan regime and the application of policing and intelligence methods to shore up defenses and to go after al-Qaeda and its leadership could probably have been sold to the public. The war in Afghanistan was widely supported, and its remarkable success – at least in the period of active warfare – makes second-guessing difficult. But it was not clearly required from a political standpoint – even less the war in Iraq – and more moderate measures could have worked politically if they showed some tangible results.

Trends in war

There is an extremely important reason for carefully differentiating war from terrorism. Like crime, terrorism can be carried out by individuals and very small groups, and therefore it cannot cease to exist. However, war, as reasonably defined, can. Indeed, it may be in the process of doing so.

Definitions

War is very commonly defined in the social science literature as an armed conflict between governments (in the case of international wars) or between a government and an at least somewhat organized domestic armed group (for civil wars) in which at least 1000 people are killed in each year as a direct consequence, or a fairly direct one (caught in the crossfire), of the fighting.

Most of the literature on war, of course, deals with very substantial conflicts like the World Wars, the American Civil War, or the Korean or Franco-Prussian Wars in which organized combatants have at each other. In such context, a 1000-battle death threshold could be considered to be very low, even minimalist. Indeed, the Falklands/Malvinas War of 1982 between Britain and Argentina, in which about 1000 battle deaths were inflicted, has gone down in history almost as something of a comic opera exercise in considerable part because of its comparatively low casualties.

Following the distinctions set out above, if an armed conflict inflicts fewer than 1000 battle and battle-related deaths in a year, there has been a tendency to call it exactly that: an armed conflict, not war.[6] Other terms that might sometimes apply are terrorism, coordinated riots, a high crime rate, brutal policing, or criminal predation.

There are also armed conflicts, particularly civil ones, in which combatants, most of them of the criminal variety, rarely actually fight each other, but

---

6   As, for example, in Gleditsch et al. (2002) and Harbom and Wallensteen (2005). The highly useful database for these studies can be found at at http://www.pcr. uu.se/database/index.php.

instead primarily prey on the civilian population. Although comparatively few battle or battle-related deaths may be inflicted, considerably more – often vastly more – than 1000 civilian deaths may result each year, consequences that often persist even after any fighting among combatants stops (Ghobarah et al., 2003). In these cases, it seems sensible to use words other than "war" to characterize what is going on – perhaps ethnic cleansing, genocide, mass killing, terrorism, or extensive criminal predation. Most clearly, following the suggestion of Peter Wallensteen, they might be designated "one-sided violence." War, in distinct contrast, is characterized by two-sided violence.[7]

Trends

Applying this approach, one can tally the number of international, colonial, and civil wars going on in each year since World War II (Mueller, 2004, 87).

International war. Most importantly, the number of wars that have taken place since 1945 between developed states is zero (or near-zero), and this must surely be the most significant statistic in the history of warfare. Shattering centuries of bloody practice, these states have substantially abandoned war as a method for dealing with their disagreements, reversing the perspective of such earlier thinkers as Immanuel Kant who held that "a prolonged peace favors the predominance of a mere commercial spirit, and with it a debasing self-interest, cowardice, and effeminacy, and tends to degrade the character of the nation."[8]

---

7   Doyle and Sambanis contrast "negative" or "sovereign" peace with "positive" or "participatory" peace (2006, 18). For the purposes of this chapter, the absence of war means only that negative peace has been achieved. Some analysts have tallied armed conflicts that inflict as few as 25 battle deaths yearly. See, for example, Gleditsch et al. (2002); Harbom and Wallensteen (2005). Others, rather than simply focusing on the frequency of wars, have applied a measure of destructiveness, weighing costly wars more heavily than ones less costly: see Marshall and Gurr (2005). Still others have tallied warfare without including casualty estimates in their definitions at all: see Gantzel and Schwinghammer (2000); Luard (1986-7). Other data sets, particularly ones developed over the last twenty years, have focused entirely on civil wars, applying various definitions about casualties and about the wars' beginning and ending dates: see Fearon and Laitin (2003): Sambanis (2004). However, no matter how defined, the basic patterns for warfare – and in particular for the remarkable decline in civil wars in recent years – are found in all these data sets. For specific commentary on this, see Mack (2005); Marshall and Gurr, (2005).

8   See Kant (1952), 113. Kant was in good philosophic company: according to Aristotle, "a time of war automatically enforces temperance and justice: a time of the enjoyment of prosperity, and license accompanied by peace, is more apt to make men overbearing" (1958), 231-22. On the remarkable decline of war among developed states, see also Howard (1991), 176; Jervis(2002), 1; Keegan (1993), 59; Kaldor (1999), 5; Mueller (1989); (2004). More generally, see Luard (1986); Mack (2002), 523; Mandelbaum (2002). For contrary perspectives, see Gray (2005); Huntington (1989).

The Cold War of 1945-1989 did generate several international wars, waged not between developed states but between developed states and states or entities in the developing world. Three of these were particularly notable and costly – the Korean War (1950-53), the American war in Vietnam (1965-75), and the Soviet Union's war in Afghanistan (1979-89). This kind of war expired, of course, with the Cold War.

In general, international war of any kind – not simply wars among developed states – has become rather rare.[9] Between 1948 and 1973, several were waged between Israel and its neighbors, but none since that period (though Israel has had armed conflicts with Arab substate groups). Nor, except perhaps for a brief, localized flareup over Kashmir in 1999, has there been a direct war between India and Pakistan over the same period of time. Indeed, of the international wars waged since the end of the Cold War in 1989, there was only one that fits cleanly into the classic model in which two countries have it out over some issue of mutual dispute, in this case territory: the almost unnoticed, but quite costly, conflict between Ethiopia and Eritrea that transpired between 1998 and 2000.

There have also been a few "policing wars" in the post-Cold War period. These are militarized efforts by developed countries designed to bring order to civil conflicts or to deal with thuggish regimes. They have often been carried out under the authorization of the Security Council of the United Nations, which appears in recent years to have developed or evolved the legal ability legitimately to authorize such interventions (Doyle and Sambanis, 2006, 10; Gray, 2004, 250-51).[10] However, this phenomenon, rather tentative at best, seems more likely to wane than to grow. There are several reasons for this, among them a lack of interest, an extremely low tolerance for casualties in military missions that are essentially humanitarian, and an aversion to long-term policing. The experience of the wars in Iraq and, increasingly, Afghanistan are likely to further magnify a reluctance to intervene. Thus, when depredations by government-inspired armed bands caused ethnic cleansing and tens of thousands of deaths in western Sudan, the international community, after ten years of mea culpa breast-beating over its failure to intervene in Rwanda, responded with little more than huffing and puffing, pressure on the Sudan government, and the setting up of inadequate and underfunded refugee camps (Mueller, 2004, chs. 7-8; 2005; Straus, 2005). The same description applies to the hybrid "peacekeeping" force.

---

9   There was a considerable expansion during this period in the number of independent states. When these states were colonies, they could not, by definition, engage in international war with each other. It is rather impressive that there have been so few international wars during a period in which the number of entities capable of conducting international war so greatly increased.

10   On this issue, see also Rawls (1999), 81, 93n; Annan (1999); and "A more secure world: Our shared responsibility," Report of the High-level Panel on Threats, Challenges and Change, United Nations, 2004, paragraph 203.

Colonial war. One of the great, if often undernoted, changes brought about by the Cold War was the final demise of the idea of empire – previously one of the great epoch-defining constants in human history (Crawford, 2002; Fazal, 2007; Keeley, 1996; Mueller, 2005; Ray, 1989). Colonialism's demise has meant, of course, an end to its attendant wars. To a considerable degree, this remarkable development is a consequence of rising war aversion that led, essentially, to demise in the acceptance of the idea of conquest.

Civil war. By far the most common type of armed conflict since World War II has been civil war, with most taking place in the poorest countries of the world. Many have been labeled "new war," "ethnic conflict," or, most grandly, "clashes of civilizations," but, in fact, most, though certainly not all, are more nearly opportunistic predation waged by packs – often remarkably small ones – of criminals, bandits, and thugs engaging in armed conflict either as mercenaries under hire to desperate governments or as independent or semi-independent warlord or brigand bands (Mueller, 2004, ch. 6).

There was a considerable rise in the number of civil wars until the early 1990s when some two dozen were being waged. This development can be attributed to several factors. With the decolonization of the late 1950s and 1960s, a group of poorly-governed societies came into being, and many found themselves having to deal with civil warfare. Moreover, as many of these civil conflicts became criminal enterprises, they tended to become longer and to accumulate in number. This pattern may have been embellished by another phenomenon: democratization which often is accompanied by a period in which governments become weak.[11] Then, in the aftermath of the Cold War in the early 1990s, there was a further increase in the number of incompetent governments as weak, confused, ill-directed, and sometimes criminal governments emerged in many of the post-Communist countries, replacing comparatively competent police states. In addition, with the end of the Cold War, the developed countries, including former colonialist France, no longer had nearly as much interest in financially propping up some third world governments and in helping them police themselves – an effect particularly noticeable in Africa (Bates, 2001, ch. 5; Gray, 2004, 215-17; Keen, 1998, 23; Reno, 1998, ch. 2; Shearer, 1998, 27-29).

To a very substantial degree, then, much civil warfare is essentially the result of inadequate government (Mueller, 2004, ch. 9). Civil wars are least likely to occur in stable democracies and in stable autocracies – that is, in countries with effective governments and policing forces (Hegre et al., 2001).[12] They

---

11   On the connection between democratization and weak government, see also Collier (2000), 98, 108; Hegre et al. (2001); Jones (2001), 164-65; Marshall and Gurr (2005), 17-20.

12   For more on this point, see also Doyle and Sambanis (2006), 19, 35; Fearon and Laitin (2003), 85, 88; (2004), 21-22; Marshall and Gurr (2003), 19-20, 25; Russett and Oneal (2001), 70.

are most common – almost by definition – in what have come to be called "failed states." In fact, many civil wars, following the patterns noted earlier, have effectively been *caused* by inept governments which tend to apply excessive and indiscriminate force to try to deal with relatively small bands of trouble-makers, often turning friendly or indifferent people into hostile ones.

Many of these civil wars endured for years. The growth pattern through the early 1990s was mostly the result of a process of accumulation, not because in each year more civil wars started than concluded (Fearon and Laitin, 2003, 77-78). In recent years, however, this process seems to have reversed itself, and the number of civil wars for the last several years has been reduced to around four. Many of the wars – or competitive criminal enterprises – eventually exhausted themselves, and new ones have failed to arise to take their place. In the process, relatively effective governments have emerged in many formerly ill-governed countries even in the poorest areas of the world (Ford, 2003; Rotberg, 2002). Moreover, lingering ideological civil wars inspired or exacerbated by the Cold War contest died out (or became transmogrified into criminal ones) with its demise (Mack, 2005). Additionally, international organizations have sometimes been able to seize the opportunity to stabilize a shaky peace when the combat-ants have become exhausted and to help keep wars from reigniting (Doyle and Sambanis, 2006; Fearon and Laitin, 2004; Fortna, 2005; Mack, 2005). However, a truly effective, long-term solution to the problems presented by civil warfare and vicious regimes lies less in the ministrations of the international community than in the establishment of competent domestic military and policing forces.

The present situation

No matter how defined, then, there has been a most notable decline in the frequency of wars over the last decade or so. Indeed, between 2002 and 2006, only one war, America's conflict in Iraq, shattered the 1000 battle death threshold. Several intermittent armed conflicts could potentially rise above the violence threshold in the future, and new wars could emerge in other places. For now, though, conventional war has become a rare phenomenon.

There is no way to be certain that the trend in warfare, particularly civil warfare, will continue on its notable, recent downward trajectory. Perhaps we have today slumped only temporarily into a similar sort of hiatus even as hideous explosions await us around the next corner (Gray, 2005; Wallensteen, 2006). However, the incredible, completely unprecedented, and now remarkably long-term absence of international war in Europe, that once most warlike of continents, suggests that something new may indeed be afoot. There were relatively peaceful periods in Europe before 1914, but these were far shorter than the present one, and they were accompanied by routine and profuse fulminations about the glories and the sublime benefits of war. Also significant is the near-absence for the last few decades of international wars in which states directly go after each other in classic manner over matters of dispute like territory. Moreover, the frequency of civil war, far the most common form of warfare over the last half-century, has now remained at low levels for several years; although it is too soon to be confident that these levels will continue, there does not seem to be a large number of countries about to descend into internal armed conflict. A continuing decline in war seems to be a reasonable prospect.

Even if war fades, however, all sorts of other calamities will persist; the decline of war hardly means that everything is perfect. There will be other problems to worry about – famine, disease, malnutrition, pollution, corruption, poverty, politics, economic travail, and the potential for climate change.

Most importantly for present purposes, crime and criminal predation will still exist, and so will terrorism. Policing such activities in order to draw down their frequency and destructiveness may be sensible policy. Seeking to eradicate them entirely, however, is illusory.

References

African Rights. (1995). *Rwanda: Death, Despair and Defiance*. (Rev ed.). London: African Rights.

Annan, K. (1999, September 18). Two concepts of sovereignty. *Economist*.

Applebaum, A. (2005, June 15). Airport security's grand illusion. *Washington Post*, A25.

Aristotle. (1958). *The politics of Aristotle*. (E. Barker, Ed. and Trans.). New York: Oxford University Press.

Bates, R. H. (2001). *Prosperity and violence: The political economy of development*. New York: Norton.

Bin Ladin Speech. (2004, October 30). *Full transcript of bin Ladin's speech*. Retrieved from http://english.aljazeera.net/archive/2004/11/200849163336457223.html

Bourke, J. (1999). *An intimate history of killing: Face-to-face killing in twentieth-century warfare*. New York: Basic Books.

Brezinski, Z. (2007, March 25). Terrorized by 'war on terror': How a three-word mantra has undermined America. *Washington Post*, B1.

Burke, J. (2003). *Al-Qaeda: Casting a shadow of terror*. New York: Tauris.

Byman, D. 2005. *Deadly connections: States that sponsor terrorism*. New York: Cambridge University Press.

Coll, S. (2004). *Ghost wars: The secret history of the CIA, Afghanistan, and bin Laden, from the Soviet invasion to September 10, 2001*. New York: Penguin.

Collier, P. (2000). Doing well out of war: An economic perspective. In Berdal, M. & Malone, D. M. (eds.). *Greed and grievance: Economic agendas in civil wars* (pp. 91-111). Boulder, Colorado: Lynne Rienner.

Congleton, R. D. (2002). Terrorism, interest-group politics, and public policy. *Independent Review*, 7(1), 47-67.

Crawford, N. C. (2002). *Argument and change in world politics: Ethics, decolonization, and humanitarian intervention*. Cambridge, UK: Cambridge University Press.

Cullison, A., & Higgins, H. (2002, August 2). Strained alliance: Al Qaeda's sour days in Afghanistan. *Wall Street Journal*, A1.

Daum, W. (2001). Universalism and the West: An agenda for understanding. *Harvard International Review*, 23(2).

Des Forges, A. (1999). *"Leave none to tell the story": Genocide in Rwanda*. New York: Human Rights Watch.

Doyle, M. W., & Sambanis, N. (2006). *Making war and building peace: United Nations peace operations*. Princeton, NJ: Princeton University Press.

Dyer, G. (1985). *War*. New York: Crown.

Eggen, D., & Solomon, J. (2007, October 17). Justice dept.'s focus has shifted: Terror, immigration, are current priorities. *Washington Post*, A1.

Ellig, J., Guiora, A., & McKenzie, K. (2006). A framework for evaluating counterterrorism regulations. Washington, D.C.: Mercatus Center, George Mason University.

Fazal, T. M. (2007). *State death: The politics and geography of conquest, occupation, and annexation*. Princeton, NJ: Princeton University Press.

Fearon, J. D., and Laitin, D. D. (2003). Ethnicity, insurgency, and civil war. *American Political Science Review, 97*(1), 75-90.

Fearon, J. D., and Laitin, D. D. (2004). Neotrusteeship and the problem of weak states. *International Security, 28*(4), 5-43.

Fortna, V. P. (2005). *Where have all the victories gone? War outcomes in historical perspective*. New York: Saltzman Institute for War and Peace Studies, Columbia University.

Friedman, B. (2004). Leap before you look: The failure of homeland security. *Breakthroughs, 13*(1), 29-40.

Gantzel, K. J., and Schwinghammer, T. (2000). *Warfare since the second world war*. New Brunswick, NJ and London: Transaction.

Ghobarah, H. A., Huth, P., & Russett, B. (2003). Civil wars kill and maim people – long after the shooting stops. *American Political Science Review, 97*(2), 189-202.

Gleditsch, N., Wallensteen, P., Eriksson, M., Stollenberg, M., and Strand, H. (2002). Armed conflict 1946-2001: A new dataset. *Journal of Peace Research, 39*(5), 615-37.

Gorman, S. (2004, March 5). On guard, but how well?. *National Journal*.

Gourevitch, P. (1998). *We wish to inform you that tomorrow we will be killed with our families: Stories from Rwanda*. New York: Farrar Straus and Giroux.

Gray, C. (2004). *International Law and the Use of Force*. (2nd ed.). Oxford, UK: Oxford University Press.

Gray, C. S. (2005). *Another bloody century: Future warfare*. London: Weidenfeld & Nicolson.

Guilmartin, J. F., Jr. (1997). Light troops in classical armies: An overview of roles, functions, and factors affecting combat effectiveness. In Bradford, J. C. (ed.). *The military and conflict between cultures: Soldiers at the interface* (pp. 17-48). College Station, TX: Texas A&M University Press.

Harbom, L., & Wallensteen, P. (2005). Armed conflict and its international dimensions, 1946- 2004. *Journal of Peace Research, 42*(5), 623-35.

Hauser, W. L. (1980). The will to fight. In Sarkesian, S. C. (ed.). *Combat effectiveness: Cohesion, stress, and the voluntary military* (pp. 186-211). Beverly Hills, CA: Sage.

Hedges, C. (1997, February, 28). On Bosnia's ethnic fault lines, it's still tense, but world is silent. *New York Times*, A1.

Hedges, C. (2002). *War is a force that gives us meaning*. New York: Public Affairs.

Hegre, H., Ellingsen, T., Gates, S., & Gleditch, N. P. (2001). Toward a democratic civil peace? Democracy, political change, and civil war, 1816-1992. *American Political Science Review, 95*(1), 33-48.

Holmes, R. (1985). *Acts of war: The behavior of men in battle*. New York: Free Press.

Howard, M. (1991). *The lessons of history*. New Haven, CT: Yale University Press.

Huntington, S. P. (1989). No exit: The errors of endism. *National Interest*, Fall, 3-11.

Ignatieff, M. (2004). *The lesser evil: Political ethics in an age of terror*. Princeton, NJ: Princeton University Press.

Jensen, R. B. (2002). The United States, international policing, and the war against anarchist terrorism, 1900-1914. *Terrorism and Political Violence, 13*(1), 15-46.

Jervis, R. (2002). Theories of war in an era of leading-power peace. *American Political Science Review, 96*(1), 1-14.

Jones, B. D. (2001). *Peacemaking in Rwanda: The dynamics of failure*. Boulder, CO: Lynne Rienner.

Kaldor, M. (1999). *New and old wars: Organized violence in a global era*. Cambridge, UK: Polity Press.

Kant, I. (1952). *The critique of judgment*. (Meredith, J. C., Trans.). London: Oxford University Press.

Keegan, J. (1987). The evolution of battle and the prospects of peace. In Cinor, J.R., & Beisner, R. L. (eds.). *Arms at rest: Peacemaking and peacekeeping in American history* (pp. 189- 201). New York: Greenwood.

Keegan, J. (1993). *A history of warfare*. New York: Knopf.

Keeley, L. H. (1996). *War before civilization: The myth of the peaceful savage*. New York: Oxford University Press.

Keen, D. (1998). *The economic functions of violence in civil wars*. London: International Institute for Strategic Studies.

Kepel, G. (2002). *Jihad: The trail of political Islam*. (Roberts, A. F., trans.). Cambridge, MA: Harvard University Press.

Lake, D. A. (2002). Rational extremism: Understanding terrorism in the twenty-first century. *Dialog-IO, Spring, 15-29.*

Larson, E. V. (1996). *Casualties and consensus: The historical role of casualties in domestic support for U.S. military operations*. Santa Monica, CA: RAND Corporation.

Larson, E. V. (2000). Putting theory to work: diagnosing public opinion on the U.S. intervention in Bosnia. In Nincic, M., & Lepgold, J. (eds.). *Being useful: Policy relevance and international relations* (pp. 174-236). Ann Arbor, MI: University of Michigan Press.

Lebow, R. N. (2003). *Contingency, catalysts, and non-linear change: The origins of world war I*. Dartmouth College, Department of Government.

Luard, E. (1986). *War in international society*. New Haven, CT: Yale University Press.

Mack, A. (2005). *Human security report 2005*. New York: Oxford University Press.

Mandlebaum, M. (2002). *The ideas that conquered the world: Peace, democracy, and free markets in the twenty-first century*. New York: Public Affairs.

Manjoo, F. (2005, September 7). *Why FEMA failed*. Retrieved from http://dir.salon.com/story/news/feature/2005/09/07/fema/index.html

Marshall, M. G., & Gurr, T. R. (2005). *Peace and conflict, 2005: A global survey of armed conflicts, self-determination movements, and democracy*. College Park, MD: Center for International Development and Conflict Management, University of Maryland.

McPherson, J. M. (1997). *For cause and comrades: Why men fought in the Civil War*. New York: Oxford University Press.

Mueller, J. (1989). *Retreat from doomsday: The obsolescence of major war*. New York: Basic Books.

Mueller, J. (2002). Public support for military ventures abroad. In Moore, J. N., & Turner, R. F. (eds.). *The real lessons of the Vietnam War: Reflections twenty-five years after the fall of Saigon* (pp. 171-219). Durham, NC: Carolina Academic Press.

Mueller, J. (2004). *The remnants of war.* Ithaca, NY: Cornell University Press.

Mueller, J. (2005). Ordering the new world. In Bothe, M., O'Connell, M. E. & Ronzitti, Natalino (eds.). Redefining sovereignty: The use of force after the Cold War (pp. 65-88). Ardsley, NY: Transnational.

Mueller, J. (2006). *Overblown: How politicians and the terrorism industry inflate national security threats, and why we believe them.* New York: Free Press.

Mueller, J. (2007, February 28). *Reacting to terrorism: Probabilities, consequences, and the persistence of fear.* Paper presented at the Annual Convention of the International Studies Association.

Pape, R. A. (2005). *Dying to win: The strategic logic of suicide terrorism.* New York: Random House.

Peterson, P. G. (2004, September/October). Riding for a fall. *Foreign Affairs,* 111-25.

Pillar, P. R. (2003). *Terrorism and U.S. foreign policy.* Washington, D.C.: Brookings Institution Press.

Rapoport, D. C. (2004). The four waves of modern terrorism. In Cronin, A. K., & Ludes, J. M. (eds.). *Attacking terrorism: Elements of a grand strategy* (pp. 46-73). Washington, D.C.: Georgetown University Press.

Rawls, J. (1999). *The law of peoples.* Cambridge, MA: Harvard University Press.

Ray, J. L. (1989). The abolition of slavery and the end of international war. *International Organization, 43*(3), 405-439.

Reno, W. (1998). *Warlord politics and African states.* Boulder, CO: Lynne Rienner.

Rosen, J. (2004). *The naked crowd.* New York: Random House.

Rotberg, R. (2002, January 9). New breed of African leader. *Christian Science Monitor,* 9.

Russett, B. M., & Oneal, J. R. (2002). *Triangulating peace: Democracy, interdependence, and international organizations.* New York: Norton.

Sambanis, N. (2004). What is a civil war? Conceptual and empirical complexities of an operational definition. *Journal of Conflict Resolution, 48*(6), 814-58.

Shearer, D. (1998). *Private armies and military intervention.* London: International Institute for Strategic Studies, Adelphi Paper Number 316.

Shils, E. A., & Janowitz, M. (1948). Cohesion and disintegration in the Wehrmacht in World War II. *Public Opinion Quarterly, 12*(2), 280-315.

Simon, J. D. (2001). *The terrorist trap: America's experience with terrorism* (2nd ed.). Bloomington, IN: Indiana University Press.

Sivak, M., & Flanagan, M. J. (2004). Consequences for road traffic fatalities of the reduction in flying following September 11, 2001. *Transportation Research Part F: Psychology and Behavior,* 301-05

Smith, M. B. (1949). Combat motivations among ground troops. In Stouffer, S. A. (ed.). *The American soldier: Combat and its aftermath* (pp. 105-91). Princeton, NJ: Princeton University Press.

Stouffer, S. A., Lumsdaine, A. A., & Lumsdaine, M. H. (1949). Attitudes before combat and behavior in combat. In Stouffer, S. A. (ed.). *The American soldier: Combat and its aftermath* (pp. 3-58). Princeton, NJ: Princeton University Press.

Straus, S. (2005, January/February). Darfur and the genocide debate. *Foreign Affairs*, 84(1), 123- 46.

Takeyh, R. (2001, May/June). The rogue who came in from the cold. *Foreign Affairs*, 80(3), 62- 72.

Turner, H. A., Jr. (1996). Hitler's impact on history. In Wetzel, D. (ed.). *From the Berlin museum to the Berlin wall: Essays on the cultural and political history of modern Germany* (pp. 109-26). Westport, CT: Praeger.

Valentino, B. (2004). *Final solutions: Mass killing and genocide in the twentieth century.* Ithaca, NY: Cornell University Press.

Wallensteen, P. (2006). Trends in major war: Too early for waning? In Väyryen, R. (ed.). *The waning of major war: Theories and debates* (pp. 80-93). New York: Routledge.

Watson, P. (1978). *War on the mind: The military uses and abuses of psychology.* London: Hutchinson.

Wright, L. (2006). The looming tower: Al-Qaeda and the road to 9/11. New York: Knopf.

B. Military and Military History

Chapter 11

Meaning of War

General Sir Michael Rose

A recent book by General Rupert Smith on modern conflict entitled 'The Utility of War' opens with the uncompromising statement that "war no longer exists."[1] This view is reminiscent of Ivan Bloch's six volume work published in 1898 entitled "War of the Future,"[2] in which he stated that war was impossible. Yet, within sixteen years of this somewhat Delphic utterance, Europe had been plunged into the greatest war the world had ever witnessed.

It might have been better had General Smith declared that "peace does not exist" – for mankind can always be found to be in a state of war somewhere on this planet. Indeed, in the case of the British Army, there has only been one year during its long history that it has not been involved in conflict. As Professor Michael Howard puts it in his book The Invention of Peace quoting a 19th century jurist, "War appears to be as old as mankind, but peace is a modern invention."[3]

Whether mankind is considered to be in a perpetual state of war or not depends, of course, upon how one defines war. At one end of the spectrum lie people like President George W. Bush, who seemed to be defining all conflict as war when he asserted post 9/11 that America was now at war with global terror. At the other end of the spectrum lie military thinkers like Clausewitz and General Smith, who more narrowly regard conflict as being absolute war in which states fight other states. In General Smith's words, war is "a massive deciding event in a dispute in international affairs"[4] and of course the two world wars of the 20th century provide obvious ostensive examples of this definition of the meaning of war.

---

1   Smith, R. (2008). *The Utility of Force: The Art of War in the Modern World.* New York: Vintage Books.

2   Bloch, I.S. (1903). *The Future of War In Its Technical Economic and Political Relations.* Boston: Ginn & Co.

3   Howard, M.E. (2001). *The Invention of Peace: Reflections on War and International Order.* (p. 1). New Haven, CT: Yale University Press.

4   Smith, R. (2008). *The Utility of Force.* (p. 3).

Mary Ellen O'Connell (ed.), What Is War? An Investigation in the Wake of 9/11.
© *2012 Koninklijke Brill NV. Printed in The Netherlands.* ISBN *978 9004 17234 0. pp. 167–176.*

Attempting to define the meaning of war is not, however, a purely academic exercise, for confusion over what constitutes war, and, therefore, what should be the necessary responses to different levels of war, has often led to deeply flawed policies and strategies being pursued by state and non state actors. This, in turn, has resulted in unnecessary loss of life as well as the prolonged suffering of entire populations. Nowhere has this been more evident than during the 1990s, when UN peacekeeping forces were continually being pressured by the international community to conduct war-like military operations, even though the UN had only been mandated to undertake peacekeeping missions. The disastrous consequence of trying to use peacekeepers in this way is well demonstrated by what happened in Somalia in 1993.

It is therefore important that the answer to the question "What is war?" is sufficiently precise to make it possible to develop meaningful rules of engagement and associated laws for the guidance of politicians, soldiers and lawmakers. This is a considerable task – given that the rapidly changing nature of conflict, but it is that very rate of change that makes the need for agreement, particularly at the international level, even more urgent.

My purpose in writing this paper, which is intended neither to be prescriptive nor exhaustive, is to identify four different levels of conflict and to suggest that a varying set of laws is needed to regulate each level of conflict because the military response to each form of conflict is so different.

I will illustrate my thesis by describing a number of past occasions where a better understanding of the meaning of war and the existence of a workable legal framework would have made conflict resolution more effective and limited the destructiveness of military operations. I use the term "war" to cover all forms of conflict that range between general war and the extremes of peace enforcement. It includes insurgency and terrorism, but it excludes initiatives to deal with drugs and crime unless military force forms a central part of the response.

General War

Clausewitz defines war as "violence pushed to its utmost bounds",[5] which is intended to compel an opponent to "fulfil our will."[6] He regards the principle of moderation in war as an absurdity – as it might well have seemed to be when he expounded his ideas in the 18th century. If wars were to be less cruel and destructive, in his view, this could happen only as a result of the condition of each warring state and their relations to each other.

Nevertheless, there were some early attempts to codify rules of war. The most significant international agreements were reached during the last century,

---

5   Von Clausewitz, C. (1949). *On War.* (Rev. ed., Vol. 1, p. 20). London: Routledge & Kegan Paul Ltd.

6   *Id.* at 18.

resulting in The Hague and Geneva Conventions and Protocols. These deal mainly with the protection of civilians, wounded personnel, property and the treatment of prisoners of war. Since then there have been continuing attempts, not all successful, to add new agreements to these basic laws of war, mostly relating to human rights, humanitarian law and war crimes.

Ongoing discussions about what constitutes war and what should constitute its governing laws have been greatly complicated by United States President George W. Bush's declaration of war on global terror in 2001. In making this declaration, President Bush conflated two distinct and separate levels of war: general war and counter-terrorism. Counter-terrorism is merely a sub class of insurgency warfare. This novel and contentious approach resulted in the U.S. Administration availing its security forces of a number of military options which have hitherto not been traditionally open to those engaged in counter-terrorist operations. These include targeted assassination, the kidnapping of enemy personnel from around the world, the designation of unlawful combatants and prolonged internment without trial. In effect, President Bush authorized the employment of means previously thought to be needed only for the conduct of general war to fight what others have regarded as an extreme form of criminality.

His strategy put into focus questions already being asked regarding the conduct of the war. Does the use of civilians to shield military objectives by Al Qaeda in Iraq or the Taliban in Afghanistan absolve the U.S. military from their general responsibility for civilian protection? If not, what is their accountability where civilians have been killed? What are the limits of military necessity and is the use of cluster bombs with time delays, for example, acceptable when used in civilian areas against military targets – as happened during the NATO bombing of Serbia in 1999? What responsibility did the U.S.-led coalition forces have as the occupying power in Iraq with regard to the prevention of the looting of Iraqi national treasures and destruction of places of worship? So far it has been impossible to answer any of these questions without knowing the limits, if they exist, of war.

What is quite clear, however, is that no matter what the level of conflict is deemed to be involved, under international law there can, never be any justification for the routine mistreatment of prisoners where this is tantamount to torture or constitutes undignified and inhumane treatment.

Limited War

Limited wars are conflicts where there are self-imposed or internationally prescribed limits to the conflict. In the Falklands conflict of 1982 for example the British Government limited itself to the objective of expelling the Argentine forces from the Falkland Islands. Nine years later, during the First Gulf War, the United Nations limited the mission of the US-led alliance to that of driving the forces of Saddam Hussein from Kuwait. At no point during either conflict did the physical invasion of the territory of the aggressor nation take place, although in the case of the First Gulf War there was significant bombing of Iraq.

In limited wars, it would seem obvious that all the laws of war, including those governing the declaration of war, the protection of civilians, property and the environment, and the humane treatment of prisoners should all be scrupulously observed. Yet, when NATO went to war against Serbia in 1999, it not only went to war without the authorization of the United Nations, but it did so before exhausting all other political options. At Rambouillet in January 1999, Milošević had acceded to all NATO's demands except one: that NATO troops should have full freedom of movement not only in Kosovo but throughout Serbia. In spite of going to war, NATO never succeeded in achieving this unnecessary and provocative demand. Going to war was certainly not the action of last resort and by ignoring this necessary requirement of a just war, NATO allowed itself to become involved in an illegal war.

By subsequently attacking civilian targets in Belgrade and using cluster bombs in civilian areas, NATO put itself further outside the laws of war, and in doing so undermined its own argument that it had only acted against Serbia and in Kosovo for humanitarian purposes. NATO's actions in Kosovo have undoubtedly set back international efforts to get wider international agreement regarding the laws of war.

Kosovo, in my view, also provides a clear justification of the argument that in limited war the entire armoury of international law, including human rights law, should be respected by the warring parties. Not doing so is likely to cause unnecessary human suffering and result in peace settlements that will not endure.

Insurgency War

By far the most difficult level of war, in discussing how the laws of war should be applied, is that of insurgency warfare. At this level of war, it is likely that there will be no formal declaration of war, there may be no territorial or political limits to the war, and in particular the insurgents may not have the status of lawful combatants under the Geneva Conventions.

Clausewitz thought that overcoming an enemy invariably involved the destruction of military force. This may be true of general war, but in insurgency war, it is rare that an enemy is defeated militarily. What most commonly causes insurgents to abandon the armed struggle – war, of course, is not over until the enemy agrees that it is over – is because the insurgents have become isolated from the people. This has happened because the political, economic social and religious grievances of the previously oppressed element of the population have now largely been met and they are now sided with the government. Throughout any such conflict, it is essential that a government defend human rights and that its security forces act within the laws of war, even where such wars are being fought transnationally. This holds true for the counter-terrorist war that is currently being waged against Al Qaeda, for terrorism is but an early phase of insurgency warfare and the principles governing counter insurgency warfare apply equally to counter-terrorism.

Governments involved in counter insurgencies are nevertheless often obliged to grant their security forces extra legislative powers that would clearly be unacceptable in peacetime. These extra powers include the ability to stop and search, impose curfews, create special criminal courts without juries in which it may be necessary to conceal the identity of witnesses, electronic interception and the seizing of funds. It may also become necessary to introduce limited internment without trial. During the Malayan Emergency between 1948 and 1950, the British colonial administration of Malaya found it necessary to move entire populations into protected villages. However, harsh measures of this sort should always be the result of parliamentary legislation and be subjected to annual renewal, otherwise they are in danger of being seen as oppressive by the general population.

At all stages of counter insurgency warfare, a continual balance has to be struck between giving people adequate security and the introduction of legislation that limits civil liberties and infringes on human rights. This is a particularly difficult balance to achieve when dealing with transnational insurgency and the problem of unlawful combatants.

Nevertheless, in 1958, a judgment by the International Committee of the Red Cross stated that every person must be either a prisoner of war or a civilian covered by the Geneva Third and Fourth Conventions respectively. There was to be no intermediate status and no prisoner could be held to be outside the law. Civilians who were directly engaged in hostilities and who were subsequently deemed to be unlawful combatants or belligerents would be prosecuted under the criminal law of the detaining state. This judgement related to all levels of conflict. The creation of the prison at Guantanamo in 2002 by the U.S. Administration ignored the ICRC judgement and President Bush inevitably faced the very problem concerning the final disposition of prisoners that the 1958 judgement sought to avoid.

In 1969 in Northern Ireland, the British Government was faced with a serious insurgency by Irish nationalists. Nevertheless, for the entire duration of the conflict, which lasted nearly 40 years, the terrorists were always treated, with one limited exception, as simple criminals by the law. Even when the IRA extended their operations elsewhere, the criminal law of the relevant nation in which they were operating was used to prosecute them. This happened many times in Éire and West Germany.

Many extra powers of course had to be granted to the British security forces to enable them to deal with what was a sophisticated, well armed and determined insurgency. On occasions, however, the British government had to be reined in by European courts. In one instance, the European courts found that the security force practice of hooding IRA terrorists and putting them into

stress positions constituted inhuman treatment and was therefore an infringement of their human rights. The practice had to be stopped. Financial compensation was furthermore paid whenever the security forces had been found to
have used excessive force.

Most important of all, any use of military force by members of the security forces was subjected to scrutiny by civil courts. Soldiers and policemen
were charged with manslaughter or murder wherever the level of force used was
considered to be unreasonable. As a result of this approach, ordinary, decent,
republican Irish people could see that the law was being operated fairly and
impartially by the British. This did much to persuade them to end their support
for the terrorists who had no such moral or legal position.

Using criminal law to defeat the IRA terrorists thus had enormous benefits
when it came to winning the hearts and minds of the Irish nationalist population. The end of the armed struggle for the IRA finally came when the IRA
could no longer operate in nationalist areas of Northern Ireland without risk of
compromise by their own compatriots. Their organization was massively infil-
trated by agents of the British and Irish governments and their main source of
funding from North America dried up. All this was achieved by the security
forces uniquely operating within UK criminal law.

In counter insurgency situations, the employment of high levels of military
force will generally prove to be counterproductive in terms of maintaining the
support of the population, – as well as often being in breach of international
law. Insurgency wars can of course escalate to the level of limited or general war
and it will then be necessary to employ all appropriate military means to achieve
success. But the civil and military responses to such an escalation will need the
endorsement of national legislatures and, if the conflict widens, ultimately that
of international bodies such as the UN. In 1999, NATO moved from attacking
military targets to civilian targets without the approval of the UN.

The national wars of liberation against the colonial powers during the past
centuries provide frequent examples of where local insurgencies whose objective was self-determination ultimately received recognition as sovereign states
with their own seats in the United Nations General Assembly. Nevertheless, at
the start of their campaigns, the insurgents were certainly unlawful combatants, as defined by international law. But, often with outside help, many became
recognised members of armies of national resistance with their own uniforms
and emblems and achieved nationhood. The emergence of the United States of
America is probably the first modern example of the successful transformation
of an insurgent movement into a state. The difficulty identifying the moment
when a struggle for self-determination becomes justified, no matter what means
have been used during that struggle, still complicates the arguments concerning what is a just war.

Seven years after 9/11 there remained great diversity of understanding between the Western powers about how most effectively to deal with Al
Qaeda, – and this plays into the Islamic terrorists' hands. The U.S. position

was that general war measures were required and that military force should be the main element of the response, whilst other countries believed that a limited set of extra powers, the use of criminal courts, and the redressing of grievances offered the best chance of success. Clearly, much work needs to be done with regards to defining the appropriate response for this level of war before there is any chance of international agreement in the critical area of counter-insurgency and counter-terrorist warfare.

Peacekeeping Operations

The term peacekeeping refers to a wide variety of military operations. They range from simple Chapter VI actions in situations where both sides have agreed to end a conflict when the UN is invited in to monitor the peace process, through to the extremes of peace enforcement operations. In the latter case, peace enforcement typically takes place when the international community has decided to intervene for humanitarian purposes in order to prevent human rights abuses or to deliver urgently needed aid. This often happens in civil wars or where a nation state has failed.

In all peacekeeping operations there is a limit, not only to the level of military force used, but also to the objectives that are pursued. Peacekeepers are not mandated, equipped, trained, or deployed to accomplish war-fighting tasks, and, therefore, they will never be able to take on a full combat role. They need some level of consent from the warring parties to the conflict, if they are to be successful. Only a war-fighting military force can impose its own conditions on the battlefield.

At the extreme end of peacekeeping lie Chapter VII peace enforcement operations which border on war fighting. Whilst commanding the United Nations forces in Bosnia in 1994, I called the line that separates peacekeeping from warfighting the "Mogadishu line" for it was in Somalia that such a line was crossed to the detriment both of the peacekeepers and the people of Somalia. This line cannot be marked out on the ground, but lies in the perceptions of the combatants and the relations that the peacekeepers maintain with them. At Annex A is the schematic diagram that I used in 1994 to explain to NATO the limits of peacekeeping.

Nevertheless, peacekeepers may be required to use relatively high levels of force if, for example, they need to ensure the passage of a convoy or maintain a weapons exclusion zone. Generally, peacekeepers will only open fire in self-defence, and they will always try to give a warning before doing so. They act impartially towards both sides, and use only the minimum level of force to achieve a specific objective. Their mandate, legal status and rules of engagement should thus reflect these limitations, but often they do not.

In Bosnia, I was frequently accused both of using too much force by those who were accustomed to Chapter VI peacekeeping missions and of using insufficient force by NATO, which wished to use the UN force as a surrogate member of the warfighting transatlantic alliance. Although millions of small arms rounds, mortars tank fire and air strikes were used by the UN peacekeepers against the recalcitrant Serbs, I always resisted the call to use greater force and, as a result, at no point during my command in 1994 were relations with the Serbs ever completely severed. I was mindful that at that time, the UN was responsible for feeding, and providing fuel, shelter and medical supplies for 2.7 million Bosnians, and that without this aid many of them would have perished. There was also an urgent requirement in early 1994 to implement a cessation of hostilities between two of the warring parties, the Muslims and the Croats.

It is to the great credit of the 23,000 young peacekeepers that they succeeded in bringing about an end to the fighting between the Muslims and Croats in 1994 and at the same time were able to meet the World Health Organization aid targets for the delivery of aid in Bosnia during that difficult year. It was their presence and persistence that finally led to the tipping of the military balance against the Serbs and ultimately to the Dayton peace agreement. The bombing of the Bosnian Serbs by NATO in September 1995, which is always claimed by NATO as having delivered Dayton was, in fact, strategically ineffective and added little to the peace process.

One of the central problems of defining the meaning of war is also to decide upon the definition of peace. During the Bosnian conflict there was an evident lack of understanding amongst international statesmen regarding the difference between the two states of war and peace. UN Security Council Resolutions, in particular Resolutions 824 and 836, which related to safe areas in Bosnia, had been carefully worded to prevent giving the peacekeepers the mission of defending the safe areas. For defence is a warfighting mission and requires warfighting capabilities. The UN resolutions therefore limited the mission of the peacekeepers to "deterring attacks against" rather than defending. Yet the world still firmly believed that it was the mission of the UN peacekeepers in Bosnia to defend the safe areas. Such misunderstandings will inevitably lead to disaster.

At the end of December 1994, a hard won four-month cessation of hostilities agreement was arranged by the UN between the Bosnian Serbs and Bosnian government. However, clear evidence soon emerged that this period was being used by both sides not to advance the peace process, – but to prepare for a return to offensive war. It was obvious early in 1995 that the UN should have withdrawn from Bosnia and the peacekeepers should have been replaced by NATO troops, for all possibilities of peacekeeping had come to an end. The ensuing disasters that occurred for the people of Bosnia after the end of the cessation of hostilities in April 1995 and in particular the appalling massacre that took place at Srebrenica in August 1995 could never have happened had NATO war fighting formations been in place at that time. Srebrenica provides a terrible example of how international misunderstanding as to what distinguishes war from peace, and what, therefore, should be the respective responses to each condition, can lead to tragedy.

Nevertheless, I believe that the UN mission in Bosnia until 1995 still demonstrates that it is possible to bring about the opportunities for peace and yet remain within the proper and legal limitations of peacekeeping.

These limitations clearly include all the basic laws of general war when it comes to the protection of civilians, property and the environment. Respect for humanitarian law and the identification of war crimes, however, are high on the list of responsibilities for peacekeepers, whereas these legal requirements may be a lower priority for those engaged in national wars of survival. Once again, greater clarity as to what constitutes peacekeeping and what constitutes war fighting will enable future UN missions to avoid the mistakes made in Bosnia.

Conclusion

Thus, each level of war needs not only to be clearly defined, but also should have its own set of legal rules. Some rules, like The Hague and Geneva Conventions and Protocols, are clearly common to all levels of war. Other laws may apply only to particular levels of conflict. The examples that I have given are by no means exhaustive, and may be factually contested, but I hope that they will open the way to further debate. It is undeniable that in the world today there is insufficient understanding of what constitutes war and peace.

Politicians and soldiers urgently need a comprehensive legal framework within which they can develop military strategy. Such a framework is vital to their endeavours to make the world a safer place.

Annex A: Meaning of War

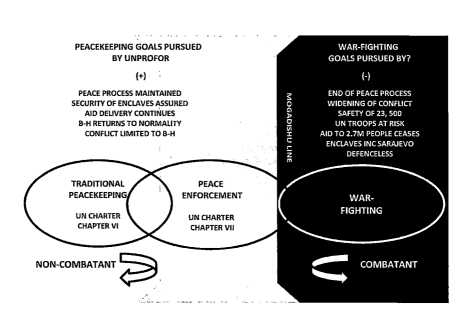

Chapter 12
What Is War?

Jeremy Black

History deals with time and its values are those of time. What that means is that definitions and understandings are transient, changing, and culturally specific. This specificity is a matter of space and time, and that cuts across, indeed, for many, invalidates attempts to provide an unchanging definition. Indeed, a failure to note the nature and impact of chronology and of chronological time is labelled ahistorical.

That such an attempt, however, is not seen as appropriate by many other disciplines, for example political science, underlines the extent to which, whatever some of them may think, historians do not own the past, nor its interpretation. Yet, other attempts to employ the past for models of wide applicability both utilise the work of historians and, also, face scrutiny in terms of the scepticism that characterises history in the Western empirical tradition.

This will be a major theme of this paper, but first it is necessary to note the salient character of the question. Aside from the key issue of the war on terror, there are now a whole host of what could be seen as 'non-traditional conflicts' to which the term war is applied. These include war on drugs, war on crime, the battle of the sexes, generational conflict, culture wars and history wars; and that is not a complete list. Moreover, it can be expanded if other languages and cultures are considered. War, if not bellicosity, has therefore entered the language as part of an assessment of all relationships as focused on power, confrontation and force.

Whether or not that is appropriate, it calls for the abstracting of warfare from the language of war. In this short paper, I propose to offer a working definition, to look at a few of the many analytical problems with defining war, and to conclude with some suggestions.

War can be seen in functional terms as organised large-scale violence, and in cultural or ideological terms as the consequence of bellicosity. The first, at once, separates war from say the actions of an individual, however violent the means or consequences (one individual poisoning a water supply could kill more than died in the Falklands War); from non-violent action, however much it is an aspect of coercion; and from large-scale violence in which the organisation

Mary Ellen O'Connell (ed.), What Is War? An Investigation in the Wake of 9/11.
© *2012 Koninklijke Brill NV. Printed in The Netherlands. ISBN 978 9004 17234 0. pp. 177–182.*

is not that of war, for example football hooliganism. Each of these points and caveats can be detailed and qualified, but they also draw attention to fundamental issues of definition.

The cultural or ideological aspects of war also repay examination. They focus on the importance of arousing, channelling and legitimating violent urges, and of persuading people to fight, kill and run the risk of being killed, without which there is, and can be, no war. The willingness to kill is crucial to the causes of war and is a conflation of long-term anthropological and psychological characteristics with more specific societal and cultural situations. Whether and to what effect these propensities to organised conflict have altered over time is an historical question.

The model of war as organised conflict between sovereign states, begun deliberately by a specific act of policy, is that which has been discussed most fully by theorists and historians. Thus, the grand title of Donald Kagan's interesting *On the Origins of War and the Preservation of Peace* (London, 1995) reveals a study only of the Peloponnesian, Second Punic, First World and Second World wars, and of the Cuban Missile Crisis. Kagan explains

> I am interested in the outbreak of wars between states in an international system, such as we find in the world today. The Greeks and the Romans of the republican era lived in that kind of a world, and so has the West since the time of the Renaissance. Most other peoples have lived either in a world without states, or in great empires where the only armed conflicts were civil wars or attempts to defend the realm against bands of invaders.

This overly restricted definition can be matched by the prominent British historian A.J.P. Taylor, who wrote of "the more prosaic origin of war: the precise moment when a statesman sets his name to the declaration of it."

Such an account of war might seem to have been made redundant by shifts through time, to the position today when non-sovereign actors play a major role, but, instructively, its clear-cut distinction between peace and war was even inappropriate for 1815-1945, the focus of Taylor's work and of much IR scholarship. It was inappropriate, for example, for much of the warfare then arising from Western imperialism. More generally, any definition of war in terms of a public monopoly of the use of force has to face both the contested nature of the public sphere and the role and resilience of 'private' warfare, both of which are issues today.

Moreover, the rulers of sovereign states did not necessarily declare war. In 1700, Augustus II of Saxony-Poland and Frederick IV of Denmark joined Peter the Great of Russia in attacking the Swedish empire, but neither declared war. In 1726-7, the British blockaded the Spanish treasure fleet in Porto Bello and kept another fleet off Cadiz, dislocating the financial structure of the Spanish imperial system, while the Spaniards besieged Gibraltar, but neither power declared war and the conflict did not spread. Indeed, the two powers became allies in 1729. Chinese intervention against the American-led United Nations forces in the Korean War (1950-3) did not lead to any declaration of war, and there were no hostile operations on Chinese soil.

The question of goals is raised when defining war in terms of intentionality, but that also poses problems. In eighteenth-century India, military operations were sometimes related to revenue collections, often indeed dictated by the need to seize or protect revenue, but it is not easy to separate such operational aspects of wars from the use of force to collect or seize revenue. The same point is relevant for many other societies. In pre-[European] contact warfare between Native North Americans, it is very difficult to define what war meant to the Natives. There was 'public' warfare, in the form of conflict between tribes, and 'private' warfare, raids with no particular sanction, often designed to prove manhood. Furthermore, there appears to have been no sharp distinction between raiding and hunting, the latter an economic necessity. They merged. In part, this may be because non-tribal members were not viewed as human beings, or at least as full persons.

The treatment of enemies as beasts or as subhuman can also be seen in European conflict, especially civil warfare, as for example the religious wars of the sixteenth and seventeenth centuries. It was also a feature in the genocidal drive of 'modern' states, most obviously Hitler's Germany. The centrality of the Holocaust to Hitler's views and, finally, goals has been increasingly emphasized in recent years, and this has helped make the Holocaust a major part of our understanding of World War Two. As such, the totally one-sided war on Jews becomes a conflict that should be considered as a war, and indeed Hitler regarded it as a meta-historical struggle. This is a point that can also be discussed for other genocides. It at once poses problems with any idea of war as inherently legal because of the fact of sovereignty or noble due to the test of battle.

There is also the need to address the issue of the relationship between war and state development. The fifth-century Church-father St Augustine's comparison, in his *City of God,* of Alexander the Great with a company of thieves – 'in the absence of justice there is no difference between Alexander's empire and a band [societas] of thieves' – was a moralist's vain attempt to argue that intentionality, not scale, was the crucial issue, and that sovereignty was not a legitimator of slaughter.

This point can be approached from a variety of directions, which can be grouped as ideological, legal and functional, without suggesting that this categorization is precise or uncontested. If a key issue with warfare is how it is possible to persuade people to kill, and to run a strong risk of being killed then, for example, there was not much functional difference, in the sixteenth century, between 'state-directed' warfare and its *ghazi* (the Muslim system of perpetual raiding of the infidel) and, indeed, piratical counterparts. The organized killing of humans was central to each, even if the objectives behind this killing was different. 'States' were inchoate, and not generally seen as enjoying the right to monopolize warfare and alone to legitimate conflict. Today, issues of legitimacy come into play, not least with the claim to the attributes of sovereignty by groups not recognized as such, but also by the rejection of the ideas that sovereign governments have a monopoly of force. This overlaps with the question of the distinction between military and civilian, one that is at the heart of the legitimization of the modem Western practice of force and the legalization of Western high-technology warfare.

The use of force by (major) states against those they deem internal opponents or international reprobates cannot be rigidly separated from war simply because the states do not accept the legitimacy of their opponents. There was a distinction between wars begun by imperial powers, such as Ottoman Turkey, Safavid Persia, Mughal India, and Ming or, later, Manchu China, and war within the empires, but the latter could be large-scale, more so than external conflict, and could be regarded by contemporaries as war. Moreover, since each of these states rested on warfulness, war and conquest, they had highly bellicose values. When I asked the Mughal specialist John Richards to explain the propensity of the Mughal rulers for war, he used the analogy of a bicyclist to describe the Mughal empire and war: if it was not fighting, it would collapse. Through fighting, it did in the end do so.

It is difficult to determine whether attempt to overthrow these or other states or to deny their authority should be regarded as sufficiently functionally and intellectually different to conflicts between sovereign powers not to be classed as wars. This raises the question whether it is only outcome that earns the designation war. Empirically, this is a question posed by the contrast between the American War of Independence (1775-83) and the Irish rebellion/revolution of 1798, and also by disagreements over whether the Indian Mutiny (1857-9) should be referred to as a mutiny, a rebellion, or a war of independence. This feeds directly into modern revolutionary claims about struggles as wars.

More generally, the absence of strong, or even any, police forces frequently ensured that troops were used to maintain order and control, as is also the case in many countries today. That, again, raises the question of a definition of war as the use of force, in other words through function rather than intention.

Turning to culture, the use of the concept of bellicosity in part overcomes the unhelpful distinction between rationality and irrationality in motivation and conduct. Bellicosity can be regarded as both, or either, a rational and an irrational response to circumstances. To refer to bellicosity as a necessary condition for, and, even, definition of war, is not to confuse cause and effect, or to run together hostility and conflict, but to assert that in many circumstances the two are coterminous. Bellicosity also helps explain the continuation of wars once begun. An emphasis on bellicosity leads to a stress on the assumptions of ruling groups, assumptions that are often inherent to their existence and role.

There is a growing reluctance to fight in many societies, certainly in comparison to the first half of the twentieth century, although the popularity of war toys, games and films suggest that military values are still seen as valuable, indeed exemplary, by many, or, at least, as an aspect of masculinity. Partly thanks to growing professionalism and the abandonment of conscription in many Western states, the military there is less integrated into society.

There has also been a 'civilization', or process of civilizing, of the military. It can no longer be an adjunct of society able to follow its own set of rules, but is expected to conform to societal standards to behaviour – a pressure that has caused scandals and court cases in the USA and UK.

Yet, it is necessary to be cautious about extrapolating from this model to the entire West, while, as recent years have shown, globalization can readily lead to the use of force. Once roused, democracies can be very tenacious in war, or at least their governments can be.

The suggestion that the 'West' has become less bellicist might also seem ironic given its nuclear preponderance, the capacity of its weapons of mass-destruction, and the role of its industries in supplying weaponry to the rest of the world. Indeed, it might almost be argued that this strength is a condition for the decline of militarism. A decline in bellicosity could also be seen as owing something to the prevalence and vitality of other forms of 'aggression', for example what might be seen as economic and cultural imperialism. If a difference in bellicosity between cultures in the present world is to be emphasized, then that suggests the continued vitality of a model of transcultural variations, and this underlines the culturally-contingent nature of definitions of war.

An emphasis on cultural contexts within which war is understood, even welcomed, as an instrument of policy and as a means and product of social, ethnic or political cohesion, is, also, in part, a reminder of the role of choice. As such, this approach is a qualification of the apparent determinism of some systemic models. A denial of determinism also opens up the possibility of suggesting that the multiple and contested interpretations of contemporaries are valuable. This underlines the importance of integrating them into explanatory models. As far as intentionality is concerned, bellicosity leads to war not through misunderstandings that produce inaccurate calculations of interest and response, but, rather, from an acceptance of different interests and a conviction that they can be best resolved through the use of force. As such, war can be the resort of both satisfied and unsatisfied powers. The resort for war is a choice for unpredictability, not simply the uncertain nature of battle, but an inherent characteristic of the very nature of war. The acceptance that risk is involved, and the willingness to confront it, are both culturally conditioned.

Bellicose factors in leadership and society can be related to the structure of international relations and to the perceived alternatives available to leaders in reaching their objectives in foreign relations. The former can owe something to the response of other powers, but the extent to which the structure shapes this response is questionable. Indeed, this underlines the extent to which analytical notions shift. The current habit is to focus on an international system, with the system treated as something that exists in the real world, and indeed has legal force and the capacity for political and judicial action; rather than simply as an analytical category. In the seventeenth and eighteenth centuries alliances and other formal agreements between states were the focus. Thus, the system was the relations between states, and these relations were the essential element.

In the nineteenth century, however, the system was presented in Europe as a mediating agent which constrained the activities of its member units and controlled the interactions between them and the system's environment. This concept was drawn from the model of a living body, and can be termed organic or biological. Such an approach, as taken today in the West, sees the bellicosity of individual states as a problem, if not a crime, and, instead, requires a moralization of war not only to mobilize public support but also to explain why conflict in some circumstances is necessary.

As such, we move to the slippage in the description of warfare referred to above. Bellicosity is thus reformulated, away from an aspect of sovereignty, and, instead, as a problem in others and a necessity in terms of international order and systemic norms. This is the background to modern ideas about the desirability of interventionist warfare. These ideas are not new, and some are the secularization of earlier religious ideas about conflict between co-religionists, but their application is very much so. It is, however, unclear whether these ideas help us in understanding and overcoming the values of those for whom compromise is unacceptable, force necessary, and even desirable, and war crucial to identity and self-respect.

Chapter 13

History and War:
The Grim Record of the Past

Williamson Murray

Nearly twenty-five centuries ago, the greatest of all military and strategic historians recorded the dark words of the Athenian negotiators at the island of Melos, who in reply to the claim of the Melians that the Gods would provide for them because of the justice of their cause:

> So far as the favor of the Gods is concerned, we think we have as much right to that as you have. Our aims and our actions are perfectly consistent with the beliefs men hold about the Gods and with the principles which govern their own conduct. Our opinion of the Gods and our knowledge of men lead us to conclude that it is a general and necessary law of nature to rule wherever one can. This is not a law that we made ourselves, nor were we the first to act upon it when it was made. We found it already in existence, and we shall leave it to exist for ever among those who come after us. We are merely acting in accordance with it, and we know that you or anyone else with the same power as ours would be acting in precisely the same way.[1]

At the start of his history Thucydides made the claim that he had written his history for "those who want to understand clearly the events which happened in the past and which (human nature being what it is) will, at some time or other and in much the same ways, be repeated in the future."[2] The basic theme of this paper then is that in almost every respect Thucydides was correct and that, to use modem terminology, the human brain was hard wired at some time in the dim past before history to make war an inevitable fact of human life. The rules and the tactics may change, but the hard realities of history – not to mention the insurgencies and wars across today's world – suggest an inevitability to war to the human condition, no less inevitable than the belief in human sin that fathers of this institution of Catholic learning quite rightly espouse.

---

1   Thucydides, *The Peloponnesian War*, trans. by Rex Warner (London, 1954), pp. 404-405.
2   Ibid., p. 48.

Mary Ellen O'Connell (ed.), What Is War? An Investigation in the Wake of 9/11.
© *2012 Koninklijke Brill NV. Printed in The Netherlands. ISBN 978 9004 17234 0. pp. 183 – 193.*

Yet the view of the Anglo-American world for over a century and a half –
and of virtually all of the First World at the beginning of the twenty-first century is very much at odds with such an understanding of how the world works
or has worked in the past. Here the influence of geography, history, and the
peculiarities of the development of Anglo-American culture played major roles.
In effect those factors created a view of the relationship between peace and war
that is fundamentally at odds with what history suggests.[3] In fact, I would go
so far as to argue that a substantial portion of our troubles in Iraq in the post-
conflict phase beyond sheer, unadulterated incompetence – has reflected how
far removed our framework and understanding of peace is from the realities of
the world beyond.

The relationship between peace and war in our world finds itself entangled
to a considerable extent in how the modem world defines peace. The modem
belief appears to be that peace is the normal order of human affairs. The irony of
such hopeful expectations lies in the fact that within living memory, the catastrophe of World War II spread horror, murder, and destruction across the face
of the world in a fashion and to a extent which had never occurred before in history and which came frighteningly close to achieving Clausewitz's theoretical
concept of total war.[4] Despite the bizarre efforts of political scientists to suggest that war is disappearing from our world, only the narrowest of definitions
makes such claims possible. The so-called decline in interstate war among the
states of the First World may indeed be occurring, but such intellectual soph-
istry entirely misses the absence of peace as we define it throughout much of the
remainder of the world.

To understand how far removed our thinking is from man's historical – and
current experiences we might begin with how we view peace in our comfortable world. Michael Howard in a wonderfully concise and insightful book, *The
Invention of Peace* has described the requirements of peace in our world in the
following terms:

> Peace... is not an order natural to man; it is artificial, intricate and highly vola-
> tile. All kinds of preconditions are necessary, not the least a degree of cultural
> homogeneity (best expressed through a common language), to make possible
> the political cohesion that must underlie a freely accepted framework of law,
> and at least a minimum level of education through which that culture can be

---

3   For a dissection of this emergence see particularly Michael Howard, *War and
    the Liberal Conscience, The George Macaulay Trevelyan Lectures in the University of
    Cambridge,* 1977 (New Brunswick, NJ, 1978).

4   For the extent of World War IT and the damage that it caused both to human
    beings and their edifices see particularly Gerhard L. Weinberg, *A World at Arms.
    A Global History of World War II* (Cambridge, 1994); and Williamson Murray and
    Allan R. Millett, *A War to Be Won. Fighting the Second World War* (Cambridge,
    MA, 2000).

transmitted. Further, as states develop they require a highly qualified elite, capable not only of operating their complex legal, commercial and administrative systems, but of exercising considerable moral authority over the rest of society.[5]

Such conditions, first noticeable in the Anglo-American world of the early to mid nineteenth century and then spreading to Europe and beyond, have required centuries to emerge. However, the ahistoricism of Americans – and to a lesser extent the British – have led most, including the intellectuals, to assume that the same preconditions exist in the external world as exist in theirs.[6] Nothing better suggests the gulf between those who presently inhabit the industrialized, global world of the United States and the world beyond, than the bizarre belief of all too many senior political and military policy makers in early 2003 that the emergence of a Western style democracy would quickly and inevitably follow the fall of Saddam's regime.[7] But then ahistoricism lies at the heart of the modern world's *Weltanschauung*, especially that of Americans.[8] Unfortunately, the comforts of modem life appear to allow for a deep-seated belief that the past has little relevance for understanding the modern world – a world where history has ended. And even those who do recognize the value of history, all too often assume that the particular history of their own nation provides a model for all situations, no matter what the political, cultural, geographic, or religious context within which they find themselves.

History and War

So what does the past suggest about the role of war and peace in human affairs? There have been long periods of peace in history, but their rarity suggests the pervasive nature of human conflict. The Romans certainly managed to create an empire, where for nearly three centuries – from 30 B.C. to 250 A.D. the *pax Romana* provided the citizens of the Empire a period of extended peace, one

---

5   Michael Howard, *The Invention of Peace, Reflections on War and International Order* (New Haven, cr, 2000), pp. 104-105.

6   What makes such conceptions so bizarre is the fact that even within their own societies there exist large pockets where the conditions for peace certainly do not exist.

7   For discussions about the planning for and the making of peace see among others Thomas Ricks, *Fiasco, The American Military Adventure in Iraq* (New York, 2006); and James Fallows, *Blind into Baghdad, America's War in Iraq* (New York, 2006).

8   Astonishingly not only civilian, but military leaders could not recall historical events within the recent past, such as December 1989 when U. S. military forces had taken down Panama's government national guard, and police forces in a matter of hours, only to watch aghast as the country dissolved into anarchy and massive looting with the general breakdown of society.

broken rarely by civil war, barbarian invasion, or rebellions. Yet there was a price to be paid, especially by those foolish enough to rebel against Roman power.

The destruction of Jerusalem in 70 A.D. and then the diaspora of the Jewish people after the second great rebellion in the 130s. As one commentator noted about Roman practices in dealing with an insurgency: "They made a desert and call it peace." Nevertheless for most of the inhabitants of an empire which stretched from the deserts of Arabia to the straits of Gibraltar and from Hadrian's Wall in northern England to the Upper Nile, there was a real peace with only the rumble of conflicts on distant frontiers that had little impact on the lives of the citizens. The upper classes may have suffered at times under the heel of paranoiac or demented emperors, but even the worst acts rarely impinged on the lives of those lower down on the food chain.

In many ways, Rome – and similar periods in the history of China – represent anomalies on history's landscape. In both those cases of enduring peace, the hegemonic power possessed the resources, manpower, and *military forces* to *impose* its concept of peace against all comers. It certainly does not speak to a world of globalized states like the European Union, which lacked the will to intervene even against a murderous petty tyrant like Slobodan Milosovich, despite the fact that his actions were threatening to destabilize the entire Balkans, *their neighborhood.*

The period that followed the fall of the Roman Empire suggests how tenuous peace has been in most periods of history. In the third and fourth centuries, the *pax Romana* collapsed, never to be restored. A series of ferocious barbarian invasions followed Rome's collapse over a period which that lasted for over six centuries and which culminated in the ferocious Viking raids of the tenth and eleventh centuries. Moreover, from the seventh century on, the Europeans confronted constant pressure from Saracen infidels on the frontiers of the Balkans, Sicily, and particularly Spain. Yet wars against external invaders only represented the tip of the iceberg, as the Europeans appeared even more willing to wage war against themselves.[9] From its earliest days, the Medieval world present a landscape of constant, unremitting conflict. Internecine wars between and among kings and great nobles, among the great nobles themselves, and among what can best describe as marauding knights and mercenaries fell on the backs of the peasants and emerging towns.[10]

---

9   In fact, William McNeil's classic study on the rise of the West argues persuasively that the constant conflicts that marked the European scene among a host of contenting powers played the decisive role on the eventual domination over the world's civilizations that the West was to achieve. See William H. McNeil, *The Rise of the West, A History of the Human Community* (Chicago, 1963).

10   The chronicler Jean Froissart present the grim landscape of a European society in which real peace hardly existed in a world in which violence of every sort was perpetrated on the weak and the helpless. One particularly revealing episode occurs as Edward Ill's army approaches Caen. Its soldiers and nobles hear confession from

Admittedly, all was not war – at least among the monarchs. The Hundred Years War between France and England did see truces between the major contestants. After all there were only three major battles – Crecy, Poitiers, and Agincourt. But the problem for the peasants and the villagers of the France was the fact that even during periods of truce among the great and mighty, there existed nothing that to our eyes would resemble peace. Bands of marauders, unemployed soldiers, and mercenaries kept the countryside in a constant state of turmoil, which at times became too much for the "Jacques," as Froissart so contemptuously referred to the French peasants. But only under the most desperate of circumstances, such as after the catastrophic defeat of the French Anny at Poitiers, were the "Jacques" willing to rise in murderous rebellion against their lords and masters, who had not only failed to stop the foreign invaders, but who had scarcely been able to keep the peace at home.

The monarchs of Europe were finally able to bring some level of order within their realms during the sixteenth and seventeenth centuries. While the level of sheer banditry, or at least irresponsible, uncontrolled violence in the countryside may have declined during this period, war between and among the European states hardly showed any decline. In fact, it became both more expensive and with the addition of religious fanaticism to the equation, it may well have become more ferocious. Nothing better elucidates the effect that religious quarrels had on war in Europe that the Thirty Years War (1618-1648), which wrecked the Germanies from the Mark of Brandenburg-Prussia to Alsace-Lorraine. The sack of Magdeburg, in which the attacking Habsburg armies slaughtered the city's 30,000 Protestants suggests the complete lack of even a humane framework for thinking about the waging of war.

Ironically, it may well have been the catastrophic ferocity of the Wars of Religion that led the Europeans to pull back from the brink and at least attempt to place some limits on the waging of war. The Treaty of Westphalia (1648), despite the shrill denunciations of the Papacy, represented a significant break with Europe's past in a number of ways. Most obviously, it removed religion from the context of wars among the European powers. Equally important it established the state and its representatives as the arbiters of war and peace. The emergent modern state of the late seventeenth century had little interest in what its citizens thought,[11] but it also had little interest in waging unlimited conflict against its neighbors, since the territories thus ravaged might well be under its

---

the army's chaplins in the morning, and then immediately proceed to march on and after slaughtering the French army in front of Caen proceeded to slaughter virtually every civilian they could get their hands on in Caen. Not satisfied with murder, the English men at arms raped every woman, including nuns. See Jean Froissart, *Chronicles,* trans. by Geoffret Brereton (London, 1978).

11   Although one should note that the "Glorious Revolution" of 1688 that overthrew James II in England for his obdurate unwillingness to pay attention to the wishes of his Protestant subjects does indicate the first stirrings of popular influences.

control after the making of peace. Thus the advantage for most Europeans was considerable, even if they had no vote in the waging of war or the making of peace, because war remained limited in its goals, conduct, and the damage that it inflicted on the landscape.[12] As for the making of peace, the major powers aimed not at insuring a long lasting solution to conflict, but rather at positioning themselves best for the next war that they all understood was coming.

All of this changed radically with the wars of the French Revolution and Napoleon. Quite simply the revolutionaries in Paris tossed out the rule book of eighteenth century war out the window. As the great theorist of war Carl von Clausewitz underlines:

> [B]ut in 1793 a force appeared and beggared all imagination. Suddenly war again became the business of the people – a people of thirty millions, all of whom considered themselves to be citizens.... The people became a partici-pant in war; instead of governments and armies as heretofore, the full weight of the nation was thrown into the balance. The resources and efforts now available for use surpassed all conventional limits; nothing now impeded the vigor with which war could be waged, and consequently the opponents of France faced the utmost peril...
>
> War untrammeled by any conventional restraints, had broken loose in all its elemental fury. This was due to the people's new share in the great affairs of state; and their participation in turn, resulted partly from the impact that the revolution had on the internal conditions of the state and partly from the danger that France posed to everyone.[13]

Driven by the popular nationalism of the French nation, the French Republic completely overturned the European balance of power. Its successor, the Napoleonic Empire, came close to establishing France's hegemony over the continent. What saved Europe was the consistent strategic and political arro-gance and France and the fact that a second great revolution in human affairs – the Industrial Revolution – was beginning across the English Channel. That revolution, which had as of yet no direct impact on the battlefield, did provide the financial support that kept the great coalitions of the anti-French powers together until Napoleon's final defeat.[14]

But the success of the French unleashed a response from the conquered. Ironically, it was in the areas furthest from the heart of Europe's enlighten-ment – Spain, Russia, the Tyrol- where resistance emerged in its most effective

---

12   None of this, of course, applied to the Balkans in the contest between the Austrian and Ottoman Empires, where religion remained on the table.

13   Carl von Clausewitz, *On War,* ed. and trans. by Michael Howard and Peter Paret (Princeton, 1975), pp. 591-593.

14   These issues are further explored in MacGregor Knox and Williamson Murray, *The Dynamics of Military Revolution, 1300-2050* (Cambridge, 2000).

form. When it was over, an exhausted Europe, led by the reactionary victors, cobbled together a peace which managed to put the genie of nationalism as well as war back in the jar for the next three decades. Moreover, one should not underestimate the possibility that Europe's exhaustion after a quarter century of devastating conflict also provided a major incentive for peace over the course of succeeding decades.

There was a major advantage that the peacemakers at Vienna enjoyed over their successors in the twentieth century. The making of peace from Westphalia to Vienna, just as with the making of war, was a matter of kings, princes, and their generals and diplomats. In many ways the making of peace resembled a cotillion among the great, while popular opinion had neither say nor vote. Thus, the complexity of negotiations reflected both the ambiguities and lack of clarity in the military results, as well as the problems involved in maximizing territorial gains as well as the desire to gain the best position for the coming peace. It certainly did not reflect public opinion outraged by its enemies. In all of this, none of the diplomats felt the slightest need to consult public opinion, which hardly existed in 1815, with the limited exception of France and Britain.[15] And so they did not. The result was that those who made the settlement were able to suppress the deep bitterness of those who had suffered under French depredations and rule in deciding how Europe would treat Napoleon's successors.

The near century of peace from 1815 through 1914 resulted from two factors: The settlement at Vienna kept a modicum of peace for nearly half a century. Then, with nationalism's re-emergence, beginning in 1848 and the late 1850s with the wars on the Italian peninsula, but in its most virulent form in the Franco-Prussian War, accident as well as incompetence conspired to limit the damage, at least until 1914. In the Franco-Prussian conflict, the incompetence of Louis Napoleon's Second French Empire, as well as the French passion for political fragmentation, resulted in a decisive Prusso-German victory, one magnified by the brilliance of Bismarck's strategy. Thus, the implications of the reappearance of nationalism as a major driver in war and the making of peace remained hidden even to the most sophisticated analysts. Moreover, the combination of the French Revolution with the Industrial Revolution, which had appeared in the American Civil War and which explains a great deal about its length and cost, only began to appear in the Franco-Prussian War, but after the catastrophic defeat of the French Armies at the war's onset, made a lengthy war impossible. The lid remained on until the catastrophe of 1914.

As Michael Howard has pointed out in two significant works, it was during this period that present conceptions of "peace" as distinct from war emerged full blown. The making of peace between the British and French on one side and the Russians on the other at the end of the

---

15   And even then the lack of speedy means of communications meant that the decisions of British negotiators in Vienna were in variably overtaken by events by the time that they reached London.

The Crimean War found an altered world. The telegraph now allowed reports from both the front, and from the negotiating table, to reach Paris and London newspapers the next day.[16] However, it did not matter until the denouement of the Franco-Prussian War, when public opinion in Prusso-Germany and France played major roles first in driving the two sides into conflict and then in making it exceedingly difficult for Bismarck and the Republic's negotiators to arrive at a settlement, even considering the decisive nature of the Prussia's and its German allies' battlefield victories throughout the course of the war.

If the hundred years of relative stability that ended in 1914 created the expectation that peace was the norm in human affairs, the catastrophe of the First World War should have disabused most of that notion.[17] Despite the horrendous slaughter of the war, it did not.

Unfortunately, after 1919 the prevailing opinion in the democracies, with the possible exception of France, was that the First World War had all been a tragic mistake, largely caused by miscalculation and error rather than deliberately set in motion by anyone power.[18] Thus, the Germans by the early 1930s had to a considerable extent escaped their culpability for unleashing the dogs of war in August 1914.[19] Such attitudes go far in explaining the fact that Britain and the United States so totally ignored the strategic and moral threat posed by the rise of Nazi Germany and its burgeoning military power in the 1930s.[20] Thus, Hitler

---

16 Interestingly, that factor exercised relatively little influence over the making of peace, but it certainly resulted in a massive public outcry in Britain over the inexcusable incompetence of the War Office in clothing, feeding, and medical services for the British soldiers in the field.

17 Perhaps nothing better underlines the illusions under which British and American intellect were working in the years immediately before the war than Norman Angel's *The Great Illusion, A Study of the Relation of Military Power to National Advantage* (London, 1912).

18 The war's literature, among the most powerful of the twentieth century was particularly important in molding Anglo-American attitudes that rejected war as something that would not again occur among the reasonable peoples of the civilized world.

19 The massive German campaign of disinformation certainly encouraged and abetted such opinions. Ironically that campaign influenced the Reich's population as much as it did Germany's opponents – with disastrous results in the Second World War. See Holger Herwig, "Clio Deceived, Patriotic Self-Censorship in Germany after the Great War," *International Security*, Fall 1987, vol. 12, no. 2.

20 In fact, the Bank of England played a major role in helping the Germans overcome their serious liquidity crisis in 1934 and 1935, decisions that prevented an economic crisis in the Third Reich that might well have brought German rearmament to a halt for a considerable period of time with huge implications for the future of European peace, as well as the ability of the Germans to wage war in 1939 with some prospect of success. Throughout the 1930s the Nazi economy, considering Hitler's massive program of rearmament, was always in a tenuous situation.

and his criminal regime were allowed a pass that allowed them to destroy all of the safe guards that Versailles had put in place – almost until it was too late.

Unlike the democracies, the ideologies of both Nazism and Communism in the Soviet Union absolutely rejected the idea that peace, whether between race or class, was the norm – the latter at least until the entire Capitalist World had been overthrown, the former until the world "biological revolution" had completely altered the world's racial balance. As General Erich Ludendorff was to argue after the Great War, peace was simply a continuation of war by other means, a complete reversal of Clausewitz's dictum. It was a dictum that Adolph Hitler's Third Reich would even manage to exceed.[21] As we now have come to understand, those two ideological definitions of the human condition came perilously close to success in the 1930s and 1940s.

At least, after the Second World War, the *Wehrmacht's* absolute defeat and the destruction and occupation of the Reich solved the German problem – and those posed by Imperial Japan and Fascist Italy. There could now be no quarrel on the part of the Germans, east or west, with the terms the victors imposed on them, as there had been in 1919, when the victors had not even reached German territory when the war ended. The German problem, at least as far as the threat the Reich represented to its neighbors, had been solved once and for all.[22] Nevertheless, the ideological conflict between Soviet Communism and American Capitalism-democracy should have followed World War II's pattern. But the existence of nuclear weapons as well as the belief on the part of Soviet ideologues in the internal contradictions of capitalism prevented the outbreak of another world war, which would have placed humanity's survival in doubt.

Of course, nuclear standoff did not mean the end of war, or for that matter the concomitant problems raised by the need to make peace. In the case of the wars of colonialism the Dutch East Indies, French Indo-China, Malaya, Cyprus, Kenya, Algeria, and the second Vietnam war, etc. – the making of peace found solution by the defeat of the colonial power (or its replacement) and absolute victory by the insurgency.[23] However, in conflicts such as the Arab-Israeli wars, the India-Pakistan conflicts, or perhaps even the Falkland Island's War of 1982, a period of neither war nor peace followed on the conduct of military operations.

For a fuller discussion of German rearmament and these issues see Adam Tooze, *The Wages of Destruction. The Making and Breaking of the Nazi Economy* (New York, 2006), particularly pp. 15-16, 18.

21   MacGregor Knox, *Common Destiny: Dictatorship, Foreign Policy, and War in Fascist Italy and Nazi Germany* (Cambridge, 2000).

22   A fact that the swift agreement of Germany's neighbors to reunification with the collapse of the German Democratic Republic in 1989 underlined.

23   No book underlines more graphically the results of a people's war of liberation than Alistair Home's *A Savage War of Peace: Algeria 1954-1962* (New York, 2006).

The defeated in each case simply refused to accept the report cards of military operations, no matter how decisive they might have appeared to outside observers. In effect, the seeds of the next conflicted found themselves firmly implanted in the soil of bitterness left after "the decisive victory of the last conflict." And that looks to be the problem the United States confronts in the aftermath of its "decisive" victory in the three week war of March-April 2003 against Saddam Hussein's Ba'athist regime.[24]

Conclusion

And so what conclusions might we draw from this dismal record of human behavior over the past 2,500 years, for thinking about war in the future. Let me again quote the words of King Archidamnus of Sparta: "war is [not] a good thing or a safe thing." It involves ferocious, murderous violence. There will never be any such thing as clean tidy, by-the-rule-book wars.
    Again Clausewitz:

Kind-hearted people might of course think that there was some ingenious way to disarm or defeat an enemy without too much bloodshed, and might imagine this is the true goal of the art of war. Pleasant as it sounds, it is a fallacy that must be exposed: war is such a dangerous business that the mistakes which come from kindness are the very worst....
    This is how the matter must be seen. It would be futile – even wrong – to try and shut one's eyes to what war is from sheer distress at its brutality.[25]

To believe that we can surround war with legalisms and constraints is the most dangerous of illusions. Military and political law may have its uses, but we should beware any claims, hopes or beliefs that a legal framework should constrain our actions, when expediency and necessity demand otherwise, much less that it will constrain the actions of our opponents. From our vantage point at the start of the twenty-first century, the strategic bombing campaign and the dropping of atomic bombs appear to be acts of unbelievable brutality. Yet the historical record, at least for those who are willing to read it with some honesty, has made it clear over the past several decades that both of those acts were absolutely necessary to avoid the slaughter on millions of more human beings, the

---

24   For the misapprehensions with which U.S. policy makers embarked on the war against Saddam Hussein's regime see among others: Ricks, *Fiasco;* and Michael Gordon and Bernard Trainor, *Cobra II* (New York, 2006). For the disastrous results in terms of how matters were actually handled on the ground by the Coalition Provisional Authority see Rajiv Chandrasekaran, *Imperial Life in the Emerald City, Inside Iraq's Green Zone* (New York, 2(06).

25   Clausewitz, *On War,* pp. 75-76.

majority of whom were citizens of Allied nations.[26] In the end war can be, and often is, about national survival. And under those circumstances, it will require hard behavior. In September 1939 the rules of engagement prevented the Royal Air Force from attacking German warships tied up in port for fear of killing civilian dockyard workers. Only four years later (three years and ten months later), the RAF was obliterating German cities in one of the most ruthless, but necessary campaigns of the Second World War.

For the soldiers and marines at the sharp end, combat is about survival, simple, sheer human survival in an arena where other human beings have no other purpose other than to kill them. In that arena there are no holds barred. Perhaps how far the American people are from that arena is suggested by the fact that in the immediate aftermath of the Gulf War of 1991, there were complaints by so-called ethicists about the number of Americans killed compared to the number of Iraqis killed.

In ending, let me suggest to you that war with all its horrors will be with us far into the future. It is crucial that we hold on to our definition of peace as long and as hard as we can. We cannot again afford to embark as casually and superficially on war again as we did in February 2003. On the other hand, we must recognize that there are others, in fact the majority of the world's population, which does not accept our conception of peace. And after Iraq is over, we will find ourselves at war with them again in the future, perhaps the near future.

---

26   For the crucial impact of the strategic bombing campaign on the German war economy see Adam Tooze, *The Wages of Destruction, The Making and Breaking of the German war Economy* (New York, 2006); for the most careful examination of all the evidence on why the dropping of the atomic bombs was necessary see Richard B. Frank, *Downfall, The End of the Imperial Japanese Empire* (New York, 2001).

C. Journalism

Chapter 14

The Meaning of War

Pamela Constable

I have been covering foreign conflicts for the past 25 years, but I have never covered a conventional war, with uniforms and flags and clear battle lines and clear codes of conduct. I have covered guerrilla conflicts and civil wars, ideological and ethnic and religious conflicts – all by definition full of moral murk, ambivalence and ambiguity. I have had to grapple with contradictory and constantly shifting versions of the truth, where one side's freedom fighters were the other's subversive delinquents.

I have seen American-backed armies committing atrocities in the name of anti-communism, and leftist or Islamic guerrillas inspiring the young and poor to kill in the name of revolutionary mystique and ideology. I have lived in post-war societies where former soldiers and security forces became a vast class of idle, armed criminals, and wars left permanent legacies of abusiveness and amorality, extending even until today.

My first conflicts were the wars of Central America, which I covered for *The Boston Globe*. In El Salvador and Guatemala, repressive military regimes backed by the Americans, battled revolutionaries inspired by the Cuban revolution. The victims were those of the democratic and reformist center – land reformers, clergy, human rights groups, and political leaders.

In Guatemala, where a US-backed coup in 1954 led to the creation of a powerful anti-communist army, a 30-year civil war led to the deaths of 200,000 people, most of them peasants killed at military hands. In the process, a world of spies and powerful state intelligence agencies was built, and its power and poison lasted long after the official peace process and the return of democracy. Political assassinations continue to mar elections., In 2007, the front runner for president was a former general whose forces were involved in the 1998 murder of a prominent bishop.

I also covered the military dictatorships and dirty wars of South America, especially Chile and Argentina. In Chile, General Pinochet seized power with a messianic belief that the army was the only force that could counter the dangers of communism. Terrible atrocities were committed in the name of extirpating that ideology. In the process, a society known for rule of law and legalism

Mary Ellen O'Connell (ed.), What Is War? An Investigation in the Wake of 9/11.

degenerated into fearful, moral cowardice. Courts and judges were subverted to justify political repression, and a deeply divided nation lost its traditional tolerance for diversity.

In Argentina, a country of cafes, intellectual discourse and European tastes, a series of military bureaucratic regimes "disappeared" thousands of people in its dirty war against the left. In Peru, Maoist rebels championed the impoverished and neglected Indian masses, but their fanatical discipline and mystique led to terrible cruelty that was mirrored by the counterinsurgency squads of the military. Extremes begat extremes and ends justified means. Village mayors were beheaded, and peasant leaders vanished inside military camps.

In more recent years, I covered conflicts in South Asia and the Arab World, again mostly ethnic and ideological struggles, but often with a volatile overlay of religious jihad and a complex love-hate attitude between East and West. These were conflicts where children were trained to become suicide bombers in the name of religion or ethnic freedom, and where moral imperatives were lost in a fog of propaganda and deceit. I lost many friends and colleagues to seemingly senseless deaths, and I narrowly escaped being killed several times myself.

In Kashmir, I saw how conflict could be viewed through totally different prisms of culture and nationality and emotion. I saw villages burned down and two instant, irreconcilable versions of the same incident immediately put out by the Indian army and the separatist Muslim leadership. I covered the invisible war in the Kargil Mountains, where everyone lied in a barrage of competing propaganda. I lost a friend, a moderate Muslim politician, who was assassinated by unknown extreme forces who stood to benefit from continued conflict and viewed moderate voices as the enemy.

In Sri Lanka, I saw child soldiers, caught up in a revolutionary mystique, taught to blow themselves up in the name of establishing an elusive utopian homeland for their Tamil ethnic group.

In Pakistan, I saw General Musharraf take power much like General Pinochet in Chile, vowing to replace corrupt civilians and sham democracy with honor and order. Instead he ended up clinging to power, as dictators inevitably do. Pakistan had been an important US ally in the anti-Soviet struggles in Afghanistan, but in the process of arming local Islamic militias, a monster was created that Musharraf proved unwilling or unable to control. Although he sided with the West after the attacks of September 11, he formed tactical alliances with religious fundamentalists, and the society slipped further into the grip of Islamic fanaticism.

Today, Pakistan is a country at war with itself, torn between a modernizing moderate vision of Islam and the traditional, tribal forces that follow conservative Islam. Many poor Muslims there have been taught to believe that their religion is under siege, that the West is out to destroy them, that democracy equals pornography and alcohol. The appeal of jihad, to be a soldier of God and reach a martyr's paradise, must be powerful to young and alienated people with few prospects in a corrupt, tightly controlled society. The clash of civilizations will ultimately be played out not between East and West, but within such bifurcated Muslim societies.

In Afghanistan, the struggle between modernism and tradition is even sharper. I first went there in 1998, under Taliban rule, and quickly discovered that many Western myths about the situation were false. The Taliban were repressive, but their forces were welcomed after the chaos and crime of civil war. We imagined women hated to cover their faces, but many felt safer that way from marauding militiamen.

After the US-led assault that liberated Afghanistan in 2001, I went to live there. A transition to democracy unfolded, with elections and a new constitution, but the society was brutalized by decades of conflict and repression, and it had become a place where only survival mattered. There was no rule of law, corruption was rampant, and opium poppy cultivation spread like wildfire. The US sided with local warlords against the Taliban and focused narrowly on hunting down Al Qaeda, allowing rapacious militiamen to regain niches in power.

As Afghans became disillusioned with the Western-backed government, the once-defeated Taliban was able to regroup and step into a void of power in many rural areas where the government could not deliver stability, services or security. Their forces intimidated people but also offered rough justice, while Islamic militia leaders with conservative views created their own pressure against Western values and modernizations. Six years after a new government was brought in by the UN, there are now thousands of foreign troops and billions of dollars invested in a country where there is no rule of law, and there is rising insurgent violence and enormous resentment against the West. In a worst-case scenario, Afghanistan could become a combination of Columbia and Saudi Arabia – an Islamist narco-state.

Finally, my work as a correspondent in Iraq proved the ultimate experience in moral confusion and multiple versions of truth. We went into Iraq to liberate it from political repression, but lost all moral authority by using torture and degradation to achieve our ends. I reported there on four different tours, each one more dangerous and less welcoming. I learned of appalling atrocities committed by Saddam and his cronies, but also realized Western forces were gaining new enemies by the day.

I embedded with the Marines during the assault on Fallujah, where I saw one side of the conflict in great personal detail, but had absolutely no access to the other side during constant and heavy combat. Our forces wiped out a bad regime, but in the process made enormous mistakes that loosened sectarian poisons and disenfranchised hundreds of thousands of soldiers and government employees and Baath Party members who became obvious recruits for insurgency. Instead of liberating Iraq, we ended up lost in the chaos of a growing civil war.

My experiences with moral ambivalence of modern conflict, as well as with the deaths of many friends and my own narrow escape from being killed in Afghanistan, made me determined to search for some deeper meaning in my work as a war correspondent and in cruel and conflicted societies themselves. In 2003, I took six months off and poured all my questions and epiphanies into a book called, *Fragments of Grace: My Search for Meaning in the Strife of South Asia.*

The book was partly an attempt to highlight incidents and individuals that were enlightening or ennobling in places full of cruelty and greed, gratuitous violence and misguided belief or passion. It singled out people who helped me when they had little themselves, moments when compassion broke through walls of cynicism and suspicion. I called it a search for dignity in the ruins of war. But much of what I learned and wrote was about the harder, sadder lessons of my time as a reporter of foreign struggles with oppression and civil conflict. In the end, I realized that the mistakes of human history always repeat themselves, that the cure for one form of oppression very often creates a new and worse one, and that in war, self-interested or self-deluded versions of the truth will almost always prevail over the facts.

Chapter 15

The Semantics of 21st Century Warfare

James Gordon Meek

When I woke up on the morning of September 11, 2001, in Arlington, Virginia, I was not a war correspondent and I had no experience as a war correspondent. I had no idea that I would become one before lunchtime. I had just moved back to Arlington from Brooklyn, New York, where I was a news editor working a couple of blocks from the World Trade Center. The only pressing matter on my mind that sunny Tuesday morning was my wedding on September 15th. I was also dreading that day having to cover a "snewzer" – a press briefing on the annual meeting of the Judicial Conference.

But everything changed at 8:46 a.m.

I turned on my TV and switched over to CNN. The network cut to the World Trade Center on fire. American Airlines Flight 11 had ripped into the North Tower, but at first they reported it as a small plane crash. Minutes later, United Airlines Flight 175 hit the South Tower. The Pentagon was struck, and I was out the door, camera and tape recorder in hand. Destiny was beckoning loudly.

In those first moments of the 9/11 attacks, my life – and my journalism career – took a hard turn. Soon enough I was spinning on my own inner axis right along with the rest of the country, forced to face challenges to the very notion of liberty and equality for which we stand as a free people. Soon the nation would have to decide where the moral compass of the Republic was pointing. Was it on the side of unambiguous justice – even for terrorists? Or was it on the side of simple pragmatism and survival, no matter the moral cost?

I got my first glimpse of war that morning as I zipped East down Arlington Boulevard toward Washington. The roadway was empty. But the westbound lanes heading away from Washington were a parking lot. It was a slow retreat. The exodus began immediately after the towers were struck. I looked up and saw a ghastly cloud of gray smoke visible above the trees of Fort Myer, the Army post that is home to Arlington National Cemetery and its "toy soldier" protectors, the fabled 3rd Infantry Regiment, known as the Old Guard. It is also the site of the first military aviation flight, in 1908 by the Wright brothers – and the scene of military aviation's first crash fatality, involving a Wright aircraft.

Mary Ellen O'Connell (ed.), What Is War? An Investigation in the Wake of 9/11.
© *2012 Koninklijke Brill NV. Printed in The Netherlands.* ISBN 978 9004 17234 0. *pp. 201–208.*

A few short steps from the Iwo Jima Memorial at the outer edge of the military cemetery and overlooking Washington's monuments and memorials, I watched ghostly military uniforms of every service streaming toward me through the white headstones, away from the Pentagon, and just ahead of the sickening green plume of smoke.

I had written about terrorism for years and had done investigative work on Al Qaeda's involvement in the Millennium Plot. That summer, I had visited the newly-dedicated Oklahoma City National Memorial on the grounds of the destroyed Alfred Murrah Federal Building, where my cousin Claudette Meek perished in a domestic terrorist bombing in 1995. It had been hard to imagine witnessing the immediate aftermath of a terrorist attack, or that I would see flaming jet fuel spitting out the windows of a building I had once worked inside of during a short-lived assignment as a defense reporter for United Press International a few years earlier. Even as I began to interview the survivors, I never imagined that four years later I would be standing on a landing zone at a desolate, windswept Green Beret camp in Zadran tribal turf along the AfPak border, only a few feet from a bound and blindfolded, English-speaking Al Qaeda prisoner.

I could not have imagined on September 11, 2001, what an important moment August 17, 2005, would represent to me, in the context of everything that had happened between those two dates. By the time I found myself in Lwara, Afghanistan, I had already spent the years since the 9/11 attacks covering the Bush administration's "Global War on Terror," its legal war on terror, and its war to redefine human rights for inhuman combatants. So I cannot forget – nor can I understate – the importance of what I heard come out of the mouth of a Special Forces sergeant that cold night in 2005. Addressing another soldier clutching the prisoner's flexicuffs as a chopper overhead thundered down on our LZ, the sergeant growled:

"If he does anything funny, *kick the shit out of him.*"

With that statement, the sergeant essentially helped define a central question for many about the Bush administration's Global War on Terror: was it not just relentless and ruthless, but also rule-breaking?

In an instant, the whole reality of this war came crashing down on me. I had written hundreds of stories on Afghanistan, Al Qaeda "central", Iraq, Al Qaeda Iraq, Abu Musab al Zarqawi, Osama Bin Laden, Ayman al-Zawahiri, KSM, the 9/11 Commission, Gitmo, Abu Ghraib, Tora Bora, enemy combatants, military commissions, Hamdan, Hamdi, Chaplain Jim Yee, Saddam Hussein and the CIA – and all of it imploded inside my head. This was where legal niceties, words on a piece of paper and thousands of phone calls by a reporter sitting at a desk in Georgetown were meaningless when it all came down to a pragmatic choice by combatants on the field of battle. I was being confronted with a hard reality, which went beyond a legal concept or a think tank theory.

This Green Beret's remark directly challenged the Pentagon's claims that its leadership had made it crystal clear to *all* the troops that prisoners be treated humanely and in the spirit – if not by the legal requirements – of the Geneva Conventions banning mistreatment of those captured on the battlefield. After four years of chronicling Team Bush's chutzpah challenging dusty international treaties as "quaint" at the least, redefining the law of armed conflict, I concluded that all the scrutiny by critics probably amounted to nothing in hotspots where bullets and shrapnel permeated the air. For in at least one foxhole of the Global War on Terror, practical military necessity demanded that if prisoners did anything "funny," their captors might "kick the shit" out of them. It could have been worse. The sergeant could have ordered his subordinate operator to meet resistance with lethal force, and he certainly did not do that.

Killing terrorists is a good thing. But, as one senior intelligence official said to me recently, "We can't kill all of them". That means we have to think beyond the trigger. We have to change people's way of thinking and thereby shrink the recruiting pool if we're serious about defeating the violent Islamic extremists and living without fear. We *must* think beyond the trigger.

Taking at face value the remark by an otherwise brave soldier on the real front line in the fight against Al Qaeda, one has to ask, did he miss the memo on prisoner abuse? By 2005, even the military commanders and intelligence officials at Guantanamo Bay had finally gotten the message and had begun to clean up their detention operation. So what happened in Afghanistan and in Iraq? Perhaps the words written or spoken banning rough treatment of detainees weren't as influential as the posture of our leaders had suggested. They said one thing publicly but conveyed another message privately, some argued.

In Afghanistan, troops were issued, as early as May 5, 2004, rules of engagement (ROE) on a laminated 4x10-inch card distributed by Combined Joint Task Force-76, the overall military command based at Bagram Airfield. Under the heading, "Rules for treatment of person under control," the document states: "Never use more force then (sic) is necessary to maintain discipline and compliance with the detaining unit's instructions."

Was the Green Beret sergeant's order to his subordinate in line with the ROE issued by CJTF-76? As a member of Special Forces under a separate command, Combined Joint Special Operations Task Force-Afghanistan (CJSOTF-A), did he feel obliged to follow CJTF-76's ROEs? I don't know the answer.

But the consequences of ignoring the ROEs were spelled out on the card and should have been plain to anyone. It said, simply: "Improper handling/treatment may result in prosecution under the UCMJ [Uniform Code of Military Justice]."

President Bush said repeatedly that the U.S. "does not torture." But he also defended "enhanced interrogation techniques" used by the CIA – which we now know included waterboarding Al Qaeda detainees, which the President claimed in a 2006 White House speech had foiled plots and saved American lives. That was classic George W. Bush: the cowboy swagger, the wide stance, hands poised over each hip; an unapologetic gunslinger with a Colt Peacemaker in one holster and a legal brief tucked into the other. The man Americans wanted to drink a beer with in the 2000 campaign looked Americans squarely in the eye after 9/11 and told them that even though Al Qaeda detainees didn't deserve the legal protections of prisoners of war covered by the Geneva Conventions, he was going to give them the same human rights and guarantee of humane treatment anyway.

But out on a desolate Afghan battlefield, there may have been some perceived ambiguity. Many Americans on the secret front lines of counterterrorism may not have cared much about what some Brooks Brothers-clad lawyers back in Washington had sweated over in an air-conditioned Executive Branch suite.

I once asked then-Attorney General Alberto R. Gonzales if he felt in any way personally responsible for documented prisoner abuses at GTMO and Iraq's Abu Ghraib prison, given that, without him in his former role as White House counsel, the modern legal concept of "unlawful enemy combatants" might not have existed.

"I don't know if I would lay that at the feet of the lawyers," Gonzales told me in a May 2005 interview published in the New York *Daily News*. Gonzales said there was a "collective judgment" by Bush's legal advisors that Al Qaeda and Taliban prisoners didn't deserve any legal rights under international law or the law of armed conflict. "It wasn't a conclusion, or an opinion, rendered solely by me," he added.

The administration called the new conflict with Al Qaeda a "global war," and it's hard to argue that it was *anything but* a war waged around the globe. The trouble was that the administration didn't always treat it purely like a war when prosecuting terror suspects. Bush's corps of lawyers wanted to have it both ways: it was a "war" when it suited rhetorical purposes to treat it as such; it *wasn't* a war when calling it that interfered with new, sweeping legal powers that the Executive Branch of government was now asserting in wartime.

President Bush's defenders once derided his predecessor, Bill Clinton, for treating terrorism as a crime and prosecuting in federal courts all manner of thugs from Omar Abdel Rahman, the "Blind Sheik" bent on destroying New York City to Ramzi Yousef, who masterminded the bombing of the World Trade Center in 1993 and who, with his uncle Khalid Sheikh Mohammed, hatched the "Bojinka" plot to bomb U.S.-bound airliners over the Pacific to the killers who murdered hundreds at the U.S. embassies in East Africa. (H unit at Florence, Colorado's Supermax prison, in other words.) After 9/11, some conservatives inside and outside the administration argued that putting terrorists on trial was too risky. Some even suggested that documents entered into evidence by the government in the 1998 East Africa U.S. embassy bombing trials had been an intelligence boon to Al Qaeda.

Subsequently, the Bush administration took an approach to prosecuting terrorists that many found confusing and inconsistent. Low-level thugs with minimal capability for pulling off an attack – particularly of the homegrown variety – saw the inside of courts, while senior Al Qaeda operatives disappeared inside secret CIA black sites across Eastern Europe.

"Hindsight is always 20/20", smirked one former Bush Justice Department senior official. The military nabbed Marin County, California-raised *jihadi* convert John Walker Lindh in "manjams" with a Kalashnikov on an Afghan battlefield. But they gave him the right to counsel – and he hired one of the best lawyers in San Francisco, who ensured Lindh got his day in court, winning a 20-year prison stretch. Yasser Hamdi – just as much a U.S. citizen as lucky Lindh – was sent straight to GTMO from the same Afghan battlefield, denied his constitutional rights and held for years by the military in a South Carolina naval brig. And then he was set free to return to Saudi Arabia. Chicago gang-banger Jose Padilla was arrested on U.S. soil at O'Hare Airport for plotting a radiological "dirty" bomb strike, was held for four years without legal rights as an enemy combatant, and then finally prosecuted and convicted in federal court – for terrorism offenses unrelated to those he was accused of publicly by Attorney General John Ashcroft and Deputy Attorney General James Comey. And consider the curious case of convicted Al Qaeda terrorist Zacarias Moussaoui, a French citizen and admitted pet goon of Osama Bin Laden, a man whom I have had the unsettling experience of looking in the eye. He was arrested at a Minneapolis flight school in August 2001, later charged in federal court, granted court-appointed defense counsel and then acquitted by a jury in his death penalty trial after pleading guilty to being part of the 9/11 conspiracy.

Why did battlefield combatant Lindh get a lawyer and his day in court, Padilla and Hamdi none of their constitutional rights as citizens, and Moussaoui – who wasn't even an American – constitutional rights, lawyers and a civil criminal trial?

The concept of "unlawful enemy combatants," a status of detention which falls far short of Prisoner of War, has been the subject of scholarly and extensive political discourse, yet remains unresolved in the legal system. Some have argued that Al Qaeda operatives fail to meet one common definition of a lawful POW: they don't wear distinctive uniforms, carry a flag or wear visible markings affiliated with a nation-state. (Neither did the Viet Cong, but we designated their detainees as POWs eventually and afforded them legal rights.)

For years after the 2003 U.S. occupation began, the Iraqi National Police and security services wore no distinctive uniforms or identifying markings. Some simply donned black fatigues and wore a kaffiyah scarf or balaclava mask. It has often been difficult for U.S. troops to make a visual distinction between "friendlies" and "Anti-Coalition Forces," particularly aggravated by the fact that insurgents frequently pose as Iraqi police by donning their uniforms and using their vehicles. (This has also occurred in Afganistan.) Where did the real Iraqi police fit into the American definition of war or "lawful" combatants? Did they deserve Common Article 3 protections if taken prisoner?

This is a photo of a U.S. Army Special Forces Sgt. First Class James Oschner, who was killed in action by an improvised explosive device during his fourth tour of duty in Afghanistan in November 2005. The picture was snapped on a combat operation. He's wearing a baseball hat, a Tommy Bahama sport shirt and he's carrying a Kalashnikov assault rifle – obviously not a standard-issue weapon in the conventional U.S. military. Many wondered, under the legal standards set by the Bush administration, where Sgt. First Class Oschner would fit in if he had been captured instead of killed by the enemy? Can we hold America's enemies to one standard and our own troops to another?

Is it really a war if *neither side* wears a uniform?

The issue of a combatant's visual identity is no small matter. It is not written anywhere in the Geneva Conventions that lawful combatants must wear a uniform, carry a flag or don other identifying markings that associate them with a nation-state. But the Bush administration relied upon a World War II-era Supreme Court decision to justify calling operatives of Al Qaeda "unlawful enemy combatants." *Ex Parte Quirin* set the stage. A group of Nazi saboteurs nabbed inside the U.S. during World War II dressed in civillian clothing. They didn't carry swastika flags, either.

Jack Goldsmith, a conservative Republican lawyer who became the assistant attorney general in charge of the powerful Office of Legal Counsel at the Department of Justice right after the 2003 Iraq invasion, wrote in his book *The Terror Presidency* about the administration's view that all violent Islamic extremist enemies of the United States were unlawful enemy combatants undeserving of Geneva Conventions rights or protections. Goldsmith agreed with then-White House counsel Gonzales, Vice President Dick Cheney's counsel David Addington and other insiders on this – but only to an extent.

"In Feb 2002, President Bush had determined, correctly in my view, that in our conflict with Al Qaeda and in Afghanistan the Third Geneva Convention, which governed prisoners of war, did not confer POW status on Al Qaeda terrorists or on members of the Taliban who did not wear uniforms or comply with the laws of war," Goldsmith writes in Chapter 1, "The New Job," page 39. The new OLC chief soon enraged the White House by advising them that Iraqi insurgents – but not foreign fighters joining the insurgency or serving under Jordanian terrorist Abu Musab al-Zarqawi, who was forming the network eventually christened "Al Qaeda in Mesopotamia" – deserved some POW protections.

Another question springs to mind: is it really a war if the enemy is in an army of God?

The United States can easily refute Al Qaeda's common charge that it is a "crusader" force bent on dominating Muslims and stealing their oil. What is undeniable is that the Global War on Terror is a religious *jihad* for Al Qaeda and their allies, associates and followers. It is also undeniable that the U.S. military, while not on any sort of religious crusade, is nevertheless a force made up almost entirely of Christians. The soldiers you meet on the downrange and "outside the wire" of this conflict without borders or DMZs see it as a holy war of some flavor. Just ask the G.I.s on the Afghanistan-Pakistan border, the fuzzy 1893 Durand Line. They hear the screams of "Allah akhbar" (God is great) when their enemy launches attacks, and they know it is their nation's Christian heritage being targeted as much as the American flag velcroed to their shoulders.

I reported from Afghanistan during the summer of 2005 when only 20,000 U.S. troops patrolled the countryside. At that time, they told us that Al Qaeda was on the ropes. They told us that Osama was living in a cave, being hunted and on the run, and that he was probably dead. Military commanders speaking on the record to reporters in the country claimed – apparently quite sincerely – that the Taliban was all but defeated and was incapable of mounting military operations.

Everyone remembers President Bush standing on the deck of an aircraft carrier on May 1, 2003 in front of a giant banner reading "Mission Accomplished" and proclaiming the successful end of major combat operations in Iraq. But no one remembers Defense Secretary Donald Rumsfeld on the same day declaring from Kabul that the mission was also accomplished in Afghanistan.

"We're at a point where we clearly have moved from major combat activity to a period of stability and stabilization and reconstruction activities," Rumsfeld told reporters that day, according to the Associated Press. By August 2005, we hit a record number of Americans killed there and Al Qaeda and the Taliban were well into a yearlong offensive, which drenched the countryside in blood.

By the summer of 2007, it was obvious that Al Qaeda was not on the ropes and that the Taliban – now introducing suicide bombings at the urging of their Arab friends – was quite capable of mounting military operations against yet another superpower.

"We assess the group [Al Qaeda] has protected or regenerated key elements of its Homeland attack capability, including: a safehaven in the Pakistan Federally Administered Tribal Areas (FATA), operational lieutenants, and its top leadership," chimed in a National Intelligence Estimate on July 17, 2007.

So, is it a war if the U.S. says it's practically over and we have all but won? Is it a war if some of the most intense fighting since the Vietnam War – taking place on the AfPak – was largely concealed from the American public? Is it a war if the CIA is running the show?

President Bush's administration was still litigating the basic questions pertaining to the Global War on Terror as they left office in early 2009. But let's face it, you can't lawyer away the carnage indelibly linked to war or its essential character. Is it really a Global War on Terror? Yes, it is war. People die in this well-armed conflict. But *terror is a tactic*. Ours is really a war on violent Islamic extremism. It is, whether we like it or not, a clash of religions.

Let us go back to the basic question. What is war? Air Force General Mike Hayden, the Director of Central Intelligence, recently characterized the fight against Al Qaeda, the Taliban and the Iraqi insurgency during a speech before the Council on Foreign Relations in New York City on Sept. 7, 2007.

"Our nation is in a state of armed conflict with Al Qaeda and its affiliates," the CIA chief said. "It's a conflict that is global in scope, and a precondition for winning that conflict is to take the fight to the enemy wherever he may be. From my vantage point, measured by the required intensity of effort or the profound nature of the threat, it's very hard to see this thing as anything less than war. I've seen public references to, quote, 'the so-called war on terrorism' or, quote, 'the Bush's administration's war on terrorism,' but for us it's simply war. It's a word we use commonly without ambiguity in the halls of the Pentagon and at Langley."

D. Ethics

Chapter 16

The Precariousness of Rules

Thomas Grassey

I have titled my remarks "The Precariousness of Rules," but were I allowed a ridiculously long, accurate title it would be, "and thus the Precariousness of Laws, Professions, Organizations, Institutions, and Societies." My fundamental thesis is that, for each of us, our thoughts about moral right and wrong inevitably threaten rules, and thus laws, professions, organizations, and institutions, including communities, nations, and societies. Our thinking about what is the morally (or ethically – I use the terms and their cognates interchangeably) right thing to do in given situations regularly understates, and thus devalues, universals, categories, classes, groups, and principles.

To illustrate this, I shall offer some examples drawn from several of the professions represented at this conference.

I begin with lawyers. Herman Horrific savagely murders a six-year old girl. Our ethical instincts tell us that Herman should be caught and punished, removed from society so that he cannot do this to anyone else. However, in our adversarial system, the duty of Herman's criminal defense attorney is to do all that is legally permitted in order to allow Herman – even though the defense attorney knows him to be guilty of the crime of which he is accused – to walk free. Volumes have been written about this duty, of course. But notice: in this case, looking at Herman Horrific who actually committed a horrendous crime, our ethical instincts are that such a person should be punished.

Now the military. For several years I have given a case to officers at the War College, all having from ten to more than twenty years' experience. The case begins by stipulating that the standing regulations prohibit them and their subordinates from crossing a certain international border for any reason. When they observe an apparent atrocity in progress across the border, and communicate with their headquarters to explain the situation, they are nevertheless re-told specifically *not* to cross the border. As you can imagine, in this case, many officers who well understand the professional importance of obedience to orders are nevertheless torn between their personal desire to prevent (at little or no cost) a considerable amount of evil, and their professional obligation to obey

Mary Ellen O'Connell (ed.), What Is War? An Investigation in the Wake of 9/11.
© *2012 Koninklijke Brill NV. Printed in The Netherlands.* ISBN 978 9004 17234 0. *pp. 211 – 215.*

perfectly clear, specific orders from authorities who fully understand the situation the soldiers have described.

Reporters, specifically war correspondents. Perhaps you recall the wonderful series of programs on ethics and the professions that professors at Harvard Law School moderated. One of them had an all-star panel of esteemed reporters with combat experience, military officers who'd served in Vietnam, and other thoughtful commentators. The moderator asked the war correspondents what they would do if, in accompanying a rebel unit in the field, they found themselves about to witness an ambush of an American unit. Mike Wallace agonized over this, first holding that as a reporter he would have to remain silent, and thus complicit in the killing of the Americans; then, under enormous pressure, changing his mind and saying he could not allow his silence to cause the deaths of fellow Americans. In this case, was he, in truth, wrong to conceive of himself (once he had made the agreement to go into the field with the rebels) as obliged to warn the Americans (almost certainly at the cost of his own life)?

Another military case, albeit a legal one as well. In the Kosovo air campaign, there were strong reasons to believe that if certain civilian objects (factories, luxury homes) owned by wealthy supporters of Yugoslav president Slobodan Milošević could be publicly threatened, those supporters almost certainly would have pressured Milošević to end the war. Even if a few of the properties had to be destroyed (when they were unoccupied, and thus at little cost in life), the war could be ended far more mercifully – it was thought – than by engaging only military targets (tanks, artillery sites, formations of young soldiers). As we all know, however, civilian properties are *not* lawful targets under the present laws of armed conflict, while tanks and the soldiers in them are. So, to fight lawfully, NATO had to kill many more people than it wanted to. Many NATO planners were unhappy about this, and a senior U.S. Air Force JAG officer – now a two-star general – wrote an article in *Strategic Review* arguing that, in this case, what we did was morally wrong.

A case for priests and other chaplains, and doctors. About a year ago, a seasoned professor of ethics at another service war college who had a doctorate from the University of Chicago Divinity School, after listening to a public discussion of a hypothetical priest hearing the confession of a man who was sexually abusing his daughter, declared without hesitation that the priest in this case should abandon the confidentiality of the confessional and report the man to the police so the daughter could be spared any further abuse.

A hoary old case for peace activists and police officers: A terrorist has been captured after placing a nuclear weapon somewhere in Chicago. He laughs and says that the weapon will go off in an hour. Notwithstanding the various rules and conventions that prohibit torture, should we authorize the police interrogators in this case to torture the terrorist if we believe that the information about the weapon's location can be extracted from him in this and no other way?

For history professors and other academics. You will recall that, during the Vietnam War, being a college student entitled most young men to a deferment from the draft, and thus often from serving in Vietnam. Some professors refused to give draft-eligible men any grade below "C" lest they lose their student status by flunking out of college. In this case, the professors reasoned, the harm that might result from a grade of "F" was so great that the morally right thing to do was to ignore the academic rules of grading standards.

Finally, another military case. For those unfamiliar with a famous work in the field of ethics and conflict, *Just* and *Unjust Wars*, Michael Walzer – who loathes utilitarian thinking – argues for the just war theory, especially what he calls "the war convention," requiring enormous respect for the rights of civilians *but*, late in the book, he introduces the idea of "supreme emergency" – and here I quote – "there is a fear beyond the ordinary fearfulness ... of war, and a danger to which that fear corresponds, and this fear and danger may require exactly those measures that the war convention bars." Walzer argues that, facing a Nazi war machine that had already overrun almost the entire European continent, and having only Bomber Command as a tool to seriously damage Germany – a tool that was technologically and operationally limited to night area bombing – Great Britain was morally permitted to bomb German cities and indiscriminately kill innocent Germans. In Walzer's words, "But it does seem to me that the more certain a German victory appeared to be in the absence of a bomber offensive, the more justifiable was the decision to launch the offensive. It is not just that such a victory was frightening, but also that it seemed in those years [1940-1942] very close; it is not just that it was close, but also that it was so frightening. Here was a supreme emergency, where one might well be required to override the rights of innocent people and shatter the war convention." In this case, Walzer believes, a supreme emergency morally justified ignoring the rules.

In all these illustrations, what seems a common compelling motive is a focus of our ethical judgment – what we think is the morally right thing to do – on the individual, on the specific situation. And let me recall for our consideration the standard definition of "conscience" as "an act of the practical intellect which judges the morality of an action in the concrete and singular." Thus, I contend, individual situations, and consultation of our conscience about those situations, regularly and inevitably depreciate rules.

I hold that this is a specific manifestation of our general desire always to consider *rules, consequences, and intentions* (or character), to want them all to be in agreement in specific situations, *and* our unwillingness in ethical reflection to give absolute or even lexical priority to any one of these. All three matter all the time.

But if we always take into account consequences and intentions when we try to make ethical judgments, what can be said *in favor* of rules? Why should I obey the rule not to torture a terrorist if a city and its populace can be saved by torturing one person, briefly and not fatally? Why should we *not* threaten to bomb a candy factory (when it is unoccupied, at night) if the owner of the candy factory, thus threatened, would compel his cronies in the government to end the war, and hundreds of lives could be saved?

In fact, why should we ever support *rules?*

I think there are three possible justifications.

First, a rule could be intrinsically meritorious. Perhaps God issued the rule. Perhaps what the rule requires is *always* superior to what would result if the rule were broken.

Second, obeying a rule in this specific situation could be superior in this specific situation to not obeying it in this specific situation. (I abusively repeated "in this specific situation" because we must exclude any appeal to the good that would generally result if this rule generally were followed as a practice. That is the next argument.)

Third, obeying a rule could be justified because of the "slippery slope" argument – that although breaking the rule in this specific situation *looks* morally right, by weakening the tendency to obey the rule, we actually would end up producing greater harm in the long run, or in the greater picture. Since more good generally will result if we honor this rule, and not honoring the rule in this specific case would weaken the general tendency to honor this rule, we must honor the rule in this case regardless of the specific results in this case.

I know of no other justification for obeying a rule than these three.

Let me conclude then by suggesting some implications of my observations, most of which you already recognize.

When we look at specific cases, rules are in trouble. We can always, or almost always, push the consequences and intentions dimensions of our thinking to make compliance with a certain rule look immoral.

If this is so, lawyers – including lawyers working in the field of international and civil conflict, or "war" however defined – must foresee that laws, being a subset of rules, are vulnerable to moral attack and criticism when examined ethically, especially by someone looking at a specific case.

Third, if my observations are correct, rules (and thus laws) are *not* the ultimate arbiters of ethics, and our reflections on what is the morally correct action in a specific situation may *properly* lead us to ignore, or break, rules (and thus laws).

Specifically, then, I hold that a military commander, and thus even an ordinary soldier, may be morally justified in breaking a law, even a good and proper law.

Fourth, a "slippery slope" is *not* a "narrow ledge." There is a difference between taking a step down from the ridge line *and* plunging all the way to the valley floor.

Even slippery slopes allow one to walk one or two or more steps very, very carefully! Similarly, to break one rule at one time in one situation for very good reasons is *not* to doom the world to perdition.

Finally, I am nevertheless anxious about my observations and their implications, because we all know that some slippery slopes *are* very dangerous, and we all make mistakes about where we may step safely without falling all the way to the bottom of the hill. For instance, while I think Walzer was right about supreme emergency, and am inclined to think – despite being a member of the ACLU – that torturing the nuclear terrorist might be morally warranted, I would argue that all the other illustrations I offered do *not* justify ignoring the rule that was under attack. So I am apprehensive about the danger of using specific cases to guide our moral judgments about rules. That danger lies in the threat to laws, professions, organizations, and institutions, including communities, nations, and societies – a threat I am sure everyone in this audience well appreciates.

Chapter 17

The Meaning of War:
An Ethical Analysis of Sanctions and
Humanitarian Intervention

Gerard Powers

There are a variety of ethical approaches to the use of force. For the most part, ethical debates about war do not revolve around attempts to define when war begins and ends. Ethicists are mostly just interested observers of the lawyers' attempts to define the meaning of "armed attack" in the UN Charter or the political scientists' debate about how many battle deaths constitute a "war". Distinctions between inter-state and intra-state war have less meaning for ethicists than they do for international lawyers. The implications of these distinctions for *jus in bello* norms are much less developed in ethics than in international law. That is not to say, however, that such distinctions do not matter in ethical analysis. Especially since the end of the Cold War, ethicists have been confronted with a number of issues that arise somewhere between the categories of war and peace. Do traditional approaches to the ethics of war provide an adequate framework for evaluating coercive measures that fall short of war? Were the UN sanctions against Iraq, for example, an alternative to war or an alternate form of war? What kind of moral reasoning is appropriate for analyzing forms of humanitarian intervention that are more like policing than war, such as the highly-restricted uses of force to protect aid convoys and safe havens?

In this essay, I will consider how the just war tradition can provide an ethical framework for evaluating economic sanctions and humanitarian intervention. I will focus especially on the approaches of those who adopt a restrictive, as opposed to a permissive, approach to the just war tradition.[1] I will show that

---

1   A restrictive approach begins with a strong presumption against the use of force; just war criteria, strictly construed, provide a basis for determining when this presumption may be overridden. A permissive approach begins with a presumption not against force but for justice. The resort to military force, in this view, is not inherently problematic but is, according to James Turner Johnson, "a tool to be employed in the proper exercise of government to combat evil and other forms of injustice in the service of the public goods of justice, order, and peace." Johnson, J.T. (2005, January). Just War As It Was and Is. *First Things*, 149, 14. These different starting points reflect different perspectives on the role of military force in international affairs. Those who begin with a presumption against the use of force assume

Mary Ellen O'Connell (ed.), What Is War? An Investigation in the Wake of 9/11.
© *2012 Koninklijke Brill NV. Printed in The Netherlands. ISBN 978 9004 17234 0. pp. 217–234.*

even those advocates of the just war tradition who are least prone to justify the use of military force, have found a just war style of reasoning to be helpful in evaluating a wide range of coercive measures that do not involve inter-state conflict and do not rise to the level of force associated with war. In exceptional cases, a restrictive just war analysis can justify humanitarian intervention in internal conflicts as legitimate acts of defense, but the clear moral obligation is to find effective forms of humanitarian intervention that involve nonviolent political and juridical measures, coercion short of force, and military deployments that are more akin to policing than war-fighting. Finally, I will argue that a just war analyst is generally more willing than an international lawyer to override norms of procedural justice (e.g., the requirement of UN Security Council authorization) when they conflict with norms of substantive justice (e.g., defending the innocent against aggression).

Sanctions: Alternative to war or an alternate form of war?[2]

The proliferation of UN-authorized economic sanctions, especially those imposed on Iraq from 1990 to 2003, led to a new debate over the ethics of sanctions. Central to this debate was the question: Are such sanctions an alternative to war, as envisioned by article 41 of the UN Charter, or an alternate form of war, a *casus belli* akin to sieges and blockades?[3] If sanctions are an alternate form of warfare, they should be governed by standard just war ethical analysis. But if they are an alternative to war, then the moral issues posed by sanctions should

---

a sharp break between war and politics, while those who begin with a presumption for justice would emphasize the continuity between the use of force and international politics. While their mode of reasoning is quite different, the strict and permissive approaches in ethics have their analogues in debates over narrow and broad interpretations of art. 51 of the UN Charter, which allows force in response to an "armed attack." A permissive ethic is more likely than a restrictive one to be at odds with art. 51, narrowly construed. That raises interesting questions of the relationship between law and ethics, such as how preemptive war, which clearly violates a narrow construction of art. 51, could promote justice, in a moral sense, while violating justice, in a legal sense. On the two main legal interpretations of art. 51, see Gray, C. (2008). *International Law and the Use of Force* (3rd ed.). Oxford: Oxford University Press, 117-119.

2   The analysis in this section is taken from a longer article by Christiansen, D., S.J., & Powers, G. (1995). Economic Sanctions and the Just-War Doctrine. In Cortright, D. & Lopez, G. (Eds.), *Economic Sanctions: Panacea or Peacebuilding in a Post-Cold War World?* pp. 97-117. Boulder: Westview Press.

3   In addition to article 41, this same distinction between sanctions and the use of military force is found in international law's treatment of countermeasures. See O'Connell, M.E. (2008). *The Power and Purpose of International Law*. Oxford: Oxford University Press, 229-294.

be examined on their own terms, perhaps drawing on some of the just war criteria, but not being limited to this analysis.

In evaluating sanctions, it is important to acknowledge the wide range
of measures used. Many sanctions now being imposed by the UN Security
Council, such as freezing bank accounts and restricting travel of key leaders,
are targeted measures that are far removed from acts of war. The sanctions that
raise issues for just war analysis are those, such as embargoes, that international
law has historically considered "acts of war." Michael Walzer argues that "it is
common sense to recognize that [these measures] are very different from actual
warfare."[4] Sanctions, according to Walzer, constitute "force-short-of-war" and
should be governed by "a theory of just and unjust uses of force .... [which]
shouldn't be an overly tolerant or permissive theory, but it will certainly be more
permissive than the theory of just and unjust war."[5]

Both conservative and liberal critics of sanctions have rightly pointed out
that comprehensive sanctions are like war in that they are enforced by military
means and can directly and indirectly cause serious civilian suffering and even
widespread death. The Iraq embargo, which activists have dubbed an act of
"genocide," is the best recent example.[6] If Walzer's distinction between sanctions as force-short-of-war and sanctions as an act of war is to be valid, three
criteria must be met.

First, sanctions must be intended to and designed to avoid war, not intended
as a prelude to war or a means to multiply the effects of war. Most, perhaps all,
UN sanctions regimes would seem to meet this criterion insofar as they are
authorized as an alternative to military action under Chapter VII. But the best
test of right intention is whether the sanctions regime is tied to an abiding commitment and robust strategy to find a political solution. Determining the intent
of governments is always fraught with difficulty, not least because there are
almost always multiple and sometimes conflicting intentions. The problem is
only multiplied in the case of sanctions, whose effectiveness depends upon collective action. Nevertheless, the difficulty in assessing intent does not diminish
its centrality to the ethical analysis. If, for example, it could be shown that the
intent of the UN embargo against Iraq in 1990 was to weaken the Iraqi regime's
capacity to resist a military intervention and to consolidate international support for war, it could be considered an act of war. If, however, the intent was, as
stated, to reverse the aggression against Kuwait without resort to military intervention, then it could be considered force-short-of-war.

---

4   Walzer, M. (1977). *Just and Unjust Wars: A Moral Argument with Historical
    Illustrations* (4th ed.). New York: Basic Books, xiv.

5   Walzer, M. (1977), xv.

6   For ethical arguments that find sanctions difficult to justify, see McGee, R.W.
    (2003, December). The Ethics of Economic Sanctions. *Economic Affairs*, 23(4),
    41; Gordon, J. (1999, March). A Peaceful, Silent, Deadly Remedy: The Ethics of
    Economic Sanctions. *Ethics & International Affairs*, 13(1), 149.

Second, even when sanctions are intended as alternatives to war, if the direct and indirect harms they cause, especially to the civilian population, are akin to the harms caused by war, Walzer's distinction fails. A morally just sanctions regime can take account of this problem in four ways: (1) assessing the assent of the population; (2) distinguishing between harms to basic rights and lesser harms; (3) giving priority to "smart" or targeted sanctions and, (4) tying sanctions to a political strategy that has reasonable prospects for success.

In war, civilian immunity is based on the fact that civilians pose no military threat. While direct and intentional attacks on civilians are prohibited, indirect and unintentional harm to civilians that are not disproportionate to the legitimate military objective is permitted. James Turner Johnson notes the morally problematic nature of some forms of comprehensive sanctions: they impose the greatest harm on the most vulnerable ("the young, sick, and elderly") and those most removed from responsibility for their government's wrongdoing – the people who are most clearly noncombatants in war.[7] In other words, civilians suffer direct injury while those who are legitimate targets suffer only indirectly.

Two aspects of assent may mitigate this problem. The first, which is not ordinarily a consideration in just war analysis, is the willingness of a population to endure suffering. South Africa is an example of how popular support for sanctions, while notoriously difficult to determine, may help justify the harms imposed on civilians. The second form of assent relates not to the imposition of sanctions but rather to widespread support for the government's unjust or aggressive policies. In cases such as the conflict in Bosnia-Herzegovina in the early 1990s, sanctions against Yugoslavia were more easily justified because of popular support for the government's policies. In cases like Iraq and North Korea, the authoritarian nature of the regimes excludes imputing responsibility to the civilian population, making comprehensive sanctions much more difficult to justify.

Another way to distinguish between sanctions as force-short-of-war and sanctions as acts of war is to distinguish between basic rights and lesser rights. The survival and health of the population may not be put at risk by sanctions, but other aspects of civilian life, such as jobs and access to oil may be degraded, at least temporarily, for the sake of protecting the basic rights of those threatened by the offending regime's policies. Military action or wartime blockades are akin to imposition of the death penalty, whereas sanctions are more like attaching assets. Sanctions might eventually place a population in crisis, but, whereas war's impact is immediate and lethal, the impact of sanctions grows over time, allowing for mitigation of its harms on civilians and more time to pursue a political solution. In cases like Iraq, where a government deliberately denies basic goods to a population in order to undermine sanctions, the sanctioning entity must reshape sanctions to include broad humanitarian provisos.

---

7   Johnson, J.T. (1991, February 6). Just-War Tradition and the War in the Gulf. *The Christian Century*, p. 134.

Given the difficulties associated with assessing popular assent to sanctions, imputing responsibility on the civilian population, and ensuring that sanctions do not cause irreversible harm to basic rights, a third element is necessary for Walzer's distinction to be valid: targeted economic and political sanctions. Just as military force must be directed against military objects, there is a prima facie obligation to target sanctions against responsible political, military and economic actors. Given the inefficacy and negative humanitarian consequences of comprehensive sanctions against Iraq and other countries, targeted sanctions have become the cornerstone of effective UN sanctions regimes in the past decade.[8]

The final element which must be present if sanctions are to be considered force-short-of-war relates to effectiveness. A sanctions regime must be "smart," not only in that it is directed as much as possible at responsible parties, but also in that it is tied to a viable political strategy that has a reasonable chance of avoiding war. This requires, first, an analysis of the political impact of sanctions themselves. If sanctions are having the unintended effects of helping targeted leaders rally their people around the flag, enriching leaders who control black markets, and undermining nascent opposition movements, they become morally problematic. Even if these unintended effects can be avoided, the efficacy of sanctions is tied to intentionality. Since there is not a direct relationship between the imposition of sanctions and changes in military and political behavior, sanctions must be just one part of a robust political and diplomatic strategy to achieve legitimate ends short of war.

As Drew Christiansen and I have argued elsewhere, a just sanctions regime that can be considered "force short of war" would meet several criteria. First, the most comprehensive forms of sanctions need not be imposed only in response to aggression, but there must be a grave injustice; less coercive sanctions would be required to respond to a lower threshold. Second, as with resort to war, sanctions must be imposed by legitimate political authorities; multilateral sanctions are usually preferable to unilateral ones. Third, those who impose sanctions should have a commitment to and reasonable prospects for reaching a political settlement short of war. Fourth, sanctions should be a penultimate resort, imposed when less coercive measures have failed. Fifth, those imposing sanctions must take robust measures to ensure that basic human needs are met. Sixth, the harms likely to be caused by sanctions must be proportionate to the good likely to be achieved.[9]

---

8   Lopez, G. & Stuhldreher, K. (2007). Sanctions as Counter-Genocide Instruments. In Totten, S. (ed.), *The Prevention and Intervention of Genocide* (pp.138). New Brunswick: Transaction Publishers.

9   Christiansen, D., S.J., & Powers, G. (1995). Economic Sanctions and the Just-War Doctrine. In Cortright, D. & Lopez, G. (eds.), *Economic Sanctions: Panacea or Peacebuilding in a Post-Cold War World?* (pp.111-113). Boulder: Westview Press.

Humanitarian intervention: a classic case of just war?

While a very few states and a larger number of international lawyers have advocated a right of humanitarian intervention, the prevailing view is that unilateral humanitarian interventions violate the norm of nonintervention and the prohibition of the use of force in Art. 2(4) of the UN Charter. Interventions for humanitarian reasons may only be authorized by the UN Security Council as part of UN peacekeeping operations or as UN enforcement measures under Chapter VII to restore international peace and security.[10]

In many respects, debates among just war ethicists about humanitarian intervention parallel those among international lawyers and political scientists. How does one weigh seemingly conflicting norms of non-intervention and non-use of force against a responsibility to protect basic human rights and vulnerable populations? Is it possible to define a threshold or just cause for humanitarian intervention that is clear and strict enough that it would not "open the door to new forms of imperialism or endless wars of altruism"?[11] Is humanitarian intervention effective in preventing or stopping genocide or other humanitarian disasters or does it only exacerbate conflicts and contribute to civilian suffering? Is it justifiable to kill and injure some innocent people in order possibly to save others?

But there can be important differences between a just war analysis and international law perspectives. To highlight those differences, I will examine the approach of the Catholic Church, which continues to play an important role in articulating and developing the just war tradition.

A Catholic approach, in my view, begins with a broader understanding as to what is encompassed by the term "humanitarian intervention" than is typically used in international law. Humanitarian intervention is not limited to military interventions to protect human rights but also includes a wide range of diplomatic and juridical measures and coercive measures short of force, such as sanctions. I define humanitarian intervention broadly as (1) a use or threat of non-violent diplomatic or substantial humanitarian activity, economic or political coercion, or various kinds of military deployments, (2) by a state(s), regional body(ies), or international organization(s), (3) in a way that impinges on a state's sovereignty, (4) on behalf of the population within that state, (5) in response to genocide, mass suffering, or widespread human rights abuses (6) caused by internal conflict, a failed state, or systemic injustice.[12]

---

10   See Gray, C. (2004). *International Law and the Use of Force* (2nd ed.). Oxford: Oxford University Press, 31-49.

11   National Conference of Catholic Bishops. (1993). *The Harvest of Justice Is Sown in Peace*. Washington, D.C.: USCCB Publishing Services, 16.

12   This is a slightly modified version of the definition in Christiansen, D., S.J., & Powers, G. (1998). The Duty to Intervene: Ethics and the Varieties of Humanitarian Intervention. In Abrams, E. (ed.), *Close Calls: Intervention, Terrorism, Missile Defense, and "Just War" Today* (p. 185).Washington, D.C.: Ethics and Public Policy Center.

Using a broad definition of humanitarian intervention, the *Compendium of the Social Doctrine of the Church* contends that there is not only a right but a duty of humanitarian intervention:

> *The international community as a whole has the moral obligation to intervene on behalf of those groups whose very survival is threatened or whose basic human rights are seriously violated.* As members of the international community, States cannot remain indifferent; on the contrary, if all other available means should prove ineffective, it is "legitimate and even obligatory to take concrete measures to disarm the aggressor." The principle of national sovereignty cannot be claimed as a motive for preventing an intervention in defence of innocent victims. The measures adopted must be carried out in full respect of international law and the fundamental principle of equality among States.[13]

In *The Harvest of Justice Is Sown in Peace*, the U.S. Catholic Bishops noted that a Catholic perspective on humanitarian intervention is rooted in several concerns. First, is a cosmopolitan understanding of international affairs that is human-centric rather than state-centric. As the bishops say, "[g]eography and political divisions do not alter the fact that we are all one human family, and indifference to the suffering of members of that family is not a moral option." Second, given this vision of a global community, sovereignty and non-intervention "remain crucial to maintaining international peace and the integrity of nations, especially the weaker ones," but they are not absolute norms. They "may be overridden by forceful means in exceptional circumstances, notably in the cases of genocide or when whole populations are threatened by aggression or anarchy." Third, consistent with an increasingly restrictive view of when military force may be justified, the bishops emphasize that "nonmilitary forms of intervention should take priority over those requiring the use of force." Fourth, the bishops acknowledge that "military intervention may sometimes be justified to ensure that starving children can be fed or that whole populations will not be slaughtered. They represent St. Augustine's classic case: love may require force to protect the innocent." They warn, however, that "military force, even when there is a just cause, must remain an exceptional option that conforms strictly to just-war norms," with careful scrutiny given the "particular difficulties involved in meeting criteria of success and proportionality" in humanitarian interventions. Finally, the bishops contend that "a right to intervene must be judged in relation to the broader effort to strengthen international law and the international community." They urge that the right to humanitarian intervention be "more clearly defined in international law" and suggest that "[m]ultilateral interven-

---

13   Pontifical Council for Justice and Peace. (2005). *Compendium of the Social Doctrine of the Church*. Washington, D.C.: USCCB Publishing Services, 220 (italics in original), quoting Pope John Paul II, Message for the 2000 World Day of Peace, 11.

tions, under the auspices of the United Nations, are preferable because they enhance the legitimacy of these actions and can protect against abuse."[14]

This analysis raises several pertinent issues. How does one deal with seemingly conflicting values of sovereignty and defense of basic rights? Is humanitarian intervention justified only when there is a threat to international peace, or is it justified on humanitarian or human rights grounds alone? Is humanitarian intervention more like war or policing, or is a wider framework of moral analysis needed? Must the UN authorize all humanitarian interventions or are unilateral interventions sometimes permissable?

May human rights trump sovereignty?

Catholic social teaching is consistent with international law in insisting that sovereignty and non-intervention "remain crucial to maintaining international peace and the integrity of nations, especially the weaker ones."[15] But, like many other ethical approaches, Catholic social teaching's cosmopolitan ethic does not consider these norms as absolute. Instead, they are instrumental norms that are important in protecting more fundamental values, such as peace, justice among nations, human rights, self-determination, and the national and international common good. While Catholic teaching differs in fundamental ways from liberalism, the notion that sovereignty and non-intervention are instrumental norms resonates with the more interventionist liberals for whom sovereignty is a "contingent" value which is "subsidiary" to human rights insofar as it does "not automatically trump other compelling claims."[16] When governments fail in their responsibility to protect human rights and the common good, they lose their legitimacy and it falls to other public authorities to fill the void.[17]

---

14 National Conference of Catholic Bishops. (1993). *The Harvest of Justice Is Sown in Peace.* Washington, D.C.: USCCB Publishing Services, 16.

15 National Conference of Catholic Bishops. (1993). *The Harvest of Justice Is Sown in Peace.* Washington, D.C.: USCCB Publishing Services, 16.

16 Smith, M.J. (1998, March). Humanitarian Intervention: An Overview of the Ethical Issues. *Ethics & International Affairs*, 12(1), 79.

17 In his address to the United Nations in April 2008, Pope Benedict XVI said: "If States are unable to guarantee such protection [of their own population from grave and sustained violations of human rights], the international community must intervene with the juridical means provided in the United Nations Charter and in other international instruments. The action of the international community and its institutions, provided that it respects the principles underlying international order, should never be interpreted as an unwarranted imposition or a limitation of sovereignty." Pope Benedict XVI. (2008, April 18). Address to the U.N. General Assembly. See also John XXIII. (1963). *Peace on Earth (Pacem in Terris)*, papal encyclical. Washington, D.C.: USCCB Office of Publishing and Promotion Services, paras 61, 132-137; Smith, M.J. (1998, March). Humanitarian Intervention: An Overview of the Ethical Issues. *Ethics & International Affairs*, 12(1), 76.

Christiansen and I have argued elsewhere that the "key question is always whether the intervention is intended and designed to restore the basic human rights and the conditions for community that are the *raison d'etre* of sovereignty and non-intervention."[18] That requires an assessment of the extent to which particular ends and means actually interfere in the internal affairs of a state, and whether that interference is consistent with the underlying humanitarian justification for intervention. Higher levels of force usually involve greater infringements of sovereignty, but not always. The deployment of UN forces to protect aid convoys is arguably less of an infringement of sovereignty than diplomatic pressures to force a tyrant to relinquish power.[19]

Must there be a threat to peace?

Pierre Laberge identifies three ethical positions on humanitarian intervention: 1) an ethics of peace and security, 2) an ethics of the right to a historical community, and 3) an ethics of human rights.[20] UN or UN-sanctioned humanitarian interventions generally fall under the first category. While they often do not have a precise legal rationale, they are usually justified as traditional peacekeeping or Chapter VII enforcement operations in response to (usually ill-defined) threats to or breaches of international peace and security. Even the unilateral "humanitarian" interventions in Bangladesh, Uganda, and Cambodia by India, Tanzania and Vietnam, respectively, were justified, at least implicitly, as necessary to maintain international peace. The common thread is that the primary justification for both UN and unilateral humanitarian interventions has been the need to preserve international peace, not the need to protect basic human rights.

Laberge's second approach is best represented by Walzer's "state moralist" argument for humanitarian intervention. Walzer's principal concern is to protect the right of self-determination of historical political communities. In most cases, according to Walzer, respect for self-determination would preclude humanitarian intervention. But in cases that "shock the moral conscience of

---

18 Christiansen, D., S.J., & Powers, G. (1998). The Duty to Intervene: Ethics and the Varieties of Humanitarian Intervention. In Abrams, E. (ed.), *Close Calls: Intervention, Terrorism, Missile Defense, and "Just War" Today* (p. 197).Washington, D.C.: Ethics and Public Policy Center.

19 Christiansen, D., S.J. & Powers, G. (1998), 196-197. In the *Nicaragua* case, the International Court of Justice determined that "the provision of strictly humanitarian aid to persons or forces in another country, whatever their political affiliations or objectives, cannot be regarded as unlawful intervention, or as in any other way contrary to international law." *Case Concerning Military and Paramilitary Activities in and against Nicaragua.* (1986). ICJ Reports, para. 242.

20 Laberge, P. (1995). Humanitarian Intervention: Three Ethical Positions. *Ethics & International Affairs*, 9, 15-35.

mankind," such as massacres, enslavement, or large-scale expulsions, unilateral humanitarian intervention is morally permissible because such acts destroy any possibility for a community to be self-determining.[21]

While it incorporates elements of the first two, the Catholic perspective on humanitarian intervention is an example of Laberge's third approach – an ethics of human rights. Catholic teaching is certainly concerned about the risks that humanitarian crises pose to international peace and security, as well as the need to ensure that responses to these crises respect international norms on self-determination, non-intervention and the non-use of force. But, as Pope Benedict XVI said in his 2008 address to the UN, "human dignity ... is the foundation and goal of the responsibility to protect."[22]

Likewise, the *Compendium of the Social Doctrine of the Church* is clear that respect for sovereignty does not preclude intervening "in defense of innocent victims." In citing Pope John Paul II's calls for disarming "the aggressor" in internal conflicts, the *Compendium* defines aggression, not just in terms of the rights of nations or self-determining political communities but as a violation of the basic human right to life. This human-centric, rights-based approach to humanitarian intervention requires a retrieval of an earlier understanding of the just war tradition. The tradition developed long before the current nation-state system, so historically it has not been applied only to inter-state wars. That is why the U.S. bishops emphasize that humanitarian intervention represents St. Augustine's classic case for justifying force to protect the innocent.

Robert Johansen contends that a human rights approach is preferable to tying humanitarian intervention to the collective security framework of Chapter VII threats to international peace and security. Failure to distinguish humanitarian intervention from Chapter VII enforcement measures erodes the protections afforded the principle of non-intervention and respect for the domestic jurisdiction of states, and allows self-interested states to justify their intervention based on the pretense that they are protecting international peace. He predicts that small states, the most likely victims of illegitimate intervention, would more likely support humanitarian intervention if it "could be authorized by the UN for genocide but not for vague claims that a threat to the peace exists."[23]

Johansen's human rights argument differs from the *Compendium's* in one critical respect. He does not want to justify humanitarian intervention as defense against aggression. "[F]ailure to distinguish between humanitarian intervention against violations of human rights, which threaten a humane domestic society, and collective security action against aggression, which threatens the interna-

21   Walzer, M. (1977). *Just and Unjust Wars: A Moral Argument with Historical Illustrations* (4th ed.). New York: Basic Books, 101-108.

22   Pope Benedict XVI. (2008, April 18). Address to UN General Assembly.

23   Johansen, R. (1996). Limits and Opportunities in Humanitarian Intervention. In Hoffmann, S. (ed.), *The Ethics and Politics of Humanitarian Intervention* (pp. 66). Notre Dame: University of Notre Dame Press.

tional order, could make reluctance to intervene against violations of human rights appear to be more dangerous, consequential, and likely to threaten international order than is warranted."[24] Defining humanitarian intervention as a justified response to aggression raises the specter of humanitarian war, an oxymoron. But, from a human-centric perspective, restricting defense against aggression to international conflicts is artificially narrow. The internal conflicts which call for humanitarian intervention involve kinds and amounts of military force, threats to civilian populations, and overall destructiveness that warrant the use of the terms "defense" and "aggression" as much as similarly destructive international conflicts do.

Is humanitarian intervention like war or policing?

Johansen's distinction between defense against aggression and humanitarian intervention is related to a distinction that he and some ethicists make between war and policing. Gerald Schlabach argues that the just war tradition has mistakenly assumed that military force is an international equivalent to policing when, in fact, there is a huge difference between the two. "Once wars have been justified [as policing]... very different psycho-social dynamics take over, which move it farther and farther away from policing."[25] His argument about the differences between war and policing can be extended to humanitarian intervention. Humanitarian wars will tend to be untethered from the common good of the country in crisis because, unlike police forces, military intervenors do not share the same commitment to protecting and being held accountable by the people of the other country. Maintaining public support for war usually involves manufacturing "war fever" in ways that policing does not. War is an inherently blunt instrument, which disproportionately harms the civilians humanitarian intervention is intended to protect. In permitting the killing of "enemy" soldiers who might not have any responsibility for the crimes of their leaders, as well as permitting the "collateral" deaths of civilians, war permits the intervenors to be both judge and executioner, something that policing does not. "Good" military strategy usually involves the decisive use of overwhelming force, while "good" policing limits the use of force.[26]

This effort to delineate the differences between war and policing is consistent with the UN's approach to peace operations, which are distinguishable from collective self-defense and collective security. It is also consistent with the diversity of types of humanitarian interventions, whether undertaken by the

24   Johansen, R. (1996), 64.

25   Schlabach, G. (2007). Warfare vs. Policing: In Search of Moral Clarity.
     In Schlabach, G. (ed.), *Just Policing, Not War* (p. 70). Collegeville, MN: Order of St. Benedict.

26   For a complete list of differences between war and policing, see Schlabach, G. (2007), 73-77.

UN and regional bodies or by individual nations. The *justifications* for intervention vary widely from stopping genocide and mass starvation to protecting refugees and promoting democracy. The *causes* of crises range from repression by a totalitarian regime and civil war to a failed state or inter-state conflict. The *objectives* or ends of intervention can be quite limited (e.g., providing humanitarian aid, monitoring abuses) or quite robust (replacing a murderous regime). And the *means* of intervention can range from non-violent (e.g., diplomacy, war crimes trials) to coercive (e.g., arms embargoes, economic sanctions) to various forms of military deployments (e.g., peacekeeping, deterrence, enforcement).[27] The International Criminal Court's indictment against Sudan's president and NATO's massive intervention in Kosovo span the spectrum of humanitarian interventions.[28]

If the focus is on objectives and means, it is easy to see the similarities between humanitarian intervention and policing. For example, ensuring the delivery of aid in Somalia or Sudan by deploying military forces with highly restrictive rules of engagement has more in common with policing than warfare. Using the military, in cooperation with local security forces, to detain war criminals in Bosnia is a police function. Enforcing economic sanctions against Iraq and no-fly-zones in Bosnia and preventive deployments of lightly-armed UN forces in Macedonia to deter an outbreak of violence fall somewhere between policing and war, but, in most cases, are closer to the former. Locating humanitarian interventions along a policing-war continuum is comparable to proposals to use "coercive protection" as a middle way between peacekeeping and military intervention.[29] The problem, according to Alex De Waal, is that "theoretical and practical attempts to create this intermediate space for coercive protection have failed to resolve basic strategic and operational issues."[30] Nevertheless, from a moral point of view, these distinctions are critically important.

While humanitarian interventions that are more akin to policing than war-fighting are far easier to justify morally, in Bosnia, Kosovo, East Timor, Rwanda, and Darfur, the level of military force that may be required to stop "ethnic cleansing" and genocide is more like war than policing. As Walzer notes:

> [H]umanitarian interventions and peace-keeping operations are first of all military acts directed against people who are already using force, breaking the

---

27   See Christiansen, D., S.J., & Powers, G. (1998). The Duty to Intervene: Ethics and the Varieties of Humanitarian Intervention. In Abrams, E. (ed.), *Close Calls: Intervention, Terrorism, Missile Defense, and "Just War" Today* (pp. 185-190). Washington, D.C.: Ethics and Public Policy Center.

28   Christiansen, D., S.J., & Powers, G. (1998), 190.

29   International Commission on Intervention and State Sovereignty. (2001). *The Responsibility to Protect.* Ottawa: International Development Research Centre.

30   De Waal, A. (2007, November). Darfur and the Failure of the Responsibility to Protect. *International Affairs*, 83(6), 1039-1054.

> peace. They will be ineffective unless there is a willingness to accept the risks
> that naturally attach to military acts – to shed blood, to lose soldiers. In much
> of the world, bloodless interventions, peaceful peacekeeping is a contradiction
> in terms: if it were possible, it wouldn't be necessary.[31]

Many UN peace operations have suffered because their mandates, rules of engagement, and force structures were not designed to deal with the magnitude of the military problem – the aggression – that their intervention was meant to stop.

The solution is not to hold to a bright-line distinction between legitimate humanitarian policing and illegitimate humanitarian war. Rather, it is to treat humanitarian intervention as a continuum of means and ends, with a strong preference (and a lower threshold of justification) given those which are more like policing than warfare, but an acknowledgement that, in some cases, war-like defense against (internal) aggression is an appropriate description of what is at stake. A moral analysis must assess humanitarian intervention along a range of very different kinds of action, from non-violent political and juridical interventions, through coercive measures short of force, to various kinds of military deployments, many, but not all of which could be considered policing, not war-fighting. The clear moral preference is for interventions short of war-fighting. The presumption against force which underlies the just war tradition erects a high, though not always insurmountable, barrier to humanitarian interventions akin to war. Such interventions should be strictly limited to cases of genocide, mass starvation, or similar mass suffering where survival of a significant segment of the population is at risk. Even when this high threshold for just cause is met, the moral legitimacy of any particular intervention will depend on whether other just war criteria are met, especially legitimate authority, last resort, probability of success, proportionality and discrimination.[32]

The *jus in bello* norms of discrimination and proportionality raise particularly challenging issues in cases of war-like types of humanitarian interventions. The dilemma is that the means needed to succeed often might seem to undermine the humanitarian ends. If humanitarian intervention is not to be an oxymoron, noncombatant immunity and proportionality must be defined more restrictively (i.e., more like policing) than what might be appropriate in other forms of warfare. The deference to military necessity in humanitarian law, the emphasis in military doctrines on overwhelming force, the primacy of force protection over avoiding harm to civilians (e.g., Libya's "zero casualty" war) are especially difficult to justify in humanitarian interventions. What is needed is a

---

31 Walzer, M. (2004). *Arguing About War*. New Haven: Yale University Press, 72.
32 Christiansen, D., S.J., & Powers, G. (1998). The Duty to Intervene: Ethics and the Varieties of Humanitarian Intervention. In Abrams, E. (ed.), *Close Calls: Intervention, Terrorism, Missile Defense, and "Just War" Today* (pp. 199).Washington, D.C.: Ethics and Public Policy Center.

recovery of the robust duty of care owed civilians which is central to the just war tradition, but which is not fully embodied in contemporary international law or military doctrine and practice. This will require a fundamental rethinking of the widely-held assumption that it is easier to justify asking a soldier to risk his life to protect national security interests than to defend basic human rights.

A related issue – one not addressed in international law or the standard just war analysis – is whether the corollary of a duty to intervene is a duty of intervenors to protect the innocent, which will almost invariably entail undertaking increased risks to themselves? UN humanitarian interventions, NATO's intervention in Kosovo, and other interventions have exhibited a pattern of lack of balance between protecting the intervenors and protecting civilians at risk. The failure to save civilians when an intervenor has the capacity to do so (sins of omission) may be less problematic morally than uses of military force that unnecessarily put civilians at risk (sins of commission), but it is still morally problematic.[33]

Must humanitarian interventions be UN interventions?

In international law, a decisive difference between illegitimate and legitimate humanitarian intervention turns on who intervenes or has authorized intervention. Only a few states and commentators have suggested that unilateral humanitarian intervention is permitted under international law.[34] Catholic social teaching, like many ethical approaches, presumes the need to strengthen the capacity of international institutions to intervene effectively, as envisioned in the UN Charter, and strongly prefers UN Security Council authorization for any interventions. But, in my view, it does not rule out unilateral intervention. This point deserves further elaboration because acknowledging the possibility of unilateral intervention, even as an exceptional case position, is not consistent with most international law perspectives.

In international law, this issue of agency is discussed in terms of who has the legal *right* to intervene. The ethical debate, however, discusses the issue more as the *Compendium* does in terms of who has the *duty* to intervene. This difference has been blurred by an emerging norm in international law, the responsibility to protect, which was adopted at the September 2005 World Summit.[35] The World Summit Outcome Document is clear that the responsibility to protect envisions "collective action... through the Security Council in accordance with the UN

---

33   See Christiansen, D., S.J., & Powers, G. (1998), 204-205.

34   For a detailed analysis that rejects the claim that there is a legal right to unilateral humanitarian intervention, see Chesterman, S. (2001). *Just War or Just Peace? Humanitarian Intervention and International Law*. Oxford: Oxford University Press, 45-87.

35   UN General Assembly. (2005). *World Summit Outcome Document*. (UN doc A/60/2005).

Charter, including Chapter VII."[36] From an ethical perspective, the problem with a *duty* to intervene is that it is an imperfect duty. It is not obvious that the UN or any individual country or groups of countries has an actual duty, in any given case, to intervene. As Terry Nardin points out, the principle of beneficience which undergirds humanitarian intervention is "general": "You shall not stand idly by, whoever you are, if you can provide effective assistance at reasonable cost and without neglecting other duties."[37] Even if justice, not beneficience, is the ultimate grounding for this duty, its imperfect nature remains. Therefore, deciding who has this duty to intervene in Darfur, for example, is a prudential judgment, not a matter of moral principle.

A variety of prudential reasons suggest the UN should be the intervenor of choice. As the bishops recognize, insisting on UN authorization for humanitarian intervention can serve the broader cosmopolitan goal of respecting and strengthening international law and institutions. Requiring UN authorization can also enhance the legitimacy of humanitarian interventions because the collective decision-making process of the UN Security Council, even with its flaws, can help ensure that "humanitarian intervention is an authentic act of international solidarity and not a cloak for great power dominance."[38] UN authorization can also generate broader support for, and therefore enhanced prospects for success of, interventions that are inherently complex and difficult.

According to the bishops and many other just war thinkers, legitimate authority does not, as a matter of moral principle, require UN authorization in every conceivable situation, however. Ought implies can. While the range, scope, sophistication and effectiveness of UN peace operations have risen dramatically in the past two decades, the unwillingness or inability of the UN Security Council and UN Member States to take timely and effective action in Darfur is symptomatic of the difficulties the UN faces in generating the political will and resources needed to respond to grave humanitarian crises in a comprehensive and long-term way.[39] There are "practical reasons" for the UN to authorize interventions, but, as Nardin argues, "to insist on such authorization is to presume a degree of justice and effectiveness at the supranational level that the world has not yet achieved."[40]

---

36   UN General Assembly. (2005). *World Summit Outcome Document*. (UN doc A/60/L.70), para 139.

37   Nardin, T. (2002). The Moral Basis of Humanitarian Intervention. *Ethics & International Affairs*, 16(2), 67.

38   National Conference of Catholic Bishops. (1993). *The Harvest of Justice Is Sown in Peace*. Washington, D.C.: USCCB Publishing Services, 16.

39   For a full discussion of the UN's lack of capacity to implement the new norm of the "responsibility to protect" in Darfur, see De Waal, A. (2007, November). Darfur and the Failure of the Responsibility to Protect. *International Affairs*, 83(6), 1039-1054.

40   Nardin, T. (2002). The Moral Basis of Humanitarian Intervention. *Ethics & International Affairs*, 16(2), 67.

Similarly, Walzer acknowledges the many benefits of international action over unilateral action, but he insists that neither is necessarily more or less free of the taint of politics or impure motives. In fact, he contends that, "[i]n recent years, there have almost certainly been more justified unilateral interventions than unjustified ones."[41] He maintains that "[t]he use of force by the UN would presumably have greater legitimacy than similar uses by single states, but it is not clear that it would be any more just or timely." The problem, in his view, is the "[n]eglect of intervention rather than any excessive resort to it." Neglect, indifference and incapacity to act can be a problem for the UN, just as it is for individual states.[42]

But what of the moral obligation to obey international law and to strengthen international norms and institutions? It is useful to distinguish between legal, political, and moral legitimacy. UN Security Council authorization clearly enhances the legal legitimacy of a humanitarian intervention. UN Security Council authorization can, subject to Walzer's concerns about mixed motives, enhance the political legitimacy of interventions to the extent that it expresses and reflects a consensus among states that humanitarian intervention is justified in a particular case. Moral legitimacy depends, in part, on legal and political legitimacy, but ultimately, it depends upon the extent to which the UN action (or inaction) is consistent with substantive moral norms. Procedural or legal justice does not supplant moral justice. As Tom Farer points out, "[b]ecause international law is both 'thinly institutionalized' and constantly evolving in ways that reflect emerging normative ideas, an appeal to the law itself cannot solve the underlying moral issues raised by humanitarian intervention."[43]

---

41   Walzer, M. (2000). *Just and Unjust Wars* (3rd ed.). New York: Basic Books, xiii.

42   Stanley Hoffmann comes to a similar conclusion. He argues that the old presumption against unilateral intervention ought to stand but would permit "unilateral coercive intervention ... if the UN has been incapable of dealing with such an issue, and whatever regional organization empowered to deal with it has also demonstrated its paralysis and impotence – as in the case of Tanzania's removal of Idi Amin from Uganda, and of Vietnam's intervention against Pol Pot." Hoffmann, S. (1996). Sovereignty and the Ethics of Intervention. In Hoffmann, S. (ed.), *The Ethics and Politics of Humanitarian Intervention* (pp. 22). Notre Dame: University of Notre Dame Press. Paul Ramsey, speaking of interventions more generally and writing in a very different international context of the Cold War, argued that "[t]he right and duty of intervention can be morally and politically withdrawn from nation-states no more rapidly than this same right and duty is perfected in its exercise by world or regional public authorities." Ramsey, P. (1983). *The Just War: Force and Political Responsibility*. Lanham, MD: Rowman & Littlefield, 27.

43   Farer, T.J. (1993). A Paradigm of Legitimate Intervention. In Damrosch, L.F. (ed.), *Enforcing Restraint: Collective Intervention in Internal Conflicts* (pp. 341). New York: Council on Foreign Relations Press, quoted in Smith, M.J. (1998, March). Humanitarian Intervention: An Overview of the Ethical Issues. *Ethics & International Affairs*, 12(1), 66.

Moreover, the UN Security Council is an oligarchical (because of the veto-wielding Permanent Members) and political decision-making body. Secretary General Kofi Annan is not alone in saying that the UN has come into disrepute because of its failure to act effectively in Rwanda and other places, in large part due to the lack of political will of member states. It would be morally perverse to insist that even willing and able nations may not intervene to stop mass killings in the name of respecting procedures of international law that are inherently imperfect. We should not lightly dismiss the moral obligation to obey international law and to do much more to strengthen international law and international institutions. But Nardin is correct in saying that that moral obligation may be overridden if international law is "manifestly unjust or because the relevant governments or international authorities are ineffective."[44] Legal and moral conceptions of justice and legal and moral conceptions of order should, ideally, be congruent. But, given the inherent imperfections of international law and institutions, and, for that matter, any legal system, we should not be surprised when they are not coterminous.

Conclusion

Sanctions and humanitarian intervention represent two cases that fall between war and peace. Sanctions can be considered force short of war and humanitarian intervention can have more in common with policing than warfare. What distinguishes them from war is the extent to which there is a fit between the means, intentions, objectives, and consequences that is truly humanitarian. At the most coercive end of a wide spectrum of evils and responses to those evils, "aggression", "defense" and "war" provide the appropriate lenses through which to view the moral legitimacy of these responses. Whether a conflict is inter-state or intra-state, or whether a response to that conflict is authorized by the UN Security Council are important questions, but ultimately are not decisive in my moral analysis.

   While only some types of sanctions and humanitarian interventions should be considered wars, a just war style of analysis can be helpful in judging coercive measures short of war. Just as the just war tradition has evolved over time to deal with new problems and new political realities, just war analysis must evolve to deal with the new role of UN sanctions and the changing need and potential for effective humanitarian intervention. The just war tradition need not be restricted to classic embargoes, armed conflict between nations or military forms of humanitarian intervention. Its criteria and style of reasoning can help answer some of the same issues that arise in sanctions and policing: What level of injustice or violence warrants what type of sanction or intervention? Who has the right or duty to respond? Is the intention really to avoid war or to

44   Nardin, T. (2002). The Moral Basis of Humanitarian Intervention. *Ethics & International Affairs*, 16(2), 69.

save lives? Is there a fit between the means used and legitimate objectives? Are the means likely to be proportionate and effective? Are appropriate efforts being made to protect civilians?

Apart from the limits or breadth of just war analysis, the categories of sanctions and humanitarian intervention make clear that a much broader ethical analysis is needed. An ethic of humanitarian intervention, in particular, must be married to an ethic of self-determination that can address the conflicting claims of secession that so often lead to humanitarian crises. An ethic of humanitarian intervention also must be married to the development of a *jus post bellum* ethic that can address the range of issues that arise after successful humanitarian interventions, from the role of forgiveness to the moral responsibilities of those charged with rebuilding these societies.

On the other end of the conflict time-line is conflict prevention. Here, international law and practice offer a rich set of instruments and experience on which to build, from early warning and mediation to the use of courts for peaceful resolution of disputes. As lawyers give more attention to the practical meaning of a "responsibility to prevent,"[45] ethicists need to devote more attention to the moral imperatives of conflict prevention and better defining a political ethic that could buttress the kind of institutions and strategies needed to meet that moral imperative.

These various challenges are all part of the ultimate challenge, which is to address in a serious and realistic way the immediate moral conundrums presented by sanctions and humanitarian intervention while, at the same time, maintaining a moral vision of a world in which strengthened international institutions and greater respect for international law dramatically reduce the cases in which these moral conundrums arise.

---

45   Bellamy, A. J. (2008). Conflict Prevention and the Responsibility to Protect. *Global Governance*, 14(2), 135-156.

Chapter 18

Uganda's "War in the North": How Clashing Religious Views Created an Armed Conflict, How Reconciling Them May End It

Todd Whitmore

Most analyses of armed conflict in Christian ethics follow the tripartite rubric of just war, pacifism, and crusade set forth in Roland Bainton's *Christian Attitudes Towards War and Peace*.[1] When the issue is the justifiability of any particular conflict, however, the language is typically that of just war thinking, with its criteria of, for instance, just cause, legitimate authority, proportionality, and non-combatant immunity. These criteria are familiar to legal scholars because, from Hugo Grotius onward, the norms of the just war tradition have been inscribed into international law. The just war tradition also shares with international law the normative presupposition that war is an activity carried out by states or state-like agents for political purposes. The broad aim of both the just war tradition and international laws on war is to set parameters around what those political purposes may be and what means that the actors can use to achieve them. The effort is to keep armed conflict political, in the broad sense, rather than an activity carried out for other – for instance, religious – reasons.

Though the separation of the political from the religious in the conduct between nations received its public imprimatur with the Peace of Westphalia (1648), the development of theology itself prepared for this moment by shifting the basis of thought on armed conflict from the virtue of charity (Augustine, Fourth Century) to the dictates of natural law (Vitoria, Fifteenth Century), with Thomas Aquinas' treatment of the topic (Thirteenth Century) as an intermediate point melding the two. Natural law thinking at the time of Vitoria and, arguably, Grotius, was indeed theologically grounded. Human law was to be based on the natural law, which in turn was a reflection of the eternal law of God. However, the split-level format of much of natural law thought allowed for ready separation of the natural law from the eternal law in later legal thought.

There is a danger, however, in this analytical separation. International actors – states and otherwise – often continue to act out of religious motivation, even where this is not explicitly articulated in the form of a well worked-

---

1   Bainton, R. (1960). *Christian Attitudes Towards War and Peace*. New York: Abingdon.

Mary Ellen O'Connell (ed.), What Is War? An Investigation in the Wake of 9/11.
© *2012 Koninklijke Brill NV. Printed in The Netherlands.* ISBN *978 9004 17234 0. pp. 235–247.*

out theology. An understandable *normative* distinction between the political and legal on the one hand and the religious and theological on the other can, if one is not careful, lead to mistakes in *empirical* analysis of what is going on in a particular conflict. The temptation then is to read the political as rational and to interpret whatever one does not understand – whatever does not fit into the Westphalian paradigm – as irrational, and even mad.

A good case in point is what in Uganda is often called "the War in the North." When current president Yoweri Museveni took power in 1986 after a five-year bush war, his National Resistance Army chased the remnants of the previous army, made up primarily of people from the northern part of the country, back home, killing, raping, and pillaging on the way. The northern-ers fought back under the leadership of spirit mediums – first Alice "Lakwena" Auma, then Joseph Kony – in a conflict that continued as of time of writing in mid-2009, and has been marked by massive abductions, mutilations, and kill-ings of the civilian populace.

The conflict has been interpreted primarily through Western news reports and media – for instance, the film *Invisible Children* has brought the situation to the attention of many Americans – and the Ugandan government itself. The government's account stresses Kony's syncretistic and often strange religious practices and claims – for instance, the smearing of shea butter on the fighters to protect them from bullets and the oft-cited statement that his aim is to rule Uganda in accordance with the Ten Commandments. Kony's motivation is reli-gious, the argument goes, and therefore cannot be political. An effect of this argument is to downplay the human rights violations of the Museveni regime. What is going on, in this view, is a legitimate war of the Ugandan government against the rationally incomprehensible and clinically mad Kony-led Lord's Resistance Army (LRA), and, aside from the killings directly carried out by the LRA, the loss of civilian Acholi life is an unfortunate, but collateral matter. The reality, however, is much more complex, with both sides drawing upon reli-giously-linked ideas to articulate their positions. The LRA has used such ideas in different ways at different stages of the conflict. I understand the conflict to have had so far four stages: political grievance, apocalyptic politics, attempted secularization, and warlordism. In what follows, I will elucidate these stages in order to highlight the complexity on the ground of the relationships between theology, ethics, and armed conflict.

1.   Stage One: Political Grievance: 1988-1994

Museveni and the National Resistance Army/Movement (NRA/M) began their insurgency in 1981 on the grounds that then president Milton Obote rigged the 1980 elections that brought him to power. The fiercest fighting was in an area called the "Luwero Triangle," north of the capitol, Kampala. All parties took part in brutal atrocities against civilians. Over 300,000 people in the region lost their lives. Acholi soldiers made up most of Milton Obote's army and, according to many accounts, committed most of the atrocities. When Museveni took power in 1986 – after overthrowing an Acholi, Tito Okello, with whom he had ostensibly agreed to share power – he directed his troops to follow Okello's retreating forces. Rape and summary executions by the NRA/M were common, and even the norm.[2] Museveni's forces also looted extensively. By 2002, the Acholi had lost over ninety percent of their cattle,[3] and were forced to carry out their agriculture largely through use of hoes made of bent sticks. Many Acholi interpret this initial surge of the NRA/M into Acholiland as an act of revenge on the part of Museveni for Acholi atrocities in Luwero, and the President's own rhetoric has reinforced this interpretation. These are the conditions – stunning defeat and loss of livelihood – that faced the Acholi in 1986. Many Acholi then joined Alice "Lakwena" Auma's Holy Spirit Movement (HSM) because it offered the only politically viable option for resistance.[4] In 1987, she and her troops reached to within sixty miles of the capitol. At this point, the Acholi resistance fits the international law paradigm and achieved what could recognizably be called "belligerent rights."[5]

The NRA/M defeated the HSM in November 1987, and Alice Lakwena went into exile. The Acholi political resistance was without a leader. Joseph Kony then became the figure through whom many Acholi manifested their grievances. As with the Holy Spirit Movement, many Acholi at least initially joined what was to become the Lord's Resistance Army (LRA) more out of the sense that it was the only viable avenue of active resistance to the Museveni regime than as a result of any commitment to the worldview Kony espoused, and elders encouraged youth to join. Still, the fact that these two – Lakwena and Kony – were the only figures around whom the Acholi could rally was already evidence that the Acholi world was under extreme stress.

2.   Stage Two: Apocalyptic Politics: 1994-2005

By the early 1990's, the LRA managed to control much of the rural area of Acholiland. The NRM and its reconstituted army, the United People Defense Forces (UPDF) seemingly did not have the will to engage in conflict in a region in which they had little stake. At the time, Uganda, despite the lack of develop-

---

2   See, for instance, Amnesty International. (1992). *Uganda: The Failure to Safeguard Human Rights*. London: Amnesty International.

3   There is debate over just how many cattle were looted by the NRM and how many were taken by the Karamajong people of northeastern Uganda who were taking advantage of the disarray of the Acholi. See Finnstrom, S, (2008). *Living with Bad Surroundings: War, History, and Everyday Moments in Northern Uganda*. Durham, NC and London: Duke University Press.

4   Finnstrom. (2008), 107.

5   On belligerent rights, see Walzer, M. (1976). *Just and Unjust Wars: A Moral Argument with Historical Illustrations*. New York: Basic Books, 86-109.

ment in the north, was reporting over seven percent annual economic growth. The years 1992-1993 brought a relative lull in the hostilities, and it looked as though the LRA and NRM were approaching a negotiated settlement in 1994. However, there seemed to be little trust between the two parties, and when the LRA asked for three more months to consider the final proposal, Museveni gave them one week. The talks broke off and a new stage of the conflict began.

Although Kony carried out abductions of Acholi as early as 1989, the extent of killing and abduction of Acholi on the part of the LRA grew significantly after the failed peace talks.[6] Kony believed – and he was largely correct – that the local populace no longer actively supported his efforts. They did not see the original political objectives as any longer achievable through force. Kony charged the elders with abandoning him, and in 1996, when two elders came to negotiate with the LRA, he had them killed. On April 22, 1995, the LRA massacred over 300 people in Atiak; in January 1997, they killed over 400 in Palabek and Lokung.

It is easy to see from the above why many observers quickly conclude Kony and the LRA as being simply mad and therefore without any discernable political agenda. However, from the beginning of the conflict, the Acholi distinguished but also related the theological and political aspects of their aims. In the early phases, they distinguished between the *mony me ngom* – the "army of earth" led by regrouping members of the defeated forces, renamed the Ugandan Peoples Democratic Army (UPDA) – and the *mony me polo* – the "army of heaven" led by the spirit medium Alice "Lakwena" Auma. Distinction does not mean separation, however, and while the two "armies" at first employed different methods, they shared the goal of, among other things, the overthrow of the Museveni government. Soon, they fused earthly and heavenly modalities and moved towards the capitol, Kampala, and Lakwena led the UPDA on a military campaign that nearly reached Kampala in 1987.

When Museveni's forces defeated Lakwena, remnants of her forces gathered around Kony, and formed what soon became the LRA. However, further defeat turned the LRA simultaneously further outward and in on the Acholi people. In a worldview that integrates the theological and the political, setback in the political/military arena can lead to a changed relationship between that and the theological. The relationship can become apocalyptic. That is, the view develops that only a radical intervention, either by God alone or by God's selected agents, can reorder earthly affairs. It is important to note, however, that the new view is not apolitical for being more overtly religious. On the contrary, the political and military metaphors continue and become more charged. The emphasis is on the *army* of God, or in traditional Christian language, the

---

6   Human Rights Watch estimates that the LRA abducted 8,000 youths between 1994 and 1997. Cited in Doom, R. & Vlassenroot, K. (1999). Kony's Message: A New Koine? The Lord's Resistance Army in Northern Uganda. *African Affairs*, 98: 390.

kingdom of God. The difference is that this kingdom, and the army that brings it about, must constitute a radical break from the present situation. They are fighting for a *new* order. The aim of the LRA became that of "purifying" the Acholi such that the latter would be made worthy of rulership, and it is this that motivated the killings and mutilations of Acholi civilians at this point in time. Adam Branch has argued, rightly, that the aim of the LRA attacks on civilians of its own ethnic group was, "an attempt to eradicate the external enemy from the inside of Acholi society."[7] The new political order does not need to march to Kampala and overthrow the NRM, at least not any time in the near future. Indeed, at this stage, virtually none of the LRA attacks are on the UPDF. Given the reluctance of the NRM either to defeat the LRA outright or enter into significant negotiations with them until recently, it seemed that the LRA, *in their reconfigured terms*, at the time had a very "reasonable chance of success." This understanding of political rationality may not fit the Westphalian model, but it is no less political for not doing so.[8]

A number of clarifying points are necessary at this point of the argument in order not to lead to a misunderstanding regarding religion and theology. First, far from all apocalyptic religions are violent. Indeed, before it joined with the UPDA, Alice Lakwena's Holy Spirit Movement was not only avowedly non-violent, it also practiced gender equality. Second, apocalyptic theologies are not the only theologies that can be drawn upon to support violence. Violence is taken up even by those who do not seek a radical break from the status quo; Yoweri Museveni may himself demonstrate such a case.

---

7   Branch, A. (2007). The Political Dilemmas of Global Justice: Anti-Civilian Violence and the Violence of Humanitarianism, the Case of Northern Uganda. (Doctoral dissertation, Columbia University, 2007), 22.

8   It is important to add here that the Acholi resistance to Museveni fragments at this point in the conflict. As indicated above, most civilians on the ground in northern Uganda lost any confidence in the military defeat of Museveni, and so, while sympathetic to the early aims of the LRA, no longer supported its tactics. However, many Acholi expatriates with the affluence to leave for England, Canada, and the United States at the start of Museveni's regime and the luxury to observe the conflict from a safe remove, continued to espouse the by now defunct rhetoric of military defeat of Museveni. Their grievance against the President ran so deep that they were willing to overlook or at least minimize the atrocities committed by the LRA lest the case against Museveni appear weakened. Sverker Finnstrom quotes an Acholi who remained behind, "They lit the candle and then left for London. Now we are left here and the bush is on fire." (Finnstrom. (2008). *Living with Bad Surroundings*, 22; cf also ch. 2). In the meantime, the government of Sudan began providing the LRA with material support and back bases in its country, so that the primary international alliance for the LRA shifted away from the Acholi diaspora. At this point, then, we have the LRA, under the stress of political defeat, turning to apocalyptic politics and supported by Sudan, the expatriates, unable or unwilling to face the realities on the ground, still stuck in the first stage of the conflict, and the Acholi civilians on the ground without either military or international political representation.

While there has been much written about the religious dimension of the LRA, there has been next to nothing about the theology resting behind Museveni's actions. Michael Twaddle refers to the Museveni's ruling style as constituting a "secularized puritanism," and Ronald Kassimir follows this up by suggesting that this style is rooted in the Anglican faith of the president's mother.[9] In both instances, the ultimate root appears to be in colonial Britain, and this is a good starting point of analysis. Of note here is that, unlike with the LRA, the theological dimensions of Museveni's thought remain constant throughout the conflict.

In *"Exterminate All the Brutes,"* Sven Lindqvist follows Hannah Arendt to make the argument that genocide on the part of fascist and totalitarian regimes in the mid-twentieth century, including the Nazi genocide of the Jews, are not unique circumstances, but rather constitute the continuation of a colonial mind-set that developed most vigorously in the exploration and subsequent occupation of sub-Saharan Africa in the late nineteenth and early twentieth-century. The book is an extended reflection on its title, which comes from the last sentence of Joseph Conrad's *Heart of Darkness.* Lindqvist states his conclusion early: "The core of European thought? Yes, there is one sentence ["Exterminate all the brutes"], a short simple sentence, only a few words, summing up the history of our continent...It says nothing about Europe as the original home on earth of humanism, democracy, and welfare. It says nothing about everything we are quite rightly proud of. It simply tells the truth we prefer to forget."[10]

Lindqvist makes clear that the colonial justification for the right to mass killing is grounded in what anthropologists call a unilinear view of social evolution. The colonial powers mapped the differences between sub-Saharan cultures and their own onto a cosmological viewpoint that had humanity evolving through pre-specified stages. Given the assumption that European culture was at the most advanced stage, the colonizers identified the cultures of Africa as belonging to earlier stages. This evolutionary scheme is what gives rise to the distinctions between civilized and barbaric, modern and primitive. Of importance here is that although the colonizers often turned to rougher, more blatant terms – "brutes," "animals," "insects," and the like – to refer to Africans, such appeals are not necessary to instigate the act of genocide. Neo-colonialism continues this trend in the post-independence era through structures that perpetuate African economic dependence on the developed world.

The theology resting behind and reinforcing the unilinear evolutionism of the colonial mindset is a heretical one: Manicheanism. The Persian prophet

---

9   Twaddle, M. (1988). Museveni's Uganda: Notes Toward an Analysis. In H. B. Hanson & M. Twaddle (Eds.), *Uganda Now: between Decay and Development* (pp. 328). London: James Currey.

10   Lindqvist, S. (1996). *Exterminate All the Brutes: One Man's Odyssey into the Heart of Darkness and the Origins of European Genocide.* (J. Tate, Trans.). New York, London: The New Press. (Original work published 1992), ix-x and 3.

Mani (AD 210-276) held, *contra* orthodox Christianity, that there was not one God, but rather that the cosmos was constructed of counterposed forces of light and darkness. The task of the adherent was to take on the quality of light and so enter into battle with darkness. St. Augustine famously first embraced and then condemned Manicheanism as a heresy. Colonialism, in contrast, whatever the claims of its practitioners to be Christian, superimposed a Manichean worldview onto society, supplementing the terms light versus dark – fortuitously allied with skin color – with those of "civilized" verses "primitive" and "modern" versus "backward." The theory of social evolution provided a crude chronological schema to reinforce the social Manichean distinctions between civilized and primitive. Colonial powers enforced this worldview through various mechanisms of regimentation of the indigenous peoples, from displacement and taxation to forced labor and genocide. The theology and worldview of Manicheanism is present in Museveni's rule today, as can be seen by tracing Manicheanism through the period of colonialism.

Prior to the arrival of the British, the people in northern Uganda who came to be known as the Acholi were loosely federated and decentralized.[11] In 1894, the British declared Uganda a protectorate. The status of Uganda as a protectorate and not a colony is critical because in the former the British dominated through "indirect" rule, that is, by designating one indigenous group to rule over the rest on behalf of the empire. Indirect rule, coupled with the British quest for bureaucratic order, hardened and reified ethnic differences by setting African over African. The British made the Buganda in the South, who already had a centralized political system that more closely resembled that of the colonizers, the administrators of the protectorate.[12]

Over one hundred ten years later, a form of indirect rule continues. President Museveni's government receives over half of its budget from foreign aid in a way that reinforces his twenty-three year presidency and lack of democratic accountability. There is little argument that Museveni is using the aid money for his own end of maintaining power. Foreign aid decreases the accountability he has to those within his own country and supports his patronage network within it. For instance one study has shown that only thirteen percent of Uganda's education budget reaches the schools. The rest is "captured by local officials and politicians."[13] The money that goes to the politicians leverages and solidifies their allegiance to Museveni.

---

11   See Atkinson, R. (1994). *The Roots of Ethnicity: The Origins of the Acholi of Uganda Before 1800*. Philadelphia: University of Pennsylvania Press.

12   On indirect rule, see Mamdani, M. (1996). *Citizen and Subject: Contemporary Africa and the Legacy of Late Colonialism*. Princeton, NJ: Princeton University Press.

13   Reinikka, R. & Svensson, J. (2004). Local Capture: Evidence from a Central Government Transfer Program in Uganda. *Quarterly Journal of Economics*, 119 (2), 679-705.

Museveni's tactics exemplify not simply a generic grab for power, but rather a form of indirect rule. This is evident not only in the amount of aid his government receives, but also in the lack of robust donor responses to his abuses. When Museveni's failure to end the conflict in the North combined with his alteration of the Ugandan constitution to allow him to run for a third term as President in a campaign in which he jailed his main opponent on trumped up charges of rape and treason, several countries temporarily withheld – but did not withdraw – portions of their donations. The United States government did not even temporarily withhold its aid donation. Rather, it increased it so as to give the impression of being in control. The U.S. has appeared more concerned about Uganda as a post-9/11 East African ally than about human rights.

The Manicheanism that undergirds indirect rule also comes through in Museveni's own discourse. As early as 1987, in reference to the fight with the Holy Spirit Movement – the Acholi precursor to Kony's LRA – Museveni claimed, "This is a conflict between modernity and primitivity."[14] As late as 2006, at the installation of Sabino Odoki as Auxiliary Bishop of Gulu, and just a month before the ceasefire with the LRA, Museveni declared, "We shall transform the people in the north from material and spiritual backwardness to modernity."[15] Thus from the beginning of the conflict up to the present, Museveni has drawn upon the colonial/neo-colonial lexicon to frame the situation. Moreover, his indebtedness to colonialism goes beyond the terms to their ideological substratum, unilinear social evolutionism. He makes clear in his autobiography that "the laws of social evolution" drive his policies.[16]

Museveni's actions have been consistent with his ideology. A 2005 Human Rights Watch report found rape and arbitrary arrest and detention on the part of the UPDF to be common. In some cases there was willful killing of civilians. The most egregious outfit was the 11th Battalion, which beat and tortured people in the Cwero and Awach IDP camps, "almost every day for the first two months of 2005."[17] According to the report, the UPDF forces have been able to carry out these actions with near impunity.

Not only did the government fail to provide sufficient counterforce to protect the Acholi from the LRA, but beginning in 1996 it also forcefully displaced them into so-called "protected" camps that actually served as magnets for LRA attack. Moreover, a 2005 World Health Organization study, after careful analysis of the situation on the ground in comparison with "non-crisis" levels in the camps in the Acholi districts of Kitgum, Pader, and Gulu,, found that there were almost 1000 excess deaths per week due to malaria, AIDS, malnutrition,

---

14   "Museveni directs final Lakwena offensive," *New Vision* (November 6, 1987).

15   *New Vision* (July 23, 2006).

16   Museveni, Y. (1997). *Sowing the Mustard Seed: The Struggle for Freedom and Democracy in Uganda*. London: Macmillan, 26.

17   Human Rights Watch. (2005). *Uprooted and Forgotten: Impunity and Human Rights Abuses in Northern Uganda*, 17,12(A), p. 26.

diarrhea, violence, and other causes. About ninety percent of the people in these districts lived in camps at the time of the report.[18] Olara Otunnu has argued that such acts on the part of the government and its forces constitute genocide.[19] There is not space to take up his argument here, but from the above it is evident that what has taken place is at minimum a willful negligence that, in my judgment, is due to the fact that in Museveni's view the Acholi are "primitive," that is, not quite fully human beings, and therefore not deserving of the government's protection.

3.   Stage Three: The Attempt to Secularize the Conflict: 2005-2008

In August 2006, after a month and a half of talks the LRA and the NRM both signed on to a Cessation of Hostilities Agreement – the first bilateral accord ever between the two parties – and over the next twenty months, representatives of each side met to work out an agenda for peace and reconstruction in northern Uganda. By early 2008, the parties had signed all five major agenda items: 1) the cessation of hostilities, 2) comprehensive solutions to the war, 3) reconciliation and accountability, 4) formal ceasefire, and 5) disarmament, demobilization, and reintegration. The impact on the ground in northern Uganda was remarkable. Abductions and killings by the LRA in Uganda became virtually non-existent. At present, about thirty percent of camp residents have returned to their original villages, while another forty percent are in intermediate "satellite" camps where the conditions are not quite as cramped and squalid.

The question thus arises as to what allowed these things to take place. In my judgment, a cluster of three events in 2005 reoriented the conflict in northern Uganda towards "earthly" perspectives on the part of both the LRA and the NRM. The first is the Comprehensive Peace Agreement (CPA) between the Sudan People's Liberation Army/Movement (SPLA/M) and the Sudan government in January. The agreement is critical because, in an exemplification of the intertwined nature of regional war in sub-Saharan Africa, the government of Sudan was supporting the LRA as a proxy army against the SPLA/M, while the government of Uganda was supporting the SPLA/M against the Khartoum government. Once the CPA was in place, the Khartoum government had no further use for the LRA, and the latter no longer had a safe haven in Sudan from which it could launch its forays into Uganda. The second event occurred in July 2005, when the International Criminal Court handed down indictments

---

18   Ministry of Health. (2005). *Health and Mortality Survey Among Internally Displaced Persons in Gulu, Kitgu, and Pader Districts, Northern Uganda.* The Republic of Uganda, ii.

19   Ottunu, O. (2006). Saving Our Children from the Scourge of War. *Speech delivered on the occasion of the 2006 Sydney Peace Prize, Part 1 and Part 2*, Retrieved from http://www.essex.ac.uk/armedcon/story_id/000290.html.

of the LRA's top five leaders. The indictments were at first sealed, but news of them leaked in October. Kony has feared prosecution at The Hague ever since, and the indictments served, at least at first, as an inducement for him to negotiate.

There is debate as to which of these two events – the CPA or the ICC indictments – was the most important,[20] but it is clear that Kony at this point was trying to change his image into that of a political leader as this is normally understood. He cut the dreadlocks and took off the sunglasses for which he was famous and donned a collared button-down shirt, tie, and jacket for news photos. Verbal changes coincided with the new sartorial trend. In a May 25, 2006 meeting with Riek Machar, the Vice President of South Sudan, Kony insisted that, in keeping with international law, he was fighting with both just cause and right intention, and that his recourse to arms was only as a last resort:

> I want peace, that is why I was in the bush… I am fighting for peace…we want to talk to Museveni but only that Museveni did not want to talk to us…I am not a terrorist, I am also a rebel in military opposition like SPLA…Because we are human beings also we know law… We are fighting for are people to be free. We are fighting for the right cause.[21]

In the debate over the relative impact of the CPA and ICC indictments in bringing the LRA to the bargaining table, most commentators overlook the question of what brought Museveni and the NRM there. There is general consensus that Museveni's ultimatum in 1994 that the LRA agree to his terms in one week was an indication of his lack of seriousness about peace talks. Jan Egeland, the international figure who has brought the most attention to the conflict, quotes an exchange he had with Museveni in November 2006. A ceasefire had been holding for about three months. Egeland had just met with the LRA leaders, and was explaining, "It was good for peace and therefore to your benefit." Museveni replied, "No, those talk were not to our benefit. Let me be categorical – there will only be a military solution to this problem."[22]

Given Museveni's general disinclination to negotiate, an account of his situation in 2006 helps explain why he did so beginning in 2006. I suggest that the threat of donor withdrawal after his breach of democratic protocols in 2001 and 2006 forced his hand. Museveni knew that his standing as a beacon of African

20   On the role of Sudan in the conflict, see forthcoming Atkinson, R. R. (2009). 'The Realists in Juba'?: An Analysis of the Juba Peace Talks. In T. Allen & K. Vlassenroot (Eds.), *Understanding the LRA*. Oxford: James Currey.

21   Nyakairu, F. (2006, May 25). I am not a terrorist, I am a freedom fighter, says Kony. *The Daily Monitor*. Retrieved from http://www.kas.de/proj/home/pub/84/1/year-2008/dokument_id-8502/index.html.

22   Egeland, J. (2008). *A Billion Lives: An Eyewitness Report from the Frontlines of Humanity*. New York/London/Toronto/Sydney: Simon and Schuster, 211.

leadership had suffered. A leaked World Bank report put it most directly: "The Government has largely failed to integrate the country's diverse peoples into a single political process that is viable over the long term."[23] The balancing act between maintaining the appearance of democratic processes and running a neo-colonial regime was off-kilter, and needed to be fixed. One ready solution was to follow up on South Sudan's offer to enter into negotiations with the LRA. This could help Museveni regain his previous luster without any cost to him. As indicated above, he thought from the beginning that the process would go nowhere, and in the meantime it would deflect international attention from the anti-democratic trends in the Ugandan government.

There were no heroes, then, in the return to "earthly" politics, but rather, just as the Westphalian model would have it, a working out of self-interest between contending groups. Moreover, though the ICC warrants were one of the factors initially bringing the LRA to negotiations, they were also a key factor in Kony ultimately pulling out. The continuing threat of prosecution kept Kony in the bush. In the meantime, the LRA stepped up abductions in DRC, South Sudan, and the Central African Republic.[24]

Interestingly, during this period where both sides were trying to appear more reasonable in secular terms, civil society organizations and a range of religious communities called for a rejuvenation of the traditional Acholi reconciliation ritual of *mato oput* as the most promising means of ending the conflict and returning to normalcy. The ritual has the accused person and the offended person (or a representative of the offended) jointly drink a liquified bitter herb (*mato oput* "to drink bitterness") out of a single bowl to signify their "swallowing" of the bitterness in their hearts. One of the strongest advocates of *mato oput* was and continues to be the Acholi Religious Leaders Peace Initiative, a consortium of Catholic, Anglican, Orthodox, and Muslim religious leaders. The great social stress resulted in neither fracture nor apocalypticism, but a grounded ecumenism such as the region has never seen before.[25] Part of the argument for *mato oput* is that the punitive approach of international law as exhibited by the ICC is not representative of the more restorative approach to justice in the Acholi tradition.

23   Busharizi, P. (2005, May 17). World Bank May Cut Aid. *New Vision*.

24   Prendergast, J. & Spiegal, J. (2008). *A New Peace Strategy for Northern Uganda and the LRA*. Retrieved from http://www.enoughproject.org/reports/uganda_lra.

25   On the efforts to restore *mato oput*, see Baines, E. (2005). *Roco Wat I Acholi: Restoring Relationship in Achloi-land: Traditional Approaches to Justice and Reintegration*. Vancouver: Liu Institute for Global Issues, Gulu Districe NGO Forum, and Ker Kwaro Acholi.

4.   Stage Four: New Warlordism and Continued
Neo-Colonialism: 2008-Present

In April and again in November 2008, Kony failed to show up at arranged
meetings where he was to sign the final peace agreement. The government of
Uganda responded with airstrikes against the LRA's primary back base in the
Democratic Republic of the Congo (DRC) in December of that year. The LRA,
in turn, went on a rampage, slaughtering an estimated 900 civilians in the DRC
and South Sudan over the next month. Even though the marauding did not
reach Uganda, camp residents ceased moving to their home villages, and some
who had gone home returned back to the camps.

From the standpoint of our analysis, the ways in which the attacks were
carried out are noteworthy. Three characteristics stand out as at odds with
previous LRA modes of engagement. They attacked on Christmas day, they
attacked churches while people were inside worshipping, and they carried out a
campaign of rape.[26] The LRA has changed. In my understanding, the period of
attempted secularization coupled with the extended time away from the Acholi
context that gave it its initial rationale has turned the LRA into a secular warlord band. The LRA is still abducting, but now in the DRC and South Sudan,
and the rationale is no longer to "purify" the Acholi. Therefore the LRA is
now a specific instantiation, with one important irregularity, of the transition
from traditional peasant-supported insurgency (here against Museveni) to "professional" soldiering under an economically-driven warlord in a resource war.[27]
The irregularity is this: unlike Liberia or the Democratic Republic of Congo,
for instance, Uganda is not rich in natural resources to be plundered. In order
to keep itself going, therefore, the LRA turned to absconding with the only
resource available – people – in order to sustain itself. Important here is the fact
that abduction and mutilation are not practices specific to the LRA, but were
also carried out, for instance, by Charles Taylor's forces, which did not have any
pretensions of religiosity.

In the meantime, consistent with the neo-colonial paradigm, Museveni has
moved to "modernize" northern Uganda by attempting to make land available
to outside sources, including members of his own clan and foreign investors. In
2007, his administration ordered that 40,000 hectares of land in the Acholi district of Amuru be given to a foreign investment group to develop a sugar cane

---

26   I am indebted to Ronald Atkinson for pointing these factors out to me. They are
     detailed in an afterward of a forthcoming new edition of his book, *The Roots of
     Ethnicity*.

27   On the shift from peasant to resource wars in Africa, see Buijtenhuijs, R. (2000).
     Peasant Wars in Africa: Gone with the Wind?. In D. Bryceson, C. Kay, & J. Mooij
     (Eds.), *Disappearing Peasantries?: Rural labor in Africa, Asia, and Latin America* (pp.
     112-121). Bourton-on-Dunsmore, Warwickshire, UK: ITDK Publishing.

plantation.²⁸ The political battle over that land continues. Moreover, Museveni's brother and aspirant successor, Salim Saleh, formed a company called Divinity Union Ltd. as early as 1999, that proposed, in its own words a "project intervention" to "make use" of traditional "communally owned lands" to form "Security and Production Units" – in other words, guarded farms – all overseen by central government agencies, including the Ministry of Defense.²⁹ These are but two key instances of a general pattern where Museveni has used the modern/primitive lexicon to leverage his own acquisitiveness.³⁰ Again noteworthy is the fact that donor nations, through the indirect rule paradigm, countenance Museveni acting in such ways: he is the contemporary version of what the Acholi call the outsider-installed and supported *rwot kalam* ("chief by the pen") who has virtual plenitude of power within the boundaries of his own country.

Conclusion: Lessons for International Law

The Westphalian settlement of 1648 established sovereign states through the mechanism of international law. The religious controversies that had fueled wars prior to Westphalia were resolved by linking the ruler's religion to his territory. That solution has done much to effectively bracket out religious considerations in the conduct and evaluation of armed conflict. It is debatable, however, as to whether it has actually reduced the incidence and severity of armed conflict. Secular functional equivalents have sprung up in the absence of religiously explicit transcendent rationales for engaging in armed conflict: witness the George W. Bush administration's initial terming of the most recent engagement with Iraq, Operation Ultimate Justice. Moreover, bracketing out religion in our analysis of armed conflict can lead to misdiagnoses of what is actually going on. In the case of Uganda's "War in the North," the Westphalian paradigm oversimplifies the motivations of the Lord's Resistance Army while leaving out of consideration altogether the theology resting behind Museveni's neo-colonialism as well as ecumenical efforts at peacebuilding that emphasize reconciliation rituals grounded in traditional Acholi culture. Aside from the criticism that the actions of the International Criminal Court are too little and too late, it is also widely argued, and I agree, that they overlook key local mechanisms for conflict resolution, mechanisms that do not fit readily into any paradigm that brackets out religion.

---

28   "Madhvani to set up second sugar plantation," *New Vision* (January 1, 2007).

29   Divinity Union, *Security and Production Program* (pamphlet). I am indebted to Ronald Atkinson for point out this and the previous source to me. See Atkinson, R. (2008). Land Issues in Acholi in the Transition from War to Peace. *The Examiner*. 4, 4-7.

30   Acholi MPs and various civil society groups did manage to resist both of these efforts by Museveni.

E. Peace Research

Chapter 19

The Meaning of War

John Darby

I am grateful for the involvement of non-lawyers in this search by the ILA committee for a more cross-disciplinary approach to the problems posed by war. If the impasse over the Ugandan peace talks between the government and the International Criminal Court in 2007-2008 illustrate anything, it is the need for a more holistic approach to these common problems, and to examine more closely the research interfaces and opportunities between our disciplines. I welcome this initiative.

I come from Northern Ireland. My first research work was an attempt to understand what was happening in my own place. Three years ago I was somewhat taken aback when I came across a list of states with the longest-lasting civil wars since the second World War, compiled by James Fearon and David Laitin.[1] Northern Ireland was placed fifth, lasting 31 years, after Burma, Colombia, Chad and the Philippines, all of which are ongoing. I lived in Northern Ireland during these years. If you have to have a civil war, I suppose it's flattering to find that you are up there with the leaders. The problem is that it does not conform to my understanding of civil wars. It seems almost fraudulent for Northern Ireland to be classified among such bloodbaths as those in England in the 17th century, the United States in the 19th and Russia in the 20th.

To add further confusion, civil wars were defined by the authors as "conflicts in which rebel groups are trying to take control of a central government or trying to secede or gain greater regional autonomy". By that soft measure – that is, including groups seeking to gain greater regional autonomy – it is easier to find countries experiencing civil wars than those not.

Internal conflicts: Changing patterns

In this chapter I want to focus on how attitudes to war and violence within my field of study – what used to be called internal conflict – have changed. Let

---

1   James D. Fearon and David Laitin, *Ethnicity, Insurgency and Civil War*, Am. Pol. Sci. Rev.(Feb. 2003).

Mary Ellen O'Connell (ed.), What Is War? An Investigation in the Wake of 9/11.
© 2012 Koninklijke Brill NV. Printed in The Netherlands. ISBN 978 9004 17234 0. pp. 251 – 259.

no one say that academic research is not subject to fashion. During the last thirty years, research into internal conflicts has progressed through three major phases: a focus on internal ethnic conflicts; a focus on comparative conflict analysis; and a current concern about the relationship between local, regional and international conflicts.

The 1970s and 1980s: Internal versus international

Like many others working at the same time in other divided societies – in South Africa, Sri Lanka, Israel – I believed that the international wars of the first half of the 20th century were being replaced by a different pattern of violence: one characterized by ethnic tensions, by armed resistance movements, and by asymmetric struggles between states and irregular militant groups. Whatever the correct term was for this phenomenon, it was different to war. If even the term "civil war" was mentioned at all, it was usually done provocatively. Of course, we recognized the imprecision of this distinction between international and internal conflicts, but we tended to avoid it, more or less uneasily.

The 1990s and 2000s: Comparative peace processes

The emergence of ethnic tensions following the collapse of the Soviet Union and Jugoslavia, seemed to resemble more traditional ethnic conflicts. Perhaps there were lessons to learn from looking at the differences and similarities between them. More positively, the peace processes that began to proliferate during the 1990s, and especially after the transfer of power in South Africa in 1994, presented approaches to peace-making that seemed novel:
–   the key negotiators were the actual parties in conflict, although they were often helped (and often hindered) by external actors;
–   they devised new approaches to negotiations;
–   they tackled new problems, including ways of acknowledging the violence that preceded the peace process.

The Current position: Uncertainty

The third phase, one of uncertainty, still pertains. The optimism of the 1990s has been succeeded by a new caution. Some peace processes that seemed promising have faltered or stalled. Peace agreements often failed to deliver peace and stability. The report card on the 40+ comprehensive peace agreements signed since 1990 might be summarized: "Could try harder". Some of the traditional conflicts – notably South Africa and Northern Ireland – could point to significant advances; others – The Basque Country; Sri Lanka – remained stubbornly unresolved. In addition, it was becoming increasingly difficult to approach some significant violent conflicts as if they were insulated within a nation state. In the last five years alone, a significant number of local disputes have become insepa-

rable from broader wars within their regions. The Liberian peace process cannot
be understood outside its regional context alongside Sierra Leone and The Ivory
Coast. The same applies to the Israeli-Palestinian conflict; all the conflicts in
the Horn of Africa; conflicts and wars in Central Africa; Afghanistan and its
neighbors.

This tour d'horizon is, of course, over-simplified and crude, but not inaccurate. I am not suggesting that the Israeli-Palestinian conflict, for example, was
ever contained within a small geographical area; Jordan, Syria, Egypt and other
neighbors have long been involved. As a result, wars in the region, most notably the current war in Iraq, have greatly complicated the search for a solution
of more local conflicts, and muddied further the definition of the term "war".

Nor is the problem confined to the internationalization of local struggles.
The War on Terror declared by the Bush administration in 2001 has mainly
been discussed in terms of international relations, human rights, and the complexity of dealing with what President Bush described as "a different type of
war". However, I would like to focus briefly on one aspect of the War on Terror
that receives less attention: its effects on traditional ethnic struggles – armed
disputes between states and those challenging their authority.

9/11 and the "War on Terror"

Developments following the events of September 11, 2001, have elevated terrorism from the local to the international stage. President Bush's declaration of a
"War on Terror" had a number of important consequences: it was declared globally, but fought locally; it became more difficult to distinguish between the war
against al-Qaeda and long-standing struggles in Indonesia, Palestine, Sudan
and other places; it has affected the behavior of states facing internal violence;
and it has affected the behavior of militants confronting states.

The effect of 9/11 on governments

Since the attacks on New York and Washington in September 2001 the United
States has toughened its internal approach to the threat of terrorism.[2] It has
also provided encouragement and support for other countries willing to take
stronger actions against violent internal groups. As a result, many governments
are adopting tougher approaches against their dissidents, rather than seek-

---

2   There has been an increased use of "enemy-combatant" status to jail and ques-
     tion some US citizens without giving them access to a lawyer. Five thousand for-
     eign citizens have been detained, with just a few being charged with terror related
     crimes. It has been alleged that the Patriot Act has been used "with increasing
     frequency in many criminal investigations that have little or no connection to ter-
     rorism." (Eric Lichtblau, US Uses Terror Law to Pursue Range of Criminals, N.Y.
     Times, Sept. 28 2003).

ing to negotiate with them, a change of approach governments often seek to justify by reference to the adoption of similar measures in the United States. Human Rights Watch (2003) claimed that "many countries around the globe cynically attempted to take advantage of this struggle to intensify their own crackdowns on political opponents, separatists and religious groups, or to suggest they should be immune from criticism of their human rights practices". It detailed seventeen such countries. Amnesty International detected a similar trend: "Exploiting the atmosphere of fear that followed 11 September, many governments ignored, undermined or openly violated fundamental principles of international human rights and humanitarian law.... Some sought to use the War against Terrorism to legitimize their repression of political dissent and their failure to address internal conflicts and grievances".[3]

The intensification of anti-terrorist measures was most evident in Muslim countries and countries with Muslim minorities. The Philippines provide one example. The Philippines was among the first countries to respond to 9/11 by offering air space to the United States. The rewards were substantial. "It's 4.6 billion dollars and still counting", acknowledged President Arroyo (*Inter Press Service*, March 25 2002). Part of the American aid came in the form of advisors, arms and military aid. Six hundred an sixty US troops were sent to Basilan to help seize control from the Abu Sayyaf group. At the same time the Philippine government reversed its policy of trying to end its war with Muslim rebels.

Stronger actions by governments against terrorists have reached far beyond groups associated with al-Qaeda (*Independent*, June 13 2003). The Spanish government cited international terror in its decision to ban the Basque independence party Batasuna, in 2002, and leaped prematurely to the conclusion that ETA had planted the Madrid bomb in March 2004. New legislation in Thailand authorized the government to use military force in emergency cases such as terrorist attacks, but also to try to deal with unrest in the southern part of the country. In other countries moves to combat violent opposition were stimulated by the prospect of American aid. The US provided $20 million military aid in an attempt to crush the Marxist rebellion in Nepal after the government offered air space to the United States following the 9/11 attacks. According to Dhruba Kumar, a strategy analyst working with Center for Nepal and Asian Studies, "The United States and other western countries showed very little interest in Nepal's internal affair before the 9/11 terrorist attacks". (*Poudel*, 2002).

The global threat cited as justification for these and similar actions was often unconvincing. As Richard Falk put it, "the anti-state armed movements that are being targeted are by and large preoccupied with their own territorial struggles of a political character against a particular government in power, and their al-Qaeda links are not significantly related to the sort of mega-terrorist vision of Osama bin Laden, but are designed to facilitate their local struggles." (Falk 2003, 12). Falk goes on to argue that one of the results of the US's approach

---

3   Amnesty International website, Annual report, 2003.

to what he terms "megaterrorism" is that violence by the state, even when deliberately directed at civilians, is not regarded as terrorism:

> This purported exemption allows governments around the world to rely on large-scale violence against their civilian populations, and avoid the stigma of terrorism, while at the same time tending to taint all reactive violence from oppressed peoples, even in resistance to foreign occupation, as terrorism (Falk 2003, 9/10).

The effect of 9/11 on militants

The most immediate effect of the War on Terror was to provide a stimulus for resistance struggles in Afghanistan, Iraq, the Philippines, Palestine and elsewhere. Suicide bombings have spread. Recruitment has risen and the level of ferocity increased.

It has had the opposite effect in other places, where sympathy for militants engaged in ethnic violence diminished. This has particularly affected those resistance groups depending on financial and other forms of support from diaspora populations living in the United States, Australia and Europe. The result, at least in the short term, has been to restrict the activities of such groups, as demonstrated in Sri Lanka. Before September 11, the war conducted by the Liberation Tigers of Tamil Eelam (LTTE) had been funded primarily by a strong Tamil diaspora. After 9/11 the pro-LTTE support has gone underground and fundraising has been much more difficult (Ganguly, 2002). Shastri Ramachandaran (2002) rated the War on Terror high in the list of factors that pushed the Tigers to the negotiating table.

> First and foremost, after 9/11, knowing that their flow of weapons and funds for weapons would get choked, they came out with a strong plea for peace.... Secondly, there was a sharp drop in the flow of funds and arms following the global War against Terrorism. (Ramachandaran, 2002)

The result was a more conciliatory posture from the LTTE, at least temporarily. Its leader, Velupillai Prabhakaran, went to great lengths to condemn the September 11 attacks in New York and Washington. Within days, he halted all attacks on Sri Lankan forces, and three months later declared a unilateral cease-fire. The situation was short-lived, but the association was explicit.

So the War on Terror appears to have had three parallel, and sometimes contradictory, effects:

1. Some governments, encouraged by the growing concern about terrorism, have distanced themselves from the possibility of negotiations with militant minorities in their own countries. Others have justified tougher security approaches as part of the War on Terror.

2. The tougher security approaches have further antagonized many Muslim groups, and violent resistance has intensified, especially but not exclusively in parts of Asia and the Middle East.
3. Some armed militants, especially those depending on diaspora support, have been forced to limit their campaigns.

One might argue about the balance between benefits and costs. What is indisputable is that the War on Terror has significantly altered the local climates within which ethnic conflicts and peace processes are conducted. The question is whether this is temporary, or represents a more permanent change.

Metaphorical dangers

There has been another effect – an increased predilection towards the use of metaphors. "Terrorism is to the twenty-first century what piracy was to an earlier era", in Joseph Nye's striking metaphor.[4] As with piracy, the elusive nature of the enemy and their ambivalent relationship with some governments continually frustrated international action against them. The events of September 2001 have added a new dimension to the problem of state violence, and the War on Terror[5] presents a novel and elusive problem. 'Where does terror live? What is its capital? Who commands its army?'[6]

In this sort of context the use of the term "war" may be becoming dysfunctional. The word has been devalued by over-generalization in other regards too. Is the War against Terror in any sense a useful conceptualization of the events following 9/11? I am not disputing the need to respond to terrorist attacks, rather underlining some of the dangerous implications of applying the term to include a conceptually different type of threat and violence; one which does not involve violence between two organized armies, or between an organized army and a rebel group, but between a group of nations threatened by violence and unable to determine how to respond. "War on Terror" is the wrong metaphor because it implies a conflict that can be won by military means. So what would victory look like? With whom would one sign a ceasefire or treaty? How would postwar society be reconstructed?

Similar objections apply to other "wars" that arose from political speeches – wars against poverty, the war against aids, the war against ignorance. I appreciate the attraction of the term as a means of mobilizing popular support ("mobilizing": observe how invasive the war metaphor is – "invasive" too, come

---

4   Joseph Nye, 2002.
5   The use of the term War on Terrorism has attracted considerable criticism. Thomas Pettigrew expressed some of the main concerns: "Nation states fight wars, and wars typically have clear end-points of victory. The so-called 'War on Terrorism' meets neither of these criteria." (Pettigrew, 2002).
6   Timothy Garton Ash, "Next Stop Syria?", Guardian, January 22 2004.

to think of it). But it seems to me that these terms are more troublesome than insightful. Would it not be beneficial to call an end, or at least observe a moratorium, on these "rhetorical wars," and start approaching the problems in more prosaic terms.

Implications for our understanding of war

To summarize, the earlier view that war and peace were easily distinguished, in law and in practice, has been undermined by an elision of the term "war" on at least two fronts.

First, the distinction between international wars and internal violent struggles, or "civil wars", has lost much of its clarity. There are different reasons for this, one of them not new: the presumption for years by militants that their liberation struggles were actually legitimate wars. In virtually every peace process initiated since 1990, one of the preconditions required by militants for entering negotiations was the release of their prisoners. The demand arises from more than comradely obligation. The release of prisoners is an acknowledgment by government that they are more than rebels or militants or criminals, but warriors engaged in a war. Consequently the violence preceding the peace process was a war rather than the plethora of other words – insurrection; rebellion; qualified terms such as guerrilla war or civil war – usually used to describe it. It provides the symmetry between governments and militants necessary for successful peace negotiations.

Further, the growing regionalization and internationalization of ethnic and other disputes previously regarded as essentially internal, are increasingly spilling over state boundaries, and disturbing the comfortable distinction between internal and external violence.

Second, the War on Terror has undermined the popular view of what constitutes "war", and also perhaps the legal view, by its increasing imprecision, and by including under the rules of war groups previously not included. For those of us who are not lawyers, this raises a number of questions:
– What have been, and are, the benefits of establishing a separate set of rules for war and peacetime?
– Do the benefits still apply in a world where the conventional understanding may be changing fundamentally?
– Has the time come for a review of their usefulness?

A Postscript: Breaching research interfaces

I am particularly pleased that we are discussing these issues as a result of an initiative from the International Law Association, and that the lawyers are involving non-lawyers in their search for a more holistic approach to the problems posed by war.

The problem is that, although disciplinary studies of peace and violence are not completely discrete, all of us – historians, sociologists, economists, peace studies scholars and human rights lawyers – often address different audiences. We use different languages and approaches. We draw on and feed into different literatures, although we are essentially working on separate aspects of the same issue of war. I think the time has come for a more interdisciplinary approach to these common problems, and to examine more closely the research interfaces and opportunities between our disciplines.

The research interface between justice and peace is starkly illustrated by the current impasse in Uganda. In 2006 the government of Uganda began negotiations with the Lord's Resistence Army (LRA) in an attempt to end the vicious war there. The LRA leaders insisted that they should be granted amnesty for crimes committed during the war, as a pre-condition for entering negotiations. The government was prepared to give the leaders amnesty in order to secure peace. Further, the Acholi community, which had suffered the worst atrocities from the LRA, also supported the amnesty. The problem was that the International Criminal Court (ICC), on behalf of the international community, had issued arrest warrants against six leaders of the LRA, including Joseph Kony. Morris Ogenga-Latigo, the head of Uganda's parliamentary opposition, summed up the dilemma well: "The ICC has become an impediment to our efforts. Should we sacrifice our peacemaking process here so they can test and develop their criminal-justice procedures there at the ICC? Punishment has to be quite secondary to the goal of resolving this conflict." (Cobban, 2006) The dilemma was stark: To overturn the warrants might save many lives and bring some stability. To overturn the warrants will overlook some appalling crimes. How is the dilemma to be resolved?

One possible route out of this dilemma is to seek an alternative accountability system to that proposed by the international community. The Acholi system of conflict resolution, called mat oput or "drinking the bitter root," requires perpetrators to acknowledge their crimes, show remorse, and ask the community for forgiveness. This has been proposed as an approach which delivers accountability, without insisting on international norms.

Clearly not every peace process faces such a stark confrontation between peace and justice as Uganda, but all of them have to confront the issue. Similarly, not all can present indigenous legal processes that may address the issue. The point is that, while it is useful to look for guidance from comparative examples, no magic template applies to all peace processes. There is need for flexibility in seeking escape routes from apparently intractable confrontations.

References

Amnesty International Report. (2003). *2002 in focus: 'Counter-terrorism' and human rights*. Retrieved from http://asiapacific.amnesty.org

Ash, T. G. (2004, January 22). Next step Syria?. *The Guardian*. Retrieved from http://www.guardian.co.uk

Cobban, H. (2006, August 24). Uganda: when international justice and internal peace are at odds. *Christian Science Monitor*. Retrieved from http://www.csmonitor.com

Falk, R. A. (2003). *The great terror war*. New York: Olive Branch Press.

Fearon, J. D., & Laitin D. D. (2003a). Additional tables for "Ethnicity, insurgency, and civil war." Retrieved from http://www.stanford.edu/ group/ethnic/

Fearon, J. D., & Laitin, D. D. (2003b). Ethnicity, insurgency, and civil war. *American Political Science Review, 97*(1), 75-90.

Fearon, J. D., & Laitin D. D. (2003c). Additional tables for "Ethnicity, insurgency, and civil war." Retrieved from http://www.stanford.edu/ group/ethnic/

Ganguly, M. (2002, February 18). Breaking off the battle. *Asia*.

Human Rights Watch. (2003). *Opportunism in the face of tragedy: Repression in the name of anti-terrorism*. Retrieved from http://www.hrw.org

Nye, J. (2002). The American national interest and global public goods. *International Affairs, 78*(2), 233-244.

Pettigrew, T. F. (2002). People under threat: Americans, Arabs, and Israelis. *Peace and Conflict 9*(1), 69-90.

Poudel, K. (September 2002). What a difference a year makes. *Nepal News 22*(12), 5. Retrieved from http://www.nepalnews.com

Ramachandaran, S. (2002, November 11). Tamil Tiger out of the woods. The Transnational Organization for Peace and Future Research. Retrieved from http://www.transnational.org

Sison, M. (2002, March 25). 'War on Terror' Vindicates U.S. Role in the Philippines. *Inter Press Service*. Retrieved from ipsnews.net/asia.asp

US uses terror law to pursue range of criminals. (2003, September 28). *The New York Times*, p. 2.

Younge, G. (2001, September 21). Bush talks of a 'different kind of war.' *The Guardian*. Retrieved from http://www.guardian.co.uk

Chapter 20

What's in a War? Insights from a Conflict Data Program

Peter Wallensteen

1.   The Importance of Understanding "War"

Waging war is one of the most destructive activities that human beings can
inflict on each other. Certainly, more people may succumb to natural disasters
or epidemics, but these are not humanly induced actions aimed at extinguish-
ing a population or making a government change its behavior. Instead, humans
have instituted measures to warn of such events and deal with the harm they
generate. There is a process of learning to improve the management of disasters
and their prevention. Similarly, traffic accidents take place at humanly constructed roads and result in large numbers of deaths, but the vehicles, roads,
and signs are not designed to kill people, but rather the reverse: to reduce incidence of violent death and damage. Wars and comparable organized activities, such as terrorism and genocide, are humanly conceived for a particular
defined purpose which allows for the killing of human beings. "Wars" are an
oddity in human experience and, even odder, they are not always regarded by
the initiators or supporters as a calamity for most victims and bystanders. It is
not "heroic" to initiate an epidemic, or to refuse to save people in an earthquake
or tsunami, or to run a car into somebody else's. "Wars," however, do have a
great number of heroes, often on opposing sides of a conflagration. "War," in
other words, requires considerable and special analysis. This contribution will
attempt to understand what a "war" actually is: how is it defined, by whom, and
for what purpose. Furthermore, having defined it, it asks what this definition
includes, and what is, as a consequence, excluded, and what impact that has on
our understanding of war. Parallel to this, the chapter asks whether there are
any discernable trends that can be detected with the help of these definitions,
and, if so, what do they say about war today?

2.   Who Defines War?

Although "war" is often seen as a pervasive phenomenon throughout history
there is little agreement on its precise definition. The outer contours are clearly

Mary Ellen O'Connell (ed.), What Is War? An Investigation in the Wake of 9/11.
© *2012 Koninklijke Brill NV. Printed in The Netherlands. ISBN 978 9004 17234 0. pp. 261–272.*

visible; cases such as World War I and World War II would be subsumed under most definitions. They have entered into history textbooks around the world and are part of a common, globally shared experience. They are understood as "wars". Even so, there are variations in that understanding among the participants, suggesting that "war" is defined differently by different parties.

For instance, there is a difference as to *when* particular wars were fought and when they ended. World War II started on September 1, 1939 according to much European writing. That is the occasion of Germany's invasion of Poland. For the Soviet Union, however, this was not the beginning, as the Soviet Union was allied with Germany at the time. Instead, the Great Patriotic War started on June 22, 1941, with Germany's attack in Operation Barbarossa. To the US the Second World War began even later, December 7, 1941, with Imperial Japan's attack on Pearl Harbor. As is often the case, those attacked united to face the enemy and that unification formed the events into a World War. In the end, in May and/or August 1945, this particular war terminated with the USSR and the USA as the primary victors. Yet, their understanding of the purpose of the war was quite different. Apart from defending themselves against attack and defeating the enemy, they were fighting for dissimilar specific *issues*. That was revealed as the War was ending. It crystallized around the question associated with one of the beginnings: Who shall rule Poland? There is a common understanding of war as the *actions* between 1941 and 1945. This framework does not necessarily extend to what went on before or what was to come after. The Allies fought the same battles but different wars.

This means that the war participants may be unlikely sources of generic definitions. Their definitions of inter-state wars, such as World War II, are likely to vary. The same is true when it comes to defining a particular internal situation as a "war." Conflicts within the same sovereignty (intra-state conflicts) will have political as well as legal consequences. There may in fact be more consensus on what constitutes a war between states than a war within a state. War between states may have legal declarations of war or other legal implications that define them as war. Such statements may be more difficult to identify when turning to internal wars. A number of war-like situations, such as the one in Northern Ireland after 1968, may not have agreed definitions by the parties. To United Kingdom officials it was not a "war" but a domestic disturbance, even some form of "troubles." Others, notably "rebels" ("freedom fighters") organized in the Irish Republican Army (IRA) may have preferred to describe it as a "liberation war." The same difficulties accrue to situations such as those the United States has confronted during the first decade of the 21st century: President George W. Bush declared a "global war on terror" in 2001, while at the same time, making clear that there was no "civil war" in Iraq by 2007. Rather it was a form of "sectarian violence." The global war was not fought against another state but against a set of non-state actors (for instance, al-Qaeda, a constellation of "terrorists.") The Iraq "war" was a matter of supporting a government to establish control within its jurisdiction. Warring parties, in other words, will describe a situation as "war" or "not war" depending on circumstances, desired public associations, and expected legal implications. Thus, using the practice of warring parties to establish generic definitions does not appear to be fruitful.

Thus, it becomes more appropriate to approach the body that is created to "save succeeding generations from the scourge of war": the United Nations (UN). The United Nations uses the term "war" in its preamble. However, its most important operative paragraphs do not. Article 39 (UN Charter, Chapter VII) identifies "threat to the peace, breach of the peace, or act of aggression." It does not mention "war." The Organization, thus, does not express its relationship to all wars, only those that meet criteria associated with forms of aggression. This might not, after all, be surprising. The UN is composed of national governments that have been parties to many wars. They were united in the UN against particular challenges (notably the expansionism of Nazi Germany and Imperial Japan). Thus, a collectively agreed definition of "war" is as likely to avoid a generic formulation as the states would by themselves. Other terms are used, as they may be more easily agreed to by the decisions-makers, for instance in the UN Security Council. A term such as inter-state "aggression" may generate more common understanding. For instance, when Iraq under Saddam Hussein invaded Kuwait in 1990 the US and USSR could quickly agree on defining this as "a breach of the peace."

As a consequence it may not be surprising to find that a new tool, for use in diplomacy and academia, the *UN Peacemaker Glossary* does not contain the word "war." It does, however, include "armed conflict," defined as "a dispute involving the use of armed force between two or more parties." It also identifies an international armed conflict as "a war involving two or more states," i.e. the notion of "war" creeps into the definition without itself being defined. A "non-international armed conflict" then is a "conflict in which government forces are fighting with armed insurgents, or armed groups are fighting amongst themselves" (*UN Peacemaker Glossary*, Jan. 3, 2008). Thus, the terms "war" and "armed conflict" become almost synonymous. Perhaps the two are only separated by the size of the conflagration, as other sources would have it: "War is any large scale, violent conflict" (Wikipedia, Jan. 3, 2008). This, however, is clearly only a diversionary move. It remains to define "large scale" as well as "violent." Furthermore, if we want to be prescriptive it is difficult to determine how a situation is going to turn out. What unfolds when one actor attacks another with armed instruments and for political reasons *may* become "large scale," but that can often not be predicted at the outset. Inevitably, the one who initiates action expects the event to be short, small-scale and successful. When that does not happen an "attack" or an "intervention" turns into a "war." Possibly, these objections may have influenced writers: by November 2008 Wikipedia had changed its definition. War was now described as "an international relations dispute, characterized by organized violence between national military units.", i.e. dropping the distinction having to do with magnitude (Wikipedia, November 10,

2008), but at the same time limiting the concept to inter-state conflicts. This underscores the volatility in definitions and inconsistencies that may emerge.

For instance, it is likely that developments following the initial use of armed force are more predictable in inter-state conflict. When two highly organized actors such as two states clash militarily it is more likely to turn "large scale" in terms of suffering, the use of resources, the public awareness of what is going on, etc. Thus, there is a common understanding of a "war" over the Falkland Islands/Malvinas between Argentina and the United Kingdom in 1982, although the casualties were limited. Many "internal wars" are, however, not described in those terms, although they may be considerably more destructive than some inter-state wars. A significant number of present challenges to international peace and security arise from internal conflicts that have become protracted and/or internationalized. Often this emerges in ways that could not be predicted from the outset.

Media may be the source of the greatest confusion. The word "war" is used in a number of contexts which do not have an immediate bearing on violence and organized confrontations. Political leaders have declared "wars" on poverty, on crime, and on drugs; media has used war descriptions of football games and other sporting events. There are also virtual war games that are downloadable, sometimes being modeled on real wars. There are fictional movies (e.g. *Star Wars*). The war metaphor is loaded and has its uses but is not ultimately helpful in defining the phenomenon in the first place.

Furthermore, there are many events that are violent, political, and have devastating human consequences that do not fit under the heading of "war." Terms such as genocide, communal violence, forced expulsions, ethnic cleansing, massacres, politicide, mass killings, etc. all aim to describe "non-war" violent phenomena, but may also be subsumed under each other. There is a need to develop a coherent approach to be able to separate "war" from other forms of politically motivated violence. That would make it possible to identify particular events and then consider which legal, political and other remedies apply.

To do that, however, we have to move a step away from the actors of a particular war. Academics can be a source of insight. By being detached from the practical implications of particular wars, peace research, security studies, political science and international law could be disciplines that throw additional light on the definitional conundrums.

3.   Peace Research and the War Definition

Standard peace research definitions depart from conflict theory and the notion of armed conflict in order to delimit the definition of war. If "war" is a large-scale armed conflict, the primary task becomes to identify "conflict". Machiavelli and Clausewitz are important writers in Western traditions of conflict analysis. Adam Smith and Karl Marx offered concepts of "competition" and "class analysis" as additional insights. In classical Chinese discourse on war Sun Tzu is a central writer, as is Kautilya in India or Ibn Khaldun in the Arab world. Thus, there is considerable thinking on the questions of conflict and how they relate to war. It is fruitful to move from "conflict" to identify "war".

The term "conflict" has many meanings in everyday life. First, we can refer to *destructive behavior* or *action*. There is conflict when a trade union goes on strike or an employer locks out its employees. Action is part of what constitutes a conflict. As we saw in the previous section, the warring parties may agree on the battles they are involved in, thus, making their actions a way of concurring on a definition. However, it would mean that a conflict ends once armed behavior ends. Few would agree with this. A cease-fire is not the end of a conflict. Actions may resume at some later stage. There may still be dissatisfaction. Conflict, and as a consequence war, is more than the behavior of the parties.

As we saw in the discussion of World War II, parties will not cease their actions until there is some movement on the issues which sparked the dispute. The "issue" refers to the incompatible positions taken by the parties, motivating their actions. This, then, is a deeper understanding of what a conflict is. It contains a serious disagreement between at least two sides, where their demands cannot be met by the same resources at the same time. This is an *incompatibility*. The goals of the primary parties are incompatible. Incompatible demands have to be handled. Incompatibility is key to the existence of conflict. If there are no actions, it is still possible to identify tensions and disagreements: there is latent conflict that may become manifest when action is taken.

In this discussion we have mentioned the actors and parties, the agents of action. They need to be included in a definition. For violence to take place actors must have access to means of violence, the more such resources, the "stronger" the actors. That is where the states enter the analysis. Conflicts involving the state or a relationship between states have more inherent danger of the use of violence than conflicts involving any other actor or sets of actors. The state is an actor with a particular status as the sole legitimate user of physical, fiscal, and legal power within a particular geographical domain, its territory. The state is also important in an ideological sense. The actions and explanations by the holders of state power are likely to be a central dimension in the life of that particular state. Thus, states are powerful actors. Remarkably, control of the state can also become the object of conflict: to control the government gives many advantages. The state, thus, is an actor with recourse to violence, but exercising its control becomes an incompatibility for others desiring to have that control.

From some perspectives, states are in constant conflict with each other (Herz 1950; Waltz 1959, 1979) as one state is a danger to any other state. This is defined as the security dilemma: the security of one state can imply the insecurity of another. As long as there is unpredictability in the system, there will be fear and, thus, conflict. For our purposes it means that *actors* or *parties* are fundamental for conflict to exist. When actors are formed, they are ready to act (they have a purpose, an organization, some resources) and if they make an analysis where their needs for survival are in conflict with other actors, then there is conflict built into the system. The history of the actors, the actors' understanding of their own role, and their resources are important elements in conflict analysis.

Let us then conclude that "conflict" consists of three components: incompatibility, action, and actors. This leads to a generic definition that a conflict is *a social situation in which a minimum of two actors (parties) strive to acquire at the same moment in time an available set of scarce resources* (Wallensteen, 2007). "Armed conflict" is the situation when the actors have weapons and use them in their "striving" for scarce resources. The notion of an "available set of scarce resources" does not refer only to economic matters. To be a prime minister, to control a particular piece of territory, to be able to propagate a particular idea can all be covered by this notion. It also includes demands for recognition, acceptance of responsibility for actions, or psychological retribution as they imply an admission affecting an actor's standing nationally or internationally. Such demands may lead to a quest for compensation and legal changes and, thus, to redistribution of material resources, as well as matters of justice, morals and attribution of guilt.

With the conflict concept clarified, we should be able to move to the most difficult of all types of conflicts: wars. They are different from all other conflicts in that they include irreversible actions. Wars involve the forceful conquest of territory, the eviction of inhabitants, the death of soldiers and civilians, the destruction of property, resources and environment, and the disruption of people's mental, physical, economic and cultural development. Such events turn into conscious elements in the history of peoples, groups, and individuals. They can become part of an identity, and color the way a state may look at itself, its subjects or it neighbors. These are events that can be ended and remedied by humans, but they cannot be undone.

War is a form of armed conflict. It is the use of violence for a political purpose reaching a certain level of destruction. The Uppsala Conflict Data Program (UCDP) has wrestled with these definitions and how to turn them into tools for mapping the world of war. The result is a generic definition of armed conflict, and war, which reads as follows: *an armed conflict is a contested incompatibility which concerns government and/or territory where the use of armed force between two parties, of which at least one is the government of a state, results in at least 25 battle-related deaths. A war is when the total number of battle-deaths between the conflict parties reaches at least 1000 in a year.* (Wallensteen, 2007).

The UCDP definition brings together the elements of "conflict." There is a basic disagreement that can be surmised from the statement of the parties. The parties are clearly distinguishable. One side is always the state, or more precisely the government, facing another state or an organized actor, which takes responsibility for its action. There is manifest armed action. When reaching a certain threshold of battle-related deaths in a specified period of time the conflict is sustained action that is identified as a war. This definition has the strength of being operationalizable. It is feasible to browse all published material globally and search for events that meet these criteria, identify and add them for each calendar year. In this way a comparable, reliable and valid definition has emerged. It can be used to describe trends in the world, and it can also be used for comparative and statistical studies. The basic unit, the armed conflict, is identifiable across culture, time and space.

When applying this definition for the entire post-World War II period, it identifies 232 armed conflicts since 1945, of which around 122 have been active in the post-Cold War period (i.e. since 1989). It can also be demonstrated graphically (e.g. in Harbom and Wallensteen, 2007). The definition permits reliable analysis of trends in world conflict patterns. As the Uppsala database includes more than 100 variables describing these armed conflicts, there is a vast potential for research.

"War" will be a small subset of all the armed conflicts. In the 2000s, so far, the number of wars has reached as many as eleven in a year, compared to a yearly average of more than thirty armed conflicts. There are a large number of conflicts that do not escalate into war. Some do, however, and that is in itself an interesting research query: which ones will remain on a lower intensity level and which ones will turn into wars? To answer this question, we would have to draw on what we have presumably learned about preventing the escalation of armed conflict.

What is the prescriptive value of a definition like this? "Armed conflict" as a basic notion is distinct from non-armed conflict: do the parties use weapons to achieve the purposes they have specified and has this resulted in the deliberate death of more than 25 persons in a year? There are a number of qualitative shifts from non-armed to armed conflict: the introduction of weapons, the use of them against the other side, and the resulting deaths of opponents. It may seem that the "war" definition does not apply to a similar qualitative shift, only a quantitative one. However, on a yearly basis the death rate increases from about one person killed every second week (resulting in 25 in a year) to some twenty every week (resulting in 1000 in a year). In terms of impact on society, this is likely to be a qualitative shift: fear will rise all over a country, hostile attitudes will form and become entrenched, financial resources will be devoted to the military, and international relations strained. It is obviously not possible to specify that all these shifts will occur exactly at the 1000 threshold of battle-related deaths. A qualitative shift may occur earlier raising fears dramatically (for instance, if the fighting takes place in the capital, as happened in Moscow in 1993). The rapid intensification of fighting between well-prepared and resourced entities certainly is an indication of a potential for war. It will quickly be reported, possibly acted upon, and thus contained. The fear of such a qualitative shift is the fear of war. Thus, there is a prescriptive value in this definition.

It has another prescriptive value as well: it serves to highlight protracted events that may have been just accepted, and led to little international attention. A case in point also played itself out in Russia: the war in Chechnya may have been deliberately underreported by Russian media in order to avoid generating fear among Russian civilians. This practice makes a problem appear less significant and more marginal. In all likelihood this increases frustration in a region that bears the brunt of the fighting, even leading to desperate acts. Thus, the definition helps to demonstrate problematic situations that do not or are not allowed to generate the same imminent fear, as would be the case with battles in a capital. The first violent event in Russia had the elements of "war" in a common sense way but did not generate many deaths. The second certainly has been a war at times but may be perceived in the capital as distant and less relevant. The systematic definition draws attention to both and makes them comparable, not as wars, but as armed conflicts.

The political and public understanding of what goes on will thus be affected by the way it is portrayed by government, concerned actors, and the media. The strength of a generic definition is, however, that it is used neutrally across time and space and thus does not change depending on how the parties themselves would want to describe a particular situation. In an uncorrupt way it will define similar situations as similar when they meet the criteria. It is the strength of an independent approach.

4.   Non-State and One-Sided Conflicts

The definition of armed conflict introduced in section 3 does not cover all types of political and deadly conflict. There are violent events between non-state actors where the state is not directly involved as a party but has to intervene in order to maintain security. There are violent events where organized parties attack innocent persons who are not themselves organized into parties or even do not perceive themselves to be in conflict with such organized parties. A fuller understanding will have to include such situations. If, furthermore, these situations can be independently defined, they can be analyzed in conjunction with armed conflict. Is there a relationship between armed conflict and other forms of organized and destructive behavior? If there is a close link, the categories can be combined becoming a unified measure of violence. If there is discussion on the link between them, they can be separated for analysis. If they are unrelated they can be studied independently of each other. The Uppsala Conflict Data Program has introduced two such definitions, in cooperation with the Human Security Report project, (Vancouver, Canada) in two categories described as non-state and one-sided conflicts.

A *non-state conflict* situation is defined as the use of armed force between two organized groups, neither of which is the government of a state, which results in at least 25 battle-related deaths in a year. The same threshold respecting deaths is maintained and thus a basis to commonly categorize events as armed conflicts. Non-state actors, however, need not be as well organized as states involved in armed conflicts. Nor is there a requirement that the cause of the armed conflict be a clearly recognizable incompatibility. This emerges both for theoretical and practical reasons. It is likely that non-state actors confronting each other do so on an understanding of such disagreements. These disagreements are not necessarily spelled out, as they are obvious to the groups: tribal clashes, communal violence, and para-military groups fighting leftist movements confront each other over issues that are formed by previous relations or by involvement in another conflagration (issues could be grazing areas, local harassments, or strategic points of importance in an armed conflict). These parties do not have the same need or wish to rally public support as state parties in armed conflicts do. A practical concern follows from this: it is not often even possible to identify statements on an incompatibility.

The conflict situation defined as *one-sided violence* is when the use of armed force by the government of a state or by a formally organized group against civilians results in at least 25 deaths. Again there is a focus on mass events involving many persons, thus meaning that extrajudicial killings in custody are excluded. The typical genocide event does not involve a confrontation between two organized actors. The Jewish population in Germany was not organized to challenge a non-state actor or the state. The Holocaust was entirely motivated by the instigator's own theories and imaginations. There was no previous history of confrontation or violent conflict. Similarly, the ethnic cleansing during the Bosnia war targeted civilians that were unprotected and unorganized. In the case of Bosnia, it was sometimes argued that the ethnic cleansing had to do with historical grievances, but again, that was in the mind of the instigator, and nothing emerging out of a stated incompatibility among the different sides. Certainly, there was a war going on parallel to these events and strategic arguments were used in some parts of the country. That may have been an excuse, but mostly the intention was the one of eviction, extermination, or humiliation of a civilian population. Terrorist acts are also included here as they target civilians, i.e. persons who are not organized into a movement or an actor. Not all actions that are branded as "terrorist" would fit with this category, notably when they are directed against military targets.

The investigations by the UCDP find for the 2000s that these two types of violence are as frequent as the armed conflicts. Events that come to mind are found in Gujarat, India, in 2002, and clashes between groups in Nigeria, ostensibly around sharia laws. The deadliness of non-state conflict is not as high as in armed conflicts. However, one-sided violence will result in high death tolls in some situations, notably the attack on the World Trade Center in New York on September 11, 2001 (Eck and Hultman, 2007, Harbom, 2007, Human Security Report Project, 2005, Kreutz, 2007).

Equipped with these three distinct definitions of violent conflict, new research questions can be formulated. They provide, for instance, for a profiling of particular situations, as many of them will contain two or three types of violence. The 2007 situation in Iraq, for instance, has elements of an armed conflict between organized actors (i.e. between the government supported by the US and its coalition on the one hand and al-Qaeda inspired groups on the other) as well as non-state conflict between Shiite and Sunni groups, and one-sided violence on people in daily pursuit of normal tasks, for instance going to the market.

Different conflict situations will have different emphases at different times. Thus, developing the definitions is not only an academic exercise, but helpful in describing particular situations and following them over time.

5.   Conflict Trends and Peacemaking

The three types of conflict that we have introduced here makes it possible to see trends in global conflict patterns over time. So far only data for the category of armed conflict is available for a period such as the post-World War II era. As the work progresses data for the other definitions will become available, thus making parallel trend observations possible. Already now it is possible to survey the conflicts in terms of how they end, the peace agreements that are concluded, and preventive measures that are taken. Some of the observations that can be made at this time include the following:

- There was a continuous rise in the number of armed conflicts from 1946 into the early post-Cold War period. The peak years were 1991 and 1992, with 52 armed conflicts in each. The number in 2006 was 32.
- Inter-state conflicts have been rare throughout the period, but intra-state conflict has often been highly internationalized thus having an inter-state dimension. Many intra-state conflicts during the Cold War saw strong commitments from the major powers. Also in the post-Cold War other actors are engaged, but more frequently these are neighbors of the country in conflict. Some countries are the battlefields of others, what could amount to regional conflict complexes.
- There have been more peace agreements since 1989 than at any comparable period in modern history; at least 150 have been identified. They are associated with the temporary or durable ending of armed conflicts.
- There is considerable activity by third parties in the early phases of conflict to prevent further escalation. The amount/level of international commitment to conflict resolution and peacemaking since 1989 is unprecedented: the use of peacekeeping, peacemaking envoys, and sanctions has increased, as have humanitarian efforts, non-governmental concern, and public support.
- Terrorist acts (suicide bombings, for instance) and counter-reactions (the formation of coalitions of the willing) in some conflicts have contributed to a dramatic erosion of the respect for established international law (protection of civilians, humane treatment of prisoners of war, due process).
- In the early 2000s the number of armed conflicts is about equal to the number of non-state conflicts and situations of one-sided violence. The general challenge to peacemaking thus includes more than 60 conflict situations. It is also likely that those situations involving the state as a driving actor are generating more deaths than any other type. At the same time

the other types of violence may escalate into state-based conflict. Thus, the agenda for international peace and security will have to include all three categories.

This chapter has underlined the importance of a definition of "war" that transcends one proposed by parties to a dispute. One such definition has been presented and its strength in describing trends and pinpointing comparable situations has been demonstrated. Its weakness has partly been remedied by adding two new categories of violence. Together these definitions provide a more comprehensive picture of the global challenge of politically motivated, organized violence.

References

Clausewitz, C. (2007). *On war.* (B. Heuser, Ed.). New York: Kessinger Publishing. (Original work published 1832).

Eck, K. and Hultman, L. (2007). One-sided violence against civilians in war: insights from new fatality data. *Journal of Peace Research, 44*(2), 233-246.

Harbom, L. (Ed.). (2007). *States in armed conflict 2006.* Uppsala University: Department of Peace and Conflict Research.

Harbom L. and Wallensteen, P. (2007). Armed conflicts 1989-2006. *Journal of Peace Research, 44*(5), 621-32.

Herz, J.H. (1950). Idealist internationalism and the security dilemma. *World Politics, 2*(2), 157-180.

Human Security Report Project. (2005). *Human security report 2005.* New York: Oxford University Press.

Khaldun, I. (1958). *The muqaddimah: an introduction to history.* London: Routledge and Kegan Paul.

Kreutz, J. (2007). Conflict without borders? A brief overview of non-state conflicts. In L. Harbom (Ed.), *States in armed conflict 2006*: 155-67. Uppsala University: Department of Peace and Conflict Research.

Machiavelli, N. (1975). *The prince.* (G. Bull, Trans.). United Kingdom: Penguin Books. (Original work published 1532).

Marx, K. (2002). *The Communist manifesto.* (G. S. Jones, Ed.). New York: Penguin Classics. (Original work published in 1848).

Rangarajan, L. N. (1992*). Kautilya – the Arthasastra*: Edited, rearranged, translated and Introduced, New Delhi: Penguin Books India (Original work published ca. 300 B.C.).

Smith, A. (1937). *An inquiry into the nature and causes of the wealth of nations.* New York: Modern Library. (Original work published 1776).

Sun-Tzu. (1963). *The art of war.* (Griffith, F. B. Trans.) New York: Oxford University Press. (Original work published in the 6th century).

UN Peacemaker Glossary. Available at http:// peacemaker.unlb.org/index.php.

Wallensteen, P. (2007). *Understanding conflict resolution: War, peace and the global system.* (2nd ed.). London: Sage Publications.

Waltz, K. N. (1959). *Man, the state and war.* New York: Columbia University Press.

Waltz, K. N. (1979). *Theory of international politics.* Reading: Addison-Wesley.

War. (2008). In *Wikipedia, the free encyclopedia.* Retrieved Jan. 3, 2008 and Nov. 10, 2008 from http://en.wikipedia.org/wiki/War.

Part IV

The ILA Reports on the Meaning of Armed Conflict in International Law (2008-10)

Chapter 21

Initial Report of the ILA Use of Force Committee on the Definition of Armed Conflict (2008)

International Law Association
Rio De Janeiro Conference (2008)
Use Of Force

Members of the Committee:

Professor Mary Ellen O'Connell (USA): *Chair*
Professor Judith Gardam (Australia): *Rapporteur*

Professor Masahiko Asada (Japan)	Professor Koichi Morikawa (Japan)
Professor Jutta Brunnee (Canada)	Professor Eric Myjer (Netherlands)
Professor James Gathii (USA)	Professor Georg Nolte (Germany)
Professor Christine Gray (UK)	Mr R K P Shankardass (India)
Professor Wolff Heintschel Von Heinegg (Germany)	Sir Michael C Wood (UK)
Dr Elzbieta Mikos-Skuza (Poland)	*Alternate:* Dr Nikolaos Tsagourias

REPORT
**Initial Report on the Meaning of Armed Conflict
in International Law**

Prepared by the International Law Association
Committee on the Use of Force

Summary

In May 2005, the Executive Committee of the International Law Association approved a mandate for the Use of Force Committee to produce a report on the meaning of war or armed conflict in international law. The report was moti-

Mary Ellen O'Connell (ed.), What Is War? An Investigation in the Wake of 9/11.
© *2012 Koninklijke Brill NV. Printed in The Netherlands.* ISBN *978 9004 17234 0. pp. 275–305.*

vated by the United States' position following the attacks of 11 September 2001 that it was involved in a "global war on terror". The U.S. position was contrary to a trend by states attempting to avoid acknowledging involvement in wars or armed conflicts. The Committee was asked to study the evidence in international law and report on how *international law* defines and distinguishes situations of war and peace. Given that important aspects of international law turn on whether a situation is properly defined as armed conflict, providing a clear understanding of what counts as armed conflict would support the proper functioning of the law in general. Most fundamentally, it would support the proper application of human rights law.

At the outset of its work, the Committee found that the term "war", while still used has, in general, been replaced in international law by the broader concept of "armed conflict". The Report focuses, therefore, on "armed conflict".

The existence of armed conflict triggers international humanitarian law (IHL) obligations, affects treaty rights, asylum rights and other important rights and duties. The Committee found no widely accepted definition in any treaty, but did find evidence that certain characteristics do define armed conflict in international law. The existence of armed conflict is not something that can be declared or denied by governments as a matter of policy.

The Committee employed standard international legal methodology. Looking to relevant treaties – in particular IHL treaties – rules of customary international law, general principles of international law, judicial decisions and the writing of scholars, as of the drafting of this Initial Report, the Committee has found evidence of at least two characteristics with respect to all armed conflict:

1. The existence of organized armed groups
2. Engaged in fighting of some intensity

These characteristics were restated perhaps most authoritatively in a 1995 decision of the International Criminal Tribunal for the former Yugoslavia in *Prosecutor v. Tadić.* That decision has been widely cited for its description of the characteristics of armed conflict.

A number of questions respecting these characteristics remain for further research in preparation of the Final Report. In particular, further clarification will be sought as to the requirements of organization and intensity. More research is needed on when armed conflict begins, when it ends, and on territorial scope. In the course of this research, additional characteristics may be found.

It should also be emphasized that the Committee's mandate is to clarify the meaning of armed conflict in international law. It is not to determine when IHL applies or what principles of IHL apply in what circumstances.

Introduction

(a) Mandate and Purpose

Since at least the time of Hugo Grotius and his seminal work, *The Law of War and Peace* (1625), international law has been organised around two contrasting situations: the presence or absence of war or what is now more commonly referred to as armed conflict. Armed conflict is, therefore, a core concept in international law, but it is also a socially constructed concept and, as such, it is not amenable to any scientific litmus test.[1] Correctly categorising situations as armed conflict has been a long-standing challenge in international law. The challenge seems to have become greater in recent years with the clash today between advocates of a broad, flexible understanding of armed conflict that affords states more rights and advocates of a narrow definition that better protects individuals. During armed conflict states have greater rights to kill without warning, detain without trial, and suspend or derogate from treaties and other obligations. Individuals may have their right to life, their right to a trial, and other important rights circumscribed in armed conflict.

Before the adoption of the United Nations Charter in 1945, states officially declared war and thereby triggered wartime law. Even then, however, states did not always declare war when war existed or refrain from declaring war when it did not exist. With the adoption of the Charter, declarations of war have become mostly irrelevant in international law. International law continues to reflect a war-peace distinction, but the division is based on whether a particular situation of violence amounts, as a factual matter, to armed conflict.

Until the 11 September 2001 attacks on the United States, states generally resisted acknowledging that fighting on their territory was armed conflict. To do so was to admit
failure, a loss of control to opposition forces.[2] Some scholars even raised the possibility that the distinction between armed conflict and peace in international law was dissolving.[3] There seems to have been little pressure to clarify the meaning of armed conflict when governments were willing to apply the higher level of rights and duties applicable in peacetime. True, the International

---

1   N Berman, *Privileging Combat? Contemporary Conflict and the Legal Construction of War* (2004) 43 Columbia Journal of Transnational Law 1.

2   See M E O'Connell, *Enhancing the Status of Non-State Actors Through a Global War on Terror* (2004) 43 Columbia Journal of Transnational Law 435.

3   See, for example, F F Martin, *Using International Human Rights Law for Establishing a Unified Use of Force Rule in the Law of Armed Conflict* (2001) 64 Saskatchewan Law Review 347; T Meron & A Rosas, *A Declaration of Minimum Humanitarian Standards* (1995) 85 American Journal of International Law 375. These authors advocate a rule prohibiting the use of lethal force except in cases of necessity in any context.

Committee of the Red Cross (ICRC) has pressed governments to acknowledge fighting as armed conflict and to apply IHL,[4] but the real pressure for clarification came with the US "declaration" of a "global war" in 2001 and its claim[5] to exercise certain rights applicable only in armed conflict, such as the right to kill combatants without warning, detain without trial, search vessels on the high seas, and seize cargo.[6]

The need is now pressing for a clarification of the distinction between armed conflict and peace. The proper application of IHL, human rights law and other international legal principles depend on an accurate understanding of the legal meaning of armed conflict. It is the mandate of the Committee to provide this clarification.

(b)   Methodology and Organisation

The Committee took up the mandate to report on the meaning of armed conflict in international law by employing standard international legal analysis. The members looked to the primary and secondary sources of international law: relevant treaties, evidence of customary international law, relevant general principles of international law, judicial decisions and the writing of scholars.[7] The Committee found no multilateral treaty that provides a generally applicable definition of armed conflict. Therefore the meaning of armed conflict is to be found in the practice of states under relevant treaties and in customary international law as evidenced by state practice and *opinio juris*.

The Report is organized around the time periods associated with major developments in IHL. IHL is the subfield of international law most concerned with the meaning of armed conflict and is, consequently, the field that provides the most evidence as to the meaning of armed conflict in general law. Since IHL is such an important part of this Report, it made sense to organize it around the timeframe of the major IHL developments that is, the 1949 Geneva Conventions, the 1977 Additional Protocols and the statutes of the international criminal tribunals of the 1990s. Reference is also made to the ICRC 2005 cus-

---

4   See, for example, the cases of Sri Lanka (International Committee of the Red Cross, *Sri Lanka*, in ICRC Annual Report 1996 (1997) 140-42, http://www.icrc. org/Web/Eng/siteengo.nsf/htmlall/section_annual_report_2006/$File/icrc_ ar_06_Full.zip), Colombia (ICRC action to protect and assist the victims of armed conflict in Colombia, 2 April 2008, http://www.icrc.org/Web/Eng/siteengo.nsf/ html/colombia-report-02042008) and El Salvador (R K Goldman, *International Humanitarian Law: Americas Watch's Experience in Monitoring Internal Armed Conflicts* (1993) 9 American University Journal of International Law and Policy 49, 89).

5   See infra.

6   See infra.

7   Statute of the International Court of Justice art. 38.

tomary international law study. This examination of the evidence cannot begin to consider all relevant state practice but does refer to many of the most significant developments since the Second World War.

The materials reviewed indicate substantial support for the conclusion that certain specified criteria are characteristic of armed conflict.

(c)   Terminology

Clarifying the meaning of armed conflict is facilitated by an appreciation of several other terms frequently used in discussions of armed conflict. In the context of the use of force, international law distinguishes between *ius ad bellum* and IHL.[8] The *ius ad bellum* regulates the resort to force by states and to a certain extent its conduct, through the requirements of necessity and proportionality.[9] Under this law, the terms "war" and "armed attack" are of particular significance.[10] First with respect to "war", in classic pre-Charter *ius ad bellum,* this was the international law term used to describe the situation of armed conflict between states, and it is still in use today. It has undergone a particular resurgence in the context of the so-called "war on terror".

In Oppenheim's classic definition, war was "a contention between two or more States through their armed forces, for the purpose of overpowering each other and imposing such conditions of peace as the victor pleases".[11] During the period when many legal scholars and states contended that the resort to force was unregulated, a declaration of war had considerable legal significance, such as bringing into operation not only the laws of war as IHL was then known but also the institution of neutrality and validating the exercise of belligerent rights. The United Nations Charter, however, prohibits all use of force except in

---

8   See generally C Greenwood, *The Relationship Between* Ius Ad Bellum *and* Ius In Bello (1983) 9 Review of International Studies 133-147, reprinted in C Greenwood, *Essays on War in International Law* 13 (London: Cameron May Ltd, 2006).

9   See generally J Gardam, *Necessity, Proportionality and the Use of Force by States* (Cambridge: Cambridge University Press, 2004).

10   For an explanation of the various terms used to describe this area of the law, see J Gardam, Introduction, in *Humanitarian Law* xi (J Gardam ed, Aldershot: Ashgate, 1999).

11   L Oppenheim, II *International Law: A Treatise* 202 (H Lauterpacht ed, London: Longman, Greens and Co, 1952).

self-defence or with Security Council authorisation.[12] After the adoption of the Charter, governments and jurists began to abandon the use of the term "war".[13]

It is still possible for states to find themselves in a state of war[14] or to make formal declarations of war.[15] Many national constitutions still require formal declarations of war in some circumstances.[16] Such a declaration is not contrary to international law unless (depending on the context) it constitutes a threat within the meaning of Article 2(4) of the United Nations Charter.[17] Political factors are obviously of considerable significance in this context and frequently will dictate whether states use the terminology of war or choose to use other more pacific terminology and strategies to deal with the problem. For example, in 2005 Eritrea used the terminology of war in its argument before the Eritrea/ Ethiopia Claims Commission but failed to report its actions to the Security Council as required under Article 51 of the Charter that governs the legal right

---

12   For recent discussions of these rules, see M E O'Connell, *Preserving the Peace: The Continuing Ban on War Between States* (2007) 38 California Western International Law Journal 41; M Wood, *The Law on the Use of Force: Current Challenges* (2007) 11 Singapore Yearbook of International Law 1; C Gray, *International Law and the Use of Force* (Oxford: Oxford University Press, 2nd ed 2004).

13   As to the relevance of 'war' in post-Charter times, see E Lauterpacht, *The Legal Irrelevance of the 'State of War'* (1968) 62 Proceedings of the American Society of International Law 58; R R Baxter, *The Legal Consequences of the Unlawful Use of Force under the Charter* (1968) 62 Proceedings of the American Society of International Law 68; A D McNair and A D Watts, *The Legal Effects of War* (New York: Cambridge University Press, 4th ed 1966); C Greenwood, *War, Terrorism and International Law* (2004) 56 Current Legal Problems 505, 529; M E O'Connell, *The Legal Case Against the Global War on Terror* (2004) 36 Case Western International Law Journal 349, 353.

14   C Greenwood, *The Concept of War in Modern International Law* (1987) 36 International and Comparative Law Quarterly 283, 302-305.

15   *Jus Ad Bellum*, Partial Award, Ethiopia Claims 1-8, Eritrea Ethiopia Claims Commission, 2006 ILM 430.

16   For example, the United States Constitution mandates that 'war' be declared by the Congress. US Constitution art. I sec. 8. The Congress has not declared a war, however, since the Second World War, despite the many uses of force in that period including cases commonly characterized as war: the Korean War, the Vietnam War, the Gulf War, and the Iraq War. See D L Westerfield, *War Powers: the President, the Congress, and the Question of War* (Westport, CT: Praeger Publishers, 1996).

17   As Brownlie writes, 'acts which would otherwise have been equivocal may be treated as offensive if one of the parties to a conflict declares itself in a state of war.' I Brownlie, *International Law and the Use of Force by States* 368 (Oxford: Clarendon Press, 1963).

to self-defence.[18] The terminology of war was also used by Israel in the 2006 conflict in Lebanon.[19]

To summarise, although the term "war" may still have some significance in a few areas such as for some national constitutions,[20] or some domestic contracts, in international law the term "war" no longer has the importance that it had in the pre-Charter period.

Another term important to distinguish from armed conflict is the phrase "armed attack". Armed attack is a term of art under Article 51 of the United Nations Charter. The occurrence of an armed attack triggers a state's right to resort to measures in self-defence. The phrase lacks an agreed definition.[21] The Committee plans further research on the term armed attack and its relationship to armed conflict.

Turning to terminology in IHL, the traditional description of the customary practices that developed into both treaty and customary IHL was "the laws and customs of war" or more generally "the law(s) of war". These terms are still in use today[22] although the "law of armed conflict" or "IHL" are more generally accepted.

---

18 *Jus Ad Bellum*, Partial Award, supra n 15.

19 See identical letters dated 12 July 2006 from Dan Gillerman, Permanent Representative of Israel to the United Nations, addressed to the UN Secretary-General and the President of the Security Council, UN Doc. A/60/937S/2006/515, 12 July 2006. However, the resolution of the US Congress House of Representatives on the conflict used the traditional terminology of armed attack and self-defence. House Resolution 921, 109th Congress, 18 July 2006.

20 See, for example, D L Westfield, *War Powers: the President, the Congress, and the Question of War*, supra n 16.

21 What constitutes an armed attack has been comprehensively examined by a number of commentators, in particular C Gray, *International Law and the Use of Force*, supra n 12, at 108-20; B Simma (ed), *The Charter of the United Nations: A Commentary* 794-803 (Oxford: Oxford University Press, 2nd ed 2002); Y Dinstein, *War, Aggression and Self-defence* 182-208 (Cambridge, Cambridge University Press, 3rd ed 2005). See also *Military and Paramilitary Activities in and against Nicaragua*, (Nicaragua v United States of America) (Merits) 1986 ICJ reports 14, 191; *Oil Platforms* (Islamic Republic of Iran v United States of America) (Merits) 2003 ICJ reports 803, 876; *Jus Ad Bellum*, Partial Award, supra n 15.

22 See, for example, Letter from J B Bellinger, III, Legal Advisor, US Department of State, and W J Haynes, General Counsel, US Department of Defence, to Dr J Kellenberger, President, International Committee of the Red Cross, Regarding Customary International Law Study, 3 November, 2006, 46 ILM 514 (2007), at fn 1 ('[t]he field has traditionally been called the 'laws and customs of war'. Accordingly, we will use this term, or the term 'law of war', throughout.'). For a comprehensive collection of relevant documents and their use of terminology see generally A Roberts and R Guelff *Documents on the Laws of War*, (eds 3rd ed Oxford: Oxford University Press, 2000).

"International" and "non-international" are also significant terms in the context of applying IHL. Traditionally "international armed conflicts" are conflicts between states and "noninternational armed conflicts" are those between states and armed groups within the territory of a state or states.[23]

In more recent times conflicts not involving a government, for example on the territory of a "failed state", can qualify as armed conflicts to which IHL applies.[24] There is nowadays thought to be growing convergence between the rules governing international and non-international armed conflicts and in the future it may be less important to classify the type of conflict.[25] The jurisprudence of the ICTY, state practice and treaties all demonstrate this convergence.[26] Nevertheless, there remain important distinctions in the rules. Which

---

23 According to Greenwood: 'A non-international armed conflict is a confrontation between the existing governmental authority and groups of persons subordinate to this authority, which is carried out by force of arms within national territory and reaches the magnitude of an armed confrontation or a civil war.' C Greenwood, *Scope of Application of Humanitarian Law*, in *The Handbook of Humanitarian Law in Armed Conflicts* 54 (D Fleck ed, Oxford: Oxford University Press, 2d ed. 2008). See also R Arnold, *Terrorism and IHL: A Common Denomination*, in *International Humanitarian Law and the 21st Century's Conflicts: Changes and Challenges* 3, 11-12 (R Arnold ed, Lausanne: Editions Interuniversitaires Suisses – Edis, 2005); R Arnold, *The ICC as a New Instrument for Repressing Terrorism* 116 (Ardsley, NY: Transnational Publishers, 2004); J Peijic, *Terrorist Acts and Groups: A Role for International Law?* (2004) 75 British Yearbook of International Law 71, citing M Sassòli, *The Status of Persons Held in Guantanamo under International Humanitarian Law* (2004) 2 Journal of International Criminal Justice 96, 100; L Moir, *The Law of Internal Armed Conflict* 30-52 (Cambridge: Cambridge University Press, 2002).

24 See discussion infra.

25 See generally J G Stewart, *Towards a Single Definition of Armed Conflict in International Humanitarian Law: A Critique of Internationalized Armed Conflict* (2003) 85 No 850 International Review Red Cross 313; E Crawford, *Unequal Before the Law: the Case for the Elimination of the Distinction between International and Non-international Armed Conflicts* (2007) 20(2) Leiden Journal of International Law 441.

26 For example, some weapons conventions do not distinguish between international and non-international armed conflict. See the Convention on the Prohibition of the Development, Production and Stockpiling of Bacteriological (Biological) and Toxin Weapons and on Their Destruction (Biological Weapons Convention), 1015 UNTS 163 (entered into force 26 March 1975); Convention on the Prohibition of the Development, Production, Stockpiling and Use of Chemical Weapons and on their Destruction (Chemical Weapons Convention), 1974 UNTS 45 (entered into force 29 April 1997); Convention on the Prohibition of the Use, Stockpiling, Production and Transfer of Anti-personnel Mines and on their Destruction (Ottawa Convention), 2056 UNTS 211 (entered into force 1 March 1999); the Convention on Conventional Weapons (and its protocols) was extended to non-international armed conflict through amendment in 2001; it came into force on 18 May 2004. See also the Second Protocol to the Hague Convention of 1954 for

set of rules applies continues to depend, as it has traditionally, first and foremost on who the parties to the conflict are – whether the organized armed groups are predominantly sovereign states or not.[27] Some rules applicable in non-international armed conflict may also depend on the fighting reaching a higher level of intensity than is required in the general understanding of armed conflict.[28]

The term "hostilities" is another common term used frequently in IHL. It is closely related to the concept of "armed conflict" but is apparently a narrower term. Hostilities are at least the

actual engagement in fighting but some take the term to mean the broader concept of "actual prosecution of the armed conflict on behalf of the parties to the conflict".[29] It is the first understanding that comports with the international legal meaning of armed conflict.[30]

---

the Protection of Cultural Property in the Event of Armed Conflict, 823 UNTS 231 entered into force 9 March 2004), which applies to all armed conflicts . There has also been convergence in the enforcement regimes and in particular in the establishment of individual criminal responsibility in internal armed conflicts, see generally Statute of the International Criminal Tribunal for Rwanda, available at http://www.un.org/ictr/statute.html, and *Prosecutor v Tadić*, Case No. IT-94-1-A, 15 July 1999.

27   See however Art 1(4) of Protocol I that treats certain conflicts involving entities other than States as international in character.

28   See discussion infra.

29   See Third Expert Meeting on the Notion of Direct Participation in Hostilities, ICRC, 18-19 (1995), available at http://www.icrc.org/Web/eng/siteengo.nsf/htmlall/participation-hostilities-ihl311205/$File/Direct_participation_in_hostilities_2005_eng.pdf (Report on Direct Participation in Hostilities). The term hostilities is also of particular significance in the context of the concept of 'direct participation in hostilities'. Under Article 51(3) of Additional Protocol I and Article 13(3) of Additional Protocol II to the 1949 Geneva Conventions, civilians are immune from direct attack 'unless and for such time as they take a direct part in hostilities'. For a discussion of the meaning of the term 'direct participation in hostilities', see *Customary International Humanitarian Law Volume I: Rules* 22-23 (J-M Henckaerts and L Doswald-Beck eds, Cambridge: Cambridge University Press, 2005). The Study regards this rule as customary. For an effort to further clarify the meaning of 'direct participation in hostilities', see Report on Direct Participation in Hostilities 17-24. This Report indicates that the greater point of disagreement among the experts is not over the meaning of 'hostilities' but of 'direct participation'.

30   See discussion infra and see Separate Opinion of Judge Simma, in *Armed Activities on the Territory of the Congo* (Democratic Republic of the Congo v Uganda) 2005 ICJ reports, paras 6-23.

II Armed Conflict in IHL and Beyond

With the adoption of the United Nations Charter, some thought major war would end and with it the need for IHL.[31] In fact, major war did not end and the ICRC was prescient enough to understand that IHL would require further development.[32] In 1949, most states in the world came together to agree to four new Conventions for the protection of victims of armed conflict.[33] For the purposes of this Report, the 1949 Conventions are particularly important because, unlike earlier IHL instruments, the 1949 Conventions deal with the issue of scope of application. In 1977 two Additional Protocols were added to the 1949 Conventions,[34] and in the 1990s, statutes for several international criminal tribunals were drafted that include provisions on war crimes committed during armed conflict. In addition to these major IHL developments, this section also surveys judicial decisions, commentary and the actual treatment of various conflicts during the time frame of each of these major developments in IHL.

(a) *The 1949 Geneva Conventions*

From 1949-77

The 1949 Geneva Conventions each include a scope provision in common Article 2. It reads:

> In addition to the provisions which shall be implemented in peacetime, the
> present Convention shall apply to all cases of declared war or of any other

---

31   For example, the International Law Commission. See, however, J L Kunz, *The Chaotic Status of the Laws of War and the Urgent Necessity for their Revision* (1951) 45 American Journal of International Law 37, 43.

32   Id. at 58-59.

33   Convention (I) for the Amelioration of the Condition of the Wounded and Sick in Armed Forces in the Field; Convention (II) for the Amelioration of the Condition of Wounded, Sick and Shipwrecked Members of Armed Forces at Sea; Convention (III) relative to the Treatment of Prisoners of War; Convention (IV) Relative to the Protection of Civilian Persons in Time of War, 75 UNTS 31 (each entered into force 21 October 1950) (hereafter 1949 Geneva Conventions).

34   Protocol Additional to the Geneva Conventions of 12 August 1949, and relating to the Protection of Victims of International Armed Conflicts, adopted in 1977 (Protocol I), 12 December 1977, 1125 UNTS 3 (hereafter Protocol I) and Protocol Additional to the Geneva Conventions of 12 August 1949, and relating to the Protection of Victims of non-international Armed Conflicts, adopted in 1977, 12 December 1977, 1125 UNTS 609, (hereafter Protocol II). See also *Commentary on the Additional Protocols of 8 June 1977 to the Geneva Conventions of 12 August 1949* (Y Sandoz et al eds, Geneva: Martinus Nijhoff Publishers, 1987).

armed conflict which may arise between two or more of the High Contracting Parties, even if the state of war is not recognized by one of them.

The ICRC Commentary to common Article 2 explains that

> [t]his paragraph is entirely new. It fills the gap left in the earlier Conventions, and deprives the belligerents of the pretexts they might in theory invoke for evasion of their obligations. There is no longer any need for a formal declaration of war, or for recognition of the state of war, as preliminaries to the application of the Convention. The Convention becomes applicable as from the actual opening of hostilities. The existence of armed conflict between two or more Contracting Parties brings it automatically into operation.
>   It remains to ascertain what is meant by "armed conflict". The substitution of this much more general expression for the word "war" was deliberate. One may argue almost endlessly about the legal definition of "war". A State can always pretend, when it commits a hostile act against another State, that it is not making war, but merely engaging in a police action, or acting in legitimate self-defence. The expression "armed conflict" makes such arguments less easy. Any difference arising between two States and leading to the intervention of armed forces is an armed conflict within the meaning of Article 2, even if one of the Parties denies the existence of a state of war. It makes no difference how long the conflict lasts, or how much slaughter takes place.[35]

Article 3 common to the four 1949 Geneva Conventions, the so-called "mini convention" dealing with non-international armed conflict, has a significantly different scope provision. It applies "[i]n the case of armed conflict not of an international character occurring in the territory of one of the High Contracting Parties".

Common Article 3 is a revolutionary provision in that it was the first international treaty provision to attempt to regulate non-international armed conflict. The ICRC Commentary, suggests criteria for determining the existence of an Article 3 armed conflict as follows:

(1)   That the Party in revolt against the *de jure* Government possesses an organized military force, an authority responsible for its acts, acting within a determinate territory and having the means of respecting and ensuring respect for the Convention.

(2)   That the legal Government is obliged to have recourse to the regular military forces against insurgents organized as military and in possession of a part of the national territory.

---

35   I *Commentary on the Geneva Conventions of 12 August 1949* 32 (footnote omitted) (J S Pictet ed, Geneva: ICRC, 1960).

(3) (a) That the *de jure* Government has recognized the insurgents as belligerents; or

(b) that it has claimed for itself the rights of a belligerent; or

(c) that it has accorded the insurgents recognition as belligerents for the
purposes only of the present Convention; or

(d) that the dispute has been admitted to the agenda of the Security
Council or the General Assembly of the United Nations as being
a threat to international peace, a breach of the peace, or an act of
aggression.

(4) (a) That the insurgents have an organization purporting to have the
characteristics of a State.

(b) That the insurgent civil authority exercises *de facto* authority over the
population within a determinate portion of the national territory.

(c) That the armed forces act under the direction of an organized
authority and are prepared to observe the ordinary laws of war.

(d) That the insurgent civil authority agrees to be bound by the provisions of the Convention.[36]

The above criteria are useful as a means of distinguishing a genuine armed
conflict from a mere act of banditry or an unorganised and short-lived insurrection.

State practice during this period indicates that states generally drew a distinction between on the one hand, hostile actions involving the use of force that
they treated as "incidents", "border clashes" or "skirmishes" and, on the other
hand, situations that they treated as armed conflicts to which IHL applied. Two
examples amongst many are the *Red Crusader* incident and the "Cod Wars". In
both instances neutral decision-makers provided opinions on international legal
aspects of the cases, but in neither case was the incident treated as an armed
conflict. The 1961 *Red Crusader* incident involved a Danish fishing enforcement
vessel and a British Navy vessel in an attempt by the Danes to arrest a British
fishing trawler.[37] A commission of inquiry found the Danes had used excessive
force in arresting the trawler, but neither that fact nor the involvement of forces
of two parties to the 1949 Conventions led to treatment of the incident as an
armed conflict. Similarly in the 1970s in the "Cod Wars" between Iceland, the
UK and Germany, naval vessels of the UK and Germany escorted fishing vessels to prevent interdiction by Icelandic fishery enforcement vessels.[38] Despite

---

36 III *Commentary on the Geneva Conventions of 12 August 1949* 36 (J S Pictet ed,
Geneva: ICRC, 1960).

37 Report of the Commission of Inquiry Into the Red Crusader Incident, 35 ILR 485
(1962).

38 For the facts of the incident, see *Fisheries Jurisdiction* (Federal Republic of Germany
v Iceland), 1974 ICJ reports 175.

applying the label "war" and the use of armed force, these were not treated as a legal matter as armed conflict. There is certainly no hint of this categorisation in the International Court of Justice decision in the cases.

Weisburd describes the following incidents as including the engagement of troops but on too limited a basis to have been treated as armed conflicts. He calls them "limited uses of force": Saudi-Arabia-Muscat and Oman (1952, 1955), United Kingdom-Yemen (1957), Egypt-Sudan (1958), Afghanistan-Pakistan (1961), and Israel-Uganda (1976).[39]

These examples are to be contrasted with the acknowledged armed conflicts of the period: India-Pakistan (1947-48), the Korean War (1950-53), the 1956 Suez Invasion, many wars of national liberation (e.g., Algeria, Indonesia, Tunisia, Morocco, Angola), the Vietnam War (1961-1975), the 1967 Arab-Israeli Conflict, the Biafran War (1967-70), El Salvador

Honduras ("the Soccer War" 1969), the 1973 Arab-Israeli Conflict, and the Turkish Invasion of Cyprus (1974).[40]

Both types of examples indicate that following the adoption of the 1949 Conventions conflicts were commonly classified on the basis of intensity of fighting and not simply as to whether the armed forces of the parties to the Conventions were engaged.

(b)   The 1977 Protocols

From 1977-93

The Biafran War in Nigeria and the Vietnam War convinced the ICRC of the need to update the 1949 Conventions in light of the growing problem of civil war and unconventional warfare. In 1977, two Protocols were adopted to the 1949 Conventions. Each has a scope provision. The Protocol Additional to the Geneva Conventions of 12 August 1949, and relating to the Protection of Victims of International Armed Conflicts (Protocol I), 8 June 1977, provides in Article 1(3):

> This Protocol, which supplements the Geneva Conventions of 12 August 1949 for the protection of war victims, shall apply in the situations referred to in Article 2 common to those Conventions.

---

39   A M Weisburd, *Use of Force: The Practice of States Since World War II* 255-56, 257-59, 260, 276-77. (University Park, PA: Pennsylvania State University Press, 1997).

40   For accounts of most of these armed conflicts and lesser incidents, see generally A M Weisburd, *Use of Force*, supra n 39. Weisburd also includes incidents in which there was no fighting and no engagement of armed forces, as well as conflicts that have been treated as armed conflicts.

Additional Protocol I added nothing to the meaning of armed conflict in the 1949 Geneva Conventions. The major development in Additional Protocol I is not in relation to the meaning of armed conflict but rather what entities can be engaged in an armed conflict to which the international rules of IHL apply. So-called "wars of national liberation" are deemed to be international in nature by Article 1(4) of the Protocol.

In response to this expansion of the parties that could be engaged in an armed conflict to which the rules of Additional Protocol I apply, the UK made the following statement upon becoming a party to the Protocol: "It is the understanding of the United Kingdom that the term 'armed conflict' of itself and in its context denotes a situation of a kind which is not constituted by the commission of ordinary crimes including acts of terrorism whether concerted or in isolation."[41] France made a similar statement on becoming a party to the Protocol.[42]

The Protocol Additional to the Geneva Conventions of 12 August 1949, and relating to the Protection of Victims of Non-International Armed Conflicts (Protocol II), 8 June 1977, provides its scope of application in Article 1:

Material field of application
1. This Protocol, which develops and supplements Article 3 common to the Geneva Conventions of 12 August 1949 without modifying its existing conditions of application, shall apply to all armed conflicts which are not covered by Article 1 of the Protocol Additional to the Geneva Conventions of 12 August 1949, and relating to the Protection of Victims of International Armed Conflicts (Protocol I) and which take place in the territory of a High Contracting Party between its armed forces and dissident armed forces or other organized armed groups which, under responsible command, exercise such control over a part of its territory as to enable them to carry out sustained and concerted military operations and to implement this Protocol.
2. This Protocol shall not apply to situations of internal disturbances and tensions, such as riots, isolated and sporadic acts of violence and other acts of a similar nature, as not being armed conflicts.

Additional Protocol II sets a higher threshold for armed conflict than Common Article 3. This was done in order to make its more detailed and demanding rules acceptable to states.[43] Consequently Additional Protocol II applies only to conflicts that more resemble traditional interstate conflict – it requires control over territory by organised armed groups. The Protocol does not cover a situation

---

41   See Reservations/Declaration 2 July 2002.
42   See Reservations/Declaration 11 April 2001.
43   See G I AD Draper, *Humanitarian Law and Internal Armed Conflicts* (1983) 13 Georgia Journal of International and Comparative Law 253, 275.

where there is no government.[44] It requires sustained and concerted operations and that the rebels be able to implement the Protocol.

Consequently there are currently two separate regimes for non-international armed conflict: those covered by Common Article 3 with its relatively low threshold of application but limited protections and conflicts falling within the scope of Additional Protocol II whose threshold of application is high but offers more protections.

According to the ICRC commentary, Article 1(2) of Additional Protocol II is intended to define the lower threshold of the concept of armed conflict.[45] Examples of the situations covered by Article 1(2) are: "riots, such as demonstrations without a concerted plan from the outset; isolated and sporadic acts of violence, as opposed to military operations carried out by armed forces or armed groups; other acts of a similar nature, including, in particular, large scale arrests of people for their activities or opinions".

The ICRC gave the following description of internal disturbances during the first session of the Conference of Government Experts in 1971 that preceded the adoption of the Additional Protocols:

> This involves situations in which there is no non-international armed conflict as such, but there exists a confrontation within the country, which is characterized by a certain seriousness or duration and which involves acts of violence. These latter can assume various forms, all the way from the spontaneous generation of acts of revolt to the struggle between more or less organized groups and the authorities in power. In these situations, which do not necessarily degenerate into open struggle, the authorities in power call upon extensive police forces, or even armed forces, to restore internal order. The high number of victims has made necessary the application of a minimum of humanitarian rules.
>
> As regards "internal tensions," these could be said to include in particular situations of serious tension (political, religious, racial, social, economic, etc.), but also the sequels of armed conflict or of internal disturbances. Such situations have one or more of the following characteristics, if not all at the same time:
> – large scale arrests; – a large number of "political" prisoners; – the probable existence of ill-treatment or inhumane conditions of detention; – the sus-

---

44   As the ICRC Commentary observes, 'the Protocol applies on the one hand in a situation where the armed forces of the government confront dissident armed forces, i.e., where there is a rebellion by part of the government army or where the government's armed forces fight against insurgents who are organized in armed groups, which is more often the case. This criterion illustrates the collective character of the confrontation; it can hardly consist of isolated individuals without co-ordination.' *Commentary on the Additional Protocols*, supra n 34, at 1351.

45   Id. at 1351-52.

pension of fundamental judicial guarantees, either as part of the promulgation of a state of emergency or simply as a matter of fact; – allegations of disappearances.

In short, as stated above, there are internal disturbances, without being an armed conflict, when the State uses armed force to maintain order; there are internal tensions, without being internal disturbances, when force is used as a preventive measure to maintain respect for law and order.

These definitions are not contained in a convention but form part of ICRC doctrine.... While designed for practical use, they may serve to shed some light on these terms, which appear in an international law instrument for the first time.[46]

A number of conflicts following the adoption of the Protocols were generally acknowledged to be armed conflicts to which IHL applied: the 1980-88 Iran-Iraq War; the Falklands Conflict (1982), the Persian Gulf War (1990-1991); and the internal conflicts in El Salvador (1980-1993), the Philippines (1991) and Bosnia-Herzegovina (1992-1994).

By way of contrast, other forceful events have not generally been characterized as armed conflict.[47] For example, in 1981 and 1982 incidents involving Soviet submarines in Swedish waters, including the use of depth charges by the Swedish Navy, were not treated as an armed conflict.[48] Also in 1981, US fighter jets engaged in a firefight with Libyan aircraft above the Gulf of Sidra, shooting them down.[49] This incident was not treated as an armed conflict. In 1985, the US intercepted an Egyptian passenger plane carrying the hijackers of the *Achille Lauro*. The Egyptian plane was forced down in Sicily.[50] No one, apparently, considered the US and Egypt to have been engaged in an armed conflict. Along similar lines in 1985, French secret agents attached bombs to the hull of the Greenpeace ship, *the Rainbow Warrior*, while docked in Auckland, New Zealand. The ship was sunk with the loss of one life. New Zealand police quickly arrested the two agents. In the subsequent arbitration to enforce a decision in the case by the Secretary-General of the United Nations, the arbitrators

---

46   *Commentary on the Additional Protocols*, supra n 34, at 1355.

47   O'Connell, *Enhancing the Status of Non-State Actors*, supra n 2, at 445-46.

48   R Sadurska, *Foreign Submarines in Swedish Waters: The Erosion of an International Norm*, in *International Incidents: The Law that Counts in World Politics* 40, 41-44 (W M Reisman and A R Willard eds, Princeton: Princeton University Press, 1988); S Schemann, *Soviet Accuses Swedes on Listening Post*, New York Times, 11 November 1981, A3.

49   S R Ratner, *The Gulf of Sidra Incident of 1981: The Lawfulness of Peacetime Aerial Engagements*, in *International Incidents*, supra n 48, at 181; A M Weisburd, *Use of Force*, supra n 39, at 289-90.

50   See C P Wallace, *Action by US 'Surprises and Saddens' Egypt*, Los Angeles Times, 12 October 1985, 1.

do not refer to the bombing as an armed conflict or that the agents were subject to IHL rather than New Zealand's criminal law.[51]

(c)   Statutes of International Criminal Tribunals

From 1993-2008

The meaning of armed conflict has undergone considerable development in the Statutes and jurisprudence of the two ad hoc tribunals established by the Security Council during the 1990s, the ICTY and the ICTR, and in the Statute of the ICC adopted by States in 1998. In 2007 the ICC delivered its first judgement considering the meaning of armed conflict.

The ICTY *Tadić* decision is nowadays widely relied on as authoritative for the meaning of armed conflict in both international and non-international armed conflicts.[52] According to the Appeals Chamber of the ICTY in the *Tadić* case an armed conflict, "exists whenever there is a resort to armed force between States or protracted armed violence between governmental authorities and organized armed groups or between such groups within a State".[53] The *Tadić* formulation has no requirement that armed groups exercise territorial control, be capable of meeting IHL obligations, or that a government be involved in the fighting.[54]

In applying the *Tadić* Appeal Chamber formulation the *Tadić* Trial Chamber focused on two aspects of a conflict: the intensity of the conflict and the organisation of the parties to the conflict. In the opinion of the Chamber, in an armed conflict of an internal or mixed character these closely related criteria are used solely for the purpose of distinguishing an armed conflict from banditry, unorganized or short-lived insurrections or terrorist activities which are not subject to IHL.[55] Many other ICTY cases follow this approach.[56] In *Kordić*

---

51   *Rainbow Warrior* (New Zealand v France) 20 RIAA 217 (1990).

52   See, for example, the Rome Statute of the International Criminal Court art. 8, 17 July 1998, 37 ILM 999; European Commission for Democracy Through Law (Venice Commission) Opinion on the International Legal Obligations of Council of Europe Member States in Respect of Secret Detention Facilities and Inter-State Transport of Persons, 17 March 2006, Op. no. 363/2005, CDL-AD (2006)009 (Venice Commission Opinion).

53   *Prosecutor v Tadić*, Case No. IT-94-1-T, Decision on Defense Motion for Interlocutory Appeal on Jurisdiction, 2 October 1995, para.70.

54   L Moir, *The Law of Internal Armed Conflict*, supra n 23, at 42, quoting *Prosecutor v Tadić*, Case No. IT-94-1A, Jurisdiction, 2 October 1995, para. 70.

55   *Prosecutor v Tadić*, Case No. IT-94-1-T, Opinion and Judgement, 7 May 1997, para. 562.

56   *Prosecutor v Blagojević and Jokić*, Case No. IT-02-60-T, Judgement, 17 January 2005, para. 536; *Prosecutor v Halilović*, Case No. IT-01-48-T, Judgement, 16 November

and Čerkez, the Appeals Chamber said that the term "protracted" is significant in excluding mere cases of civil unrest or single acts of terrorism in cases of non-international conflicts.[57]

The *Mucić* case elaborated on the *Tadić* test in relation to international conflicts stating that, "the existence of armed force between States is sufficient of itself to trigger the application of international humanitarian law" and furthermore that it was "guided by the Commentary to the Fourth Geneva Convention, which considers that 'any difference arising between two States and leading to the intervention of members of the armed forces' is an international armed conflict and 'it makes no difference how long conflict lasts, or how much slaughter takes place'".[58]

The question as to whether there was a non-international armed conflict came before the ICTY again with regard to the conflict in Kosovo; the Tribunal had to decide whether there was a non-international armed conflict or mere internal unrest. In *Milošević*, an *amici curiae* motion was brought that there was no armed conflict in Kosovo at the relevant times and so no case to answer for war crimes under Article 3 of the ICTY Statute.[59] It was argued that the armed conflict began on 24 March 1999 when the NATO bombing campaign began. Before then, the conflict did not involve protracted armed violence; it was only "acts of banditry, unorganized and short-lived insurrections or terrorist activities". The Trial Chamber held that *Tadić* had set out the test for the existence of an internal armed conflict. The Chamber was of the view that the *Tadić* test was "not inconsistent" with the ICRC's Official Commentary to Common Article 3 of the Geneva Conventions set out above. The Commentary, however, was of persuasive value only; although it does offer a more extensive list of criteria, these are not definitive or exhaustive. Thus the Chamber dismissed the more

---

2005, para. 24; *Prosecutor v Limaj et al*, Case No IT-03-65-T, Judgement, 30 November 2005, para. 84; *Prosecutor v Galić*, Case No. IT-98-29-T, Opinion and Judgement, 5 December 2003, para. 9; *Prosecutor v Stakić*, Case No. IT-97-24-T, Judgement, 31 July 2003, paras. 566-68. See also Venice Commission Opinion, supra n 52: 'sporadic bombings and other violent acts which terrorist networks perpetrate in different places around the globe and the ensuing counter-terrorism measures, even if they are occasionally undertaken by military units, cannot be said to amount to an 'armed conflict' in the sense that they trigger the applicability of International Humanitarian Law.'

57   *Prosecutor v Kordić and Čerkez*, Case No. IT-95-14/2-A, Judgement, 17 December 2004, para. 341.

58   *Prosecutor v Mucić et al*, Case No. IT-96-21-T, Judgement, 16 November 1998, paras. 184, 208.

59   See *Prosecutor v Milošević*, Case No. IT-02-54-T, Decision on Motion for Judgement of Acquittal *Under Rule 98 bis*, 16 June 2004.

restrictive criteria of the ICRC in relation to Common Article 3 in favour of the broader approach of the Court in *Tadić*.[60]

As for the factors that should be taken into account in assessing intensity, the Trial Chamber in the *Milošević* case considered a large body of evidence: the size of the Serbian response to the actions of the Kosovo Liberation Army (KLA) was treated as evidence of the nature of the conflict; account was taken of the spread of the conflict over territory, the increase in number of government forces and of the weapons used. The Chamber said that control over territory by insurgents was not a requirement for the existence of a non-international armed conflict.

Reference was also made to the decisions of other Chambers that had considered such factors as the seriousness of attacks and whether there had been an increase in armed clashes, the spread of clashes over territory and over a period of time, any increase in the number of government forces, mobilisation and the distribution of weapons among both parties to the conflict, as well as whether the conflict has attracted the attention of the Security Council and whether any resolutions have been passed.

The Trial Chamber also held that fighters must exhibit organisation, but only "some degree of organisation will suffice".[61] It rejected the argument that in order to be bound by IHL a party must be able to implement IHL.[62] The Chamber referred to the fact that other Chambers had

taken into account factors "including the existence of headquarters, designated zones of operation, and the ability to procure, transport, and distribute arms".[63] The Chamber pointed to the fact that the KLA had a general staff that appointed zone commanders, gave directions to units and issued public statements. Unit commanders gave orders and subordinate units generally acted in accordance with those orders. Steps had been taken to introduce disciplinary rules and military police and to recruit, train and equip new members.[64]

The criteria of intensity and organisation in a non-international armed conflict were considered in detail again in 2008 in the case of *Haradinaj*. The Trial Chamber, after a survey of the practice reviewed in previous ICTY decisions, observed that the criterion of protracted armed violence in practice had been interpreted as referring more to the intensity of the armed violence than to its duration.[65]

---

60   The same approach to the ICRC criteria was adopted in the *Limaj* case (*Prosecutor v Limaj et al*, supra n 56, at para. 85. The Trial Chamber in that case also observed that the drafting history of Common Article 3 shows a clear rejection of more detailed criteria (para. 86) and moreover that Article 8 of the Rome Statute of the International Criminal Court adopted the *Tadić* approach (para. 87).

61   Id. at para. 89.

62   Id. at paras. 88-89.

63   Id. at para. 90, citing *Milošević* Rule 98 *bis* Decision, supra n 59, at paras. 23-24.

64   Id. at paras. 94-134.

65   Prosecutor v Ramush Haradinaj, Case No. IT-04-84-T, 3 April 2008, at para. 49 (

The ICTR[66] has followed the approach of the ICTY on Common Article 3. In *Akayesu*,[67] the Tribunal considered the nature of the conflict in Rwanda at some length.[68] The Chamber quoted the *Tadić* case on the definition of armed conflict; it also noted the ICRC commentary on Common Article 3, which ruled out mere acts of banditry, internal disturbances and tensions and unorganized and short-lived insurrections.[69] Because the definition of an armed conflict is abstract, the question whether or not a situation can be described as an armed conflict, meeting the criteria of Common Article 3, was to be decided on a case-by-case approach. The ICTR suggested an "evaluation test", evaluating the intensity of the conflict and the organisation of the parties.[70] Intensity did not depend on the subjective judgment of the parties; it was objective.[71]

The Inter-American Commission on Human Rights had to determine whether IHL applied in *Abella v Argentina*.[72] The Commission's determination depended, in turn, on whether the petitioners had been involved in an armed conflict with Argentine authorities. The Commission found that an armed conflict had indeed occurred despite the fact that fighting lasted only thirty hours. The Commission considered the following factors: "the concerted nature of the hostile acts undertaken by the attackers, the direct involvement of governmental armed forces, and the nature and level of the violence attending the events in question. More particularly, the attackers involved carefully planned, coordinated and executed an armed attack, i.e., a military operation against a quintessential military objective -a military base."[73]

The Rome Statute of the International Criminal Court, 17 July 1998, provides in Article 8 for War Crimes. War crimes include serious violations of Common Article 3, which "applies to armed conflicts not of an international character and thus does not apply to situations of internal disturbances and

---

for the factors relevant to assessing intensity see para. 49 and for organisation see paras 64-89).

66   See Human Rights Watch, *Case Law of the International Criminal Tribunal for Rwanda*, February 2004, available at http://www.hrw.org/reports/2004/ij/ictr/index.htm.

67   *Prosecutor v Akayesu*, ICTR-96-4-T, 2 September 1998, paras. 619-27.

68   See also *Prosecutor v Kayishema and Ruzindana*, ICTR-95-1-T, 21 May 1999, paras. 170-72.

69   See also *Prosecutor v Akayesu*, supra n 67, at paras. 619-21; *Prosecutor v Kayishema and Ruzindana*, supra n 74, at para. 155-90.

70   Id. at para. 620.

71   *Prosecutor v Akayesu*, supra n 67, at para. 603.

72   *Juan Carlos Abella v Argentina*, Case 11.137, Report No. 55/97, Inter-Am. C.H.R., OEA/Ser.L/V/II.98, Doc. 6 rev., 18 November 1997, paras. 149-51 (distinguishing "internal disturbances" from armed conflict on the basis of the nature and level of violence).

73   Id. at para. 155.

tensions, such as riots, isolated and sporadic acts of violence or other acts of a similar nature".[74] Article 8(2)(e) applies to other serious violations of the laws and customs applicable in armed conflict not of an international character. It "applies to armed conflicts that take place in the territory of a State when there is protracted armed conflict between governmental authorities and organised armed groups or between such groups". The Rome Statute is not limited to conflicts between governments and armed groups; it omits the condition that dissident armed forces or other organised groups should be "under responsible command or exercise such control over a part of its territory as to enable them to carry out sustained and concerted military operations".[75]

The extent to which the *Tadić* test is consistent with the ICC Rome Statute was considered by the Trial Chamber of the ICTY in the judgment on the *Milošević amici curiae* motion. The Chamber was of the view that the *Tadić* case definition of internal armed conflict was consistent with Article 8 of the ICC Statute.[76]

The Pre-Trial Chamber of the ICC for the first time considered the meaning of armed conflict in the ICC Rome Statute in the 2007 case of *Prosecutor v Thomas Lubanga Dyilo*.[77] The Chamber focused on the criteria of intensity, organisation and protraction. The criteria of organisation and protraction are linked by the Chamber: "protracted armed conflict...focuses on the need for the armed groups in question to have the ability to plan and carry out military operations for a prolonged period of time".[78]

Other developments during this period include the Secretary-General's adoption in 1999 of the *Bulletin on Observance by United Nations Forces of International Humanitarian Law*.[79] IHL applies when United Nations forces are in situations of armed conflict, actively engaged as combatants, to the extent and for the duration of their engagement.[80] National courts in the United

---

74　This language is the same as Art 1(3) of Protocol I and Art 1(2) of the Convention on the Prohibition of the Use, Stockpiling, Production and Transfer or Anti-Personnel Mines and on Their Destruction (entered into force 1 March 1999) (Mine Ban Treaty), 36 ILM 1507 (1997).

75　D Willmott, *Removing the Distinction between International and Non-International Armed Conflict in the* Rome Statute of the International Criminal Court (2004) 5 Melbourne Journal of International Law 196, 218. See also H Spieker, *The International Criminal Court and Non-International Armed Conflicts* (2000) 13(2) Leiden Journal of International Law 395, 409.

76　*Milošević* Rule 98 *bis* Decision, supra n 59, at para. 20.

77　Case no ICC-01/04-01/06, 29 Jan 2007.

78　Id. at para 234.

79　*UN Secretary General's Bulletin on Observance by United Nations Forces of International Humanitarian Law*, UN Doc ST/SGB/1999/13, 6 August 1999, available at http://www.un.org/peace/st_sgb_1999_13.pdf.

80　C Greenwood, *International Humanitarian Law and UN Military Operations* (1998)

Kingdom,[81] Canada, Italy and Belgium have struggled with cases turning on the legal status of peacekeeping operations and the applicability of IHL to their conduct.

In a case particularly on point, *Brocklebank*,[82] the Canadian Court Martial Appeal Court considered the torture and beating to death of a Somali teenager during Canada's participation in the UN peacekeeping mission in Somalia. The Court did not find evidence of an armed conflict in Somalia at the material time and, on that basis, found the criminal counts inapplicable because they were based on the Fourth Geneva Convention, which does not apply to peace operations. However, other authorities, such as the Commission of Inquiry of 1995[83] and the Simpson Study of the law applicable to Canadian forces in Somalia in 19921993,[84] arrived at the opposite conclusion.

An Italian Commission of Inquiry looking into the conduct of Italian peacekeeping troops in Somalia apparently also found it difficult to define the nature of the conflict. "It appears evident from the Report that it is truly difficult to ascertain whether the events reported can be set within a legal context of war or within that of a police operation aiming at restoring public order. Therefore, the Commission failed to express any legal evaluation of the facts, particularly from the perspective of international humanitarian law."[85] Similarly a Belgian Military Court denied the applicability of IHL in Somalia and Rwanda. It found that IHL did not apply to operations with humanitarian aims in situations of internal conflicts instituted under Chapter VII of the UN Charter. Consequently it rejected the argument that Belgian troops were either "combatants" or "occupying forces" in either crisis.[86]

I   Yearbook of International Humanitarian Law 24. See also M Zwanenburg, *Accountability under International Humanitarian Law for United Nations and North Atlantic Treaty Organization. Peace Support Operations* ch. 3 (Leiden: Martinus Nijhoff Publishers, 2004).

81   See *R v Ministry of Defence; ex parte Walker*, UKHL 22 [2000] 2 All ER 917 (House of Lords) (6 April 2000).

82   *The Queen v Brocklebank*, Court Martial Appeal Court of Canada, 2 April 1996, 106 Canadian Criminal Cases (3d); see also K Boustany, *Brocklebank: A Questionable Decision of the Court Martial Appeal Court of Canada* (1998) 1 Yearbook of International Humanitarian Law 371.

83   Although the Commission of Inquiry did not reach any definitive conclusions on the issue of applicability, 87% of its general recommendations were supported and implemented by the Department of National Defence.

84   J M Simpson, "Law Applicable to Canadian Forces in Somalia" 1992/93: A study prepared for the Commission of Inquiry into the Deployment of Canadian Forces to Somalia (Ottawa: Minister of Public Works and Government Services Canada, 1997).

85   N Lupi, *Report by the Enquiry Commission on the Behaviour of Italian Peace-Keeping Troops in Somalia* (1998) 1 Yearbook of International Humanitarian Law 375, 379.

86   Belgium, Military Court, *Violations of IHL in Somalia and Rwanda*, Case Nr. 54

The 2004 United Kingdom Manual of the Law of Armed Conflict provides as follows in relation to international armed conflict: "The law of armed conflict applies in all situations when the armed forces of a state are in conflict with those of another state or are in occupation of territory. The law also applies to hostilities in which some of those involved are acting under the authority of the United Nations and in internal armed conflicts. Different rules apply to these different situations."[87] The Manual observes that the expression "armed conflict" remains undefined and cites the ICRC Commentary[88] and the *Tadić* case as guidance. In relation to the question of the threshold of armed conflict the Manual says that:

> whether any particular intervention crosses the threshold so as to become an armed conflict will depend on all the surrounding circumstances. For example, the replacing of border police with soldiers or accidental border incursion by members of the armed forces would not, in itself, amount to an armed conflict, nor would the accidental bombing of another country. At the other extreme, a full-scale invasion would amount to an armed conflict.[89]

The International Law Commission is considering a proposed definition of armed conflict for the purposes of its work on "Effects of Armed Conflicts on Treaties." The draft definition (on which opinions continue to be divided as to the inclusion of non-international armed conflicts) is based on the formulation adopted by the Institute of International Law in its resolution of the 28th of August 1985:

> "Armed conflict" means a state of war or a conflict which involves armed operations which by their nature or extent are likely to affect the operation of treaties between States parties to the armed conflict or between States parties to the armed conflict and third States, regardless of a formal declaration of war or other declaration by any or all of the parties to the armed conflict.[90]

A. R., 20 November and 17 December 1997. The French report on military engagement in Rwanda also does not offer any practical solutions. Rapport d'information No. 1271, available at http://www.assembleenationale.fr/11/dossiers/Rwanda/r1271. asp. However, the Indonesian report on investigations and prosecution of atrocities in East Timor seems to be different. Executive Summary Report on the investigation of human rights violations in East Timor, Jakarta, 31 January, 2000, available at http://www.etan.org/news/2000a/3exec.htm.

87   The Manual of the Law of Armed Conflict 27 (UK Ministry of Defence, 2004).

88   III *Commentary on the Geneva Conventions of August 12 1949*, supra n 34.

89   The Manual of the Law of Armed Conflict, supra n 87, at 29 (footnote omitted).

90   ILC Report on the work of its fifty-ninth session (7 May to 5 June and 9 July to 10 August 2007) GAOR Sixty-second Sess Supp No 10 (A/62/10), para 284-288.

The 2005 Report of the International Commission of Inquiry on Darfur to the United Nations Secretary-General accepted the *Tadić* definition of armed conflict.[91]

Also in 2005 the ICRC published a major study on the customary status of IHL.[92] The aim of the study was first to assess what elements of IHL are now reflected in customary law, in particular the more recent humanitarian treaties that do not have the same level of acceptance as the 1949 Geneva Conventions. Secondly, given the limited nature of the treaty rules applicable to non-international armed conflict, it was desirable to determine if in fact customary international law regulates non-international conflict in more detail than treaty law.[93] The study does not contain a definition of armed conflict, however, despite the evident usefulness of including one.

Relevant state practice on the definition question of armed conflict following the adoption of the international criminal court statutes and the ICRC study included the following: In February 1995, a Canadian naval vessel fired across the bow of a privately owned Spanish fishing vessel on the high seas to prevent over-fishing of Greenland Halibut. Spain brought a case against Canada before the ICJ, complaining against Canada's "measures of coercion and the exercise of jurisdiction over [the *Estai*] and its captain"; Spain claimed that Canada's actions violated Article 2(4) of the UN Charter among other treaties as well as customary law obligations.[94] The ICJ found it had no jurisdiction in the case, so no ruling on the question was ever made. The "Herring War" in 1994, between Iceland and Norway, also involved the engagement of official vessels of states, as well as limited use of armed force.[95] These incidents were not treated as armed conflicts.

---

91   See *Report of the International Commission of Inquiry on Darfur to the United Nations Secretary-General, Pursuant to Security Council Resolution 1564 of 18 September 2004,* Geneva, 25 January 2005, para. 74, available at http://www.un.org/news/dh/sudan/com_inq_darfur.pdf.

92   *Customary International Humanitarian Law,* supra n 31. Consider in connection with this part *Perspectives on the ICRC Study on Customary International Humanitarian Law* (E Wilmshurst and S Breau eds, Cambridge: Cambridge University Press, 2007) and see ICRC Opinion Paper, March 2008, "How is the Term 'Armed Conflict' Defined in International Humanitarian Law?".

93   See J-M Henckaerts, *Assessing the Laws and Customs of War: The Publication of Customary International Humanitarian Law* (2006) 13 Human Rights Brief 8.

94   Fisheries Jurisdiction (Spain v Canada) (Jurisdiction), 1998 ICJ reports 432, 437.

95   B Maddox, *Fleets fight in over-fished waters: Fishing disputes have risen up the diplomatic agenda,* Financial Times (London), 30 August 1994, at 4. The first two cases before the International Tribunal for the Law of the Sea concerned arrest of fishing vessels. See *Panama v France* (the *Camouco* case), International Tribunal for the Law of the Sea, 7 February 2000, available at http://www.itlos.org/cgibin/cases/case_detail.pl?id=4&lang=en; *Saint Vincent and the Grenadines v Guinea* (the *M/V Saiga* case), International Tribunal for the Law of the Sea, 37 ILM 360 (1998).

Rioting, even when it is widespread, resulting in deaths or serious destruction is not considered armed conflict because of the lack of organisation. Such rioting occurred in the United Kingdom (esp. 1985, 2001, 2005), Los Angeles (1992), Albania (1997), France (2005) and Kenya (2007-8). These have not been classified as armed conflicts. In the case of Los Angeles, United States Marines were deployed to help quell the violence. They operated under police rules.[96]

States have on occasion fired on civil aircraft.[97] While many of these cases involved mistaking passenger planes for enemy attack aircraft, in 1996 Cuba intentionally shot down two civil aircraft flown by persons opposed to the Castro regime after the aircraft made illegal incursions into Cuban airspace. The debate around this incident was over whether the aircraft were over international waters or not.[98] The case was described as an "incident," not an armed conflict.

The US has argued that it entered into a worldwide war on terrorism as of the attacks of 11 September 2001.[99] Terrorist attacks since 11 September, however,

---

See also J P E Hijos, *S A v Canada* (Attorney General) (the *Estai* case), FC 1011 (Federal Court of Canada, 2005). See also E Cowan, *Oil and Water: the Torrey Canyon Disaster* (Philadelphia: Lippincott, 1968).

96 Rwanda in 1994 may be another example. The Tutsis inside Rwanda were not an organized armed group at the time Hutu leaders ordered their deaths. Most charges against Hutu leaders later were for genocide and crimes against humanity, not war crimes. The Swiss Military Court of Cassation, however, found Niyonteze, the mayor of a Rwandan town, guilty of war crimes. See B H Oxman and L Reydams, *Niyonteze v Public Prosecutor*, Tribunal militaire de cassation (Switzerland), 27 April 2001 96 AJIL 231 (2002).

97 See A F Lowenfeld, *AGORA: The Downing of Iran Air Flight 655: Looking Back and Looking Ahead* (1989) 83 American Journal of International Law 336; C. Morgan, *The Shooting of Korean Air Lines Flight 007: Responses to Unauthorized Aerial Incursions*, in *International Incidents*, supra n 48, at 202.

98 M Clary, *Cuban Fighters Down 2 Planes Owned by Exiles*, Los Angeles Times, 25 February 1996, A1.

99 G W Bush, President's Address to the Nation on the Terrorist Attacks, 37 Weekly Comp. Pres. Doc. 1301 (11 September 2001); President's Address to Joint Session of Congress on the United States Response to the Terrorist Attacks of September 11, 37 Weekly Comp. Pres. Doc. 1432 (20 September 2001). (Bush said the US was in a 'war on terror' that would last 'until every terrorist group of global reach has been found, stopped and defeated'.) US Deputy National Security Adviser S. Hadley, in remarks at The Ohio State University, explained that the US was in a war as of 12 September, because the 11 September attacks were 'an act of war'. S Hadley, Remarks at the Moritz College of Law of the Ohio State University (24 September 2004). See also A Dworkin, Official Examines Legal Aspects of Terror War: Interview with Charles Allen, US Department of Defense Deputy General Counsel for International Affairs (on file with author); A Dworkin, *Law and the Campaign against Terrorism: the View from the Pentagon*, Crimes of War Project (16 December 2002), available at http://www.crimesofwar.org/print/onnews/pentagon-print.html at 6; J B Bellinger,

including the attacks in London, Madrid and Bali, have been characterized as crimes, not armed conflict.[100]

In 2002, a 21-minute exchange of fire between North and South Korea resulted in a patrol boat being sunk and four South Korean sailors being killed. It was referred to as an "incident", "armed provocation", "border incursion", "clash" and the like, but not an armed conflict.[101] North Korean naval submarines have also been detected in Japanese territorial waters, neither in transit nor on the surface – two violations of the right of innocent passage.[102] These incursions have not been treated as armed conflict.

By contrast, there were many conflicts not already mentioned above during this period that were widely recognized as armed conflicts, including in Angola, Bougainville, Congo, Liberia, Sierra Leone, Colombia, the Philippines, Indonesia, and Sri Lanka.[103]

In December 2006, Israel's Supreme Court considered the meaning of armed conflict and found that Israel is engaged in an armed conflict in the Palestinian Territories. The most important factor for the Court in reaching this determination was the number of persons who have died on both sides. It did not take into account the sporadic nature of the violence against Israel.[104]

The requirement that armed conflict must meet some sort of threshold of intensity is supported by the 2007 consultation paper issued by the UK Ministry of Justice on *War Powers and Treaties: Limiting Executive Powers*. The Paper observes "there may be difficult questions about when violence has reached the threshold where there can be said to be a state of 'armed conflict' between the participants".[105]

   Legal Issues in the War on Terrorism, London School of Economics (31 October 2006), available at http://www.lse.ac.uk/collections/LSEPublicLecturesAndEvents/pdf/20061031_JohnBellinger.pdf.

100 O'Connell, *Enhancing the Status of Non-State Actors, supra* n 2.

101 D Kirk, *North and South Korea Trade Charges Over Naval Clash*, New York Times, 30 June 2002, 12.

102 See *The Call to Arms*, Economist (London), 27 February 1999, 23; *The Koreas: the Money Factor*, Economist (London), 31 October 1998, 45.

103 For a discussion of several of these conflicts see M E O'Connell, *Humanitarian Assistance in Non-International Armed Conflict: The Fourth Wave of Rights, Duties and Remedies* (2000) 31 Israel Yearbook on Human Rights 183.

104 Public Committee Against Torture in Israel v Israel, HCJ 769/02 (Dec. 14, 2006). But see the ICJ Advisory Opinion on the Wall, finding Israel to be in occupation in the Occupied Palestinian Territory, and not in an armed conflict. The Court found Israel must confine itself to security measures consistent with the law of occupation. *Legal Consequences of the construction of a Wall in the Occupied Palestinian Territory*, Advisory Opinion, 2004 ICJ reports 196.

105 United Kingdom Ministry of Justice, The Governance of Britain: War Powers and Treaties: Limiting Executive Powers, Consultation Paper CP26/07, 25 October 2007, 25, available at http://www.officialdocuments.gov.uk/document/cm72/7239/7239.

Also in 2007, Iran detained the crew of a small British naval vessel claiming that the vessel was in Iranian territorial waters.[106] The British claimed they were in Iraqi waters. This case, again, involved the intervention of the armed forces of two states. It was not apparently considered an armed conflict. Britain complained when its troops were shown on television, and a spokesperson for the Prime Minister said doing so was a violation of the Third Geneva Convention.[107] The UK did not take an official position, however, as to whether the Convention applied. It was certainly consistent with the spokesperson's statement that the UK hoped the higher standard regarding protection from public displays found in the Geneva Convention would be honoured (Third Geneva Convention, Article 13) even if Iran were not obligated to apply it. No similar protection appears to exist in peacetime human rights law.[108] Iran, however, treated the matter as one of illegal entry and indicated it might put the crew on trial. Iran made no reference to the Geneva Conventions that was reported in the English-language press.

Election-related violence in Kenya in late 2007 and early 2008 has consistently been described as rioting, civil unrest, and criminality, not armed conflict.[109] Colombia's 2008 incursion into Ecuador was determined by the Organization of American States to have violated the principle of non-intervention and to have posed a threat of armed conflict, without reaching the level of actual armed conflict.[110]

Finally in early 2008, Swedish and British immigration tribunals assessed the conflicts in Iraq and Somalia for purposes of determining whether asylum seekers from those states could continue to receive asylum from armed con-

---

pdf. See also the White Paper, The Governance of Britain-Constitutional Renewal (Cm 7342, March 2008).

106   See, for example, M Stannard, *What Law Did Tehran Break? Capture of British Sailors a Gray Area in Application of Geneva Conventions*, San Francisco Chronicle, 1 April 2007, A1.

107   Id.

108   The Foreign Office reports the United Kingdom did not take an official position on the Geneva Conventions. E-mail message of 17 May 2007 (on file with the Committee).

109   For example, the Global Partnership for the Prevention of Armed Conflict refers to the situation in Kenya in late 2007 and early 2008 as 'violence' and 'escalating violence', not armed conflict. See Kenya Update 22 January 2008, available at http://www.gppac.net/page.php?id=1837.

110   See, for example, S Romero, *Files Released by Colombia Point To Venezuelan Bid to Arm Rebels*, New York Times, 30 March 2008, A1 ("Colombia's relations with its two Andean neighbours veered suddenly toward armed conflict after Colombian forces raided a FARC camp inside Ecuador on March 1, killing 26 people, including a top FARC commander, and capturing the computers, according to the Colombians.")

flicts.[111] In other words, the tribunals had to determine whether there were armed conflicts occurring in Somalia and Iraq. In *HH & Others*, an appeal of three asylum cases, decided 22 January 2008, a UK immigration tribunal found that the conflict in Somalia was a non-international armed conflict that was occurring in Mogadishu.[112] Individuals from areas beyond Mogadishu did not have a right to seek asylum from armed conflict. The decision is highly detailed respecting the situation in Somalia. It uses the *Tadić* criteria to determine the meaning of armed conflict in international law.[113] The tribunal found the parties to the conflict sufficiently organized, and the intensity of fighting sufficient in the Mogadishu area.[114] It also stated that "the Tribunal should endeavour to identify both the territorial area in respect of which international humanitarian law applies (following the identification of an internal armed conflict) and, where feasible, the parameters of the actual zone of conflict".[115]

The tribunal noted the differences in IHL that depend on whether a conflict is international or non-international, but provided virtually no analysis of why it considered Somalia a non-international armed conflict, despite the fact that Ethiopia and the United States were involved in intense fighting beginning in early 2007. By October, 6000 people were dead. The US position respecting its role in Somalia is that it was aiding Ethiopia in collective self-defence as well as using force in respect of its own "global war on terror".[116]

III   Criteria And Characteristics of Armed Conflict

The above discussion supports the position that armed conflict is to be distinguished from "incidents"; "border clashes"; "internal disturbances and tensions such as riots, isolated and sporadic acts of violence";[117] "banditry, unorganised and short lived insurrections or terrorist activities"[118] and "civil unrest, [and]

---

111   See also Swedish cases.

112   *HH & Others (Mogadishu: Armed Conflict: Risk) Somalia v Secretary of State for the Home Department.* CG [2008] UKAIT 00022. United Kingdom: Asylum and Immigration Tribunal / Immigration Appellate Authority. 28 January 2008. Online. UNHCR Refworld, available at: http://www.unhcr.org/cgibin/texis/vtx/refworld/rwmain?docid=47dfd9172.

113   Id. at para. 318.

114   Id. at para. 337.

115   Id. at para. 330.

116   See J E Frazer, Assistant Secretary, Department of State, Policy Options in the Horn of Africa, Congressional Testimony, 11 March 2008.

117   Additional Protocol II art 1(2).

118   *Tadić*, supra n 55, at para. 562. Other cases have adopted this terminology: see, for example, *Blagojević and Jokić,* supra n 56, at para. 536; *Halilović,* supra n 56, at para. 24; *Galić,* supra n 56, at para. 9; *Stakić,* supra n 56, at para. 560.

single acts of terrorism".[119] The distinction between these situations and armed conflict is achieved by reliance on the criteria of organisation and intensity. IHL also uses these criteria in distinguishing between different types of armed conflicts to which different categories of IHL apply.[120]

The criteria of organisation and intensity are clearly related and should be considered together when assessing whether a particular situation amounts to an armed conflict. It seems that the higher the level of organisation the less degree of intensity may be required and vice versa.

Over the years there have been various other characteristics that have been put forward as integral to armed conflict. The majority of these have related to the level of organisation of dissident groups. For example, the requirement that the conflict take place between governmental forces and rebel forces and for the latter to control part of the territory, to have a responsible command and to be capable of implementing the requirements of IHL. However, it appears that none of these are reflected in the treaty or customary law meaning of armed conflict although they are integral to the application of Additional Protocol II.

The criterion of organisation: the evidence discussed above indicates clearly that armed conflicts involve two or more organized armed groups. Violence perpetrated by the assassin or terrorist acting essentially alone or the disorganized mob violence of a riot is not armed conflict. This criterion is reflected in treaty instruments,[121] mentioned explicitly or implicitly in decisions of several courts and tribunals,[122] as well as in the commentary of international law scholars. The significance of organisation for the existence of an armed conflict is also reflected in United Nations peacekeeping practice. As outlined above, peacekeeping forces respect peacetime human rights protections unless a force opposing them is, *inter alia*, an organized armed group.

The organisation factor is readily met in conflicts involving states, but is a more complex issue in the context of non-international armed conflict. Reaching the requisite level of organisation indicates, as a practical matter, that armed conflicts will commonly feature opposing groups controlling enough territory to organise. Trial Chambers of the ICTY have relied on several indicative factors to determine whether the organisation criterion is fulfilled. None of them, however, is central in themselves.[123] As mentioned in the *Milošević* case, organi-

---

119   See *Kordić and Čerkez*, supra n 57, at para. 341.

120   For example, a higher degree of organisation is required for the application of Additional Protocol II; see discussion supra.

121   See Common Article 2 of the 1949 Geneva Conventions (referring to High Contracting Parties); Common Article 3 of the Geneva Conventions ("organised military forces"); Article 1 of Additional Protocol II ("or other organised armed groups") and Rome Statute 8(2) (e).

122   In particular the *Tadić* case.

123   See Case no IT-04-84-T, 3 April 208 at para. 60 (for an analysis of the factors taken into account by the Tribunal in applying the organisation criterion).

sation is dependent on a command structure, space to train, storage of weapons and supplies, or space to rest – all aspects of armed conflict not seen in less-organized violence. While more recent decisions of the ICTY and the Rome Statute do not emphasize control of territory, the actual cases indicate that this criterion may well be an aspect of organisation. The Committee will undertake additional research on the organization question, including the issue of control of territory and the related question of the geographic extent of armed conflict.

The criterion of intensity: State practice, judicial opinion and the majority of commentators support the position that a certain level of hostilities is charac-teristic of all armed conflict. This is the case with respect to both international and non-international armed conflict, although some commentators support the view that there is no intensity requirement for the former.

In the context of international armed conflict the intensity requirement takes the form of requiring more than a minor exchange of fire or an isolated or insignificant border clash. The duration of the particular event is apparently not a determinate factor. Yet, this distinction is difficult to establish in state practice. Fighting that does not last for some period of time is less likely to be "intense" enough to meet the intensity criterion of international armed conflict.

The decision in the *Tadić* case also indicates that the level of intensity of non-international armed conflicts must be protracted. In other words, in order to constitute a non-international armed conflict there must be a certain level of armed violence over a protracted period. The additional requirement helps to distinguish armed conflict from "banditry, riots, isolated acts of terrorism, or similar situations".[124] The two concepts, intensity and protraction, are clearly linked and a lesser level of duration may satisfy the criterion if the intensity level is high.[125] The reverse is also the case.[126] The idea of "protraction" is also linked with the "organisation" criterion as it requires a certain level of organisation to undertake protracted hostilities.[127]

Additionally, the intensity criterion raises the issue of location of an armed conflict. In *HH & Others*, the tribunal found an armed conflict in the capi-tal, Mogadishu, but not the rest of Somalia. The IHL rules for non-interna-tional armed conflict applied only there. If the conflict had been characterized as an international armed conflict, some might argue that IHL rules presum-ably would have applied throughout Somalia, Ethiopia and the US. The intense fighting would still have only taken place in Mogadishu, however. It seems that few States apply IHL beyond the zone of intense fighting, whether the fighting

---

124   *Tadić* Jurisdiction Decision, para. 70.

125   This may be the explanation for the finding by the Inter-American Commission in *Abella*, discussed above, that fighting lasting only 30 hours was protracted enough for IHL to apply in a non-International armed conflict.

126   See Case no IT-04-84-T, 3 April 208 at para. 49.

127   See Case no ICC-01/04-01/06, 29 Jan 2007.

is an international or non-international armed conflict.[128] The US has certainly not recognized IHL as applicable in the US, despite applying it in Iraq and Afghanistan since 2003 and 2001 respectively and presumably in Somalia since early 2007.

As the IHL rules on international and non-international armed conflict converge, the argument for a distinction between the intensity level required for international versus non-international armed conflict will presumably lose its purpose. Indeed, as the cases show, making a meaningful distinction between the two types of conflicts is increasingly difficult. The distinction that appears to remain important is between armed conflict – of whatever type – and peace.

Conclusion

The 2001 US "declaration" of a "war on terror" has highlighted the lack of clarity as to the meaning of armed conflict in international law. Are states at liberty to declare "war" and does this change the pre-existing legal regime governing armed conflict? It is the view of the Committee that a "declaration" of war is meaningless from the international law perspective. It is the factual existence of a state of armed conflict that marks the transition from the law of peace to the law of armed conflict. A state of armed conflict exists if the criteria of organised armed groups and intensity of the hostilities are satisfied. This is the case in relation to both international and non-international armed conflicts. Once armed conflict exists IHL is triggered. Relevant principles of human rights law and other rules of international law, however, continue to apply to the situation. Forceful actions that do not satisfy these criteria remain governed by domestic criminal law, human rights law, refugee law and other general rules of international law.

---

128 Under the rules on the use of force there are geographical limits on States hostile activities 'The extent to which a belligerent today is justified in expanding the area of operations will depend upon whether it is necessary for him to do so in order to exercise his right of self-defense....' C Greenwood, *Scope of Application of Humanitarian Law*, supra n 23, at 53. See also Gardam, *Necessity, Proportionality and the Use of Force* 16263 supra n 9 and C Greenwood, *Self-Defence and the Conduct of International Armed Conflict*, in *International Law at a Time of Perplexity: Essays in Honour of Shabtai Rosenne* 273, 276-78 (Y Dinstein and M Tabory eds, Dordrecht: Martinus Nijhoff Publishers, 1989). But see Y Dinstein, *War, Aggression and Self-Defence* 19-20 supra n 21.

Chapter 22

Defining Armed Conflict, The Work of the ILA Committee on the Use of Force
(2005-2008)

Mary Ellen O'Connell[1]

13 Journal of Conflict & Security Law 393-400
Winter 2008*

In May 2005, the Executive Committee of the International Law Association (ILA) asked the ILA Use of Force Committee to report on the definition of armed conflict in international law. The ILA recognized the need for such a report following the United States declaration of a "global war on terrorism" after the attacks of 11 September 2001. At that time, no widely accepted definition of armed conflict was recognized by international law scholars. Nevertheless, there was plenty of evidence awaiting examination on what definition international law supports. The Use of Force Committee spent three years in research and discussion. It presented its Initial Report on "The Meaning of Armed Conflict in International Law" in August 2008 at the ILA biennial meeting in Rio de Janeiro.[2] The final report is scheduled to be submitted in 2010 at the ILA biennial in The Hague. This brief comment discusses why the Report was mandated, how the Report was prepared, its conclusions, and the additional topics to be included in the final report.

The Problem

On 11 September 2001 in the United States – a day of tragedy, chaos, and confusion, the President of the United States announced the country was at war.[3] The United States had yet to fire any bullets in anger. Military jets had scrambled, but they engaged no targets. It was not confirmed who was responsible for the attacks. The possibilities discussed on the day included home-grown terrorists, terrorists sponsored by a foreign state, and terrorists belonging to an

---

* Reprinted with permission.
1 Robert and Marion Short Chair in Law, University of Notre Dame and Chair of the International Law Association Committee on the Use of Force.
2 The Initial Report is posted at the Website of the ILA: <www.ila-hq.org/en/committees/index.cfm/cid/1022>.
3 George W. Bush, Address to the Nation (Sept. 11, 2001); Address to a Joint Session of Congress and the American People (Sept. 20, 2001).

Mary Ellen O'Connell (ed.), What Is War? An Investigation in the Wake of 9/11.
© *2012 Koninklijke Brill NV. Printed in The Netherlands.* ISBN *978 9004 17234 0. pp. 307–313.*

unsponsored non-state actor. These and other important issues remained open when nevertheless the President said the United States was at war all over the world. He said it was "global war against terrorism". Many scholars, especially specialists in the law of armed conflict, assumed the President's statement was rhetorical, a rallying cry to galvanize the nation. United States presidents had declared wars on drugs and poverty. The perception was that now the United States would wage a similar campaign of determined opposition to the scourge of terrorism. Slowly over the next months, however, as the United States and United Kingdom mounted a major military campaign in Afghanistan start-ing on 7 October 2001, it became apparent that the United States was claiming rights available to a state only during a *de jure* armed conflict afflicting all parts of the globe. Individuals were detained far from any battlefield and declared "unlawful enemy combatants" if they were suspected of association with ter-rorist organisations.[4] Six men were killed without warning in Yemen where no fighting was taking place because of their suspected ties to al Qaeda.[5]

The U.S. position was a departure from that taken more typically by gov-ernments since the adoption of the UN Charter and the outlawing of the use of force except in self-defense and with Security Council authorization. For the most part governments have preferred to deny being engaged in armed con-flicts even when they plainly are. Armed conflict, particularly internal armed conflict, is a sign that a government has failed to keep order. It is a sign that opponents have reached a level of strength where they may challenge the gov-ernment militarily.[6] Once that threshold is crossed, international humanitarian law applies and domestic law is circumscribed. In international armed con-flicts, the regular armed forces of a state become legitimate targets. In all armed conflict, the International Committee of the Red Cross (ICRC) may demand the right to visit detainees and to demand that certain standards applicable to detention are maintained.

Thus, the ICRC had pressed El Salvador, Sri Lanka and other states to treat conflicts on their territory as rising to internal conflicts, but it met resistance.[7]

---

4   Memorandum from William J. Haynes II, General Counsel of the Department of Defense, Enemy Combatants, http://www.cfr.org/publication.php?id=5312 (last visited June 15, 2006).

5   Doyle McManus, *A U.S. License to Kill, a New Policy Permits the C.I.A. to Assassinate Terrorists, and Officials Say a Yemen Hit Went Perfectly. Others Worry About Next Time,* L.A. TIMES, Jan. 11, 2003, 2003 WLNR 15125740; Jack Kelley, *U.S. Kills al-Qaeda Suspects in Yemen,* USA TODAY, Nov. 5, 2002, 2002 WLNR 4504127; John J. Lumpkin, *Administration Says That Bush Has, in Effect: a License to Kill; Anyone Designated by the President as an Enemy Combatant, Including U.S. Citizens, Can Be Killed Outright, Officials Argue,* ST. LOUIS POST-DISP., Dec. 4, 2002, 2002 WLNR 1198949.

6   For a discussion of this phenomenon, see, Mary Ellen O'Connell, *Enhancing the Status of Non-State Actors Through a Global War on Terror,* 43 COL. J. TRANS. LAW 435 (2005).

7   A number of cases of internal armed conflict and the efforts of the ICRC to get

The United Kingdom argued against demands that the conflict in Northern Ireland be labelled an armed conflict. Nevertheless, in these cases and in the U.S. case following 9/11, the issues could not be resolved by simply pointing to the accepted definition of armed conflict as found in a major treaty or influential decision of the International Court of Justice. The Geneva Conventions of 1949, for example, while stating in Common Article 2 that they apply in "armed conflict", do not define armed conflict.

When states argue against characterising situations as armed conflict, peacetime law continues to apply with, arguably, greater protections for individuals. True, the ICRC does not have the same rights to monitor situations other than armed conflict, but the right to kill without warning and detain without trial are far more limited in peacetime than during fighting amounting to armed conflict. The lack of a widely accepted definition of armed conflict did not, therefore, become a pressing issue until the United States moved against the prevailing trend and declared an armed conflict where specialists doubted there was one. The expanded wartime rights to kill and detain were claimed in a way that appeared to violate international law.

This new situation motivated the ILA to study the meaning of armed conflict in international law. In May 2005, the ILA Executive Committee mandated the ILA's Use of Force Committee to report on the question. The mandate asked for the general meaning of armed conflict in international law, not just the meaning with respect to the triggering of international humanitarian law (IHL). Plainly, the definition of armed conflict is also important for the proper application of neutrality laws, asylum laws, war risk clauses and the like.

The Initial Report

The author of this comment chaired the Use of Force Committee tasked to report on the meaning of war. Professor Judith Gardam was the Committee's Rapporteur.[8] The Committee undertook background research, held six meetings, and held e-mail exchanges prior to the completion of the initial report.

The Committee's approach to its research followed standard international legal analysis. The members looked to the primary and secondary sources of international law: relevant treaties, evidence of customary international law, rel-

---

governments to apply international humanitarian law are discussed in Mary Ellen O'Connell, *Humanitarian Assistance in Non-International Armed Conflict, The Fourth Wave of Rights, Duties, and Remedies*, 31 Is. YBK. ON HUMAN RIGHTS 183 (2001).

8   The other members of the Committee at the time of the presentation of the Initial Report were: Masahiko Asada (Japan), Jutta Brunnée (Canada), James Thuo Gathii (USA), Christine Gray (UK), Wolff Heintschel von Heinegg (Germany), Elzbieta Mikos-Skuza (Poland), Koichi Morikawa (Japan), Eric Myjer (The Netherlands), Georg Nolte (Germany), RKP Shankardass (India), and Sir Michael Wood (UK).

evant general principles of international law, judicial decisions and the writing of scholars. Situations were examined and official statements about them noted. Research papers on the factors triggering the law respecting international armed conflict, non-international armed conflict, peacekeeping operations, and neutrality were prepared, as well as examination of the *jus ad bellum*, human rights law, the law relevant to terrorism, and the historical development of the question.

The most significant meeting occurred at the end of a two-day interdisciplinary conference on the meaning of war held at Notre Dame University, 13-14 September 2007. In addition to members of the Committee, speakers at the conference included war correspondents, military historians, soldiers, peace researchers, ethicists, and political scientists. All were asked to address the meaning of armed conflict from their respective discipline.

Following the conference, the Committee convened for its sixth meeting, the third formal meeting of the committee as a whole. The objective was to move forward from the draft report submitted to the committee in August 2007 by Committee Rapporteur, Judith Gardam, in light of the papers presented at the conference from other disciplines dealing with the phenomenon of armed conflict.[9] The Committee developed a revised outline for the report. Judith Gardam produced a new draft report in March 2008, which the chair made available for general discussion of the Committee in April 2008.

Through this process, Committee members reached consensus on the existence of two primary criteria for the existence of an armed conflict for general purposes of international law: organized groups who are engaged in intense fighting.

The Committee had not been in agreement on the criteria of "intensity" prior to the Notre Dame meeting, but was able to agree after full discussion of the point. Some members of the Committee had focused particularly on the Pictet commentary on Common Article 2 that the 1949 Geneva Conventions suggesting that the Conventions are triggered by any engagement of the armed forces of high contracting parties – regardless of the intensity of that engagement:

> The Convention becomes applicable as from the actual opening of hostilities. The existence of armed conflict between two or more Contracting Parties brings it automatically into operation.
>
> It remains to ascertain what is meant by "armed conflict". The substitution of this much more general expression for the word "war" was deliberate. One may argue almost endlessly about the legal definition of "war". A State can always pretend, when it commits a hostile act against another State, that it

---

9　These papers and those of the Use of Force Committee are being published: *The Meaning of Armed Conflict in International Law* [renamed *What Is War?*] (Mary Ellen O'Connell ed., Martinus Nijhoff, forthcoming).

> is not making war, but merely engaging in a police action, or acting in legiti-
> mate self-defence. The expression "armed conflict" makes such arguments less
> easy. Any difference arising between two States and leading to the interven-
> tion of armed forces is an armed conflict within the meaning of Article 2, even
> if one of the Parties denies the existence of a state of war. It makes no differ-
> ence how long the conflict lasts, or how much slaughter takes place. [10]

The ICRC has long supported this view. Some have, therefore, concluded that
if Article 2 states the Conventions apply during armed conflict and if the commentary says they apply with any engagement of armed forces, this means an
armed conflict may be any engagement of armed forces.

During the Committee's discussion, however, it was pointed out that the
ICRC argues for a very low threshold for the triggering of the Conventions in
order to encourage their wide application. The ICRC wishes to discourage states
using formalistic arguments to avoid applying the Conventions. In other words,
the ICRC position is based on policy rather than, perhaps, its view of what the
Conventions require as a matter of law. In fact, as the Initial Report indicates,
there are few if any examples of states treating minor engagements with other
states as armed conflict. The evidence supports a higher threshold. Colleagues
from political science and peace studies confirmed this from their own disciplinary perspectives: an incident that does not include at least the intense use of
weapons and incident in fighting, will not be labelled an armed conflict. Indeed,
the other disciplines generally require that a certain number of deaths occur
before a situation is counted as an armed conflict. International law does not go
this far but does incorporate a criterion of intensity.

The Committee also agreed at Notre Dame to continue to research whether
the level of intensity is different in "international" versus "non-international"
armed conflict. Some members believe that the intensity of fighting may be
less in the case of an international armed conflict. Others believe that the core
meaning of armed conflict is the same and that "international" versus "non-
international" armed conflicts are distinguished by other factors, primarily the
level of cross-border activity.

After additional research and discussion following the Notre Dame meeting and extensive commentary by e-mail on a draft initial report, the Committee
included in the Initial Report presented at Rio the following conclusion as to
the two core characteristics of any armed conflict:

> Looking to relevant treaties – in particular IHL treaties – rules of custom-
> ary international law, general principles of international law, judicial deci-
> sions and the writing of scholars, as of the drafting of this Initial Report, the

---

10   I *Commentary on the Geneva Conventions of 12 August 1949* 32 (footnote omitted) (J
     S Pictet ed, Geneva: ICRC, 1960).

Committee has found evidence of at least two characteristics with respect to all armed conflict:

1.   The existence of organized armed groups
2.   Engaged in fighting of some intensity

The Initial Report was presented during a working session of the Rio biennial. There was wide support among the discussants for the Committee's conclusions. Participants also suggested topics to include and expand upon for the final report. These suggestions are discussed in the next section.

The Final Report

The Final Report of the Committee is scheduled for submission in The Hague in 2010. Final reports may be longer than the initial reports. The Committee will have the opportunity to go into more detail respecting the conclusions reached to date and to add at least three new sections.

The first new section recommended by the participants in the Rio discussion will be a more detailed discussion respecting human rights and the intersection/overlap with IHL. While the Committee task is to report on armed conflict and not what triggers IHL *per se*, because IHL is triggered by armed conflict, the Committee's Report will clearly be relevant to that issue. The Final Report will make clearer that while armed conflict triggers IHL, some human rights continue to apply in armed conflict. The Report needs to underscore that despite its recognition of a war/peace distinction, important legal rules, especially fundamental human rights are not affected by the distinction.

The Initial Report does not discuss when armed conflict begins. Some members of the Committee support the view that they begin with a significant unilateral, armed attack. Others support the view that the beginning must be when an initial attack is responded to by a significant counter-attack that it takes a counter-attack to initiate fighting. This topic will obviously be essential to an understanding of armed conflict in international law and will be the subject of a new section of the Final Report.

Similarly, the Final Report will contain a section on when armed conflict ends. While it may seem logical that armed conflict ends when there is no longer intense, organised inter-group fighting, the Committee has yet to confirm this with research.

The concern that launched the Use of Force Committee's work was the "global war on terrorism." In some official U.S. government statements the argument that the United States is involved in a global war is based on the view that individuals fighting in Afghanistan and Iraq or those who are members of organizations fighting in Afghanistan or Iraq are combatants wherever they are found. This view touches on the territorial scope of armed conflict. If there is intense, organized inter-group fighting in some parts of Afghanistan or Iraq, how widespread is the *de jure* armed conflict? Do people leaving a zone of armed conflict, who have been combatants, remain combatants when they are well beyond the zone? Are people who are members of the regular armed forces remain combatants wherever they are? The evidence remains to be examined and compiled for the Final Report. The Committee will no doubt be aided by the publication of the study of direct participation in hostilities undertaken by the T.C. Asser Instituut and the ICRC.[11]

Additionally, the Initial Report promises to provide more details on the two primary criteria of armed conflict in the Final Report. The Committee expects the Final Report to contain new or expanded discussions of:

1. Human rights and armed conflict

2. When armed conflict begins

3. The criterion of intensity

4. The criterion of organization

5. The territorial scope of armed conflict

6. When armed conflict ends

Conclusion

With the adoption of the United Nations Charter certain principles of international law relevant to armed conflict changed. It was no longer the case that the declaration of war created the *de jure* fact of war. Rather, the facts on the ground, the facts of fighting, determined whether a situation was one of armed conflict or peace. What those facts were remained vague as states generally tried to resist acknowledging engagement in armed conflict. This trend shifted dramatically on 9/11 when the United States declared it was in a global war on terrorism that justified the right to kill without warning anywhere and detain without trial persons it designated enemy combatants. The U.S. position is not consistent with the Use of Force Committee's report. Intense inter-group armed fighting does not characterise the entire globe. Claiming the combatant's privilege outside zones of armed conflict appears unjustifiable. Further research on the start, end, and scope of armed conflict should indicate the accuracy of this initial conclusion.

---

11   At the time of writing, the ICRC had not yet issued its final report on 'Direct Participation in Hostilties'. See documents on direct participation in hostilities at the ICRC website, <http://www.icrc.org/web/eng/siteeng0.nsf/htmlall/participation-hostilities-ihl-311205?opendocument>.

Chapter 23

Excerpts from a Memo by the Chair to the Committee on Submitting the Final Report (June 2010)

...The Report resulted from a sustained effort over five years by an 18-member committee representing 15 countries. The last six weeks have been particularly demanding, but, thanks to so many of you, we believe the Final Report will make an important contribution to international law.

Throughout the five years, Judith and I have been guided by the initial decisions taken by the Committee. In particular, the Committee decided in Berlin in 2006 that we would follow standard international law methodology. We have also remained cognizant of the ILA mandate to us, formulated in 2005, and we have recognized that the conclusions of our Initial Report were accepted at a well-attended working session at the Rio de Janeiro meeting in 2008. We have borne these three parameters in mind at all times in our own research, in incorporating your research and comments, and in writing and revising the Final Report. As a result, we have high confidence in the Report, and believe it will be accepted with the same high level of support in The Hague as our Initial Report was in Rio.

In producing the final version, we were able to incorporate almost all of the comments sent by almost all of you on the penultimate version. We heard from fourteen of you respecting the final draft – probably an ILA record for Committee participation. We included all of your suggestions except where we found them inconsistent with one of the parameters. In the case of one suggestion that called for a major change, I will make some additional comments given that four other Committee members may also support the change.

[One new committee member suggested that] we define international armed conflict as Pictet indicated in his 1952 commentary on the Geneva Conventions: That an international armed conflict is any engagement of the armed forces of sovereign States. Of course the Committee is well aware of the Pictet comment. We quote it at the outset of our review of State practice and have discussed it at various times prior to submitting our Initial Report. We point out, however, in our Initial Report and in our Final Report that the Committee's mandate is different from Pictet's. We have not been asked to discuss what triggers IHL rules, but rather what is the definition of armed conflict in general international law.

Mary Ellen O'Connell (ed.), What Is War? An Investigation in the Wake of 9/11.
© 2012 Koninklijke Brill NV. Printed in The Netherlands. ISBN 978 9004 17234 0. pp. 315–317.

[The member offered two arguments in favor of making this change in the Final Report: first, that the Report "relies heavily on non-international armed conflict but is determined to be indicative of international conflicts as well" and "treaty rules on international armed conflict do not contain a high intensity threshold."

The Report, in fact, reviews *more* international conflict than non-international. We discuss at least 48 cases of international conflict versus about 24 cases of non-international. The international cases show that States do not treat minor engagements of their armed forces as armed conflict. [The Committee received] no examples of State practice with *opinio juris* in which the contrary is true. As for [the] second point, the Geneva Conventions themselves only say they apply in "armed conflict" with no definition – they say nothing about intensity one way or the other. It is Pictet who adds the notion that an armed conflict can be any engagement regardless of intensity. He does so for the well-known policy reasons we discuss in the Report. He thought it was better to create a very low-threshold for what counts as armed conflict. (Although he also says that armed conflict begins with "hostilities," which appears to contradict the "any engagement" phrase.) By 2010, the clear weight of state practice and *opinio juris* is not in support of that very low threshold. As we discuss in the Report, even the ICRC no longer uses the Pictet formula to define armed conflict, although it still has a clear policy of applying IHL widely. ...

...[T]wo explanations [are offered] for why there is no state practice to support Pictet. ... States prefer to keep their opinions confidential and that, as a matter of policy, we should not be placing weight on the publicly expressed views of States for the application of IHL.

As ...[the] second explanation [recognizes], States do in fact express opinions about the status of violent situations. The Report shows this clearly. Moreover, States also know that communications in confidence to the ICRC or otherwise about situations cannot count as *opinio juris* because *opinio juris* must be accessible to other States and courts in order to assess customary international law. If States wish to rebut a prevailing rule of custom, they must do so publicly.

Whether the Committee should or should not give weight to the views of States as a matter of policy is not within our mandate. Our Committee has not been asked to propose a change to the definition of armed conflict in international law based on policy concerns. The Committee was asked to assess what definition international law supports. Having found no authoritative treaty on the subject, the Committee turned to customary international law. We found significant evidence of the definition that we present in the Report. We received virtually no evidence to either rebut our conclusion or to support an alternative definition.

Indeed, both showings would need to be made before we could change the Report: 1.) The Committee's evidence would have to be negated with contrary evidence and 2.) The alternative definition would have to be supported with sufficient evidence of State practice and *opinio juris* to support it as the definition in customary international law. Two years after our Initial Report went on-line, 18-months after an on-line article became available about the Report, and five years after the research efforts of 18 Committee members, we do not have evidence opposed to our definition, let alone evidence to support a different definition.

Again, we recognize that there are different types of armed conflict. We recognize that fact throughout the report. We have added new emphasis of the point to the Final Report ... (see, e.g., new footnotes 7 and 205), but we suggest that a future committee work on the details of what those differences are if that is thought to be needed. (There are arguably more than two types of armed conflict.)

Others at the meeting in The Hague who encounter our Report for the first time and are familiar with the Pictet commentary may have a similar concern .... It is important to have a well-considered answer if they do, so it has been helpful to think through and carefully consider [the] suggestion. I hope my response allays any remaining concerns. We have done extensive research; we have followed sound methodology; we have offered our results publically for a two-year period; specifically vetted the Report with the ICRC and other experts outside of our Committee, and can have, as I said above, high confidence in our Report.

I also hope this memo conveys the seriousness with which Judith and I took all the comments. Working through a committee never results in the outcome that a single author would reach on his own, but as I believe is true in this case, the result is usually stronger. We hope that there is general satisfaction in the contribution our Committee has been able to make to the better functioning of international law in taking on the mandate to define the concept of armed conflict. We believe the Report will have a positive impact, in particular, in the area clarifying when states may lawfully claim belligerent rights at the expense of otherwise prevailing peacetime human rights but in many other important areas of international law as well.

Let me just also add a word about how very fortunate our Committee has been in having Judith Gardam as our rapporteur. She, of course, has expertise in the areas of greatest importance to our Report: the *jus ad bellum, jus in bello*, and human rights. She has also worked extremely hard and at inconvenient times to meet our important deadlines. She has been an ideal rapporteur without whom we would not have produced this Final Report. My sincere thanks to her and to all of you.

I look forward to seeing many of you in The Hague, to presenting our Report, and to discussing the future work of one of the ILA's most important committees.

Chapter 24

The ILA Use of Force Committee's Final Report on the Definition of Armed Conflict in International Law (August 2010)*

International Law Association
The Hague Conference (2010)
Use Of Force

Members of the Committee:

Professor Mary Ellen O'Connell (USA): *Chair*
Professor Judith Gardam (Australia): *Rapporteur*

Dr Constantine Antonopoulos (Hellenic)	Dr Elzbieta Mikos-Skuza (Poland)
Professor Masahiko Asada (Japan)	Professor Koichi Morikawa (Japan)
Professor Jutta Brunnée (Canada)	Dr Josef Mrazek (Czech Republic)
Professor James Gathii (USA)	Professor Eric Myjer (Netherlands)
Professor Christine Gray (UK)	Professor Georg Nolte (Germany)
Professor Wolff Heintschel Von Heinegg	Professor Inger Osterdahl (Sweden)
(Germany)	Mr R K P Shankardass (India)
Dr Noam Lubell (Ireland)	Sir Michael C Wood (UK)
Anternate: Professor Wladyslaw Czaplinski	*Alternate:* Dr Nikolaos Tsagourias

Final Report on the Meaning of Armed Conflict in International Law

Summary

In May 2005, the Executive Committee of the International Law Association (ILA) approved a mandate for the Use of Force Committee to produce a report on the meaning of war or armed conflict in international law. The report was

---

*   Editor's Note: The page references are internal to the Report.

Mary Ellen O'Connell (ed.), What Is War? An Investigation in the Wake of 9/11.
© *2012 Koninklijke Brill NV. Printed in The Netherlands. ISBN 978 9004 17234 0. pp. 319–367.*

motivated by the United States' position following the attacks of 11 September 2001 that it was involved in a "global war on terror". In other words, the U.S. has claimed the right to exercise belligerent privileges applicable only during armed conflict anywhere in the world where members of terrorist groups are found. The U.S. position was contrary to a trend by states attempting to avoid acknowledging involvement in wars or armed conflicts. The Committee was asked to study the evidence in international law and report on how *international law* defines and distinguishes situations of armed conflict and those situations in which peacetime law prevails. Given that important aspects of international law turn on whether a situation is properly defined as armed conflict, providing a clear statement about the definition of armed conflict in international law would support the proper functioning of the law in general. Most fundamentally, it would support the proper application of human rights law (HRL).

At the outset of its work, the Committee found that the term "war", while still used, has, in general, been replaced in international law by the broader concept of "armed conflict". The Report focuses, therefore, on "armed conflict".

The Committee also found that the existence of armed conflict has many significant impacts on the operation of international law beyond the well-known fact that during armed conflict international humanitarian law (IHL) will apply and states party to an armed conflict (or other emergencies) may have the right to derogate from some human rights obligations. In addition, states that provide asylum to persons fleeing the violence of armed conflict will have the duty to do so; treaty obligations may be implicated; the law of neutrality may be triggered; arms control agreements are affected, and United Nations forces engaged in armed conflict will have rights and duties not applicable in operations outside of armed conflict. These are just some of the areas of international law that are affected by the outbreak of armed conflict. Plainly, the existence of armed conflict is a significant fact in the international legal system, and, yet, the Committee found no widely accepted definition of armed conflict in any treaty. It did, however, discover significant evidence in the sources of international law that the international community embraces a common understanding of armed conflict. All armed conflict has certain minimal, defining characteristics that distinguish it from situations of non-armed conflict or peace. In the absence of these characteristics, states may not, consistently with international law, simply declare that a situation is or is not armed conflict based on policy preferences.

The Committee confirmed that at least two characteristics are found with respect to all armed conflict:
1) The existence of organized armed groups
2) Engaged in fighting of some intensity

In addition to these minimum criteria respecting all armed conflict, IHL includes additional criteria so as to classify conflicts as either international or non-international in nature.[1] These additional criteria will be discussed briefly below, but the main focus of the Report is on the basic characteristics of armed conflict rather than the classification of armed conflict under IHL.

The Committee followed standard international legal methodology in identifying these basic characteristics. It examined treaties; state practice and *opinio juris*; and, as subsidiary means, judicial decisions, and the writing of scholars. The Committee also considered the definitions of armed conflict used by other disciplines.[2] The Committee collected evidence from mid-1945 through mid-2010. The 1945 starting date was natural as the United Nations Charter was adopted in June of that year. The Charter all but eliminated the importance of declarations of war for international law purposes. After 1945, such declarations no longer were determinative of the *de jure* existence of war or armed conflict. Just four years later, the 1949 Geneva Conventions were adopted. In these treaties, too, the term "armed conflict" is significant. Article 2 common to all four Conventions states that the Conventions apply in all situations of "armed conflict" – not just in declared wars.[3]

The Committee's research indicates that since the Second World War our world has been characterized by much violence. Nevertheless, a distinction is made between the violence that gives rise to the right of a state to claim the belligerent's privileges to kill without warning, detain without trial, or seize cargo on the high seas. The violence must be organized and intense – even between sovereign states – before the otherwise prevailing peacetime rules are suspended. States, international organizations, courts, and other legitimate actors in the international legal system distinguish lower level or chaotic violence from armed conflict. The International Committee of the Red Cross (ICRC) Commentary to the Conventions refers to "any engagement of the armed forces of High Contracting Parties" as an armed conflict for purposes of applying the Conventions. The Committee, however, found little evidence to support the view that the Conventions apply in the absence of fighting of some intensity. For non-state actors to move from chaotic violence to being able to chal-

---

1   For example, it is often stated that for IHL to apply to a non-international armed conflict, the fighting must be "protracted". See *infra* pp 19, 37.

2   In September 2007, the Committee participated in an inter-disciplinary conference on the meaning of armed conflict at the University of Notre Dame. Members of the military, war correspondents, military historians, political scientists, just war ethicists, and peace studies scholars all made presentations on the definition of armed conflict from the perspective of their discipline. The presentation by Peter Wallensteen, a peace studies scholar, was particularly helpful as he drew on a major database on armed conflict developed at Uppsala University in Sweden. See *infra* n 44. See also the collected papers from the conference in The Meaning of Armed Conflict in International Law (M E O'Connell ed. forthcoming Martinus Nijhof.)

3   I *Commentary on the Geneva Conventions of 12 August 1949* 32 (footnote omitted) (J S Pictet ed, Geneva: ICRC, 1952).

lenge the armed forces of a state requires organization, meaning a command structure, training, recruiting ability, communications, and logistical capacity. Such organized forces are only recognized as engaged in armed conflict when fighting between them is more than a minimal engagement or incident. The Inter-American Commission on Human Rights characterized an engagement of Argentina's armed forces with organized, armed militants that lasted thirty hours and resulted in casualties and property destruction as an armed conflict.[4] The Committee found no other examples more minimal than this as being described by a court, the Security Council, other organizations, states, or scholars as an armed conflict. Among the many other situations of violence widely acknowledged to be armed conflict, the Inter-American Commission's finding in the Argentine case appears to involve the least amount of fighting.

It is well known that criminal gangs can perpetrate considerable levels of violence even against the armed forces of a state. Still, states have rejected recognizing such situations as "armed conflict". Criminals generally do not organize themselves to carry out armed conflict with government military forces. It is also common knowledge that the well-organized armed forces of states often clash, for example, at disputed land or maritime boundaries. States do not, however, classify such incidents as armed conflicts unless they reach a certain level of intensity.

Many will recognize the characteristics of intensity and organization from a 1995 decision of the International Criminal Tribunal for the former Yugoslavia in *Prosecutor v. Tadić*, a decision widely cited for its description of the characteristics of armed conflict. The International Criminal Tribunal for the former Yugoslavia (ICTY) found that both a certain amount of organization among all fighting groups and a certain level of intense fighting distinguished armed conflict from other violence, such as riots and border incidents. While the *Tadić* criteria are well known, the Committee found significant additional evidence supporting the decision.

The Committee submitted its findings to the ILA in June 2008 as an Initial Report. That Report was presented at the ILA Biennial in Rio de Janeiro. The Report was received favorably with suggestions for the final report. In particular, ILA members asked that care be taken to emphasize that even during armed conflict certain fundamental human rights continue to apply. IHL is not the only law relevant to armed conflict. That point is reflected throughout this Final Report. The Committee also undertook to add more details to the final report respecting the criteria of organization and intensity and at least some discussion as to the commencement, termination, and territorial scope

---

4   *Juan Carlos Abella v Argentina*, Case 11.137, Report No. 55/97, Inter-Am. C.H.R., OEA/Ser.L/V/II.98, Doc. 6 rev., 18 November 1997, paras. 149-51 (distinguishing 'internal disturbances' from armed conflict on the basis of the nature and level of violence). See also *infra* pp 19, 37.

of armed conflict. These complex topics require additional in-depth research. These topics could well be the focus of future Committee reports.

The Initial Report and a report of the Working Session at the Rio Biennial are included in the 2008 Proceedings of the ILA. The Initial Report has remained posted on the Website of the ILA since June 2008. Also, the Committee's Chair publicized the Initial Report in an article published in 2008 that is also available online.[5] Since the posting of the Report, the Rio Biennial, and the publication of the article, the Committee has received no evidence of state practice to support a different conclusion than that reached in its Initial Report. The U.S. appears to continue to recognize a "global war on terror," although in somewhat modified form. It is now characterized as an "armed conflict with al-Qaeda, the Taliban and associated forces".[6] Yet, many other examples came to the Committee's attention in the same time period supporting the Committee's initial conclusions. The new evidence is included in this Final Report. The Report continues to conclude that all armed conflict involves, at a minimum, intense fighting among organized armed groups.[7]

I   Introduction

(a)   Mandate and Purpose

Since at least the time of Hugo Grotius and his seminal work, *The Law of War and Peace* (1625), international law has been organised around two contrasting situations: the presence or absence of war, now more commonly referred to as armed conflict. Armed conflict is, therefore, a core concept in international law, but it is also a socially constructed concept and, as such, it is not amenable to any scientific litmus test.[8] Nevertheless, whether or not armed conflict exists depends on the satisfaction of objective criteria. Identifying these criteria has been a long-standing challenge in international law. The challenge seems

---

5   M E O'Connell, *Defining Armed Conflict* (Winter 2008) 13 Journal of Conflict & Security Law 393.

6   H H Koh, *The Obama Administration and International Law*, Annual Meeting of the American Society of International Law, Washington, D.C., March 25, 2010, www.state.gov. Available at: http://www.state.gov/s/l/releases/remarks/139119.htm.

7   As stated above the Committee recognizes that international law distinguishes between different types of armed conflict relying on criteria additional to the common characteristics of organization and intensity. The Committee's mandate, however, was to report on the general definition of armed conflict. Consequently, the different categories of armed conflict, although identified throughout the Report are not its particular focus. They, too, might well be a topic for a future Committee.

8   N Berman, *Privileging Combat? Contemporary Conflict and the Legal Construction of War* (2004) 43 Columbia Journal of Transnational Law 1.

to have become greater in recent years with the clash today between advocates of a broad, flexible understanding of armed conflict that affords states belligerent rights and advocates of a narrow definition that better protects individuals. During armed conflict states have expanded rights to kill without warning, detain without trial, and suspend or derogate from treaties and other obligations. Individuals may have their right to life, their right to a trial, and other important rights circumscribed in armed conflict. Therefore, the existence of armed conflict not only triggers the application of IHL, but can also have a wide reaching impact on the international legal norms regulating relations between states including asylum obligations, HRL, neutrality law, UN operations, and treaty practice.[9]

Until the 11 September 2001 attacks, states generally resisted acknowledging that even intense fighting on their territory was armed conflict. To do so was to admit failure, a loss of control to opposition forces, and could be seen as recognizing a status for insurgents.[10] Some scholars even raised the possibility that the distinction between armed conflict and peace in international law was dissolving.[11] There seems to have been little pressure to clarify the meaning

---

9   See, e g, Report of the Special Rapporteur on extrajudicial, summary or arbitrary executions, Philip Alston, UN Doc A/HRC/14/24/Add.6 at 9, 28 May 2010 ('Whether or not a specific targeted killing is legal depends on the context in which it is conducted: whether in armed conflict, outside of armed conflict, or in relation to the inter-state use of force.' Citing UN Doc A/61/311, paras. 33-45 (detailed discussion of 'arbitrary' deprivation of life under human rights law)).

10   See, e g, the position of the Russian government with respect to the conflict in Chechnya in the 1990s. Arguments of Russia in *Isayeva, Yusopova and Bazayeva v Russia*, nos. 57947/00, 57948/00 and 57949/00, ECHR 24 February 2005 [hereinafter *Isayeva I*]. But see decision of the Russian Constitutional Court finding that a non-international armed conflict was occurring between Russian forces and Chechen rebel forces in the mid-1990s: *Presidential Decrees and the Resolutions of the Federal Government Concerning the Situation in Chechnya*, Judgment of July 31, 1995. Available at http://www.venice.coe.int/docs/1996/CDL-INF(1996)001-e.pdf. See examples of states refusing to recognize armed conflict on their territory, in M E O'Connell, *Humanitarian Assistance in Non-International Armed Conflict: The Fourth Wave of Rights, Duties and Remedies* (2002) 31 Israel Yearbook on Human Rights 183, 196. See also *infra* n 12.

11   See, for example, the arguments for the principle of necessity to govern all uses of lethal force in F F Martin, *Using International Human Rights Law for Establishing a Unified Use of Force Rule in the Law of Armed Conflict* (2001) 64 Saskatchewan Law Review 347; and T Meron & A Rosas, *A Declaration of Minimum Humanitarian Standards* (1991) 85 American Journal of International Law 375. See also, International Committee of the Red Cross, *Interpretive Guidance on the Notion of Direct Participation in Hostilities under International Humanitarian Law* (2009) at 78-82 [hereinafter ICRC, *Interpretive Guidance on Direct Participation in Hostilities*] (indicating a common rule of necessity for all uses of lethal force). Available at http://www.icrc.org/Web/Eng/siteengo.nsf/htmlall/p0990/$File/ICRC_002_0990.pdf.

of armed conflict when governments were willing to apply the higher level of rights and duties applicable in peacetime. True, the International Committee of the Red Cross (ICRC) has consistently pressed governments to acknowledge fighting as armed conflict and to apply IHL,[12] but the real pressure for clarification came with the U.S. declaration of a "global war" in 2001 and its claim to exercise certain rights applicable only in armed conflict, such as the right to kill combatants without warning, detain without trial, search vessels on the high seas, and seize cargo.[13] Subsequently, European Union member states have also been grappling with the definition of armed conflict after the adoption of an EU Directive affording asylum rights to persons fleeing armed conflict.[14]

The need now clearly exists for a clarification of the distinction between armed conflict and peace. The proper application of IHL, HRL, asylum rights, and other international legal principles depends on an accurate understanding of the legal meaning of armed conflict. It is the mandate of the Committee to provide this clarification.

(b)   Methodology

The Committee took up the mandate to report on the meaning of armed conflict in international law by employing standard international legal analysis. The

---

12   See, for example, the cases of El Salvador, Sri Lanka, and Colombia. Re Sri Lanka, see International Committee of the Red Cross, *ICRC Annual Report 1996* 140-42 (1997); re Colombia see ICRC action to protect and assist the victims of armed conflict in Colombia, 2 April 2008, http://www.icrc.org/Web/Eng/siteengo.nsf/html/colombia-report-02042008, and re El Salvador see R K Goldman, *International Humanitarian Law: Americas Watch's Experience in Monitoring Internal Armed Conflicts* (1993) 9 American University Journal of International Law and Policy 49, 89.

13   G W Bush, President's Address to the Nation on the Terrorist Attacks, 37 Weekly Comp. Pres. Doc. 1301 (11 September 2001); G W Bush, President's Address to Joint Session of Congress on the United States Response to the Terrorist Attacks of September 11, 37 Weekly Comp. Pres. Doc. 1347 at 1348 (20 September 2001) (Bush said the US was in a 'war on terror' that would last 'until every terrorist group of global reach has been found, stopped and defeated'). For references to particular U.S. claims of belligerent rights to target, detain, and search, see, M E O'Connell, *Ad Hoc War*, in Krisensicherung und Humanitärer Schutz – Crisis Management and Humanitarian Protection 405 (Horst Fischer et al, eds., 2004). See also *infra* pp 30-31.

14   See Council Directive 2004/83/EC of 29 April 2004 on minimum standards for the qualification and status of third country nationals or stateless person as refugees or as person who otherwise need international protection and the content of the protection granted, (30 September 2004) Official Journal of the European Union L 304, [hereinafter EU Qualification Directive].

members looked to the primary and secondary sources of international law.[15] The Committee found no multilateral treaty that provides a generally applicable definition of armed conflict. Therefore the meaning of armed conflict is to be found in customary international law as evidenced by state practice and *opinio juris*, as well as subsidiary sources, judicial decisions and scholarly commentary.

IHL, judicial decisions applying IHL, and the writing of scholars on IHL were particularly helpful to the Committee, given, as stated above, that the 1949 Geneva Conventions apply, according to Common Article 2, during "armed conflict". HRL, judicial decisions applying HRL and scholarly writing on HRL also proved helpful, although in this area, scholars and courts are noting the increasing convergence of fundamental protection rules that apply in both situations of armed conflict and peace.[16] In the *Nuclear Weapons* Advisory Opinion the International Court of Justice (ICJ) dealt with the argument that the use of nuclear weapons constituted a violation of the right to life contrary to Article 6 of the International Covenant on Civil and Political Rights (ICCPR) in these terms:

> The Court observes that the protection of the International Covenant on Civil and Political Rights does not cease in times of war, except by operation of Article 4 of the Covenant whereby certain provisions may be derogated from in a time of national emergency. Respect for the right to life is not, however,

---

15   Statute of the International Court of Justice, art 38.
16   Indeed, the treaty provisions of IHL already incorporate some aspects of human rights norms that are applicable in times of armed conflict. Art 72 of Additional Protocol I specifically requires that the fundamental guarantees in art 75 are to be applied in addition to 'other applicable rules of international law relating to the protection of fundamental human rights during international armed conflict'. Protocol Additional to the Geneva Conventions of 12 August 1949, and relating to the Protections of Victims of International Armed Conflicts (Protocol I) of 8 June 1977, 1125 U.N.T.S. 3 (1979). *See also* Protocol Additional to the Geneva Conventions of 12 August 1949, and relating to the Protections of Victims of Non-International Armed Conflicts (Protocol II) of 8 June 1977, 1125 U.N.T.S. 609 (1979). Art 75 of Additional Protocol I defines fundamental guarantees as prohibition of murder, torture, inhuman and degrading treatment, taking of hostages, corporal punishment and collective punishment. Additional Protocol II makes express reference to human rights ('Recalling ... that international instruments relating to human rights offer a basic protection to the human person') while Arts 4-6 of Protocol II elaborate on the protection of the basic human rights already the object of Common Article 3. See generally, F Hampson, *The Relationship between International Humanitarian Law and Human Rights Law from the Perspective of a Human Rights Treaty Body*, 90 No 871 IRRC 549 (2008). See also C Antonopoulos, *The Relationship Between International Humanitarian Law and Human Rights*, 63 Revue Hellenique de Droit International (2010), issue 2 [forthcoming]; W Schabas, Lex Specialis? *Belt and Suspenders? The Parallel Operation of Human Rights and the Law of Armed Conflict, and the Conundrum of* Jus Ad Bellum, (2007) 40 Israel Law Review 592 (no. 2).

such a provision. In principle, the right not arbitrarily to be deprived of one's life applies also in hostilities. The test of what is arbitrary deprivation of life, however, then falls to be determined by the applicable *lex specialis*, namely, the law applicable in armed conflict which is designed to regulate the conduct of hostilities. Thus whether a particular loss of life, through the use of a certain weapon in warfare, is to be considered an arbitrary deprivation of life contrary to Article 6 of the Covenant, can only be decided by reference to the law applicable in armed conflict and not deduced from the terms of the Covenant itself. ...'[17]

However, in applying the right to life provision of the European Convention of Human Rights in more recent cases, the European Court of Human Rights (ECHR) has not felt the need to categorize situations as armed conflict or peace in order to assess the legality of the use of force by authorities.[18] Indeed, commentators are finding that as HRL develops it is of increasing importance in

---

17   *Legality of the Threat or Use of Nuclear Weapons*, Advisory Opinion, 8 July 1996, ICJ Rep. 1996, 226, para. 25. See also *Legal Consequences of the Construction of a Wall in the Occupied Palestinian Territory*, Advisory Opinion, 9 July 2004, ICJ Rep. 2004, 196, para. 106 and *Armed Activities on the Territory of the Congo* (Congo v Uganda), 19 December 2005, ICJ Rep. 2005, 168, para. 216 (to the effect that the protections offered by human rights conventions continue to apply in cases of armed conflict).

18   Convention for the Protection of Human Rights and Fundamental Freedoms, art 2, opened for signature 4 November 1950, available at http://www.echr.coe.int/NR/rdonlyres/D5CC24A7-DC13-4318-B457-5C9014916D7A/o/EnglishAnglais.pdf. It provides:

   1.   Everyone's right to life shall be protected by law. No one shall be deprived of his life intentionally save in the execution of a sentence of a court following his conviction of a crime for which this penalty is provided by law.

   2.   Deprivation of life shall not be regarded as inflicted in contravention of this article when it results from the use of force which is no more than absolutely necessary:

     (a)   in defence of any person from unlawful violence;

     (b)   in order to effect a lawful arrest or to prevent escape of a person lawfully detained;

     (c)   in action lawfully taken for the purpose of quelling a riot or insurrection.

   In several cases arising out of the Chechen conflict in Russia, the European Court of Human Rights found violations of art 2 but did not specify that these were violations of IHL and so not excused even in the case of armed conflict. See, *Isayeva I*, supra n 10; *Isayeva v Russia*, no. 57950/00, ECHR 24 February 2005 [hereinafter *Isayeva II*]; and *Khashiyev & Akayeva v Russia*, nos. 57942/00 and 57945/00, ECHR 24 February 2005.

   Similarly, in *Ergi v Turkey*, no. 66/1997/850/1057, ECHR 28 July 1998, the ECHR considered Turkey's use of force to repress the Kurdish Worker's Party. The ECHR cited only art 2 of the Convention when determining that there was insufficient evidence to prove a Turkish violation of art 2.

the context of armed conflict, and, as a consequence, the need to define armed conflict carefully so as to exclude the application of human rights is declining. Nevertheless, some older decisions concerned with HRL, such as the *Nuclear Weapons* case and the Inter-American Commission on Human Rights decision *Abella v. Argentina* have been helpful.[19]

In addition to IHL and HRL, other relevant subfields of international law are examined in the Report as well as many examples of conflict. Often a court, commission or other authoritative decision-maker will state whether or not a particular situation is an armed conflict. In the absence such evidence, the Committee examined other indications such as application of IHL by the parties, involvement of the ICRC, reference to the Security Council, official statements of the parties involved, scholarly commentary, and references in the media to determine the status of a conflict. It is an impossible task to examine all relevant legal developments or to comprehensively assess all relevant jurisprudence. Nor was it practical to review all conflicts since the adoption of the U.N. Charter. Nevertheless, the Report considers a significant amount of material and, as mentioned above, no omissions have been brought to the Committee's attention after two years.

(c)   Terminology

Clarifying the meaning of armed conflict is facilitated by an appreciation of several other terms frequently used in discussions of armed conflict. In the context of the use of force, international law distinguishes between *ius ad bellum* and IHL.[20] *Ius ad bellum* regulates the situations in which states can lawfully resort to force. Under this law, the terms "war" and "armed attack" are of particular significance. First with respect to "war", in classic pre-Charter *ius ad bellum*, this was the international law term used to describe the situation of armed conflict between states, and it is still in use today. It has undergone a particular resurgence in public discourse in the context of the so-called "war on terror".

In Oppenheim's classic definition, war was "a contention between two or more States through their armed forces, for the purpose of overpowering each other and imposing such conditions of peace as the victor pleases".[21] During the period when many legal scholars and states contended that the resort to force was unregulated, a declaration of war had considerable legal significance, such

---

19   *Abella v Argentina*, supra n 4.

20   See generally C Greenwood, *The Relationship Between* Ius Ad Bellum *and* Ius In Bello (1983) 9 Review of International Studies 133-47, in C Greenwood, Essays on War in International Law 13 (London: Cameron May Ltd, 2006) and for an explanation of the various terms used to describe this area of the law, see J Gardam, *Introduction*, in Humanitarian Law xi (J Gardam ed, Aldershot: Ashgate, 1999).

21   L Oppenheim, II *International Law: A Treatise* 202 (H Lauterpacht ed, London: Longman, Greens and Co, 1952).

as bringing into operation not only the laws of war, as IHL was then known, but also the institution of neutrality and validating the exercise of belligerent rights. The United Nations Charter, however, prohibits all use of force except in self-defence or with Security Council authorisation.[22] After the adoption of the Charter, governments and jurists began to abandon the use of the term "war".[23]

It is still possible for states to find themselves in a state of war[24] or to make formal declarations of war.[25] Many national constitutions still require formal declarations of war in some circumstances.[26] Such a declaration is not contrary to international law unless (depending on the context) it constitutes a threat within the meaning of Article 2(4) of the United Nations Charter.[27] Political factors are obviously of considerable significance in this context and frequently will dictate whether states use the terminology of war or choose to use other more pacific terminology and strategies to deal with the problem. For example, in 2005 Eritrea used the terminology of war in its argument before the Eritrea/Ethiopia Claims Commission but failed to report its actions to the Security Council as required under Article 51 of the Charter that governs the legal right

---

22 For recent discussions of these rules, see C Gray, *International Law and the Use of Force* (Oxford: Oxford University Press, 3rd ed 2008); M E O'Connell, *Preserving the Peace: The Continuing Ban on War Between States* (2007) 38 California Western International Law Journal 41; M Wood, *The Law on the Use of Force: Current Challenges* (2007) 11 Singapore Yearbook of International Law 1.

23 As to the relevance of 'war' in post-Charter times, see E Lauterpacht, *The Legal Irrelevance of the 'State of War'* (1968) 62 Proceedings of the American Society of International Law 58; R R Baxter, *The Legal Consequences of the Unlawful Use of Force under the Charter* (1968) 62 Proceedings of the American Society of International Law 68; Lord McNair and A D Watts, *The Legal Effects of War* (New York: Cambridge University Press, 4th ed 1966); C Greenwood, *War, Terrorism and International Law* (2004) 56 Current Legal Problems 505, 529, in Greenwood, Essays on War in International Law, supra n 20 at 431-32.

24 C Greenwood, *The Concept of War in Modern International Law* (1987) 36 International and Comparative Law Quarterly 283, 302-5 in Greenwood, Essays on War in International Law, supra n 20 at 54-59.

25 *Jus Ad Bellum*, Partial Award, Ethiopia Claims 1-8, Eritrea Ethiopia Claims Commission, 2006 ILM 430.

26 For example, the United States Constitution mandates that 'war' be declared by the Congress. U.S. Constitution art I sec. 8. The Congress has not declared a war, however, since the Second World War, despite the many subsequent uses of force including cases commonly characterized as war: the Korean War, the Vietnam War, the Gulf War, and the Iraq War. See D L Westerfield, *War Powers: the President, the Congress, and the Question of War* (Westport, CT: Praeger Publishers, 1996).

27 As Brownlie writes, 'acts which would otherwise have been equivocal may be treated as offensive'. I Brownlie, *International Law and the Use of Force by States* 368 (Oxford: Clarendon Press, 1963).

to self-defence.[28] The terminology of war was also used by Israel in the 2006 conflict in Lebanon.[29]

To summarise, although the term "war" may still have some significance in a few areas such as for some national constitutions,[30] or some domestic contracts, in international law the term "war" no longer has the importance that it had in the pre-Charter period.

Another term important to distinguish from armed conflict is the phrase "armed attack". Armed attack is a term of art under Article 51 of the United Nations Charter. The occurrence of an armed attack triggers a state's right to resort to measures in self-defence. The phrase lacks an agreed definition.[31] Irrespective, however, of what constitutes such an event under *ius ad bellum*, an armed attack that is not part of intense armed fighting is not part of an armed conflict.[32]

Turning to terminology in IHL, the traditional description of the customary practices that developed into both treaty and customary IHL was "the laws and customs of war" or more generally "the law(s) of war". These terms are still in use today[33] although the "law of armed conflict" or "IHL" are more generally accepted.

---

28   *Jus Ad Bellum*, Partial Award, supra n 25.

29   See Identical Letters Dated 12 July 2006 from the Permanent Representative of Israel to the United Nations Addressed to the Secretary-General and the President of the Security Council, UN Doc A/60/937-S/2006/515, 12 July 2006. However, the resolution of the US Congress House of Representatives on the conflict used the traditional terminology of armed attack and self-defence. House Resolution 921, 109th Congress, 18 July 2006.

30   See, for example, D L Westerfield, *War Powers: the President, the Congress, and the Question of War*, supra n 26.

31   What constitutes an armed attack has been comprehensively examined by a number of commentators, in particular, C Gray, *International Law and the Use of Force*, supra n 22 at 128-48; B Simma (ed), *The Charter of the United Nations: A Commentary* 794-803 (Oxford: Oxford University Press, 2nd ed 2002); Y Dinstein, *War, Aggression and Self-Defence* 182-208 (Cambridge, Cambridge University Press, 4th ed 2005). See also *Military and Paramilitary Activities in and against Nicaragua*, (Nicaragua v United States of America), Merits, 27 June 1986, ICJ Rep. 1986, 14, para. 191; *Case Concerning Oil Platforms* (Islamic Republic of Iran v United States of America), Merits, 6 November 2003, ICJ Rep. 2003, 161, para. 51; *Jus Ad Bellum*, Partial Award, supra n 25.

32   The distinction between armed attack and armed conflict is also relevant to the question of when an armed conflict begins. See *infra* pp 37-38.

33   See, for example, Letter from J B Bellinger, III, Legal Adviser, US Department of State, and W J Haynes, General Counsel, US Department of Defence, to Dr J Kellenberger, President, International Committee of the Red Cross, Regarding Customary International Law Study, 3 November, 2006, 46 ILM 514 (2007), at fn 1 ('[t]he field has traditionally been called the 'laws and customs of war'. Accordingly,

"International" and "non-international" are also significant terms in the context of applying IHL. Traditionally, "international armed conflicts" are conflicts between states and "non-international armed conflicts" are those between states and armed groups within the territory of a state or states.[34] In more recent times conflicts not involving a government, for example on the territory of a "failed state", can qualify as armed conflicts to which IHL applies.[35] There is thought to be growing convergence between the rules governing international and non-international armed conflicts and in the future it may be less important to classify the type of conflict.[36] The jurisprudence of the ICTY, state practice and treaties all demonstrate this convergence.[37] Nevertheless, there remain

---

we will use this term, or the term 'law of war', throughout'). For a comprehensive collection of relevant documents and their use of terminology see generally A Roberts and R Guelff (eds.) *Documents on the Laws of War,* (3rd ed Oxford: Oxford University Press, 2000).

34 See, M E O'Connell, *Saving Lives through a Definition of International Armed Conflict,* Proceedings of the 10th Bruges Colloquium, 22-23 October 2009: '[A]n international armed conflict involves a confrontation of two or more states. ... An armed conflict may be an international armed conflict, involving two or more states even if the organized armed groups are not the regular armed forces of the states involved' (paragraph break omitted). According to Greenwood: 'A non-international armed conflict is a confrontation between the existing governmental authority and groups of persons subordinate to this authority or between different groups none of which acts on behalf of the government, which is carried out by force of arms within national territory and reaches the magnitude of an armed confrontation or a civil war'. C Greenwood, *Scope of Application of Humanitarian Law,* in The Handbook of Humanitarian Law in Armed Conflicts 54 (D Fleck ed, Oxford: Oxford University Press, 2d ed. 2008). See also R Arnold, *Terrorism and IHL: A Common Denomination,* in *International Humanitarian Law and the 21st Century's Conflicts: Changes and Challenges* 3, 11-12 (R Arnold ed, Lausanne: Editions Interuniversitaires Suisses – Edis, 2005); R Arnold, *The ICC as a New Instrument for Repressing Terrorism* 116 (Ardsley, NY: Transnational Publishers, 2004); J Pejic, *Terrorist Acts and Groups: A Role for International Law?* (2004) 75 British Yearbook of International Law 71, 86, citing M Sassòli, *The Status of Persons Held in Guantanamo under International Humanitarian Law* (2004) 2 Journal of International Criminal Justice 96, 100; L Moir, *The Law of Internal Armed Conflict* 30-52 (Cambridge: Cambridge University Press, 2002).

35 See *infra* pp 13, 19, 23, 28.

36 See generally J G Stewart, *Towards a Single Definition of Armed Conflict in International Humanitarian Law: A Critique of Internationalized Armed Conflict* (2003) 85 No 850 International Review Red Cross 313; E Crawford, *Unequal Before the Law: the Case for the Elimination of the Distinction between International and Non-international Armed Conflicts* (2007) 20(2) Leiden Journal of International Law 441.

37 For example, some weapons conventions do not distinguish between international and non-international armed conflict. See the Convention on the Prohibition of

important distinctions in the rules. Which set of rules applies continues to depend, as it has traditionally, first and foremost on who the parties to the conflict are – whether the organized armed groups are predominantly sovereign states or not.[38] Some rules applicable in non-international armed conflict may also depend on the fighting reaching a higher level of intensity than is required in the general understanding of armed conflict.[39]

The term "hostilities" is another term closely related to the concept of "armed conflict". The ICRC Interpretive Guidance on the Notion of Direct Participation in Hostilities under International Humanitarian Law defines the term as "the (collective) resort by the parties to the conflict to means and methods of injuring the enemy...".[40] The term refers to the actual fighting of an armed conflict and is relevant to at least two important principles of IHL: civilians who take direct part in hostilities are no longer immune from attack by lawful combatants[41] and at the end of active hostilities prisoners of war should be released.[42]

---

the Development, Production and Stockpiling of Bacteriological (Biological) and Toxin Weapons and on Their Destruction (Biological Weapons Convention), 1015 UNTS 163 (entered into force 26 March 1975); Convention on the Prohibition of the Development, Production, Stockpiling and Use of Chemical Weapons and on their Destruction (Chemical Weapons Convention), 1974 UNTS 45 (entered into force 29 April 1997); Convention on the Prohibition of the Use, Stockpiling, Production and Transfer of Anti-personnel Mines and on their Destruction (Ottawa Convention), 2056 UNTS 211 (entered into force 1 March 1999); the Convention on Prohibitions or Restrictions on the Use of Certain Conventional Weapons which may be deemed to be Excessively Injurious or to have Indiscriminate Effects (with Protocols I, II and III), 1342 UNTS 137 (entered into force 2 December 1983) was extended to non-international armed conflict through amendment in 2001 (entered into force 18 May 2004). See also the Second Protocol to the Hague Convention of 1954 for the Protection of Cultural Property in the Event of Armed Conflict, 823 UNTS 231 (entered into force 9 March 2004), which applies to all armed conflicts. There has also been convergence in the enforcement regimes and in particular in the establishment of individual criminal responsibility in internal armed conflicts. See generally Statute of the International Criminal Tribunal for Rwanda, available at http://www.un.org/ictr/statute.html, and *Prosecutor v Tadić,* Case No. IT-94-1-A, Judgment (Appeals Chamber), 15 July 1999.

38   See however art 1(4) of Additional Protocol I to the 1949 Geneva Conventions that treats certain conflicts involving entities other than States as international in character.

39   See discussion *infra* pp 19, 37.

40   See ICRC, *Interpretive Guidance on Direct Participation in Hostilities,* supra n 11 at 43.

41   According to art 51(3) of Additional Protocol I and art 13(3) of Additional Protocol II to the 1949 Geneva Conventions, civilians are immune from direct attack 'unless and for such time as they take a direct part in hostilities'.

42   1949 Geneva Convention III, art 118.

II   Evidence Of Armed Conflict

As explained above, a new era with respect to armed conflict began in 1945 with the adoption of the United Nations Charter and the prohibition on the use of force in Article 2(4). This Article does more than prohibit war; it generally prohibits the use of force in international relations. Under the Charter states are permitted to use force only in self-defence against an armed attack (Article 51) or if the Security Council authorizes a use of force as a necessary measure to restore international peace and security. International law does not, however, expressly restrict the resort to force within states – though rebellion and the like are usually prohibited under national law.

With the adoption of the Charter, some thought major war would end.[43] In fact, large scale conflicts continued and so did lesser uses of force. The majority of armed conflicts since 1945 have in fact been internal armed conflicts, often with the intervention of outside powers. Numerous inter-state conflicts have occurred as well. Using a definition of armed conflict compatible with that of this Report, Cherif Bassiouni identifies 313 such conflicts during the period 1945 to 2008.[44]

In this section, we review violent conflicts through three periods: 1945–1980, 1980-2000, and 2000-2010. We consider major legal developments of each period relevant to the definition of armed conflict as well as evidence relevant to how particular conflicts were classified.[45] While no single indicator is usually determinative in classifying a situation, a number of indicators taken together do provide an understanding of how the international community regarded a situation.[46]

---

43   See discussion in J L Kunz, *The Chaotic Status of the Laws of War and the Urgent Necessity for their Revision* (1951) 45 American Journal of International Law 37, 43.

44   The 313 are categorized as 'international war': 96, 'non-international war': 152, and 'purely internal conflict': 65. M. Cherif Bassiouni (ed.) *The Pursuit of International Criminal Justice: A World Study on Conflicts, Victimization, and Post-Conflict Justice* 79 (vol. 1, 2010): for the purposes of the study he defines an armed conflict as the clashing of interests (positional differences) over national values of some duration and magnitude between at least two parties (organized groups, states, groups of states, organizations) that are determined to pursue their interests and achieve their goals and/or a 'contested incompatibility which concerns government and/ or territory where the use of armed force between two parties, of which at least one is a state, results in 25 battle-related deaths' and/or 'protracted armed conflict between such groups.'
  Ibid. at 75 (footnotes omitted.) See also Uppsala Conflict Data Program, www. ucdp.uu.se and Peter Wallensteen, *What's in a War? Insights from a Conflict Data Program*, in The Definition of Armed Conflict in International Law supra n 2.

45   See discussion supra pp 6-7 respecting the Report's methodology and sources of evidence.

46   It is also important to note that violent situations may wax and wane, beginning,

1945-1980

In this first period for review, in addition to the U.N. Charter, the major contemporary IHL agreements were concluded, namely the four 1949 Geneva Conventions and the two 1977 Additional Protocols. Common Article 2 of the four 1949 Conventions sets out their scope:

> In addition to the provisions which shall be implemented in peacetime, the present Convention shall apply to all cases of declared war or of any other armed conflict which may arise between two or more of the High Contracting Parties, even if the state of war is not recognized by one of them.

The ICRC Commentary to common Article 2 indicates the view of the ICRC respecting the scope of the Conventions:[47]

> This paragraph is entirely new. It fills the gap left in the earlier Conventions, and deprives the belligerents of the pretexts they might in theory invoke for evasion of their obligations. There is no longer any need for a formal declaration of war, or for recognition of the state of war, as preliminaries to the application of the Convention. The Convention becomes applicable as from the actual opening of hostilities. The existence of armed conflict between two or more Contracting Parties brings it automatically into operation.
>
> It remains to ascertain what is meant by "armed conflict". The substitution of this much more general expression for the word "war" was deliberate. One may argue almost endlessly about the legal definition of "war". A State can always pretend, when it commits a hostile act against another State, that it is not making war, but merely engaging in a police action, or acting in legitimate self-defence. The expression "armed conflict" makes such arguments less easy. Any difference arising between two States and leading to the intervention of armed forces is an armed conflict within the meaning of Article 2, even if one of the Parties denies the existence of a state of war. It makes no difference how long the conflict lasts, or how much slaughter takes place.[48]

As the Commentary emphasizes, the Geneva Conventions were intended to apply in all situations of armed conflict not just declared wars. By de-emphasiz-

---

for example, as civil unrest or a border incident, then developing into an armed conflict or receding to non-violence.

47   The Trial Chamber in *Prosecutor v Milošević*, Case No. IT-02-54-T, Decision on Motion for Judgement of Acquittal *Under Rule 98 bis*, 16 June 2004, para. 19 stated 'the ICRC Commentary is nothing more than what it purports to be, *i.e.*, a commentary, and only has persuasive value'.

48   I *Commentary on the Geneva Conventions of 12 August 1949*, supra n 3 at 32 (footnote omitted).

ing any formal definition of armed conflict, the Commentary to Article 2 aimed at encouraging wider application of IHL than was the case before 1949.

Article 3 common to the four 1949 Geneva Conventions, the so-called "mini convention" dealing with non-international armed conflict, has a significantly different scope provision to Article 2. It applies "[i]n the case of armed conflict not of an international character occurring in the territory of one of the High Contracting Parties".

Common Article 3 is a revolutionary provision in that it was the first international treaty provision to attempt to regulate non-international armed conflict. The ICRC Commentary, in the words of the ICTY, provides criteria that are "useful" indicators of the sort of factors to take into account in determining the existence of an Article 3 armed conflict and distinguishing it from lesser forms of violence such as "banditry, unorganised and short-lived insurrections, or terrorist activities", [49] viz:

(1) That the Party in revolt against the *de jure* Government possesses an organized military force, an authority responsible for its acts, acting within a determinate territory and having the means of respecting and ensuring respect for the Convention.

(2) That the legal Government is obliged to have recourse to the regular military forces against insurgents organized as military and in possession of a part of the national territory.

(3) (a) That the *de jure* Government has recognized the insurgents as belligerents; or

(b) that it has claimed for itself the rights of a belligerent; or

(c) that it has accorded the insurgents recognition as belligerents for the purposes only of the present Convention; or

(d) that the dispute has been admitted to the agenda of the Security Council or the General Assembly of the United Nations as being a threat to international peace, a breach of the peace, or an act of aggression.

(4) (a) That the insurgents have an organization purporting to have the characteristics of a State.

(b) That the insurgent civil authority exercises *de facto* authority over the population within a determinate portion of the national territory.

(c) That the armed forces act under the direction of an organized authority and are prepared to observe the ordinary laws of war.

(d) That the insurgent civil authority agrees to be bound by the provisions of the Convention.[50]

---

49   *Prosecutor v Boskoski & Tarculovski*, Case No. IT-04-82-T, Judgement (Trial Chamber) 10 July 2008 at paras. 175, 176.

50   III *Commentary on the Geneva Conventions of 12 August 1949* 36 (J S Pictet ed, Geneva: ICRC, 1960).

In 1977, two Protocols were added to the 1949 Conventions. Each has a scope provision. The Protocol Additional to the Geneva Conventions of 12 August 1949, and relating to the Protection of Victims of International Armed Conflicts (Protocol I), 8 June 1977, provides in Article 1(3):

> This Protocol, which supplements the Geneva Conventions of 12 August 1949 for the protection of war victims, shall apply in the situations referred to in Article 2 common to those Conventions.

Additional Protocol I includes so-called "wars of national liberation", deeming them to be international in nature.[51]

In response to this expansion of the parties that could be engaged in an armed conflict to which the rules of Additional Protocol I apply, the U.K. made the following statement upon becoming a party to the Protocol: "It is the understanding of the United Kingdom that the term 'armed conflict' of itself and in its context denotes a situation of a kind which is not constituted by the commission of ordinary crimes, including acts of terrorism, whether concerted or in isolation".[52] France made a similar statement on becoming a party to the Protocol.[53]

In addition, in a commentary on Additional Protocol I, Karl Josef Partsch explains that low level uses of force between states comparable to internal disturbances and tensions within states "should also be excluded from the concept of armed conflict as this term is used in Art. 1 of the first Protocol".[54]

Additional Protocol II is also intended to apply only to intense armed fighting and not mere incidents. The Protocol Additional to the Geneva Conventions of 12 August 1949, and relating to the Protection of Victims of Non-International Armed Conflicts (Protocol II), 8 June 1977, provides for its scope of application in Article 1:

Material field of application
1.   This Protocol, which develops and supplements Article 3 common to the Geneva Conventions of 12 August 1949 without modifying its existing conditions of application, shall apply to all armed conflicts which are not covered by Article 1 of the Protocol Additional to the Geneva

---

51   Art 1(4) of the Protocol.

52   See Reservations/Declaration, 2 July 2002. Available at http://www.icrc.org/ihl. nsf/NORM/0A9E03F0F2EE757CC1256402003FB6D2?OpenDocument.

53   See Reservations/Declaration, 11 April 2001. Available at (in French) http://www. icrc.org/ihl.nsf/NORM/D8041036B40EBC44C1256A34004897B2?OpenDocum ent.

54   M Bothe, K J Partsch, & W A Solf, *New Rules for Victims of Armed Conflicts: Commentary on the Two 1977 Protocols Additional to the Geneva Conventions of 1949* 46 (Nijhoff, 1982).

Conventions of 12 August 1949, and relating to the Protection of Victims of International Armed Conflicts (Protocol I) and which take place in the territory of a High Contracting Party between its armed forces and dissident armed forces or other organized armed groups which, under responsible command, exercise such control over a part of its territory as to enable them to carry out sustained and concerted military operations and to implement this Protocol.

2.   This Protocol shall not apply to situations of internal disturbances and tensions, such as riots, isolated and sporadic acts of violence and other acts of a similar nature, as not being armed conflicts.

Additional Protocol II sets a higher threshold for application than Common Article 3. This was done in order to make its more detailed and demanding rules acceptable to states.[55] Consequently Additional Protocol II applies only to conflicts that more resemble traditional interstate conflict – it requires control over territory by organised armed groups. The Protocol does not apply to a situation where there is no government.[56] Non-state actor armed groups must engage in sustained and concerted operations and be able to implement the Protocol.

Consequently, after 1977 there were two separate regimes for non-international armed conflict: those covered by Common Article 3 with its relatively low threshold of application but limited protections and conflicts falling within the scope of Additional Protocol II whose threshold of application is high but offers more protections.

According to the ICRC Commentary, Article 1(2) of Additional Protocol II is intended to indicate the lower threshold of armed conflict.[57] Article 1(2) excludes from the coverage of Protocol II "riots, such as demonstrations without a concerted plan from the outset; isolated and sporadic acts of violence, as opposed to military operations carried out by armed forces or armed groups; other acts of a similar nature, including, in particular, large scale arrests of people for their activities or opinions".

---

55   See G I A D Draper, *Humanitarian Law and Internal Armed Conflicts* (1983) 13 Georgia Journal of International and Comparative Law 253, 275.

56   As the ICRC Commentary observes, 'the Protocol applies on the one hand in a situation where the armed forces of the government confront dissident armed forces, i.e., where there is a rebellion by part of the government army or where the government's armed forces fight against insurgents who are organized in armed groups, which is more often the case. This criterion illustrates the collective character of the confrontation; it can hardly consist of isolated individuals without co-ordination'. J Pictet, C Pilloud et al., International Committee of the Red Cross, *Commentary on the Additional Protocols of 8 June 1977 to the Geneva Conventions of 12 August 1949* 1351 (Y Sandoz et al. eds., Nijhoff 1987).

57   Ibid. at 1351-52.

The ICRC gave the following description of internal disturbances during the first session of the Conference of Government Experts in 1971 that preceded the adoption of the Additional Protocols:

> This involves situations in which there is no non-international armed conflict as such, but there exists a confrontation within the country, which is characterized by a certain seriousness or duration and which involves acts of violence. These latter can assume various forms, all the way from the spontaneous generation of acts of revolt to the struggle between more or less organized groups and the authorities in power. In these situations, which do not necessarily degenerate into open struggle, the authorities in power call upon extensive police forces, or even armed forces, to restore internal order. The high number of victims has made necessary the application of a minimum of humanitarian rules.
>
> As regards "internal tensions," these could be said to include in particular situations of serious tension (political, religious, racial, social, economic, etc.), but also the sequels of armed conflict or of internal disturbances. Such situations have one or more of the following characteristics, if not all at the same time:
> – large scale arrests;
> – a large number of "political" prisoners;
> – the probable existence of ill-treatment or inhumane conditions of detention;
> – the suspension of fundamental judicial guarantees, either as part of the promulgation of a state of emergency or simply as a matter of fact;
> – allegations of disappearances.
>
> In short, as stated above, there are internal disturbances, without being an armed conflict, when the State uses armed force to maintain order; there are *internal tensions*, without being internal disturbances, when force is used as a preventive measure to maintain respect for law and order.
>
> These definitions are not contained in a convention but form part of ICRC doctrine.... While designed for practical use, they may serve to shed some light on these terms, which appear in an international law instrument for the first time.[58]

State practice during this period indicates that states generally drew a distinction between on the one hand, hostile actions involving the use of force that they treated as "incidents", "border clashes" or "skirmishes" and, on the other hand, situations that they treated as armed conflicts. The following armed conflicts of the period have been classified as "wars" or invasions: India-Pakistan (1947-48), the Korean War (1950-53), the 1956 Suez Invasion, many wars of national

---

58   *Commentary on the Additional Protocols*, supra n 56 at 1355 (footnotes omitted).

liberation (e.g., Algeria, Indonesia, Tunisia, Morocco, Angola), the Vietnam War (1961-1975), the 1967 Arab-Israeli Conflict, the Biafran War (1967-70), El Salvador-Honduras (the "Soccer War" 1969), the 1973 Arab-Israeli Conflict (the "Yom Kippur War"), and the Turkish Invasion of Cyprus (1974).[59] The ICRC was active with respect to these conflicts. They involved high casualty rates, and appeals were made to the Security Council for help in ending the fighting.

By contrast, the following armed clashes during the period involved the engagement of armed forces of two or more sovereign states but on too limited a basis to have been treated as armed conflicts. They are described rather as "limited uses of force": Saudi-Arabia-Muscat and Oman (1952, 1955), United Kingdom-Yemen (1957), Egypt-Sudan (1958), Afghanistan-Pakistan (1961), and Israel-Uganda (1976).[60] These situations had few or no casualties and requests to the Security Council did not concern on-going fighting.

Other examples of armed incidents between states that were not treated as armed conflicts are the *Red Crusader* incident and the "Cod Wars". In both instances neutral decision-makers provided opinions on international legal aspects of the cases, but the cases were treated as incidents, not armed conflict, despite the fact they involved "engagement" of state armed vessels. The 1961 *Red Crusader* incident involved a Danish fishing enforcement vessel, the *Niels Ebbesen*, and a British fishing trawler. [61] After the Danish vessel fired upon the trawler, a British Naval vessel, HMS *Trowbridge*, escorted both the *Niels Ebbesen* and the *Red Crusader* to port in Aberdeen. A naval vessel escorting a fishing enforcement vessel would seem to fit the phrase "any engagement" used in the ICRC Commentary to define international armed conflict.[62] An official inquiry into the incident, however, gave no indication that either of the parties or the professors of international law on the commission considered it an armed conflict. The Commission found the Danes had used excessive force in arresting the trawler, but neither that fact nor the involvement of two parties to the 1949 Geneva Conventions led to treatment of the incident as an armed conflict.

Similarly in the 1970s in the "Cod Wars" between Iceland, the U.K. and Germany, naval vessels of the U.K. and Germany escorted fishing vessels to prevent interdiction by Icelandic fishery enforcement vessels.[63] Despite applying the label "war" and the use of armed force, these were not treated as a legal

---

59   For accounts of most of these armed conflicts and lesser incidents, see generally A M Weisburd, *Use of Force: The Practice of States Since World War II*, 98, 103, 29, 74-75, 68, 70-71, 71-73, 77-79, 255, 257-58, 258-59, 260, 276 (University Park, PA: Pennsylvania State University Press, 1997).

60   A M Weisburd, *Use of Force*, supra n 59 at 255, 257-58, 258-59, 260, 276.

61   *Report of the Commission of Inquiry Into the Red Crusader Incident*, (1962) 35 ILR 485.

62   See Ibid.

63   For the facts of the incident, see *Fisheries Jurisdiction* (Federal Republic of Germany v Iceland), 25 July 1974 ICJ Rep. 1974, para. 175.

matter as armed conflict. There is certainly no hint of this categorisation in the International Court of Justice decision in the cases.

1980–2000

The most important legal development in this period relevant to the definition of armed conflict was the creation of the two *ad hoc* international criminal tribunals by the Security Council during the 1990s, the ICTY and the ICTR, and the establishment of the International Criminal Court by the Rome Statute of the ICC adopted by States in 1998.

The ICTY *Tadić* decision is widely relied on as authoritative for the meaning of armed conflict in both international and non-international armed conflicts.[64] According to the Appeals Chamber of the ICTY in the *Tadić* case an armed conflict,

> exists whenever there is a resort to armed force between States or protracted armed violence between governmental authorities and organized armed groups or between such groups within a State... These hostilities [fighting among groups within the former Yugoslavia] exceed the *intensity requirements* applicable to *both international and internal* armed conflicts. There has been protracted, large-scale violence between the armed forces of different States and between governmental forces and organized insurgent groups. [65]

The *Tadić* formulation has no requirement that armed groups exercise territorial control, be capable of meeting IHL obligations, or that a government be involved in the fighting.[66]

In applying the *Tadić* Appeals Chamber formulation the *Tadić* Trial Chamber focused on two aspects of a conflict: the intensity of the conflict and the organisation of the parties to the conflict. In the opinion of the Chamber, "[i]n an armed conflict of an internal or mixed character, these closely related criteria are used solely for the purpose, as a minimum, of distinguishing an armed conflict from banditry, unorganized and short-lived insurrections, or

---

64   See, for example, the Rome Statute of the International Criminal Court, art 8, 17 July 1998, 37 ILM 999; European Commission for Democracy Through Law (Venice Commission), Opinion on the International Legal Obligations of Council of Europe Member States in Respect of Secret Detention Facilities and Inter-State Transport of Prisoners, 17 March 2006, Op. no. 363/2005, CDL-AD (2006)009 [hereinafter Venice Commission Opinion].

65   *Prosecutor v Tadić*, Case No. IT-94-1-T, Decision on Defence Motion for Interlocutory Appeal on Jurisdiction, 2 October 1995, para.70 (emphasis added) [hereinafter *Tadić Jurisdiction Decision*].

66   L Moir, *The Law of Internal Armed Conflict*, supra n 34 at 42, quoting *Tadić Jurisdiction Decision*, supra n 65 at para. 70.

terrorist activities, which are not subject to international humanitarian law".[67] Many other ICTY cases follow this approach.[68]

The *Mucić* case, however, did not emphasize the need for intense hostilities in international conflicts stating that, "the existence of armed force between States is sufficient of itself to trigger the application of international humanitarian law".[69]

The ICTR[70] has followed the approach of the ICTY respecting Common Article 3. In *Akayesu*,[71] the Tribunal considered the nature of the conflict in Rwanda at some length.[72] The Chamber quoted the *Tadić* case on the definition of armed conflict; it also noted the ICRC commentary on Common Article 3, which ruled out mere acts of banditry, internal disturbances and tensions and unorganized and short-lived insurrections.[73] Because the definition of an armed conflict is abstract, the question whether or not a situation can be described as an armed conflict, meeting the criteria of Common Article 3, was to be decided on a case-by-case approach. The ICTR suggested an evaluation test, assessing

---

67 *Prosecutor v Tadić*, Case No. IT-94-1-T, Opinion and Judgement (Trial Chamber),7 May 1997, para. 562 [hereinafter *Tadić Trial Judgement*].

68 *Prosecutor v Blagojević and Jokić*, Case No. IT-02-60-T, Judgement (Trial Chamber), 17 January 2005, para. 536; *Prosecutor v Halilović*, Case No. IT-01-48-T, Judgement (Trial Chamber), 16 November 2005, para. 24; *Prosecutor v Limaj et al*, Case No IT-03-66-T, Judgement (Trial Chamber), 30 November 2005, para. 84; *Prosecutor v Galić*, Case No. IT-98-29-T, Judgment and Opinion (Trial Chamber), 5 December 2003, para. 9; *Prosecutor v Stakić*, Case No. IT-97-24-T, Judgement (Trial Chamber), 31 July 2003, paras. 566-68. See also Venice Commission Opinion, supra n 64: 'sporadic bombings and other violent acts which terrorist networks perpetrate in different places around the globe and the ensuing counter-terrorism measures, even if they are occasionally undertaken by military units, cannot be said to amount to an 'armed conflict' in the sense that they trigger the applicability of International Humanitarian Law'.

69 *Prosecutor v Mucić et al*, Case No. IT-96-21-T, Judgement (Trial Chamber), 16 November 1998, para. 184.

70 See Human Rights Watch, *Case Law of the International Criminal Tribunal for Rwanda*, February 2004. Available at http://www.hrw.org/reports/2004/ij/ictr/index.htm.

71 *Prosecutor v Akayesu*, ICTR-96-4-T, Judgement, 2 September 1998, paras. 619-27.

72 See also *Prosecutor v Kayishema and Ruzindana*, ICTR-95-1-T, 21 May 1999, paras. 170-72.

73 See also *Prosecutor v Akayesu*, supra n 71 at paras. 619-21; *Prosecutor v Kayishema and Ruzindana*, supra n 72 at para. 155-90.

both the intensity of the conflict and the organisation of the parties.[74] Intensity did not depend on the subjective judgment of the parties; it was objective.[75]

The Rome Statute of the International Criminal Court, 17 July 1998, provides in Article 8 for war crimes. War crimes include serious violations of Common Article 3, which "applies to armed conflicts not of an international character and thus does not apply to situations of internal disturbances and tensions, such as riots, isolated and sporadic acts of violence or other acts of a similar nature".[76] Article 8(2)(e) applies to other serious violations of the laws and customs applicable in armed conflict not of an international character. It "applies to armed conflicts that take place in the territory of a State when there is protracted armed conflict between governmental authorities and organised armed groups or between such groups".[77] The Rome Statute is not limited to conflicts between governments and armed groups; it omits the condition of Additional Protocol II that dissident armed forces or other organised groups should be "under responsible command or exercise such control over a part of its territory as to enable them to carry out sustained and concerted military operations".[78]

The Inter-American Commission on Human Rights considered the meaning of armed conflict in *Abella v Argentina*.[79] The Commission had to determine whether IHL applied, which in turn depended on whether the petitioners had been involved in an armed conflict with Argentine authorities. The Commission found that an armed conflict had indeed occurred despite the fact that fighting lasted only thirty hours. The Commission considered the following factors: "the concerted nature of the hostile acts undertaken by the attackers, the direct involvement of governmental armed forces, and the nature and level of the violence attending the events in question. More particularly, the attackers involved carefully planned, coordinated and executed an armed attack, i.e., a military operation against a quintessential military objective – a military base".[80]

---

74   *Prosecutor v Akayesu*, supra n 71 at para. 620. The court also said, as a general matter: "The term 'armed conflict' in itself suggests the existence of hostilities between armed forces organized to a greater or lesser extent". Ibid.

75   *Prosecutor v Akayesu*, supra n 71 at para. 603.

76   See art 8(2)(d). This language is the same as art 1(2) of Additional Protocol II.

77   See art 8(2)(f).

78   D Willmott, *Removing the Distinction between International and Non-International Armed Conflict in the* Rome Statute of the International Criminal Court (2004) 5 Melbourne Journal of International Law 196, 218. See also H Spieker, *The International Criminal Court and Non-International Armed Conflicts* (2000) 13(2) Leiden Journal of International Law 395, 409.

79   *Abella v Argentina*, supra n 4 at paras. 149-51.

80   Ibid. at para. 155.

A number of other judicial decisions (national and international) contributed to defining armed conflict. Courts in the United Kingdom,[81] Canada, Italy and Belgium have struggled with cases turning on the legal status of peacekeeping operations and the applicability of IHL to their conduct. In the *Brocklebank* case the Canadian Court Martial Appeal Court considered the torture and beating to death of a Somali teenager during Canada's participation in the UN peacekeeping mission in Somalia.[82] The Court found no evidence of an armed conflict in Somalia at the material time and, on that basis, found the criminal counts inapplicable because they were based on the Fourth Geneva Convention.[83]

An Italian Commission of Inquiry looking into the conduct of Italian peacekeeping troops in Somalia apparently also found it difficult to define the nature of the conflict. "It appears evident from the Report that it is truly difficult to ascertain whether the events reported can be set within a legal context of war or within that of a police operation aiming at restoring public order. Therefore, the Commission failed to express any legal evaluation of the facts, particularly from the perspective of international humanitarian law".[84] Similarly a Belgian Military Court denied the applicability of IHL in UN peacekeeping operations in Somalia and Rwanda during the same period. It found that IHL did not apply to operations with humanitarian aims in situations of internal conflicts instituted under Chapter VII of the United Nations Charter. Consequently it rejected the argument that Belgian troops were either "combatants" or "occupying forces" in either crisis.[85]

---

81   See *R v Ministry of Defence; ex parte Walker*, UKHL 22 [2000] 2 All ER 917 (House of Lords) (6 April 2000).

82   *The Queen v Brocklebank*, 106 Canadian Criminal Cases (3d); 134 D.L.R. (4th) 377 (Court Martial Appeal Court of Canada) (2 April 1996); see also K Boustany, *Brocklebank: A Questionable Decision of the Court Martial Appeal Court of Canada* (1998) 1 Yearbook of International Humanitarian Law 371.

83   However, other authorities arrived at the opposite conclusion. See, e g, the Report of the Somalia Commission of Inquiry, by The Department of National Defence and the Canadian Forces (1997), available at http://www.forces.gc.ca/somalia/somaliae.htm; and J M Simpson, Law Applicable to Canadian Forces in Somalia 1992/93, study prepared for the Commission of Inquiry into the Deployment of Canadian Forces to Somalia (Ottawa: Public Works and Government Services, 1997). See also *Ministre public and Centre pour l'égalité des chances et la lutte contre le racisme v C... et B...*, Belgium, Military Court, Judgment of 17 December 1997, *Journal des Tribunaux*, 4 April 1998, p. 286-89 [hereinafter Decision of Belgian Military Court].

84   N Lupi, *Report by the Enquiry Commission on the Behaviour of Italian Peace-Keeping Troops in Somalia* (1998) 1 Yearbook of International Humanitarian Law 375, 379.

85   Decision of Belgian Military Court, supra n 83 at 286-89. See also, the French report on military engagement in Rwanda: Rapport d'information No. 1271, available at http://www.assemblee-nationale.fr/11/dossiers/Rwanda/r1271.asp; and the Indonesian

During this period the European Court of Human Rights heard a number of claims for violation of both human rights and IHL in situations involving armed clashes. The Court did not, however, analyze the definition of armed conflict or clearly classify situations as armed conflicts or not. Rather, it tended to focus on whether or not violations had occurred of Article 2 of the European Convention on Human Rights that protects the right to life in war and peace.[86]

Other developments during this period include the 1994 United Nations Convention on Safety of United Nations and Associated Personnel. The Convention makes it a crime to attack UN personnel and others covered by the Convention and Article 2(2) provides "This Convention shall not apply to a United Nations operation authorised by the Security Council as an enforcement action under Chapter VII of the Charter of the United Nations in which any of its personnel are engaged as combatants against organized armed forces and to which the law of international armed conflict applies".[87] As Greenwood observes the effect of this provision "is that the threshold for the application of international humanitarian law is also the ceiling for the application of the Convention".[88] If a low threshold of hostilities is adopted for the application of the Convention this will have the effect of rendering virtually non-existent the protections offered by the Convention. An associated development is the Secretary-General's 1999 *Bulletin on Observance by United Nations Forces of International Humanitarian Law.*[89] IHL applies when UN forces are in situations of armed conflict, actively engaged as combatants and to the extent and for the duration of their engagement.[90]

A number of conflicts during this period were generally acknowledged to be armed conflicts: the Iran-Iraq War (1980-88); El Salvador (1980-1993); the Falklands Conflict (1982); Turkey-Kurdistan (1984-1992); the Persian Gulf War (1990-1991); the Philippines insurgency (1991); Bosnia-Herzegovina (1992-1994); Russia-Chechnya (1994-1996); Ecuador-Peru (1995). In the case of the Chechnya

---

report on investigations and prosecution of atrocities in East Timor: Executive Summary Report on the investigation of human rights violations in East Timor, Jakarta, 31 January, 2000. Available at http://www.etan.org/news/2000a/3exec.htm.

86   See, e g, *Ergi v Turkey*, supra n 18 and *Khashiyev & Akayeva v Russia*, supra n 18.

87   Convention on the Safety of United Nations and Associated Personnel, art 2(2), 2051 UNTS 363 (opened for signature 9 December 1994).

88   Greenwood, Handbook, supra n 34 at 53.

89   *UN Secretary General's Bulletin on Observance by United Nations Forces of International Humanitarian Law*, UN Doc ST/SGB/1999/13, 6 August 1999. Available at http://www.un.org/peace/st_sgb_1999_13.pdf.

90   C Greenwood, *International Humanitarian Law and United Nations Military Operations* (1998) 1 Yearbook of International Humanitarian Law 3, 24. See also M Zwanenburg, *Accountability under International Humanitarian Law for United Nations and North Atlantic Treaty Organization Peace Support Operations* ch. 3 (Leiden: Martinus Nijhoff Publishers, 2004).

conflict the Constitutional Court of the Russian Federation emphasised the fact that the disarmament of the irregular armed units could not be achieved without the use of army forces.[91]

In one minor incident, namely the 1988 shooting down and capture of a U.S. pilot by Syrian forces over Lebanon, U.S. officials at first said the pilot was entitled to be treated as a prisoner of war under the Third Geneva Convention.[92] President Reagan called that into question when he said, "I don't know how you have a prisoner of war when there is no declared war between nations. I don't think that makes you eligible for the Geneva Accords".[93]

Other minor incidents, in terms of duration and casualties, were not classified as armed conflicts even though they involved a clash between forces of two states.[94] For example, in 1981 and 1982 incidents involving Soviet submarines in Swedish waters, including the use of depth charges by the Swedish Navy, were classified by scholars as incidents not armed conflict.[95] Also in 1981, U.S. fighter jets engaged in a fire fight with Libyan aircraft above the Gulf of Sidra, shooting them down.[96] Scholars have classified this case as an incident, not an armed conflict.[97] In 1985, French secret agents attached bombs to the hull of the Greenpeace ship, *the Rainbow Warrior*, while docked in Auckland, New Zealand. The ship was sunk with the loss of one life. New Zealand police quickly arrested the two agents. In the subsequent arbitration to enforce a decision in the case by the Secretary-General of the United Nations, the arbitrators do not refer to the bombing or the arrest of the agents as an armed conflict or indicate that the agents were subject to IHL rather than New Zealand's criminal law despite the fact that armed forces and law enforcement officers of two sovereign states were involved.[98] The "Herring War" in 1994, between Iceland

---

91 *Presidential Decrees and the Resolutions of the Federal Government Concerning the Situation in Chechnya*, supra n 10 at para. 6.

92 See Proceedings of the American Society of International Law 82 (1988), 602-3, 609-11. See also, M Asada, *International Armed Conflict and International Humanitarian Law*, in The Meaning of Armed Conflict in International Law, supra n 2.

93 Proceedings of the American Society of International Law, supra n 92 at 610.

94 M E O'Connell, *Enhancing the Status of Non-State Actors Through a Global War on Terror*, (2004) 3 Columbia Journal of Transnational Law 435, 445-46.

95 R Sadurska, *Foreign Submarines in Swedish Waters: The Erosion of an International Norm*, in International Incidents: The Law that Counts in World Politics 40, 41-44 (W M Reisman and A R Willard eds, Princeton: Princeton University Press, 1988); S Schmemann, *Soviet Accuses Swedes on Listening Post*, New York Times, 11 November 1981, A3.

96 S R Ratner, *The Gulf of Sidra Incident of 1981: The Lawfulness of Peacetime Aerial Engagements*, in International Incidents, supra n 95 at 181; A M Weisburd, *Use of Force*, supra n 59 at 289-90.

97 Ibid.

98 *Rainbow Warrior* (New Zealand v France), 20 RIAA 217, 1990.

and Norway, also involved the engagement of official vessels of states, as well as limited use of armed force.[99] These incidents were not treated as armed conflicts.

Based on the reaction of states to several serious cases of rioting, it is apparent that states do not treat such events as armed conflict. This is the case even when the rioting is widespread resulting in deaths or serious destruction, and the armed forces are involved. The primary factor distinguishing riots from armed conflict is that rioters lack organisation. Such rioting occurred in the United Kingdom (1985), United States (1992), and Albania (1997). In the case of the United States, Marines were deployed to help quell violence in Los Angeles. They operated under police rules.[100]

2000–2010

One of the most prominent relevant developments in international law in this period was the publication by the ICRC in 2005 of a comprehensive study of customary international humanitarian law.[101] The Study identifies a large body of customary law rules that apply in both international and non-international armed conflicts. The Study also identifies a set of rules that apply only in international armed conflict. The Study does not provide a definition of either category of armed conflict, however, nor does it define armed conflict.

In 2008 the ICRC posted a paper on its Website, *How is the Term "Armed Conflict" Defined in International Humanitarian Law?* The paper defines the cat-

---

99   B Maddox, *Fleets fight in over-fished waters: Fishing disputes have risen up the diplomatic agenda*, Financial Times (London), 30 August 1994, at 4. The first two cases before the International Tribunal for the Law of the Sea concerned arrest of fishing vessels. See *Panama v France* (the *Camouco* case), International Tribunal for the Law of the Sea, 7 February 2000, available at http://www.itlos.org/cgi-bin/cases/case_detail.pl?id=4&lang=en; *Saint Vincent and the Grenadines v Guinea* (the *M/V Saiga* case), International Tribunal for the Law of the Sea, 37 ILM 360 (1998). Available at http://www.itlos.org/start2_en.html. See also J P E Hijos, *S A v Canada* (Attorney General) (the *Estai* case), FC 1011 (Federal Court of Canada) (2005). See also E Cowan, *Oil and Water: the Torrey Canyon Disaster* (Philadelphia: Lippincott, 1968).

100 Rwanda in 1994 may be another example. The Tutsis inside Rwanda were not an organized armed group at the time Hutu leaders ordered their deaths. Most charges against Hutu leaders later were for genocide and crimes against humanity, not war crimes. The Swiss Military Court of Cassation, however, found Niyonteze, the mayor of a Rwandan town, guilty of war crimes. See B H Oxman and L Reydams, *Niyonteze v Public Prosecutor, Tribunal Militaire de Cassation (Switzerland), 27 April 2001* (2002) 96 American Journal of International Law 231.

101 J-M Henckaerts and L Doswald-Beck, *Customary International Humanitarian Law* (Cambridge University Press 2005). Available at http://www.cicr.org/web/eng/siteengo.nsf/htmlall/pcustom.

egories of international and non-international armed conflict and indicates the current understanding of the ICRC regarding armed conflict in general:

> International armed conflicts exist whenever there is *resort to armed force between two or more States.* ... Non-international armed conflicts are *protracted armed confrontations* occurring between governmental armed forces and the forces of one or more armed groups, or between such groups arising on the territory of a State. The armed confrontation must reach *a minimum level of intensity* and the parties involved in the conflict must show *a minimum of organization*.[102]

The phrase defining international armed conflict has certain differences from the Commentary to the 1949 Conventions. To describe international armed conflict, the ICRC now uses the phrase "resort to armed force" in place of "any engagement" of the armed forces of two or more High Contracting Parties. It also omits the Commentary phrase "regardless of duration or intensity".[103]

In 2009 the ICRC published the *Interpretive Guidance on the Notion of Direct Participation in Hostilities under International Humanitarian Law* and utilized the concept of organised armed groups to identify the armed forces of a non-state party to a non-international armed conflict.[104] The report refers to organised armed groups as those that "develop a sufficient degree of military organisation to conduct hostilities on behalf of a party to the conflict, albeit not always the same means, intensity and level of sophistication as State armed forces".[105]

The meaning of armed conflict continued to be developed in the jurisprudence of the ICTY during this period. A number of cases followed the approach of *Tadić* as to the meaning of armed conflict.[106] In *Kordić and Čerkez*, the Appeals Chamber said that the term "protracted" in the *Tadić* case is significant in

---

102   ICRC, *How is the Term 'Armed Conflict' Defined in International Humanitarian Law?* 5 (2008). Available at http://www.icrc.org/web/eng/siteengo.nsf/htmlall/armed-conflict-article-170308/$file/Opinion-paper-armed-conflict.pdf   (emphasis in the original).

103   See also, J Pejic, *Terrorist Acts and Groups: A Role for International Law?*, supra n 34 at 73 ('International humanitarian law is the body of rules applicable when armed violence reaches the level of armed conflict, whether international or non-international').

104   ICRC, *Interpretive Guidance on Direct Participation in Hostilities*, supra n 11 at 27.

105   Ibid. at 32.

106   *Prosecutor v Blagojević and Jokić*, supra n 68 at para. 536; *Prosecutor v Halilović*, supra n 68 at para. 24; *Prosecutor v Limaj et al*, supra n 68 at para. 84; *Prosecutor v Galić*, supra n 68 at para. 9; *Prosecutor v Stakić*, supra n 68 at paras. 566-68. See also Venice Commission Opinion, supra n 64.

excluding mere cases of civil unrest or single acts of terrorism in cases of non-international conflicts.[107]

The question as to whether there was a non-international armed conflict came before the ICTY again with regard to the conflict in Kosovo; the Tribunal had to decide whether there was a non-international armed conflict or mere internal unrest. In *Milošević*, an *amici curiae* motion was brought that there was no armed conflict in Kosovo at the relevant times and so no case to answer for war crimes under Article 3 of the ICTY Statute.[108] It was argued that the armed conflict began on 24 March 1999 when the NATO bombing campaign began. Before then, the conflict did not involve protracted armed violence; it was only "acts of banditry, unorganized and short-lived insurrections or terrorist activities". The Trial Chamber held that *Tadić* had set out the test for the existence of an internal armed conflict. The Chamber was of the view that the *Tadić* test was "not inconsistent" with the ICRC's Official Commentary to Common Article 3 of the Geneva Conventions set out above. The Chamber pointed out that the Commentary was of persuasive value only, so that while the Commentary offered a more extensive list of criteria, these are not definitive or exhaustive. Thus the Chamber dismissed the more restrictive criteria of the ICRC in relation to Common Article 3 in favour of the broader approach of the Tribunal in *Tadić*.[109]

As for the factors that should be taken into account in assessing intensity, the Trial Chamber in the *Milošević* case considered a large body of evidence: the size of the Serbian response to the actions of the Kosovo Liberation Army (KLA); the spread of the conflict over territory; the increase in number of government forces and the type of the weapons used. The Chamber said that control over territory by insurgents was not a requirement for the existence of a non-international armed conflict.

Reference was also made to the decisions of other Chambers that had considered such factors as the seriousness of attacks and whether there had been an increase in armed clashes, the spread of clashes over territory and over a period of time, any increase in the number of government forces, mobilisation and the distribution of weapons among both parties to the conflict, as well as whether the conflict had attracted the attention of the Security Council and whether any resolutions had been passed.

---

107 *Prosecutor v Kordić and Čerkez*, Case No. IT-95-14/2-A, Judgement (Appeals Chamber), 17 December 2004, para. 341.

108 See *Prosecutor v Milošević*, supra n 47.

109 The same approach to the ICRC criteria was adopted in the *Limaj* case (*Prosecutor v Limaj et al*, supra n 68 at para. 85). The Trial Chamber in that case also observed that the drafting history of Common Article 3 shows a clear rejection of more detailed criteria (para. 86) and moreover that art 8 of the Rome Statute of the International Criminal Court adopted the *Tadić* approach (para. 87).

The Trial Chamber in *Limaj* also held that fighters must exhibit organisation, but only "some degree of organisation will suffice".[110] It rejected the
argument that in order to be bound by IHL a party must be able to implement IHL.[111] The Chamber referred to the fact that other Chambers had taken
into account factors "including the existence of headquarters, designated zones
of operation, and the ability to procure, transport, and distribute arms".[112] The
Chamber pointed to the fact that the KLA had a general staff that appointed
zone commanders, gave directions to units and issued public statements. Unit
commanders gave orders and subordinate units generally acted in accordance
with those orders. Steps had been taken to introduce disciplinary rules and military police and to recruit, train and equip new members.[113]

The criteria of intensity and organisation in a non-international armed conflict were considered in detail again in 2008 in the cases of *Haradinaj*[114] and
Boskoski & Tarculovski.[115] In *Haradinaj* the Trial Chamber, after a survey of the
practice reviewed in previous ICTY decisions, observed that the criterion of
protracted armed violence in practice had been interpreted as referring more to
the intensity of the armed violence than to its duration.[116]

In *Boskoski & Tarculovski* the Trial Chamber identified the following factors that previous decisions had regarded as relevant to the determination of the
intensity of the conflict:

---

110   *Prosecutor v Limaj et al*, supra n 68 at para. 89. The Court cited a study by the ICRC
      in support of its position:

> The ascertainment whether there is a non-international armed conflict does
> not depend on the subjective judgment of the parties to the conflict; it must be
> determined on the basis of objective criteria; the term 'armed conflict' presupposes
> the existence of hostilities between armed forces *organised to a greater or lesser
> extent*; there must be the opposition of armed force and a certain intensity of the
> fighting.

      Ibid. citing ICRC, Working Paper, 29 June 1999 (submitted by the ICRC as a ref-
      erence document to assist the Preparatory Commission in its work to establish the
      elements of crimes for the ICC) (emphasis in the original).

111   Ibid. at paras. 88-89. However later cases have established that 'the leadership group
      must, as a minimum, have the ability to exercise some control over its members so
      that the basic obligations and Common Article 3 of the Geneva Conventions may
      be implemented'. *Prosecutor v Boskoski & Tarculovski*, supra n 49 at para. 196.

112   *Prosecutor v Limaj et al*, supra n 68 at para. 90, citing *Prosecutor v Milošević*, supra n
      47 at paras. 23-24.

113   Ibid. at paras. 94-134.

114   *Prosecutor v Ramush Haradinaj*, Judgement (Trial Chamber) Case No. IT-04-84-T,
      3 April 2008.

115   *Prosecutor v Boskoski & Tarculovski*, supra n 49.

116   *Prosecutor v Ramush Haradinaj*, supra n 114 at para. 49.

the number of civilians forced to flee from the combat zones; the type of weapons used, in particular the use of heavy weapons, and other military equipment, such as tanks and other heavy vehicles; the blocking or besieging of towns and the heavy shelling of these towns; the extent of destruction and the number of casualties caused by the shelling or fighting; the quantity of troops and units deployed; existence and change of frontlines between the parties; the occupation of territory, and towns and villages; the deployment of government forces to the crisis area; closure of roads; cease fire orders and agreements, and the attempt of representatives from international organisations to broker and enforce cease-fire agreements.[117]

As for the factor of organisation the Trial Chamber in *Haradinaj* concluded that: "an armed conflict can exist only between the parties that are sufficiently organised to confront each other with military means"[118] and suggested a number of indicative factors that should be taken into account "none of which are, in themselves, essential to establish whether the 'organisation' criterion is fulfilled".[119]

In *Boskoski & Tarculovski* the Trial Chamber identified, from previous decisions of the Chamber, the following five broad groups of factors as relevant to the requirement of organisation: first, those factors that indicate the presence of a command structure;[120] secondly, factors that indicate whether the group can carry out operations in an organised manner;[121] thirdly, factors indicating the level of logistics;[122] fourthly, factors that determine whether an armed group possesses the level of discipline and the ability to implement the basic obligations of Common Article 3;[123] and finally, those factors that indicate whether the armed group was able to speak with one voice.[124]

The Trial Chamber also considered a number of national decisions on the meaning of armed conflict and remarked that "national courts have paid particular heed to the intensity, including the protracted nature, of violence which has required the engagement of the armed forces in deciding whether an armed conflict exists. The high number of casualties and extent of material destruction have also been important elements in their deciding whether an armed conflict existed".[125] Other factors that the Trial Chamber found provided "useful practical guidance to an evaluation of the intensity criterion in the particular factual

---

117 *Prosecutor v Boskoski & Tarculovski*, supra n 49 at para. 177 (footnotes omitted).

118 *Prosecutor v Ramush Haradinaj*, supra n 114 at para. 60.

119 Ibid.

120 *Prosecutor v Boskoski & Tarculovski* supra n 49 at para. 199.

121 Ibid. at para. 200.

122 Ibid. at para. 201.

123 Ibid. at para. 202.

124 Ibid. at para. 203.

125 Ibid. at para. 183.

circumstances of the case" were the way that "organs of the State such as the police and the military use force against armed groups" and how certain human rights are interpreted such as the right to life and the right to be free from arbitrary detention.[126]

The Pre-Trial Chamber of the ICC for the first time considered the meaning of armed conflict in the ICC Rome Statute in the 2007 case of *Prosecutor v Thomas Luangwa Diylo*.[127] The Chamber focused on the criteria of intensity, organisation and protraction. The criteria of organisation and protraction are linked by the Chamber: "protracted armed conflict...focuses on the need for the armed groups in question to have the ability to plan and carry out military operations for a prolonged period of time".[128]

In early 2007 and 2008, Swedish and British immigration tribunals assessed the conflicts in Somalia and Iraq for purposes of determining whether asylum seekers from those states could continue to receive asylum from armed conflicts.[129] The European Union had adopted a directive that required the grant of asylum in cases of "a serious and individual threat to a civilian's life or person by reason of indiscriminate violence in situations of international or internal armed conflict".[130]

The tribunals, therefore, had to determine whether there were armed conflicts occurring in Somalia and Iraq. In *HH & Others*, an appeal of three asylum cases, decided 28 January 2008, a U.K. immigration tribunal found that the conflict in Somalia was a non-international armed conflict that was occurring in Mogadishu.[131] Individuals from areas beyond Mogadishu did not have a right to seek asylum from armed conflict. The decision is highly detailed respecting the situation in Somalia. It uses the *Tadić* criteria to determine the meaning of armed conflict in international law.[132] The Tribunal found the parties to the conflict sufficiently organized, and the intensity of fighting sufficient in the Mogadishu area.[133] It also stated that "the Tribunal should endeavour to identify both the territorial area in respect of which international humanitarian law

---

126   Ibid. at paras. 178, 193.

127   *Prosecutor v Thomas Luangwa Diylo*, Case no ICC-01/04-01/06, Decision, 29 January 2007.

128   Ibid. at para. 234.

129   Mål nr UM 23-06, Kammarrätten I Stockholm, Migrationsöverdomstolen, Avd.5; and *HH & Others (Mogadishu: Armed Conflict: Risk) Somalia v Secretary of State for the Home Department*. CG [2008] UKAIT 00022 (Asylum and Immigration Tribunal) (28 January 2008). Available at http://www.unhcr.org/cgi-bin/texis/vtx/refworld/rwmain?docid=47dfd9172.

130   Art 15(c) of the EU Qualification Directive, supra n 14.

131   *HH & Others*, supra n 129.

132   Ibid. at para. 318.

133   Ibid. at para. 337.

applies (following the identification of an internal armed conflict) and, where feasible, the parameters of the actual zone of conflict".[134]

The Tribunal noted the differences in the applicable provisions of IHL that depend on whether a conflict is international or non-international, but provided virtually no analysis of why it considered Somalia a non-international armed conflict, despite the fact that from early 2007 Ethiopia and Somalia were involved in intense fighting. By October 2007, there were 6000 casualties from the conflict.

Other European Union member states also have had to decide what constitutes an armed conflict for purposes of granting asylum. On 17 February 2009, the Court of Justice of the European Union handed down a significant decision clarifying when states should grant asylum in the case of armed conflict. In *Elgafaji v. Staatssecretaris van Justitie*, the ECJ rejected reliance on IHL for this determination. The ECJ made two determinations relating to Article 15(c) of the EU Qualification Directive:

– the existence of a serious and individual threat to the life or person of an applicant for subsidiary protection is not subject to the condition that that applicant adduce evidence that he is specifically targeted by reason of factors particular to his personal circumstances;

– the existence of such a threat can exceptionally be considered to be established where the degree of indiscriminate violence characterizing the armed conflict taking place – assessed by the competent national authorities before which an application for subsidiary protection is made, or by the courts of a Member State to which a decision refusing such an application is referred – reaches such a high level that substantial grounds are shown for believing that a civilian, returned to the relevant country or, as the case may be, to the relevant region, would solely on account of his presence on the territory of that country or region, face a real risk of being subject to that threat.[135]

In *QD and AH v. Secretary of State for the Home Department*,[136] the United Kingdom Court of Appeal considered the impact of *Elgafaji* on prior U.K. decisions respecting Article 15(c). It confirmed that reliance on IHL is misplaced. The purposes of asylum must be considered. Asylum should be granted where a high level of violence is present. "[T]he phrase 'situations of international or internal armed conflict' in article 15(c) has an autonomous meaning broad enough to capture any situation of indiscriminate violence, whether caused by

---

134   Ibid. at para. 330.

135   *Elgafaji v Staatssecretaris van Justitie*, C-465/07, Eur. Ct. Justice, 17 February 2009.

136   [2009] EWCA Civ 620.

one or more armed factions or by a state, which reaches the level described by the ECJ in *Elgafaji*".[137]

The Swedish appeal court for migration has also reconsidered earlier Swedish decisions under Article 15(c) of the EU Qualification Directive. In October 2009, the Court looked to a variety of IHL sources and literature for the meaning of armed conflict in asylum cases. The Court decided that in cases of internal armed conflict:

> [T]he severe antagonism between different sections of the population includes protracted and still continuing fighting between the armed forces of the government and one or more other organized armed groups or between two or more such groups ... the violence the conflict entails is indiscriminate and so serious that there is well-founded reason to believe that a civilian person by his or her mere presence would run the veritable risk of being exposed to a serious and personal threat against life and limb.[138]

The new emphasis in European asylum law is to examine the actual violence being carried out by organized armed groups. It is from that violence that asylum seekers need protection. Given this purpose, despite the fact that the courts to date have only considered non-international armed conflicts, international armed conflict would equally need to be characterized by serious violence for there to be a reason for European states to provide protection.

Late in the period under review, the International Law Commission debated a definition of armed conflict for its Draft Articles Relating to the Effects of Armed Conflicts on Treaties. Draft Article 2(b), defining armed conflict involving states, provides: "'Armed conflict' means a situation in which there has been a resort to armed force between States or protracted resort to armed force between governmental authorities and organized armed groups".[139]

Other state practice includes the 2004 United Kingdom Manual of the Law of Armed Conflict that provides as follows in relation to international armed

---

137 Ibid. at para. 35.

138 Mål nr UM 133-09, Kammarrätten I Stockholm, Migrationsöverdomstolen, Avd.1 (Translation by Committee member Inger Österdahl).

139 UN Doc/ A/CN.4/627 (22 March 2010). The article was referred to the Drafting Committee in June 2010. This definition replaces one proposed in 2008 and based on the formulation adopted by the Institute of International Law in its resolution of the 28 August 1985:

> 'Armed conflict' means a state of war or a conflict which involves armed operations which by their nature or extent are likely to affect the operation of treaties between States parties to the armed conflict or between a State party to the armed conflict and a third State, regardless of a formal declaration of war or other declaration by any or all of the parties to the armed conflict

Report of the International Law Commission to the General Assembly, 60 UNGAOR Supp (No 10) at 83, UN Doc A/63/10 (2008).

conflict: "The law of armed conflict applies in all situations when the armed forces of a state are in conflict with those of another state or are in occupation of territory. The law also applies to hostilities in which some of those involved are acting under the authority of the United Nations and in internal armed conflicts. Different rules apply to these different situations".[140] The Manual observes that the expression "armed conflict" remains undefined and cites the ICRC Commentary[141] and the *Tadić* case as guidance. In relation to the question of the threshold of armed conflict the Manual says:

> whether any particular intervention crosses the threshold so as to become an armed conflict will depend on all the surrounding circumstances. For example, the replacing of border police with soldiers or accidental border incursion by members of the armed forces would not, in itself, amount to an armed conflict, nor would the accidental bombing of another country. At the other extreme, a full-scale invasion would amount to an armed conflict.[142]

The requirement that armed conflict must meet some sort of threshold of intensity is also supported by the 2007 consultation paper issued by the U.K. Ministry of Justice on *War Powers and Treaties: Limiting Executive Powers*. The Paper observes "there may be difficult questions about when violence has reached the threshold where there can be said to be a state of 'armed conflict' between the participants".[143]

The Supreme Court of Israel found in 2006 that Israel was engaged in a "continuous state of armed conflict" with various "terrorist organizations" due to the "unceasing, continuous and murderous barrage of attacks" and the armed

---

140   *The Manual of the Law of Armed Conflict* 27 (UK Ministry of Defence, 2004). In addition to the U.K., the Committee found that some states have no publicly available manual (Greece, Japan, Kenya) or the manual has no definition of armed conflict (USA). The 2001 Canadian Forces' Law of Armed Conflict Manual: At the Operational and Tactical Levels, B-GJ-005-104/FP-021 (2001-08-13), available at http://www.forces.gc.ca/jag/publications/Training-formation/LOAC-DDCA_2004-eng.pdf, includes the following in the "glossary" at the end of the document: 'An armed conflict is a conflict between states in which at least one party has resorted to the use of armed force to achieve its aims. It may also embrace conflict between a state and organized, disciplined and uniformed groups within the state such as organized resistance movements'.

141   III *Commentary on the Geneva Conventions of August 12 1949*, supra n 50.

142   *The Manual of the Law of Armed Conflict*, supra n 140 at 29 (footnote omitted).

143   United Kingdom Ministry of Justice, The Governance of Britain: War Powers and Treaties: Limiting Executive Powers, Consultation Paper CP26/07, 25 October 2007, 25. Available at http://www.official-documents.gov.uk/document/cm72/7239/7239.pdf. See also the White Paper, The Governance of Britain-Constitutional Renewal (Cm 7342, March 2008).

response to these. The most important factor for the Court in reaching this determination was the number of persons who have died on both sides.[144]

Some mistakenly believe that the 2006 U.S. decision *Hamdan v. Rumsfeld* supports the possibility of an armed conflict in the absence of fighting.[145] The Court did not in fact make such a finding. In *Hamdan*, the Supreme Court found the Bush administration's special military commissions for trials at Guantánamo Bay unconstitutional because they did not comply with the Uniform Code of Military Justice (UCMJ). The Court ruled that while the president had the right to create military commissions, they had to comply with the UCMJ. The UCMJ permitted the creation of military commissions that complied with the laws of war. For purposes of testing the compliance of the Guantánamo commissions with the laws of war, the Court accepted the Bush administration's argument that the U.S. was in a "non-international armed conflict with al-Qaeda". The Court found that Common Article 3 of the 1949 Geneva Conventions covers even that purported conflict. The Court did not find, however, that the U.S. *was* in a worldwide-armed conflict with al-Qaeda.[146]

The U.S. Executive Branch, in contrast to U.S. courts, has spoken unequivocally about being in a "global war on terror" or an "armed conflict" against certain terrorists groups wherever found. The US has argued that it entered into a worldwide war on terrorism as of the attacks of 11 September 2001.[147] State Department Legal Adviser, Harold Koh, however, spoke to the American Society of International Law in March 2010. Koh made clear that the Obama Administration was not using the term "global war on terror". Rather, it would base its actions on the view that the U.S. is in an "armed conflict with al-Qaeda,

---

144 *Public Committee Against Torture in Israel v Israel*, HCJ 769/02, para. 16 (14 December 2006). See also the *Legal Consequences of the construction of a Wall in the Occupied Palestinian Territory*, supra n 17.

145 548 U.S. 557, 628-29 (2006); *accord* D Amann, Remarks, Panel: Same or Different? Bush and Obama Administration Approaches to Fighting Terrorists, Annual Meeting of the American Society of International Law, 26 March 2010.

146 In an earlier decision, Justice O'Connor looked to such factors as the number of troops and the fact of active combat to find an armed conflict in Afghanistan. See *Hamdi v Rumseld*, 542 U.S. 507, 521 (2004).

147 See supra n 13; US Deputy National Security Adviser S. Hadley, in remarks at The Ohio State University, explained that the US was in a war as of 12 September, because the 11 September attacks were 'an act of war'. S Hadley, Remarks at the Moritz College of Law of the Ohio State University (24 September 2004) (on file with Committee). See also A Dworkin, *Law and the Campaign against Terrorism: the View from the Pentagon*, Crimes of War Project (16 December 2002), available at http://www.crimesofwar.org/print/onnews/pentagon-print.html; J B Bellinger, *Legal Issues in the War on Terrorism*, London School of Economics (31 October 2006). Available at http://www.lse.ac.uk/collections/LSEPublicLecturesAndEvents/pdf/20061031_JohnBellinger.pdf.

the Taliban, and associated forces".[148] Under the new term, however, the U.S. is carrying out many actions that would only be lawful during the hostilities of actual armed conflict, including killing without warning and detention without trial.[149]

Other terrorist attacks since 11 September 2001 have not been treated as armed conflict, but rather have been characterized as crimes.[150] Police methods, not military force, have been used in response. For example, in 2008, terrorists based in Pakistan carried out coordinated attacks at a number of sites in Mumbai, India, that left 174 persons dead.[151] Within a year of the attacks, civil trials were underway in India and Pakistan of persons suspected of involvement.[152] The indications are that most states recognized that these attacks belonged in the same category as those that have occurred subsequent to 11 September in London, Madrid, and Bali, all of which have been characterized as crimes, not armed conflict. Police methods, not military force, have been used in response.

According to the Venice Commission:

78.   ... [T]he organised hostilities in Afghanistan before and after 2001 have been an "armed conflict" which was at first a non-international armed conflict, and later became an international armed conflict after the involvement of US troops. On the other hand, sporadic bombings and other violent acts which terrorist networks perpetrate in different places around the globe and the ensuing counter-terrorism measures, even if they are occasionally undertaken by military units, cannot be said to amount to an "armed conflict" in the sense that they trigger the applicability of International Humanitarian Law.

79.   The Venice Commission considers that counter-terrorist measures which are part of what has sometimes been called "war on terror" are not part of an "armed conflict" in the sense of making the regime of International Humanitarian Law applicable to them. It considers that further reflection is necessary to consider whether any additional instrument may be

---

148   H H Koh, *The Obama Administration and International Law*, supra n 6.

149   It is unclear at present whether the armed conflict against al Qaeda et al extends to the United States and other Western countries. During the Bush administration, officials did claim that the "global war on terror" extended to the U.S., Germany and other countries not experiencing armed conflict.

150   O'Connell, *Enhancing the Status of Non-State Actors,* supra n 94. Terrorist attacks are not automatically excluded, however, when considering the evidence as to the existence of armed conflict, see *Prosecutor v Boskoski & Tarculovski,* supra n 49 at paras. 184-91.

151   *Mumbai attacks: One year on,* 26 November 2009. Available at http://news.bbc.co.uk/2/hi/8379828.stm.

152   Ibid.

> needed in the future to meet or anticipate the novel threats to interna-
> tional peace and security.[153]

Similarly, Greenwood observes:

> In the language of international law there is no basis for speaking of a war
> on Al-Qaeda or any other terrorist group, for such a group cannot be a bel-
> ligerent, it is merely a band of criminals, and to treat it as anything else risks
> distorting the law while giving that group a status which to some implies a
> degree of legitimacy.[154]

The first decade of the 21st century has also seen a number of conflicts that were,
generally, acknowledged to be armed conflicts, including the Afghanistan War
(2001-), the Iraq War (2003-), the Israel-Lebanon War (2006), and the South
Ossetia War between Russia and Georgia (2008). These conflicts were brought
to the Security Council, involved claims and counter-claims regarding IHL,
and, in all cases, involved organized, intense armed fighting that resulted in
many casualties. The conflict of shortest duration was the Russia-Georgia War
that lasted about one week. The 2006 UN Commission of Inquiry on Lebanon
concluded "the hostilities that took place from the 12 July to the 14 August constitute an international armed conflict" but noted that the actual hostilities only
took place between Israel and Hezbollah fighters.[155]

There were also non-international armed conflicts in the period that were
widely recognized as armed conflicts. The Security Council has been involved
in the armed conflict in Congo for many years. In its Resolution of 28 May
2010, it urged the restoration of peace and security, the protection of civilians,
accountability for war crimes, and for peacekeepers to have appropriate rules
of engagement for the "conflict".[156] Similar references are found in Security
Council resolutions on the armed conflict in Sri Lanka. The 2005 Report of
the International Commission of Inquiry on Darfur to the United Nations
Secretary-General accepted the *Tadić* definition of armed conflict for determining that the fighting in that region was indeed armed conflict.[157]

---

153 Venice Commission Opinion, supra n 64.

154 C Greenwood, *War, Terrorism and International Law*, supra n 23 at 529.

155 Report of the Commission of Enquiry on Lebanon pursuant to Human Rights
     Council Resolution S-2/1, UN Doc A/HRC/3/2, 23 November 2006, paras. 8-9 and 57.

156 See the Website of the Security Council and the many resolutions adopted in the
     cases of both countries. E g, S.C. Res. 1925 (2010) (Congo). Available at http://
     www.un.org/Docs/sc/.

157 See *Report of the International Commission of Inquiry on Darfur to the United Nations
     Secretary-General, Pursuant to Security Council Resolution 1564 of 18 September 2004*,
     Geneva, 25 January 2005, para. 74,. Available at http://www.un.org/news/dh/
     sudan/com_inq_darfur.pdf.

By contrast, the Committee found evidence indicating that a number of exchanges between armed forces of states were not recognized as armed conflict. North Korea has been involved with Japan and South Korea in numerous incidents during this period. In 2001, Japanese Coast Guard vessels exchanged fire with a North Korean vessel in Japan's exclusive economic zone. The North Korean vessel exploded and sank. Japan did not consider the incident an armed conflict because it involved coast guard vessels that carry out only law enforcement duties.[158] In 2002, a 21-minute exchange of fire between North and South Korea resulted in a patrol boat being sunk and four South Korean sailors being killed. It was referred to as an "incident", "armed provocation", "border incursion", "clash" and the like, but not an armed conflict. It was not reported to the Security Council.[159] On 26 March 2010, a South Korean warship sank in waters disputed between North and South Korea. Forty-six South Korean sailors perished in the incident. North Korea denied responsibility. If it is established that North Korea is responsible for this attack, South Korea has indicated no plans to counter-attack with armed force, but will consider other non-forceful measures.[160]

In 2004, the Japanese Coast Guard discovered a Chinese submarine in its territorial waters. Japanese Coast Guard vessels and helicopters took part in a "maritime security operation" – presumably observing the submarine. No shots were fired. The sub left Japanese waters.

Again, as the incident involved the Coast Guard, Japan's official position was that it engaged its vessels and helicopters in a law enforcement effort.[161]

In 2007, Iran detained the crew of a small British naval vessel claiming that the vessel was in Iranian waters.[162] The British claimed they were in Iraqi waters. This case, again, involved the intervention of the armed forces of two states. It was not apparently considered an armed conflict. Britain complained when its troops were shown on television, and a spokesperson for the Prime Minister said doing so was a violation of the Third Geneva Convention.[163] The U.K. did not take an official position, however, as to whether the Convention applied. It was

158   K Morikawa, Comments on the Draft Initial Report on the Meaning of Armed Conflict in International Law, 20 August 2008 (on file with the committee.)

159   D Kirk, *North and South Korea Trade Charges Over Naval Clash*, New York Times, 30 June 2002, 12.

160   C Sang-Hun, *North Korea Denies Role in Sinking of Warship*, N.Y. Times, 18 April 2010. See also, Letter dated 6 April 2009 from the Permanent Representative of the Republic of Korea to the United Nations addressed to the President of the Security Council, UN Doc S/2009/186, 7 April 2009 (referring to UN SC Res. 1718).

161   Morikawa, supra n 158.

162   See, for example, M Stannard, *What Law Did Tehran Break? Capture of British Sailors a Gray Area in Application of Geneva Conventions*, San Francisco Chronicle, 1 April 2007, A1.

163   Ibid.

certainly consistent with the spokesperson's statement that the U.K. hoped the higher standard regarding protection from public displays found in the Geneva Convention would be honoured (Third Geneva Convention, Article 13) even if Iran were not obligated to apply it. No similar protection appears to exist in peacetime HRL.[164] Iran, however, treated the matter as one of illegal entry and indicated it might put the crew on trial. Iran made no reference to the Geneva Conventions that was reported in the English-language press.

Colombia's 2008 armed incursion into Ecuador was determined by the Organization of American States to have violated the principle of non-intervention and to have posed a threat of armed conflict, without having reached the level of actual armed conflict.[165] Also in 2008, Thailand and Cambodia clashed over a boundary dispute in the vicinity of the Temple of Preah Vihear. Soldiers from the two states exchanged rifle and rocket fire for about an hour leaving two Cambodian soldiers dead and seven Thai soldiers and two Cambodian soldiers wounded.[166] There was a further five minute clash in April 2009, leaving two Thai soldiers dead and ten injured. Two Cambodian soldiers were also injured as well as nine "others".[167] Neither state has referred to the clashes as an armed conflict. The Security Council has not acted in the case.

During this period high intensity rioting by unorganised groups continued to be distinguished from armed conflict as in the case of the U.K. and France in 2005. Similarly election-related violence in Kenya in late 2007 and early 2008 has consistently been described as rioting, civil unrest, and criminality, not armed conflict.[168] Violence in Thailand in 2010 was also generally regarded as civil unrest but appeared to be moving toward armed conflict until

---

164 The Foreign Office reports the United Kingdom did not take an official position on the Geneva Conventions. E-mail message of 17 May 2007 (on file with the Committee).

165 See, for example, S Romero, *Files Released by Colombia Point To Venezuelan Bid to Arm Rebels*, New York Times, 30 March 2008, A1 ('Colombia's relations with its two Andean neighbours veered suddenly toward armed conflict after Colombian forces raided a FARC camp inside Ecuador on March 1, killing 26 people, including a top FARC commander, and capturing the computers, according to the Colombians'.)

166 *2 Killed on Thai-Cambodia Border*, New York Times, 15 October 2008. Available at http://www.nytimes.com/2008/10/16/world/asia/16cambo.html.

167 *Soldiers Die as Thai, Cambodian Troops Trade Fire*, 3 April 2009, CNN.com. Available at http://edition.cnn.com/2009/WORLD/asiapcf/04/03/cambodia.thai.tensions/index.html.

168 For example, the Global Partnership for the Prevention of Armed Conflict refers to the situation in Kenya in late 2007 and early 2008 as 'violence' and 'escalating violence', not armed conflict. See Kenya Update 22 January 2008. Available at http://www.gppac.net/page.php?id=1837. But see the ICC Pre-Trial decision discussed *infra* n 184-86 and accompanying text.

20 May 2010, when the military effectively re-gained control and dispersed the opposition.[169]

Mexico has experienced high levels of violence perpetrated by organized crime groups since 2006. Mexico military forces have been involved in the attempt to control well-financed and well-armed criminal groups involved in drug trafficking. Mexico's military forces follow law enforcement rules of engagement. There is no indication that persons are being held without trial until the end of hostilities. If the criminal gangs decided to challenge civil authorities for the right to govern, as opposed to fighting to prevent the break-up of their criminal activities, Mexico could become the scene of a non-international armed conflict.[170] This was not the case as of early 2010.

In sum, the evidence overwhelmingly supports the observation of Greenwood that "many isolated incidents, such as border clashes and naval incidents, are not treated as armed conflicts. It may well be, therefore, that only when fighting reaches a level of intensity which exceeds that of such isolated clashes will it be treated as an armed conflict to which the rules of international humanitarian law apply".[171]

III   Characteristics of Armed Conflict

The discussion above supports the position that armed conflict is to be distinguished from "incidents";[172] "border clashes";[173] "internal disturbances and tensions such as riots, isolated and sporadic acts of violence";[174] "banditry, unorganised and short lived insurrections or terrorist activities"[175] and "civil unrest, [and] single acts of terrorism".[176] The distinction between these situations and armed conflict is achieved by reliance on the criteria of organisation and intensity.

Over the years there have been various other characteristics that have been put forward as integral to armed conflict. The majority of these have related to the level of organisation of dissident groups. For example the requirement that the conflict take place between governmental forces and rebel forces and for the latter to control part of the territory, to have a responsible command and to be capable of implementing the requirements of IHL. Some definitions

---

169   *Bangkok Counts its Losses After Downtown Rioting,* 20 May 2010, npr.org.

170   See *Mexican President: We're Not Losing the Drug War,* 26 February 2009, msnbc.com. Available at http://www.msnbc.msn.com/id/29413556/print/1/displaymode/1098/.

171   Greenwood, Handbook, supra n 34 at 48.

172   See state practice supra at pp 16-17.

173   Ibid.

174   Additional Protocol II art 1(2).

175   *Tadić Trial Judgement,* supra n 67 at para. 562.

176   See, e g, *Kordić and Čerkez,* supra n 107 at para. 341.

specify that the parties must be pursuing particular political goals; other defini-tions require that a specific number of persons must have died in the fighting.[177] However, it appears that none of these are essential characteristics of either the treaty or customary law meaning of armed conflict although several are integral to the application of Additional Protocol II.

The criterion of organisation: the evidence discussed above indicates clearly that armed conflicts involve two or more organized armed groups. Violence perpetrated by the assassin or terrorist acting essentially alone or the disorgan-ized mob violence of a riot is not armed conflict. This criterion is reflected in treaties;[178] other State practice; mentioned explicitly or implicitly in decisions of several courts and tribunals;[179] as well as in the commentary of international law scholars. The significance of organisation for the existence of an armed conflict is also reflected in United Nations peacekeeping practice. As outlined above, peacekeeping forces respect peacetime human rights protections unless a force opposing them is, *inter alia*, an organized armed group.

The organisation factor is readily met in conflicts involving states, as the majority of armed conflicts between states involve their regular armed forces. The issue may however, be relevant along with the rules on attribution in the case of paramilitary and irregular forces. The satisfaction of the criterion of organisation is more complex in the context of non-international armed conflict. The Trial Chambers of the ICTY have relied on several indicative factors out-lined in detail above to determine whether the organisation criterion is fulfilled. The underlying theme is that there must be a sufficient level of organisation through a command structure in order for the basic requirements of Common Article 3 to the 1949 Geneva Conventions to be implemented.[180] None of the fac-tors in itself is central.[181] Factors relevant to assessing organisation include com-mand structure; exercise of leadership control; governing by rules; providing military training; organized acquisition and provision of weapons and supplies; recruitment of new members; existence of communications infrastructure; and space to rest.[182] As a practical matter opposing groups will in most cases control

---

177 See supra n 44.
178 See Common Article 2 of the 1949 Geneva Conventions (referring to High Contracting Parties); Common Article 3 of the Geneva Conventions ('organised military forces'); art 1 of Additional Protocol II ('or other organised armed groups') and Rome Statute art 8(2)(e).
179 In particular the *Tadić* case.
180 See *Prosecutor v Boskoski & Tarculovski*, supra n 49 at para. 196.
181 See *Prosecutor v Ramush Haradinaj*, supra n 114 at para. 60.
182 See *Prosecutor v Milošević*, supra n 47; see also M Bothe, Direct Participation in Hostilities in Non-International Armed Conflict, Expert Paper, Second Expert Meeting on the Notion of Direct Participation in Hostilities, The Hague, 25-26 October 2004. Available at http://www.icrc.org/Web/eng/siteengo.nsf/htmlall/direct-participation-article-020709/$File/2004-05-expert-paper-dph-icrc.pdf.

enough territory to organize. Control of territory is an affirmative requirement for the application of Additional Protocol II.[183]

The criterion of organisation was considered in a pre-trial decision of the International Criminal Court in the ICC's Investigation into the Situation in the Republic of Kenya.[184] A majority of the Pre-Trial Chamber applied a flexible test to the requirement that a non-state actor group be organized as a condition of a finding of an armed conflict. In a dissent, Judge Hans-Peter Kaul suggested specific factors to consider in investigating organization. He wrote that "groups of organized crime… a mob, groups of (armed) civilians or criminal gangs,"[185] generally fail to meet the criterion of organization. He further pointed out that "the acts of the members of the 'organisation' must be linked to the 'organisation'. Several factors may be indicative. A specific collectivity of persons with some kind of policy level and hierarchical structure, the capacity to impose the policy on its members and to sanction them, induces a particular relationship between the policy level of that 'organization' and its members…".[186]

The criterion of intensity: The assessment here of state practice and *opinio juris*, judicial opinion, and the majority of commentators support the position that hostilities must reach a certain level of intensity to qualify as an armed conflict.

Factors relevant to assessing intensity include for example the number of fighters involved;[187] the type and quantity of weapons used;[188] the duration and territorial extent of fighting;[189] the number of casualties;[190] the extent of destruction of property;[191] the displacement of the population; and the involvement of the Security Council or other actors to broker cease-fire efforts. Isolated acts of violence do not constitute armed conflict. The intensity criterion requires more than, for example, a minor exchange of fire or an insignificant border clash. None of the factors identified above is necessarily determinate in itself. A lower level with respect to any one may satisfy the criterion of intensity if the level of another factor is high.[192]

---

183   Art 1(1).
184   *Situation in the Republic of Kenya*, no. ICC-01/09, (Pre-Trial Chamber) Decision Pursuant to art 15 of the Rome Statute on the Authorization of an Investigation into the Situation in the Republic of Kenya, 31 March 2010.
185   Ibid. at para. 52 (Dissent of Judge Hans-Peter Kaul).
186   Ibid. at para. 69.
187   See, e g, *Prosecutor v Boskoski & Tarculovski*, supra n 49 at para. 177.
188   Ibid.
189   Ibid.
190   Ibid.
191   Ibid.
192   See, e g, *Abella v Argentina*, supra n 4 and *Prosecutor v Ramush Haradinaj*, supra n 114 at para. 49.

The jurisprudence of the ICTY indicates that the requirement of intensity will normally have a temporal aspect in the case of non-international armed conflicts for the purposes of the application of Common Article 3 to the Geneva Conventions.[193] In other words, in order to constitute a non-international armed conflict there must be a certain level of armed violence over a protracted period. The two concepts, intensity and protraction, are linked and a lesser level of duration may satisfy the criterion if the intensity level is high.[194] The reverse is also the case. The idea of "protraction" is also relevant to the "organisation" criterion, as it requires a certain level of organisation to undertake protracted hostilities.[195]

Nevertheless, according to the ICTY in *Haradinaj*, intensity is the more important criterion: "The criterion of protracted armed violence has therefore been interpreted in practice, including by the *Tadić* Trial Chamber itself, as referring more to the intensity of the armed violence than to its duration".[196]

Commencement, Termination, and Territorial Scope of Armed Conflict: If armed conflict exists when organized armed groups are engaged in intense fighting, then, logically, armed conflict does not begin until these criteria are present; armed conflict ends when the criteria are no longer present, and armed conflict extends to territory where organized armed fighting is occurring. The Committee undertook only preliminary research into whether international law confirms these observations. We found these are complicated issues in need of thorough research.

For example if armed conflict commences when both the criteria of intensity and organisation are met, this raises the question of whether a single, significant armed attack constitutes an armed conflict irrespective of any response.

Respecting international armed conflicts, among the conflicts lasting for the shortest periods was the 1969 Soccer War between El Salvador and Honduras. It lasted four days. It involved the military forces of both sides using tanks, aircraft, and heavy artillery. 1000 soldiers and 2000 civilians were killed and 300,000 civilians were displaced. The OAS intervened to help bring about an end to the fighting. See T P Anderson, *The Hundred Hours War*, 107-28 (1981).

The 2008 South Ossetia War between Georgia and Russia lasted one week. It involved the military forces of both states using aircraft and heavy artillery. Estimates are that between 600 and 800 persons died, about half of whom were civilians, and 158,000 persons were displaced. France mediated a ceasefire. See T Bahrampour, *An Uncertain Death Toll in Georgia-Russia War*, Washington Post, 25 August 2008. Available at http://www.washingtonpost.com/wp-dyn/content/article/2008/08/24/AR2008082402150.html.

193   *Tadić Jurisdiction Decision*, supra n 65 at para. 70 and see *Prosecutor v Ramush Haradinaj*, supra n 114 at paras. 40-49 (for a consideration of how the term 'protracted armed violence' has been interpreted by the ICTY).

194   See, e g, *Abella v Argentina*, supra n 4.

195   *Prosecutor v Thomas Luangwa Diylo*, supra n 127.

196   Ibid. at para. 49.

Some who argue that armed conflict begins with a significant armed attack do so in the belief that otherwise IHL would not apply to such attacks because IHL is only triggered by armed conflict. The issue is not so simply resolved, however. Even in the absence of armed conflict, a member of the armed forces may invoke IHL to justify the use of lethal force. The case of the South Korean warship *Cheonan* provides an example. The *Cheonan* sank on 26 March 2010 in the vicinity of the disputed maritime boundary between North and South Korea. Forty-six sailors perished.[197] After a six-week investigation, South Korea concluded that a North Korean torpedo had sunk the ship.[198] This type of attack could give rise to a right to respond in self-defence under Article 51 of the United Nations Charter, given either additional information about likely future attacks or Security Council authorization. Nevertheless, South Korea has not responded with military force. To date there has been no exchange of fighting and so no armed conflict. If South Korea's facts are correct, the North Korean leaders who ordered the attack have committed a serious violation of international law and may someday be held accountable. North Korea had no right to attack the South Korean ship, and it is no justification that its leaders believed that the ship was a military target. The sailors on the North Korean submarine who implemented the order, however, may have a defence if they believed in good faith that they were following a lawful order to attack a military objective as permitted under IHL. In such a case, IHL may be invoked regardless of the existence of an armed conflict.

IHL may also be applied outside a situation of an armed conflict by analogy with the military law that normally governs members of a state's armed forces. There are a number of examples of members of the armed forces who while carrying out duties in peacetime trespass into another state's territory or territorial waters. These are not considered cases of armed conflict, but as the usual law applicable to members of the armed forces is their national state's military law, by analogy, it is possible and probably preferable to apply IHL. The case of the American pilot shot down by Syria in 1988 and the British sailors detained by Iran in 2007 are examples of states requesting application of IHL even where they did not recognize the existence of an armed conflict.

Thus, it appears possible to allay the concern about the application of IHL. It could be applicable to military operations even in the absence of armed conflict without redefining "intense fighting" to include significant one-sided first strikes IHL could be applicable to soldiers who follow lawful orders or who are carrying out official duties. IHL would not apply to the leadership, however, who order first strikes without Security Council authorization. Such strikes are

---

197 Security Council to Receive Briefing on South Korea Ship Probe, 10 June 2010, http://www.globalsecuritynewswire.org/gsn/nw_20100610_6582.php.

198 J Sudworth, *How South Korean Ship Was Sunk*, 20 May 2010, BBC News. Available at http://news.bbc.co.uk/2/hi/world/asia_pacific/10130909.stm.

unlawful under the *jus ad bellum* and do not become lawful by following IHL and proclaiming that the action is within an "armed conflict".

With respect to cessation of armed conflict our preliminary observations are that it is rare for parties to end armed conflicts today with formal agreements.[199] More usual is the cessation of hostilities for a long enough period of time so that the parties and the international community recognize that the conflict is at an end. If a sufficient period elapses before the hostilities resume a new conflict would be presumed. International law contains no rule, however, as to how long the cessation needs to last for an armed conflict to be considered legally at an end. A number of factors would appear to be relevant. For example, even if hostilities cease, are the parties maintaining battle positions? Is it plain that fighting could recommence at any time or are forces being pulled back or even sent home? Are peacetime activities resuming such as trade, commerce, agriculture, and manufacturing? Are refugees who fled the fighting returning home? Some provisions of IHL may continue to apply after the cessation of hostilities, so IHL may not be a helpful indicator in indentifying the end of armed conflict.[200]

The territorial scope of armed conflict is also a complex issue. As a general rule, armed conflict occurs where organized armed groups are engaged in intense armed fighting. Again, the actual territorial scope may or may not be co-extensive with the reach of IHL. IHL may well extend beyond the area of actual fighting for certain purposes. For example war crimes may occur at some distance from the actual fighting.[201] On the other hand, the territorial extent of armed conflict is critical to know for the correct application of *ius ad bellum* requirement of proportionality.[202] The United Nations Charter limits the right to use force to self-defence or with Security Council authorization. According to Greenwood:

---

199 On peace agreements generally, see Christine Bell, *Peace Agreements and Human Rights* (2000).

200 E.g., according to Common Article 2 the 1949 Geneva Conventions apply '...to all cases of partial or total occupation of the territory of the High Contracting Parties, even if said occupation meets with no armed resistance'. See also *Tadić Jurisdiction Decision*, supra n 65 at para. 70 ('[i]nternational humanitarian law applies from the initiation of such armed conflicts and extends beyond the cessation of hostilities until a general conclusion of peace is reached; or, in the case of internal conflicts, a peaceful settlement is achieved. Until that moment, international humanitarian law continues to apply in the whole territory of the warring States or, in the case of internal conflicts, the whole territory under the control of a party, whether or not actual combat takes place there').

201 See *Tadić Jurisdiction Decision* ibid. and Separate Opinion of Judge Simma in *Armed Activities on the Territory of the Congo* (Congo v Uganda) supra n 17 334 at para. 20-21.

202 See J Gardam, *Necessity and Proportionality and the Use of Force by States* 162-67 (Cambridge: Cambridge University Press 2004).

Military operations will not normally be conducted throughout the area of war. The area in which operations are actually taking place at any given time is known as the 'area of operations' or 'theatre of war'. The extent to which a belligerent today is justified in expanding the area of operations will depend upon whether it is necessary for him to do so in order to exercise his right of self-defence. While a state cannot be expected always to defend itself solely on ground of the aggressor's choosing, any expansion of the area of operations may not go beyond what constitutes a necessary and proportionate measure of self-defence. In particular, it cannot be assumed – as in the past – that a state engaged in armed conflict is free to attack its adversary anywhere in the area of war.[203]

State practice is consistent with this position. States rarely recognize armed conflict beyond the zone of intense fighting, whether the fighting is in an international or non-international armed conflict.[204]

Conclusions

In 2005, the International Law Association decided that a study of the concept of armed conflict should be undertaken to determine the meaning of this term in international law. Despite the importance of the issue over the years, as highlighted by the U.S. "declaration" of a "war on terror" in 2001, the meaning of armed conflict in international law has not been the subject of comprehensive analysis. This was the task of the Committee.

1.   The Committee found that the term "armed conflict" had become especially significant with the adoption of the U.N. Charter in 1945 when the term "war" declined in importance. Nevertheless, neither the Charter nor any other important treaty currently defines armed conflict despite the fact that in many subfields of international law it is critical to determine whether or not a situation is one of armed conflict. The Committee, therefore, undertook extensive research into hundreds of violent situations since 1945 and identified significant state practice and *opinio juris* establishing that as a matter of customary international law a situation of armed conflict depends on the satisfaction of two essential minimum criteria, namely:
     a.   the existence of organized armed groups
     b.   engaged in fighting of some intensity.[205]

The Committee's assessment of this evidence is confirmed directly or indirectly in many judicial decisions and in scholarly commentary. These

---

203 Greenwood, Handbook, supra n 34 at 61-62.
204 Ibid.
205 As to different categories of armed conflict, see n 7 supra.

sources also indicate that the following conclusions respecting the concept of armed conflict are confirmed in customary international law:

2. In international law the concept of armed conflict has largely replaced the concept of war.

3. The earlier practice of states creating a *de jure* state of war by a declaration is no longer recognized in international law. Declarations of war or armed conflict, national legislation, expressions of subjective intent by parties to a conflict, and the like, may have evidentiary value but such expressions do not alone create a *de jure* state of war or armed conflict.

4. The *de jure* state or situation of armed conflict depends on the presence of actual and observable facts, in other words, objective criteria.

5. The accurate identification of a situation of armed conflict has significant and wide-ranging implications for the discipline of international law. Armed conflict may have an impact on treaty obligations; on U.N. operations; on asylum rights and duties, on arms control obligations, and on the law of neutrality, amongst others. Perhaps most importantly states may only claim belligerent rights during an armed conflict. To claim such rights outside situations of armed conflict risks violating fundamental human rights that prevail in non-armed conflict situations, i.e., in situations of peace.

Chapter 25

Report on the Adoption of the Committee's Final Report on the Definition of Armed Conflict (September 2010)

Mary Ellen O'Connell

Memorandum

To: The International Law Association Committee on the Use of Force
From: Mary Ellen O'Connell, Chair
Date: 29 September 2010

Re: ILA Biennial Meeting in The Hague, 15-20 August

Key documents mentioned in this memo are available on the website of the ILA at the Use of Force Committee page:
http://www.ila-hq.org/en/committees/index.cfm/cid/1022

On 21 June 2010, Judith Gardam, the Use of Force Committee's *rapporteur*, and I sent a draft or our *Final Report on the Meaning of Armed Conflict in International Law* to ILA Headquarters in preparation for the 74th Conference of the ILA in The Hague. The draft was posted on the ILA website. Judith and I also prepared a draft resolution for presentation at the Conference.

On Wednesday, 18 August, at an Open Working Session at the ILA Conference chaired by Professor Duncan French, I presented the draft report for discussion, including a history of the Committee's work and a summary of the draft Final Report. As many as 50 ILA members participated in all or part of the Working Session. Eight members of the Use of Force Committee participated: Christine Gray, Noam Lubell, Koichi Morikawa, Josef Mrazek, Eric Myjer, Michael Wood, and me. Jutta Brunnée was at the Conference but had to leave before the Open Working Session for family reasons. She spoke with me to express her support for the Final Report.

The Working Session discussion was recorded and a detailed report will appear in The Hague Conference proceedings. I will provide only a brief description here because of the delay before the publication of the proceedings and to let you know about the proposed next mandate for the Committee. The

Mary Ellen O'Connell (ed.), What Is War? An Investigation in the Wake of 9/11.
© 2012 Koninklijke Brill NV. Printed in The Netherlands. ISBN 978 9004 17234 0. pp. 369 – 372.

proposal will likely go to the Executive Council at its meeting in November, which is prior to the likely publication date of the proceedings.

The Working Session began with an introduction by Duncan French and my thanks to him for chairing the session. I then proceeded to outline the Committee's mandate; to provide a history of our work toward fulfilling the mandate, and to give a summary of our conclusions in the draft Final Report. I emphasized that the Report reflected a substantial effort by an outstanding 18-member Committee from 15 countries during a five-year period. We were privileged to have Judith Gardam as our rapporteur, someone expert in the *jus ad bellum, jus in bello,* and human rights law. We were also very fortunate to have had Christine Gray and Michael Wood with us throughout the five years, including at our meeting in The Hague. The Committee was guided at all times by the initial decisions taken by the Committee at our 2006 meeting in Berlin, hosted by Georg Nolte and attended by Jutta Brunée, Christine Gray, Elzbieta Mikos-Skuza, Michael Wood, and me. In particular, the Committee agreed to follow standard international law methodology and to adhere carefully to the Committee's mandate. The mandate was to consider the evidence in international law as to the definition of armed conflict for general purposes with respect to terrorism, asylum rights, neutrality, treaty law, arms control, combatant privileges, and the like. We were not asked what conditions trigger international humanitarian law. We did not seek to answer that question or to define different types of armed conflict.

We found that no treaty contained a general definition of armed conflict. Following standard methodology, therefore, required investigating evidence of state practice and *opinio juris.* We reviewed hundreds of conflicts in the course of our research. The Report specifically refers to 72 conflicts.

In 2007, the Committee participated in a multidisciplinary conference on the meaning of armed conflict at the University of Notre Dame. We found that in political science and peace studies a certain number of fatalities are necessary for a conflict to count as an armed conflict, such as 25 or 1000 deaths per year. In peace studies, the intentions of the fighters are also an important criterion. The Committee did not find that a certain number of fatalities or any fatalities at all are necessary for a conflict to amount to an armed conflict, nor did we find that the intentions of the party are a *sine qua non* of armed conflict. Nevertheless, the perspective of other disciplines did support our finding that the international community recognizes armed conflict as a definable situation, distinctive from situations in which peacetime law prevails.

In 2008, the Committee presented its Initial Report at the ILA's 73rd Conference in Rio de Janeiro. The Initial Report was also discussed in an Open Working Session and was well received. In the two years between the Rio Conference and the conference in The Hague, the Committee's Initial Report remained posted on the ILA website. I wrote an article about the Initial Report that was published in the *Journal of Conflict and Security Law.* The article was also posted on-line. During 2009, the Committee received valuable reports from Constantine Antonapolous on human rights and armed conflict and from Eric Myjer on the distinction between armed attack and armed conflict. I published a short article looking into the question of territorial extent of armed conflict and traveled to Australia to work with Judith Gardam on the final draft. In 2010, Michael Wood and Inger Oesterdahl brought to the Committee's attention new developments respecting the European obligations to provide asylum to persons fleeing armed conflict. In May and June 2010, the Committee engaged in an intensive period of commentary, involving nearly the entire Committee. The draft was revised and the final version submitted on 21 June.

At the Open Working Session in The Hague, I expressed my view that the Report is needed as much in 2010 as in 2005 despite significant new developments in international relations implicating the use of force. The United States, for example, despite the election of Barack Obama and the assumption by Dean Harold Koh of the top international law position in the U.S. government continues to operate under a concept of armed conflict not consistent with the definition reached in the Committee's Final Report. The U.S. government has adopted new terminology. It no longer uses the expression "global war on terror." Today it employs worldwide "armed conflict against al Qaeda, the Taliban, and associated forces." Under the new concept, however, many of the same practices previously associated with the "global war on terror" are continuing. A *New York Times* report of 15 August 2010, described U.S. military operations in 12 states that included killing and detention without trial regardless of the presence of intense fighting by organized armed groups.

I then read the concluding section of the Report and the general discussion began. All Committee members present contributed. It was generally acknowledged that more work could be done on the topic, but that the Committee had made a valuable contribution with this first major effort to identify the definition of armed conflict in international law. It was also the view of many non-Committee members that the Report should be widely disseminated.

We then discussed the proposed resolution which emphasized sending the Report to many relevant persons, states, and organizations.

The discussion moved on to a new Committee mandate. I made the point that the Use of Force Committee is clearly one of the strongest in the ILA and should continue with a new mandate. I made several suggestions of possible new topics for the Committee to take up, including, further research on topics raised in the course of our work on the definition of armed conflict; an examination of the concept of necessity in the *jus ad bellum* and the *jus in bello*; an examination of the prohibition of aggression in the *jus ad bellum* following the Kampala review conference of the ICC and its work on the crime of aggression and individual accountability, and, finally, a report cyber war.

In addition to the above, participants raised a number of topics related to self-defense and humanitarian intervention. An engaging discussion ensued and a consensus emerged that most of the suggested topics could be examined under the following mandate: The Use of Force Committee will report on the prohibition of aggression and the international law on the use of force. This mandate would lead to a comparison of the prohibition of aggression in the *jus ad bellum* and the ICC crime of aggression. It would require review of self-defense and such related topics as when, if ever, a response to a cyber-attack could involve military force; how long the right to resort to self-defense lasts following an armed attack; whether there is ever a right of anticipatory self-defense; what obligation the principle of necessity imposes on states, and whether states may respond in self-defense to attacks by non-state actors when those attacks are not attributable to a state. The proposed mandate would also require investigation of any changes in the law with respect to resort to force without Security Council authorization or with respect to internal armed conflict.

Duncan French then called for a vote on the Final Report on the Meaning of Armed Conflict in International Law and the draft resolution. Both were adopted without opposition.

I will submit the proposal for a new mandate to the Executive Council, which next meets in November. I discussed the proposal with Christine Chinkin, Director of Studies, during her meeting with me as Committee Chair. I told her that I thought with a new mandate, a new committee chair should take over but that I am willing to remain as Chair until a replacement is found. Judith Gardam has expressed the need to end her service as rapporteur owing to other pressing obligations.

Postscript

This book is being completed within weeks of the 1 May 2011, killing of Osama bin Laden, the mastermind of the 9/11 killings.[1] The world might well have expected that with bin Laden's death President Obama could end the policy known as the "global war on terror" and, thereby, end the controversy that has swirled since President Bush first declared it.[2] This book and the ILA Use of Force Committee's Final Report on the Meaning of Armed Conflict in International Law could have become documents of a troubled time in the history of international law without significant relevance for the future.

President Obama, however, did not end the "war on terror", which his administration has renamed, the "armed conflict against al Qaeda, the Taliban and associated forces." Within days of bin Laden's death, the U.S. again engaged in what is arguably the most egregious conduct of the "war on terror" – the targeted killings of terrorist suspects far from any armed conflict hostilities. Even as top United Nations human rights officials demanded to know the details of the killing of bin Laden[3] and reminded the U.S. that terrorism is generally a matter for the criminal law, not the law of armed conflict,[4] the U.S. carried

---

1   *See* White House Press Release, http://www.whitehouse.gov/the-press-office/2011/05/02/remarks-president-osama-bin-laden.
2   Evidence of the controversy associated with the so-called "global war on terror" is found throughout this book and in the ILA Final Report. One document that has not been cited in the book but contains yet another critique is the Club of Madrid, International Summit on Democracy, Terrorism, and Security, 8-11 March 2005, at 9-10, available at http://www.clubmadrid.org/img/secciones/new_consensus.pdf.
3   *See U.N. Rights Boss Asks U.S. for Facts on bin Laden Killing*, REUTERS, May 3, 2011, http://www.reuters.com/article/2011/05/03/us-binladen-un-rights-idUSTRE7425PR20110503
4   Osama bin Laden: Statement by the UN Special Rapporteurs on Summary Executions and on Human Rights and Counter-Terrorism: "Acts of terrorism are the antithesis of human rights, in particular the right to life. In certain exceptional cases, use of deadly force may be permissible as a measure of last resort in accordance with international standards on the use of force, in order to protect life,

Mary Ellen O'Connell (ed.), What Is War? An Investigation in the Wake of 9/11.
© *2012 Koninklijke Brill NV. Printed in The Netherlands. ISBN 978 9004 17234 0. pp. 373 – 374.*

out more targeted killing. On 7 and 8 May, the U.S. conducted drone attacks in Pakistan killing as many as 15 persons and in Yemen killing an unknown number.[5] The reputed target of the Yemeni attack was a Muslim cleric, Anwar al-Awlaki, who was, reportedly, not killed.[6]

The fact Awlaki was targeted is particularly stunning evidence of the Obama administration's continuing commitment to the "war on terror." In October 2010, two human rights NGOs, the American Civil Liberties Union and the New York-based Center for Constitutional Rights, relying on the ILA Report, petitioned on behalf of Awlaki's father for a court order to prevent the U.S. government from killing his son. The petition explained the situation in Yemen, Awlaki's role in al-Qaeda, and other significant facts that simply could not add up to a right to intentionally kill Awlaki. Basic documents from the case are found in the Appendix that follows this Postscript. The court refused to take jurisdiction, ruling, among other things, that the father did not have standing, and the father did not appeal.[7] Nevertheless, the case shows dramatically the importance of a definition of armed conflict for the proper functioning of international law, especially the fundamental human right to life. To kill someone who is not participating in armed conflict hostilities with the use of military force is a violation of international law. It is important that the world community have this vital principle and the definition of armed conflict clearly before it, to bring pressure to bear on the U.S. or any other state or armed group which disrespects it.

It is hoped that the publication of this book will support greater compliance with international law in general and International Law Association Resolution No. 6/2010 that "calls on all states to observe carefully the distinction between situations of armed conflict as defined in international law and situations of peace in developing and carrying out policies involving the use of lethal force; detention and trials; asylum obligations, and other relevant State action." This is the Resolution passed in plenary session at the ILA Biennial meeting in August 2010, to support the Use of Force Committee's Final Report on the Meaning of Armed Conflict in International Law.

including in opertions against terrorists. However, the norm should be that terrorists be dealt with as criminals, through legal processes of arrest, trial and judicially decided punishment." 6 May 2011, http://www2.ohchr.org/english/issues/terrorism/rapporteur/srchr.htm.

5   Mark Mazzetti, *American Drone Strike in Yemen Was Aimed at Awlaki*, N.Y. Times, May 7, 2011, at A9; Pir Zubair Shah, *Drone Strike Said to Kill At Least 8 In Pakistan*, id.

6   Mazzetti, *supra* note 3.

7   Al-Aulaqi v. Obama et al, US District Court District of Columbia, Civ. Action No. 2010-1469 (7 Dec. 2010).

Appendix

United States District Court
for the District of Columbia

NASSER AL-AULAQI,
on his own behalf and as Next Friend of
Anwar Al-Aulaqi Al-Zubairi Street
Al-Saeed Center
Sana'a, Yemen,
Plaintiff,
v. No. 10-cv- _____

BARACK H. OBAMA,
in his official capacity as President of
the United States
1600 Pennsylvania Avenue NW
Washington, DC 20500;

LEON C. PANETTA,
in his official capacity as Director of
the Central Intelligence Agency
Central Intelligence Agency
Washington, DC 20505;

ROBERT M. GATES,
in his official capacity as Secretary of Defense
1000 Defense Pentagon
Washington, DC 20301-1010,

Defendants.

Complaint for declaratory and injunctive relief
(Violation of constitutional rights and international law – targeted killing)

Introduction

1. This case concerns the executive's asserted authority to carry out "targeted killings" of U.S. citizens suspected of terrorism far from any field of armed conflict. According to numerous published reports, the government maintains lists of suspects – "kill lists" – against whom lethal force can be used without charge, trial, or conviction. Individuals, including U.S. citizens, are added to the lists based on executive determinations that secret criteria have been satisfied. Executive officials are thus invested with sweeping authority to impose extrajudicial death sentences in violation of the Constitution and international law.

2. The right to life is the most fundamental of all rights. Outside the context of armed conflict, the intentional use of lethal force without prior judicial process is an abridgement of this right except in the narrowest and most extraordinary circumstances.

3. The United States is not at war with Yemen, or within it. Nonetheless, U.S. government officials have disclosed the government's intention to carry out the targeted killing of U.S. citizen Anwar Al-Aulaqi, who is in hiding there. In early 2010, several newspapers reported that U.S. government officials had confirmed Anwar AlAulaqi's placement on government kill lists; these lists amount to standing authorizations to use lethal force. Numerous subsequent reports have corroborated those accounts. According to one media report, there have already been as many as a dozen unsuccessful attempts on Anwar Al-Aulaqi's life. Anwar Al-Aulaqi has been in hiding since at least January 2010. Plaintiff Nasser Al-Aulaqi is Anwar Al-Aulaqi's father; he brings this action on his own behalf and as next friend to his son.

4. Outside of armed conflict, both the Constitution and international law prohibit targeted killing except as a last resort to protect against concrete, specific, and imminent threats of death or serious physical injury. The summary use of force is lawful in these narrow circumstances only because the imminence of the threat makes judicial process infeasible. A targeted killing policy under which individuals are added to kill lists after a bureaucratic process and remain on these lists for months at a time plainly goes beyond the use of lethal force as a last resort to address imminent threats, and accordingly goes beyond what the Constitution and international law permit.

5. The government's refusal to disclose the standard by which it determines to target U.S. citizens for death independently violates the Constitution: U.S. citizens have a right to know what conduct may subject them to execution at the hands of their own government. Due process requires, at a minimum, that citizens be put on notice of what may cause them to be put to death by the state.

6. Plaintiff seeks a declaration from this Court that the Constitution and international law prohibit the government from carrying out targeted killings outside of armed conflict except as a last resort to protect against concrete, specific, and imminent threats of death or serious physical injury; and an injunction prohibiting the targeted killing of U.S. citizen Anwar Al-Aulaqi outside this narrow context. Plaintiff also seeks an injunction requiring the government to disclose the standards under which it determines whether U.S. citizens can be targeted for death.

Jurisdiction and venue

7. Jurisdiction is proper pursuant to 28 U.S.C. § 1331 (federal question jurisdiction) over causes of action arising under the Fourth and Fifth Amendments to the U.S. Constitution, and 28 U.S.C. § 1350 (Alien Tort Statute) over a cause of action arising under customary international law and treaty law. Jurisdiction is also proper pursuant to 5 U.S.C. § 702 *et seq.* (Administrative Procedure Act) and 28 U.S.C. § 2201 *et seq.* (Declaratory Judgment Act).
8. Venue is proper in this district pursuant to 28 U.S.C. § 1391.

Parties

9. Plaintiff Nasser Al-Aulaqi is the father of Anwar Al-Aulaqi, a U.S. citizen whose targeted killing Defendants have authorized. Nasser Al-Aulaqi is a citizen and resident of Yemen. He acts on his own behalf and as next friend to his son. He acts in the latter capacity because his son is in hiding under threat of death and cannot access counsel or the courts to assert his constitutional rights without disclosing his whereabouts and exposing himself to possible attack by Defendants. He brings the Alien Tort Statute claim on his own behalf to prevent the injury he would suffer if Defendants were to kill his son.
10. Defendant Barack H. Obama is President of the United States. As President, he is Commander-in-Chief of the U.S. armed forces and serves as Chair of the National Security Council, which authorizes the targeted killing of suspected terrorists who are U.S. citizens. President Obama is sued in his official capacity.
11. Defendant Leon C. Panetta is the Director of the Central Intelligence Agency ("CIA"). As CIA Director, he has ultimate authority over the CIA's operations worldwide. Upon information and belief, Defendant Panetta approves the addition of individuals to the kill list maintained by the CIA, and signs off on individual targeted killing operations conducted by the CIA outside of armed conflict, including those against U.S. citizens. Director Panetta is sued in his official capacity.
12. Defendant Robert M. Gates is the Secretary of Defense. As Defense Secretary, he has ultimate authority over the U.S. armed forces world-

wide, including the Joint Special Operations Command ("JSOC"). Upon information and belief, JSOC is involved in carrying out targeted killings, including of U.S. citizens outside of armed conflict. In his capacity as Secretary of Defense, Defendant Gates is also a statutory member of the National Security Council, which authorizes the targeted killing of U.S. citizens. Secretary Gates is sued in his official capacity.

Factual Allegations

Targeted Killings by the United States Outside of Armed Conflict

13. Since 2001, the United States has carried out targeted killings in connection with the "war on terror." While many of these killings have been conducted by the U.S. military in the context of the armed conflicts in Afghanistan and Iraq, the United States has also carried out targeted killings outside the context of armed conflict, and it is these killings that are at issue here. Upon information and belief, both the CIA and JSOC are involved in authorizing, planning, and carrying out targeted killings, including of U.S. citizens, outside the context of armed conflict.

14. The first reported post-2001 targeted killing by the U.S. government outside Afghanistan occurred in Yemen in November 2002, when a CIA-operated Predator drone fired a missile at a suspected terrorist traveling in a car with other passengers. The strike killed all passengers in the vehicle, including a U.S. citizen. The United Nations Special Rapporteur on Extrajudicial Killings later stated that the strike constituted "a clear case of extrajudicial killing" and set an "alarming precedent." Since 2001, there has been an increase in targeted killings by the United States against terrorism suspects outside of Afghanistan and Iraq.

15. The government has publicly claimed the authority to carry out targeted killings of civilians, including U.S. citizens, outside the context of armed conflict. For example, in February 2010, then-Director of National Intelligence Dennis Blair, in response to a question by a member of Congress about the targeted killing of U.S. citizens, stated that the United States takes "direct action" against suspected terrorists and that "if we think that direct action will involve killing an American, we get specific permission to do that." In June 2010, Deputy National Security Advisor John Brennan responded to questions about the targeted killing program by stating, "If an American person or citizen is in Yemen or in Pakistan or in Somalia or another place, and they are trying to carry out attacks against U.S. interests, they will also face the full brunt of a U.S. response."

16. Although the government has publicly claimed the authority to carry out targeted killings of civilians outside the context of armed conflict, it has not explained on what basis individuals are added to kill lists, or the circum-

stances in which the asserted authority to carry out targeted killings will actually be exercised.

Specific Authorization to Kill Plaintiff's Son Anwar Al-Aulaqi

17. Plaintiff Nasser Al-Aulaqi moved to the United States in 1966 to pursue his studies as a Fulbright scholar at New Mexico State University. Plaintiff's son, Anwar Al-Aulaqi, was born in New Mexico in 1971. Plaintiff remained in the United States with his family for the next seven years, until 1978, when they moved back to Yemen. Plaintiff went on to serve as Minister of Agriculture and Fisheries in the Government of Yemen, and later founded and served as president of Ibb University and served as president of Sana'a University. Plaintiff currently resides in Yemen with his wife, who is an American citizen, and their family.

18. In 1991, Plaintiff's son Anwar Al-Aulaqi returned to the United States to attend college at Colorado State University. Anwar Al-Aulaqi went on to obtain his master's degree at San Diego State University and later enrolled in a Ph.D. program at George Washington University, which he attended through December 2001. He married and had three children while living in the United States. He moved to the United Kingdom in 2003, and to Yemen in 2004.

19. In January 2010, the Washington Post reported that Anwar Al-Aulaqi had been added to "a shortlist of U.S. citizens" that JSOC was specifically authorized to kill. The same article reported that Anwar Al-Aulaqi had survived a JSOC-assisted strike in Yemen in late December 2009. That strike reportedly killed 41 civilians, mostly children and women. Another January 2010 news report stated that Anwar Al-Aulaqi was "all but certain" to be added to a list of suspects that the CIA was specifically authorized to kill. In April 2010, the Washington Post and other media sources reported that Anwar Al-Aulaqi had been added to the CIA's list.

20. Numerous news reports have corroborated that Defendants have authorized the targeted killing of Anwar Al-Aulaqi and are actively pursuing him. According to one media report, he has already been the target of as many as a dozen unsuccessful strikes. One U.S. official stated that "he's in everybody's sights." In the context of a discussion about targeted killing, Defendant Panetta stated that Anwar AlAulaqi is "someone that we're looking for" and that "there isn't any question that he's one of the individuals that we're focusing on."

21. Defendants added Anwar Al-Aulaqi to the CIA and JSOC kill lists after a closed executive process. In the course of that process, Defendants and other executive officials determined that Anwar Al-Aulaqi satisfied secret criteria that determine whether a U.S. citizen can be killed by his own government. Upon information and belief, Anwar Al-Aulaqi is now subject to a standing order that permits the CIA and JSOC to kill him. Upon

information and belief, the authorization for Anwar Al-Aulaqi's killing by the CIA and JSOC involved the approval or recommendation of all Defendants.

22. Upon information and belief, individuals placed on the CIA and JSOC targeted killing lists remain on those lists for months at a time. An intelligence official who was questioned about the CIA's kill list stated that individuals would be removed from the kill list if their names "hadn't popped on the screen for over a year, or there was no intelligence linking [them] to known terrorists or plans."

23. Upon information and belief, Defendants have authorized the CIA and JSOC to kill Anwar Al-Aulaqi without regard to whether, at the time lethal force will be used, he presents a concrete, specific, and imminent threat to life, or whether there are reasonable means short of lethal force that could be used to address any such threat.

24. Executive officials have condemned Anwar Al-Aulaqi's public statements and sermons; they have also alleged that he has "cast his lot" with terrorist groups and taken on an "operational" role in a terrorist organization. The U.S. government has not, however, publicly indicted Anwar Al-Aulaqi for any terrorism-related crime.

25. In response to reports that the United States has placed Anwar Al-Aulaqi on kill lists, Yemeni officials, including the Prime Minister, the Foreign Minister, and the Director of the National Security Agency, have publicly stated that their government's security forces are taking measures to arrest Anwar Al-Aulaqi for possible charge and trial. Yemeni cabinet members have also publicly requested that the United States provide the Yemeni government with any evidence against Anwar Al-Aulaqi to support arresting him and bringing him to trial. The Yemeni government has prosecuted other residents of Yemen for terrorism-related crimes, and the Yemeni government is currently prosecuting at least one U.S. citizen who is alleged to be a member of a terrorist organization. Anwar Al-Aulaqi has in the past been detained by the Yemeni government and was imprisoned for 18 months in 2006 and 2007.

26. Anwar Al-Aulaqi has been in hiding in Yemen since at least January 2010. Plaintiff has had no communication with his son during that time. Anwar Al-Aulaqi cannot communicate with his father or counsel without endangering his own life.

Causes of action

First Claim for Relief
Fourth Amendment: Right to be Free from Unreasonable Seizure

27. Defendants' policy of targeted killings violates the Fourth Amendment by authorizing, outside of armed conflict, the seizure, in the form of tar-

geted killing, of U.S. citizens, including Plaintiff's son, in circumstances in which they do not present concrete, specific, and imminent threats to life or physical safety, and where there are means other than lethal force that could reasonably be employed to neutralize any such threat. Plaintiff brings this claim as next friend for his son.

Second Claim for Relief
Fifth Amendment: Right Not to be Deprived of Life Without Due Process

28. Defendants' policy of targeted killings violates the Fifth Amendment by authorizing, outside of armed conflict, the killing of U.S. citizens, including Plaintiff's son, without due process of law in circumstances in which they do not present concrete, specific, and imminent threats to life or physical safety, and where there are means other than lethal force that could reasonably be employed to neutralize any such threat. Plaintiff brings this claim as next friend for his son.

Third Claim for Relief
Alien Tort Statute: Extrajudicial Killing

29. Defendants' policy of targeted killings violates treaty and customary international law by authorizing, outside of armed conflict, the killing of individuals, including Plaintiff's son, without judicial process in circumstances in which they do not present concrete, specific, and imminent threats to life or physical safety, and where there are means other than lethal force that could reasonably be employed to neutralize any such threat. Plaintiff brings this claim in his own right to prevent the injury he would suffer if Defendants were to kill his son.

Fourth Claim for Relief
Fifth Amendment: Due Process Notice Requirements

30. Defendants' policy of targeted killings outside of armed conflict violates the Fifth Amendment by authorizing the killing of U.S. citizens, including Plaintiff's son, on the basis of criteria that are secret. Plaintiff brings this claim as next friend for his son.

Prayer for relief

For the foregoing reasons, Plaintiff Nasser Al-Aulaqi requests that the Court:
a. Declare that, outside of armed conflict, the Constitution prohibits Defendants from carrying out the targeted killing of U.S. citizens, including Plaintiff's son, except in circumstances in which they present concrete,

specific, and imminent threats to life or physical safety, and there are no means other than lethal force that could reasonably be employed to neutralize the threats.

b. Declare that, outside of armed conflict, treaty and customary international law prohibit Defendants from carrying out the targeted killing of individuals, including Plaintiff's son, except in circumstances in which they present concrete, specific, and imminent threats to life or physical safety, and there are no means other than lethal force that could reasonably be employed to neutralize the threats.

c. Enjoin Defendants from intentionally killing U.S. citizen Anwar Al-Aulaqi unless he presents a concrete, specific, and imminent threat to life or physical safety, and there are no means other than lethal force that could reasonably be employed to neutralize the threat.

d. Order Defendants to disclose the criteria that are used in determining whether the government will carry out the targeted killing of a U.S. citizen.

e. Grant any other and further relief as is appropriate and necessary.

Respectfully submitted,

/s/ Arthur B. Spitzer
Arthur B. Spitzer (D.C. Bar No. 235960)
American Civil Liberties Union of the Nation's Capital
1400 20th Street, N.W., Suite 119 Washington, DC 20036
Tel. 202-457-0800 Fax 202-452.1868 artspitzer@aol.com

Jameel Jaffer (to be admitted *pro hac vice*)
Ben Wizner (to be admitted *pro hac vice*)
Jonathan M. Manes
American Civil Liberties Union Foundation
125 Broad Street, 18 Floor New York, NY 10004
(212) 519-7814 jjaffer@aclu.org

Pardiss Kebriaei (to be admitted *pro hac vice*)
Maria C. LaHood (to be admitted *pro hac vice*)
William Quigley
Center for Constitutional Rights
666 Broadway, 7th floor New York, NY 10012
(212) 614-6452 pkebriaei@ccrjustice.org

August 30, 2010

United States District Court
for the District of Columbia

NASSER AL-AULAQI,
Plaintiff,
v.
No. 10-cv-01469 (JDB)
BARACK H. OBAMA, et al.,
Defendants.

Reply Memorandum in Support of Plaintiff's Motion for a Preliminary Injunction and in Opposition to Defendants' Motion to Dismiss

Jameel Jaffer (admitted *pro hac vice*)
Ben Wizner (admitted *pro hac vice*)
Jonathan M. Manes
American Civil Liberties Union Foundation
125 Broad Street, 18th Floor New York, NY 10004
Tel.: (212) 519-7814 jjaffer@aclu.org

Pardiss Kebriaei (admitted *pro hac vice*)
Maria C. LaHood (admitted *pro hac vice*)
William Quigley Center for Constitutional Rights
666 Broadway, 7th floor New York, NY 10012
Tel.: (212) 614-6452 pkebriaei@ccrjustice.org

Arthur B. Spitzer (D.C. Bar No. 235960)
American Civil Liberties Union
of the Nation's Capital
1400 20th Street, N.W., Suite 119
Washington, DC 20036
Tel.: (202) 457-0800 artspitzer@aol.com

October 8, 2010

Table of contents

Introduction

Argument

I.   Plaintiff has standing to bring this suit

A. Plaintiff has satisfied the requirements of article III
B. Plaintiff has standing to bring this suit as next friend for his son
C. Plaintiff has third-party standing to raise his son's constitutional claims
D. The court does not lack authority to grant the relief that plaintiff requests

II.   Plaintiff's claims are not barred by the political question doctrine

A. The text of the constitution clearly commits the resolution of plaintiff's claims to the judiciar
B. Claims asserting individuals' constitutional rights are justiciable even if they implicate foreign policy and national security
C. Courts routinely adjudicate claims implicating war powers and national security
D. The existence and scope of the armed conflict is not a political question

III. Plaintiff has asserted a proper cause of action for extrajudicial killing under the alien tort statute

A. Plaintiff's claim is well recognized under the ats
B. Plaintiff's claim is not barred by sovereign immunity

IV.   Litigation of plaintiff's claims is not foreclosed by the state secrets privilege

Conclusion

Introduction

The government's brief seeking the dismissal of this case runs to nearly sixty pages but can be summed up in a single sentence: No court should have any role in establishing or enforcing legal limitations on the executive's authority to use lethal force against U.S. citizens whom the executive has unilaterally determined to pose a threat to the nation. The government has clothed its bid for unchecked authority in the doctrinal language of standing, justiciability, equity, and secrecy, but the upshot of its arguments is that the executive, which must obtain judicial approval to monitor a U.S. citizen's communications or search his briefcase, may execute that citizen without any obligation to justify its actions to a court or to the public. While the Constitution designates the President Commander-in-Chief of the nation's armed forces, it does not provide him with a blank check over the lives of its citizens.

The government would exclude the courts from any role in determining when lethal force may be used against American citizens, whether lethal force has been applied unlawfully, whether the United States is engaged in an armed conflict, and whether there are limitations on the scope of that conflict. To reach this drastic outcome, the government distorts long-settled standing doctrine by insisting that an American citizen whose extrajudicial death sentence has been broadcast to the world through coordinated government leaks cannot establish a "case or controversy" because his fears are speculative and his father is an inappropriate representative of his interests. But by the government's reasoning, Plaintiff's claims will become non-speculative only after his son has been killed – and even then, the government would seek to repel any legal challenge by invoking the "state secrets" and "political question" doctrines. If the government's theories are adopted, no American (or his estate) will ever be in a position to seek protection from the courts when faced with credible threats of assassination (or actual assassination) by his or her own government.

The sum and substance of the government's demand for judicial abdication is perhaps best articulated by one of its amici:

> Amici do not mean to suggest that American citizens such as Al-Aulaqi are not entitled to the protections afforded by the U.S. Constitution. They most certainly are entitled to such protections. But under the Constitution, it is the province of the political branches of government, not the federal courts, both to determine the extent of those constitutional rights and to ensure that those rights are protected.

See Amicus Br. of Jack W. Klimp et al.("Klimp Amicus Br.") 23. Plaintiff respectfully suggests that, in the face of executive assertions that a U.S. citizen may be targeted for death away from a battlefield and without due process, "[i]t is emphatically the province and duty of the judicial department to say what the law is." *Marbury v. Madison*, 5 U.S. (1 Cranch) 137, 177 (1803). If this Plaintiff is not permitted to raise these claims in this context, it is difficult to conceive of any plaintiff who will be, and the courts will have been categorically excluded from any role in resolving profound and critical questions involving the constitutional rights of US citizens. Adjudicating Plaintiiff's claims will do no harm to the nation's security; ratifying the government's extreme theories will do lasting harm to the nation's values and institutions.

Argument

I. Plaintiff has standing to bring this suit

A. Plaintiff has satisfied the requirements of Article III

The Court should reject the government's argument that Plaintiff lacks standing. To satisfy the standing requirements of Article III, a litigant seeking to invoke the authority of the federal courts need only show that he has suffered a "concrete and particularized" injury that is "actual or imminent" rather than "conjectural" or "hypothetical"; that there is a causal connection between his injury and the conduct or policy he challenges; and that it is "likely" that his injury would be redressed by a favorable decision. *Lujan v. Defenders of Wildlife*, 504 U.S. 555, 560-61 (1992); *see also Whitmore v. Arkansas*, 495 U.S. 149, 163 (1990). These requirements are satisfied here.[1]

At the most basic level, the injury here could not be clearer, or more profound: Plaintiff's suit is based on his fear that the government will kill his son. The government does not argue that Plaintiff's fear lacks foundation. To the contrary, it declares that Plaintiff's son is a leader of Al-Qaeda in the Arabian Peninsula ("AQAP"), and it asserts that the Authorization for the Use of Military Force ("AUMF") invests the executive branch with the authority to use "necessary and appropriate force" against that organization. Defs.' Mem. in Opp. to Pl.'s Mot. for Prelim. Inj. ("Gov't Br.") 6. It declines to disavow any of the government statements indicating that Plaintiff's son is on government kill lists. Declaration of Ben Wizner ("Wizner Decl.") ¶¶ 11-13. It also implicitly confirms that it is trying to kill Plaintiff's son by stating that he can avoid lethal force by surrendering himself to authorities. Gov't Br. 13. In these circumstances, it is beyond dispute that Plaintiff has standing. He asserts an injury – his son's death. The injury would be caused by the government's conduct – specifically, its decision to authorize the use of lethal force. And the feared injury would be redressible by the relief requested – an injunction prohibiting the government from using lethal force except in accordance with constitutional and human rights standards.

---

[1]   The government does not challenge Plaintiff's standing to raise his claim under the Alien Tort Statute.

The government argues that Plaintiff has not established a constitutionally cognizable injury because he has not demonstrated that the government will kill his son "without regard to whether, at the time lethal force will be used, he presents a concrete, specific, and imminent threat to life, or whether there are reasonable means short of lethal force that could be used to address any such threat." Gov't Br. 16 (quoting Compl. ¶ 23). This argument is misguided for several reasons. First, the government is wrong to suggest that Plaintiff must demonstrate to a certainty that the injury he fears will be realized. To satisfy Article III, a plaintiff need only demonstrate a "realistic danger" of injury. *Babbitt v. United Farm Workers Nat'l Union*, 442 U.S. 289, 298 (1979); *see also Biggerstaff v. FCC*, 511 F.3d 178, 183 (D.C. Cir. 2007). Second, the government conflates the standing inquiry with the merits. To satisfy Article III, Plaintiff must demonstrate that his injury results from the government's conduct, but he need not show that his injury results from the government's *unlawful* conduct – otherwise every case in which a plaintiff had standing to sue the government would necessarily result in a judgment in plaintiff's favor.

In any event, Plaintiff has shown precisely what the government says Article III requires him to show – he has shown a realistic danger that the government will kill his son in contravention of constitutional and human rights principles. Government officials have stated to the press that both the Central Intelligence Agency ("CIA") and Joint Special Operations Command ("JSOC") maintain lists of individuals who can be targeted and killed, that the lists include American citizens, that individuals added to the lists can remain on the lists for months at a time, that placement on the lists creates a standing authorization for use of lethal force, that Anwar al-Aulaqi has been added to the lists, and that the government has already conducted at least one missile strike with the intent of killing him. Wizner Decl. ¶¶ 4-13. These statements show not only a realistic danger that the government will kill Plaintiff's son, but a realistic danger that the government will kill him without compliance with constitutional and human rights standards.[2]

---

2   In adjudicating the government's motion to dismiss, the Court must take the allegations in the Complaint as true and draw all inferences in favor of Plaintiff. *Warth v. Seldin*, 422 U.S. 490, 501 (1975); *Ctr. for Law & Educ. v. Dep't of Educ.*, 396 F.3d 1152, 1156 (D.C. Cir. 2005). In adjudicating Plaintiff's motion for a preliminary injunction, the Court can rely on the government's public statements quoted, and the facts asserted, in the myriad news reports cited in the record. *See, e.g.*, Wizner Decl. ¶¶ 3-18. This is the case both because the news reports are relevant for their existence as well as their truth, and because in the context of a preliminary injunction motion even inadmissible evidence can be considered, *see, e.g., Univ. of Tex. v. Camenisch*, 451 U.S. 390, 395 (1981) ("[A] preliminary injunction is customarily granted on the basis of procedures that are less formal and evidence that is less complete than in a trial on the merits. A party thus is not required to prove his case in full at a preliminary injunction hearing."); Charles Alan Wright, Arthur R. Miller, Mary Kay Kane & Richard L. Marcus, 11A Federal Practice & Procedure

If there were any doubt about this point, the government's own brief dispels it. The government labels Plaintiff's son a leader of AQAP, labels AQAP "an organization against which the political branches have authorized the use of all necessary and appropriate force," and finds support for the use of lethal force against AQAP leaders in, among other things, the law of war. Gov't Br. 4. But the authorization to use lethal force is broader under the law of war than it is under constitutional and human rights standards. Declaration of Mary Ellen O'Connell ("O'Connell Decl.") ¶¶ 6-8. The government's repeated invocation of the law of war only confirms the possibility that Plaintiff's son will be killed without compliance with constitutional and human rights standards.[3]

For these reasons, the Court should reject the government's argument that Plaintiff lacks standing. Even if the Court agrees with the government that Plaintiff lacks standing to challenge his son's targeted killing, however, it should find that Plaintiff has standing to press his son's notice claim. That claim does not turn on the lawfulness of the standards under which the government adds U.S. citizens to government kill lists. Whether or not the government's standards are lawful, and whether or not Plaintiff can demonstrate a realistic danger that his son will be killed unlawfully, Plaintiff's U.S. citizen son has a constitutional right to know the standards under which the government has authorized his killing.[4]

---

§ 2949 (2d ed. 2010) ("[i]n practice affidavits usually are accepted on a preliminary injunction motion without regard to the strict standards of Rule 56(e), and ... hearsay evidence also may be considered"); *id.* ("the trial court should be allowed to give even inadmissible evidence some weight when it is thought advisable to do so in order to serve the primary purpose of preventing irreparable harm before a trial can be had").

3   To be sure, one of the questions in dispute in this case is whether the government can permissibly rely on the law of war to carry out the targeted killing of a U.S. citizen in Yemen. But the government cannot invoke the law of war as a justification for the use of lethal force against Plaintiff's son and then contend that Plaintiff lacks standing because the government may abide by the narrower limits that apply outside the context of armed conflict.

4   If this Court finds that Plaintiff has standing to assert his son's notice claim but lacks standing at this time to assert his son's targeted killing claims, it should stay the targeted killing claims until it has adjudicated the notice claim. If Plaintiff prevails on the notice claim, the government will be required to disclose the standard under which the government adds U.S. citizens to government kill lists. (As Plaintiff has explained, this standard must be stated with sufficient specificity to allow individuals to conform their behavior to the law. Pl.'s Mem. in Supp. of Mot. for Prelim. Inj. ("Pl. Br.") 32-34). Once the government has disclosed its standard, it will be clear whether the government's standard is broader than Plaintiff contends it should be under the Constitution and international human rights law. If the government's standards are the same as those Plaintiff contends should apply, Plaintiff's targeted killing claims can be dismissed.

B. Plaintiff has standing to bring this suit as next friend for his son

The government argues that Plaintiff cannot permissibly bring this suit as next friend for his son. But as the government acknowledges, Gov't Br. 11, a litigant has standing to raise claims as "next friend" if he is truly dedicated to the best interests of the person whose rights he seeks to assert, and if that person is unable to assert his rights himself. *Whitmore*, 495 U.S. at 163. Plaintiff meets both of these requirements.

First, Plaintiff is dedicated to his son's best interests. One federal circuit has observed that "[t]here is essentially a *per se* rule that a parent meets this prong of the next friend standing test." *Vargas ex rel. Sagastegui v. Lambert*, 159 F.3d 1161, 1168 (9th Cir. 1998) (holding that mother could act as next friend for adult son, and collecting cases). Here, Plaintiff has declared that he is dedicated to his son's best interests, Declaration of Nasser Al-Aulaqi ("Al-Aulaqi Decl.") ¶ 11, and the government has not introduced evidence to the contrary.

Second, Defendants' own actions prevent Plaintiff's son from accessing the courts himself. The government has declared that it is trying to kill Plaintiff's son, and it has tried to kill him at least once already. Wizner Decl. ¶¶ 11-13. Since the government made its intentions known, Plaintiff's son has gone into hiding. Al-Aulaqi Decl. ¶ 8 ("My son is currently in hiding in Yemen. He has been in hiding continuously since at least January 2010, when the United States' intention to kill him became clear."). Plaintiff's son has been out of contact with even his closest family members. Al-Aulaqi Decl. ¶ 9 ("Since the time my son went into hiding, neither I nor any of my family members have had any contact or communication with him."). Plaintiff himself has not attempted to locate his son for fear that doing so will jeopardize his son's life. Al-Aulaqi Decl. ¶ 9. Even the government's *amici* appear to acknowledge that Plaintiff's son is not in a position to file a lawsuit in U.S. courts. *See* Klimp Amicus Br. 15 n.5.[5]

The government's contention that next friend standing "has not been recognized outside of the habeas context to a mentally competent adult," Gov't Br. 12, is misguided. While the cases in which the courts have conferred next

---

5 The government cites *Coalition of Clergy, Lawyers & Professors v. Bush*, 310 F.3d 1153 (9th Cir. 2002) for the proposition that "even if [Plaintiff's son's] access to the courts were somewhat constrained by circumstances not of his own making … that would not suffice to establish next friend standing." Gov't Br. 14 n.6. But *Coalition of Clergy*, a case involving Guantánamo detainees, supports the opposite proposition. The court in that case emphasized that "detainees are not able to meet with lawyers, and have been denied access to file petitions in United States courts on their own behalf" before concluding that "from a practical point of view the detainees cannot be said to have unimpeded or free access to court." 310 F.3d at 1161. The court thus suggested that the detainees might indeed satisfy the inaccessibility prong as a result of the obstacles imposed on them by the government. The court, however, declined to decide the issue because the other *Whitmore* prong – the requirement of a "significant relationship" – had not been satisfied.

friend standing have generally involved individuals who were detained, minors, or mentally incompetent, the courts have made clear that the relevant question is not whether the real party in interest falls into one of these categories but whether there is some impediment to that party's bringing suit. *See, e.g.*, *Whitmore*, 495 U.S. at 165 (stating that a next friend must show "that the real party in interest is unable to litigate his own cause due to mental incapacity, lack of access to court, or other similar disability"). The courts have taken a flexible, non-formalistic approach to this inquiry. *See, e.g., id.* at 163 (stating that next friend must provide *"an adequate explanation* ... why the real party in interest cannot appear on his own behalf" (emphasis added)); *Bismullah v. Gates*, 501 F.3d 178, 191

(D.C. Cir. 2007) ("whether a would-be next friend has standing is necessarily a matter to be determined case by case"). That no court has conferred next friend standing in a case precisely like this one, *see* Gov't Br. 12, is a testament not to the novelty of Plaintiff's standing theory, but to the extraordinary facts of this case. To Plaintiff's knowledge, the government has never before claimed the authority to carry out targeted killings of its own citizens.

The government also errs in proposing that next friend standing is available only where authorized by statute or regulation. Before it was amended in 1948, the federal habeas statute did not authorize next friend suits. 28 U.S.C. § 454 (1940) ("Application for writs of *habeas corpus* shall be made to the court, or justice, or judge authorized to issue the same, by complaint in writing, *signed by the person for whose relief it is intended* ... ." (emphasis added)). Courts nonetheless entertained next friend suits filed for the benefit of individuals in detention. *See, e.g., United States ex rel. Funaro v. Watchorn*, 164 F. 152, 153 (C.C.N.Y. 1908)

("Notwithstanding the language of [the *habeas* statute], it has been the frequent practice in this district to present habeas corpus petitions in deportation cases signed and verified by others than the person detained."); *Whitmore*, 495 U.S. at 162-63 & nn.3-4 (surveying history of next friend standing in habeas and other contexts); *United States ex rel. Bryant v. Houston*, 273 F. 915, 916 (2d Cir. 1921) (characterizing next friend doctrine as "ancient and fully accepted"). The argument that the government advances here – that next friend standing requires congressional authorization – is one that the Supreme Court expressly declined to endorse in *Whitmore*. 495 U.S. at 164-65 (declining to hold that next friend standing is limited to contexts in which authorized by statute, and noting that federal habeas statute merely "codified the historical practice").

The government's argument that Plaintiff's son could avoid death by "surrender[ing] or otherwise present[ing] himself to the proper authorities," Gov't Br. 13, is flawed on several levels. As an initial matter, the government lacks authority to summarily execute fugitives from the law. The government cannot kill its own citizens simply because they refuse to present themselves to the proper authorities. But in any event Plaintiff's son is not a fugitive from the law, because neither the United States nor Yemen has publicly charged him with any crime. The government's argument that Plaintiff's son should "surrender" is predicated on the contention that Plaintiff's son is a participant in an armed conflict against the United States, but this is a contention that Plaintiff disputes. Plaintiff disputes that the United States is engaged in armed conflict in Yemen, and he disputes that the U.S. government has authority to kill his son in connection with any armed conflict. To accept the government's argument that Plaintiff's son should surrender to the proper authorities would require the Court to accept at the standing stage what is disputed on the merits.

In fact, it would be particularly inappropriate to deny next friend standing in the circumstances of this case. The action that Plaintiff seeks to challenge – the government's contemplated targeted killing of his son – is the same action that deprives his son of access to the courts. The government should not be permitted to rely on the very conduct that Plaintiff alleges is unlawful in order to insulate that conduct from judicial review.

The government's contention that "there are good reasons to doubt that this suit reflects [Plaintiff's son's] wishes" is equally groundless. Gov't Br. 14-15. The government says that Plaintiff's "son's public pronouncements indicate that he has no desire to avail himself of protections afforded by the Constitution and courts of a nation that he deems an enemy deserving of violent attacks." Gov't Br. 15 (citing Public Clapper Decl. § 16). But no "pronouncement" cited in the paragraph comes even remotely close to saying what the government asserts. Plaintiff's public silence with respect to the present lawsuit supports an inference in his favor. This suit has received media attention throughout the world, *see, e.g., Rights Groups Sue Over Kill List*, Al Jazeera, Aug. 31, 2010,[6] but Plaintiff's son has issued no statement disavowing or condemning it.[7]

---

6   Available at http://english.aljazeera.net/news/americas/2010/08/2010831134842819 315.html.

7   The government cites a series of cases in which litigants were denied next friend standing because they could not establish that they were acting in accord with the wishes of those whose rights they sought to assert. In each of these cases, however, the real parties in interest repudiated the suit, failed to bring suit themselves even though there were no obstacles to doing so, or were not even identified by name and could not be represented by next friends who did not know their identities, let alone their interests. *See Idris v. Obama*, 667 F. Supp. 2d 25 (D.D.C. 2009) (Guantánamo detainee's brother denied next friend standing to bring *habeas* petition where detainee had repeatedly refused to meet with counsel who were seeking to represent him directly); *Hauser ex rel. Crawford v. Moore*, 223 F.3d 1316 (11th Cir. 2000) (death row inmate's mother denied next friend standing because her lawsuit was contrary to the express wishes of inmate, who had repeatedly declined to assert any potential claims and who had consistently been found mentally competent); *Davis ex rel. Potts v. Austin*, 492 F. Supp. 273, 276 (N.D. Ga. 1980) (death row inmate's cousin denied next friend standing because he had only a small amount of contact with inmate, there was no impediment to such contact, and cousin appeared motivated by philosophical and religious opposition to capital punishment rather than inmate's wishes); *Does 1-570 v. Bush*, No. 05-CV-313, 2006 WL 3096685 (D.D.C.

Even if it were a close case whether Plaintiff can bring this lawsuit as next friend, it bears emphasis that the requirements of next friend standing are strictly "prudential" and are not mandated by the Constitution. *See, e.g., Elk Grove Unified School Dist. v. Newdow*, 542 U.S. 1, 11-12, 17-18 (2004). Given that Plaintiff's son's life hangs in the balance, prudential concerns weigh heavily in favor of conferring next friend standing. *Cf. Rosenberg v. United States*, 346 U.S. 273, 294 (1953) (Clark, J. concurring for six Justices) ("Human lives are at stake; we need not turn this decision on fine points of procedure or a party's technical standing to claim relief"); *id.* at 290-91 (Jackson, J. concurring for the same six Justices) (joining Justice Clark's decision on the merits even though the person bringing the petition was "a stranger to the Rosenbergs and to their case" and even though "[h]is intervention was unauthorized by them and originally opposed by their counsel").

C. Plaintiff has third-party standing to raise his son's constitutional claims

Plaintiff also has third-party standing to raise his son's constitutional claims. Under *Powers v. Ohio*, 499 U.S. 400 (1991), a litigant can assert the rights of another when: (i) the litigant has "suffered an injury in fact, thus giving him or her a sufficiently concrete interest in the outcome of the issue in dispute"; (ii) the litigant has a "close relation to the third party"; and (iii) there is "some hindrance to the third party's ability to protect his or her own interests." *Id.* at 411 (internal quotation marks and citations omitted).[8] All three prerequisites are satisfied here.

The injury threatened here – the killing of Plaintiff's son – is plainly sufficient to satisfy *Powers'* first requirement. Plaintiff would suffer a profound injury if the government carried out its threat, and the government's actions have already deprived Plaintiff of the ability to talk or meet with his son. These injuries give Plaintiff a "concrete interest" in the outcome of the case. *Cf. Jones v. Prince George's County*, 348 F.3d 1014 (D.C. Cir. 2003) (holding that daughter whose father had been killed had suffered injury in fact); *Pub. Citizen, Inc. v. Nat'l Highway Traffic Safety Admin.*, 489 F.3d 1279, 1292-96 (D.C. Cir. 2007) (holding, in the context of challenge to agency's failure to implement automobile safety measure, that threat of "death, physical injuries, and property damage" could constitute an injury in fact where the increased "risk of harm"

Oct. 31, 2006) (attorneys did not have next friend standing for anonymous class of Guantánamo detainees that counsel could not identify by name, with whom counsel had no relationship, whose very existence was unclear, and whose best interests and wishes counsel could only speculate about).

8   The latter two requirements are prudential considerations, while the first is a constitutional prerequisite to standing. *Sec'y of State of Md. v. Joseph H. Munson Co.*, 467 U.S. 947, 955-56 (1984).

was from agency's failure to act); *Reed v. Islamic Republic of Iran*, 439 F. Supp. 2d 53, 58 (D.D.C. 2006) (holding that father's alleged imprisonment and torture constituted an injury in fact to his son); *Yaman v. U.S. Dep't of State*, --- F. Supp. 2d ---, No. 10-CV-537, 2010 WL 1783300 (D.D.C. May 5, 2010) (holding that non-custodial mother whose daughter had been denied a passport had suffered injury in fact). Plaintiff also clearly satisfies *Powers'* second factor. As this Court has previously stated, "the relationship between a son and his father constitutes the requisite close relationship for the second prong of the third party standing test." *Reed*, 439 F. Supp. 2d at 62 (citing *Miller v. Albright*, 523 U.S. 420 (1998) (finding a father-child relationship sufficiently close to satisfy the second prong of *Powers*)).

More broadly, the first two prongs of the *Powers* test are intended to ensure that "the relationship between the litigant and the third party [is] such that the former is fully, or very nearly, as effective a proponent of the right as the latter." *Singleton v. Wulff*, 428 U.S. 106, 115 (1976); *see also Lepelletier v. FDIC*, 164 F.3d 37, 43 (D.C. Cir. 1999) ("[T]he reason for the 'close relation' factor is to ensure that the plaintiff will act as an effective advocate for the third party." (internal quotation marks omitted)). In this case, father's and son's interests and objectives are identical – to prevent the unlawful killing of the latter. If any proof were required of Plaintiff's earnest concern for his son's well being, the court need look no further than Plaintiff's advocacy on his son's behalf immediately after it was disclosed that the government had authorized his son's execution, and well before the present litigation was contemplated. *See* Al-Aulaqi Decl. ¶ 6 (discussing letter to President Obama); Paula Newton, *Al-Awlaki's Father Says Son Is 'Not Osama Bin Laden'*, CNN, Jan. 10, 2010 (discussing his son's targeting and pleading with the U.S. government not to carry out its threat).[9]

This Circuit has been particularly inclined to grant third-party standing "when the third party's rights protect that party's relationship with the litigant." *Haitian Refugee Ctr. v. Gracey*, 809 F.2d 794, 809 (D.C. Cir. 1987); *see also Fair Employment Council of Greater Wash., Inc. v. BMC Marketing Corp.*, 28 F.3d 1268, 1280-81 (D.C. Cir. 1994) (observing that "the Court has allowed litigants to assert third parties' rights in challenging restrictions that do not operate directly on the litigants themselves, but that nonetheless allegedly disrupt a special relationship – protected by the rights in question – between the litigants and the third parties"). In this case, a father seeks to preserve the very existence of a relationship with his son by protecting his son's right to life. In such circumstances, "the court ... can be sure that its construction of the right is not unnecessary in the sense that the right's enjoyment will not be unaffected by the outcome of the suit." *Singleton*, 428 U.S. at 114-15.[10]

---

9   Available at: http://articles.cnn.com/2010-0110/world/yemen.al.awlaki.father_1_awlaki-qaeda-yemeni-officials.

10 It is possible that *Haitian Refugee Center* establishes a basis for third-party standing separate and independent from the *Powers* test. *See Am. Immig. Lawyers Ass'n*

The third prong of the *Powers* test – the existence of some "hindrance" to the thirdparty's assertion of his own rights – is also easily satisfied here. As discussed above, Plaintiff's son is under threat of death and cannot contact counsel, much less access the courts, without exposing himself to death or, at the very least, indefinite detention without charge. Notably, the "hindrance" requirement under *Powers* has been more liberally construed and is significantly less stringent than the analogous consideration under the doctrine of next friend standing. In the latter context, Plaintiff must show that "the real party in interest is *unable* to litigate his own cause." *Whitmore*, 495 U.S. at 150 (emphasis added). By contrast, the Supreme Court and D.C. Circuit have routinely found that a "hindrance" exists – and third-party standing is appropriate – even in cases where it was clearly possible for the third-party to sue on his or her own behalf. *See, e.g., Powers*, 499 U.S. at 415 (holding that the "small financial stake involved [in litigation] and the economic burdens of litigation" were sufficient hindrance); *Singleton*, 428 U.S. at 117-18 (holding that privacy concerns of women who wish to seek an abortion, along with concerns about "imminent mootness" of claims raised by pregnant women, were sufficient hindrance); *Campbell v. Louisiana*, 523 U.S. 392, 398 (1998) (holding that third parties' lack of incentive to file suit was sufficient hindrance); *United Auto Workers v. Nat'l Right to Work Legal Def. & Educ. Found.*, 590 F.2d 1139 (D.C. Cir. 1978) (holding that union contributors' desire to remain anonymous was sufficient hindrance). The Supreme Court has even approved third-party standing in a case where it found no cognizable obstacle at all to the third-party's ability to raise his own constitutional claim. *See Caplin & Drysdale, Chartered v. United States*, 491 U.S. 617, 623 n.3 (1989). The Court in that case reasoned that the absence of any hindrance was outweighed by the other factors relevant to the third-party standing analysis. *Id.*

---

v. Reno, 199 F.3d 1352, 1362 (D.C. Cir. 2000) ("It could be that *Haitian Refugee* and *Powers* now coexist and a party can establish third party standing by meeting either standard."). Under *Haitian Refugee Center*, a litigant has third-party standing "[i]f the government has directly interfered with the litigant's ability to engage in conduct together with the third party, for example, by putting the litigant under a legal disability with criminal penalties, and if a statute or the Constitution grants the third party a right to engage in that conduct with the litigant." *Haitian Refugee Ctr.*, 809 F.2d at 808. Plaintiff satisfies this standard too: the government's contemplated killing of Plaintiff's son "has directly interfered" with Plaintiff's ability "to engage in conduct together with" his son. Further, the father-son relationship that the government would end is clearly protected by the Constitution not only through its protection for the right to life – which Plaintiff asserts here – but also in its protection of fundamental rights. *See, e.g., Franz v. United States*, 707 F.2d 582, 594-95 (D.C. Cir. 1983) ("Among the most important of the liberties accorded ... special treatment [as a fundamental liberty interest protected by the Constitution] is the freedom of a parent and child to maintain, cultivate, and mold their ongoing relationship.").

Where, as here, Plaintiff would be profoundly injured if the government were to act on its expressed intention to kill his son, and Plaintiff's son is not simply hindered but all but foreclosed from accessing the courts himself, it would be wholly inappropriate to deny Plaintiff the opportunity to assert his son's rights.

D. *The Court does not lack authority to grant the relief that Plaintiff requests*

The government makes a series of other arguments in support of the contention that the Court cannot or should not grant the relief that Plaintiff requests. These arguments, too, lack merit.

The government argues that Plaintiff has requested relief that is "untethered to any particular fact situation." Gov't Br. 17. This is decidedly not a case, however, in which a plaintiff seeks to reform a law or policy in which he has no direct stake apart from a special interest in the subject matter. *See, e.g., Lujan v. Defenders of Wildlife*, 504 U.S. 555 (1992). Plaintiff seeks to prevent the government from killing his son. His claims arise out of the government's past and contemplated actions with respect to his son. Although there is no doubt that this case raises questions of broad importance, the relief Plaintiff requests is very much tethered to a particular fact situation: it would limit the circumstances in which the government can use lethal force against a specific American whom the government has labeled an enemy of the state.

The government also argues that equitable relief is inappropriate because there is "[no] basis for assuming that the United States would otherwise disregard applicable legal constraints." Gov't Br. 17. The government's brief itself, however, provides ample basis for this assumption. The government repeatedly references the law of armed conflict, making clear its belief that this body of law provides the framework under which the targeted killing of Plaintiff's son should be evaluated. Plaintiff disputes, however, that the law of war governs this case. Accordingly, while it may be true that the government does not intend to "disregard [what it believes are the] applicable legal constraints," Gov't Br. 17, there is a dispute about which legal constraints are applicable, and there is plainly a basis for assuming that the government will, absent an injunction, apply a standard different from the one that Plaintiff believes should apply. That was true even before the government filed its brief, *see* Wizner Decl. ¶¶ 4-9; it is all the more true now. This is precisely why a judicial declaration of "what the law is" is necessary.

The government also argues that the injunction Plaintiff seeks is "extremely abstract – simply a command that the United States comply with generalized constitutional standards." Gov't Br. 17; *see also id.* at 18 & n.18 (suggesting that the requested relief is insufficiently specific). The government is mistaken. The general rule is "that an injunction may not be so broad or imprecise as to leave one subject to it in doubt as to the conduct actually prohibited." *SEC v. Savoy*

Indus., Inc., 665 F.2d 1310, 1317 (D.C. Cir. 1981). This Circuit has held that an injunction is appropriate even if it does no more than parrot the language of governing statute, so long as the language of the statute itself "is sufficiently specific to pass muster." *Id. at* 1318; *see also United States v. Miller*, 588 F.2d 1256, 1261 (9th Cir. 1978) ("[T]he mere fact that the injunction is framed in language almost identical to the statutory mandate does not make the language vague."). The injunction and declaration that Plaintiff seeks certainly meet this standard. Indeed, the relief Plaintiff seeks is no more "abstract" than the command issued by the Supreme Court in *Tennessee v. Garner*, 417 U.S. 1 (1985); *see also* Pl. Br. 10-12 (discussing legal standard). The government has been held to the standard in countless excessive force cases, and the government should not now be heard to argue that the standard that governs the use of force by every law enforcement agency in the country is too "abstract" or "imprecise" to govern the CIA and Department of Defense. Plaintiffs do not ask this Court to order the government simply to comply with the Constitution, but rather to require its compliance with the specific legal constraints that apply in the specific circumstances presented here: the government's avowed intent to use lethal force against a citizen outside armed conflict.

The government also argues that Plaintiff's proposed injunction would be unenforceable because the Court would be "ill-equipped to evaluate whether such standards are satisfied in any particular circumstances," Gov't Br. 17, and because enforcement would require the Court to evaluate "real-time, heavily fact-dependent decision made overseas by military and other officials on the basis of complex and sensitive intelligence, tactical analysis, and diplomatic considerations." Gov't Br. 18-19. But Plaintiff does not propose that the Court should engage in real-time evaluation of the government's targeting decisions. If the relevant standard incorporates an "imminence" requirement, as Plaintiff submits that it does, then real-time judicial review – that is, prior judicial review of the government's compliance with the injunction – is infeasible by definition; exigency forecloses it. That real-time judicial review is infeasible, however, does not mean that the requested injunction would be unenforceable. The injunction could be enforced through an after-the-fact contempt motion, or an after-the-fact damages action (in which the injunction would preclude the government from arguing that the law was not clearly established)."

The government's argument is actually far broader than it first appears, because the government's true objection is not to the *timing* of judicial review, but to its *existence*. Gov't Br. 19 (arguing that courts are ill-equipped to "assess[] whether a particular threat to national security is imminent and whether reasonable alternatives for the defense of the Nation exist to the use of lethal military force. Courts have neither the authority nor expertise to assume these

---

11   While Plaintiff submits that entry of injunctive relief is appropriate and necessary
      here, it is open to the Court to issue declaratory relief as an alternative. *Steffel v.*
      Thompson, 415 U.S. 452, 466 (1974).

tasks."). The government's extraordinary proposition is that the President's power to carry out targeted killings of suspected terrorists, including American citizens, is beyond the authority and competence of the judiciary to police – that this power is subject to judicial review neither before it is used nor after. But the government's arguments about "authority" and "competence" simply do not stand up. The courts routinely evaluate claims that executive officials used excessive force. Pl. Br. 10-16 (discussing cases). And the courts in this district have become accustomed to evaluating information that is sensitive for reasons of foreign policy, military strategy, and national security. In the Guantánamo detention cases, judges in this district routinely evaluate the decisions that executive officers made in the context of armed conflict. *See, e.g., Parhat v. Gates*, 532 F.3d 834 (D.C. Cir. 2008); *Khan v. Obama*, --- F. Supp. 2d ---, No. 08-CV-1101, 2010 WL 3833917, at *2-3 (D.D.C. Sept. 3, 2010). If the courts have authority and competence to conduct this kind of review for non-citizens detained by the government in the context of armed conflict, they surely have authority and competence to conduct this kind of review for Americans killed by the government outside the context of armed conflict.

Gilligan v. Morgan, 413 U.S. 1 (1973), which the government contends is "analogous," is not. In that case, which involved the aftermath of the Kent State University shootings in 1970, plaintiffs filed suit seeking a sweeping injunction that would have prohibited the Governor from "prematurely ordering National Guard troops to duty in civil disorders" and "restrain[ed] leaders of the National Guard from future violation of the students' constitutional rights." 413 U.S. at 3. By the time the case arrived at the Supreme Court, the National Guard had new use-of-force regulations and training that plaintiffs did not "quarrel" with, *id.* at 11 n.15, and plaintiffs (who were no longer students) only sought "[c]ontinued judicial surveillance to assure compliance with the changed standards." *Id.* at 6. The Court looked at a combination of justiciability doctrines involving the advisory nature of the opinion sought, mootness, standing, and the political question doctrine, and found that these doctrines together rendered plaintiffs' claims nonjusticiable. *Id.* at 10.

This case is not like *Gilligan*. The Supreme Court expressly distinguished the claims in that case – "a broad call on judicial power to assume continuing regulatory jurisdiction over the activities of the Ohio National Guard" – from "an action seeking a restraining order against some specified and imminently threatened unlawful action." *Id.* at 5-6. Moreover, the injunctive relief requested in *Gilligan* was to monitor governmental compliance with new regulations that were already in place and that no one contended had been violated. The *Gilligan* Court was also concerned that the judicial relief sought would impermissibly interfere with the "complex[,] subtle, and professional decisions as to the composition, training, equipping, and control of a military force." *Id.* at 10. But the present case does not seek to interfere with such matters.[12] Plaintiff does not ask

---

12   Here and elsewhere, the government and one of its *amici* suggest that the injunc-

this Court to supervise the military's real-time decisions, or its internal organization or processes. While the government seeks to rely on *Gilligan* for the
proposition that the judiciary cannot enforce compliance with the Constitution
in military matters, Gov't Br. 17-19, the *Gilligan* Court explicitly disclaimed
that notion. 413 U.S. at 11-12 ("[W]e neither hold nor imply that the conduct
of the National Guard is always beyond judicial review or that there may not
be accountability in a judicial forum for violations of law for specific unlawful conduct by military personnel, whether by way of damages *or injunctive
relief*" (emphasis added)). *Gilligan* therefore does not suggest that the "specific
unlawful conduct" at issue here – unlawful targeted killing of citizens outside
of armed conflict – is beyond judicial review.

Equally unpersuasive is the government's contention that the Court does
not have the power to enjoin executive officers. The government argues that this
Court should not exercise its equitable discretion to issue an injunction against
the President, Gov't Br. 37, and then extends that argument to the completely
insupportable proposition that the Court must also refrain from enjoining the
Secretary of Defense and Director of the CIA on the grounds that "any action
taken by these subordinate officials in the context of this case necessarily implicates the President's own authority and discretion in directing the use of force,"
Gov't Br. 38-39. Nothing in the law supports the proposition that the courts'
traditional reluctance to issue an injunction directly against the President can
cloak subordinate officers with a similar immunity against injunctive or declaratory relief. This Court is bound not only by common sense but by clear precedent to reject the government's novel theory. *See, e.g., Franklin v. Massachusetts*,
505 U.S. 788, 803 (1992) ("[W]e need not decide whether injunctive relief against

---

tion or declaration sought would inhibit the ability of the President to command
the armed forces, and otherwise interfere with the orderly and effective operation
of the military. *See, e.g.,* Gov't Br. at 18-19, 23-24, 27-28; Amicus Br. of Veterans
of Foreign Wars ("VFW Amicus Br."). But the military's own internal targeting process already recognizes that there are legal limits to the circumstances in
which the government can use lethal force – even in the context of armed conflict.
See Declaration of Jonathan Manes ("Manes Decl."), Ex. A at 8-10 (briefing slides
from Joint Chiefs of Staff which exhaustively describe the process by which the
armed forces select, vet, plan, approve, engage, and assess targets). The government's targeting operations already incorporate internal legal review at specific,
defined points. *Id.* Ex. A at 9-10 (indicating that legal review for compliance with
"Law of War (LOW)/Law of Armed Conflict (LOAC) and Rules of Engagement
(ROE)" occurs during the "Target Development and Prioritization"); *id.* Ex. A
at 8 (indicating that even before specific targets are identified and vetted, senior
military leadership – the President, Secretary of Defense, Combatant Commander
or Joint Forces Commander – establish "ground rules/policies" and "scope/restric-
tions" on targeting). With respect to "real-time" targeting decisions, an injunction
from this Court would simply ensure that the legal standard being applied by the
Defense Department is the correct one.

the President was appropriate, because we conclude that the injury alleged
is likely to be redressed by declaratory relief against the Secretary alone."");
Massachusetts v. Mellon, 262 U.S. 447, 488 (1923) ("If a case for preventive relief
be presented, the court enjoins ... the acts of the official ... ."); *Swan v. Clinton*,
100 F.3d 973, 979 (D.C. Cir. 1996) (stating that "[i]f [plaintiff's] injury can be
redressed by injunctive relief against subordinate officials, he clearly has standing; moreover this approach would make it unnecessary to determine whether
... the President can be enjoined to perform a ministerial duty"); *Newdow v.
Bush*, 391 F. Supp. 2d 95, 105-07 (D.D.C. 2005).

The government's reliance on *Mississippi v. Johnson*, 71 U.S. 475 (1866), is
misplaced. That case concerned an attempt to enjoin the President from carrying into effect two of the Reconstruction Acts enacted in the wake of the
Civil War. The Court declined to issue such an injunction on the grounds that
such an order would enjoin the "purely executive and political" duties of the
President. *Id.* at 499. But while *Johnson* may remain good law for the proposition
that the President should not be enjoined from carrying out "purely executive
and political" duties, this lawsuit does not trench on questions reserved to the
exclusive judgment of the executive branch. *See* Section II, infra; *see also Minn.
Chippewa Tribe v. Carlucci*, 358 F. Supp. 973 (D.D.C. 1973) (interpreting *Johnson*
as a forerunner of the modern political question doctrine). *Johnson* does not and
could not stand for the proposition that subordinate officials are not amenable
to injunctive relief, still less that the executive branch can authorize the killing
of a citizen in violation of the Fourth and Fifth Amendments immune from any
and all judicial scrutiny. Richard H. Fallon, Jr. et al., Hart & Wechsler's Federal
Courts and the Federal System 1137 (5th ed. 2003) ("[E]xecutive officials in general have no immunity from suit for prospective relief – a conclusion supported
by the entire history of suits against officers as a means of ensuring governmental accountability.").

Insofar as the government asks this court to stay its hand because the case
implicates "the authority of the President ... to protect the national security
from a terrorist threat," Gov't Br. 39, the government presses a proposition
that the courts have already rejected. *See, e.g., Boumediene v. Bush*, 553 U.S. 723
(2008); *Hamdan v. Rumsfeld*, 548 U.S. 557 (2006); *Hamdi v. Rumsfeld*, 542 U.S.
507 (2004); *Rasul v. Bush*, 542 U.S. 466 (2004); *Youngstown Sheet & Tube Co. v.
Sawyer*, 343 U.S. 579 (1952); *Ex Parte Milligan*, 71 U.S. (4 Wall.) 2 (1866); *Ex Parte
Endo*, 323 U.S. 283 (1944). As the Supreme Court wrote in *Hamdi*, "a state of war
is not a blank check for the President when it comes to the rights of the Nation's
citizens." 542 U.S. at 536.[13]

---

13 The government cites *Sanchez-Espinoza v. Reagan*, 770 F.2d 202 (D.C. Cir. 1985),
    as contrary authority. But that case is entirely inapposite. There, the court with-
    held discretionary relief because the case involved "the conduct of ... diplomatic
    relations with [a] foreign state[]." This case, by contrast, involves only the con-
    duct of the United States with respect to one of its citizens. Furthermore, *Sanchez-*

II. Plaintiff's claims are not barred by the political question doctrine

The government argues that the issues raised by this case pose non-justiciable political questions. But the question of whether and in what circumstances the government may target and kill an American citizen in Yemen is no less justiciable than the question of whether the executive branch could indefinitely detain an American citizen captured in Afghanistan, a question the Supreme Court addressed in *Hamdi*; or indefinitely detain non-citizens at Guantánamo Bay, a question the Supreme Court addressed in *Rasul* and *Boumediene*; or charge and try suspects in ad-hoc military commissions, a question the Supreme Court addressed in *Hamdan*. In each of these cases and others, the Supreme Court and other federal courts flatly rejected the government's claims of unreviewable war powers over individuals suspected of terrorism. As Justice O'Connor wrote for the plurality in *Hamdi*:

> [W]e necessarily reject the Government's assertion that separation of powers principles mandate a heavily circumscribed role for the courts in such circumstances. ... Whatever power the United States Constitution envisions for the Executive in its exchanges with other nations or with enemy organizations in times of conflict, it most assuredly envisions a role for all three branches when individual liberties are at stake.

Plaintiff asserts claims concerning the right of his United States citizen son not to be killed in violation of the Constitution, claims which are undoubtedly committed to the judiciary, even where adjudicating them might implicate the areas of foreign policy and national security. The question of the proper legal framework that applies to the planned targeting here – the threshold question of the existence or absence of an armed conflict – is also squarely a question for the courts. Indeed, to the extent the executive's claimed authority to use force is pursuant to the AUMF, the question is one of statutory interpretation, which is quintessentially a judicial task.

A. The text of the Constitution clearly commits the resolution of Plaintiff's claims to the Judiciary

The Supreme Court has relied on the political question doctrine only twice in the last fifty years, *El-Shifa Pharm. Indus. v. United States*, 607 F.3d 836, 856 (D.C. Cir. 2010) (*en banc*) (Kavanaugh, J., concurring in the judgment) (citing *Nixon v. United States*, 506 U.S. 224 (1993) and *Gilligan*, 413 U.S. 1), *petition*

Espinoza did not allege the infringement of any individual's constitutional rights, let alone the violation of a citizen's constitutional right not to be killed in violation of the Fourth and Fifth Amendments.

for cert. filed, No. 10-328 (Sept. 7, 2010), invoking it in cases implicating the first two factors identified in *Baker v. Carr,* 369 U.S. 186, 217 (1962). *Baker* outlined six formulations describing a political question, at least one of which must be inextricable from the case in order to dismiss on nonjusticiability grounds. The "dominant consideration in any political question inquiry is [the first *Baker* factor,] 'whether there is a textually demonstrable constitutional commitment of the issue to a coordinate political department.'" *Lamont v. Woods,* 948 F.2d 825, 831 (2d Cir. 1991) (citation omitted) (finding challenge to foreign aid program did not usurp political branches' foreign policy).

Plaintiff asserts the rights of his U.S. citizen son under the Fourth and Fifth Amendments of the Constitution.[14] These rights are not "textually committed" to the political branches. To the contrary, the judiciary is charged with the responsibility of interpreting and ultimately safeguarding legal rights. "It is emphatically the province and duty of the judicial department to say what the law is." *Marbury,* 5 U.S. (1 Cranch) at 177. The judiciary is the "ultimate interpreter of the Constitution," *Baker,* 369 U.S. at 211, and "the final authority on issues of statutory construction." *Chevron, U.S.A., Inc. v. NRDC, Inc.,* 467 U.S. 837, 843 (1984). It is also the judiciary's role to ascertain international law. *The Paquete Habana,* 175 U.S. 677, 700 (1900). The court has "no more right to decline the exercise of jurisdiction which is given, than to usurp that which is not given." *Union Pac. R.R. Co. v. Bhd. of Locomotive Eng'rs and Trainmen,* 130 S. Ct. 584, 590 (2009) (citation omitted).

Defendants do not assert that resolution of Plaintiff's claims is vested in the political branches by a specific provision of the Constitution, but argue broadly that the judiciary cannot interfere in decision-making in the areas of foreign policy and national security, relying generally on the numerous powers vested in Congress under Article I, Section 8, and on the President's Commander in Chief power. U.S. Const., art. II, § 2; Gov't Br. at 23-24. But Plaintiff's constitutional claims are undoubtedly justiciable, even where adjudicating them might implicate foreign policy and national security.[15]

---

14   *Amici* Klimp et al. concur that U.S. citizens are entitled to constitutional protection, but assert that it is the role of the political branches to determine the extent of those rights and ensure their protection. Klimp Amicus Br. 8. This extraordinary assertion — one that is essential to Defendants' case — merely highlights the absurdity of the government's position.

15   Notably, in reviewing Israel's targeted killing policy, the Israeli High Court of Justice rejected the Israeli government's argument that the issues were non-justiciable, finding that the doctrine did not apply to the enforcement of human rights; that the questions were legal, not political (despite the likelihood of political implications), including the question regarding norms of proportionality; that international courts had decided the same types of questions; and that judicial review would ensure that objective *ex post* examinations functioned appropriately. HCJ 769/02 *Pub. Comm. against Torture in Israel v. Gov't of Israel* [2006] IsrSC 57(6) 285 ¶¶ 47-54.

B. Claims asserting individuals' constitutional rights are justiciable even if they implicate foreign policy and national security

Defendants acknowledge that claims asserting constitutionally protected interests may require the court to address the powers of the political branches in the area of foreign policy and national security, yet assert that the Court should have no role here. Gov't Br. 23. But claims asserting the constitutional rights of U.S. citizens are justiciable even when they implicate these areas. In *Committee of United States Citizens Living in Nicaragua v. Reagan*, U.S. citizens living in Nicaragua sought to enjoin U.S. funding of the Contras, alleging that it violated their Fifth Amendment rights of liberty and property because Americans were targets of the Contras. 859 F.2d 929, 935 (D.C. Cir. 1988). The court found plaintiffs' claims and request for injunctive relief justiciable, noting that "the Supreme Court has repeatedly found that claims based on [citizens' fundamental liberty and property rights] are justiciable, even if they implicate foreign policy decisions." *Id.* (citing *Regan v. Wald*, 468 U.S. 222 (1984); *Dames & Moore v. Regan*, 453 U.S. 654 (1981)); *see also, Marbury*, 5 U.S. (Cranch) 166 (political questions "respect the nation, not individual rights"); *Reid v. Covert*, 354 U.S. 1, 5 (1957) (plurality opinion) (rejecting "the idea that when the United States acts against citizens abroad it can do so free of the Bill of Rights").[16]

"The Executive's power to conduct foreign relations free from the unwarranted supervision of the Judiciary cannot give the Executive *carte blanche* to trample the most fundamental liberty and property rights of this country's citizenry." *Ramirez de Arellano v. Weinberger*, 745 F.2d 1500, 1515 (D.C. Cir. 1984) (en banc), *vacated on other grounds*, 471 U.S. 1113 (1985). In *Ramirez*, a U.S. citizen sought to enjoin the Secretaries of Defense and State from occupying and destroying his ranch in Honduras by operating a military training camp on it, alleging a Fifth Amendment deprivation of the use and enjoyment of his property. The court rejected the government's political question argument, finding plaintiffs' claims were "not exclusively committed for resolution to the political branches," but were "narrowly focused on the lawfulness" of defendants' deprivation of his private property. *Id.* at 1512; *see also Linder v. Portocarrero*, 963 F.2d 332, 336-37 (11th Cir. 1992) (finding torture and murder claims justiciable even though a civil war was in progress and the acts were allegedly "part of an overall design to wage attacks ... as a means of terrorizing the population" because the complaint was "narrowly focused on the lawfulness of the defendants' conduct

---

16   Defendants misplace reliance on *Bancoult v. McNamara*, as it affirmed this principle. 445 F.3d 427, 435 (D.C. Cir. 2006) ("claims based on 'the most fundamental liberty and property rights of this country's citizenry,' such as the Takings and Due Process Clauses of the Fifth Amendment, are 'justiciable, even if they implicate foreign policy decisions.'" (citations omitted)); *see also id.* at 437 ("the presence of constitutionally-protected liberties could require us to address limits on the foreign policy and national security powers assigned to the political branches").

in a single incident"). Plaintiff's claims here are likewise narrowly focused on the constitutional deprivation of his son's life; he does "not seek judicial monitoring of foreign policy" or to "challenge United States relations with any foreign country." *Id.* at 1513. It cannot be that a constitutional claim to enjoin the destruction of Plaintiff's son's property in Yemen would be justiciable but a constitutional claim to enjoin the taking of his life would not be.

As this Court found in *Abu Ali v. Ashcroft*, "[t]here is simply no authority or precedent ... for respondents' suggestion that the executive's prerogative over foreign affairs can overwhelm to the point of extinction the basic constitutional rights of citizens of the United States to freedom from unlawful detention by the executive." 350 F. Supp. 2d 28, 61-62 (D.D.C. 2004). This statement surely applies with even greater force in the circumstances presented here. Plaintiff challenges "the United States' alleged actions against a citizen in violation of certain constitutional duties."[17] *Id.* at 64. "[T]he D.C. Circuit has left little doubt that the political question doctrine will not trump the due process rights that lie at the heart of this dispute." *Id.* at 65.[18]

Gilligan v. Morgan is not to the contrary. As discussed above, *see* Section I.d, *supra*, the facts in *Gilligan*, the nature of the relief sought, and the posture of the case bear no resemblance to those here. The Court did not decide that the political question doctrine alone warranted dismissal of plaintiffs' claims, but looked at a combination of justiciability doctrines.[19] In any case, the *Gilligan*

---

17 Amici Klimp et al. argue that deference is due to the government's political question argument. Klimp Amicus Br. 21-22. But the government's legal arguments "merit no special deference." *Republic of Austria v. Altmann*, 541 U.S. 677, 701 (2004). As this Court noted with regard to the Act of State doctrine in *Abu Ali*, "[w]hatever limited bearing the ... doctrine has on this case in light of the above analysis is only diminished further by the fact that the doctrine is being invoked here by the United States in an attempt to shield itself from judicial inquiry for its own allegedly unconstitutional acts against one of its citizens." *Abu Ali*, 350 F. Supp. 2d at 60.

18 Other circuits agree. "[A]n area concerning foreign affairs that has been uniformly found appropriate for judicial review is the protection of individual or constitutional rights from government action." *Flynn v. Shultz*, 748 F.2d 1186, 1191 (7th Cir. 1984) (citing *Mathews v. Diaz*, 426 U.S. 67, 81-82 (1976)); *see also Pangilinan v. INS*, 796 F.2d 1091, 1096 (9th Cir. 1986) (political question doctrine does not bar court from hearing cases involving individual rights to equal protection and due process). "This protection of the individual unquestionably extends to cases involving United States Government action taken against our citizens abroad." *Flynn* at 1191. "The pervasive influence of political-question doctrine in fields touching on foreign affairs has not led courts to surrender their power to protect individuals against government action." 13C Charles Alan Wright et al., Federal Practice & Procedure § 3534.2 (3d ed. 2008).

19 To the extent that *Gilligan* analyzed plaintiffs' claims under the political question doctrine, it noted that the relief sought would "embrace critical areas of responsibility" in the political branches given that Congress has the power to "provide for organizing, arming, and disciplining" the National Guard, 413 U.S. at 6 (quoting

Court itself made clear that it neither held nor implied "that there may not be accountability in a judicial forum for violations of law or for specific unlawful conduct by military personnel, whether by way of damages or injunctive relief." *Gilligan*, 413 U.S. at 1112; *see also Laird v. Tatum*, 408 U.S. 1, 16 (1972) ("There is nothing in our Nation's history or in this Court's decided cases, including our holding today, that can properly be seen as giving any indication that actual or threatened injury by reason of unlawful activities of the military would go unnoticed or unremedied.").

Nor does *El-Shifa* alter this fundamental principle: the "political question doctrine does not bar a claim that the government has violated the Constitution simply because the claim implicates foreign relations." 607 F.3d at 841 (citing *INS v. Chadha*, 462 U.S. 919 (1983)). In *El-Shifa*, plaintiffs brought tort claims for a military strike on their pharmaceutical plant in Sudan, which the President had asserted was a chemical weapons factory associated with Osama bin Laden. However, the plaintiffs in *El-Shifa* were noncitizens. *See El-Shifa*, 607 F.3d at 844 ("the courts cannot assess the merits of the President's decision to launch an attack on a *foreign* target" (emphasis added)). Upholding the constitutional rights of a U.S. citizen is clearly the judiciary's role, which cannot be abdicated.[20]

Moreover, in finding plaintiffs' claims nonjusticiable, the D.C. Circuit explained that it had "distinguished between claims requiring us to decide whether taking military action was 'wise' – 'a policy choice and value determination constitutionally committed for resolution to the halls of Congress or the confines of the Executive Branch – and claims presenting purely legal issues' such as whether the government had legal authority to act." *El-Shifa*, 607 F.3d at 842 (citations omitted). Plaintiff does not seek a determination that carrying out a targeted killing against his U.S. citizen son would be unwise as a matter of policy. His claims present purely legal issues – whether the targeted killing of his U.S. citizen son outside of armed conflict, and in the absence of an imminent threat that cannot be addressed with non-lethal means, violates the Constitution and international law.[21]

U.S. Const., Art. I, § 8, cl. 16), and that Congress had expressly authorized the President "to prescribe regulations governing the organization and discipline of the National Guard," *id.* at 7. In other words, the precise role that plaintiffs asked the court to play in *Gilligan* was a role that the Constitution expressly and exclusively committed to the political branches.

20 Plaintiffs in *El-Shifa* sought a declaration that the government's failure to compensate them violated international law and that the statements made about them were defamatory, as well as an injunction requiring retraction of the statements. *El-Shifa*, 607 F.3d at 840. They did not seek to enjoin an impending execution in violation of the Constitution.

21 *El-Shifa* is also distinguishable because, as discussed further below, Plaintiff's claims involve the government's use of lethal force outside the context of armed

C. Courts routinely adjudicate claims implicating war powers and national security

Plaintiff's claims would be justiciable even if this case involved armed conflict. *See Hamdi,* 542 U.S. at 636 ("We have long ... made clear that a state of war is not a blank check for the President when it comes to the rights of the Nation's citizens."). Since 9/11, the Supreme Court has routinely adjudicated issues implicating national security and the President's war powers. *See Hamdi,* 542 U.S 507; *Rasul,* 542 U.S. 466; *Boumediene,* 553 U.S. 723; *Hamdan,* 548 U.S. 557.

The Supreme Court has also historically permitted actions against U.S. soldiers and officials for wrongful or tortious conduct taken in the course of warfare. *See, e.g., Mitchell v. Harmony,* 54 U.S. (13 How.) 115 (1851) (U.S. soldier sued for trespass while in Mexico during Mexican War); *Ford v. Surget,* 97 U.S. 594 (1878) (soldier was not exempt from civil liability for actions that were not in accordance with the usages of civilized warfare); *The Paquete Habana,* 175 U.S. 677 (1900) (court imposed damages for seizure of two Spanish fishing vessels by U.S. forces during Spanish American War because they had not been authorized by Congress). Other claims arising in the context of U.S. military operations have been adjudicated by the Supreme Court as well. *See Youngstown Sheet & Tube Co.,* 343 U.S. at 596 (enjoining President Truman's seizure of steel mills during the Korean War); *N.Y. Times Co. v. United States,* 403 U.S. 713 (1971) (rejecting foreign relations objections to publication of the Pentagon Papers); *Brown v. United States,* 12 U.S. (8 Cranch) 110 (1814) (rejecting executive power to seize domestic property of enemy alien during War of 1812).

Defendants' argument that problems of enforceability render Plaintiff's claims non-justiciable is based on a misapprehension of the relief Plaintiff seeks. *See, e.g.,* Gov't Br. 24.[22] As discussed above, *see* Section I.d, *supra,* Plaintiff does not ask the court to intervene in real-time decision-making by the executive regarding the use of lethal force. Again, if the relevant standard incorporates an "imminence" requirement, real-time judicial review is infeasible by definition. But if the government were to execute Plaintiff's son with an injunction in place, this Court could be asked to review the legality of the government's actions, including whether its actions violated the injunction.[23] As *"Youngstown*

---

conflict. *See El-Shifa,* 607 F. 3d at 845 (relying on Congress's power to declare war (U.S. Const., art. I, § 8, cl. 11), and the Executive's power as commander in chief (U.S. Const., art. II, § 2, cl. 1)).

22   As to Plaintiff's request for disclosure of the criteria the Government uses in deciding whether to target a U.S. citizen for killing, Plaintiff seeks the operative legal standards used by the executive branch – the equivalent of the information that would appear in a federal statute; he does not seek targeting criteria or policy judgments.

23   Defendants also argue that no judicially manageable standards exist to determine whether Anwar Al-Aulaqi poses a concrete, specific, and imminent threat, and

illustrates, when the enjoined defendant is a responsible government officer residing in the nation's capital ..., questions of evaluating and guaranteeing compliance are not insurmountable." *Ramirez*, 745 F.2d at 1511. The role of the judiciary in such circumstances would be no different than in any of the cases above, any action for damages, or any case seeking review of the reasonableness of a killing in a law enforcement context.[24]

To be clear, Plaintiff does not propose that *ex post* judicial review would be sufficient in this context. *Cf. Ramirez*, 745 F.2d at 1511 ("[M]ere monetary relief would be insufficient under any concept of justice."). To say that the Court cannot supervise the executive's real-time targeting decisions is not to say that this Court has no role to play until Plaintiff's son has been killed. This Court should, and must, ensure that the government's real-time targeting decisions are being made with reference to the appropriate legal standard. It has a crucial role to play in ensuring, *before* the government takes the life of an American citizen, that the government is interpreting the law correctly.[25]

---

whether means other than lethal force are available. Gov't Br. 27. The "concept of a textual commitment to a coordinate political department is not completely separate from the concept of a lack of judicially discoverable and manageable standards for resolving it," *Nixon v. United States*, 506 U.S. 224, 228 (1993), which is the second *Baker* factor. It is the judiciary's role to interpret the Constitution, and there are manageable standards for doing so. *See, e.g., Powell v. McCormack*, 395 U.S. 486, 549 (1969). Moreover, "universally recognized norms of international law provide judicially discoverable and manageable standards for adjudicating suits brought under the" ATS. *Kadic v. Karadzić*, 70 F.3d 232, 249 (2d Cir. 1995) (citing *Nixon*, 506 U.S. at 227-29).

24 Defendants further argue that a judicial pronouncement might interfere with presidential commands, giving rise to multifarious pronouncements "to officials in the field with respect to the real-time use of force against AQAP." Gov't Br. 24. The sixth *Baker* factor, "the potentiality of embarrassment from multifarious pronouncements by various departments on one question," *Baker*, 369 U.S. at 217, is the least important of the factors. *Vieth v. Jubelirer*, 541 U.S. 267, 278 (2004). Again, Plaintiff is not seeking relief that would require real-time judicial supervision of the government's conduct. Moreover, "[o]ur system of government requires that federal courts on occasion interpret the Constitution in a manner at variance with the construction given the document by another branch. The alleged conflict that such an adjudication may cause cannot justify the courts' avoiding their constitutional responsibility." *Powell*, 395 U.S. at 549; *see also, Alperin v. Vatican Bank*, 410 F.3d 532, 558 (9th Cir. 2005) ("[f]ulfilling our constitutionally-mandated role to hear controversies properly before us does not threaten to cause embarrassment or multiple pronouncements.").

25 Defendants cite no authority for the proposition that their motion to dismiss on political question grounds is properly brought under Rule 12(b)(1) for lack of subject matter jurisdiction, and *Hwang Geum Joo v. Japan*, 413 F.3d 45 (D.C. Cir. 2005), cited by Amici Klimp et al. at 10-11, is not dispositive. *See Oryszak v. Sullivan*, 576 F.3d 522, 527 (D.C. Cir. 2009) (Ginsburg, J., concurring); *see also Baker*, 369 U.S.

D. *The existence and scope of the armed conflict is not a political question*

The government additionally claims that it is beyond the competence of the courts to determine whether the targeting of Plaintiff's son in Yemen is properly evaluated under the law of armed conflict.[26] Gov't Br. 32. Supreme Court precedent proves otherwise, and to the extent the government relies on the AUMF as authority for the expansive reach of its "war against Al-Qaeda," the scope of the force authorized by the statute is squarely a question for the judiciary.[27] In *Hamdan*, the Supreme Court responded to the government's claim of unbounded authority to create ad-hoc military commissions with which to prosecute "enemy combatants" by applying the laws of war and determining the threshold question of the existence and nature of the conflict between the United States and Al-Qaeda in Afghanistan. 548 U.S. at 629-31. The Court described the conflict as a non-international armed conflict and found that the government's authority was thus circumscribed by the rules applicable to such conflicts. *Id.* at 630-32; *see also Hamdi*, 542 U.S. at 521 (finding a state of armed conflict in Afghanistan in 2004, referencing active military operations and thousands of U.S. troops on the ground).

To the extent the government claims the AUMF as the source of its authority to target Plaintiff's son in Yemen, the question of whether and under what circumstances such force is authorized is a matter of statutory interpretation. Indeed, since the AUMF was passed, the courts have repeatedly pronounced upon the meaning of the statute – and rejected the government's arguments for unreviewable discretion – in addressing questions concerning the scope of

---

at 198. In any event, a constitutional claim cannot be dismissed on jurisdictional grounds unless it is "unsubstantial and frivolous." *Baker*, 369 U.S. at 199.

26 Even if the government is correct that the law of armed conflict applies here, there are still limitations on the circumstances in which the government can use lethal force against a civilian – even a suspected terrorist. Civilians may be targeted with lethal force only if they are directly participating in the armed conflict. *See, e.g.,* Geneva Convention Relative to the Protection of Civilian Persons in Time of War (IV) art. 3, Aug 12, 1949, 75 U.N.T.S. 287. Even civilians who are directly participating in hostilities can be targeted only in accordance with principles of military necessity, proportionality and precaution. *See* Nils Melzer, *Targeted Killing in International Law* 397-411 (2008). The authority to kill is narrower than the authority to detain.

27 The government vaguely asserts "other legal bases under U.S. and international law for the President to authorize the use of force against al-Qaeda and AQAP, including the inherent right to national self-defense recognized in international law." Gov't Br. 24. To the extent the Executive invokes a right to self-defense, however, the question of whether the use of force by one state within the territory of another is lawful is separate and distinct from the question of whether the targeting of the individual himself is lawful, as Plaintiff explained in his opening brief. *See* Pl. Br. 30-31.

the executive's authority. *See, e.g., Padilla v. Hanft*, 423 F.3d 386 (4th Cir. 2005); *Hamdi*, 542 U.S. 507; *Hamlily v. Obama*, 616 F. Supp. 2d 63 (D.D.C. 2009).

In construing the terms of the AUMF, the Supreme Court has interpreted the statute in light of "longstanding law-of-war principles," including the Geneva Conventions. *Hamdi*, 542 U.S. at 521.[28] While the laws of war provide standards regarding the categories of persons and the types of conduct that render individuals subject to military force, which the courts have applied in interpreting the AUMF in the detention context, they similarly provide standards for determining the existence and type of an armed conflict, which is an essential precondition to the application of the laws of war. *See* O'Connell Decl. ¶ 9-13. Contrary to the government's claim about the lack of "judicially manageable standards," Gov't Br. 34, courts have regularly applied and evaluated these criteria in addressing the threshold question of the existence or absence of armed conflict, as discussed below.

The decision of the International Criminal Tribunal for the former Yugoslavia ("ICTY") in *Prosecutor v. Tadić* provides a widely accepted standard for determining the existence of an armed conflict. *Tadić*, Case No. IT-94-1-T, Decision on Defence Motion for Interlocutory Appeal on Jurisdiction (Appeals Chamber), ¶ 70 (Oct. 2, 1995). The *Tadić* tribunal found that an armed conflict existed – noting that the hostilities at issue exceeded certain "intensity requirements" and there had been "protracted, large-scale violence between the armed forces of different States and between governmental forces and organized insurgent groups" – and in so doing, the tribunal distilled two key criteria for determining the existence of an armed conflict: 1) its intensity and 2) the organization of the parties to the conflict.[29] With respect to non-international armed conflicts in particular, "these closely related criteria are used ... for the purpose, as a

---

28   This Court and others have followed suit, *see e.g., Hamlily*, 616 F. Supp. 2d 63, and the administration itself has taken the position in the courts and the public that its authority pursuant to the AUMF should be informed by the laws of war. *See* Resp'ts' Revised Mem. Regarding the Government's Detention Authority Relative to Detainees Held at Guantanamo Bay, *In re Guantanamo Bay Detainee Litig.*, No. 08-442 (D.D.C. Mar. 13, 2009) (TFH); Speech of Harold Koh, Legal Adviser, U.S. Dep't State, Annual Meeting of the American Society International Law, Washington, DC (Mar. 25, 2010) ("Let there be no doubt: the Obama Administration is firmly committed to complying with all applicable law, including the laws of war, in all aspects of these ongoing armed conflicts" (referring to conflicts in Iraq, Afghanistan and against Al-Qaeda)).

29   *See also* ICRC, III *Commentary on the Geneva Conventions of 12 August 1949* 36 (J.S. Pictet ed., 1960); Rome Statute of the International Criminal Court, July 17, 1998, U.N. Doc. A/CONF. 183/9, reprinted in 37 I.L.M. 999; European Commission for Democracy Through Law (Venice Commission), Opinion on the International Legal Obligations of Council of Europe Member States in Respect of Secret Detention Facilities and Inter-State Transport of Prisoners, Op. no. 363/2005, CDL-AD (2006)009 ("Venice Comm'n Op.").

minimum, of distinguishing an armed conflict from banditry, unorganized and short-lived insurrections, or terrorist activities, which are not subject to international humanitarian law." *Tadić*, Case No. IT-94-1-T, Opinion and Judgment, ¶ 562 (May 7, 1997).[30]

Subsequent decisions of the ICTY and other courts have applied and interpreted these criteria in evaluating whether various situations of violence constituted armed conflict. With respect to the level of organization of a party, courts have looked to, *inter alia*, the existence of a headquarters and command structure; territorial control by the group; and the extent of the group's ability to access military equipment to recruit and provide military training to members, to use military tactics, and to speak with one voice. Regarding the level of intensity of a conflict, indicators have included, *inter alia*, the number and frequency of attacks, the extent of civilian casualties and displacement, and the severity of the state's response. *See Prosecutor v. Ramush Haradinaj, Idriz Balaj and Lahi Brahimaj*, Case No. IT-04-84-T, Judgment, ¶¶ 90-99 (Apr. 3, 2008) (citing evidence of a group's membership of hundreds to thousands of soldiers, considerable control of territory, and sophisticated access to arms to find that it was "organized," and evidence of nearly 1,500 attacks by the group, daily shelling and clashes involving state forces and the group, deployment of state forces numbering 1,500 to 2,000, and the flight and disappearances of civilians to find the requisite "intensity" of fighting); *see also, e.g., Prosecutor v. Halilović*, Case No. IT-01-48-T, Judgment (Nov. 16, 2005); *Prosecutor v. Kordić and Cerkez*, Case No. IT-95-14/2-A, Judgment (Dec. 17, 2004); *Prosecutor v. Thomas Lubanga Dyilo*, Case No. ICC-01/04-01/06, Decision on the Confirmation of Charges (Jan. 29, 2007).

Courts at the national level have similarly addressed this question. *See, e.g,* HCJ 769/02 *Pub. Comm. against Torture in Israel v. Israel* [2006] IsrSC 57(6) 285, ¶16 (finding an armed conflict and citing evidence of "severe combat," the use of "military means" by the parties, and thousands of civilian casualties); *HH & Others*, CG [2008] UKAIT 00022 (U.K. Asylum and Immigration Tribunal) (Jan. 28, 2008) (relying on criteria used in *Tadić* to determine that the violence in Somalia constituted a non-international armed conflict for purposes of determining a claim for asylum).

As these cases show, there are indeed "judicially manageable standards" for courts to apply in addressing questions concerning the existence and scope of armed conflict, as well as "access to the requisite information," contrary to the government's assertion. Gov't Br. 34. Indeed, evidence relied upon in cases discussed above came from publicly available sources. *See, e.g., Prosecutor v. Thomas*

---

30   *See also* Venice Commission Op. ("[S]poradic bombings and other violence acts which terrorist networks perpetrate in different places around the globe and the ensuing counterterrorism measures, even if they are occasionally undertaken by military units, cannot be said to amount to an 'armed conflict' in the sense that they trigger the applicability of International Humanitarian Law.").

Lubanga Dyilo, ¶¶ 235-236 (relying on news reports, human rights organization analyses, and United Nations reports).

For its contrary argument, the government relies on two distinguishable Second Circuit cases. In *DaCosta v. Laird*, the Second Circuit refused to hear the case on political question grounds only after "[h]aving previously determined, in accordance with our duty, that the Vietnamese war has been constitutionally authorized." 471 F.2d 1146, 1157 (2d Cir. 1973). In the prior decision cited by the *DaCosta* court, the Second Circuit had expressly rejected the government's argument that determining the legality of the Vietnam war was foreclosed by the political question doctrine. *Orlando v. Laird*, 443 F.2d 1039, 1042 (2d Cir. 1971) ("[T]he constitutional delegation of the war-declaring power to the Congress contains a discoverable and manageable standard imposing on the Congress a duty of mutual participation in the prosecution of war. Judicial scrutiny of that duty, therefore, is not foreclosed by the political question doctrine."). Even in terms of escalation of a previously-determined lawful war, the *DaCosta* court wrote that the issue may be justiciable if "litigants raising such a claim ... [could] present to the court a manageable standard which would allow for proper judicial resolution of the issue." 471 F.2d at 1156. In *Holtzman v. Schlesinger*, 484 F.2d 1307 (2d Cir. 1973), the court recognized that the "role of the Judiciary is to determine the legality of the challenged action," *id.* at 1309, while ultimately finding that the challenged action constituted a non-justiciable "tactical decision," *id.* at 1310. But the legal determination sought here, of the permissible bounds of the AUMF, is not a tactical decision but a question of law on which courts have pronounced upon many times before.

While the government is correct that the existence of an armed conflict between the United States and Al-Qaeda in one location "does not mean it cannot exist outside this geographic area," that does not mean it exists everywhere. *See* O'Connell Decl. ¶ 13 ("[A]rmed conflict has a territorial aspect. It has territorial limits."). Nine years ago Congress authorized the President to use force against those "nations, organizations, or persons" responsible for the attacks of September 11, pursuant to which the President launched a military campaign against Al-Qaeda and the Taliban regime in Afghanistan. But the AUMF was not "a blank check." *Hamdi*, 542 U.S. at 536. The existence of an armed conflict is governed by the laws of war and depends upon objective criteria, namely, the existence of organized parties and intense conflict. *See* O'Connel Decl. ¶¶ 9-12. Those criteria are not met here. *See id.* ¶¶ 14-17.

As the declaration of Bernard Haykel describes, Al-Qaeda in the Arabian Peninsula ("AQAP") is a fragmented group with differing interests and no unified strategy, and numbers no more than a couple of hundred individuals. *See* Declaration of Bernard Haykel ("Haykel Decl.") ¶ 7. Attacks by the group have been sporadic and numbered some two dozen since 2006. *See id.* ¶ 11. In contrast, a war has been waged in the north of the country since 2004 between the Yemeni government and a group called the Huthis, which has resulted in thousands of casualties, tens of thousands of refugees, destroyed villages and depopulated entire areas, employed all types of armaments, and involved international groups and countries offering mediation services to reach a cease fire and a resolution to the hostilities. *See id.* ¶ 11. According to Haykel, the government's military engagements with AQAP do not compare in terms of the number of victims, refugees, destruction, and the use of armaments; the nature of the battle against elements of AQAP is in the nature of a police action. *See id;* O'Connell Decl. ¶ 15 (concluding that there is no armed conflict in Yemen).

In addition to being constrained by the laws of war, by its plain terms the AUMF also requires a nexus to the individuals and organizations responsible for the September 11 attacks.[31] While Al-Qaeda and the Taliban fall under this rubric, AQAP is a separate and distinct group that is not known to have any actual association with Al-Qaeda, whether in terms of command structure or activities, and no connection to September 11. *See id.* ¶ 13; *see also, e.g., Hamlily,* 616 F. Supp. 2d at 75 n.17 (holding that "'[a]ssociated forces' do not include terrorist organizations who merely share an abstract philosophy or even a common purpose with al Qaeda – there must be an actual association in the current conflict with al Qaeda or the Taliban"). Thus, the use of force against AQAP is not authorized by the AUMF.

While the government's claimed authority for targeting Plaintiff's son appears to be premised largely on a purported relationship between AQAP and Al-Qaeda, evidence of this crucial link appears nowhere in its declarations. Indeed, it is remarkable that while the government relies heavily and repeatedly on the assertion that "AQAP is an organized armed group that is either part of al-Qaeda or, alternatively, is an organized associated force, or cobelligerent, of Al-Qaeda," it provides absolutely no support for this claim in its declaration or elsewhere.[32] Gov't Br. 8, 24, 32-33. In the face of the evidence provided by the Plaintiffs as to the nature of AQAP, the situation in Yemen, and the non-

---

31 The legislative history confirms that such a nexus is required. *See, e.g.,* 147 Cong. Rec. S9417 (Sen. Feingold) (AUMF is "appropriately limited to those entities involved in the attacks that occurred on September 11") (daily ed. Sept. 14, 2001); *id.* at S9416 (Sen. Levin) ("[The AUMF] is limited to nations, organizations, or persons involved in the terrorist attacks of September 11. It is not a broad authorization for the use of military force against any nation, organization, or persons who were not involved in the September 11 terrorist attacks."). Moreover, President Bush specifically proposed – and Congress rejected – an earlier version of the AUMF that would have authorized the President to use force to "deter and pre-empt any future acts of terrorism or aggression against the United States" that are unrelated to the September 11th attacks. Richard F. Grimmett, *Authorization for Use of Military Force in Response to the 9/11 Attacks (P.L. 107-40): Legislative History,* CRS Report for Congress (Jan. 16, 2007).

32 It is also worth pointing out that the government does not appear to have decided whether it regards AQAP as "part of al-Qaeda" or as an "organized associated force or cobelligerent."

existence of an armed conflict, the government's bald assertion to the contrary cannot stand. *See generally* Haykel Decl.; O'Connell Decl.

III. Plaintiff has asserted a proper cause of action for extrajudicial killing under the alien tort statute

The government moves to dismiss Plaintiff's ATS claim on the grounds that it presents a "novel" cause of action and is barred by sovereign immunity. The government misunderstands Plaintiff's claim, and misapplies the law on sovereign immunity.

A. Plaintiff's claim is well recognized under the ATS

The government characterizes Plaintiff's claim as one for intentional infliction of emotional distress, arguing that such a tort "is not even universally recognized under domestic law, let alone international law," Gov't Br. 41. But this is not the claim Plaintiff brings. Plaintiff alleges that Defendants' authorization for the targeted killing of his son in Yemen would constitute an extrajudicial killing – a *jus cogens* violation of international law, and a tort consistently recognized by U.S. courts since the beginning of modern ATS litigation and indeed codified in domestic law under the Torture Victim Protection Act. *See* Pl. Br. 25-26. While Plaintiff certainly will suffer harm if Defendants succeed in killing his son, which the government misconstrues as the basis for his claim, he brings the claim to enjoin the extrajudicial killing of his son.[33] Thus, while the Supreme Court in *Sosa v. Alvarez-Machain*, 542 U.S. 692 (2004) urged caution when recognizing new causes of action under the ATS,[34] there is nothing new about the international norm – the prohibition of extrajudicial killing – upon which Plaintiff bases his ATS claim.

Nor is the injunctive and declaratory nature of the relief Plaintiff seeks unprecedented under the ATS. As an initial matter, nothing in the plain language of the ATS limits the type of relief courts may grant.[35] 28 U.S.C. § 1350

---

33   If Plaintiff's son was indeed subject to an extrajudicial killing and Plaintiff sought damages under the ATS, he would be the appropriate party to bring the claim under applicable law. He is therefore the appropriate party to bring this claim for injunctive relief.

34   One consideration behind the caution *Sosa* urged was the fear that U.S. courts would overly intrude upon the treatment of foreign citizens by their own governments. *Sosa*, 542 U.S. at 728 ("It is one thing for American courts to enforce constitutional limits on our own State and Federal Government's power, but quite another to consider suits under rules that would go so far as to claim a limit on the power of foreign governments over their own citizens."). By contrast, Plaintiff's claim concerns the United States' treatment of one of its own citizens.

35   Compare with the relief provided under the Federal Tort Claims Act ("FTCA"), 28

("The district courts shall have original jurisdiction of *any civil action* by an alien for a *tort* only, committed in violation of the law of nations or a treaty of the United States." (emphasis added)); *see also City of Monterey v. Del Monte Dunes*, 526 U.S. 687, 726 n.1 (1999) (Scalia, J., concurring) ("Since the merger of law and equity, any type of relief, including purely equitable relief, can be sought in a tort suit."); *see also* Restatement (Second) of Torts § 933(1) (injunctions are available "against a committed or threatened tort" if appropriate).

Furthermore, courts have previously granted equitable relief for ATS claims. In *Von Dardel v. Union of Soviet Socialist Republics*, the district court in this circuit issued a default judgment against the Soviet Union, granting injunctive, declaratory and compensatory relief under the ATS, and ordering the Russian government to release a political prisoner or otherwise account for his whereabouts. 623 F. Supp. 246 (D.D.C. 1985), *vacated on other grounds*, 736 F. Supp. 1 (D.D.C. 1990). As noted in Plaintiff's opening brief, in *Kadic v. Karadzić*, the district court granted a permanent injunction against Radovan Karadzić, enjoining him from committing or facilitating extrajudicial killings among other acts.[36] Pl. Br. 24 n.8.

B. Plaintiff's claim is not barred by sovereign immunity

Sovereign immunity does not bar Plaintiff's ATS claim because the claim falls within the APA's waiver of sovereign immunity for non-monetary relief. *See* 5 U.S.C. § 702 (waiving sovereign immunity for "[a]n action in a court of the United States seeking relief other than money damages and stating a claim that an agency or an officer or employee thereof acted or failed to act in an official capacity or under color of legal authority"). "The APA's waiver of sovereign immunity applies to any suit whether under the APA or not." *Trudeau v. FTC*, 456 F.3d 178, 186 (D.C. Cir. 2006) (citation omitted); *see also Sanchez-Espinoza*, 770 F.2d at 207 (Scalia, J.) (noting that the APA's waiver of sovereign immunity may be available for ATS claims against federal defendants "in their official capacity for *nonmonetary* relief ").

Alternatively, Plaintiff's ATS claim may proceed under the *"Larson-Dugan"* exception to sovereign immunity. The Supreme Court in *Larson v. Domestic & Foreign Commerce Corp.*, 337 U.S. 682 (1949), and later in *Dugan v. Rank*, 372 U.S. 609 (1963), held that "sovereign immunity does not apply as a bar to suits alleging that an officer's actions were unconstitutional or beyond statutory

---

U.S.C. § 1346(b)(1) (limiting recovery to monetary damages) and the Administrative Procedure Act ("APA"), 28 U.S.C. § 702 (limiting recovery to equitable relief).

36   *Kadic v. Karadzić*, No. 93-1163, at 2 (S.D.N.Y. Aug. 16, 2000) ("Under the equitable powers of this Court and the Court's authority under the Alien Tort Claims Act ... the defendant [and defendant's forces] ... are hereby immediately and permanently ENJOINED and RESTRAINED from ... committing or from aiding, abetting, directing or facilitating others to commit, any acts of ... extrajudicial killing ... .").

authority." *Swan*, 100 F.3d at 981 (citation omitted); *Larson*, 337 U.S. at 690 (sovereign immunity does not attach where the "order conferring power upon the officer to take action in the sovereign's name is claimed to be unconstitutional"). "Actions for *habeas corpus* against a warden and injunctions against the threatened enforcement of unconstitutional statutes are familiar examples of [the constitutional] type [of excepted cases]." *Larson*, 337 U.S. at 690.

In fashioning this exception, the *Larson* Court reasoned that in cases of unconstitutional acts, "the conduct against which specific relief is sought is beyond the officer's power and is, therefore, not the conduct of the sovereign." *Larson*, 337 U.S. at 690; *see also id.* ("The only difference [from a claim alleging *ultra vires* conduct] is that in this case the power has been conferred in form but the grant is lacking in substance because of its constitutional invalidity."). The *Larson* exception applies to official capacity actions such as this. *See, e.g., Doe v. Wooten*, 376 F. App'x 883, 885 (11th Cir. 2010) (agreeing that a "plaintiff may be able to obtain injunctive relief against a federal officer acting in his official capacity when the officer acts beyond statutory or constitutional limitations" (citing *Larson*)); *Simmat v. U.S. Bureau of Prisons*, 413 F.3d 1225, 1233 (10th Cir. 2005) (holding *Larson* rule waives sovereign immunity in suit against prison officials in their official capacity). Regardless of this Court's conclusions regarding Defendants' waiver of immunity under the APA, therefore, Defendants are not entitled to sovereign immunity because the conduct Plaintiff's ATS claim seeks to enjoin – targeted killings outside of armed conflict, in the absence of judicial process or where lethal force is not a last resort to prevent an imminent threat to life, Compl. ¶ 29 – is both a violation of international law and unconstitutional. *See Swan*, 100 F.3d at 981 ("[S]overeign immunity does not apply as a bar to suits alleging that an officer's actions were unconstitutional or beyond statutory authority." (citing *Larson*)); *Am. Policyholders Ins. Co. v. Nyacol Prods.*, 989 F.2d 1256, 1265 (1st Cir. 1993) (the "case's underlying merits" must fall within scope of *Larson* exceptions).

While Defendants are correct that the President may not be enjoined pursuant to a waiver under the APA, Gov't Br. 40-41, he may be enjoined under the *Larson* exception described above. *See Made in the USA Found. v. United States*, 242 F.3d 1300, 1309 n.20 (11th Cir. 2001) (sovereign immunity does not bar injunctive action against President where conduct falls under *Larson* exception). "It is now well established that 'review of the legality of Presidential action can ordinarily be obtained in a suit seeking to enjoin the officers who attempt to enforce the President's directive.'" *Chamber of Commerce of the U.S. v. Reich*, 74 F.3d 1322, 1328 (D.C. Cir. 1996) (quoting *Franklin v. Massachusetts*, 505 U.S. at 828 (Scalia, J., concurring in part and concurring in the judgment)); *see also Soucie v. David*, 448 F.2d 1067, 1072 n.12 (D.C. Cir. 1971) ("[C]ourts have power to compel subordinate executive officials to disobey illegal Presidential commands."). While President Obama may be enjoined under the *Larson* exception, he need not be enjoined for Plaintiff to receive his desired relief. *Cf. Made in the*

USA Found., 242 F.3d at 1309 (APA waiver of sovereign immunity would not be available because *only* the President could carry out act sought to be enjoined).

The government further argues that the FTCA bars the APA's waiver of sovereign immunity. While the APA "excludes from its waiver of sovereign immunity … claims seeking relief expressly or impliedly forbidden by another statute," *Fornaro v. James*, 416 F.3d 63, 66 (D.C. Cir. 2005) (citation omitted), the government's assertion that the FTCA "comprehensively addresses" suits against the United States for personal injury and death is incorrect. The plain language of the FTCA confirms that it is solely "exclusive of any other civil action or proceeding *for money damages* by reason of the same subject matter against the employee whose act or omission gave rise to the claim or against the estate of such employee." 28 U.S.C. § 2679(b)(1) (emphasis added); *see also id.* ("Any other civil action or proceeding *for money damages* arising out of or relating to the same subject matter against the employee or the employee's estate is precluded." (emphasis added)).[37] As such it does not address – expressly or impliedly – whether *equitable* relief may be sought under a separate statute.

This Circuit has confirmed this view. In *U.S. Info. Agency v. Krc*, 989 F.2d 1211 (D.C. Cir. 1993), the court held that sovereign immunity did not bar plaintiff's injunctive claim even though the plaintiff could not proceed under the FTCA. The Court contrasted the FTCA to the Tucker Act and the Little Tucker Act, which comprehensively address contract cases, finding that the "FTCA specifically bars money damages as a remedy for [plaintiff's] claim, which by parity of reasoning implies that injunctive relief is available." 989 F.2d. at 1216. Defendants' reliance on *Moon v. Takisaki*, 501 F.2d 389 (9th Cir. 1974) is misplaced. In *Moon*, the Ninth Circuit merely noted that it was not possible to seek injunctive relief for an FTCA claim, 501 F.2d at 390, and not that the FTCA precluded injunctive relief – even impliedly – in other statutes. *See also Hui v. Castaneda*, 130 S. Ct. 1845, 1851 (2010) ("Congress follows the practice of explicitly stating when it means to make FTCA an exclusive remedy." (quoting *Carlson v. Green*, 446 U.S. 14, 20 (1980))). Because the government cannot identify any statute that impliedly or expressly prohibits injunctive relief for a claim of extrajudicial execution, the APA provides a waiver of sovereign immunity for Plaintiff's ATS claim.[38]

---

37 Indeed, because of the constitutional and statutory exceptions in the act, 28 U.S.C. § 2679(b)(2)(A)-(B), which provide that the FTCA's exclusivity provision does not preclude claims for relief for violations of the Constitution or another statute, the FTCA does not even "comprehensively address" monetary claims for personal injury or death resulting from U.S. official conduct.

38 The government relies on *Sanchez-Espinoza v. Reagan*, 770 F.2d 202 (D.C. Cir. 1985) for the argument that the Court should not exercise its discretion to enjoin or declare illegal a "military operation" that receives the approval of the President, Secretary of Defense and the Director of the CIA, and purportedly implicates foreign relations. Gov't Br. at 41. But the equitable relief plaintiffs sought in *Sanchez-*

IV. Litigation of plaintiff's claims is not foreclosed by
the state secrets privilege

finally, the government moves to dismiss this suit without any adjudication of its merits on the ground that litigation of Plaintiff's claims would force the disclosure of state secrets and result in "significant harm to the national security of the United States." Gov't Br. 43. The government's assertion of an evidentiary privilege to foreclose judicial consideration of a U.S. citizen's claim that, absent requested relief, he faces extrajudicial execution is without precedent and should be rejected.

The government's sweeping invocation of the state secrets privilege to shut down this litigation is as ironic as it is extreme: that Anwar Al-Aulaqi has been targeted for assassination is known to the world only because senior administration officials, in an apparently coordinated media strategy, advised the nation's leading newspapers that the National Security Council had authorized the use of lethal force against him. *See, e.g.,* Scott Shane, *U.S. Approves Targeted Killing of American Cleric,* N.Y. Times, Apr. 6, 2010; Greg Miller, *Muslim Cleric Aulaqi is 1 U.S. citizen on List of those CIA Allowed to Kill,* Wash. Post, Apr. 7, 2010. Had the government itself adhered to the overriding secrecy concerns so solemnly invoked in its pleadings, those senior officials would *not* have broadcast the government's intentions to the entire world, and intelligence officials, speaking on the record, would have refused all comment rather than providing tacit acknowledgement that Plaintiff's son is being targeted. Thus, the Defense Secretary's assertion that "disclosure of whether or not lethal force has been authorized to combat a terrorist organization overseas, and, if so, the specific targets of such action" would provide the nation's enemies with "critical information needed to evade hostile action," Public Declaration of Robert M. Gates ("Gates Public Decl.") ¶ 7, must be taken here with a grain of salt: any harm associated with such disclosures in this instance has already occurred, and the government has only itself to blame.[39] Now that the government has placed its asserted authority to kill Plaintiff's son into the public debate, its attempt to

---

Espinoza – ranging from "end[ing] appellees' alleged disregard of Congress's right to declare war and of a prohibition against supporting the Contras imposed by Congress through statute" to "enjoin[ing] an alleged nuisance created by the maintenance and operation of paramilitary camps," *id.* at 205 – is clearly distinguishable from the relief Plaintiff seeks here, namely, preventing the execution of a U.S. citizen in violation of the Fourth and Fifth Amendments and applicable international law. Even the D.C. Circuit in *Sanchez-Espinoza,* while wary of intruding on military operations approved by senior officials, noted that the "consequences [of such an intrusion] are tolerated when the officer's action is unauthorized because contrary to statutory or constitutional prescription." *Id.* at 207.

39   There is no indication that the senior government officials who disclosed this information to the world are being criminally investigated for risking "exceptionally grave harm" to the nation's security.

preclude judicial consideration of the limits of that authority is both impermissible and unseemly.

Even if the government had not itself generated the very public controversy it seeks now to extinguish, invocation of an evidentiary privilege to prevent a court from adjudicating a litigant's potentially meritorious claims related to the executive's asserted authority to kill him would be unconscionable. "[T] he action of the sovereign in taking the life of one of its citizens ... differs dramatically from any other legitimate state action." *Gardner v. Florida,* 430 .S. 349, 357-358 (1977). For that reason, the common-law privilege recognized by the Supreme Court in *United States v. Reynolds,* 345 U.S. 1, 12 (1953), whereby a private litigant's right of redress must in some cases yield to the executive's obligation to safeguard military secrets, takes on an altogether different dimension when the interest at stake is not the recovery of property but the preservation of life. The singularity of this situation "is a natural consequence of the knowledge that execution is the most irremediable and unfathomable of penalties; that death is different." *Ford v. Wainwright,* 477 U.S. 399, 411 (1986) (Marshall, J., plurality opinion). Indeed, the unique circumstances of this case raise serious questions about the propriety of the any reliance on the state secrets privilege as a basis for declining to adjudicate Plaintiff's claims.[40]

In his public declaration in support of the government's state secrets assertion, the Director of National Intelligence alleges that Plaintiff's son has engaged in conduct that, if supported by evidence, would be prosecutable under numerous criminal statutes. It is beyond dispute that were the government to prosecute Plaintiff's son criminally, rather than execute him without charge or trial, invocation of the state secrets privilege would be categorically impermissible. Rather, under the ample protections offered by the Classified Information Procedures Act, the government would be required to present evidence derived from intelligence sources in support of its allegations that Plaintiff's son is an "operational" terrorist who has conspired in terrorist plots against the United States. That is because, as the Supreme Court held in *Reynolds,* it would be "unconscionable to allow [the government] to undertake prosecution and then invoke its governmental privileges to deprive the accused of anything which might be material to his defense." 345 U.S. at 12.

The present circumstances raise an even more grave concern: the government is seeking to impose the ultimate penalty *without* trial while claiming a secrecy privilege that would be unavailable *with* trial. It would be an odd and remarkable rule that would permit the government to avoid all judicial scrutiny simply by electing to bypass trial in favor of summary execution. In that regard,

---

40 *See, e.g.,* Charlie Savage, *U.S. Debates Response to Targeted Killing Lawsuit,* N.Y. Times, Sept. 15, 2010 (quoting "David Rivkin, a lawyer in the White House of President George H. W. Bush," expressing concern that "if someone came up to you and said the government wants to target you and you can't even talk about it in court to try to stop it, that's too harsh even for me.").

the government's widely publicized intent to kill Plaintiff's son places him more in the position of "the accused," *Reynolds*, 345 U.S. at 12, than of an ordinary civil litigant in cases in which courts have upheld invocations of the state secrets privilege. The government can cite to no remotely similar case in which it has been permitted to block a citizen's access to court even as it proceeded with ongoing efforts to deprive him of his life, or even his liberty.

In fact, with regard to Plaintiff's claim that the government's refusal to disclose the standards by which it targets U.S. citizens for death violates the notice requirement of the Due Process Clause, the government's argument is, if anything, even more extreme. As Plaintiff has argued, due process requires at a minimum that citizens be put on notice of what may cause them to be put to death. Just as due process prohibits the government from convicting a person on the basis of a secret law, so, too, does it prohibit killing him pursuant to secret legal standards. The constitutional right to meaningful notice cannot be trumped by an evidentiary privilege. Put otherwise, the government's invocation of the state secrets privilege with respect to Plaintiff's due process notice claim is itself a constitutional violation: the very information the government seeks to suppress is the information to which Plaintiff is constitutionally entitled.[41]

By broadcasting its intent to target a U.S. citizen for death, the government has initiated an extraordinary controvery about the limits on executive authority to use lethal force, the scope of the armed conflict in which the United States is now engaged, and the rights of U.S. citizens who are suspected of involvement with terrorist organizations. Plaintiff's interest in establishing these limits in accordance with constitutional and international standards is manifestly different and more direct than that of others who may share a generalized concern about U.S. policy. Plaintiff is trying to protect his son against unlawful killing by the U.S. government. By invoking the state secrets privilege to terminate this litigation at its very outset, the government seeks to exclude from this controversy the only branch of government that can provide an authoritative reso-

---

41   The government's contention that disclosure of "any criteria or procedures that may be utilized in connection with [operations in Yemen]" would reveal state secrets, Gov't Br. 49-50, is untenable in light of the documents that it recently disclosed in response to a FOIA request. *See* Manes Decl. Ex. A. On October 1, 2010 – after the government filed its brief in this case – the government disclosed a set of 47 Department of Defense briefing slides that set out in detail the various steps that occur before and after targeting operations. Among other details, the slides identify the types of targets that may be identified, *id.* Ex. A at 6; the considerations taken into account in deciding whether to prioritize a target, *id.* Ex. A at 9-10, 23, 25; the process for determining what weapons system to use against a specific target, *id.* Ex. A at 11; the considerations that factor into approval of particular operations, *id.* Ex. A at 12; and a remarkably detailed description of the considerations that guide the operational decision to launch a strike in light of potential civilian casualties, *id.* Ex. A at 13, 15-20, 24, 26-38.

lution. There can be no question that Plaintiff's complaint raises profound and difficult questions concerning the relationship between liberty and security. But "[s]ecurity subsists, too, in fidelity to freedom's first principles." *Boumediene v. Bush*, 553 U.S. at 797. And no principle can be more firmly embedded in our constitutional system than the centrality of the right to life, and the gravity of its deprivation at the hands of the government. This Court should reject the government's effort to declare these matters off-limits for judicial review.

Conclusion

For the foregoing reasons, this Court should deny Defendants' Motion to Dismiss and grant Plaintiff's Motion for a Preliminary Injunction.

Respectfully submitted,

Jameel Jaffer (admitted *pro hac vice*)
Ben Wizner (admitted *pro hac vice*)
Jonathan M. Manes
American Civil Liberties Union Foundation
125 Broad Street, 18th Floor New York, NY 10004
Tel.: (212) 519-7814 jjaffer@aclu.org

Pardiss Kebriaei (admitted *pro hac vice*)
Maria C. LaHood (admitted *pro hac vice*)
William Quigley
Center for Constitutional Rights
666 Broadway, 7th floor
New York, NY 10012 Tel.: (212) 614-6452 pkebriaei@ccrjustice.org

s/ Arthur B. Spitzer
Arthur B. Spitzer (D.C. Bar No. 235960)
American Civil Liberties Union
of the Nation's Capital
1400 20th Street, N.W., Suite 119 Washington, DC 20036
Tel.: (202) 457-0800 Fax: (202) 452-1868 artspitzer@aol.com

October 8, 2010

United States District Court
for the District of Columbia

NASSER AL-AULAQI,
Plaintiff,
No. 10-cv-01469 (JDB)
v.
BARACK H. OBAMA, *et al.,*
Defendants.

Declaration of prof. Bernard Haykel

I, Bernard Haykel, pursuant to 28 U.S.C. § 1746, declare as follows:

1. I am a Professor of Near Eastern Studies at Princeton University with tenure. I have held this position since July 2007 and the areas I teach, at both the graduate and undergraduate levels, pertain to the history and politics of the Middle East, Islamic law, Islamic political movements and Islamic political thought. My particular area of research is the Arabian Peninsula and the countries of Yemen and Saudi Arabia.

2. Before joining the faculty at Princeton University, I was an associate professor at New York University with tenure. I joined NYU's faculty in 1998 and before that I was a post-doctoral research fellow at Oxford University in Islamic studies. It is from Oxford University that I obtained my MA, M.Phil. and D.Phil. (=Ph.D.) in Islamic and Middle Eastern studies. I obtained my undergraduate Bachelor's degree in International Politics from the Georgetown University 's School of Foreign Service.

3. I have lived and traveled extensively in the Middle East and South Asia and was awarded a Fulbright Fellowship in Yemen in 1992–1993. My doctoral dissertation was a study of the Salafi movement in Yemen from its roots in the 18th century until modern times. I revised this for publication and it was published as a book entitled "Revival and Reform in Islam" (Cambridge University Press, 2003). I have also published extensively on Islamic political movements in major refereed journals as well as in the press. The book project I am presently completing is a history of the Salafi movement as it has emerged in modern times in Saudi Arabia. I have conducted fieldwork research in both Yemen and Saudi Arabia and regularly visit both countries for this purpose.

4. I have native fluency in Arabic and French. I have taught Arabic at both the advanced undergraduate and graduate levels, in Oxford, New York and Princeton Universities.

5. In the course of my research and academic publications I regularly read Al-Qaeda's various websites, publications and all media output, including all that Al-Qaeda in the Arabian Peninsula (AQAP) has produced. I also follow the political situation in Yemen very closely and am regularly consulted by the US government on this matter.

6. Since the tragic events of September 11, 2001, I have regularly advised the CIA, the State Department and the US armed forces on matters relating to al-Qaeda and Islamic terrorism.

7. Al-Qaeda in the Arabian Peninsula (AQAP) is a fragmented group numbering no more than a couple of hundred men at most. The divisions among its members are generational, regional, and by nationality of origin. A majority of its members are Yemeni by origin but it also includes a small number of Saudi nationals. AQAP is best understood as a group consisting of separate distinct gangs with differing interests and no unified strategy. Some, for example, wish to reach an accommodation with the Yemeni government, others wish to fight the Saudi royal family and still others want to attack the Yemeni government in Sanaa. Unlike Al-Qaeda in Mesopotamia or Al-Qaeda in Pakistan, AQAP does not have an organizational chart that lays out its various levels of leadership, command and control or the various committees that manage if different affairs. The movement is not sufficiently coherent to be organized in a stable fashion. What is known are the names of some of the individual members, including its alleged leader Nasser al-Wuhayshi, but not how these relate to one another.

8. The situation with AQAP is further complicated by two additional factors. First, the government in Yemen has a dubious relationship with members of this group. It has struck deals with them, released them from prison at different times, and at others times co-opted them into the fight against its various domestic enemies. Furthermore, the government has and continues to inflate the threat posed by AQAP as well as its membership numbers. It does this in order to generate support (financial and military) from Western nations, especially the United States. The US has given Yemen considerable sums of money and has a small number military personnel in Yemen training its counter-terrorism force. The Yemeni government's own internal financial resources are dwindling because oil is running out and because support from oil-rich Arab neighbors has been reduced significantly. The external support that the Yemeni government generates from its claims about Al-Qaeda is not used exclusively against AQAP. Rather, the regime in Sanaa seeks to have this financial and military support in order to strengthen itself against its numerous local enemies and competitors and to assure its survival. AQAP, in other words, is not the Yemeni government's principal enemy nor is it its top priority in terms of whom to fight. Second, individual members of AQAP have created links with various tribes in Yemen, either because they as individu-

als hail from these tribes or because they have married into them. The tribes, all of whose members are heavily armed, essentially promise to give protection to an individual or a group, as is the custom in Arabia. This tribal offer of safety is not due to any ideological affinity with AQAP's views and tactics, but rather because of a bond of blood or marriage. Furthermore, tribes are made up of large numbers of people and they control specific territory in Yemen, and if one of these offers safety to an individual or individuals from AQAP, this might give the mistaken appearance that AQAP is larger than it actually is and in control of territory which it is not. Moreover, tribal violence against the government, which is a regular feature of Yemeni politics, might be easily attributed to AQAP by Sanaa. It is important to note that AQAP does not control any territory in Yemen, but that individuals or small groups take advantage of the tribal system and inhabit areas where they are afforded a degree of protection.

9. In terms of organization, AQAP appears most organized on the Internet due to its publication entitled Sada al-Malahim (Echo of Battles), the first issue of which appeared in January 2008 and has since erratically appeared on various online jihadi forums. The last issue (no. 12) was produced in January 2010. In these we find interviews with members of the AQAP, statements by Nasir al-Wuhayshi, its putative leader, and various pieces on points of theology or law. Individual members of this movement, such as al-Wuhayshi, have issued video statements, but the entire online operation is amateurish and is likely to be the effort of a few dedicated individuals, not that of an organization that has a media and public relations arm such as we have seen with Al-Qaeda in Saudi Arabia before it joined forces with AQAP or Al-Qaeda in Mesopotamia (Iraq).

10. Another feature that has given AQAP a more organized appearance than its reality of a fragmented and internally divided group is that it has issued statements, again on the Internet, claiming to have joined forces with the movement's survivors from Saudi Arabia and to have changed its name from "Al-Qaeda Organization in the Southern Arabian Peninsula" (AQSAP) to "Al-Qaeda Organization in the Arabian Peninsula" (AQAP). This allegedly took place in January 2009 and the number of Saudis is not more than a handful of individuals. Several members of this group have since handed themselves over to the Yemeni and Saudi governments, while others have vowed to continue their campaign of terror against all enemies of Islam.

11. This campaign has taken various forms, notably ideological tracts, speeches and videos on the Internet. More perniciously, however, violent attacks have taken place against tourists, diplomats, oil sector workers and oil installations and facilities, and individuals within the Yemeni security and intelligence services. These attacks, some two dozen in number since 2006, have been an irritant and dangerous feature of life in Yemen, but they do not rise up to the level of a war between the Yemeni government and AQAP. By way of contrast, a war has been waged since 2004 between the Yemeni government and a group called the Huthis in the north of the country who have been critical of the regime's poli-

cies and have resisted its attempts to control their territory. This war against the Huthis produced thousands of injured and killed victims, civilian and military, as well as tens of thousands of refugees. Many villages were destroyed and entire areas depopulated. All types of armaments, from tanks to canons to airplanes and mines, have been used in this war, which the Yemeni government as well as international groups and countries (Saudi Arabia, Qatar, the Arab League) have considered to constitute a war and have offered mediation services to reach a cease fire and resolution to all hostilities. The military engagements with AQAP do not compare with this war between the Huthis and the government in Sanaa. The number of victims, refugees, destruction wrought in the campaign against AQAP is considerably less and the use of armaments is much more limited. The number of civilian casualties has been relatively small and there has been virtually no destruction to infrastructure or homes in what amount to small arms skirmishes and AQAP suicide attacks. The nature of the struggle against elements of AQAP is more in the nature of a police action. The most recent skirmish that took place in the last week of September 2010 in a village called Hawta involved a few AQAP fighters, who fled after a botched attempt to blow up a gas pipeline. The bulk of the fighting, which lasted three days, was between government forces and southern separatist elements and local tribesmen.

12. One important feature of the AQAP is that the government in Sanaa is fearful that elements within AQAP might link up with the southern secession-ist movement in the country, which is known as the "Southern Mobility Movement." Most of the oil in Yemen is in the south and a strong independence movement has emerged here as a result of the poor governance and abuse of power by Yemen's President Ali Saleh. This is another element complicating the situation in Yemen, because it is not clear when the government claims to be attacking AQAP, that it is not in fact fighting this secessionist movement. The US appears to have been drawn in by the Yemeni government in either drone or cruise missile attacks in 2009 and 2010 and this has resulted in the injury and death of civilian tribesmen. These attacks have in turn led to tribes rebelling militarily against the government in Sanaa.

13. The relationship between Al-Qaeda Central, that is the movement's original leadership along the Pakistan-Afghan border, and AQAP is not organizationally close. AQAP uses the same language and ideology, but it is not subordinate to it. There is no example since the bombing of the USS Cole in 2000 of any member of Al-Qaeda in Yemen taking orders or following through on specific instructions from Al-Qaeda's leadership in the Afghan-Pakistan region. It is a group that has taken independent action.

I declare under penalty of perjury under the laws of the United States that the foregoing is true and correct.

Executed on October 7, 2010

Bernard Haykel

United States District Court
for the District of Columbia

NASSER AL-AULAQI,
Plaintiff,
No. 10-cv-01469 (JDB)
v.
BARACK H. OBAMA, *et al.,*
Defendants.

Declaration of prof. Mary Ellen O'connell

I, Mary Ellen O'Connell, pursuant to 28 U.S.C. § 1746, declare as follows:

1. I hold the Robert and Marion Short Chair in Law and am Research Professor of International Dispute Resolution-Kroc Institute at the University of Notre Dame. My area of specialty is the law of armed conflict. I have unique expertise respecting the definition of armed conflict. This expertise has developed over a thirty-year period that began in 1980 at Cambridge University in the United Kingdom where I was pursuing an advanced degree in international law as a Marshall Scholar. I took a specialized course on the law of armed conflict with the prominent expert, Judge Sir Christopher Greenwood. For two summers following my graduation from Cambridge with first class honors, I researched legal aspects of the Falkland Islands War with Sir Elihu Lauterpacht. While earning my JD at Columbia University, I continued to study, research, write, and teach on the subject of armed conflict. My first published article was on the Afghanistan conflict of the 1980s. My second article, published while I was an associate attorney at Covington & Burling, was on the Central American armed conflicts of the 1980s.

2. In 1989, I entered the academy and began teaching a course on international law and the use of force. In 1993 I published with Thomas Ehrlich my first book on the subject, *International Law and the Use of Force* (Little, Brown 1993). In 1995, I was asked to serve the United States as a professional military educator at the George C. Marshall European Center for Security Studies, a program developed jointly by the United States and German defense departments. I served for three years as a Title X associate profes-

sor, earning the Army's Certificate of Achievement upon my return to the academy. During my years with the Department of Defense, I continued to teach and write about the law of armed conflict. I regularly lectured at the NATO School at Oberammergau, Germany, and I was part of a NATO expert team advising the Albanian Defense Ministry in the aftermath of civil unrest in that country. Also, while in Germany, I married U.S. Army interrogator and decorated combat veteran, Peter Bauer.

3. Upon returning to the United States and joining The Ohio State University, I became the William B. Saxbe Designated Professor of Law and a senior fellow of the Mershon Center for International Security. For three years, I worked with an expert group of the International Institute of Humanitarian Law, San Remo, Italy, to produce a manual on the law of non-international armed contıict. In 2005, I published a new book, *International Law and the Use of Force* (Foundation 2005). In 2005, I joined the faculty of the University of Notre Dame, where I continue to teach, research, speak, and publish on the law of armed conflict. In 2008, I published *The Power and Purpose of International Law* (Oxford University Press) and in 2009, I published the second edition of *International Law and the Use of Force*.

4. Most relevantly, I have chaired a five-year study of the definition of armed conflict for the International Law Association (ILA). In June 20Io, the ILA's 18 member Committee on the Use of Force submitted its final report, which was adopted without opposition by the full membership of the ILA at its biennial conference in The Hague on August 19, 2010. International Law Association, Final Report of the Use of Force Committee, The Meaning of Armed Conflict in International Law (Aug. 20Io, The Hague) www.ilahq.org. *See also,* Mary Ellen O'Connell, *Defining Armed Conflict,* 13 I. CONFLICT & SECURITY LAW (2008).

5. In *Hamdi* v. *Rumsfeld,* the United States Supreme Court concluded that in 2004, the United States was engaged in an armed conflict in Afghanistan. Justice O'Connor pointed to the fact the U.S. had 20,000 troops in Afghanistan conducting intensive military operations. *Hamdi,* 542 U.S. 507, 521 (2004). The domestic legal basis for U.S. participation in the armed conflict in Afghanistan is the Authorization for the Use of Military Force. 115 Stat. 224 (2001). In the AUMF, Congress refers to the U.S. exercising "its rights of self-defense" in authorizing the president to "use all necessary and appropriate force." The rights of self-defense encompass the right to engage in armed conflict outside the state's own territory. It is a right provided in international law. In light of these facts, plaintiff's counsel has asked me to discuss the definition of "armed conflict" under international law.

6. The definition of armed conflict is crucial because during an armed conflict, and only during an armed conflict, regular members of a state's armed forces who respect the law of armed conflict (LOAC) may kill without warning. They may use lethal force without fear of prosecution for the deaths they

cause. Knut Ipsen, *Combatants and Non-Combatants, in* THE HANDBOOK OF HUMANITARIAN LAW IN ARMED CONFLICT 68 (Dieter Fleck ed., 1995). Outside armed conflict, law enforcement officials are authorized to use lethal force but only in personal self-defense or the defense of others facing an immediate threat to life or serious physical injury. Office of the U.N. High Commission for Human Rights, Basic Principles on the Use of Force and Firearms by Law Enforcement Officials, art. 9, adopted by the Eighth United Nations Congress on the Prevention of Crime and the Treatment of Offenders, Havana, Cuba, 27 August to 7 September 1990, *available at* http://193.194.138/htmllmenu3/b/h_comp43.htm.

7. It is only during the intense fighting of an armed conflict that international law permits the taking of human life on a basis other than the immediate need to save life. In armed conflict, a privileged belligerent may use lethal force on the basis of "reasonable necessity"; outside armed conflict, the relevant standard is "absolute necessity." *See* NILS MELZER, TARGETED KILLING IN INTERNATIONAL LAW 243 (2008). The combatant's privilege is necessitated by the exigencies of military conflict. Therefore, the expanded right to kill during an armed conflict may be invoked in only the most exceptional circumstances--actual armed conflict in which regular law enforcement operations are difficult to maintain because of regular firefights, bombings, and the like. The Israeli Supreme Court described the condition as an "unceasing, continuous and murderous barrage of attacks." *Public Committee Against Torture in Israel* v *Israel,* HC] 769/02, para. 16 (14 December 2006). It is in such conditions that the combatant's privilege applies. The combatant's privilege to kill "in reality, exists under limited conditions and may only be exercised by lawful combatants and parties to armed conflict." Gabor Rona, *Interesting Times for International Humanitarian Law: Challenges from the 'War on Terror,'* 27 FLETCHER FORUM OF WORLD AFFAIRS 64 (2003).

8. Absent an armed conflict, domestic criminal law, as regulated by international human rights law, applies to persons suspected of participating in criminal conduct such as organized crime or terrorism. Individuals may not be killed on suspicion of membership in such groups or on suspicion that they have carried out criminal acts. Rather, authorities must attempt to arrest the suspect and provide a criminal trial to determine guilt or innocence. Criminal suspects are presumed innocent. It is these rules that generally prevail. Situations of armed conflict are exceptional. As discussed below, international law establishes clear criteria for determining when the normal peacetime criminal law may be suspended and the extraordinary right to kill in circumstances where there is no strictly immediate threat may be claimed.

9. Under international law, an armed conflict does not exist unless certain conditions are met. In particular, armed conflict does not exist except when organized armed groups engage in intense armed fighting.

10.   The ILA's Use of Force Committee surveyed state practice and *opinio juris*
      (the two components of customary international law) from 1945 through
      mid-2010 regarding the definition of armed conflict. Hundreds of conflicts
      were considered; 72 were specifically discussed, along with dozens of judi-
      cial decisions that considered the definition of armed conflict, including
      decisions of the International Court of Justice, the Inter-American Court
      of Human Rights, the European Court of Human Rights, the International
      Criminal Court, the International Criminal Tribunals for Yugoslavia and
      Rwanda, the Ethiopia-Eritrea Claims Tribunal, as well as decisions of the
      national courts of the United States, United Kingdom, The Netherlands,
      Sweden, Italy, Israel, Canada, Bulgaria, Belgium, and others.
11.   The ILA Committee's conclusions are as follows:

   a.   The Committee undertook extensive research into hundreds of violent
        situations since 1945 and identified significant state practice and *opinio
        juris* establishing that as a matter of customary international law a situa-
        tion of armed conflict depends on the satisfaction of two essential mini-
        mum criteria, namely:
        i.   the existence of organized armed groups
        ii.   engaged in fighting of some intensity.
        The Committee's assessment of this evidence is confirmed in many judi-
        cial decisions and in scholarly commentary. These sources also indicate
        that the following conclusions respecting the concept of armed conflict
        are confirmed in customary international law:
   b.   In international law the concept of armed conflict has largely replaced
        the concept of war.
   c.   The earlier practice of states creating a *de jure* state of war by a declara-
        tion is no longer recognized in international law. Declarations of war or
        armed conflict, national legislation, expressions of subjective intent by
        parties to a conflict, and the like do not alone create a *de jure* state of war
        or armed conflict.
   d.   The *de jure* state or situation of armed conflict depends on the presence of
        actual and observable facts, in other words, objective criteria.
   e.   The accurate identification of a situation of armed conflict has signif-
        icant and wide-ranging implications for the discipline of international
        law. Armed conflict may have an impact on treaty obligations; on U.N.
        operations; on asylum rights and duties; on arms control obligations, and
        on the law of neutrality, amongst others. Perhaps most importantly states
        may only claim belligerent rights during an armed conflict. To claim
        such rights outside situations of armed conflict risks violating fundamen-
        tal human rights that prevail in non-armed conflict situations, i.e., in
        situations of peace.
        Final Report on the Meaning of Armed Conflict, *supra*, at p. 32-33 (foot-
        note omitted).

12. Thus, not all violence meets the definition of armed conflict. Terrorist violence and the instigation of terrorist violence involving intermittent attacks or hostage situations do not rise to the level of armed conflict. Nor does sporadic, one-sided violence, or mere instigation of violence. Hostilities that last only a short period of time generally do not amount to armed conflict. Moreover, to be able to engage in armed conflict, groups need to control territory for purposes of training, storage of weapons and supplies, for rest, and the like.

13. Armed conflict has a territorial aspect. It has territorial limits. It exists where (but only where) fighting by organized armed groups is intense and lasts for a significant period.

14. It is my understanding that the government has argued that the armed conflict against al Qaeda is a global conflict, and that the law of armed conflict governs the detention, prosecution, and killing of suspected al Qaeda associates wherever they are found. This conception of armed conflict is inconsistent with the one recognized by international law. That the United States is engaged in armed conflict against al Qaeda in Afghanistan does not mean that the United States can rely on the law of armed conflict to engage suspected associates of al Qaeda in other countries. The application of the law of armed conflict depends on the existence of an armed conflict. Armed conflict exists in the territorially limited zone of intense armed fighting by organized armed groups.

15. Based on my review of the declaration of Bernard Haykel, and on my own knowledge of the situation in Yemen, I conclude that the United States is not engaged in armed conflict in Yemen. Yemen is facing insurrectional and secessionist challenges in the north and south of the country. These challenges have at times reached a level of armed conflict and may do so again, but the United States is not engaged in these hostilities. In addition, AQAP is not an organized armed force within the meaning of international law.

16. My views respecting the existence of armed conflict in Yemen today are consistent with a report provided in January 2003 to the United Nations Commission on Human Rights with respect to a killing carried out by the CIA of six persons, including a U.S. citizen, traveling in a passenger vehicle in Yemen. *See* Doyle McManus, A *U.S. License to Kill, a New Policy Permits the C.I.A. to Assassinate Terrorists, and Officials Say a Yemen Hit Went Perfectly. Others Worry About Next Time,* L.A. TIMES, Jan. 11, 2003, at A1. The Commission's special rapporteur on extrajudicial, summary, or arbitrary killing found that the U.S. killing was "a clear case of extrajudicial killing." The U.S. killing of persons today in Yemen would occur in a similar factual setting to 2002. The killings were not justified by the combatant's privilege then; they cannot be so justified now. UN Doc. E/CNA/003/3, paras. 37-39. Following the attack on the *USS Cole* in 2000, the United States sent agents of the Federal Bureau of Investigation to work

with Yemeni authorities to investigate. They used law enforcement methods rather than military force. Conditions in Yemen at the time of the 2002 missile strike against a passenger vehicle have not changed markedly from the time of the *Cole* attack.

17. Because the United States is not engaged in armed conflict in Yemen, its use of force in that country is properly evaluated under international human rights standards applicable to law enforcement operations, and, where applicable, the Constitution.

18. It is also my understanding that the government has suggested, in distinction to its argument respecting a global armed conflict, that the law of self-defense may permit it to use lethal force against suspected terrorists in Yemen. It is true that, even absent armed conflict, states have a limited right to use military force in self-defense under Article 51 of the UN Charter. Mary Ellen O'Connell, *Lawful Self-Defense to Terrorism,* 63 U. PITT. L. REV. 889 (2002). Article 51 permits the use of force in response to an armed attack. The right recognized by Article 51, however, is not engaged unless the state in question is responsible for the armed attack. Armed Activities on the Territory of the Congo (Congo v. Uganda) 2005 I.C.J. para. 301 (Dec. 19). Moreover, even where Article 51 is engaged, the use of force is permitted only insofar as it is necessary and proportional. The restriction on permissible force extends to both the quantity of force used and the geographic scope of its use. Christopher Greenwood, *Scope of Application of Humanitarian Law, in* THE HANDBOOK OF HUMANITARIAN LAW IN ARMED CONFLICTS 53 (Dieter Fleck ed., 1995). In other words, self-defense, like armed conflict, has a territorial dimension. International law requires the U.S. to work with Yemen using law enforcement methods to arrest and prosecute persons suspected of terrorist activity.

I declare under penalty of perjury under the laws of the United States that the foregoing is true and correct.

Executed on October 8, 2010

Mary Ellen O'Connell

Exhibit A

Joint Targeting Cycle
and
Collateral Damage Estimation
Methodology (CDM)

General Counsel
10 Nov 2009

Briefing is Unclassified//FOUO

Derived From: CJCSI 3160.01, CJCSI 3122.06C

Agenda

- Background
- References
- Targeting and Collateral Damage
  - Definitions
  - Targeting Overview
  - Targeting Cycle key elements
  - Collateral Damage Estimation
- Summary
- Questions/Discussion

2

References

- DOD Directive 2311.01, 9 May 2006, "DoD Law of War Program"
- CJCSI 5810.01, "Implementation of the DOD Law of War Program"
- CJCSI 3160.01, "No-Strike and Collateral Damage Estimation Methodology"
- CJCSI 3122.06, "Sensitive Target Approval and Review (STAR) Process"
- Joint Publication 3-60, 13 April 2007, "Joint Targeting"
- DIA Instruction 3000.002, 15 July 2008, "U.S./Allied Targeting Analysis"
- JTCG-ME Publication, 61 JTCG/ME-05-4, 29 September 2008", Collateral Damage Estimation (CDE) Table Development"
- JTCG-ME Accredited CDE Tables, 9 January 2009

3

Joint Targeting Definitions and Processes

4

Targeting and Fires Definitions

- Targeting: the process of selecting and prioritizing targets and matching the appropriate response to them, considering operational requirements and capabilities

  - The purpose of targeting is to integrate and synchronize fires into joint operations

  - Targeting supports the process of linking desired effects of fires to actions and tasks at the joint force component level

- Fires: the use of weapon systems to create a specific lethal or nonlethal effect on a target (JP 1-02)

UNCLASSIFIED//FOUO

5

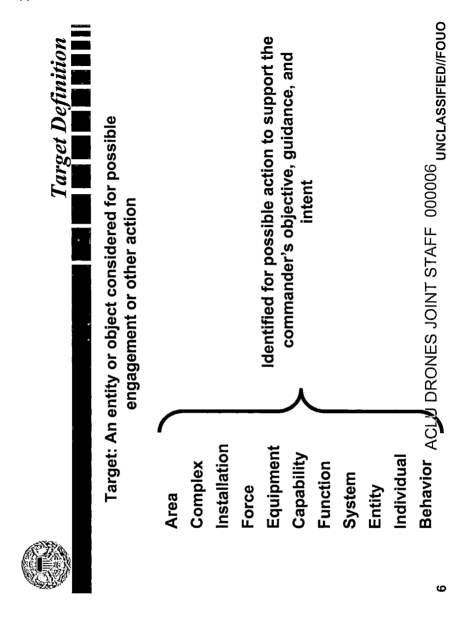

Target Definition

Target: An entity or object considered for possible engagement or other action

Area
Complex
Installation
Force
Equipment
Capability
Function
System
Entity
Individual
Behavior

Identified for possible action to support the commander's objective, guidance, and intent

ACLU DRONES JOINT STAFF 000006

6

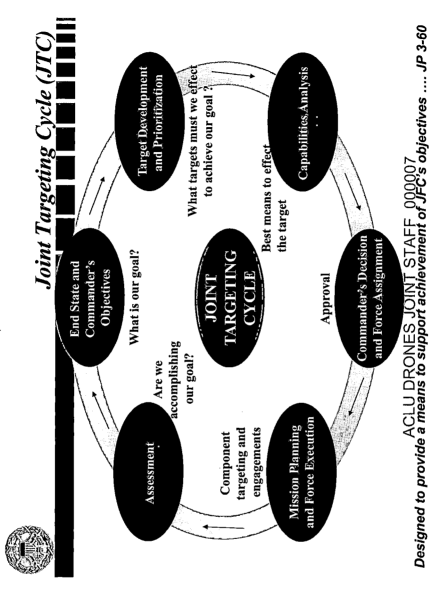

Joint Targeting Cycle (JTC)

End State and Commander's Objectives

What is our goal?

Target Development and Prioritization

What targets must we effect to achieve our goal ?

Capabilities Analysis

Best means to effect the target

JOINT TARGETING CYCLE

Commander's Decision and Force Assignment

Approval

Mission Planning and Force Execution

Component targeting and engagements

Assessment

Are we accomplishing our goal?

Designed to provide a means to support achievement of JFC's objectives .... JP 3-60

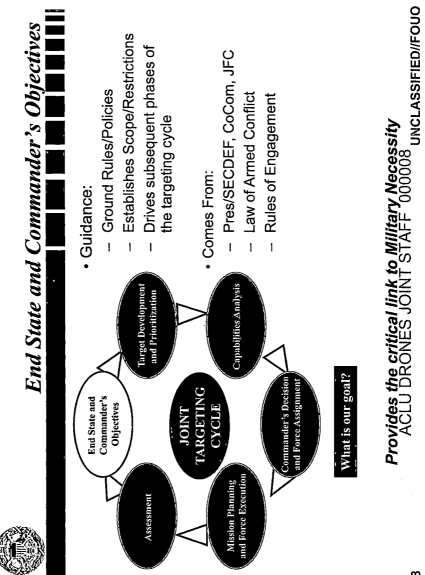

End State and Commander's Objectives

- Guidance:
  - Ground Rules/Policies
  - Establishes Scope/Restrictions
  - Drives subsequent phases of the targeting cycle

- Comes From:
  - Pres/SECDEF, CoCom, JFC
  - Law of Armed Conflict
  - Rules of Engagement

JOINT TARGETING CYCLE

- End State and Commander's Objectives
- Target Development and Prioritization
- Capabilities Analysis
- Commander's Decision and Force Assignment
- Mission Planning and Force Execution
- Assessment

What is our goal?

Provides the critical link to Military Necessity

8

Target Development and Prioritization

- Target Vetting
  - Collective effort of the Intelligence Community
  - Examines
    - Target Identification, location, function, description, significance, critical elements, target expectation, functional characterization/collateral objects of concern, intel gain/loss
  - IC votes and provides advice on each target

- Target Validation
  - Compliance with commander's objectives
  - Law Of War (LOW)/Law Of Armed Conflict (LOAC) and Rules of Engagement (ROE)
    - Target's relevancy within the Targeting System

Target Development and Prioritization

Capabilities Analysis

End State and Commander's Objectives

JOINT TARGETING CYCLE

Commander's Decision and Force Assignment

Assessment

Mission Planning and Force Execution

What targets must we engage to achieve our goal ?

ACLU DRONES JOINT STAFF **UNCLASSIFIED//FOUO**

9

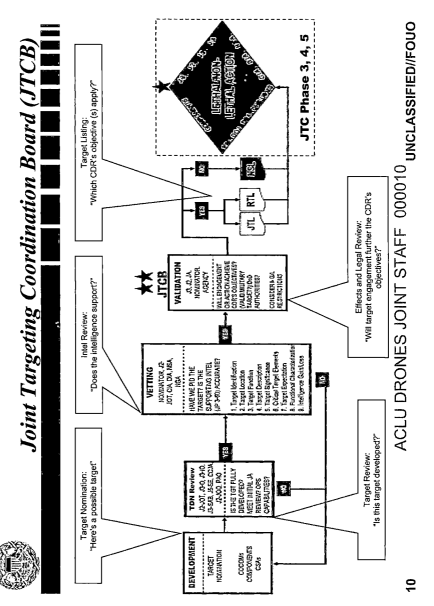

Joint Targeting Coordination Board (JTCB)

10

Capabilities Analysis

- Evaluate available capabilities vs. desired effects to determine options
  - Effectiveness & efficiency of forces
  - Estimate the effects of attacks (kinetic & non-kinetic)
  - Weighs available forces w/ COAs
  - Inline with JFC's Objectives
- Weaponeering:
  - Weapon/system to achieve effect
  - Efficient & effective use of resources
  - Objectives and desired effects
- Collateral Damage Estimation:
  - Unintended or incidental damage to persons or objects not the intended target and are not lawful targets

JOINT TARGETING CYCLE

- End State and Commander's Objectives
- Target Development and Prioritization
- Capabilities Analysis
- Commander's Decision and Force Assignment
- Mission Planning and Force Execution
- Assessment

Best means to engage the target

ACLU DRONES JOINT STAFF 000011   UNCLASSIFIED//FOUO

11

Cdr's Decision and Force Assignment

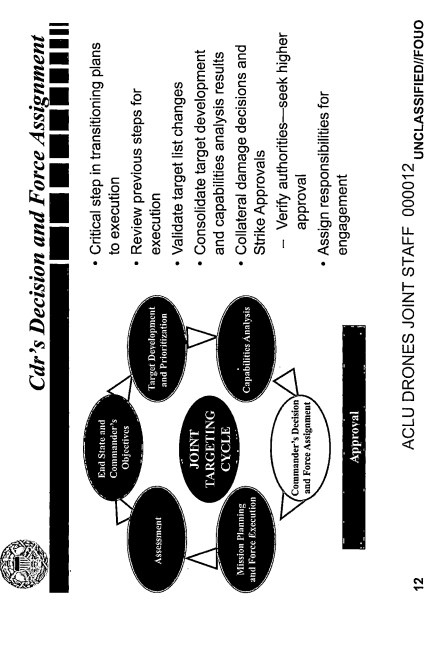

- Critical step in transitioning plans to execution
- Review previous steps for execution
- Validate target list changes
- Consolidate target development and capabilities analysis results
- Collateral damage decisions and Strike Approvals
  - Verify authorities—seek higher approval
- Assign responsibilities for engagement

Target Development and Prioritization

Capabilities Analysis

End State and Commander's Objectives

JOINT TARGETING CYCLE

Commander's Decision and Force Assignment

Assessment

Mission Planning and Force Execution

Approval

ACLU DRONES JOINT STAFF 000012 **UNCLASSIFIED//FOUO**

12

Mission Planning and Force Execution

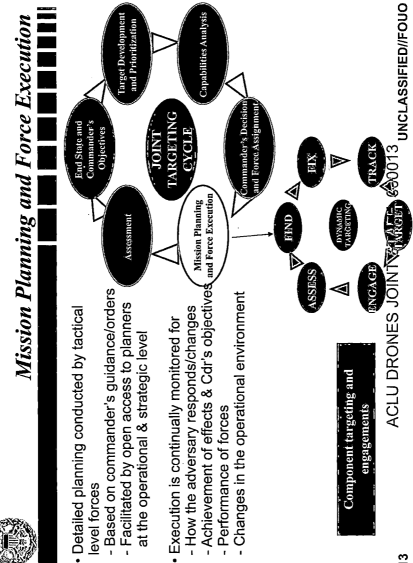

- Detailed planning conducted by tactical level forces
  - Based on commander's guidance/orders
  - Facilitated by open access to planners at the operational & strategic level

- Execution is continually monitored for
  - How the adversary responds/changes
  - Achievement of effects & Cdr's objectives
  - Performance of forces
  - Changes in the operational environment

JOINT TARGETING CYCLE

End State and Commander's Objectives

Target Development and Prioritization

Capabilities Analysis

Commander's Decision and Force Assignment

Mission Planning and Force Execution

Assessment

FIND
FIX
TRACK
TARGET
ENGAGE
ASSESS

DYNAMIC TARGETING

Component targeting and engagements

ACLU DRONES JOINT STAFF 00013 UNCLASSIFIED//FOUO

13

Combat Assessment

- Measures progress toward achieving the commander's objectives
  - MOP / MOE

- Provides:
  - Status
  - Benchmark for validating actions
  - Munitions effects assessment
  - Collateral Damage Assessment

- Generally the level at which a specified operation, task, or action is planned and executed should be the level at which such activity is assessed.

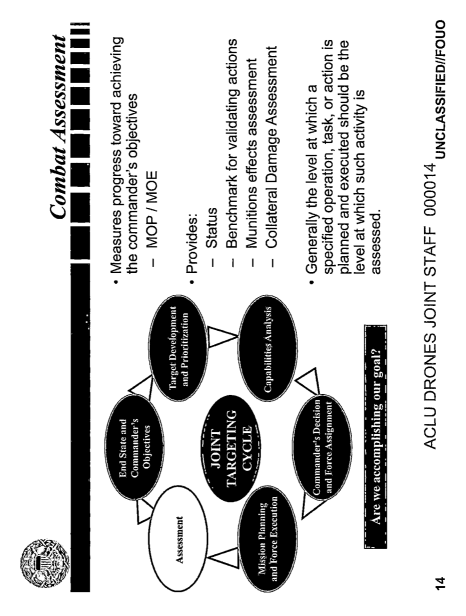

Are we accomplishing our goal?

ACLU DRONES JOINT STAFF 000014 UNCLASSIFIED//FOUO

14

Collateral Damage Estimation (CDE)

- Commanders must conduct a proper proportionality analysis to use the amount of force required to achieve a direct and concrete military advantage

- CDE Methodology provides the process to predict and mitigate collateral damage from conventional, non-nuclear kinetic strikes

  – Facilitates risk estimation and mitigation

  – Identifies target engagement's sensitivity and associated risks

  – Required on every target in accordance with Rules of Engagement

  – Target is weaponeered to balance accomplishing the mission with the risks to U.S. forces and the risk for collateral damage

15

UNCLASSIFIED//FOUO

CDE Methodology - Technical Facts

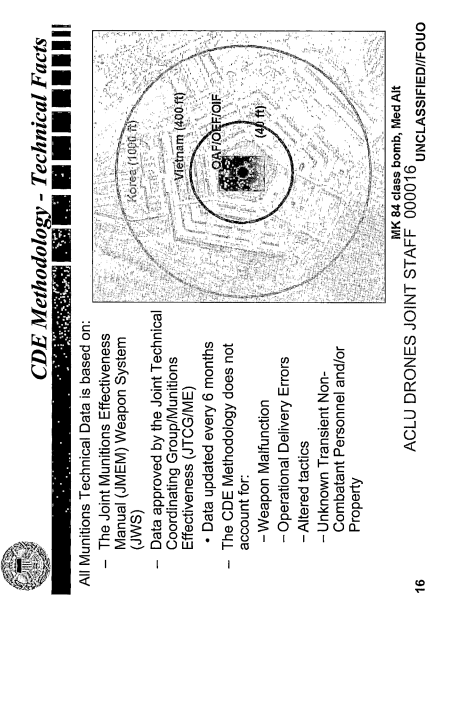

MK 84 class bomb, Med Alt

Korea (1000 ft)

Vietnam (400 ft)

OAF/OEF/OIF

(40 ft)

All Munitions Technical Data is based on:

– The Joint Munitions Effectiveness Manual (JMEM) Weapon System (JWS)

– Data approved by the Joint Technical Coordinating Group/Munitions Effectiveness (JTCG/ME)

   • Data updated every 6 months

– The CDE Methodology does not account for:

   – Weapon Malfunction

   – Operational Delivery Errors

   – Altered tactics

   – Unknown Transient Non-Combatant Personnel and/or Property

The 5 Basic Questions of CDE

CDE methodology is five questions to be answered before engaging a target:

1. Can I PID the object I want to affect?

2. Are there protected or collateral objects, civilian or noncombatant personnel, involuntary human shields, or significant environmental concerns within the effects range of the weapon I would like to use to attack the target?

3. Can I mitigate damage to those collateral concerns by attacking the target with a different weapon or with a different method of engagement, yet still accomplish the mission?

4. If not, how many civilians and noncombatants do I think will be injured or killed by the attack?

5. Are the collateral effects of my attack excessive in relation to the expected military advantage gained and do I need to elevate this decision to the next level of command to attack the target based on the ROE in effect?

17

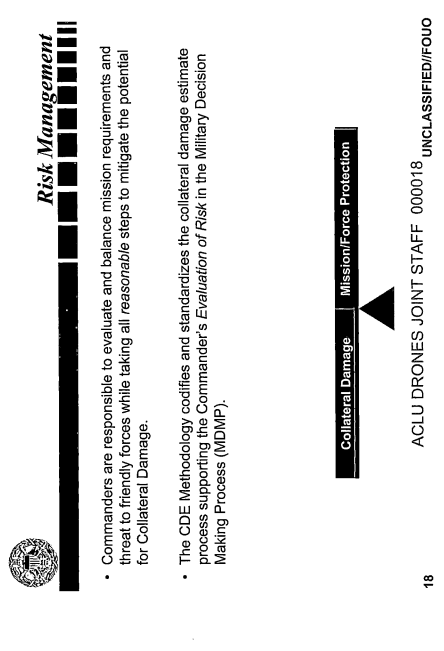

Risk Management

- Commanders are responsible to evaluate and balance mission requirements and threat to friendly forces while taking all *reasonable* steps to mitigate the potential for Collateral Damage.

- The CDE Methodology codifies and standardizes the collateral damage estimate process supporting the Commander's *Evaluation of Risk* in the Military Decision Making Process (MDMP).

| Collateral Damage | Mission/Force Protection |

ACLU DRONES JOINT STAFF 000018

18

CDM Process Guide

CDE Level 1

Positive ID	Yes / No
Defined Facility Boundary	Yes / No
Authorized by ROE	Yes / No
Dual-Use Facility	No / Yes
CoIlateral Objects in CHA	No / Yes
CBR Plume Hazard	No / Yes
Environmental Hazard	No / Yes
CDE Level 1 Assessment	

CDE Level 2

Minimum Target Size Feasibility (CDE 2B/2C) ASUGM or SSBM	Yes / No
Yes – Proceed to CDE Level 3 / No – Consider PGM Only	
PGM General Assessment, (CDE 2A Unitary or Cluster) CoIlateral Objects in CHA?	No / Yes
CDE Level 2 Assessment	

CDE Level 3

Measure and record distance from aimpoint(s), ASUGM EZ or SSBM sheaf to nearest CoIlateral concern(s)	Yes / No
Is an Unmitigated Weaponeering Solution required to achieve desired effect?	No / Yes
Is there a Mitigated Weaponeering Solution using CDE Level 3 CER Tables to achieve desired effect with a CER less than the distance in Level 2?	Yes / No
CDE Level 3 Assessment	
Weapon/Fuse Restrictions	

CDE Level 4

Assess and record collateral concern structure type(s)	
Select and enter CDE Level 4 Weaponeering Solution	
Is CDE Level 4 CER for the weaponeering solution less than the distance calculated in CDE	Yes / No
CDE Level 4 assessment	
Delivery heading restrictions	
Other mitigation techniques	

CDE Level 5

Record each unshielded collateral concern on the CDE Level 5 Casualty Estimate (CE) Worksheet (functionality, dimensions, total area)	
Determine the percent of area affected and affected sq ft of each unshielded collateral concern and record on the CDE Level 5 CE Worksheet	
Record the Day, Night and Episodic estimated population density for each unshielded collateral concern using the AOR's population density reference table on the CE worksheet.	
Determine the appropriate casualty factor for each unshielded collateral concern and record on the CE worksheet.	
Compute the casualty estimate, adding any DTRA / NCMI casualty estimate or human shields (involuntary/status unknown).	Day: / Night:
Is the total casualty estimation less than or equal to the NCV?	Episodic: / Yes / No
CDE Level 5 assessment	

Refer to ROE & STAR Process

DTRA and/or NCMI Analysis

CDE Level	Low/High	Weapon Class	Weaponeering Restriction	Heading Restriction	Casualty Estimate
CDE		(PGM/ASUGM/SSBM)			D_ N_ E_

19

Summary of CDE in Joint Targeting

- Never before has a nation taken such measures and resources to reduce the likelihood of civilian casualties

  - Our processes and procedures are rigorous

  - The methodology is derived from physics based computer modeling backed up by weapons testing data and direct combat observations

  - Estimates are applied by commanders exercising informed judgment to mitigate civilian casualties while balancing their responsibility to accomplish the mission while defending themselves and their forces

ACLU DRONES JOINT STAFF   000020   UNCLASSIFIED//FOUO

20

Questions/Discussion

21

Back-Up
(Vignette)

22

Target Value Analysis Definitions

- High Value Target: A target the enemy commander requires for the successful completion of the mission. The loss of high-value targets would be expected to seriously degrade important enemy functions.

- High Payoff Target: A high value target whose loss to the enemy will significantly contribute to the success of the friendly course of action. High-payoff targets are those high-value targets that must be acquired and successfully attacked for the success of the friendly commander's mission.

- Time Sensitive Target: A joint force commander designated target requiring immediate response because it is a highly lucrative, fleeting target of opportunity or it poses (or will soon pose) a danger to friendly forces.

23

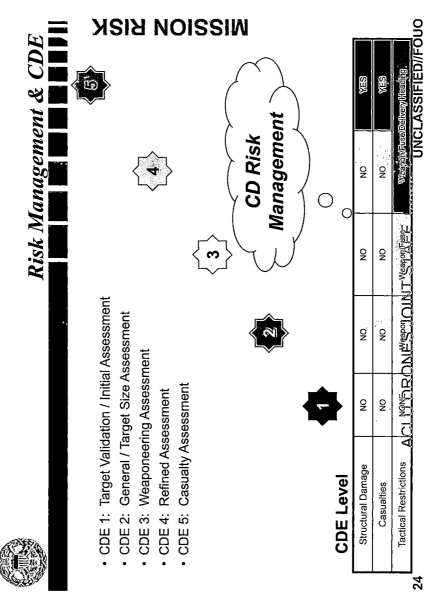

Lawful Military Objectives

- Lawful Military Objectives
  - Contribute to the enemy's warfighting/war sustaining effort and its destruction would constitute a definite military advantage
  - Four elements that allow targets to be lawful military objectives:
    - Nature
    - Location
    - Purpose
    - Use

Each target is assessed holistically on these elements

Critical Analytical Component in CDE Methodology

ACLU-DRONES-JOINT STAFF 000025

25

Positive Identification

"It is an inherent responsibility of all commanders, observers, air battle managers, weapons directors, attack controllers, weapons systems operators, intelligence analysts, and targeting personnel to (CJCSI 3160.01):

– Establish Positive Identification (PID) and to accurately locate targets consistent with current military objectives and mission specific Rules of Engagement.

– PID is defined as the <u>reasonable certainty that a functionally and geospatially defined object of attack is a legitimate military target</u> in accordance with the Law of War and applicable Rules of Engagement.

– Identify potential collateral concerns prior to munitions release and target engagement (provide function and geospatial delimitations if able)

– Apply the Collateral Damage Methodology (CDM) with due diligence to mission objectives, force protection, and collateral damage."

26

Dual-Use

- Targets characterized as having both a military and civilian purpose/function are considered dual-use.

- In most cases, dual-use Targets consist of facilities/structures associated with providing support to the civilian population and the military effort (eg. senior governmental level command and control, media centers, public utilities)

- Commanders are responsible to determine the predominant functionality of LOW Protected Structures, based on current intelligence, and decide if the target is dual-use or not.

- ROE provides the authorizations and prohibitions regarding targeting Dual-Use Facilities.

- Regardless of the ROE in effect, civilian personnel working within the boundary of dual-use targets must be considered as noncombatant casualties for the purposes of casualty estimation

27

No-Strike Policy

- Combatant Commanders identify, develop, maintain, and distribute to subordinate and supporting commands a list of No-Strike Objects for each Country within Area of Responsibility (AOR) and each OPLAN/OPORD Areas of Operation (AO)

- The National Intelligence Community will support and assist the COCOMs with No-Strike Object research, development, and production; validate additions to COCOM generated No-Strike Lists (NSL)

- A NSL is a list of all identified objects within a specified geographic area (Country or AO) functionally characterized as non-combatant / civilian in nature.

Updated and disseminated daily

28

Categories of Collateral (No Strike) Objects

- Category 1:

  – Diplomatic Facilities

  – Religious/Cultural/
    Historical

  – Non-Governmental Orgs.

  – Medical Facilities

  – Public Education Facilities

  – Civilian Refugee Camps

  – Prisoner of War (POW) Camps

  – Facilities with Environmental Concerns

  – Dams and dikes

- Category 2:

  – Non-Military Billeting (Housing,
    Hotels/Motels)

  – Civilian Meeting Places (Arenas,
    Theaters, Parks, Stadiums, Markets,
    Convention Centers)

  – Public Utilities (Power, Water,
    Electric, Gas, Fire & Police Stations,
    Banks, etc.)

  – Agricultural Storage or Processing
    Facilities

  – Facilities whose functionality is
    unknown

29

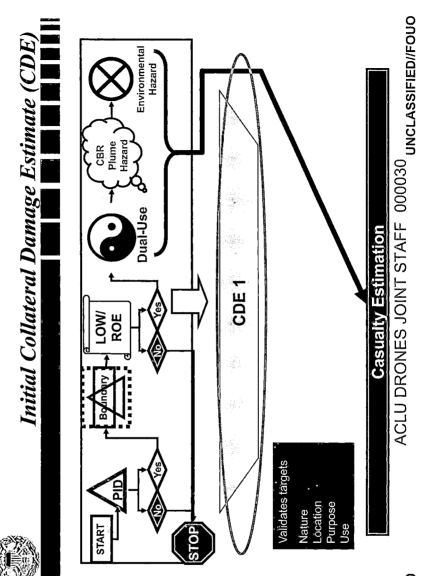

Initial Collateral Damage Estimate (CDE)

Casualty Estimation

ACLU DRONES JOINT STAFF 000030 UNCLASSIFIED//FOUO

30

CDE Level 1

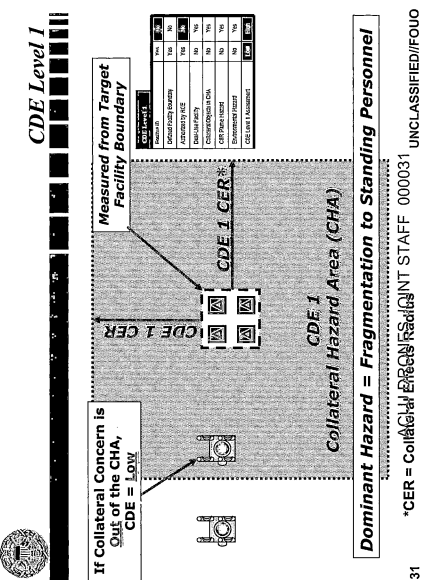

Measured from Target Facility Boundary

CDE Level 1		
Positive ID	Yes	Yes
Defined Facility Boundary	Yes	No
Authorized by RCE	Yes	Yes
Dual-Use Facility	No	Yes
Collateral Object/s in CHA	No	Yes
CBR Plume Hazard	No	Yes
Environmental Hazard	No	Yes
CDE Level 1 Assessment	Low	High

CDE 1 CER*

CDE 1 CER

If Collateral Concern is
Out of the CHA,
CDE = Low

CDE 1
Collateral Hazard Area (CHA)

Collateral Effects Radius

Dominant Hazard = Fragmentation to Standing Personnel

*CER = Collateral Effects Radius

31

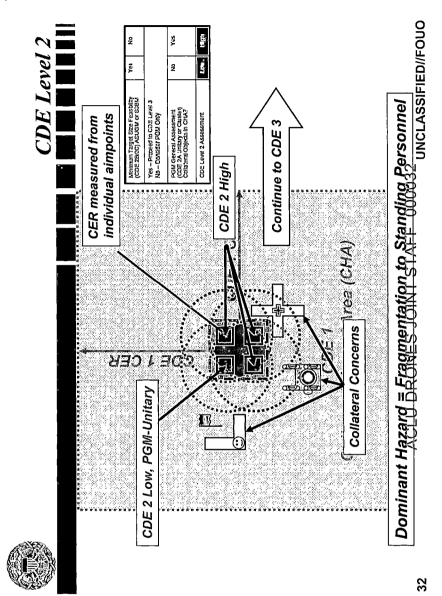

CDE Level 2

Minimum Target Size Feasibility (CDE 2BCC) ACUGM or SGBM	Yes	No
Yes – Proceed to CDE Level 3 No – Consider PGM Only		
PGM General Assessment (CDE 2A Unitary or Cluster) Collateral Objects in CHA?	No	Yes
CDE Level 2 Assessment	Low	High

CER measured from individual aimpoints

CDE 2 High

Continue to CDE 3

CDE 2 Low, PGM-Unitary

Collateral Concerns

CDE 1 CER

Collateral Hazard Area (CHA)

Dominant Hazard = Fragmentation to Standing Personnel

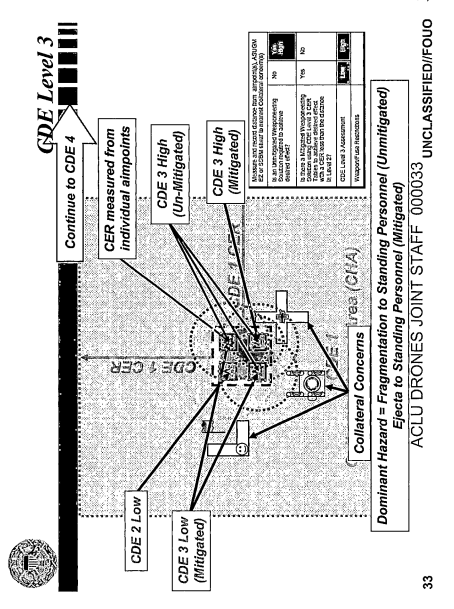

CDE Level 3

Continue to CDE 4

CER measured from individual aimpoints

CDE 3 High (Un-Mitigated)

CDE 3 High (Mitigated)

CDE 2 Low

CDE 3 Low (Mitigated)

Collateral Concerns

Dominant Hazard = Fragmentation to Standing Personnel (Unmitigated)
Ejecta to Standing Personnel (Mitigated)

Measure and record distance from aimpoint(s), ASUGM EZ or SGBM sheaf to nearest Collateral concern(s)		
Is an Unmitigated Weaponeering Solution required to achieve desired effect?	No	Yes, High
Is there a Mitigated Weaponeering Solution using CDE Level 3 CER Tables to achieve desired effect with a CER less than the distance in Level 2?	Yes	No
CDE Level 3 Assessment	Low	High
Weapon/Fuze Restrictions		

33

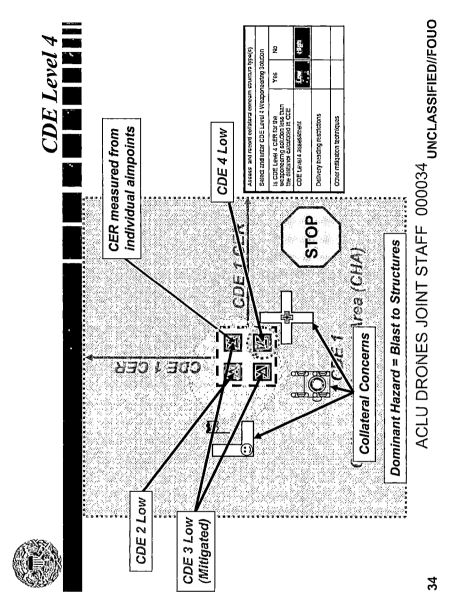

CDE Level 4

CER measured from individual aimpoints

CDE 4 Low

CDE 1 CER

STOP

CDE 1 CER

CDE 1

Collateral Concerns Area (CHA)

Dominant Hazard = Blast to Structures

CDE 2 Low

CDE 3 Low (Mitigated)

	Yes	No
Assess and record collateral concern structure type(s)		
Select and enter CDE Level 4 Weaponeering solution		
Is CDE Level 4 CER for the weaponeering solution less than the distance collected in CDE		
CDE Level 4 assessment	Low	High
Delivery heading restrictions		
Other mitigation techniques		

CDE Level 5

- Casualty Estimation is not an exact science—pattern of life assists
- There are no precise means to predict non-combatant demographics
- Combatant Commanders are responsible to develop estimated non-combatant demographic factors
  - Factors for Day and Night are based on socialized cultural norms for the applicable AOR/Country
- Casualty Estimates are computed based on three key factors
  - Affected Area of collateral concerns
  - Estimated Population Density of the effected collateral concerns
  - Casualty Factor (Multiplier)

35

CDE Level 5 (cont'd)

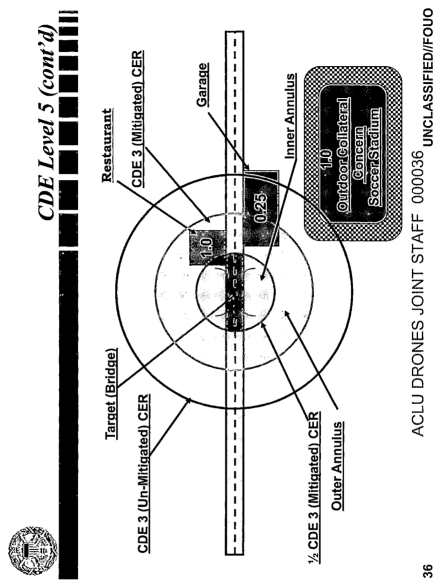

Restaurant

CDE 3 (Mitigated) CER

Garage

Inner Annulus

Target (Bridge)

CDE 3 (Un-Mitigated) CER

½ CDE 3 (Mitigated) CER

Outer Annulus

1.0

0.25

1.0

Outdoor Collateral Concern Soccer Stadium

36

Population Density Tables

Valid for: (AOR/Country)

CDEN Level 5 Population Density Reference Table

Collateral Structure Functionality	Estimated Population Density		
	Day	Night	Episodic Events
Residential Structures			
Single Family Urban or Small Town, Upper and Middle Class			
Single Family Urban or Small Town, Lower Class and Slum			
Single Family Village or Rural Scattered, Lower Class			
Multi-Family Unit (Apartment, Condominium, Dormitory)			
Institutions/Public Service			
Religious			
Museum			
Library			
School			
College/University			
Hospital			
Public Service Outlet			
Store			
Restaurant			
Hotel/Motel			
Office Building/Industrial Facility			
Light Manufacturing			
Heavy Manufacturing			
Chemical, Refining, Cement			
Heat Processing (i.e. foundry)			
Craftworks			
Transportation Facility			
Station (Air, Rail, Bus, Subway, Gas)			
Transportation Repair (Garage, Hangar)			
Warehouse			
Recreation/Entertainment			
Indoor (Theater, Gymnasium)			
Outdoor Intensive (Stadium, Racetrack)			
Outdoor Extensive (Park, Zoo)			
Auction			
Indoor			
Outdoor/Intensive (Theater, Gymnasium, Casino)			

Notes:
1. The table is based on population density per 1000 square feet.
2. Combatant commands are responsible for tables for their assigned AOR. Combatant commands may use multiple tables to account for the disparity in population density throughout different regions of various countries.
3. Day and night refer to socialized cultural norms for daytime/nighttime functional activities. Special consideration must be given to unique cultural practices and periodic events (i.e. religious holidays) that may influence the population density during impromptu events or during episodic events.

37

Sensitive Target Approval and Review Process (STAR)

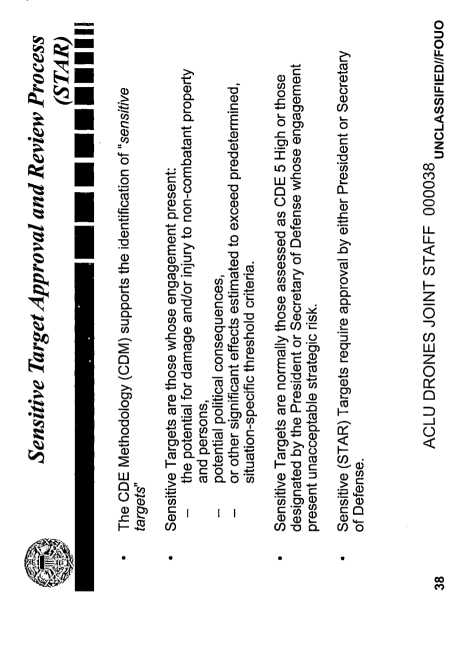

- The CDE Methodology (CDM) supports the identification of "*sensitive targets*"

- Sensitive Targets are those whose engagement present:
  - the potential for damage and/or injury to non-combatant property and persons,
  - potential political consequences,
  - or other significant effects estimated to exceed predetermined, situation-specific threshold criteria.

- Sensitive Targets are normally those assessed as CDE 5 High or those designated by the President or Secretary of Defense whose engagement present unacceptable strategic risk.

- Sensitive (STAR) Targets require approval by either President or Secretary of Defense.

CDE in the Joint Targeting Cycle

Methods to prevent civilian casualties permeates the cycle

39

Mitigating Weapon Effects

Effect	Delay Fuzing	Proximity Fuzing	Shielding	Delivery Heading	Aimpoint Offset
Frag.	✓	✓	✓	✓	✓
Blast	✓	✓	✓		✓
Debris		✓	✓		✓
Pen. & Cratering	✓	✓			
Thermal		✓	✓		
CBR		✓	✓		✓
Delivery Error				✓	

Weapon Effects & Risks

CDE Level	Intended Use	Dominant Hazard	CERUCHA Criteria and Weapon Restrictions
1	Initial assessment for all conventional weapons	Fragmentation versus personnel	Less than 10% probability of serious or lethal injury to standing personnel
2A	General assessment for unitary and cluster PGMs		
2B	Minimum target size assessment for ASUGM based on delivery platform	Delivery error only	Less than 10% probability of serious or lethal injury to standing personnel / No low or high assessment – feasibility only
2C	Minimum target size assessment for SSBM based on weapon system		
3A	Assessment for each PGM warhead in an unmitigated case	Fragmentation versus personnel (or blast if no weapon fragments/debris exist)	Less than 10% probability of serious or lethal injury to standing personnel / Fuze for surface or air detonation
	Assessment for each PGM warhead in a mitigated case	Crater ejecta/debris versus personnel (or blast if no ejecta/debris exist)	Less than 10% probability of serious or lethal injury to standing personnel / Fuze for complete detonation below grade
3B	Assessment for each ASUGM based on delivery platform and warhead in an unmitigated case	Fragmentation versus personnel (or blast if no weapon fragments/debris exist)	Less than 10% probability of serious or lethal injury to standing personnel / Fuze for surface or air detonation / Heading restriction for multi-warhead delivery
3C	Assessment for each SSBM weapon system/shell/fuze for Observer Adjusted method	Fragmentation versus personnel (or blast if no weapon fragments/debris exist)	Less than 10% probability of serious or lethal injury to standing personnel / Fuze for surface or air detonation
	Assessment for each SSBM weapon system/shell/fuze for Predicted method		
4A	Refined assessment for each PGM warhead based on collateral structure type in a mitigated case	Blast versus structures leading to blunt trauma injury to personnel	Less than 1% structural damage to collateral structure / Delay fuze for complete detonation below grade or complete detonation within target structure
4B	Refined assessment for each ASUGM warhead and associated delivery platform based on nearest collateral structure in a mitigated case		Excludes cluster munitions / Requires delivery heading restrictions
4C	Refined assessment for each SSBM weapon system/shell/fuze based on nearest collateral structure using Observer Adjusted method		Less than 1% structural damage to collateral structure / Excludes ICM, RAP and enhanced range munitions
	Refined assessment for each SSBM weapon system/shell/fuze based on nearest collateral structure using Predicted method		

41

CDE Program of Instruction

1.   CDE Methodology Program of Instruction – Overview   (1 hr)

2.   CDE Methodology - Introduction   (3 hrs)

3.   Measuring and Mitigating Weapons' Effects   (4 hrs)

4.   CDE Level 1 – Target Validation / Initial Assessment   (2 hrs)

5.   CDE Level 2 – General / Target Size Assessment   (2 hrs)

6.   CDE Level 3 – Weaponeering Assessment   (2 hrs)

7.   CDE Level 4 – Refined Assessment   (2 hrs)

8.   CDE Level 5 – Casualty Estimation / Assessment   (4 hrs)

9.   CDE Automation – JADOCS CDE Wizard   (4 hrs)

10. Practical Exercises   (8 hrs)

11. CDE Methodology - Review   (4 hrs)

12. Examination   (4 hrs)

ACLU DRONES JOINT STAFF 000042 UNCLASSIFIED//FOUO

42

Resource Allocation – Find/Fix versus Engage

Better intelligence and proportional precision engagement allows us to better discriminate valid military objectives from civilian population

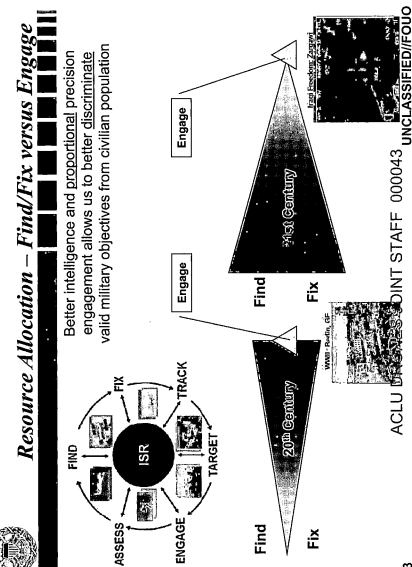

Engage

Engage

Find

Fix

Find

Fix

21st Century

20th Century

FIND

FIX

TRACK

TARGET

ENGAGE

ASSESS

ISR

Iraqi Freedom: Zarqawi

WWII - Berlin, GE

43

USCENTCOM Strike Approval Authorities

- Rules of Engagement give the appropriate permissions to approve strikes based on Collateral Damage Estimation (CDE) call and target type

- Approvals, Rules of Engagement, and Collateral Damage Estimation (CDE) for strikes in Afghanistan are driven by nationality of the selected strike platform:

  – United States Rules of Engagement apply to all U.S. assets when used to strike targets

  – Other Rules of Engagement apply to all non-US assets when used to strike targets

44

Collaborative CDE Process

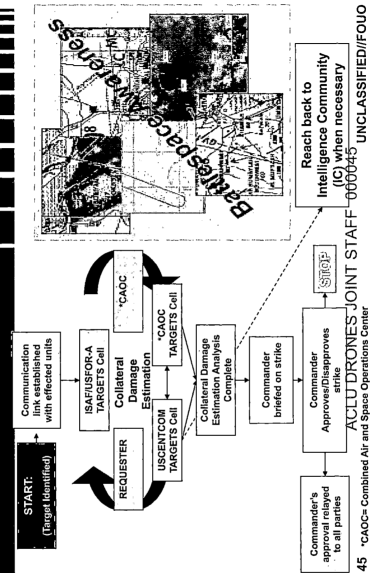

Battlespace Awareness

START: (Target Identified)

Communication link established with effected units

ISAF/USFOR-A TARGETS Cell

*CAOC

Collateral Damage Estimation

REQUESTER

USCENTCOM TARGETS Cell

*CAOC TARGETS Cell

Collateral Damage Estimation Analysis Complete

Commander briefed on strike

Commander Approves/Disapproves strike

Commander's approval relayed to all parties

Reach back to Intelligence Community (IC) when necessary

45 *CAOC= Combined Air and Space Operations Center

Mission Planning and Force Execution

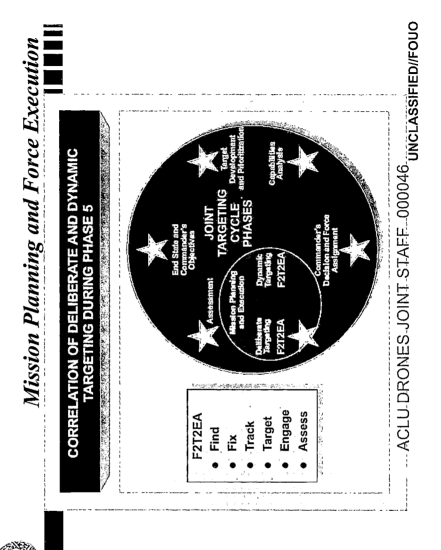

CORRELATION OF DELIBERATE AND DYNAMIC TARGETING DURING PHASE 5

JOINT TARGETING CYCLE PHASES

End State and Commander's Objectives

Target Development and Prioritization

Capabilities Analysis

Commander's Decision and Force Assignment

Dynamic Targeting F2T2EA

Mission Planning and Execution

Deliberate Targeting F2T2EA

Assessment

F2T2EA
- Find
- Fix
- Track
- Target
- Engage
- Assess

46

Dynamic Targeting Cycle

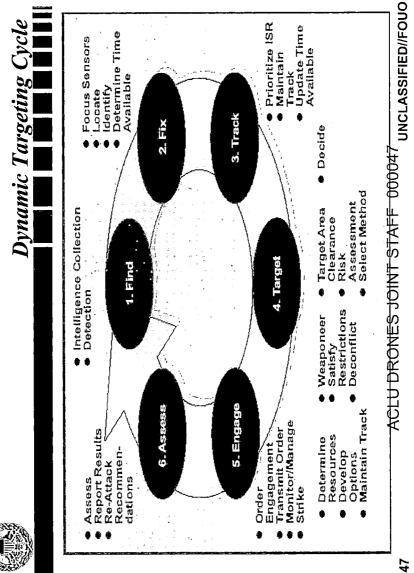

- Intelligence Collection
- Detection

1. Find

- Focus Sensors
- Locate
- Identify
- Determine Time Available

2. Fix

- Prioritize ISR
- Maintain Track
- Update Time Available

3. Track

- Target Area Clearance
- Risk Assessment
- Select Method
- Decide

4. Target

- Weaponeer
- Satisfy Restrictions
- Deconflict

5. Engage

- Order Engagement
- Transmit Order
- Monitor/Manage
- Strike
- Determine Resources
- Develop Options
- Maintain Track

6. Assess

- Assess
- Report Results
- Re-Attack Recommen-dations

47

Exhibit B

DEPARTMENT OF DEFENSE
OFFICE OF GENERAL COUNSEL
1600 DEFENSE PENTAGON
WASHINGTON, DC 20301-1600

OCT 0 1 2010

Jonathan Manes
National Security Project
American Civil Liberties Union Foundation
125 Broad Street, 18th Floor
New York, NY 10004

Dear Mr. Manes,

Please find enclosed the first release from the Department of Defense (DoD) pursuant to our agreement in the case of *ACLU v. DOJ, et al.*, No. 1:10-cv-00436-RMC (D.D.C.).

Your original request sought the release of "records relating to the use of unmanned aerial vehicles—commonly known as 'drones'—for the purpose of targeting and killing individuals since September 11, 2001." Through the Department of Justice, we have informed you that, generally speaking, weapons fired by drones are treated identically to weapons fired by other aircraft. DoD instead attempted to identify the unclassified information most likely to be of interest to the ACLU on this topic. DoD proposed to process one or more sets of unclassified briefing slides that describe the Joint Targeting Cycle including selection and prioritization criteria, no-strike and collateral damage estimation methodology, and the sensitive target approval and review (STAR) process. By agreement, the date of release was extended to October 4, 2010. The enclosed document contains 47 briefing slides from the Joint Staff regarding the agreed upon information.

These slides would not be responsive to your original FOIA request, because they are not specific to "drone strikes" as defined in your request. These slides are being produced solely pursuant to our negotiated production agreement.

DoD will continue to conduct the remaining searches as detailed in our agreement.

Sincerely,

Mark H. Herrington
Associate Deputy General Counsel
Office of Litigation Counsel

Index